Fight or Pay

Studies in Canadian Military History

The Canadian War Museum, Canada's national museum of military history, has a three-fold mandate: to remember, to preserve, and to educate. It does so through an interlocking and mutually supporting combination of exhibitions, public programs, and electronic outreach. Military history, military historical scholarship, and the ways in which Canadians see and understand themselves have always been closely intertwined. Studies in Canadian Military History builds on a record of success in forging those links by regular and innovative contributions based on the best modern scholarship. Published by UBC Press in association with the Museum, the series especially encourages the work of new generations of scholars and the investigation of important gaps in the existing historiography, pursuits not always well served by traditional sources of academic support. The results produced feed immediately into future exhibitions, programs, and outreach efforts by the Canadian War Museum. It is a modest goal that they feed into a deeper understanding of our nation's common past as well.

1 John Griffith Armstrong, *The Halifax Explosion and the Royal Canadian Navy: Inquiry and Intrigue*
2 Andrew Richter, *Avoiding Armageddon: Canadian Military Strategy and Nuclear Weapons, 1950-63*
3 William Johnston, *A War of Patrols: Canadian Army Operations in Korea*
4 Julian Gwyn, *Frigates and Foremasts: The North American Squadron in Nova Scotia Waters, 1745-1815*
5 Jeffrey A. Keshen, *Saints, Sinners, and Soldiers: Canada's Second World War*
6 Desmond Morton, *Fight or Pay: Soldiers' Families in the Great War*

FIGHT OR PAY

Soldiers' Families in the Great War

DESMOND MORTON

UBCPress · Vancouver · Toronto

15 14 13 12 11 10 09 08 07 06 05 04   5 4 3 2 1

Printed in Canada on acid-free paper.

Library and Archives Canada Cataloguing in Publication

Morton, Desmond, 1937-
   Fight or pay : soldiers' families in the Great War / Desmond Morton.

   Includes bibliographical references and index.
   ISBN 0-7748-1108-0

   1. Canadian Patriotic Fund. 2. World War, 1914-1918 – Civilian relief – Canada. I. Title.

FC557.M66 2004   940.4'77871   C2004-904598-9

Canadä

UBC Press gratefully acknowledges the financial support for our publishing program of the Government of Canada through the Book Publishing Industry Development Program (BPIDP), and of the Canada Council for the Arts, and the British Columbia Arts Council.

This book has been published with the help of a grant from the Canadian Federation for the Humanities and Social Sciences, through the Aid to Scholarly Publications Programme, using funds provided by the Social Sciences and Humanities Research Council of Canada.

Publication of this book has been financially supported by the Canadian War Museum.

UBC Press
The University of British Columbia
2029 West Mall
Vancouver, BC V6T 1Z2
604-822-5959 / Fax: 604-822-6083
www.ubcpress.ca

To the late Janet Lillian Smith Morton
and to Gael Eakin Morton,
two wonderful women
and inspirations for this book.

Our slogan has always been "Fight or pay."
We call upon the people to enlist or help others to enlist.
    We sometimes say:
"If you cannot put the 'I' into fight,
    put the 'pay' into patriotism,"
and that serves as a slogan on any platform.

—Sir Herbert Ames in the House of Commons,
    29 February 1916

Contents

Illustrations / VIII

Preface / XI

Abbreviations / XVIII

1   War and Families / 1

2   Pay and Allowances / 25

3   The Patriotic Fund / 50

4   Choices and Responsibilities / 89

5   Homecomings / 133

6   Grumbling and Complaining / 170

7   Victory for Whom? / 201

8   Never Again / 239

Appendix / 243

Notes / 246

Bibliography / 292

Index / 306

Illustrations

FOLLOWING P. 204

If you cannot put the "I" into fight, you can put the "pay" into patriotism by giving to the Canadian Patriotic Fund, *Howell, Lith, CWM 19900348-025*

French army reservists in St. Boniface, 11 August 1914, *Foote Collection no. 2185, Manitoba Archives*

Italian army reservists in Toronto, 1915, *R. D'Angelo, Library and Archives Canada, PA-091096*

Sergeant François-Xavier Maheux, his wife, Angeline, and their children, *Library and Archives Canada, PA-120121*

Two soldiers, one with his wife and infant, *James Collection no. 777F, City of Toronto Archives*

A Canadian soldier chats with the young French woman who looks after the railway crossing gates, *Library and Archives Canada, PA-01449*

Lily Fields Mackinnon, wife of a corporal in the PPCLI, and her two children, *courtesy and permission of Gordon Mackinnon*

Women collecting soldiers' comforts, Toronto, *James Collection no. 879, City of Toronto Archives*

Women holding bazaar for war aid, *James Collection no. 872, City of Toronto Archives*

Miss Helen Reid, of the Montreal branch of the Canadian Patriotic Fund, *From Philip Morris, The Patriotic Fund, facing p. 246*

Sir Herbert Ames, MP, honorary secretary, Canadian Patriotic Fund, *From Philip Morris, The Patriotic Fund, facing p. 14*

A knitting circle for soldiers' wives and mothers, Toronto, *James Collection no. 873, City of Toronto Archives*

"Christmas, 1917," *The Canadian Liberal Monthly, Ottawa, December 1917*

Mrs. W.E. Oliver, *BC Archives, MS 2685 Box 4, file 12, William Edgar Oliver Papers, 1914-1919*

"Boys to the farm," advertisement for Soldiers of the Soil uniform, *E. Henderson, Library and Archives Canada, C-095289*

"Moo-che-we-in-es" advertisement for the Canadian Patriotic Fund, c. 1912-16, *Library and Archives Canada, C-121137*

"Time for a Hog-Killing!" *The Vancouver Daily Sun, 23 July 1917*

The Children's Story of the War, Ontario school textbook, *Thomas Nelson and Sons*

Boy Scouts in front of the Patriotic Relief Fund headquarters, Toronto, September 1914, *William James Topley, Library and Archives Canada, PA-042857*

"Salvage, save what you can, where you can," *G.P. Ltd., CWM 19720121-065*

"Are you breaking the law?" *Library and Archives Canada, C-095280*

"If you cannot join him, you should help her," advertisement for the Canadian Patriotic Fund, *CWM 19890086-530*

"G-Bye Mary. The Patriotic Fund will care for you," *CWM 19890086-900*

Letter from the Minister of Militia and Defence for Canada to Ida May Dowling, 20 September 1917, *property of the author*

"These four mothers gave to their country 28 brave sons," *James Collection no. 727, City of Toronto Archives*

Military amputee in invalid chair with daughter, *Department of Veterans' Affairs, Military Hospitals Commission*

Death notice from the Director of Records to Ida May Dowling, 1917

Preface

A decade ago, I wrote a book about what I thought it was like to be a Canadian soldier in the First World War. I tried to explain why a million young Canadians – one in eight in the entire population – thought they had to volunteer for the war. Only half were accepted into the wildly improvised Canadian Expeditionary Force (CEF). Only about three-fifths of them actually went overseas to fight. One shocking fact about this country in 1914 is that less than half of its keenest volunteers could meet the modest physical standards of its army. I went on to look at how the volunteers learned to be soldiers, how some of them became officers, and how they experienced trench warfare. Perhaps the hardest question for me was what persuaded men, when the time came, the whistles blew, and the officers shouted, to climb out of their trench and walk forward to face death or agonizing and permanent injury. One of the best answers was a sheer fatalism that a soldier would live until "his number came up" in the lottery of life. What else explained why some died and others survived in situations that seemed utterly fatal – or as utterly safe as any battlefield allows.

At some point while studying the soldiers through their diaries and letters and through the acres of documents that recorded their training and service and ultimate demobilization, I promised myself to write a similar book about the wives and children and parents they left behind in Canada when they went off to war. Lots of people knew at least a little about an uncle or a grandfather or a school teacher or an elderly colleague at work who had fought in the Great War, but who could remember what happened to their grandmother or an orphaned uncle or the old lady who had never found another beau to match the one lost in the war? Somewhere out there was another set of experiences that was a story in its own right.

I soon discovered more to that story than curiosity satisfied. Soldiers' wives and mothers were as much a part of Canada's war effort as nurses, munition workers, "conductorettes," and other women normally featured in war art, history books, and museums. To fight the war, governments needed affordable armies of men willing to risk their lives at an unskilled labourer's wages. To persuade them to volunteer, a husband's obligation to support his wife and their children, or a son's duty to his widowed mother, had to be satisfied as cheaply as possible. Not even the government pretended that a twenty-dollar separation allowance would be enough. To save the government from paying even more, powerful men devised a source of family funding that would reassure any woman who released her man for war and would legitimate a responsible man's decision to leave her and his children. The "Patriotic" was their solution. Men must "fight or pay."

The architects of the Canadian Patriotic Fund and of Canada's Board of Pension Commissioners correctly insisted that their allowances and pensions were not charity. They were entitlements, established by an unwritten contract between Canadians and those, male and female, who provided them with an army. The core question of this book is how well that contract was fulfilled. Opinions will differ. Based on the grumbling and even despair among the wives and mothers who had let their men go to war, readers may conclude that the contract was broken. Others will note that the specifics of several different contracts proved more complex than they initially seemed. The rich and powerful do not grant entitlement easily, particularly to those much poorer and weaker than themselves. Although its chief architect insisted the Canadian Patriotic Fund was not a charity, it surprisingly resembled one in its submissiveness to powerful donors and its manipulative approach to its beneficiaries.

In this book, I argue that the Fund was designed by Sir Herbert Ames at least partly to demonstrate how systematic thrift, and counselling on domestic sanitation and child rearing, could liberate working-class families from the burden of poverty. Like most social experiments, too many conflicting personalities and beliefs and too many real-life complications undermined a project that Ames could not even publicly acknowledge. Only after the Second World War were Canadians willing to reduce poverty's prevalence from being the daily reality of the majority to being the fate of only one Canadian in six by 1960.

During and after the First World War, however, the principle of entitlement had to do battle with older convictions that allowances to soldiers' families and pensions to the disabled were a charity bestowed on the needy, well-behaved, and politically supportive. Women as well as men fought for their rights to both pensions and "The Patriotic" with pertinacity and a sturdy sense of their vital contribution to a desperate national struggle. Munition workers might arm the troops, nursing sisters might care for them, but mothers brought soldiers into the world, nursed and raised them, and sent them off to fight and to die. Women's struggle for entitlement against heavy odds is the unifying theme of this sometimes sad and ultimately unresolved story.

The favourite slogan of the Patriotic Fund as it addressed itself to the pockets of wealthy subscribers was "Fight or Pay." Women, of course, were condemned to pay, though some were compelled to fight for the meagre sums the government and its chartered charity allowed them. They paid in the loneliness of raising families without a husband's support, they paid a toll of anxiety for his survival and return, and they paid many times over when a son or husband returned disabled in mind or body. Condemned to the poverty inherent in a fractional disability pension, their fate was to be untrained nurses, sharing in the pain and humiliation of a husband or son. All history is unfinished, but a logical extension from this book would be a study of the wives and families of war veterans and the evolution of the War Veterans' Allowance by 1930 as a cautious, poverty-level pension for that vague but undeniable set of symptoms first labelled "shell shock."

ANY HISTORIAN wonders why a particular story has not been told before. This can encourage whining about the shocking negligence of other historians that, in fact, has allowed the scholar a thesis or book topic. As someone who has frequently cultivated relatively fallow patches of Canadian experience in the First World War, I have come to a more benign conclusion. Kindly colleagues have generously left me an interesting topic and, for the most part, backed off to see what I would do with it. Thus I have written about Canadian generals and politicians, the Overseas Ministry, French Canadians in the CEF, veterans' policies during and after the Great War, Canadian prisoners of war in Germany in 1914-18, and much else that had otherwise slipped beneath my colleagues' radar. I am solely to blame for the time this book has taken to appear. I got distracted by the chance to come to McGill University and to Quebec in 1994 in time to participate in the 1995 referendum campaign. Thanks to the vision and generosity of Charles R. Bronfman, I was able to launch McGill's unique Institute for the Study of Canada and to share its first seven years.

When I set out to fulfill the pledge I had made to myself in 1993 to write about soldiers' wives and families, I began to appreciate a sad reality. Perhaps my colleagues had stayed away from soldiers' wives out of unadulterated common sense. The sources for this story had largely been obliterated. During the war, Canadian soldiers and their families had bridged the Atlantic with their letters, but those letters met very different fates. A soldier's letters came home to be saved as potentially the last relic of his life. Countless mothers, wives, and relatives patiently collected letters and anything else a soldier could send home. True, a soldier's letters were carefully censored, first by his own officers and then by official censors at the base. Anything that could remotely be considered a military secret, from the name of a nearby village to an upcoming move, was ruthlessly blacked out. So were reactions to enemy shelling or grumbles about army rations or visiting generals. However, soldiers' letters have survived, along with tiny (and illegal) pocket diaries and snapshots, as well as the poetry and prose in trench newspapers. And more comes to light regularly as descendants recognize that ancestral treasures can be shared with archives and museums, sometimes for a convenient tax deduction.

The letters that went the other way have virtually all vanished, although wives and mothers wrote at least as faithfully as their menfolk. Most censored themselves, reluctant to add their anxieties and sufferings to those of men at the front. Others, we can infer, shared all or most of their problems. It is not hard to imagine the letter that led a Toronto soldier to explain to his wife precisely how to take their son to his cousin's house, where the boy would get a dose of the discipline an absent dad could not apply. However, the letter that inspired the father's advice has disappeared, and so have all the other letters the soldiers' kinfolk sent overseas. The reason is no mystery. Regulations required a soldier to read and then destroy personal letters in case they fell into enemy hands.[1] Even if he ignored the rules, an ordinary soldier had to lug all he owned on his own back. Issued far more kit than he could ever carry, much of it was stuffed into his kitbag for storage and near-certain pilferage. A letter from home was shoved into a tunic pocket or laid smoothly on the bottom of a haversack. A cherished photo might be glued into a soldier's pay book. Then the soaking rains of England or Flanders fell, drenching men to their skin and reducing paper to pulp.

We have a rich sampling of women's letters to officials and politicians as proof of their eloquence. Some, like their men, were virtually illiterate; few had experienced long or thorough schooling, but their passion, logic, and persuasiveness still speak to us across most of a century. The tragedy is that so much relating to these women and their story has simply vanished.

So has much else that might have illuminated their lives and experience. During the war, local relief committees of the Canadian Patriotic Fund conducted thousands of investigations into the home life of applicants. A form used by the Patriotic Fund in Ontario's Frontenac County demands intensely personal details. What is the household income and how much did the soldier contribute before and after he enlisted? Was his former employer continuing his wages in whole or in part? What debts, bank accounts, and insurance policies did the soldier leave? What is the character of the neighbourhood? A relief investigator would ask the same questions, perhaps without being adjured to use "tact and friendliness."[2]

A scattered handful of these investigations have survived in the archives of war-time politicians and officials. Why had Mrs. X been denied support by the Patriotic Fund, or why had she been treated with such generosity that she provoked the indignation of her jealous neighbours? Occasionally, a copy of the evidence has survived, pinned to the bland official letter. As Professor Margaret McCallum discovered when she tracked down the records of the Patriotic Fund, however, almost all the local branches transferred their records and case files to Ottawa after the end of the war. The Fund then sought a home for them. In 1932 it was the turn of the Ontario Archives: for two additional staff members, the provincial archivist reported to his superiors, he would take them. Instead, his staff was cut, and over sixty boxes of CPF records were simply destroyed.[3] I persist in the hope that some CPF branches defied the central edict. I still suspect that, somewhere, local records hide in an attic or a basement, but, apart from a few false leads, my suspicion remains baseless.

Of course, as historians of women have regularly demonstrated, any story worth telling leaves sources. Having made its case in wartime with scores of posters, pamphlets, and a monthly *Bulletin,* the Canadian Patriotic Fund ensured that its record would survive, immune from external comment or criticism, by commissioning its full-time secretary, Philip Morris, to produce a handsome, well-illustrated volume as a tribute to its volunteers. William Raynsford, a war orphan, recalled his own experiences in the Toronto orphanages operated by Ontario's Soldiers' Aid Commission. In 1934 a new Liberal government fired the staff, robbed the children of their names so that brothers and sisters could never be reunited, and dispatched them as cheap labour for Ontario farmers.[4] In 1981 the University of Toronto Press published Grace Morris Craig's *But This Is Our War,* a reminder that women other than nurses and factory workers had gloried and worked and ultimately suffered in the war.

Thanks to the accident of coming to McGill, I also discovered the archives of the McCord Museum of Canadian History, then cared for by Pamela Miller. Thanks to her guidance and encouragement, and to the McCord's resources, I was able to see how much the national Fund was the invention of Montrealers and how far Montreal had provided both funds and experience for a Canadian institution.

MORE THAN MOST of my books, this has been a team effort, involving family, friends, audiences in a dozen cities, and at least ten years of teaching and learning from students at all levels. Among the contributors was Margaret McCallum, now a professor of law at the University of New Brunswick, whose career as a professional historian and student of public policy began with a thorough and perceptive study of public provision for soldiers' dependants, particularly in Nova Scotia. If Montreal has a central place in this book, it is partly due to the research of Gibran van Ert, who made evident the city's importance in shaping the Patriotic Fund. Manitoba, chief provincial holdout from the national Fund, was explored by Cheryl Smyth, generously diverting time she would otherwise have devoted to her history of the professional ballet in Canada. Adrian Lomaga did all that he could to bring the Toronto and York Patriotic Fund to life, and Ulric Shannon spent days in the Oxford County archives exploring the work of the county's Patriotic Association.

In addition to his meticulous eye for detail, Cabot Yu enlightened me on the Canadian Patriotic Fund in northern Alberta. Tanya Gogan struggled to educate me on feminist theory, while Jenny Clayton covered British Columbia, from the devoted women of the Florence Nightingale chapter of the IODE to the patriotic citizens of Hedley, not to mention the indefatigable Mrs. Janet Kemp. Thanks to the patient and omniscient Barbara Wilson, Jeff Osweiler found the files that mattered in the vast National Archives holdings on the CEF.

Each historian stands gratefully on the shoulders of many others. While Margaret McCallum's articles exposed the potential significance of wartime family policies on the development of government programs for single mothers and for alleviating family poverty, others have developed our understanding of gender and politics. An obvious landmark is Nancy Christie's *Engendering the State: Family, Work, and Welfare in Canada*, though readers will note a few differences on factual detail. Lacking their own experience of war, Canadians depended heavily on the British example, sometimes in imitation and more occasionally by reaction. Family policy had both elements. Graham Wootton's *The Politics of Influence: British Ex-Servicemen, Cabinet Decisions and Cultural Change (1917-57)* has been an invaluable guide to both fact and theory. And Canada had another influential model: American experience balanced the British, though we entered the Great War long before our neighbours. Theda Skocpol's *Protecting Soldiers and Mothers: The Political Origins of Social Policy in the United States* led me to a more kindly view of the American pension experience than in my earlier work with Glenn Wright on Canadian veterans, *Winning the Second Battle*. Skocpol's work reinforced the view that wartime attitudes and policies could shape the future, as Margaret Jane Hillyard Little acknowledged in her account of mothers' allowances in post-Great War Ontario, *No Car, No Radio, No Liquor Permit: The Moral Regulation of Single Mothers in Ontario, 1920-1997*.

After Morris's inevitably self-congratulatory institutional account, the first major attempt to tackle the history of the Patriotic Fund was a 1992 master's thesis by David Laurier Bernard, "Philanthropy vs. the Welfare State: Great Britain's and Canada's Response to Military Dependants in the Great War." A doctoral thesis by Ian Miller, published in 2001 as *Our Glory and Our Grief: Torontonians and the Great War,* is a little disappointing since, as usual, soldiers' families and their supporters are allowed a very obscure role in the history of the city's wartime life. The apparent limitations of archives in Toronto compared to the McCord archives in Montreal, however, provide a partial explanation.

During the past ten years, I have shared this topic with scores of friends and strangers, gaining insights and memories and learning more than I could have imagined – and probably far less than I needed – about that complex and ever-changing institution called the family. One of the highlights of this experience came through a respected Toronto historian, Gordon Mackinnon, whose grandfather, Archie, had served and died in Princess Patricia's Canadian Light Infantry. Archie's widow, Lily, and her two small children became symbols of the wives and children I could never see, read about, or interview. The son, in the uniform of a PPCLI corporal, went on to serve in the Second World War; his tiny sister died, tragically, during the great influenza epidemic at the end of the First World War. Lily chose to remarry, forfeiting her pension in the hope of providing her son with a father. Her second marriage was not very happy, but only Hollywood promises happy endings. Any book is a team project. This one has been guided by the devoted and patient Camilla Gurdon.

Writing a book about families grows inevitably out of one's own experience. I was born and grew up in a Canadian soldier's family, barely old enough to understand my mother's lonely anxiety during the long years of her husband's absence overseas. My first wife died at the end of 1990, and this book is dedicated both to her memory and to the woman who replaced her in my heart and life seven years later. In envisioning the often voiceless women who inspired this book, Jan and Gael have been the reality that filled my mind and my imagination.

Abbreviations

ANV	Army and Navy Veterans
AP	Assigned Pay
BPC	Board of Pension Commissioners
CAMC	Canadian Army Medical Corps
CAPC	Canadian Army Pay Corps
CEF	Canadian Expeditionary Force
COS	Charity Organization Society
CPF	Canadian Patriotic Fund
DSCR	Department of Soldiers' Civil Re-establishment
GWVA	Great War Veterans' Association
IMB	Imperial Munitions Board
IODE	Imperial Order, Daughters of the Empire
MHC	Military Hospitals Commission
MPF	Manitoba Patriotic Fund
MSA	Military Service Act
NCWC	National Council of the Women of Canada
OPA	Oxford Patriotic Association
SA	Separation Allowance
SSFA	Soldiers' and Sailors' Families Association
SWL	Soldiers' Wives League
VTLC	Vancouver Trades and Labour Council

FIGHT OR PAY

1
War and Families

On a broiling August weekend in 1914, the Great War came to Canada. Most people had barely noticed its approach. Canada was a rural country, where any news short of gossip travelled slowly. Decent country folk had too much to do, even in midsummer, to go lollygagging into town to find out what foreigners were up to. Cities, of course, were different. The first Monday in August was a public holiday in many places. For their health, the rich escaped the summer heat to Muskoka, Lake of the Woods, or the Lower St. Lawrence, and a long weekend allowed the menfolk a little extra time to join their families. The vast majority could only dream of escaping their airless rooms and the odour of pit privies and horse manure. Many wandered the streets on a holiday, looking for excitement. On the 1914 August holiday, the rulers of Europe obliged.

The war was neither expected nor an entire surprise. After all, for the previous decade European war scares had been as common as summer thunder and about as dangerous. For the three previous years in the Balkans, Serbia, Bulgaria, Greece, Turkey, and Montenegro had fought their enemies and then, without much pause, fought their allies. Meanwhile, Europe's major powers postured and threatened and enlarged their armies and fleets. Did the murder of Archduke Franz Ferdinand and his wife at Sarajevo by a Serb terrorist really make any difference? Pundits might debate but the Canadian media gave them short shrift. Drought on the prairies, the collapse of British Columbia land prices, and other symptoms of a continuing depression worried Canadians more than a European war. Though few then argued that governments caused or cured depressions, bad times reassured many Liberals that Canadians would repent their Tory votes in 1911. With elections due in 1915, a newly knighted Sir Robert Borden and his Tories would have little to show for their time in office. Liberals hoped Canadians would let old Sir Wilfrid Laurier finish his work.

Suddenly, as August began, newspaper editors cleared domestic news from their front pages. Hapsburg Austria had ignored Serbia's concessions and apologies, mobilized its armies, and declared war. As defender of all Slavs and Serbia's sworn ally, Russia had to respond, prompting Germany to follow Austria. An 1894 treaty bound France to support Russia against Germany. For years, Germany had prepared for this threat: it would cross a neutral Belgium, knock France out of the war in a few weeks, as it had in 1870, and then turn eastward against the huge, incompetent czarist army. At midnight on Friday, 1 August, the Russian czar declared war on Germany. Berlin's ultimatum to France to cancel its mobilization expired. When Belgium's King Albert refused to yield to Germany's invasion, Great Britain, guarantor of Belgian neutrality for eighty years, felt obliged to intervene with an ultimatum to Berlin that expired at noon on August 4th.

Early on 2 August, Saturday morning in Canada's largest, richest, and most cosmopolitan city, French immigrants remembered their status as army reservists and gathered outside their consulate on Montreal's Place Viger to wait for orders.[1] Through the day, their numbers grew to an orderly throng in straw boaters and cloth caps. A few women stood on the edges, but this was not a gathering for wives and children. Montreal journalists pestered Louis Raynauld, the French consul, for names of French Canadians who had volunteered, or the name of "the distinguished doctor who had offered his services." It was enough, Raynauld insisted, to declare his pride at "cette marque d'attachement et de sympathie." Names of French reservists could be published if they desired. *La Presse* reported that many of the men were members of Montreal's fire department. The press corps then moved over to the Coristine Building, where Belgium's honorary consul, Clarence de Sola, encouraged his reservists to lead the singing of "La Brabançonne," the Belgian national anthem. Belgium, de Sola explained, would fight, but 300,000 of its 400,000 soldiers had to be summoned from the reserves. Among them, *La Presse* noted, was the wealthy Sir Vincent Meredith's chauffeur, a married man.[2]

Earlier that morning, local militia regiments had acted on prewar emergency plans and mounted guards on canal locks and at the harbour gates. Maj. Pierre-H. Bisaillon boasted that his 85th Regiment was eager for overseas service.[3] Lt.-Col. J.T. Ostell of the 65th Carabiniers de Mont-Royal, the city's senior francophone regiment, was more sober: "War is not an outing to Saint Irene, it's a calamity."[4]

That evening, separate French- and English-speaking crowds marched through their Montreal neighbourhoods, bellowing out "La Marseillaise," "Rule Britannia," and "God Save the King." A city policeman told a group to quit singing "O Canada"; the nationalistic anthem favoured by the Société St-Jean-Baptiste seemed a little too provocative. They obliged.[5] On Sunday, 3 August, rain and cooler temperatures discouraged such patriotic demonstrations, though a cheerful mob invaded the Windsor Hotel in pursuit of the German consul. Mobs bellowed abuse outside the Germania Club on Dorchester and the German consulate on McGill. Monday, 4 August was a civic holiday in Montreal. *Le Devoir* reported to its *nationaliste* readers that French troops had slaughtered 3,000 Germans at Longwy, and that French warships had captured a German convoy with $10 million in gold. Montrealers also learned that Britain's ultimatum to Germany had expired at dawn, local time, and the Empire was at war. It would be the biggest war in history, *La Presse* warned its readers, with 15 million soldiers, regular and reserve, ready to fight.[6] Crowds took on fresh energy.

Two days after the British ultimatum expired, Canadians learned of their official share in the distant struggle. On 6 August the minister of militia, Col. Sam Hughes, announced a Canadian Expeditionary Force of 20,000 men. Scrapping his department's official mobilization plans, Hughes telegraphed militia colonels from coast to coast, commanding them to bring volunteers to Valcartier, an undeveloped sandy expanse outside Quebec City. Thousands of volunteers gathered outside armouries and discovered that militia officers could not provide uniforms or information about pay and allowances. Few of the would-be warriors quibbled. Excitement, escape, bravado, and all the spices that draw men closer to death prevailed. The drab burdens of wage earning, family, and loved ones were easily forgotten or answered by the confidence that others would now provide the necessities of life.

Families and War

Families, seemingly, were not part of war. For millennia war was an activity primarily reserved for young men, whether the mass of humble, poorly armed, ill-rewarded spear carriers who filled the ranks of the Greek or Persian myriads, the Roman legion, and the medieval host, or the highly trained, well-capitalized, professional warrior-specialists like the knights of medieval Europe. Periodically, religion or barbarian invasions could rouse entire populations to fight, flight, or massacre. Then, for a time, the memory of terror and horror would suffice to make war a minority activity. The scourge of Europe's Thirty Years War was followed through most of the eighteenth century by limited dynastic wars, waged by European monarchs with professional armies recruited among the least productive of their subjects, and with foreign mercenaries. Brutally drilled until they obeyed their officers more readily than their fears, such soldiers mastered the movements necessary to load, prime, and fire their flintlock muskets, no small task in a premechanical age. Then they were marched into battle, carefully aligned, and commanded to fire volleys with weapons that could barely hit a barn door at a hundred paces. With luck, practice, and immense discipline, they could do more damage than they suffered from the enemy. At the end of the battle, the corpses were hurriedly counted and buried in mass graves. Most of the wounded soon followed, as infection painfully achieved what the day of battle had failed to accomplish. Indeed, germs were almost always more successful in killing soldiers than bullets. The Russo-Japanese War of 1904-5 was the first major war in which the soldiers killed in battle outnumbered those who perished of disease.

From such wars, the rest of the population was largely exempt, unless they lived on the line of march, close to the battlefield, or in a fortified city under siege. Their fate in such circumstances might be appalling, since soldiers released from discipline by defeat or victory promptly degenerated into ruthless, murderous freebooters. Indeed, the ruthless enforcement of discipline was the best guarantee that a civilian would survive a passing army. Eighteenth-century commanders did their best to provide sufficient food and supervised camps for their field armies less for the sake of the local population than to limit the crippling effects of desertion. Given the chance to flee the likely alternatives of flogging or death, soldiers made themselves scarce. Marching an army through a forest or into a large city entailed such a high risk of it melting away that Prussia's Frederick the Great forbade his generals to do so.

The era of small, brutally disciplined armies ended soon after the French Revolution of 1789. Suddenly radical notions of popular sovereignty, national identity, and individual rights and responsibility, hitherto limited to self-absorbed intellectuals, became the official doctrine of Europe's most advanced and influential country. People of the new French republic took up arms as proud citizens, not as half-starved scum, desperate for dinner. True, the ragged levies of the early French revolution were initially no match for the traditional armies sent by Europe's reigning monarchs, but once stiffened by the troops and artillery of what had been Europe's best army, and commanded by generals chosen for aptitude, not bloodlines, the tables turned. Once successful, France's citizen army became a model that every European power, except Great Britain, had to embrace. The Napoleonic wars, with as many as a million men marching and dying across Europe, forced almost every country with a claim to modernity to create some form of mass citizen army.

Even regimes like Prussia and Russia that despised the claims of popular sovereignty learned that they could match and defeat Napoleon only if they based their armed forces on some form of universal military service by their country's young men. The postrevolutionary ideology of nationalism became the fuel that persuaded young Prussians, Frenchmen, Danes, Austrians, Swiss, Wurttembergers, Italians, Swedes and, much later, Russians, Japanese, Romanians, and even Turks that several years of their lives had to be sacrificed to the hardships and discipline of military service. Success against Denmark, Austria, and finally France allowed the army of the new German Empire to set the European standard: two years of full-time training and front-line service, followed by a several years of potential call-up to first-line divisions. In their later years, men were subject to call-up to reserve formations of lower quality and readiness. Shrinking demographically in the early twentieth century, but desperate to match the strength of its dangerous

German neighbours, France by 1914 had extended its period of full-time service to three years. Once their active service was complete, male citizens transferred to a "reserve," and waited, with varying degrees of enthusiasm, for the call to mobilize for war.

Because the size of the annual "class" of conscripts was anxiously scrutinized by its army's general staff – and by nosy neighbours – nineteenth-century regimes had powerful incentives to improve the health, welfare, and education of the population. European progress towards universal elementary education, improved housing, safe drinking water, and other public welfare measures owed little to socialist oratory and much to military authorities complaining about recruits too malnourished, debilitated, or ignorant to become useful soldiers. No trade unionist ever preached as powerfully against the evils of unsafe and unhealthy factories, or the fetid industrial slums growing up around them, as did generals facing a shortfall of cannon fodder for the next war. The spread of public education guaranteed soldiers who could read, write, and count and who had been thoroughly imbued with a patriotic version of their national history.

Mass armies were possible only because industrial methods allowed military conscripts to be cheaply fed, housed, clothed, and equipped. As unskilled young men, conscripts were paid a pittance, soon squandered on gambling, cheap wine, cigarettes, prostitutes, and other comforts of a garrison town. The rituals of military service underlined a citizen's devotion to a duty-demanding, maternally nourishing state. Only after his compulsory military service was a young man expected to marry, build a career, and acquire serious family and economic responsibilities. Once his full-time duty to the state was satisfied, a man assumed his private duty as *paterfamilias* and breadwinner, although his civilian life might be interrupted at any time by the call to duty.

Since it stripped young and not-so-young men from every kind of employment, mobilization imposed huge costs and disruption on entire countries. War in the planting or harvest season could threaten starvation. Yet to be caught demobilized by a better-organized neighbour guaranteed defeat. If a soldier-breadwinner's absence led to domestic crisis, local authorities were prepared to meet the immediate needs of soldiers' families. Exemptions for reservists working in strategic industries like railways or munitions factories preserved economic essentials. Above all, experience seemed to suggest, any modern war waged by efficient professionals would be short. Prussia had taken only weeks to crush Denmark in 1864, the Hapsburg Empire in 1866, and France in 1870. The sole nineteenth-century exception, the four-year Civil War in the United States, had been waged, Prussia's great nineteenth-century strategist Helmut von Moltke explained, by armed bands of civilians chasing each other through the wilderness.

Universal conscription and military training was no respecter of individual rights, though the rich and well-born usually found ways to modify the rigours of the system. Some regiments proved more congenial to the better-off than others; and those with connections could meet the need for large numbers of "cadets" for officers' commissions.

Men did not escape their obligations by emigration from their demanding homeland. As Canadian immigration agents discovered to their cost in the years before 1914, some European countries, notably Germany, forcefully discouraged emigration. And distance did not alleviate the duty to serve. In 1914 the French and Belgian consulates expected their reservists to report for orders and passage homeward; by early August, patriotic Germans and Austrians began slipping discreetly over the Canadian border to the neutral United States to find passage home. In Winnipeg, Bishop Nicholas Budka, the city's Ruthenian Catholic prelate, earned his Hapsburg-paid salary by reminding his flock of their military obligations to the Austro-Hungarian Empire. Swiftly reminded in turn of his local allegiances, the bishop changed his message, but the principle remained.

Women, naturally, were not conscripted. The thought was almost literally unthinkable. Women were not really citizens, either, and if the issue of their rights was ultimately raised, their immunity from conscription was an obvious and irrefutable answer. Women's role in national defence was as wives and mothers. If they benefited from public education, their literacy and patriotic indoctrination would persuade them to breed and raise their sons to be loyal defenders of the Mother- or Fatherland. A sentimental age recognized that women suffered from battlefield casualties almost as much as men. A Canadian poet, Wilson Macdonald, mustered the symbols of their sorrow in a verse inspired by the war:

Ah! The battlefield is wider than the cannon's sullen roar
And the women weep o'er battles lost or won,
For the man a cross of honour; but the crepe upon the door
For the girl behind the man behind the gun.[7]

Some women went to war as nursing sisters – famously with Florence Nightingale in 1855 at Scutari and in Canada's case as early as the North-West campaign of 1885, and more formally during the South African War. Like the United States Army but unlike Great Britain, Canada granted commissions to its nursing sisters, claiming that they enjoyed the appropriate social status.[8] It also presumed, as did most of the nursing profession, that sisters would be single women and, unlike men, would not have dependants, although in practice a few married and continued to serve. While it is conceivable that some nursing sisters may have qualified for allowances to support a widowed mother, it was inconceivable in 1914-18 that any could claim a dependent husband.

Reservists in Canada

On 6 August, the same day that Hughes announced a Canadian contingent, the Allan Line steamer *Victorian* cleared Montreal harbour with French and British reservists wealthy enough to arrange their own homeward passage. Among them was the French aviator the Comte de Lesseps and his wife, a daughter of railway magnate Sir William Mackenzie. De Lesseps announced he was eager to volunteer as a pilot in France's aviation service. As Consul Raynauld confidently proclaimed: "In present circumstances, where the very existence of the homeland is at stake, there is no doubt that each Frenchman will do his duty."[9] Belgium's Clarence de Sola also assured the press that his tiny country would put up a valiant and effective resistance, and called on reservists to come forward. By 21 August Raynauld had dispatched 1,800 French soldiers through Montreal.[10] De Sola loaded 800 Belgians on the Allan Line's *Ionian*, 308 of them Montrealers and most of the rest from the United States. Russia, the earliest Allied belligerent, characteristically made no effort to collect its reservists until November 1914, and even then it soon had second thoughts.[11]

One country in Europe had conspicuously and consistently ignored the European military model. Even in the Napoleonic era, Great Britain had rejected European-style conscription as a typically "foreign" imposition on freedom. More substantively, conscription was an extravagance for a country whose real bulwark was the Royal Navy. Possessing the world's most powerful fleet allowed Britain to launch an army on whatever maritime shore it chose, rather than joining massive and costly land battles. Throughout most of the nineteenth century, the British Army remained an eighteenth-century force of ill-paid long-service volunteers under aristocratic officers, financially dependent on Parliament but owing its true allegiance to the sovereign. Not all Britons approved. For all its loyalty and success in remote imperial wars, the British Army's poor performance in the Crimean War inspired the Victorian urge for institutional reform. After 1870, moreover, the evolution of Prussia into an aggressive German empire changed the power balance in Europe. Even more alarming was Germany's transformation under Kaiser Wilhelm II from Britain's historical ally into a menacing industrial and imperial rival.

In 1868 Edward Cardwell, the colonial secretary who had forced British North America to confederate, became Great Britain's secretary of state for war. For 200 years, the British Army had recruited its soldiers from men willing to sign away the rest of their lives for a bed in a barrack room and a pound of beef, a pound of bread, and a shilling a day. The rise of Prussia and fears of involvement in a European war gave Cardwell the backing for long-overdue reform. To the dismay of conservatives, he abolished recruiting bounties and the sale of officers' commissions and promotions. In 1870 Parliament passed the Short Service Act. Henceforth, a recruit signed on for a "short-service" engagement of twelve years, six of them "with the colours" and the rest with his regiment's "reserve." For the first time, the British began to build a trained cadre of reservists to expand the army if it engaged in a serious war. In return for a small monthly allowance, former soldiers agreed to return to service in the event of mobilization.[12] Once British employers and communities accepted that regular service helped transform young men into steady, responsible, and reasonably sober workers, unlike the illiterate, drunken "old sweats" of the old army, reservists could marry, apply army-learned skills, make their way in civilian life, and even emigrate. In the pre-1914 years, thousands of British army and navy reservists came to Canada as part of a tide of immigration from the British Isles. Some transferred to Canada's Permanent Force, especially after it was expanded in 1906 to take over the defences of Halifax and Esquimalt from the British.

In 1914 Britain's army remained small, recruited from volunteers, and scattered around the world in imperial garrisons. Ideally, half its units were located in Britain itself and available for an expeditionary force, but only in remote garrisons were units kept close to full strength. Most units required hundreds of reservists before they could take the field. Even then, 40 million British could mobilize a field army of only six or seven divisions, compared to the fifty to sixty available to major European powers. A furious prewar campaign for "National Service," led by the venerable field marshal Lord Roberts, had changed many British minds about conscription, although it was not instituted until 1916.[13] The British example was followed elsewhere in the Empire. Antipodean fears of the "Yellow Peril" led Australia and New Zealand into their own elaborate schemes of universal military training. From 1909 to 1914, a Canadian Defence League led by ardent imperialists urged universal military training and a Swiss-style militia for Canada, while the Laurier Liberals extended compulsory high school cadet corps to every province but Saskatchewan.[14]

Historically, Britain had made little provision for its soldiers to marry and none at all for its sailors. "In the Navy," reported James Gildea, "they know of no such useless appendage or encumbrance as a sailor's wife."[15] The reason was simple: by recruiting its soldiers and sailors from rural and urban slums and paying them a pittance, the British had created an army of such foul-mouthed, violent, drunken wretches that few self-respecting women would even consider marrying them.

Since a soldier who wanted a bride existed in virtual lifetime serfdom to his colonel, he required his colonel's approval to marry. In Wellington's (or Marlborough's) army, a wife who married "on the strength" (i.e., with the commanding officer's approval) was entitled to do laundry, mending, cooking, and nursing for her husband and his barrack mates. Her income for these services (done in India by male "dhobies") came from part of the "off-reckonings" deducted from a soldier's meagre pay for his clothing, medical care, and old age. An early barrack regulation, soon hardened into custom, permitted six wives per company of infantry or troop of cavalry, or approximately one wife for fifteen soldiers.[16] When a British battalion was sent overseas, surplus wives and their children were simply turned off and abandoned to the mercy of the Poor Law. Sometimes the abandoned wives were simply selected by lot. Irish regiments were "much married." When one such battalion was cut back to its regulation sixty wives, more than 400 women and their children were marched to Bristol to be returned to their native soil. After the Duke of Wellington's army reached Bordeaux in 1814, the same fate befell the Portuguese and Spanish "war brides" his soldiers had acquired during years of campaigning. The women were left to make their own way home across the Pyrenees.[17] The accompanying wretchedness was well known to authorities, reports Richard Glover, but the official response was to attempt to suppress matrimony: "Marriage is to be discouraged as much as possible. Officers must explain to the men the many miseries that women are exposed to, and by every sort of persuasion they must prevent their marrying if possible."[18]

Were their sisters "on the strength" more fortunate to share the hardships and dangers of campaigning? The domestic duties of soldiers' wives continued in any foreign garrison, and extended during campaigning to recovering and nursing the wounded. Fortress orders at Gibraltar directed the six regiments in garrison each to find six soldiers' wives to nurse the sick and wounded. No training or qualifications were expected.[19] If their husbands died in the field, women usually remarried quickly.[20] De Watteville reports that 300 wives, separated from their husbands in Egypt, found themselves camped on Minorca when news arrived that their husbands had been massacred. They promptly remarried members of the local garrison which, in its turn, was sent to Egypt. Once there, they learned that the massacre had been a rumour but, of the original husbands, only one man took back his wife "to become the laughing stock of his regiment."[21] During the Peninsular War, Mrs. Growell, wife of a sergeant in the 47th Foot, lay down under a tree and gave birth to twins. Several soldiers shared their coats with her but two days later, when the army marched, Mrs. Growell tramped with them, bearing her babies in her arms. Accounts of the war include a description of a wife watching without a murmur while her husband suffered 200 lashes. After helping him put on his shirt and coat, she picked up her man's musket and pack, shouldered his load, and trudged off beside him when the battalion resumed its march.[22]

After 1798, when military barracks began to be built in Britain, a married soldier usually hung a sheet or blankets across a corner of his barrack room to hide the two single cots to which he and his wife were entitled. Their children joined them there, sharing the atmosphere of shouting, swearing, fighting and roughhousing customary in a room full of soldiers. Daughters shared the slight shelter; sons were free to occupy any empty bed in the barrack room. Such customs dropped slowly into abeyance in Queen Victoria's reforming times. As with other military reforms, the Crimean War of 1854-5 proved a turning point. Never again would British soldiers' wives accompany their husbands to the battlefield. Florence Nightingale displaced them from their nursing role by insisting that soldiers in hospital deserved trained, disciplined, and professional nursing. Instead of sharing their family lives with a barrack room, regiments were ordered to bunk wives and children together in one or more rooms. After such communal family life proved a substantial source of friction, separate married quarters finally became a feature of barrack construction. In London, officers of the Brigade of Guards had raised enough money in 1852 to build a block of flats for fifty-four of their married soldiers. The War Office decided that officers should not be landlords and bought the building at less than the officers had paid for it.[23] Revelations of soldiers' living conditions, publicized during the Crimean War, accelerated construction of separate married quarters. However, complaints of overcrowding, quarrelling, drunkenness, and infidelity continued. A much larger reform was needed.

It came, quite incidentally, with Sir Edward Cardwell's short-service reforms. After 1870 the much younger private soldiers who filled the ranks seldom married or formed families before transferring to the reserve. Soon, most of the army's wives were married to better-paid and "steadier" noncommissioned or warrant officers.[24] Married quarters, together with a share of rations, fuel, and candles, became part of their compensation for accepting a soldier's low status, hard service, and frequent transfers. If appropriate married quarters were not available or a soldier was separated from his family by his duties, a small monthly "separation allowance" was paid to his wife. In 1914, in an army of about 200,000 regulars, the pay services in Britain's War Office recorded only 1,500 such accounts.[25] Improved pay made it easier to support a wife, even "off the strength."

The British Army served as a model for the Canadian Militia in virtually every aspect of its organization, administration, and operations. The links had even been formalized in 1907 when Canada and other self-governing Dominions agreed that the British would set the standards for tactics, training, weapons, and equipment so that colonial armed forces could easily become interoperable. In the wake of the South African War, British and colonial politicians found such an arrangement completely appropriate. In Canada, it was the natural outcome of half a century of self-conscious imitation of every detail of British military traditions, uniforms, and etiquette, from the gold lace on senior officers' sword belts to the titles chosen by socially ambitious city militia battalions. Wealthy Montrealers had transformed the 5th Royal Scots into the Royal Highlanders or Black Watch, with a huge expenditure on Scottish military dress. Soon after, the city's lacklustre 1st Prince of Wales Regiment blossomed into the Canadian Grenadier Guards after another huge investment in British uniforms largely financed by mining millionaire Col. John Wallace Carson. In 1914, Lt.-Col. Arthur Currie of Victoria's newly created 50th Gordon Highlanders of Canada ordered $10,000 worth of kilts, sporrans, and whatever else men needed to resemble their British models from a Glasgow firm that advertised in Canada's quarterly Militia List.[26]

Canada's tiny Permanent Force of about 4,000 men in 1914 adopted regulations and financial provisions for its married members similar to the British Army's. Officers' rates of pay were somewhat lower than in the British service, but other ranks fared better in a country with significantly higher living costs than Great Britain. All ranks could claim quarters, rations, fuel, light, and medical attention, or allowances in lieu of them, that ranged from $0.75 a day for a private to $2.00 for a lieutenant-colonel. Like the British Army, the Permanent Force reluctantly accepted that some of its soldiers would marry, first requiring them to obtain permission. "Subaltern officers may be permitted to marry by the Militia Council," said the regulations, but only after a commanding officer was satisfied that "the officer's means are such as will enable him to maintain himself and family in a manner befitting his position as an officer."[27] For other ranks, permission was delegated to the applicant's commanding officer, but "such permission will not be given unless a vacancy exists on the married establishment and the C.O. is satisfied that the applicant is financially able to marry and that the woman is a desirable character."[28]

Until 1914 the "married establishment" had been 12 percent of the unit's authorized strength, but that year the rule was changed to allow all warrant officers and sergeants to marry, plus 8 percent of the remainder. The chief benefit of marriage "on the strength" was the right to occupy married quarters – two rooms in barracks for a couple with one child, three rooms with two or three children, and four for four or more children if any above the age of 10 were of different sexes.[29] The bulk of Canada's defenders, however, belonged to the part-time Militia: 40,000 in 1900 compared with 60,000 in 1914.[30] Their marital arrangements were of no interest to the Militia Department, which went no further in its regulations than to direct that "women of loose character should be carefully excluded from the camp; they are often employed as spies."[31]

What provision did the British or Canadians make for families or "next of kin" if a soldier was killed or died on active service? Like other British military institutions, pensions reflected a conviction that the gulf between officers and other ranks was unbridgeable. Officers were gentlemen whose status, even in adversity, must be sustained; soldiers had presumably enlisted for a temporary escape from starvation. An officer who lost an arm, a leg, or an eyeball in the service of his king or queen was entitled to a year's pay as a gratuity, followed by half-pay for the rest of his life. If he had purchased his commission, its sale was one of his retirement assets. A private "so disabled as to be incapable of earning his livelihood" could be offered up to twenty pounds a year. Since their families were expected to look after them, most got far less.[32] In Canada, pensions for militia were a local responsibility, initially provided by donations to the 1812 version of the Patriotic Fund and then, very frugally, from tax revenues. In peacetime, official militia pensions were recommended by the boards of officers appointed to investigate the cause of injury or death. A board report was reviewed by higher officials and politicians. Such a system sufficed for the Rebellions of 1837-8, for the Fenian Raids, and for the intermittent mishaps and illnesses of militia training camps.

Modern Canada faced its first militia casualties in 1866, at the time of the Fenian Raids. Among them was Ensign Malcolm MacEachren of Toronto's 2nd Queen's Own Rifles, shot and left dying at Ridgeway on a hot June morning while the bulk of his comrades fled in panic. Home in Toronto, the newly wed Caroline MacEachren was left a widow. She never remarried, and until she died in Montreal in 1922 her annual pension of $184 was faithfully recorded in the federal government's estimates. So were other Fenian Raid pensions, including that of her husband's friend and fellow ensign William Fahey, whose disability earned him $200 a year. Even in 1866 these were modest amounts. In 1890 the annual Fenian Raid pension burden on Canada was $3,086.[33]

In 1885, faced with claims from casualties from the North-West campaign against Louis Riel and his Métis and First Nations allies, the federal government reviewed pension arrangements inherited from the War of 1812. Ottawa made a few concessions to changing times and Victorian values. Disabled officers and officers' widows received a full year's pay for their suffering plus a pension based on the full pay of their rank, ranging from $2.80 a day for a lieutenant to $1,200 a year for a lieutenant-colonel. Ordinary soldiers killed in action earned their widows more than those whose husbands had died of disease. A wholly disabled private who needed an attendant could be pensioned at $0.45 to $0.60 a day, or at $0.30 to $0.55 if he could manage for himself.[34] Since an unskilled labourer required $1 a day to support himself and his family, a disabled veteran needed kindly relatives, generous friends, and very abstemious habits to survive. Advised that prior earnings had justified a higher pension for a disabled ex-sergeant, a Conservative back-bencher warned that such a principle would land the government in no end of confusion.[35] In 1890 a crippled veteran vented his frustration from the galleries of the House of Commons. He acted in vain.[36]

Fifteen years before the British, Ottawa broke with the tradition of leaving the widows of ordinary soldiers to a Royal Patriotic Fund raised from charitable do-nations. Widows of Permanent Force soldiers who died during the 1885 North-West campaign were granted pensions: half the late husband's pay of $0.40 a day if he was killed in action, and three-eighths if he died of disease. Maria Neely's hus-band, Pte. George Neely of the Infantry School Corps, died during the campaign. When a Toronto Liberal MP investigated why she had not received a pension, To-ronto's police chief discreetly explained to the minister of militia that both Mrs. Neely and her husband, an ex-policemen, had been bad characters, and some of their four children had been born out of wedlock. Widows' pensions in Canada, explained the minister, were not a right; they depended on both financial need and good behaviour.[37] Why, Sir Richard Cartwright asked, did Lieut. Swinford's father get a pension of $750 a year while Capt. Brown's widowed mother got only $250? Although he and fellow MPs suspected political influence, the minister of militia belatedly argued that Mrs. Brown had been left a Manitoba farm by her late husband; Swinford could leave his parents nothing.[38] A widow's pension, in short, was state charity.

Pensions also depended on rank, age, and continued widowhood. After Lt.-Col. A.T.H. Williams, an MP commanding the Midland Battalion, died (either of a broken heart because General Middleton was rude to him or, more prosaically, from typhoid fever), Parliament voted Mrs. Williams a pension of $1,200.[39] Capt. John French died leading the assault on Batoche. His widow, Mary, received $2,397 as a gratuity and a pension of $342 for herself and $102.95 for each of her four children. When Mary French remarried in 1887, she lost her pension, but her sons received theirs until they were eighteen and her daughter until she was twenty-one. Capt. John Morton left his wife Anne a pension of $500 a year and a $1,000 gratuity. Each of their three children got a $333 gratuity and $100 a year. The Williamses, Mortons, and Frenches fared better than Mary Ryan, whose husband had died of pleurisy just after the 1885 campaign. After his unheroic death, Gun-ner John F. Ryan could leave his wife a pension of only $68.49, plus $14.69 for their infant daughter.[40] If Ryan had died in battle, her pension might have reached $106.36 per year. Théo Marois of St-Sauveur died in much the same way, and his widow, Octavie, also collected $68.49. However, pensions reflected family size: the five Marois children added $70.19 a year to the family income until they grew up.

Until the South African War, 1899-1902, the British left soldiers' widows to the generosity of private patriotic charities, frequently inspired by the current imperial campaign.[41] The extent and cost of the war in South Africa persuaded the British government that it would have to intervene, but for regimentally approved wives only. State-funded pensions for other dependants or for wives married "off the strength" remained unthinkable. Since many of its Permanent Force soldiers had transferred from the British Army, Ottawa decided to follow the British example and pay a "separation allowance" to soldiers frequently absent from home for months in their role of training the Militia. Two might live cheaper than one, but not if they lived under separate roofs.

Maternalism and War

After two centuries of brutal indifference to the lives of soldiers and their families, what had changed? Why had conditions that were seemingly invisible for generations suddenly been described in painful detail and considered intolerable? What made the Victorian era synonymous with the reform of institutions that previous generations had taken for granted? It would be attractive to associate reform with the queen whose name described the years between 1837 and 1900, and Victoria had, no doubt, supported modest reforms in her youth. In practice, she lacked the real power either to effect change or to prevent it, and her instincts grew steadily more conservative. "Women's Rights" she notoriously described as a "mad wicked folly," which she was most anxious to check. "God created men and women different," she insisted, "then let them remain, each in their own position."[42]

Most women in Victorian England or Canada would not necessarily have differed with Her Majesty. Even feminists divided on whether women were the equals of men, or whether men and women were so different that they properly occupied different spheres. What was new, thanks to the discoveries of conventional science and approved literature, was the importance of women's maternal role in shaping the nation and its people. For women to seek rights for their own selfish benefit might indeed be as mad and wicked as Queen Victoria believed, but the essence of maternalism was selflessness; to claim authority for the protection of the family and for the safety and well-being of the next nation-forming generation might well be women's divinely ordained duty and responsibility, and their claim to authority. Men might be endowed with superior physical strength and with the habit of authority, but one need only see them return from a tavern on pay night to know how easily their wisdom and selflessness could be impaired.

Mothering had plenty of scope for improvement in Canada in 1914. In 1900, Cynthia Comacchio claims, one baby in five died before it was two, and childbirth remained highly hazardous to mother and baby. When medical knowledge linked these deaths to slums, malnutrition, and filth, the losses seemed tragic, wasteful, and unnecessary. A radical analysis might have blamed chronic poverty, slum landlords, and ruthless exploitation of workers, but maternal feminism had few links with socialism. Radical claims that infant mortality was the fault of industrial capitalism or that the state must interfere fell generally on deaf ears. Like Americans, Canadians were reluctant to find poverty in their midst. Instead, social reformers claimed, working people only behaved as though they were poor. If they ignored hygiene, proper nutrition, and other requirements of a healthy lifestyle, and endured the wholly preventable tragedies that ensued, the fault was theirs and the solution lay in their own transformation, preferably through education and good example.[43]

While the British and Americans pioneered an assault on infant mortality during the opening years of the twentieth century, Canadians had the benefit of their leadership. In 1910 Dr. Helen MacMurchy published the first of a series of studies for the government of Ontario, in which 6,932 of the 52,629 babies born in 1909 were dead within twelve months. In Toronto the death rate was 230 per thousand live births. Montrealers were told that infant mortality was worse in their city than in Calcutta. MacMurchy's conclusions were blunt: what killed babies was not infantile cholera or "summer complaint," but ignorance, poverty, and inadequate medical attention.[44] A year later, Dr. C.A. Hodgetts insisted that epidemic diarrhea, a major baby killer, was the result of maternal neglect, unclean food storage, and the "industrial occupation of mothers."[45] Dr. MacMurchy was more blunt: "When the mother works, the baby dies."[46] Neglect and ignorance, claimed the *Canadian Public Health Journal* in 1915, were "more important than poverty as causative factors in the cause of infant illness and death." Only maternal care really mattered: "Intelligent motherhood alone can give to the infant that which neither wealth nor state nor yet science can offer, with equal benefit to mother and child."[47]

Maternalists could not place all the blame on working-class mothers. Science in the period was directed primarily at examining infant feeding, and particularly the effects of unsafe cows' milk. Since Robert Koch's 1882 discovery of the tubercle bacillus, science had identified milk as a carrier of typhoid, scarlet fever, and diphtheria. By 1910 Canadian medical practice linked tuberculosis and diarrhea to impure milk. Gouttes de lait, founded in France in the 1880s as a source of safe milk for children, reached Montreal in the 1900s. Pressed by Liberal W.K. McNaught, Ontario appointed a Milk Commission in 1910 and gave municipalities the power to license and regulate milk sales – according to their own standards of purity. Ontario passed a Dairy Standards Act in 1917 but delayed enforcement for over a year in the face of farm protests.[48]

Though some cities and some charities did their best to make safe, affordable milk available, the obligation rested on mothers to find it and feed it to their children. Equally, communities and charities provided growing numbers of clinics to collect data and dispense advice, but mothers were expected to find the time and energy to benefit from them. Experts insisted that only visiting nurses, who took their teaching and record keeping directly to mothers and children in their homes, made a real difference to infant mortality, but the price was intrusion on the family's private life and the appalling risk that the community would assume responsibility for child rearing. That was a breach with tradition that only the most ardent maternalist was yet willing to contemplate. As Comacchio concluded,

> Child welfare advocates never interpreted the rhetoric of "child as national asset" to mean that the state was to have direct responsibility for the health of children. Rather, it meant that there was a new obligation to make mothers more responsible to the state. If the state was obliged to act, always on medical advice, all were reminded that "whatever we do we must not be too ready to relieve [mothers] of their responsibility."[49]

War in 1914 gave added urgency to the prewar struggle to reduce infant mortality. The mounting casualty tolls – a million men in the first year of the war – made children military as well as civil assets. France's military weakness during and after the war was directly attributed to its lagging birth rate. Canada, too, needed people to fill its vast spaces and provide markets for its industries and railways. The tens of thousands of women who became soldiers' wives between 1914 and 1918 became a publicly salaried, privately managed demonstration project for the maternalist cause.

Maternal feminism was shrewdly conservative. It laid no claim to identity or even equality with the men who had hitherto exercised all power. Instead, its advocates embraced the selfless purity and innocence that men had long and cheerfully conceded to the "weaker sex," and then exploited it to achieve an alliance with those who cared as deeply as any good woman for the welfare of society. As in the sport of jujitsu, the heavy burden of an opponent's hypocrisy could be used to overturn his self-importance and harness him to maternalist goals, from child welfare to the prohibition of saloons.

For many women in the early twentieth century, one uniting cause had been peace. The Hague Conventions banned cruel new weapons like poison gas, restricted submarines, and required humane treatment for the sick, wounded, and prisoners. They had been followed by the establishment of the International Court of Justice at the Hague. The dream that weapons would be burned or scrapped and war appropriations be diverted to science, education, commerce, and the relief of suffering was exploded in 1914. With a few resolute exceptions such as Flora Denison, Canadian feminists accepted that the German kaiser was an abominable villain who had barred the road to perfect peace. As victims of his aggression, Belgium, France, and Britain had to fight. As for the Russian czar, had he not, in his mystic Orthodox way, been the author and inspiration of the Hague Conventions? Fighting "the monstrous Moloch called militarism" might be a task for men, wrote Mrs. Arthur Murphy, but women must give their all to the struggle so that "brute strength being no longer the supreme arbiter, women may cease to suffer from the disability of a lesser muscular development and so may attain to their due economic, legal and political status as human beings of the mother sex."[50]

Better known to contemporaries as "Janey Canuck" and to posterity as Emily Murphy, the Alberta author was one of a dozen prominent women invited by the Toronto magazine *Everywoman's World* to comment on the war for its April 1915 issue. Some women refused: Mrs. A.E. Gooderham, head of the Toronto IODE, was too busy to compose her thoughts; so was Mrs. Willoughby Cummings of the Toronto Women's Patriotic League. Perhaps Helen Merrill, honorary general secretary of the United Empire Loyalists of Canada, spoke for them when she urged the desirability of scout and cadet training for boys and girls, even if girls "form no more menacing corps than Broom Brigades."[51] Lucy Maud Montgomery, creator of Anne of Green Gables, was an early supporter of the war, bravely insisting from the outset that there were things even more horrible than war: "Moral degradation, low ideals, sordid devotion to money-getting, are worse evils than war, and history shows us that these evils invariably overtake a nation which is a long time at peace."[52] She also doubted that the war would affect the interests of women, though she hoped that "it will in some measure open the eyes of humanity to the truth that the women who bear and train the nation's sons should have some voice in the political issues that may send those sons to die on battlefields." In contrast, the veteran British feminist Millicent Fawcett insisted that women were challenged to help in

an almost infinite variety of ways by preventing waste. Waste of the spirit of helpfulness by letting it run into the wrong channels; waste of precious lives, the lives of soldiers, lives of young girls, lives of mothers, lives of infants. We can help to prevent waste of health through alcoholism and immorality, and through diseases which follow poverty and semi-starvation. We can check waste of charitable impulse, which when wrongly directed, curtails the volume of employment at the very moment when there is so much necessity for extending it. As housekeepers and managers we can set our face against waste of food in all its many ramifications.[53]

Defeating Poverty

Feminists, family advocates, and reformers in 1914 were the heirs of dramatic re-versals in thinking about poverty, need, family welfare, and the nature of women. The early nineteenth century had seen a revolution in social welfare on both sides of the Atlantic. The first phase in the revolution, starting in the 1790s, had been systematic "outdoor relief," tax-funded income supplements based on rural wages and the cost of bread sometimes described as the Speenhamland system.[54] By the 1830s, conventional wisdom claimed that such payments had reduced the lower classes across rural England to pauperism. The blame was applied to land owners who taxed everyone to subsidize their own labour costs. The poor, of course, could be denounced for accepting "the dole" instead of rising in violent revolt or starv-ing in quiet dignity. Certainly the remedy would come at their expense.

The second part of the revolution, poor law reform, began in England in the 1830s with the abolition of outdoor relief and its replacement by the workhouse and the principle of "lesser eligibility."[55] In other words, anyone who worked must be better off than anyone who was paid relief. Rather the destitute poor being paid cash, they were institutionalized in grim establishments called workhouses, care-fully designed to be so miserable that no one who worked for wages would ever envy the inmates. Workhouse food was meagre and tasteless, the clothing shabby and coarse, the work harsh and unremitting. Beds were hard and so narrow that inmates often fell on the floor during the night. Families were split and the sexes carefully segregated. The workhouse, or the "poorhouse," spread to North America, though impoverished frontier counties in Canada and the United States usually invested only in a common jail to accommodate criminals, the destitute, and the insane. Eventually, more prosperous communities could boast of hospitals, luna-tic asylums, poorhouses, orphanages, and "homes for friendless women." An insti-tution was the Victorian answer for the unfortunate.

But the answers of one era often become problems for the next. The insane in asylums seldom improved and the sick in hospital, like the orphans in orphan-ages, usually died. Once institutionalized in poorhouses, few inmates ever gradu-ated back to self-sufficiency. Even in efficiently managed orphanages, children perished in shocking numbers. Those who survived were dogged by their back-ground. Once reforming feminists examined social issues with a fresh eye, they reverted to the solution that had been forgotten: paying people enough to live. Women saw a problem that men usually took for granted. Wages, already in-adequate to house, clothe, feed, and warm a family, were often squandered on such manly vices as beer, tobacco, and gambling, not to mention more colourful sins. Even an occasional woman was known to drink and gamble, and either gen-der might fail to be a good manager.

However, with supervision and instruction, and the power of her maternal instinct, a woman might be trained to become a better manager provided she had the means. Helpful visiting was the goal of the Charity Organization Society, begun in Britain in the 1870s and soon spread to the United States. COS advocates insisted that good advice from kindly middle-class visitors, plus rigorous control of generosity, could help the poor to rebuild satisfactory lives.[56] Secure in her own home, free to apply her intellect and instincts under the oversight of wiser sisters, a mother would provide the ideal environment for her children and the nation's future citizens. In the years before the 1914-18 war, this became the family policy of most Canadian feminists, whether they sought votes for women or simply the respectable influence of Canada's "Parliament of Women," the National Council of the Women of Canada.

In Winnipeg, as Veronica Strong-Boag has pointed out, the city's Mothers' Association proved the point when they found the money to pay a woman to "stay at home and look after her children." The experiment ended when the woman found a husband, but Winnipeg's Associated Charities contributed money to provide income subsidies for other impoverished mothers. In 1915 the city's new Social Workers' Club examined the state of 124 widows being helped by the Associated Charities and published a glowing report called "State Salaries for Mothers."[57] Manitoba's new, reform-minded Norris government, elected by women's votes in 1916, embraced a Mothers Allowances Bill in its first session as a reward for its newest supporters. Other western provinces followed between 1916 and 1920.

After August 1914, the mothers' allowance debate was intertwined with the question of support for soldiers' families. By allocating a separation allowance as part of a soldier's income, the government acknowledged that ordinary military pay scales did not match the "family wage" needed for a man to support his wife and children: even the allowance provided was sufficient only to maintain a wife, without any provision for children. Based on the maternalist claim that, given adequate income, mothers were the ideal people to raise soldiers' children, particularly if they could benefit from guidance from appropriately selected and trained female volunteers, supplemental support was seen to be necessary.[58] In 1914, this program still seemed better managed by a private charity, exercising discipline and discretion, than by a government compelled to treat the deserving and the undeserving alike.[59] The result was the Canadian Patriotic Fund.

By no accident, the educated middle-class women who defined and guided maternal feminism soon devised yet another career opportunity to add to teaching and nursing. Initially as volunteers, and soon as trained social workers, women provided low-cost and instinctually qualified supervisors for the mothers of the poor. If, as a 1921 Ontario report suggested, "the mother is regarded as an applicant for employment as a guardian of future citizens of the state," the social worker would be her supervisor and disciplinarian.[60] The Canadian Patriotic Fund would eventually provide both mothers and volunteers with plenty of experience in working out a new (or revised) experience with a form of "outdoor relief" plus advice.

The "Voluntarist" Urge

In Montreal, Toronto, Winnipeg, and wherever reservists gathered to re-enlist, families had little public role. The pain of parting was a private emotion, ill-fitted to the public mood of patriotic defiance and romantic valour. For soldiers' wives, the pain of separation was all the greater once they realized that, without their bread-winner, their abandoned families faced destitution. The social institutions that underpinned conscription in European countries simply did not exist in Canada. The plight of reservists' families was soon on many minds in Montreal and across Canada. A dockside reporter dutifully reported to *La Presse* that he had been over-come by "the sobs of a mother and her children who saw the dearest being in their lives depart."[61] In Montreal, Consul Raynauld announced to reservists that he had authority to pay mothers $0.25 a day, plus $0.10 per child, too little even to cover their rent; de Sola confessed that he could distribute to Belgian families only what he received in charity.[62] Without private means, significant savings or public char-ity, the families of French and Belgian reservists faced hunger and eviction.

By 7 August, Raynauld had created a Comité de Secours. Montreal's new mayor, Médéric Martin, the wealthy Liberal senator Raoul Dandurand, Dr. Emmanuel-Persillier Lachapelle, dean of the Laval medical faculty, and Trefflé Berthiaume, publisher of *La Presse*, joined other pillars of the local French community.[63] De Sola followed suit, with Montreal's best-known Belgian, veteran labour leader Gustave Francq, as president of his committee. Soon the French and Belgians pooled their resources. On 10 August, Paul Brisset des Nos, president of l'Union Nationale Française, laid out the challenge to a public meeting at the Monu-ment National: "It is necessary that our fellow countrymen who leave Canada to fulfill their duty as soldiers leave without anxiety about their families; that they feel certain that those they leave amongst us will be surrounded by our deepest concern."[64] By nightfall the new Franco-Belgian Committee could report an of-fice in the former *Le Devoir* offices, $9,000 in pledges, and a scheme to sell silk flags printed with national emblems. Mme Brisset des Nos had formed a cloth-ing committee to sew for families "dans la plus grande indigence."[65] To much applause, Mayor Martin proclaimed that city employees summoned to the colours would continue to receive their municipal salaries. Other major employers later imitated this example.

Across Canada, the departure of French and Belgian reservists and the predicament of their families became a painful local by-product of the distant European war, even before the British ultimatum expired on 4 August. In Cape Breton, Northern Ontario, Alberta, and British Columbia, French miners remembered their duty as reservists. In turn, the families of French and Belgian reservists inspired local civic action. Outside Montreal, the larger and emotionally more congenial problems of British reservists soon exercised more influence, but Allied reservists were not forgotten. In Vancouver, Kingston, and Saint John, New Brunswick, mayors took the lead in summoning influential citizens to resolve an obvious social problem. Elsewhere local government was outpaced by local women's organizations. In Edmonton and Victoria, the young Imperial Order Daughters of the Empire (IODE) quickly mobilized its chapters to visit reservists' families and minister to their needs.[66] While accustomed to helping young mothers with layettes and baby furniture, visitors soon reported that the real need was money and the need would be large. In Winnipeg, where business leaders tended to direct the affairs of their fast-growing city, the executive of the Industrial Bureau met on 10 August and directed their paid officials to divide the city into a hundred districts and locate soldiers' relatives and dependants, as well as victims of war-related unemployment and distress. There would be no support, the Bureau declared, without "personal investigation."[67]

As of 4 August, thousands of British ex-soldiers and sailors around the world faced the obligation to report to their naval or regimental depot in Britain. A British officer had been stationed in Ottawa to pay Canadian-based reservists their pensions; he had records of 3,232 British ex-soldiers. They were ordered to report to a special camp at Lévis, opposite the Citadel in Quebec City, where transport to England would be arranged. By the end of August, 2,006 had embarked for England. The 153 British reservists in the Canadian Permanent Force were exempted, and 106 others eventually sailed with the First Contingent of the Canadian Expeditionary Force. Trained British veterans were worth their weight in gold to the Canadian contingent Col. Sam Hughes was forming at Valcartier. Since the fighting might well be over before any official Canadian contingent saw action, a Montreal millionaire, Hamilton Gaunt, proposed to form a Canadian battalion of British reservists and former soldiers under the name of the governor general's daughter: Princess Patricia's Canadian Light Infantry. It was ready by 28 August, though the War Office commanded that it disembark and accompany the main Canadian contingent.[68]

Separation Allowance

In many ways the British Army was dramatically better prepared for war in 1914 than anyone who had known it during the South African War might have expected. As secretary of state for war in a cost-cutting Liberal government, Sir Richard Haldane's prewar reforms had helped strip away costly traditions to create a highly trained, well-equipped professional army that survived months of brutal fighting and savage losses from Mons to Ypres. However, in Britain as in Europe, little thought had been given to soldiers' families. On 10 August 1914 Britain's Liberal prime minister, Herbert Asquith, declared that each British soldier, married with or without his commanding officers' permission, would be able to count on a weekly separation allowance of at least fifteen shillings for his family, graded only by rank.[69] Even when the payment was interpreted to include "unmarried wives" and the archbishop of Canterbury rose in indignant horror, Asquith robustly stuck by his original commitment.[70]

The results of his promise were initially chaotic. By the end of August, the same small office that had handled the monthly claims of 1,500 separated wives faced at least 250,000 such files once a week. As the British Army grew to 2.3 million soldiers at the end of 1915, the paper burden exploded. How could a soldier's claims to dependants even be collected from battalions fighting for their lives against an advancing German army, much less be verified in countless cities, towns, and villages? War Office officials turned to the network of military charities fostered in the Victorian era of self-help, notably the Soldiers' and Sailors' Families Association, an agency established after the Boer War as a support for military families. However, even if the SSFA had possessed the qualified staff to conduct door-to-door visits, it had little or no contact with the high-wage industrial and mining regions that had contributed few peacetime recruits to the navy or army but now filled its wartime ranks. Instead, the task had to be left to local government officials, working on their own time or bearing the stigma of Poor Law administrators. Meanwhile, the Royal Navy found itself with no machinery at all to pay separation allowances to the tens of thousands of sailors' wives who, thanks to Asquith's announcement, expected them for the first time in history.[71] The resulting administrative chaos, concealed as discreetly as the British could manage, provided the few Canadians in the know with nothing but cautionary tales.

On mobilization, explained the Imperial Pension Office in Ottawa, a reservist's wife could expect thirteen pence a day plus two pence per child in separation allowance; from his own pay, a private would be obliged to contribute six pence for his wife and a penny per child. A British private's wife and her three children would thus have to live on the equivalent of $17.10 a month.[72] The $1.10 a day per private that Hughes had announced as base pay for Canadian Expeditionary Force soldiers might be half a labourer's wage in Canada, but it was four times more than the approximately $0.25 a day a British private could expect, and he was well off compared to a French private at $0.055 a day or a Russian at $0.01.[73] No soldier in 1914 earned enough to support a wife, much less children or any other dependent relative. In the armies of 1914, conscript or volunteer, a private soldier's salary was hardly more than pocket money.

Summoned back to the colours in the early days of August, reservists faced a conflict between their patriotic duty to defend the nation and their traditional primary role as breadwinners for their families. In a modern age of shared parental responsibilities and double-income families, the role of the lonely breadwinner now seems unfashionable or discounted, but in the typical Canadian family economy of 1914, a father's competence was primarily measured by the quality of support he could offer his family. A marriage could survive many strains, even violence, but non-support was a woman's best grounds for divorce. A son was taught at home, church, and school that his first duty was to his parents, and particularly to his mother and unmarried sisters; after marriage, that duty shifted to his wife and their offspring. What example could a man provide for his children, what virtues could he transmit to the next generation, if he failed in this elementary test? Sadly, in the depression-ridden Canada of 1914, layoffs, short-time working, and other causes beyond their control forced many working men to fail this test. One reason for the crowding at local armouries in the wake of 4 August was men's hope of escaping economic failure by enlisting. Whatever the rate of pay, a man could argue, Canada would not leave his family to starve. Wives who gave their approval to enlist knew that they were possibly sending their husband to his death in return for immediate support for themselves and their offspring. A few men, ill-intentioned or desperate, believed instead that enlistment in the Canadian Expeditionary Force would enable them to desert their families and escape their obligations.

Systematic unemployment statistics were still unknown in Canada in 1914, but contemporary estimates suggested that one worker in six was unemployed and therefore incomeless.[74] A variety of causes, from inflation to overproduction, had helped end the Laurier boom even before Robert L. Borden's Conservatives won power in September 1911. When the two new transcontinental railways finally reached completion, the economic surge that had justified their construction was long since exhausted. Instead of earning enough to retire their huge construction debts, the Grand Trunk and the Canadian Northern faced falling traffic and revenues, plus a new government with close ties to the well-established Canadian

Pacific and a record on the opposition benches of criticizing overexpansion. Thousands of construction workers, inevitably laid off on the completion of construction, found no alternative market for their strength and skills.

A familiar blame game attributed unemployment and its resulting misery to assorted personal failings: drink, idleness, immorality, gambling, and general "feck-lessness." The unemployed were its villains, and their families the victims. Municipal governments, assigned the thankless task of poor relief by provincial governments, looked at shrinking revenues, borrowed a little, and sponsored work projects that paid humiliating wages for often humiliating labour. Local taxpayers, of course, complained about subsidizing idleness or busywork. Optimists claimed that a recovery was around the corner. No one anticipated that it might take the form of a major war. Instead, conventional wisdom insisted that a European war would devastate markets, send credit crashing, and magnify economic problems sufficiently to force all belligerents to sue for peace.

Although they were needy, the wives and children of recruits of the Canadian Expeditionary Force were identified as hapless but patriotic victims of a proper and manly response. It would be a shame if would-be soldiers and dutiful reservists were deterred from offering their lives to the Allied cause because they might also be neglecting the wife and kiddies. The war forced respectable Canadians to share a burden they had solemnly and irrevocably assigned to the men of their species: family support. Of course, once they assumed even a share of the costs, the community also gained a share of another male responsibility: family leadership. Even in their divinely ordained role, mothers could be imperfect. The most maternal of feminists acknowledged that a few of their sex could be irresponsible and false to their trust. Instinctively averse to regulating private matters of personal choice, Sir Robert Borden's government assigned the major role in family policy to a federally chartered private agency, the Canadian Patriotic Fund or CPF. When Parliament met in special session in August 1914, creating the CPF and approving the War Measures Act were the MPs' most significant statutory responsibilities.[75] Understandably oblivious to the possibility that the war would continue for more than four years and strain almost every familiar institution and value, the country's elected representatives asked few questions, did as they were told, and went home to do further patriotic duty.

2
Pay and Allowances

In Ottawa, the advent of a European war delighted no one more than the minister of militia. From late July, Col. Sam Hughes had feared that the British government, led by Liberals, would, in his words, "skunk it." In a moment of despair, he had even commanded that the Union Jack flying over Militia Headquarters be hauled down as a symbol of impending disgrace. When the British ultimatum to Berlin expired on 4 August, Hughes exploded with joy. The day he had sought with an eagerness matched by only the most doctrinaire of Prussian militarists had finally dawned. Finally the railway promoter, newspaper publisher, and amateur soldier was in his element.

A former school teacher, lacrosse champion, marathon runner, and commanding officer of the 45th Victoria Battalion of the volunteer militia, Hughes had been the Conservative MP for Ontario's Victoria County since 1892 and a dedicated militarist all his life. He had forced his way into Canada's first contingent to South Africa in 1899, wangled staff positions, and reported his valiant feats to Cape Town and hometown newspapers until the British, exasperated by his insubordination, sent him home. Sam Hughes lived, breathed and preached every military virtue except obedience. Since Hughes had generally been loyal to his leader during the long Tory years in opposition, Sir Robert Borden reluctantly chose him as minister of militia, the first and perhaps the only devout militarist ever to hold the portfolio.

As minister, Hughes promoted rifle clubs and armouries as leisure centres for Canada's men. Like his older brother, James, he believed in compulsory cadet training for high school boys – and girls too.[1] Despite troubled public revenues, Hughes secured the funds to expand the Militia to 60,000 members. Militia officers laughed when Hughes, an ardent foe of booze, denounced their Permanent Force colleagues as "barroom loafers." They were less pleased, though moralists and temperance enthusiasts cheered, when the new minister banned even beer from militia messes and summer camps. Hughes insisted that all a Canadian needed to be a super soldier was enough range practice with the Canadian-made Ross rifle to hit the target every time. While he was eager to prove the point against any country, including the United States, on 4 August his enemy of preference, Germany, was finally in his sights.[2]

Military spending had never bulked large in Canada's budget. For the first quarter-century after Confederation, Ottawa kept defence costs at or below $1 million a year. This budget was quite sufficient for a country bent on disproving the British thesis that Canada was vulnerable to an American attack. On the contrary, Sir John A. Macdonald had recognized that if Americans felt secure on their northern frontier, Canada would be safe. If Americans felt insecure, Canada would be indefensible. The result was a military establishment capable of controlling threats of disorder, but no threat to anyone, particularly after a few hundred North West Mounted Police had gone west in 1874 to keep the prairie frontier peaceful. Under Laurier, defence spending had risen to suit the new imperial mood in English-speaking Canada and to pay for a degree of operational integration with the British Army, but a prospering Canada barely noticed. In 1914 Ottawa felt so secure that it happily mobilized all the soldiers it could to show itself "Ready, Aye Ready" for Britain's call. Thousands of "Home Service" troops were called out from Militia units to guard ports, railways, and canals from marauding German cruisers and suspected saboteurs, and 25,000 men were summoned to Valcartier to form a Canadian Expeditionary Force (CEF) for "Overseas Service."[3] More than 33,000 volunteers appeared.

Hughes and his prime minister agreed that any Canadian force would be voluntary. Canada's Militia Act provided for conscription and even a "levée en masse" of virtually every able-bodied man in case of emergency, but both were legislative dead letters, particularly for a foreign war. In Montreal on 14 August, Hughes delivered his message: "I call for volunteers – volunteers, mark you. I have insisted that it shall be a purely volunteer contingent. Not a man will be accepted or leave Canada on this service but of his own free will, and, if I know it, not a married man shall go without the consent of his wife and family."[4]

Three days later, the militia's adjutant general, Brig.-Gen. Victor Williams, sent out the instructions to give effect to his minister's wishes: men must be "fit for service in the field," at least 5'3" with a minimum chest measurement of 33 ½ inches, under 45 and over 18, with a preference for Militia men and unmarried men, married men without children and, as a last option, married men with families.[5] Volunteers would have to be paid, of course, and the $1.00 a day Sam Hughes proposed for a private was higher than the $0.75 a militiaman could expect or the $0.50 a day paid during the South African War. He also added field pay, from $0.10 a day for a private up to $4.00 a day for a general. To encourage the example set by the railways and Montreal, federal civil servants who volunteered for the CEF would continue to collect their government salaries.[6] Since a soldier also received free food, free clothing, and free shelter, he would be virtually free to spend his money on personal pleasures. Of course, a soldier could "assign" up to 95 percent of his pay to anyone he chose, from a bank or insurance company to his mother or wife or children. In addition, thanks to Asquith's example, a married soldier felt assured of a separation allowance. After all, Canadians would be "Imperial" troops under the British Army Act; British regulations would apply to them.

What more could the government do? By recognizing the added cost of having a wife, it had already gone far beyond what any private employer would be expected to do. The real expenses of a soldier-as-breadwinner varied enormously with family size, location, and social expectations. Obviously a family with five or seven children needed more money than a childless wife. The government's *Labour Gazette* demonstrated monthly that it cost far more to live in Vancouver or Edmonton than in Toronto or Montreal, and rather less to live in Halifax or Charlottetown. In Britain, Asquith himself had been so troubled by the plight of better-off families whose father had joined the army that he proposed to link separation allowance to pre-enlistment earnings. As we shall see, Borden and Hughes found themselves spared from such anxieties by an ancient institution under new management: the Canadian Patriotic Fund or CPF. Meanwhile, they should have been preoccupied by what few appreciated and even fewer could admit in August 1914: the practical difficulty of adapting the pay arrangements of the peacetime Canadian Militia to a hurriedly improvised Canadian Expeditionary Force.

In 1914 the largely British practices and procedures for paying Canadian soldiers were known to only the minority of the few Canadians involved with the prewar militia and the tiny Permanent Force. During the routine two weeks of annual summer camp, a Militia private enjoyed "rations and quarters" – the traditional camp fare of beef stew and freshly baked bread, a leaky tent, and threadbare army blankets – and earned between $0.50 and $0.75 a day, depending on his length of service and his "efficiency," usually measured by marksmanship. Permanent Force soldiers usually earned less, though they could depend on heated barracks and meals during the winter, at a time when the unskilled labouring men with whom they were commonly compared usually experienced short commons. To attract the skilled tradesmen needed as farriers, shoeing smiths, blacksmiths, saddlers, fitters, wheelers, motor-car drivers, cooks, bakers, and butchers, both the Militia and Permanent Force offered additional "working pay" at rates of $0.50 to $1.00 per day depending on skill and experience.[7]

Until the 1900s, civil servants had administered the Militia's stores and finances. "Departmentalization" – transferring these tasks to uniformed personnel who could serve in the field – began in 1900, largely at the behest of Laurier's reforming militia minister, Sir Fred Borden.[8] That year saw a Canadian Army Medical Corps to care for the sick and wounded and protect the army's health in the field, and an Army Service Corps to provide both supplies of food, fuel, and ammunition and the transport that carried them. In September 1905 male civilian clerks were transferred to a Corps of Military Staff Clerks, composed of noncommissioned officers familiar with regulations and routine. Sixteen months later, a Canadian Army Pay Corps (CAPC) followed, with ten detachments located wherever Permanent Force units were stationed. In August 1914 the entire corps consisted of only fifteen officers.[9]

Peacetime militia units each appointed their own paymaster, often a local bookkeeper or accountant who accepted an honorary commission and the social distinction of an officer's rank in return for a few days spent preparing the regimental pay list at the end of the annual training camp and disbursing the earnings at pay parade. Once the list was signed by the commanding officer, the paymaster collected the necessary cash from an authorized bank and the soldiers willingly formed up for pay parade. Each man approached the pay table, saluted, received his earnings in cash, and departed with another salute. Minus the military trappings, it was more or less what happened on pay day at his mill, mine, or factory. Like most of his working-class contemporaries, a soldier was unlikely to have a bank account or much opportunity to cash a cheque. Payment in actual cash was a big improvement on the company scrip paid by some employers and recognized only at the company store.

When war came in 1914, few militia paymasters could easily abandon their civilian careers; even fewer could bring extensive familiarity with Militia regulations to the camp at Valcartier. Little in their prior experience had required such arcane knowledge. Canada's prewar mobilization plan had proposed that expeditionary force units would recruit, organize, and train in their home districts, where the local Militia paymasters could help out. Meanwhile the CAPC would select, collect, and train unit paymasters and pay sergeants so that when the expeditionary force finally mustered at Petawawa or Quebec City to move overseas, pay staff could rejoin their units, ready to exploit their new expertise in military regulations, forms, and jargon. It was not perfect but no one had a better plan.

However, when Sam Hughes scrapped the mobilization plan on the first day of war, pay arrangements were the last thing on his mind or anyone else's. He directed militia colonels to come directly to Valcartier with their volunteers. He would organize them there. From that moment, Militia Department officials had to struggle to catch up while Hughes and the rest of the country sneered at bureaucratic incompetence. A flood of additional telegrams explained that soldiers were to be enlisted as of 12 August, at Militia rates of active service pay. Local contingents made their way by rail to Valcartier, where, in an atmosphere of high enthusiasm and administrative chaos, thousands of volunteers were formed and re-formed into artillery brigades and batteries, cavalry regiments, field ambulances, wagon trains and, ultimately, seventeen infantry battalions, not to mention other elements of a standard British-style infantry division, plus a motor machine-gun brigade and an aeronautical section with a Burgess-Dunne biplane. In uniform and in full command, Hughes himself promoted, demoted, appointed, and disappointed as he saw fit, struggling to find appropriate volunteers for hundreds of specific appointments among the 33,000 men who crowded into the camp.[10]

On 3 September the cabinet approved Hughes's daily pay scales for the CEF. They were, he suggested, "in most cases the same as those now in force for annual training." By far the largest category, privates (as well as gunners, drivers, and sappers) would earn $1.00 a day plus a field allowance of $0.10; corporals could expect $1.10 and the same $0.10; sergeants would be paid $1.35 and $0.15 for field allowance. Thereafter, scales got more complex, with special rates for pay sergeants and quartermaster-sergeants and orderly room clerks, not to mention the rates of working pay. More senior officers might claim command pay, and a unit staff officer or adjutant earned $0.50 a day in addition to the pay of his rank. In a divisional headquarters, each senior staff position had its own rate, from $20 a day for the general officer commanding to $8 for the deputy assistant director of veterinary services, but only $5 for a deputy assistant director of ordnance services or an assistant provost marshal. The divisional paymaster collected $5 a day, as much as a lieutenant-colonel, though his rank was normally major, and a unit paymaster was paid as a captain. A lieutenant, the lowest officer rank, earned $2 a day, and so did a warrant officer, the highest noncommissioned rank.[11]

On 22 September, the volunteers at Valcartier formally switched from being members of the active Militia to become members of the Canadian Expeditionary Force. Each man's pay was at least slightly changed, and each man needed a fresh dose of documentation. Material considerations had weighed lightly on most of the men who crowded armouries and recruiting centres in the hot August days of 1914. Many volunteers had been unemployed victims of a serious depression. Close to 70 percent were British born, many of them recent arrivals in Canada. Joining the CEF, cynics claimed, guaranteed them a cheap passage home to England and away from signs warning: "No English need apply." Most volunteers, and ideally almost all of them, would have been carefree bachelors, with siblings enough at home to support infirm and indigent parents and other dependent family members. In camp, men with money to spend found clusters of makeshift shops selling food, soft drinks, ice cream, socks, sweaters, and anything a soldier could want, short of liquor. Conscious that wives and mothers were worried about the moral health of lonely sons and husbands, Colonel Hughes kept the vast camp dry, though Quebec City's bars and taverns were close at hand for those permitted to go there on leave.

Col. Hughes's call had not excluded married men. The force badly needed trained and experienced officers and noncommissioned officers. Older, British-trained veterans would stiffen the ranks of raw recruits. Many officers moved their families to Quebec to enjoy their last few days together. Some arranged for their families to join them in England. The same order that notified the CEF of its rates of pay assured soldiers that they could "assign" up to four-fifths of their pay to be paid to their families.[12] A committed feminist and brother of Canada's leading male supporter of women's suffrage, Sam Hughes had insisted that any married volunteer must have his wife's written permission to enlist.

It was soon apparent that a good many Valcartier volunteers had ignored their wives' feelings. A doctor's wife from Chatham ignored diplomacy: her husband had left "without obtaining my *written consent*," she informed Hughes, "and I *forbid* you to allow him to go to War in Europe."[13] Helen Geddes's husband from Simcoe, Ontario, had a signature, but it was not hers, she insisted, and she and her child had been left to starve, adding as a sad hint about their home life, "if he went to England he would never want to return."[14] Mary Elizabeth Agnew wanted her husband back because he had left her and their two children "totally unprovided for."[15] Tom Humphreys' wife soon repented giving him permission: "When I signed for him to go they did not give me time to think what I was doing, however I am sick in bed & Tom is all I have, he is my husband and I do sincerely wish he was here with me. I have only been married 7 weeks and I am out in Canada all alone."[16] Mrs. Murray had given her husband permission to go on the promise that she and her baby would be well provided for, but she had been deceived: "I have made myself sick worrying over financial matters; therefore my husband is worth more to me at home than away."[17] Lieut. Dayton of the 12th York Rangers had done the same to his wife and three children.[18] On the other hand, Mrs. A.E. Hall was almost eager for her husband to go, as long as he provided for her: "whatever his faults he is a good loyal soldier." Lieut. Hall of Toronto's Governor General's Body Guard had deserted her for an adulterous relationship before seeking a commission with Toronto's 48th Highlanders.[19]

Unless they could prove their son was underage, anxious mothers had less leverage with the minister, though they tried their best. Marion Presnail sought Hughes's mercy "for a poor widow mother whose heart is almost broken over this impetuous act of a boy." As added weight, she recalled a mutual friend, "the late William Campbell of Coboconk."[20] Mrs. John Quinney of Gananoque, widowed only six months before, had lost both her sons to the First Contingent of the CEF. She persuaded her local grand master, W.J. Thompson, to intercede with the minister as a fellow pillar of the Orange Lodge. A little flexibility, Thompson suggested, would see Mrs. Quinney through her state of mourning and the boys would do their duty later. He knew them as members of his Sunday School class.[21] Mary O'Meara appealed as a "poor orphan" to the governor general for her brother: "He is only a mere boy and my only support as I am an invalid having severe nervous prostration and unable to earn my own living."[22] Garfield Boyling's mother and wife combined in asking Hughes to send him home. All the minister had to do was to examine the boy to see that he was unfit for service, and he need never know that his women had meddled in his life.[23]

Before the First Contingent sailed on 1 October, no less than seven officers and 372 other ranks were sent home after a parent or wife protested.[24] Others, to avoid such a humiliating fate, neglected to report their wedded state.[25] Edith Donaldson of Toronto suspected that her husband Sam had signed up as a widower, and offered to send her marriage lines: "I am his wife. And I have three children, 2 sons and one little girl which I have to care for."[26] By no means all women got their loved ones back. Mrs. Gerald Wharton was stranded in Buffalo on 9 August after a fight with her husband: "I told him I would be better off without him for I worked most of the time to support my child and I think you will agree that I am better off without him but I do not think that he should go free and me be tied down to work to keep myself and his child as well as mine."[27] She was too late. Whether as Wharton or under the assumed name of Curry, her husband had already left Canada. So had Roy Hunter of Kamloops. Mrs. Hunter had said goodbye to her husband when he allegedly left to join the First Contingent. His wife appealed in vain to the army but Mr. Hunter had kept on travelling.[28] When Miss Boyle of Prescott failed to have her "happiness restored" by the return of her brothers Austin and Gus, George Boyle wrote to the minister in the sterner tones appropriate to the boys' father. It was too late: the contingent had already sailed.[29]

Soldiers who were sent home complained that volunteering had left them penniless. A veteran of British imperial wars, Sydney Hart enlisted at Fredericton as a sergeant but when he was sent home from Valcartier for poor health, his civilian job had vanished, "and I have a wife and two small children to support."[30] H.T. Eggleton admitted he was deaf when he joined a field artillery battery at Toronto but an officer assured him it did not matter. At Valcartier, however, he could not hear the word of command and was sent home. Like Hart's, his job had vanished, his wife had moved to Ayr, and "now I find myself out of work and with no immediate prospect of getting any. I have also ruined a good suit of clothes at camp, & my wife has not been able to receive any relief."[31]

Organizing Separation Allowance

The welcome rush of volunteers to Valcartier had left families unprovided for. How many families, no one could possibly guess. Faced with an obvious but hitherto unconsidered problem, the government almost reflexively improvised a Canadian version of a British policy. On 4 September 1914, in imitation of the British government's decision, the Borden cabinet officially approved the separation allowance (SA) for families of CEF members who were not still receiving their peacetime salaries from governments or patriotic private employers.[32] The cost of SA would be high, but surely the war would be short.[33]

Unlike the British, who paid weekly, Canada's government proposed to pay the allowance only monthly, at rates ranging from $20 for the wife of a private and $25 for a sergeant's wife, to a maximum of $60 a month for a lieutenant-colonel's lady. Initially, SA was denied to soldiers who were still being paid by their previous employer.[34] Why pay for families that were already appropriately provided for? By early September, the government could promise the wife of a CEF private $20 in separation allowance and up to $15 of her husband's pay, if he decided to assign it.[35]

But how could the money reach her without sufficient staff and organization to collect the necessary documents, verify the details, write the cheques, and mail them? Months passed before separation allowance cheques began to arrive systematically. Meanwhile, embarrassed wives were obliged to fend off landlords, extend their "tick" at the local grocery store, drain away their scarce savings, and blame their husband and his new employer. What had gone wrong? Simply put, Col. Hughes's Valcartier adventure might, as he claimed, be a marvel to the world, but it was an administrative nightmare for the men caught up in it and for their families.

As senior officer of the CAPC in 1914, Lt.-Col. W.R. Ward had devised the prewar plan to train wartime paymasters. In minutes his proposal had been completely derailed. When Ward, four CAPC officers, and seven military clerks reached Valcartier in late August, they found themselves almost paralyzed. Until the minister of militia settled down to form official units and appoint their commanding officers, no one had authority to appoint unit paymasters, much less to begin the documentation on which pay and allowances were based. Once Hughes approved a unit's commanding officer, he needed time to find a suitable paymaster – too frequently an officer unsuited for more demanding work. Given the CEF's modest level of literacy and bureaucratic experience, finding competent pay staff was hardly easier. Even after units were authorized, their composition kept changing. Soldiers were remustered, officers were transferred, and infantry battalions were reorganized from eight companies to four companies, and back again to eight. Any pay or records officers ambitious enough to have started documentation then had to repeat some of their work. Meanwhile visiting civilians either praised everything about Valcartier or Hughes expelled them. And to an utterly unmilitary people, the camp, with all its dusty bustle and excitement, was impressive.

The challenges of arranging for soldiers to assign part of their pay or of validating a soldier's claim to separation allowance proved too complex for Valcartier and for peacetime administrators. Was the task a responsibility for a soldier's company or battery commander, his battalion commanding officer, for headquarters in Ottawa, or for some authority in between? Could a soldier be trusted not to invent a fictitious dependant? Who could knock on his door and verify the existence of a wife, married or otherwise, or of a mother in need? If a soldier died or deserted, his pay ceased, but what if an office in distant Ottawa innocently continued to issue cheques to his family? Who would then recover the public funds? One theme was clear from the flood of administrative directives: a commanding officer or paymaster who authorized an improper payment would pay for it from his own pocket – or worse. All rules and peacetime experience encouraged prudence, caution, double-checking. The best that Ward and his CAPC officers could manage was to pay all soldiers up to 21 September, the date when they officially became part of the CEF and qualified for its different pay scales. When the First Contingent left for England at the end of September, Colonel Duguid's *Official History* acknowledged: "Assignments of pay to families or relatives and establishment of claims to separation allowance were matters which in the majority of cases were still unsettled." Indeed, not until December 1914 were separation allowance cheques worth $61,815 put in the mail.[36]

Though Colonel Ward implored his novice paymasters to use the two-week voyage to England to complete documentation, even with calm weather many of his subordinates proved unequal to the task. "It is terribly discouraging to me to realize that all the work I have done in the last few months and one's best efforts are defeated by the neglect of other people," he complained.[37] Ward spent his own voyage compiling a set of financial instructions for the CEF, spelling out the duties of paymasters, rates of pay, and accounting procedures. These were rushed into print in England as the first stage of training his pay organization. Pay Office paperwork continued in England, for the first few days under clear, pleasant weather, then under the cold, driving, endless rain that marked the CEF's first winter overseas. Attestation papers were barely complete and verified before the end of February 1915, when the Canadians left for France. Only then could Ward withdraw unit pay sergeants for training.[38] By then, Ward had concluded that "a large number of the married men in the force must have enlisted as single men not, I think, with any idea or desire to deprive their families of support, but, possibly, dictated by the desire to service in the contingent well knowing that it was more difficult for a married man to enlist in the Force." If soldiers did not come forward and confess their deception, their families would suffer.[39]

Capt. C.M. Ingalls, a CAPC officer and a twenty-three-year Militia veteran, had crossed on the *Franconia*. He soon found himself with six clerks packed into a fourteen-square-foot hut on Salisbury Plain, with orders to create 33,000 pay accounts for members of the First Contingent. Ingalls insisted on moving to a large attic in Salisbury, and finally set up his office in London. There he wrestled with record keeping for a force that included 287 Smiths, many of them named John. To assist him, he was sent five officers who knew nothing of accounting, and a civilian accountant who, he complained, "could not and would not interpret military regulations."[40] Ten months later, in August 1915, the Canadian Pay and Records office in London had expanded to 740 personnel, with fourteen branches including distinct Separation Allowance and Assigned Pay branches. Divided that August, the separate Canadian Pay and Records offices in London had grown by September 1916 to a combined strength of 2,841 soldiers and civilian staff.[41]

Early in November, the Militia Department tried to avoid administrative delays by sending an immediate $20 payment whenever a separation card had been received, regardless of rank.[42] Wives entitled to more soon expressed their grievance, but a final settlement of arrears was only possible in January 1915.[43] A flood of correspondence developed over early discharges, changes of address and rank, and proof of identity for foreign-born recruits. "Do not pay Separation Allowance to wives of Russians," directed J.W. Borden, the Militia Department's accountant and paymaster general, "unless proof of marriage is produced."[44] When they could, pay officials gave prompt answers. On 2 December, Mrs. Edwards, wife of a Permanent Force soldier, wrote to complain that her husband had promised her his full pay of $54.74 a month but now she was to receive only $50.00. Within a week, Maj. A.O. Lambert had written to explain that her husband's pay had risen from $0.95 to $1.00 a day but he was not allowed to assign her more than $25.00 a month, plus $25.00 in SA. Her husband had been sent the same explanation "and possibly he may mention this matter to you in his next letter."[45]

Meanwhile many soldiers' families struggled on far less. How did Mrs. Smith or Madame Untel cope when left for weeks and even months without income? One answer was family and neighbourhood solidarity and generosity; another was a basic artifact of working-class culture, retail credit. Families were familiar with the ups and downs of income and unemployment, and with jobs where payday was often delayed. The landlord and the grocer often had to wait for payment in winter and other periods of widespread unemployment, and the soldier wage-earner had as reliable a paymaster as any merchant or apartment owner could imagine, the government itself. As weeks of "tick" turned to months, creditors might grow rude and restrictive, but who really wanted the certain opprobrium of cutting off a soldier's wife or mother from her groceries or putting her, her children, and her few sticks of furniture on the street? After all, there was a war on, and what was more likely to undermine the national effort than gratuitous reports, perhaps from chronic complainers, that soldiers or their families were not getting their pay?

Indeed, reports from the First Contingent in England suggested that Canadian soldiers had altogether too much money to spend. With $1.10 a day, a private in the CEF had just over four times the "King's shilling" still deemed appropriate for his British counterpart. As Canadians quickly converted to the mysteries of pounds, shillings, and pence, English pubs near the rain-sodden Canadian camps on Salisbury Plain converted soldiers' pay into large quantities of the powerful British beer soldiers had discovered on their first landing at Plymouth. The beer, in turn, was transformed into loud voices, short tempers, fist fights, damaged furniture, and a general rowdiness that began to give the Canadians a bad name. His troops, complained their new British commander, Maj.-Gen. Sir Edmund Alderson, were grossly overpaid. What could be done about it?

When the CEF pay scales were first approved, some spoilsports had proposed holding back half the money as a trust fund for soldiers on their demobilization. How better to provide for men who would have more money in their pockets than they really needed, and who would certainly experience a period of postwar unemployment? Compulsory savings would allow veterans to pay down their debts, reduce mortgages, and invest in farm implements or a new business. Not incidentally, it would also cut Ottawa's wartime spending and reduce the short-term burden on Canada's credit. In 1915 the idea was deferred. The explosive effect on morale and therefore on recruiting was an obvious consideration. Imagine promising a man $1.10 a day and then paying him only $0.55! The discrimination between married and single men was equally evident. A bachelor would be building a nest-egg while his comrade was dutifully, if voluntarily, "assigning" half his pay to a wife or mother. Above all, Col. Hughes was firmly opposed to fiddling with the pay. In this respect, if in few others, Hughes was a libertarian: it was not his business to tell a man how to spend his money.

The problem of the "overpaid" Canadians, however, continued to trouble British and Canadian authorities. If married soldiers could be compelled to transfer their pay, so could the unmarried. In 1916 an amended *Financial Instructions and Allowances* directed that soldiers overseas "defer" half their pay if it had not otherwise been assigned. It remained to the credit of his pay account until his discharge. By the end of the war, in 1918, the paymaster general had accumulated about $300 million, averaging $1,000 each for CEF members on their release.[46]

Not until 1917 were any of the administrative problems of the opening weeks of the war explained to Canadians through a committee of the House of Commons, and by then Hughes had been dismissed to the back benches.[47] In 1914 Valcartier was portrayed as a model of Canadian ingenuity and efficiency. Canadian soldiers were young heroes, valiantly responding to the "Old Country's" danger. While Hughes presided over the Militia Department and cultivated adoring journalists, no one was allowed to know that the professionals might have handled matters better.

The plight of penniless wives and mothers was no fit counterpoint to the national patriotic chorus. Few editors were eager to rain on any parades. Northern Ontario's *Haileyburian* was an exception in denouncing Militia Department red tape. One wife in the mining community, the newspaper reported, had burned her furniture for heat; another was in an asylum and her four children were scattered.[48] In Cape Breton, a former Tory mayor of Glace Bay, John Douglas, made it his patriotic duty to visit soldiers' wives and report their grievances to the Militia Department by collect telegram. He was bluntly told to stop.[49]

Nor did all the fault lie with the CAPC. Some soldiers behaved like rogues. John Clovis Martin enlisted as a widower and assigned his pay to another woman. The real Mrs. Martin wanted it back. Howard Ferry's mother demanded his support, but it took weeks to locate which battalion Ferry had joined. Certainly Mrs. Ferry had no idea. Wesley Peters left his child with his parents when he joined the First Contingent but made no financial provision for her. "This man is an Indian," an investigator scornfully explained, "and, evidently, he did not know enough to apply for any allowance for his mother."[50] In 1917 Maj. J.W. Margeson, a paymaster from Nova Scotia, returned from overseas to head a new Militia Department Separation Allowance Board to judge claims.[51] In 1918, summoned to a special House of Commons committee on pensions, Margeson recalled soldiers who had secured separation allowance for their Canadian wife, rediscovered their earlier family in Britain, and wished to switch the allowance. "We keep the woman in Canada, who has suffered by the enlistment," Margeson explained, "and we look after her and her children." The English wife was left to her "disappointment."[52]

As 1915 turned warmer, the CEF pay system finally seemed to be functioning. By the end of March 1915, according to its official history, members of the CEF had earned $6,896,290.40 and paid out $1,255,372.70 in pay assignments to families and relatives. Despite the predominance of British-born soldiers, three-quarters of the money, $916,154.31, went back to Canada.[53] Col. Ward and his staff had trained paymasters and clerks, published regulations, established procedures, printed forms, and developed dossiers and records for each overseas member of the CEF. To document each Canadian soldier from his arrival at Liverpool to the distribution of his personal property if he died in Flanders, an extensive bureaucracy had developed in a made-over school on London's Horseferry Road. Inevitably, it became the focus for a range of complaints and criticism, from those who resented delays and insufficient service to those who denounced its bloated size and accused the staff of shirking their duty in the trenches.

Nothing for Home Service Soldiers

On 22 September 1914, as the Canadian Expeditionary Force formally began life as the organization for Canadian soldiers going overseas to fight, other Canadian soldiers stood on guard in Canada itself, defending fortresses at Halifax, Quebec, and Esquimalt from German cruisers and commerce raiders, or guarding railway bridges, docks, the Welland and Lachine canals, and other potential targets of Germans or "Fenian" sabotage. When thousands of Germans and Austro-Hungarians were interned in the fall of 1914, members of the Militia were called out to serve as their guards.[54] Even after the German seaborne threat faded with the sinking of Admiral von Spee's Far East squadron at the Battle of the Falklands, British Columbia insisted on keeping its defenders mobilized. So did the prime minister's Halifax constituents.

Many of these Home Service soldiers had families; indeed, proportionately more than in the CEF, since the approval of wives or parents (for underage soldiers) was not required. Militia pay was similar to the CEF's, but only soldiers proceeding overseas were eligible for the CEF's separation allowance. Their neighbours assumed that families of Home Service soldiers were as well off as any CEF soldier, and even better off because the risks were negligible. Keeping a family on whatever a Home Service soldier could spare from his pay, however, was as difficult for his wife as it would have been for the wife of an overseas soldier. Even his subsistence allowance (provided in lieu of quarters and army rations) was intended only to cover his wife's added cost in providing him with food and shelter, and was withdrawn when soldiers lived away from home.[55]

The added costs of a large family, a high-cost region, illness, or misfortunes, which the Patriotic Fund helped cover for families of men "at the front," also affected the families of Home Service soldiers, who were not assisted by the Fund. "We merely exist on $1.55 per day," complained Mrs. F.J. Taylor in British Columbia. "We are sick in Our family a great deal & need Doctor's attention but how can we ever pay! ... We are already head over heels in debt."[56] Lyllian Macgregor's husband bore the scars of beatings by patients at the notoriously unruly Khaki Convalescent Home in Montreal where he did night duty. Though partially blind, she abandoned her insurance premiums, broke up furniture to heat her Outremont home, and moved in with her married sister to keep herself and her six-year-old child from starving. When she complained of her plight, her husband was paraded and abused by his superior officer for failing to curb her. "If it is possible," she pleaded, "could somebody start a fund for the poor soldiers wives somewhat similar to the Patriotic fund, it would be a blessing and stop an awful lot of misery and do a world of good. [U]s soldiers' wives at home have an awful lot to put up with and are not allowed to receive any help from the various funds because we don't happen to have our men overseas."[57]

Maj.-Gen. Willoughby Gwatkin, the Militia's chief of general staff and senior officer, was no supporter of inflated home-defence garrisons. He saw the injustice and struggled to change the rules that impoverished Home Defence soldiers' families. In October 1917 he received a memo from an anonymous member of the Patriotic Fund in Halifax, citing the latest sad story of Home Service hardship: "I am moved to write this letter by a visit I have had from a woman today. She came down to the office with four children, the youngest in the baby carriage, the eldest about four years of age. I have gone into the case very carefully and for what she pays for rooms, she cannot live. As a matter of fact, the reason she came to see me was because she was turned out on the street, for non-payment of rent."[58] Needless to say, Gwatkin failed: on the eve of conscription in 1917 it did not seem necessary to grant Home Service soldiers the same separation allowance as soldiers overseas.

Debating Entitlement

Separation allowance had been launched with a brief order-in-council, but it did not stay simple for long. Acting for an absent Col. Hughes, Sir James Lougheed, Borden's Senate leader and a minister without portfolio, reported in October on the plight of widows "whose sons were sole support and went to the front." His cabinet colleagues dutifully agreed that "families be considered to include such." A month's reflection also convinced ministers that, except for pay from the federal or provincial government, "other income" should not be deducted from a soldier's separation allowance.[59] Private employers were unlikely to continue their generosity if they or their employees felt penalized. Because former civil servants and Permanent Force soldiers also collected their peacetime salary from federal or provincial governments, they were denied separation allowance. Another privilege, important to some, had been built into the Dominion Lands Act of 1908, providing that military service "in defence of the British Empire against a foreign power" counted for homestead residence purposes. This privilege was extended in a series of orders-in-council and by May 1915 included soldiers prevented by wounds or illness from meeting homesteading requirements.[60] For homesteaders and their families, such protection was almost as reassuring as a monthly flow of cash.[61]

Harried officials and politicians who had devised separation allowance in August and early September of 1914 had little idea of the complexity of family relations in Canadian society. Like their British counterparts, Militia Department officials initially balked at countenancing common-law relationships for purposes of financial support, and insisted on documented proof of marriage. Neither Borden nor Hughes echoed Asquith's robust insistence that a soldier's marital arrangements were his own business. However, Canadian military authorities eventually accepted evidence of cohabitation "on a bona fide permanent domestic basis for at least two years prior to his enlistment" as the equivalent of a marriage licence, and in 1916 this principle was endorsed in a controversial order-in-council.[62]

The few widowers in the CEF were allowed separation allowance for their motherless children, but only if the children had a defined guardian and were obviously too young for employment (initially under fourteen years for boys and sixteen for girls, but extended in 1915 to fifteen and seventeen years respectively). Divorce in Canada in 1914 was costly and rare, but separations were more common. Could a soldier apply for separation allowance to meet his support payments? Militia Department legal advisors approved – but only if the payments were court ordered. Once the First Contingent reached England, officials soon discovered that soldiers who had left a wife and family in England had sometimes started another family in Canada. Life in a new country could be lonely and a bachelor homesteader faced an almost impossible task. Initially, the CEF accepted the priority of the first wife, if she could make a satisfactory case, but that left the Canadian wife and children bereft of all but the sympathy of her neighbours and, as we have seen, the policy was reversed.[63]

Once the cabinet agreed that a widowed mother could create a claim for SA, the applicant had to prove that he was unmarried and his mother's sole support. A soldier might assign pay to more than one member of his family, but he had only one separation allowance to allocate. Support from other siblings, whether it was real or merely judged appropriate by the Militia Department, disqualified a claim; a certificate from a clergyman, the Canadian Patriotic Fund, or a local authority was required to confirm any claim.

An even more painful problem was that young men joined the army at an age when they might well be switching their financial responsibilities from their mother to a bride. For many families, this had serious consequences, since the father's income was often also in decline as he aged, and poverty faced an otherwise comfortable family. Belatedly, the Militia Department did its best to close a loophole that might pour its allowances into undeserving pockets. Having agreed that a soldier could pay his SA to his wife or, under specific circumstances, to his wid-owed mother, "applications for the allowance from parties who do not come un-der the above provisions cannot be considered."[64]

Though many mothers needed support from their children before they were widowed, a husband, however elderly and incapable, was still deemed to be the family breadwinner, and taxpayers had no obligation to relieve him of his re-sponsibility. Evelyn Moor, an anemic invalid, was assured by her brother, on whom she was wholly dependent, that she would benefit from his separation allowance when he enlisted. He was wrongly advised: sisters did not count as dependants until a painfully wrought compromise in 1917.[65] Nor did the women who married a soldier *after* he enlisted. As the CPF's historian later recalled, in 1915-16 there was "a tremendous number of marriages among members of the Expeditionary Force and it was evident that many of them were contracted in moments of irre-sponsibility." That men and women might seek a last, desperate moment of hap-piness was merely imprudence in the eyes of those who might inherit a financial burden. Soldiers were firmly warned that only those who were married at the time of enlistment could claim SA. Without the allowance, the Patriotic Fund refused to acknowledge need. "The great majority of [wives] had been earning their living prior to their marriages," wrote the assistant secretary, "and there was no reason why they should not continue to do so subsequent to the departure of their husbands."[66]

Inevitably, some couples went ahead with marriage, fully aware that the new wife could claim no immediate benefits. After he had made his friend pregnant, Pte. A. Clymer of Toronto "married me like a gentleman would do," explained Mrs. Clymer. However, after three weeks of trying to support herself and their new baby, she recognized her plight. If her husband was not discharged, she claimed, she and their child would be left penniless as well as friendless. "I would like to have him bought out," she explained to Maj.-Gen. John Hughes, the minister's brother, concluding desperately, "trusting to God you will do something as I am in urgent need of help."[67] Viola Young of Little Bras, Cape Breton Island, pregnant with the child of Pte. Sidney Edwards, was on her way to be married until his parents put a stop to it. The military authorities could do nothing for her but they reminded young Edwards of his responsibility. He had assigned her $15 from his pay but at the end of January 1917 the assignment stopped. "There has to be some-thing to come in to keep his child of course I am only a poor girl myself," wrote Miss Young. The sad truth was that Pte. Edwards had already been persuaded to switch the assignment to his mother in Joggins Mines.[68]

Separation allowance was not extended to meet such tragic cases because in 1915 the government was already appalled at the spiralling costs and duration of the war. SA had been devised solely to reassure married men and their wives when enlistment was a choice. Was it necessary to do more to encourage recruiting when targets were easily being met? Was it fair to insist that soldiers, once enrolled, should remain celibate? No doubt some ministers and officials suspected that a $20 separation allowance would persuade gold-digging harpies to suck innocent young soldiers into their arms, at extra expense to Canadian taxpayers. Certainly that was the impression of Col. John Wallace Carson, sent to England as the minister of militia's personal representative and gradually exercising increasing authority over Canadian soldiers overseas. "There is no doubt at all but that we are being 'soaked' with many men that are getting married," he warned his friend Hughes in June 1916, and it was time to put a stop to it "if only in the interests of economy." This job was given to Lt.-Col. H.A.C. Machin of the defunct 94th Battalion, an Ontario Tory MPP and future enforcer of the Military Service Act.[69]

Eventually, a modest compromise was found for men who claimed to be engaged to be married but who had set aside wedding plans in order to enlist. "The sudden call for volunteers," a Militia Department memorandum argued, had separated couples who might well have exchanged vows to marry. On 28 January 1915 a cautious order-in-council approved marriages for soldiers who applied at the moment of enlistment and who were recommended by their officer commanding, "but if not married within twenty days hereafter, the permission [would] be cancelled."[70]

In the summer of 1916, two years into the war, the Patriotic Fund, which restricted its benefits to those in receipt of separation allowance, yielded a little more. If a wife who had married after enlistment became pregnant, she could be granted the $5 a month accorded to a childless wife and, after the birth, whatever was due to a wife with one child. The married Mrs. Clymer could have claimed the modest CPF benefit if she ever heard about it; the unmarried Miss Young could not.

When the prime minister visited England in the spring of 1917, Charles Green tried to persuade him to grant separation allowance to his son-in-law, Pte. W.H. Simpson of the Ontario Military Hospital at Orpington. Doris Green had accepted the terms when she first married but now "she is to become the mother of a potential Canadian citizen" and would have to sustain the child on nothing until the war was over. "Is it assumed by Canada that these young soldiers will remain chaste and sterile during the lustiest years of their manhood?" Green asked.[71] He had picked an opportune moment; Sir Robert Borden was actually reading his mail. Sir George Perley, simultaneously minister of Canada's overseas military forces and high commissioner in London since 1914, had wrestled with many versions of Green's question, including 800 unanswered applications for separation allowance. His advice, appropriately conservative, was to recognize marriages approved by a commanding officer and after "proof has been provided that the woman is of good character and worthy of the allowance." A clergyman's certificate, a police report, or advice from a Soldiers' Aid Society or "other reputable source" would suffice. Thanks to Doris Green Simpson, Canada finally acknowledged her wartime brides.[72]

Among the beneficiaries were Pte. and Mrs. Walter Kerr. A Scottish-born soldier with a severe stutter, he went to the Wesleyan Chapel canteen in the Canadian camp at Bramshott and the cook liked him at first sight. "Her shyness, though, was about as acute as my own," Kerr recalled, "but the brief conversation we had together was more than enough to kindle a spark of liking for each other." His commanding officer gave permission, they were married at Hadley parish church on 15 September 1917, and the marriage lasted until Mrs. Kerr died in 1973.[73]

Apart from their husbands' claim to separation allowance, war brides in England and the very few in France and Belgium imposed no expense on Canadians and, given their comparatively high Canadian benefits, only exceptional costs on the corresponding British patriotic charities such as the Soldiers' and Sailors' Families Association, which reciprocated the Canadian Patriotic Fund's involvement with British reservists' families by promising to look after Dominion soldiers' families in Great Britain.[74] By the end of the war, the CEF had close to 40,000 wives and children overseas, a substantial part of its small army of dependants.[75]

As the separation allowance system grew more refined, the Militia Department had to define a "wife," or in some cases more than one of them, in ways that conformed to nine distinct provincial legal systems. In November 1915 officials granting separation allowance were provided with a definition in which the ingenuity of several lawyers was apparent:

> For the purpose of the provision of Separation Allowance, "wife" means the woman who has been married to the officer or the soldier in question under the laws of the country in which the marriage was solemnised and who has not been separated from her husband by a judicial decree or "separation from bed or board" or some similar decree parting her from her husband's home and children, but where a wife so separated is entitled either by the agreement or by an order of a competent court to alimony, such wife shall be entitled to the extent of such payments or alimony, to the separation allowance.[76]

Family support, public or private, was exclusively for women and children. Grown men could look after themselves. Or could they? George Robinson of Parry Sound complained to Sam Hughes that he had lost his wife and all his money "through misfortune," and was reduced to living in a boxcar and depending on strangers.

With winter approaching, he was too sick to work but if his son in the 12th Canadian Mounted Rifles were discharged, he could work in a local ammunition factory "and he would thus be able to help his country as well as myself."[77] Apart from advice to write to his son's commanding officer and to apply to the local patriotic charities for assistance, Robinson got no help.

Mr. and Mrs. John Grant lived in Sault Ste-Marie. Because of an accident at work, he had been paralyzed since 1902; his wife, a nurse, cared for him and supported their family by taking in boarders. By 1915 they had two sons serving with the First Contingent overseas. Mrs. Grant died suddenly on 22 May 1915, leaving her husband alone, penniless, and helpless. Surely, claimed the local MP, this was a case for separation allowance. So it might be, agreed the Militia Department's J.W. Borden, but not without testing the regulations. It was August before the Treasury Board reached even a tentative conclusion: "Instead of dealing with the individual case it would be preferable to have submitted for consideration a general recommendation dealing with cases of this character." By then, the problem was theoretical: "As both Mr. & Mrs. Grant have died of want since this case was submitted to Treasury Board," J.W. Borden minuted, "there is no need for an O/C now."[78]

Fresh Contingents

Upon the departure of the 30,000-member First Contingent at the beginning of October 1914, including close to half the prewar Canadian Army Pay Corps, the government had immediately authorized an identical Second Contingent. Mobilized on much the same plan that Colonel Hughes had scrapped in August, units were scattered across Canada, recruited during the fall and early winter, and trained locally until they embarked for Britain in the spring. Though much of the country's limited military expertise had already left for England, and the Canadian winter restricted soldiers to their improvised barracks, the chaos of Valcartier was generally not reproduced. A leaflet explained soldiers' benefits and obligations, and improvised courses taught hurriedly selected administrative personnel as much of their responsibilities as they could absorb.

The CEF kept on growing. On 1 December 1914, after Turkey had joined the Central Powers, Hughes offered to raise four battalions of Canadian Mounted Rifles as the most suitable force to defend British interests in the Middle East. When the British asked for more, thirteen battalions were authorized, each half the strength of a normal infantry battalion. In January 1915 the minister of militia announced a Third Contingent, with a further dozen battalions of infantry. "I could raise three more contingents in three weeks," Hughes boasted.[79] Between

January and June 1915, Hughes authorized thirty-five colonels to recruit infantry battalions. Others organized artillery batteries, field ambulances, companies for the Army Service Corps, and a miscellaneous collection of cyclist companies, machine-gun batteries, and signals sections inspired more by private initiative than an official plan. In the summer of 1915 the Borden government set the target strength for the CEF at 150,000.

At Valcartier, Hughes had allowed wives to order their husbands home. Soon, they were required to pay for the privilege and had to persuade a soldier's commanding officer that a husband should be discharged. When Mrs. Clements tried to recover her husband from the 7th Canadian Mounted Rifles, Col. L.W. Shannon abruptly dismissed her case: "The woman is evidently making a misrepresentation of facts, and it would appear, therefore, the best for all parties if her husband were permitted to remain in the 7th Regiment, C.M.R., C.E.F., as he desires."[80] After all, the colonel of the regiment explained, "it takes a long time to train a mounted soldier as he has to acquire horsemanship in addition to his other duties and I have, therefore, been very reluctant to discharge men without good cause."[81] On the other hand Nora Howl, friendless in Toronto with two small children and expecting a third, could have her husband back from the 59th Battalion in Kingston for only $20 – if the colonel agreed. Emma Everley of Grand Forks, British Columbia, paid $50 to get her husband out of the 54th Battalion at Vernon, but then he promptly went to Vancouver and enlisted in the 72nd Highlanders. Was she not entitled to a refund?[82]

By the summer of 1915 the pay services became more efficient and the Patriotic Fund was well established. In August, as pressed by patriotic feminists, the government cancelled the need for a wife's permission for a husband to enlist.[83] Mrs. Frank Harvey of Perth, Ontario, felt herself a victim of the change. During her absence to visit her dying mother, Frank had enlisted in the local 130th Battalion. Now her mother was dead, she was left "under doctor's care" with four children and a fifth on the way, and she saw no sign of separation allowance or CPF assistance. "I think it is of as much importance to look after a woman & her family in this country," she wrote to Hughes, "as to go across to England or France to protect them there."[84] The minister did not agree.

After Sir Robert visited Britain and France in September and discovered a dismaying lack of "earnestness" in Asquith and his British cabinet colleagues, he further boosted Canada's enlistment target to 250,000 soldiers. Still exasperated by his British allies, the prime minister used his New Year's message for 1916 to emphasize Canada's commitment. Doubling Canada's pledge to 500,000 soldiers, he insisted, would display "an unflinchable resolve to crown the justice of our cause with victory and with an abiding peace."[85] Perhaps surprisingly, this was not an unrealistic number. By war's end, a million Canadian men, one-eighth of the population, had offered themselves for service. Half a million volunteers were accepted before conscription was imposed by the Military Service Act of 1917. Even Hughes's boast proved to be no exaggeration. Of 142 infantry battalions authorized by the minister during 1915, 80 of them took more than 1,000 volunteers overseas and only 25 enlisted fewer than 700 men.[86]

Each new battalion posed problems of inexperience. Earlier units were usually raised by existing Militia regiments and could draw on their pool of experience, however shallow. With those pools drained by mid-1915, Hughes turned to fellow politicians, community leaders, and organizations to raise battalions of "Sportsmen," "Vikings," or "Bantams" (men too short for the CEF's height standard). A retired Indian agent raised a battalion of "Cowboys and Indians" in Manitoba. Some colonels simply promised that men from the same town or county would serve together.[87] Recruits were attracted by invitations to wear kilts and enter battle to the skirl of bagpipes. More influential was the pledge that volunteers would serve with fellow athletes or Scandinavians or Irishmen, and especially with pals from their own home town or county.

Though most recruits shared both unfamiliarity with and suspicion of bureaucracy, they and their families were determined to be paid and to collect whatever entitlements their new employer provided for them. Mr. H. Plume, home on harvest leave from Saskatchewan's 229th Battalion, suffered a severe eye ailment and spent a further two weeks at home. Mrs. Plume took him to an eye specialist in Moose Jaw, nursed him back to health, and then demanded her separation allowance for the weeks he had been sick. When his captain and colonel said that Plume could not be paid because he had not applied for sick leave, she consulted her father, a British Army veteran, and took her case, successfully, to the minister of militia. After all, a soldier was never "out of service."[88] From Edmonton, Alice Watts waged a seven-month struggle with her bank, the Post Office, and the Militia Department to recover a missing assigned paycheque. She, too, won, though she resented spending so much on postage at three cents a letter.[89]

Inexperienced colonels of newly authorized CEF battalions gave administration a low priority, negligently reproducing the confusion and delays associated with Valcartier. Recruits spent as much as a year in Canada, often billeted in their own homes, which raised questions about whether separation allowance should be paid to families that saw a lot of them. A typical battalion, a pay official explained to a parliamentary committee, required at least 50,000 documents; all should have been checked, and often were not. New regulations and last-minute scrambles for recruits meant that many units still left Canada with incomplete records. Major Ingalls cited the 257th Railway Construction Battalion, whose swift mobilization brought its colonel great praise. Troop trains carrying the unit reached Halifax with only half an hour to embark close to 1,000 men – and 3,300 signatures still needed. A Pay Corps officer had to sail to England with the unit to get the job done. Its predecessor, the 256th Battalion, embarked without sending in a single card for assigned pay or separation allowance. Naturally, when wives and mothers complained, the Pay Office got the blame.[90]

Regulations, properly executed, allowed the army to locate a soldier day or night. Regulations ignored, scorned, or evaded allowed some men who deserted or had been left behind as sick to be reported as having gone overseas. Months followed before the records were corrected. Confusion was often compounded when a soldier who enlisted in his hometown or county battalion was transferred to another CEF unit to bring it up to sufficient strength to go overseas. Increasingly, battalions reaching England from Canada were broken up to bring earlier arrivals up to strength. Prior to 1917, a soldier once in England might find himself on a draft to France to replace losses in any of the forty-eight original battalions of the First, Second, Third, or Fourth Divisions. In theory, orderly rooms and records clerks could handle the documentation smoothly; in practice, haste and confusion led to misunderstandings and mistakes.

As Helen Reid explained the Canadian pay system in 1917, a soldier and his family depended on four distinct pay offices, beginning with the paymaster of a man's original battalion, continuing with the paymaster general in Ottawa who paid separation allowance and, once the soldier had gone overseas, his assigned pay, on the basis of a payroll and records maintained by the Canadian paymaster general in London. By then the man also depended on the paymaster and staff of his new CEF battalion in France. If a sick or wounded soldier was invalided from France to England, he was paid by the Canadian headquarters in London, and if he was sent home to Canada as an invalid, he faced another paymaster who had to wait for the soldier's records to reach him from England. The potential for error and delay by ill-qualified personnel in a pre-electronic era was fully realized. A paymaster or clerk could easily lose a soldier or his family simply by making an error in his address. If a soldier was allowed to overdraw his pay account, his family innocently and without warning shared the resulting penalty. A desperate wife or mother who found herself owing half a substantial and unexpected debt had no recourse but the Patriotic Fund.[91]

For most Canadians, the army was a first experience with formal bureaucracy. How many civilians understood the distinctions between battalions, companies, and divisions, or the administrative significance of a soldier's regimental number? Every MP had examples of families left destitute because separation allowances and assigned pay never arrived, claimed E.M. MacDonald, a Cape Breton Liberal

MP: "How can you expect enthusiasm among the plain people of the country when you have cases like this right under their noses?"[92] As a government MP, Herbert Ames downplayed the problem; as the Patriotic Fund's leading official, he blamed paymasters and soldiers themselves for failing to fill out the necessary forms correctly: "Where avoidable mistakes occur, as they do occur sometimes, and when it is brought to the attention of one of our branches that a woman is not getting her assigned pay or separation allowance, through some reason not explained, she need not suffer, because the Patriotic Fund will give her all the money she needs until the rectification is made."[93] Ames could hardly admit that the "Patriotic" itself was a robust bureaucracy with its own regulations, procedures, and awe-inspiring gatekeepers.

The two bureaucracies were designed to mesh. In Canada, Militia pay officials depended heavily for their information on the rapidly expanding Patriotic Fund while the Fund, after some delays, gained access to military nominal rolls as an aid in identifying eligible families.[94] While the Fund could offer an income supplement to any military dependant it judged to be in need, receipt of separation allowance soon became a necessary qualification. The Fund needed current CEF records to protect itself against fraudulent claims from families whose breadwinner had been discharged or had deserted the CEF, or sometimes had never even joined.

Most cases seemed straightforward enough. Frank Amato joined the 180th Overseas Battalion in October 1916, shortly before it embarked, leaving his wife Mary and five children, aged eighteen months to eight years, at 68 Mansfield Avenue in Toronto. His mother Angeline, a widow, had other sons to support her. His colonel signed Amato's application, and both AP and SA were established by mid-November.[95] Edith Pearl Carey of Kingston should have had no complaints since her husband, a former Canadian Pacific trainman, continued to receive his railway pay after enlistment, and she received his separation allowance. She was annoyed, though, that because of her CPR income, the CPF cut off its initial allowance. She was not, in their view, "in need."[96] She was in a majority. While the Patriotic Fund had helped about 50,000 military families across Canada by 1916, about 150,000 families had to manage on their own.[97]

Many wives and mothers were dismayed to learn that their husband's military offences affected them too. When a soldier deserted or when a military court sentenced him to detention, his pay was stopped. His pay also stopped if he was admitted to a special hospital for venereal disease.[98] If the stoppage hurt his family, surely that would give him second thoughts about misbehaving. The army took six months to explain to a seventy-year-old British Columbia mother that her son's assigned pay had stopped after a court martial sentenced him to fifteen months imprisonment with hard labour for being "drunk on the line of march." Bleak poverty added to her shame.[99] Blanche Cushman pleaded in vain for news of Private Fuisse, a Second Contingent soldier who had "left me his unmarried wife and baby, 3 months old, and both homeless and pennyless [sic] ... He has never tried to deny the baby which is a beautiful child and his image a baby girl."[100] Private Fuisse was not compelled to reply, and no record was found that he did.

Building a Bureaucracy

As voluntary recruiting collapsed in 1916, the Borden government forgot its boastful 1914 promises and turned reluctantly to conscription to fill the ranks of the CEF. That would end, for a time, the need to ease the worries of soldiers' families, but the political struggle for the Military Service Act eventually demanded new allies. Under the Wartime Elections Act passed late in the summer of 1917, the female relatives of soldiers won the right to vote and many Canadians with recent roots in enemy countries lost it.

Faced with a general election in which soldiers' wives and mothers would be first-time voters, Sir Robert Borden and members of his new Union government paid attention to a variety of letters and petitions from hurriedly organized Next of Kin Associations and soldiers' wives.[101] A hurried guess from the accountant and paymaster general that a $5 increase would cost $5,400,000 a year persuaded the government to raise the minimum separation allowance from $20 to $25 from 1 December 1917, three weeks before the election.[102] As justification, the government explained that soldiers were frequently promoted to sergeant and then demoted. The documentation took so long to reach Ottawa that wives were slow to get a sergeant's SA of $25. If their husband lost his stripes, women were overpaid and had to repay. Levelling up all separation allowance to $25 alleviated the problem. Besides, pension increases in 1917 gave a private's childless widow $40 a month while the previous rates of SA and AP guaranteed a childless wife only $35.[103]

Over time, a huge office grew in Ottawa to meet the paper-bound requirements of drawing, signing, recording, and distributing tens of thousands of SA and AP cheques. By the end of 1915, the Separation Allowance and Assigned Pay Division needed 240 clerks to handle 44,842 AP and 40,258 SA accounts monthly. A year later, the SA accounts had doubled and the AP accounts had tripled to 148,049, bound in 2,055 huge alphabetical ledgers. The staff had doubled to 504 but, to set an example of chasing able-bodied men into the CEF, the office had to recruit and train 442 new employees, mostly women and, increasingly, disabled veterans.[104] When Maj. Ingalls took command of the office at the end of March 1917, he found a staff of 638 (131 women and 507 men). To increase efficiency and cut labour costs, the department invested in 46 primitive cheque-writing machines and six scriptographs to sign the cheques. The 10,000 recipients in the Ottawa area felt free to come in and discuss their problems, Ingalls reported, but there were no offices where they could do so privately. To make room, his staff was squeezed and in "the consequent vitiated state of the atmosphere ... the health of the young lady employees is impaired."[105]

Between eighty and a hundred SA applications arrived daily, mostly from Canadian dependants of soldiers who had gone overseas, and the original regulations had grown to forty-two paragraphs of legal prose. Turning to the Patriotic Fund for advice, particularly after the government opened up the difficult discretionary issues of supporting soldiers' sisters and mothers, confessed Margeson, was no help. "There are no two Patriotic Fund Committees that run it on the same principle, particularly in the country districts," he recalled later; a national body was needed.[106] Accordingly, an order-in-council in February 1917 created a Separation Allowance Board to rationalize the Militia Department responses to claims and complaints. Colonel Margeson and another officer qualified as "officials learned in the law," while Philip Morris joined the Board "as an advisor only" to add his experience of the CPF's families.[107]

Though the Board channelled most of its inquiries through the Patriotic Fund, and appointed CPF branch officials as "commissioners" to receive evidence,[108] the department also recruited its own investigators, with women preferred. A sad little trickle of malefactors followed. Mrs. Diprose, who had pretended to be Mrs. Jones, went to jail for six months. Agnes Mahoney signed the certificate on the back of her cheque and cashed it. She was charged because Private Mahoney had deserted. A judge threw out the case: what proof did the department present that she knew her husband had fled the CEF?[109]

Not all investigators found fraud. Mrs. Smith, widow of a Bank of Commerce messenger, called on May Morris, Margeson's Toronto investigator, to share her plight. When her eldest son joined up, he applied for SA to support his mother but it was denied: another younger son could support her. When that son enlisted, SA was still denied because the Bank had given Mrs. Smith a three-year annuity of $450. Now the annuity had expired, leaving Mrs. Smith with an elderly mother, a daughter in school, and a fifteen-year-old son who had left school to support the family. Suitably backed by a certificate from the rector of St. John's Norway Anglican Church, it was, the Board agreed, "a very deserving case."[110]

Still, government allowances were fixed, limited, and acknowledged to be inadequate for more than a very small family free of costly crises. Families needed more than the Militia Department regulation could allow even to the "deserving cases" who made their needs known to MPs or journalists.

3
The Patriotic Fund

When the paralyzed John Grant apparently starved to death in Sault Ste-Marie in 1915, there should have been a better solution. A branch of the Patriotic Fund existed in the Soo at the time of the tragedy, with the standard task of serving soldiers' dependants in need. While a father, however disabled, might not command the generosity due to an archetypical mother, John Grant's plight troubled contemporaries, as it shocks posterity. In the absence of his enlisted sons, his wife's death had left him in childlike dependence on his community, but his community ignored him.

An obvious contrast with Grant's treatment was the response to a tragedy at Saskatchewan River, a remote community in Alberta. With her husband absent in uniform, a woman decided to hitch the family team to a set of disc harrows and put in the spring crop herself. The horses bolted and the woman fell under the machinery, emerging with her arm broken, her face terribly mangled, and an eye put out. When the awful news reached Edmonton, a doctor and nurse were dispatched to the scene. They saved her life, and the nurse remained with the woman and her three children for six weeks until she could be transferred to a hospital. Apart from the first $500, all her expenses were paid. The explanation was, of course, action by the Canadian Patriotic Fund. As the Fund's historian and assistant secretary, Philip Morris, later observed, "It was worth it and brought in many subscriptions wherever the story was told or known."[1]

In 1914 Montreal, Canada's largest city and centre of its corporate wealth, was a little poorer than its ambitious rival on Lake Ontario. Statistical yearbooks reported that Toronto had 72.3 percent of Montreal's population. Toronto had 79 percent of Montreal's area and 78.8 percent of its taxable value, but 120 percent of its revenue.[2] While Montreal's Protestants (and Jews) taxed themselves for free, if underfunded, elementary schools, most Catholic parents still paid fees. Attendance was "customary," not compulsory.[3] If parents needed their children's meagre wages, it was because the city's labour market was continually saturated by immigration from the countryside and from Europe. A monopoly kept the cost of heat, light, and transit high. Chronic unemployment kept even hard-working families poor.[4] Inflation led to overcrowding. An 1897 study had found occupancy rates of 0.86 to 1.09 persons per room; by 1914, the overcrowding was increasing.[5] Montreal

Catholics, Protestants, and Jews also looked after their own sick, disabled, and poor, whether through the parish-based Société de Saint-Vincent-de-Paul, St. Andrew's Society for impoverished Scots, or the Baron de Hirsch Institute, opened in 1914 for Jews.[6]

Social services in Montreal depended heavily on men like Herbert Brown Ames. Born to American parents in Montreal in 1851, Ames was a graduate of Amherst College and of postgraduate studies in Paris. By 1892 he was also the heir of Ames-Holden, one of Montreal's biggest boot and shoe manufacturers. Ames had long since tired of the footwear business, and he now felt free to turn to the fashionable field of urban social reform. Struck by the example of Charles Booth's survey of the London poor, and by earnest imitations in large, troubled American cities, Ames decided to explore Montreal's working-class districts. He prepared questionnaires, recruited agents, and collected data on housing conditions in the ethnically mixed southwestern quarter he described as the "city below the hill." Then he wrote newspaper articles on his work, collected them into a book in 1897, and focused on the need to invest in efficient and potentially profitable working-class housing. Ames avoided ethnic slurs and moral righteousness. Instead, his data correlated the worst housing conditions with the lowest incomes and the earliest mortality.[7] Ames was persuaded that education, healthy living conditions, and self-discipline could offer working-class families a satisfactory life without resort to either socialism or the ban-the-bottle righteousness common among contemporary middle-class do-gooders.

In 1899 George and Julia Drummond had introduced the Charity Organization Society (COS) to Montreal's Protestant benevolent associations. Without organization and cooperation among charities, unscrupulous beneficiaries could exploit several overlapping charities, incidentally reinforcing the character defects which, contemporaries believed, had made them poor in the first place. Scientific methods applied by professionals, claimed the COS, could both save the donors' dollars and redeem their recipients: "The welfare of souls and characters," said its first report, "is of more concern than freedom from physical suffering." The COS promoted "Friendly Visiting" and "the alms of good advice," a comforting philosophy for the wealthy families that inhabited the slopes of Mount Royal.[8] Montreal reformers had also made some progress in cutting infant mortality and typhoid fever, partly by encouraging distribution of safe milk through Gouttes de lait or milk depots, and by municipal takeover of water delivery. Montreal death and infant mortality rates were still much higher than in other major North American cities, and they reflected income disparities: while ten infants per thousand died in their first year in the affluent St. Antoine ward in 1914, the rate in Hochelaga was twenty-six per thousand.[9]

In 1914 Montreal was enduring harsh, divisive times. Beginning in 1906, the cost of living had begun a dramatic rise, all the more remarkable after decades of relative stability. Since 1912 the city had been gripped by severe economic depression, triggered by the overexpansion of Canada's railway systems, almost all of which had their headquarters in Montreal. Most aspects of city trade, from textile and clothing manufacturing to the Port of Montreal, experienced a painful hangover after a decade of unprecedented growth. Many businesses, new and long-established, faced ruin or merger; layoffs bred layoffs. According to Rufus Smith of the COS, the worst depression since the 1890s had left 20,000 Montrealers out of work in 1914, many of whom were homeless and hungry.[10]

Wealthy Montrealers had an obvious explanation for the city's failings: municipal administration was corrupt. As elsewhere in North America, Montreal reformers had had their day in the first decade of the century. Discreetly partnered with French-Canadian businessmen like Hormisdas Laporte, Ames had applied his knowledge of door-to-door polling to purge padded voters' lists and helped defeat "Boss" Raymond Préfontaine and his Liberal-backed City Hall machine in 1902. Like contemporary American municipal progressives, Montreal reformers battled for a board of control, elected citywide, to limit the power of "ward-heeling" aldermen, a planning commission to protect city amenities, improved police and fire services, and sharp cuts in public spending to balance the books. Most of their spending cuts fell on the city's poor.

Despite allies like Laporte and Henri Bourassa, the reformers looked too English for a city where most people now spoke French. Reform support soon faded. In 1904 Ames switched to the federal Parliament as Conservative MP for the downtown business district of St-Antoine. Municipal reform returned in 1910, backed by Bourassa's newly founded *Le Devoir,* but "le règne des honnêtes gens" was short lived.[11] Hard times, coinciding with Robert Borden's Conservative victory in 1911, aggravated the city's perennial fiscal crisis. In 1914 reformers confidently presented the former provincial treasurer, George Washington Stephens, as mayoral candidate. In Montreal's long-standing tradition of English-French alternation, it was the turn of an English-speaking mayor. Instead, by a margin of 5,000, Montreal voters gave the job to Médéric Martin, a former cigar maker who had been removed as alderman for corruption in 1910. Never again would the English elect a mayor of Montreal.[12]

Despite falling revenues, Martin did what he could for the city's poor. On borrowed money, he set 18,000 men to labour on public works. When war broke out, he insisted over council opposition that city employees summoned as reservists by the French or Belgian armies would keep their salaries. A bigger question was whether banks, panicked by chaotic financial markets, would continue to lend

Montreal money. Quebec laid off its road gangs as a precaution, reported *Le Devoir*, while *La Presse* announced that the Bank of Montreal could meet only half of the city's $6 million loan.[13] Could the same people who condemned Martin's administration for profligacy, corruption, and living on debt also urge City Hall to spend money on soldiers' families?

Architects of the CPF

The hardy perennial response to a variety of wartime needs when Canada or its Empire went to war was the creation of a Patriotic Fund. It had happened early in the War of 1812, again during the Crimean War in 1854, and most recently in 1900, after fresh contingents of Canadians left to serve Britain in the South African War. In between, smaller funds financed help for the widows and orphans of British imperial campaigns.

The original Loyal and Patriotic Society of Upper Canada had raised £13,481, largely in Britain as well as in British North America and even the United States, to clothe the Upper Canadian Militia, care for their sick and wounded and their families, and even to pay for a medal for their leaders. In 1854, led by Col. Étienne-Paschal Taché, adjutant general of the militia and future prime minister of the Confederation government, British North America launched a second Patriotic Fund that raised £46,575 for the widows and orphans of sailors or soldiers who lost their lives in the war with Russia, and even shared £655 with Britain's French allies.[14]

The South African War, 1899-1902, inspired the third iteration, the Canadian Patriotic Fund Association (CPFA), headed by Col. D.T. Irwin of the Permanent Force artillery and J.M. Courtney, the deputy federal finance minister. It was launched on 12 January 1900 and incorporated by Canada's Parliament on 23 May 1901. After two official Canadian contingents returned from South Africa in early 1901, thousands more Canadians departed in contingents organized and financed by Britain, at the normal low British military pay scales. The CPFA collected donations and spent about $32,000 on 344 of the volunteers' wives, orphans, and other dependants. It also supplemented the meagre British pensions paid to families of those who never returned, and provided help for 639 volunteers who came home disabled by wounds, injuries, or sickness.[15] The most famous of these, Lorne Mulloy, "the Blinded Trooper," managed to have his way paid through Queen's and Oxford Universities at a cost exceeding $4,000. Mulloy's ability, courage, and charm, reinforced by the patronage of Sir Sanford Fleming, overcame the protests of the CPFA executive who had assumed "that all sufferers should receive similar treatment."[16] The CPFA still existed in 1914, though it had long since exhausted its functions, if not its funds.

Herbert Ames left no memoirs, but his claim to be chief architect of the fourth, largest, and final Canadian Patriotic Fund appears unchallenged.[17] Ideas are seldom unique or wholly original, and their success depends on context more than ingenuity, but someone has to formulate and defend them. The idea of a national fund had ample precedents, but the previous CPFA had never managed to overcome the Canadian tendency to fragmentation and localism. Most local funds raised and spent their own money. If the 1914 version of the CPF was to equalize very different regional levels of wealth, commitment, and living costs across Canada, it would need to be strong enough to persuade local branches to collect funds and transfer them to a national organization that would then remit them on a basis widely accepted as fair. It could not hope to do so unless its burden was specific. Ames was responsible for limiting the 1914 CPF to the actual needs of soldiers' dependants. By addressing only the more impoverished dependants, perhaps with some of "the alms of good advice" and attention to problem solving as well as opportune cash, Ames reasoned, a national CPF could make beneficial use of the wartime crisis to undermine a major sector of Canadian poverty.

With such ideas already taking shape in his mind, Ames travelled to Ottawa in early August to find a place in the crowded waiting rooms of the prime minister and the minister of militia. He found both men gratefully responsive. Ames was, after all, Borden's kind of progressive conservative, while Hughes was delighted to be relieved of a problem he easily recognized but had never apparently considered. Yes, the prime minister agreed, there would have to be a special allowance for wives and even dependent mothers. And no, Col. Hughes agreed, pensions and care for the disabled should not be left to the whims of private charity. Anything linked to patriotic zeal instinctively delighted the flamboyant minister. How better to serve the special needs of families while their men served in a short and glorious war? As the Mulloy case had underlined after the Boer War, paying pensions and compensating disability from charity could bring political difficulties, but nothing could be more appropriate for a wartime charity than serving families deprived of a patriotic breadwinner. The obvious alternative, higher pay for all soldiers, would let the possible needs of a minority inflate the pay scales of the great majority. No responsible, business-minded government would do that!

Another generation might argue for a "family wage," that a soldier's pay, like any other salary or wage, should be sufficient to support a family. Had any employer, public or private, ever guaranteed extra wages to a married employee, and still more pay when the employee became a parent? However, Sir Robert Borden had quietly confessed to Ames, the brand-new separation allowance would meet no more than the needs of a single dependant. Other expenses, from children to high local costs of living to medical bills, would be left to the Patriotic Fund. A government could never discriminate; a charity had every right and duty to do so. On 10 August, Hughes called the press and seized the credit: "We propose a special fund, in addition to any that may be raised for widows or disabled soldiers. It will be for the purpose of generating regular pay to the people dependent upon our volunteers when they are away. It is not charity or a relief fund that is proposed, but a straight business proposition which I do not doubt will appeal to the patriotism and common sense of our people."[18]

When key members of Montreal's commercial and social elite gathered at the Board of Trade at noon on 10 August, the MP for St-Antoine was among them. With practised efficiency R.J. Dale, president of the Board of Trade, called the meeting to order. Col. A.E. Labelle, vice-president of St. Lawrence Flour Mills and chairman of Montreal's Patriotic Fund during the Boer War, explained that his fund had spent as much as $30,000 on local families, and warned that the new war might require as much as $100,000. Next, Ames reported on the government's intention to create a Canadian Patriotic Fund when Parliament met in emergency session on 18 August. This time, Ames reported, the fund would limit its scope to soldiers' cash-strapped families. Meeting long-term needs like pensions and hospital care with cash raised from wartime patriotism did not work. The prime need was not charity or relief for families, Ames cited Sam Hughes, but a way of "generating regular pay to the people dependent upon our volunteers when they are away."[19]

After the applause came Senator Raoul Dandurand. In a businesslike, bipartisan, and bicultural spirit, he pledged that the $9,000 already collected by the Franco-Belgian Committee would be merged with the new fund, and he seconded Ames's motion to transfer the business to an executive committee. Most participants then adjourned for lunch or business, but the executive committee stayed in session. It included Ames as president, Dale, Labelle, Arthur R. Doble of Royal Securities, shipping magnate R.W. Reford, and Sir Hugh Graham of the *Montreal Daily Star*. Bishop Farthing represented the Anglicans; a clothing merchant, David Friedman, spoke for the Jewish community; others included Lt.-Col. F. Minden Cole, an insurance broker whose wife ran the Soldiers' Wives League. The Catholic archbishop, Paul-Napoléon Bruchési, and newly elected Mayor Martin were absent, but Dandurand, Dr. Lachapelle, J.R. Genin, Alfred Tarut, and Gustave Francq from the Franco-Belgian Committee all were present.

Ames took the chair while John W. Ross of the accounting firm of P.S. Ross agreed to be honorary treasurer, a role he had often played in other Montreal campaigns. Doubts raised by the general meeting about whether French and Belgian reservists should be included vanished in the executive. Bishop Farthing was deputed to compile a list of British reservists, other duties were briskly assigned, and the meeting concluded within an hour.[20] Meanwhile, the *Star*, Montreal's dominant English-language newspaper, spread the desired message to its readers:

WIVES AND CHILDREN OF THOSE WHO GO TO WAR WILL BE CARED FOR BY MONTREAL CITIZENS.[21]

Later that day, society women gathered under the presidency of Mrs. J.A. Henderson of the Local Council of Women to provide Ames with another audience. After the earnest MP had expounded his proposal, Lady Drummond warned the Council: "We shall have to give up dances, dinner parties and fashionable luncheon parties this year, and spend our money, not on luxuries for ourselves, but on necessaries for our soldiers' families ... Even if it means personal deprivation, not a soldier's family should suffer in Montreal." In the wake of this stern message, Ames invited the gathering to nominate three ladies for the board of Montreal's new Patriotic Fund.[22]

At 11 a.m. on 14 August, Col. Labelle and the remnant of the old South African War Patriotic Fund committee met at the Board of Trade for the first time since 1904, dissolved the organization, and handed $771.22 to the new fund. Much of the brief meeting was devoted to thanking the Soldiers' Wives League, an organization dominated by militia officers' wives, who, Labelle boasted, had carefully investigated each wife and family that had benefited from the Fund. The president, June Busteed, another colonel's wife, and her successor, Florence Cole, had adopted approved COS practices and established a model for the future.[23]

At noon on the same day, Ames welcomed a fifty-member general committee of the new Fund, including six women led by Mrs. Henderson. This time, Mayor Martin and the Catholic archbishop, Msgr. Bruchési, made an appearance, though Bruchési promptly deputed a canon to represent him. Eleven of the fifty members bore French names.[24] A representative of the French consul reported 1,100 reservists' families being supported, at a rate of $0.60 for the wife per day and $0.25 for each child. Consul de Sola claimed up to 300 Belgians, but only 70 British reservists had yet been found. "Were married men handing over part of their pay?" demanded Dr. Milton Hersey, a millionaire mining magnate. The government should insist on at least half. Some employers, reported Col. Starke, were covering all or part of a man's former wages. Such firms, agreed Ames, should join an Honour Roll.[25]

The Montreal executive met again on 17 August. Serious work had begun. Ames and Ross appointed the wealthier members to a finance committee under jeweller

William M. Birks. Members favoured a cheaper uptown location for Fund offices. Mrs. Busteed volunteered the Soldiers' Wives League to staff the office and to visit families. The Manufacturers Association agreed to give names of all patriotic employers who offered pay in full or in part to men who enlisted. The Fund could ensure that their families received no further help. Some landlords, Ames hoped, might "allow families to remain on rent free while the breadwinner was away." Responding to Dr. Hersey, the executive again agreed that the government should compel married men to "assign a portion of their pay to be retained and paid direct to the wife."[26]

Responding across Canada

As in Montreal, eminent citizens, business organizations and respectable women across Canada seldom waited for politicians to solve problems but instead seized the initiative. As men thronged local armouries from Halifax to Victoria, responsible citizens recognized the implications. On 17 August, Winnipeg's Industrial Bureau again took the initiative and summoned representatives of the city's charities. Buoyed by the self-confidence of Canada's fastest-growing city and the capital of its potentially richest region, the Bureau was soon well on its way to creating a distinct Manitoba Patriotic Fund. On 19 August, Mayor J.H. Frink of Saint John and a few prominent citizens met to launch a Soldiers' and Families Patriotic Fund. In Edmonton, Calgary, and Victoria, chapters of the 40,000-member Imperial Order Daughters of the Empire (IODE) began seeking out soldiers' dependants almost as soon as the war began. In some towns, like Sherbrooke, Quebec, and Belleville, Ontario, veteran militia officers recognized the problem and took the lead. Col. S.S. Lazier of Hastings County's 15th Argyle Light Infantry made himself chairman of a fund for Belleville and the surrounding county. In Chatham, Ontario, a Relief Fund already established for the local unemployed agreed to accept victims of wartime disruption as part of its mandate.

Almost everywhere, the distinction between soldiers' families and other victims of war-induced unemployment became a matter of debate. Poverty, after all, looked and felt the same, and who could really be blamed if the war was the cause? Yet could the dramatic appeal of patriotism be mobilized to feed those who had merely lost their jobs? Or would donors be indignant that their dollars helped soldiers' wives in a distant province and not poverty-stricken families in their own town? Charles Magrath of the national executive of the CPF seldom lacked an opinion: the two causes, he insisted, must not be mixed. "We must remember," he soon warned Ames, "that the public at times is a loose thinker, and when dealing with its funds – trust monies – don't give it any tendency to change its opinion from time to time as to what it intended should be done with its monies."[27] Ames accepted the advice.

Relief of the poor was not the only patriotic diversion that autumn. In Toronto, Canada's most British and Empire-minded city, the IODE was so captivated by a project to find $100,000 for a Canadian hospital ship that it had no time for lesser causes.[28] Fortunately for Ames, Sir William Mulock, a prominent jurist and former Laurier minister, later claimed that the idea of a patriotic fund had struck him on 10 August, and he had shared it immediately with E.R. Wood, millionaire president of Central Canada Loan & Savings. The two men had been planning a capital campaign on behalf of the Young Men's Christian Association (YMCA), which they sidetracked at once. Next day, they summoned an invited meeting of selected financiers, bankers, and newspaper publishers to lay out their plans for a "Toronto Citizens' Association for the purpose of raising a patriotic fund for the relief of wives, children and other dependants of residents in Canada who are enlisting in the cause of the Empire in connection with the present war."[29] Mulock and Wood emerged from the meeting as president and honorary treasurer respectively. A second meeting in Toronto's city council chamber on 14 August added Mayor Hocken, provincial opposition leader Newton W. Rowell, and more notables. It also extended coverage to the surrounding county of York. As in Montreal, management was left to an executive committee of fifty, chosen largely from elected politicians, presidents of business, trade, and labour associations, and the local military district commander. A significant decision was to launch an early appeal for funds. "No family member of a departing hero could be allowed to 'go wanting,'" claimed the *Toronto Daily Star,* "It was not a burden but a privilege" to support the fund.[30]

Ten days later, the 3,500 people who packed Toronto's Massey Hall noisily agreed. Amid brass bands, patriotic speeches, and deafening applause, Mulock welcomed "the greatest combination of public men who have ever been associated for a public purpose in Ontario." The *Mail and Empire* claimed, "Never before had the great heart of Toronto throbbed and pulsated with more patriotic enthusiasm or been thrilled with a greater loyalty to the mother country."[31] When launched on 24 August, the Toronto campaign generated over $250,000 in contributions during its first three hours, and more than $700,000 in its first three days, with an ultimate five-day total of $882,000.

This was impressive for a city hard hit by the prewar depression and experiencing significant layoffs as companies hedged their production targets against unpredictable war risks. With most of its substantial German exports shipped but unlikely to be paid for, the farm machinery firm of Massey-Harris ordered 2,500 layoffs. Still, Toronto city council voted a flat $50,000 donation, and the Toronto-based Bank of Commerce promptly matched the pledge. Not to be outdone in warlike zeal, department-store magnate John C. Eaton offered $100,000 to equip a Vickers machine-gun battery and contributed his lake steamer, the *Florence*, and his wireless radio station for Canada's defence.

Selling the Principles

The newest Canadian Patriotic Fund was officially launched on 18 August 1914, at a meeting in the prime minister's office. The governor general, His Royal Highness, Arthur, Duke of Connaught and Strathearn, had been on the verge of completing his term at Rideau Hall and returning to England. When the war intervened, the prestige of a son of Queen Victoria and the experience of a lifetime career in the army, including an early year as a subaltern in garrison at Quebec's Citadel, was redirected towards Canada's imperial war effort. Soon wearied by the stream of viceregal military advice, the government of Sir Robert Borden was delighted to invite the duke and provincial lieutenant governors to organize the country's prime wartime charity. Perhaps then the government's ministers could get on with more urgent business.

Viceregal patronage attracted a galaxy of political, commercial, and social ambition, from Sir Edmund Walker of the Bank of Commerce and Montreal magnate Senator Raoul Dandurand to young William Lyon Mackenzie King, Laurier's former minister of labour and, until August 1914, chief Canadian promoter of the Centenary of Peace along the US-Canadian border. However, the key figure on hand that day was the government backbencher who had finally found something he wanted to do. Having made himself president of Montreal's Patriotic Fund, Herbert Ames could act with a knowledge and assurance most others in the room lacked. He saw that a nationwide Patriotic Fund could become a custom-made vehicle for his ideas and his energy.

Once he had quietly established his view that the fund must include the needs of both British and Allied reservists, the duke opened the meeting with a proposal for a single national organization "to deal with any voluntary provincial, local or other association which might be in existence."[32] The government or some other fund would have to deal with the sick, the wounded, and survivors' pensions. The new Patriotic Fund "could do no more than ensure for soldiers' dependants a reasonable standard of comfort during the absence of the breadwinner."[33] Obviously, poorer provinces and some depression-hit regions would be hard pressed to pay their share. If potential volunteers were not to be deterred from enlisting by fear of leaving their families destitute, there would have to be a nationwide organization, with common standards and pooling of funds. Already some communities and regions were proceeding independently, as they had during the South African War. There could be no further delay. By applying the duke's royal prestige to enlist provincial lieutenant governors, unity might still be achieved.

The meeting broke up at noon. Ames had already been designated honorary secretary. He and a drafting committee remained to meet with parliamentary counsel to draft legislation. Other members of the inner committee included Walker, Dandurand, and King as Liberals, and Thomas Chase Casgrain, a veteran Quebec Tory lawyer. By 5 p.m. they had settled on a draft bill.[34]

When Parliament met in emergency wartime session on 18 August, it had two major tasks. Britain had declared war for all its colonies, but Canadian MPs agreed to approve a War Measures Act so sweeping that it surely satisfied an Opposition MP's demand that nothing be left out that a wartime government might need. Next, almost as an afterthought, Parliament accepted the full costs of Canada's war effort – in 1899 Canada had paid only to deliver its men to South Africa – through a War Appropriation Act and a Finance Act that suspended redemption in gold of Canadian currency.[35] On 21 August, Manitoba's Bob Rogers, the minister of public works, introduced the first reading of Bill 7, which incorporated the Canadian Patriotic Fund. Much of the language was drawn from the earlier 1901 legislation, but the purpose or "objects" of the new CPF had been more carefully limited than MPs may have realized: "The objects of the Corporation shall be to collect, administer, and distribute the fund hereinbefore mentioned for the assistance in case of need of the wives, children and dependent relatives of officers and men, resident in Canada, who, during the present war, may be on active service with the naval and military forces of the British Empire and Great Britain's Allies."[36]

As defined by its chief architect, the Patriotic Fund corporation was both more and less than it was believed to be. No definitions accompanied the act to help the Fund interpret "in case of need" or "dependent relatives" or "active service." Parliament is an undependable instrument for legislative oversight at the best of times. When the Patriotic Fund bill was introduced in the hectic atmosphere of a wartime emergency session, it was surprising that any MP even recognized an issue. The few Liberal critics were soon reminded that their complaints would have applied equally to the Laurier-era Patriotic Fund Act adopted in 1901, and accordingly, they subsided. Instead of listing the board members by name, William Pugsley won the sensible modification that provincial premiers should belong by reason of occupying the office. His further proposal that wealthy benefactors like Montreal's John Kenneth Leveson Ross and Toronto's Sir John Eaton be included on the executive was rejected.[37] Eaton's money had been offered for machine guns, not to support families, while Ross's generosity primarily took the form of offering his yacht as a destroyer for Canada's tiny navy. Col. H.H. McLean, a New Brunswick

Liberal and militia veteran, recalled the rivalries that helped frustrate the earlier fund. This time, he hoped for a fund so representative "that all the provinces, all private individuals, all municipalities should be able to subscribe to it."[38] Cape Breton Liberal MP E.M. Macdonald worried predictably that the Maritimes were insufficiently represented on the board.

Who could benefit from the Fund? D.D. McKenzie, another Liberal, warned that the word "relatives" might, under Nova Scotia law, exclude the parents of an adopted son. Manitoba cabinet minister Bob Rogers recalled that the word "dependant" in the 1901 legislation had raised problems, though he could not remember what they were. The prime minister promised to look into it.[39] Emmanuel Berchmans Devlin, a Liberal member from the Ottawa Valley riding of Wright, asked whether the Fund would cover families of men on Canada's two cruisers, the *Niobe* and the *Rainbow,* as well as "men who may be on active service not outside the Dominion of Canada." Reassurance came immediately from Sir Robert Borden, promptly echoed by Rodolphe Lemieux: "That was the view taken the other day at the first meeting of the committee – that it applies to any man on active service during the present emergency."[40] Devlin persisted, even during third reading: perhaps there could be at least the promise of an amendment that "active service" might apply to "men in, as well as outside of the Dominion." Rogers was categorical: just before the unanimous vote on 22 August, he wanted it "to be clearly understood by the members that it was the intention of the committee drafting this Bill that it should be wide enough to cover the services of Canadians at home."[41] If not, the prime minister assured Devlin, "I am sure that the committee will ask the House to remedy that at another session."[42] One feature of the Fund was not discussed: as a national body with subordinate branches, every cent contributed was vested in the national Fund, not in its branches. To underline the point, Ottawa's auditor general would be the CPF's auditor.[43] By 28 August, the Patriotic Fund had Senate approval and the status of law.

The government had quickly and neatly handed off much of the financial responsibility for soldiers' families and dependants to a charity. The CPF would be overseen, to be sure, by some of the most eminent Canadians, and it would be managed by a self-taught expert on the urban poor and by the like-minded people who would soon expand the Canadian Patriotic Fund into a near-nationwide organization. But regardless of the prime minister's assurances, the families Devlin had worried about would be consciously and deliberately excluded from the CPF's benevolence. Convinced that patriotic generosity would not extend to the families of militia members on garrison duty, Patriotic Fund administrators refused to consider the families of Home Service soldiers. Or they devised rules that would make Fund allowances unnecessary. As the British Columbia secretary, C.H.

Bonnor, explained to the local military commander: "Under the regulations of the Canadian Patriotic Fund, a man who is on Home Service is expected to assign his wife 80 cents per diem from his Regimental Pay, or $24.00 per month, and the Subsistence Allowance of 45 cents per diem, or $13.50 per month, making her total income $37.50, and such wife is therefore not entitled to any assistance from this Fund."[44]

Creating a Nationwide Fund

On 25 August the Duke of Connaught formally became president and Ames the honorary secretary and de facto manager of the new Canadian Patriotic Fund.[45] Once the Canadian Patriotic Fund bill became law, the governor general's prestige was engaged at once. In a nationally distributed advertisement proclaiming the existence of the new organization, his open letter invited every city and town across Canada to start a branch, and warned that "unless generous-minded citizens come to their aid, there will be, during the coming winter, much hardship in many families owing to the absence of the breadwinner." In an early intimation of the "Fight or Pay" slogan that would dominate CPF publicity, the duke concluded, "I am convinced that all Canadian hearts will go out to their brave fellow citizens who have gone to the front. A prompt and hearty response to this appeal will put all anxiety at rest about those near and dear to them, and will also afford to those who cannot go an opportunity of doing their duty to Canada and the Empire."[46]

Ames's role was more than honorary. In addition to presiding over the Montreal fund, he had a national office to open, staff to recruit, and a host of complex issues to resolve, with or without committees of prominent Canadians who had their own affairs to manage. Philip Morris was recruited as Ames's executive secretary, to help develop an organization and to manage records that included a card file for each soldier benefited by the Fund. Under Sir Thomas White, Borden's minister of finance and a somewhat detached honorary treasurer, E.L. Brittain from the finance department acted as the real treasurer, keeping the accounts under the supervision of the federal auditor general.[47] Meanwhile, responses to the duke's messages flooded in to Ottawa. So did offers from inexperienced volunteers, demanding opportunities of service. Perhaps the biggest cities could be managed, but who knew Canada's smaller communities well enough to know whether an offer of local leadership should be accepted or perhaps deferred in hope of a stronger or more respected alternative? A national organization operating through local branches needed simple, reasonable, and standard definitions of "need" and "dependency" in a country that was continent-wide and highly diverse.

National averages for wages and the cost of living in 1914 were not only primitive by later standards, but highly misleading. Anyone who travelled west knew that most Winnipeggers and Vancouverites paid a lot more for rent or potatoes than most Torontonians and Montrealers, and the *Labour Gazette* published monthly reports on local or seasonal variations on living costs.[48] Yet rates set for a national fund would be closely scanned for regional discrimination. Toronto and Montreal were homes to Canada's biggest companies and wealthiest individuals: would they contribute generously if their soldiers' families complained about being less well treated than their counterparts in Regina or Revelstoke? Alternatively, would it be fair to give people more money than they really needed while others in the West might have barely enough?

Defining dependency had seemed easy in the first days of the war. Married men left behind their wives and children. In most Canadian communities in 1914, a married woman who worked was publicly admitting that her husband was a poor provider. If she had children, it was her whole duty to care for them: mothers who worked were almost automatically assumed to be neglecting their central responsibility. If the war had imposed such a desperate situation, it was an obvious evil that Canadian society must set right. Equally, grown children were expected to support their aging parents, and particularly their mother, as their return on the family's social contract. Of course, the father's duty as wage-earner did not end with old age. Systematic superannuation, like widespread old-age pensions, was still a radical and foreign idea in 1914 Canada. Siblings were to share the parental burden. While the enlistment of one member of a large and grown-up family was hardly grounds for concern, if a soldier was his mother's sole support, she was as much his dependant as any wife.

The devil, as usual, was in the details. What if a soldier's siblings were young, disabled, or unemployed? What if a soldier had been supporting his adolescent sisters or even a younger brother attending school? Would they also be treated as dependants by the Canadian Patriotic Fund? And if so, would hard-nosed subscribers agree? Many Canadians in 1914 believed that no respectable man took charity, and that if a woman was too plain or ill tempered to find a husband, she must find work instead. Because it was dependent on the prejudices of its major donors, the Fund was as susceptible to opinion as any politician, and because it depended most heavily on the affluent, it was even more subject to the prejudices of the wealthy. In Britain, the prime minister might brave the frowns of church and aristocracy to give "unmarried wives" separation allowance; as a charity dependent on elite approval and financial support, the Patriotic was susceptible to its donors. Ames's solution was to shift responsibility to the bureaucracy. Once the

Canadian Expeditionary Force granted separation allowance to a dependant, even an "unmarried wife," she or he was automatically eligible for Patriotic Fund assistance if needed.[49] Additional cases might be considered and even accepted at a meagre rate, but the missing SA would not be replaced.[50]

In turn, that resolved an even bigger dilemma, already raised in the brief parliamentary debate. Could all of Canada's defenders rely on the Patriotic Fund to meet their family's needs, or only those who were committed to overseas service? The assurances offered Emmanuel Devlin implied full and equal coverage, whether a soldier went to Valcartier with the CEF, watched for German or Fenian saboteurs along the Welland Canal, or peered through the dense fog around Halifax's fortifications. Ames had a much narrower view and, as a lawyer like Devlin appreciated, "active service" was not the same as providing for domestic security. Moreover, public opinion generally agreed: heroes willing to sacrifice their lives in France or Flanders inspired generosity; Militia guards on railway bridges or outside an internment camp of Ukrainian "enemy aliens" did not.

Passing legislation and distributing the governor general's letter did not in themselves create a national organization. Loading direct responsibility onto provincial lieutenant governors was a start, where those largely nominal officials had the will and the energy. Elsewhere, Ames could direct his influence at members of Parliament and provincial legislatures, at mayors, reeves, and county wardens, and at business and civic leaders eager for some practical outlet for their patriotic fervour. Ames's Montreal experience provided him with the model he commended to other communities. As in Montreal, boards should be as broadly based, influential, and as multipartisan as possible. Not all offers were welcome. As Philip Morris, the Fund's assistant secretary, later recalled, "It was felt unwise that any existing society, however zealous, with a limited membership should undertake, unaided, so large an enterprise. Those who professed themselves ready to take the lead in the movement were exhorted to secure the co-operation of leading men in all lines of commercial and professional activity, not to confine their search for helpers to men of one political or religious faith, but to win the interest of men of varying political opinions, of different religious beliefs."[51]

On 24 August Ames had summoned the sixty-four-member general committee of the Montreal Patriotic Fund to become the first branch of the new national organization.[52] Since Ames had largely embodied the Montreal terms of reference in the national charter, there was no need to restructure the branch. An immediate benefit of the change was a $100,000 pledge from the Bank of Montreal channelled to Ottawa through the local branch, half of it immediately. The prickly question of whether the local or the national organization actually owned the funds was neatly skirted. Afterwards, Ames shared the truth with the smaller executive committee: the national CPF expected branches to forward their receipts to Ottawa; the local treasurers would then draw on the central fund according to national policies.[53]

The Montreal branch already had clients. Rufus Smith had moved over from the Charity Organization Society to apply his experience at the formative stage. On 24 August he reported over a hundred applicants for aid. Something, he insisted, must be done to separate the deserving from the undeserving. On 26 August the executive appointed a relief committee under Clarence Smith, vice-president of Ames, Holden, McCready, and a man Ames obviously trusted.[54] His committee members included John W. Ross, Bishop Farthing, J.R. Genin, Gustave Francq, Dr. Lachapelle, and Mayor Martin. After debating uptown and downtown locations, the executive approved offices in the uptown Drummond Building. Rufus Smith announced that he had started a card index of applicants, while Ross arranged with the Bank of Montreal that all payments would be made by cheque and countersigned by him.

As they had during the South African War, Mrs. Cole and Mrs. Busteed urged home visits to confirm both the bona fides and the needs of claimants. This was work that busy professional and business men could hardly be expected to do. While Rufus Smith, Bishop Farthing, and Dr. Lachapelle agreed to oversee the work, Ames turned to the women he had met in the fund's earliest days. They guided him to Helen Reid. One of McGill University's first woman graduates or "Donaldas," Reid had combined foreign study and travel with service for the National Council of the Women of Canada. Her growing familiarity with social issues led her, by 1914, to be volunteer supervisor of social work for the Victorian Order of Nurses in Montreal. Elected convenor at a meeting of the Fund's "women's auxiliary," Reid rapidly made herself the Montreal Patriotic Fund's most powerful woman.[55]

By 4 September the relief committee's Clarence Smith reported a budget and card system in place for the Montreal branch, 250 applicants, and $1,500 already paid out in temporary relief. Smith's committee had appointed a paid office staff under Mr. N. Rough at $100 a month, with two male assistants at $75 and $50 respectively, and three female secretaries at $30 a month each.[56] Ames returned to Ottawa, confident in a dependable Montreal branch and convinced that any new branch essentially needed only two committees, one to collect the funds and the other to distribute them, as well as, if possible, a ladies' auxiliary.

Ames hoped to use provincial associations as umbrellas for organizing local branches of the national Fund. Saskatchewan became the first to satisfy this ideal. Less than nine years old, a large pioneer province with hundreds of small, scattered rural communities, Saskatchewan could never be organized from Ottawa.

Yet 1,800 of its men had thronged to Valcartier and they dominated two of the CEF's seventeen infantry battalions. Many had left wives and children to face winter on lonely prairie homesteads. Responding to the challenge, Premier Walter Scott turned to his lieutenant governor, George William Brown, a Regina lawyer, Qu'Appelle Valley rancher, and veteran Liberal politician. Brown, in turn, summoned prominent citizens to a meeting in Regina on 31 August and emerged as president of a provincial Patriotic Fund executive. Commissioner A.B. Perry of the Royal North West Mounted Police and W.C. Murray, president of the University of Saskatchewan in Saskatoon, became vice-presidents. Premier Scott and his Conservative rival, Sir Frederick Haultain, headed an executive committee. An advisory committee provided representation for other voices and regions. The Scott government provided the provincial CPF an office in the new Legislature Building and agreed to absorb all the administrative costs, including wages for a secretary, Thomas M. Bee of Regina. With a strong central committee focused on organization, local community-based branches soon followed.

By February 1915 Saskatchewan boasted 260 branches, all affiliated with the national CPF. Ultimately, from Abbey to Zealandia and from Eyebrow to Waldeck, the province claimed 418 functioning local branches. Only Prince Albert and Maple Creek insisted on their independence from the organization, and even they eventually succumbed.[57] In November 1914 Saskatchewan's CPF issued its first cheque, to a French reservist's wife near Assiniboia. No province fulfilled the CPF's plan more completely. Ames's faith in home visiting was equally reciprocated: by early 1915, the Regina branch had even hired a full-time woman visitor. The next step was a Dependants' League, with weekly meetings for soldiers' wives and mothers. Farm communities, enjoying some of their best cash returns in years in 1915, shared their good fortune with the Patriotic Fund, and Thomas Bee reported "on good authority, that the File Hills Indian Reserve contributed, both in men and money, the highest per capita of any community in our province."[58]

Alberta and Manitoba might have followed the same pattern, but Winnipeg's Industrial Bureau had already led its province too far to contemplate submission to Ottawa. By 26 August 1914 an executive committee under the Bureau's W.J. Bulman had mustered most of Winnipeg's leading industrialists and an impressive selection of prominent citizens. A finance committee under the forceful Augustus M. Nanton mustered only the city's wealthy. Smaller medical and legal committees fulfilled the promises of their respective professions that deserving dependants could count on free services. On 31 August an "approval committee," with Nanton as chair, Bulman, John Galt, Judge H.A. Robson, and the Bureau's Charles Roland as secretary, began meeting with men eager to enlist if assured that their families would be cared for. By 12 September effective fundraising had amassed a mixture of gifts and pledges totalling $249,518.

Ames was in Winnipeg when the local executive met to consider a request from the suburban municipality of West Kildonan for inclusion. A committee recommended that the Winnipeg body constitute itself a Manitoba-wide organization. At the same time, after some debate, the executive also decided to ignore Ames's plea. Manitoba "should stand separate from the Canadian Patriotic Fund in the way of raising and administering funds although quite willing to follow the national organization in general work and policy."[59] With the whole province contributing, by 19 October after two months of work, the Manitoba fund boasted a total of $632,999.98. Recruiters credited the fund with a flood of CEF volunteers, though more cynical observers noted that the flood of harvest labour annually released through Winnipeg after the prairie freeze-up now headed to a patriotic destination after they had squandered their wages on Main Street's downtown attractions.

One reason Manitoba refused to trust its funds to Ottawa was a local insistence that the Patriotic Fund had to deal with other consequences of the war than penniless dependants. Nervous about the impact of a European war on markets and prices, Winnipeg's industrialists had slashed their payrolls and, if public charity did not ease the resulting poverty, municipal welfare costs might soar. For his part, Ames was determined that the Patriotic Fund must stick to its specific patriotic purpose of helping soldiers' families. His own Montreal municipal experience would have strengthened his aversion. Unemployment, he and many others believed, was a misfortune that provident families prepared for with their savings; national service in time of war was a totally different matter. Perhaps his Winnipeg hosts might have agreed with the distinction, but Ames was not solving their problem. As a result, the Manitoba Patriotic Fund felt free to spend $70,023.91 on unemployed civilians, and Mrs. Nanton, assisted by scores of wives of other influential Winnipeggers, distributed over 15,000 items of clothing to the city's needy families as well as to the impoverished dependants of soldiers. Like Ames, they might have appreciated a little discrimination but, like beggars, they were not choosers. In another traditional response to unemployment, the Manitoba fund opened a wood camp, under the supervision of hardware merchant J.H. Ashdown and Winnipeg's city controller, R.D. Waugh. At an expense of $15,843, it provided work chopping firewood for 357 men.[60]

By the time Alberta started to organize in early October, it was already divided by the bitter rivalry of its two principal cities. Organization was heralded by a pre-session announcement by Premier Arthur L. Sifton that the legislature would require all provincial civil servants to contribute 5 percent of their salaries to the

Patriotic Fund – and 10 percent from those earning over $1,500. This would constitute a guaranteed income of $8,000 per month. Faculty and staff at the provincial university dutifully followed suit. Once he and the province's chief justice had accepted the same 10 percent tax on their official salaries, Lieutenant Governor George H. Bulyea and Premier Sifton promised a provincewide organizing meeting for 7 October. Meanwhile, Bulyea summoned a public meeting in Edmonton on 12 September with Premier Sifton, cabinet ministers, and prominent citizens. Veteran *Edmonton Bulletin* publisher and federal MP Frank Oliver emerged as honorary president of an Edmonton branch of the CPF, A.F. Ewing, an Edmonton MLA, as president, and John Blue, the provincial librarian, as honorary secretary.

Independently, Mrs. W.D. Ferris of the Beaver House chapter of the IODE had summoned members of other chapters to her home on 29 August to consider the needs of soldiers' dependants. Their task was not made easy. Military authorities refused to supply either a list of the men who had enlisted or the addresses of their dependants. The truth, too embarrassing to be shared, was that the authorities did not have such a list! IODE members were reduced to posting notices at drug and grocery stores and the post office. When they met again at the Edmonton YWCA, a number of soldiers' wives showed up. For the first time, the IODE women learned to their horror that departing soldiers had left their families penniless. Using reserve funds and the proceeds of a hurriedly organized rummage sale, Mrs. Ferris soon collected $1,600. By then, the Patriotic Fund had taken over, but the IODE's eight-member relief committee was a ready-made auxiliary, visiting homes, reporting cases of illness, and recommending special grants.

Though handicapped by the lack of any estimate of how long the war would last, or how much money would be needed, Oliver's finance committee promptly planned a fundraising campaign for Edmonton. When a wealthy local businessman phoned the campaign on the day of the main collection and asked how much would be needed for a year, the hurried response was $250,000 for a year. Nonsense, the man responded; that much money would not be needed over five years. In fact, the Edmonton target was $125,000 and the campaign was perhaps fortunate to raise $40,000 over the first three days. Herbert Ames arrived in Edmonton on 28 September, fresh from Regina where he had advised on rates of eligibility and benefits. It was the fourth day of the Northern Alberta canvass, and Ames was rushed across the city to speak to the Canadian Club and a variety of associations, as well as a public meeting in the evening. With his vision of the CPF consolidated, Ames was in his element, and audiences, eager to set aside partisanship and localism, warmed to his earnest practicality. Morris, the Fund's official historian, reported on Ames's speech: "The national nature of the work was explained and emphasized, and all patriotic effort on behalf of the soldiers' dependants was consolidated under its leadership. Confidence was thereby inspired in the minds of the public that there would be no overlapping of relief nor waste of organizing power in the community."[61]

Once the Edmonton finance committee had done its work, the relief committee took over. Working initially from City Hall and, by the end of October, from a donated office, the Edmonton committee had issued its first cheque on 18 October. By the end of the month, it had paid $7,869.41 to ninety-eight families. The task of visiting beneficiaries had already been accepted by Mrs. Ferris and her IODE members, and her husband, Dr. Ferris, shared the task of rounding up drivers and automobiles for the visitors, no luxury in a city as spread out and as cold as Edmonton in winter. The original eight visitors grew within a year to 230, paying over 800 visits a month, as Alberta's contribution to the CEF grew. As Morris recorded, "Layettes without number were provided. Sick children were taken to the home of the visitor in cases where the mother died, and sometimes the children were taken home until the mother recovered from her illness."[62]

Ames remained in Edmonton to join Sifton and Bulyea and to meet two Calgary representatives, R.B. Bennett, the city's MP, and T.M. Tweedie, MLA for Calgary-Centre. Both were Tory lawyers and ex-Maritimers, who arrived to make their case for a distinct organization for their city and region. In the nonpartisan mood of the times, Bulyea and Sifton cheerfully conceded, and on 30 September a South Alberta branch of the CPF was established, with Bennett as president, Tweedie as vice-president, J.S. Dennis of the CPR's Department of Natural Resources as secretary, and W.M. Connacher, local manager of the Bank of Nova Scotia, as treasurer. For an executive, they simply listed all the MLAs of the twenty-seven legislative seats south of the line between Alberta's Townships 35 and 36. Soon after, they added southern Alberta's MPs and senators.

While Calgary's three provincial constituencies were treated as a unit, the other ridings were left to their local MLA to organize, a quick solution if not a perfect one, since six of the MLAs joined the CEF and soon had other matters on their minds.[63] With 60 percent of the region's soldiers, Calgary had to be organized first. A local office opened on 10 October and a fundraising campaign was launched with the same target for the South as for the North: $125,000. It was far from an immediate success. Calgary, still hardly more than a ranch town in 1914, was reeling from the prewar depression, and the slightly more prosperous rural districts were largely unorganized. After a week of campaigning, local organizers had come up with $33,916 in cash and pledges from Calgary, and $30,195 from the other twenty-four constituencies. Sifton's decision to split his levy on civil servants and university staff equally between the two sections gave the South Alberta branch $43,748 or 38.3 percent of its 1914 receipts.[64]

In Edmonton on 7 October, Bulyea and Sifton convened a meeting of senators, MPs, and MLAs, plus a few mayors, at the legislative buildings, and proclaimed a North Alberta branch with jurisdiction extending as far north as Herschel Island in the Beaufort Sea. The premier suggested that the Edmonton executive function as officers of the new branch and George P. Smith, the MLA for Camrose, and Mayor Ellis of Wetaskiwin moved that each member be responsible for organizing his own constituency. Once appointed, the three officers of a branch would constitute a quorum for administering funds. Depending on MLAs had the disadvantage of delaying progress until Sifton prorogued the legislature at the end of October. As in the south, not all members had their minds on the Patriotic Fund. George Smith, in contrast, was a perfect model; even with over 60 percent foreign-born residents, his Camrose riding regularly raised more than any other constituency in the province, twice doubling its assigned quota. Some MLAs organized a single committee for their whole district and turned to women's institutes, the United Farmers, and municipal councils for fundraising and relief activity; others created separate committees in the towns and villages of their districts. The former, as George Smith's Camrose demonstrated, appeared to give more generous results. To Ames's satisfaction, no Alberta communities remained outside the CPF network.

War came especially close to British Columbia in August 1914. Germany's Far East squadron, with its two huge battle cruisers, was rumoured to be heading for Canada's west coast, and Sir Richard McBride's provincial government frantically armed itself by buying two submarines from a Seattle shipyard to reinforce the Canadian navy's ill-armed and undermanned light cruiser *Rainbow*. Several hundred militia had spent the previous year at Nanaimo, guarding coal mines and strikebreakers from striking members of the United Mineworkers.[65] Other troops had been called out in Vancouver in July 1914, to bar Sikh would-be immigrants from coming ashore from the *Komagata Maru*. Nowhere had Canada's economic depression fallen more heavily than on British Columbia, where fortunes had vanished in a general collapse of land and property values. In the self-consciously British outpost on the Pacific, the distant war would doubtless have inspired a fervid patriotic response, but recent mass immigration and ensuing unemployment and dismal job prospects also helped pack the sidewalks in front of Militia armouries.

Close to 2,000 British Army reservists left their homes in British Columbia, and by 3 September 2,500 British Columbians had gone to Valcartier. Months and even years of unemployment had long since drained savings and brought many families close to destitution, while rent, food, and other living costs were among the highest in Canada. Hard times on the prairies had shrunk the main markets for the province's few manufacturing industries, agriculture still chiefly struggled to serve local markets, and natural resources were proverbially uncertain sources of wealth. British Columbia, in short, was the perfect illustration of why the Canadian Patriotic Fund had to be a national organization. When Helen Reid later described districts as "rich in men to serve but poor in means to give," she had the west coast in mind.[66] Its people were willing to fight for the Empire, but it seemed unlikely that they could afford to pay the full cost of supporting their soldiers' families.

Lieutenant Governor Thomas Wilson Paterson, Scottish-born and Ontario-raised, had made his career as a railway builder, constructing lines in the BC interior and on Vancouver Island before settling into a retirement life of Liberal politics and raising shorthorn cattle. With Premier McBride and Frank Barnard, a successful Victoria businessman and mining promoter and Paterson's designated successor, a British Columbia branch of the Patriotic Fund was formed on 8 September. Barnard began as secretary-treasurer but took the chair when he became lieutenant governor at the beginning of 1915.[67] Paterson's first step was to write to every mayor and reeve and to the government agents who performed their functions in unorganized areas, urging them to summon "the leading men" to form branches. Some branches had already come into being; others followed, and by the end of November the province had forty-four either raising money or planning to do so.

Hedley, a tiny mining community near the US border in the interior, may have been typical. G.P. Jones, the local mine manager, assembled local businessmen in a donated hall on 21 September. J.R. Brown, the government agent from Fairview, "addressed the assembly at considerable length," to explain the purpose and scope of the Fund. The outcome was an agreement to hold a public meeting in a larger hall: "We wish to repeat that this meeting is for everybody, men and women alike. It is our one great opportunity of showing if our patriotism is more than skin deep, and aiding the Empire in its hour of need."[68]

Organizing across British Columbia was never simple. By the end of November, fourteen communities had organized outside the official Fund. The biggest was Vancouver. Throngs of British reservists gave early notice of a serious problem of family destitution, and Vancouver's mayor had convened a public meeting on 11 August. The Vancouver Citizens' War Fund emerged, under the joint management of groups including the Board of Trade, the IODE, the Local Council of Women, the Red Cross Society, the Conservative and Liberal Clubs, and Vancouver's militant Trades and Labour Council. An immediate campaign raised $156,000, plus substantial donations of food and fuel. After a year of depression and mass unemployment, desperate poverty was already evident. On the first day of the campaign, a British reservist's wife walked to the city centre from South Vancouver with her newborn baby. A neighbour had given her a little tea but she had no food.[69]

To provide official visitors for its 10,000 applicants and 7,500 recipients, Vancouver turned to the Women's Patriotic Guild, a wartime association led by Mrs. J. Fyfe Smith. As in Winnipeg, local leaders initially rebuffed suggestions of national affiliation until the city's suburbs, Richmond and North and West Vancouver, sought inclusion. On 4 February 1915 Vancouver affiliated directly with the national campaign as a branch, but remained outside the British Columbia branch.

In Victoria, the IODE had taken an early lead, collecting $15,670 in the first days of the war, a third of it for the Hospital Ship Fund and the rest for work among soldiers' dependants. A meeting convened at the BC Parliament Buildings by Lieutenant Governor Paterson led to the Victoria Patriotic Aid Society, whose jurisdiction rapidly spread to the southern end of Vancouver Island and to the Gulf Islands. The president was Alfred Cornelius Flumerfelt, an Ontario-born philanthropist whose career until 1909 had been spent building the Ames-Holden shoe business, first in Winnipeg and then in British Columbia. He had since been associated with a wide variety of local businesses and worthy causes, among them the new McGill College of British Columbia.[70] Flumerfelt's chief coadjutor was Robert H. Swinerton, the honorary secretary-treasurer. The new society promptly incorporated under British Columbia law, adopting the CPF's objects with the added power to relieve families "whose breadwinners were, in the opinion of the Trustees, out of employment or in need of assistance through the effects of the war."[71] Trustees met weekly and, as elsewhere, depended on the IODE as their "ladies' auxiliary," to do their visiting and social work. A patriotic service committee, headed by Mrs. R.S. Day, with Mrs. W.E. Oliver as honorary secretary-treasurer, organized the monthly visits the trustees required as a prerequisite to any payment. The two women became virtually full-time volunteers until an exhausted and ailing Mrs. Oliver eventually had to retire. She was replaced by Dorothy King, described as having "previous training in social service work."[72]

British Columbia's third city, New Westminster, initially also went its own way. Mayor A.W. Gray launched a War Relief Fund and distributed what he and his colleagues could collect. After all, the war was supposed to be short, Ottawa was distant, and communities were jealous of their autonomy. But the war, of course, was not short, autonomy is expensive, and Ottawa's willingness to send British Columbia rather more than it received from the west coast was persuasive. In December 1915 Mayor Gray became president of a CPF sub-branch within the British Columbia branch. The addition of a claims committee, chaired by the Rev. A.E. Vert, provided all the structure Herbert Ames required.[73]

Far to the north of British Columbia, the Yukon Territory experienced its own wartime economic stresses as gold mining collapsed. The population, 5,000 at the beginning of the war, faded to only 3,000 by 1918, and 600 of them left to enlist. A public meeting in Dawson on 30 September 1914 considered a Patriotic Fund but, for lack of definite information, nothing was done until 21 December. Isolation confirmed a decision to form an independent association but to forward any surplus collected to Ottawa. The IODE, a force in the Territory, took the lead in patriotic fundraising, and the Patriotic Fund rivalled the Red Cross as the major beneficiaries of an initial $6,716 campaign. Since many of the Yukon's active political and business leaders, such as Joe Boyle, Alfred E. Thompson, and George Black, left the territory to join the war effort, most of the work fell on G.A. Jeckell, the treasurer, and S.F. Chamberlain, the secretary. Community pressure ensured that virtually everyone with a steady job signed up as a monthly contributor. Ultimately, the Yukon CPF raised $88,633 from Yukoners, paid $46,534 to its soldiers' dependants, remitted $41,216.45 to Ottawa, and spent the tiny balance on administration.[74]

If British Columbians felt threatened by the war, Maritimers knew from their history that the seas could bring enemies. After Ottawa accepted Halifax's dockyard and fortresses from the British in 1906, it had nervously created a small garrison of 2,000 Permanent Force troops, and in 1914 3,000 local Militia were called out to defend the harbour fortifications from a German attack. Col. Hughes wreaked further vengeance on the despised Permanent Force by sending the local battalion of the Royal Canadian Regiment to defend Bermuda in response to a British request.[75] Thousands of local families found themselves dependent on military pay and allowances and concerned about whether the benevolence of the Patriotic Fund extended to them.[76]

Prominent Haligonians met to establish a Patriotic Fund on 2 September 1914 with Lieutenant Governor J.D. MacGregor in the chair. Nova Scotia's veteran Liberal premier, George H. Murray, agreed to become honorary secretary for the provincial branch of the CPF, and Edgar N. Rhodes, MP for Cumberland and a leading Nova Scotia Tory, agreed to be chairman of the county branches. Headed by the provincial chief justice and the mayors of Halifax and Dartmouth, a galaxy of thirty-seven local worthies filled out Halifax's branch executive. Other notables were named as convenors for their counties. A former journalist, Arthur S. Barnstead, head of the provincial government's new Industries and Immigration Department, was appointed secretary, and Horace A. Flemming, manager of the Bank of Nova Scotia, became treasurer.[77]

Two days later, the executive met, set a fundraising target of $250,000, and proposed to raise 20 percent of it at once. The war, after all, might not go on long enough for all the money to be needed. The executive also authorized Barnstead's expenses so that he could go out and organize sub-branches across the province.[78] On 12 September the executive met to discuss how much to pay its needy families. Hector McInnes, a prominent local lawyer, civic improver, and Tory, somewhat in the Herbert Ames mould, became chairman of the Halifax relief committee. His advice, "a living sustenance," was ultimately accepted.[79]

For a time in October and November, a competing charity, Belgian Relief, distracted the Nova Scotia CPF. The plight of thousands of Belgian refugees who had fled to Britain and France before the German invasion had sent waves of shock and sympathy as far as Canada, and Halifax was an obvious port for sending emergency supplies of food, clothing, and cash. On the whole, the Fund's managers managed to divert and separate their concerns from those involved in meeting the conjectural needs of distant refugees. A subcommittee explored the possibilities of buying two carloads of flour, 1,000 barrels of beans, and 500 cases of dried apples. Buying fish, a member warned, might not be wise: Belgian preferences in fish were different from those of Nova Scotians.[80]

With thousands of uniformed soldiers occupying the city's coastal fortifications, and their families living in the vicinity, the Nova Scotia and Halifax branches felt family needs much sooner than communities whose soldiers were far away in Valcartier or in England. The concern that no money should pass to the undeserving could only be met by investigation, but by 16 September the Nova Scotia executive was aware that Militia members were resentful about queries from the CPF relief committee. Perhaps, the executive suggested, "more of a military character could be given to the visitations of the committee, having an agent in military attire to represent the committee in their investigations."[81] Did being sent to Bermuda constitute "active service" for the families of members of the Royal Canadian Regiment, hitherto part of the city's peacetime garrison? Could members of the local Militia be forced to accept pay deductions for the benefit of their families? When these questions were referred to Ottawa, Ames had no answers; instead he sent an explanation of the Alberta organization. Surely Nova Scotia would find it a useful model.

New Brunswick moved more slowly than its eastern neighbour. While militia were mobilized at Saint John for local defence, there were no fortifications for them to defend. Only about 500 New Brunswickers had hastened to Valcartier, though many more followed with the second and ensuing contingents. The province reluctantly recognized that it was one of the poorest in Confederation. Large regions depended on subsistence agriculture and ill-paid seasonal work in the forests. In the underpopulated north, few towns had as many as 2,000 people. When a provincial branch of the CPF was formed early in October 1914, it was on the initiative of Senator Josiah Wood, a Sackville businessman and Conservative, who met with Borden's minister of marine, the Hon. J.D. Hazen, Senator W.H. Thorne, a Saint John hardware merchant, and other New Brunswick members of the CPF's national executive. Local mayors and other notables were added later, but a real organization was slow to develop outside Fredericton and Saint John.

In Saint John, Mayor Frink's original organizing meeting had produced a Soldiers' and Families Patriotic Fund managed by a committee of 100, reduced by 19 August to a fifteen-member executive. A women's auxiliary, modelled on Montreal's and convened by Mrs. W.D. Forster, emerged on 28 August, and accepted responsibility for visiting homes, caring for neglected children, comforting the sick, and managing an office. The Saint John organization formally joined the national CPF on 30 September and soon extended its jurisdiction to the surrounding counties, King's, Queen's, Albert, and St. John, which contained about a quarter of province's population and a rather larger share of the 18,000 New Brunswickers who ultimately enlisted. Similarly, Fredericton's branch extended into the surrounding counties of Sunbury and York, and imitated Montreal's organization, with finance and relief committees and a women's auxiliary to do the bulk of the daily work. At the end of 1914, the rest of New Brunswick remained to be organized.[82]

Without the province's two largest English-speaking cities, both determined to deal directly with Ottawa, the energy and resources to create an effective New Brunswick branch were scarce. F.W. DesBarres, a professor at Mount Allison University in Sackville, volunteered as an organizer, but his wife became sick and his university demanded more of his time for teaching. Faced with lagging donations, New Brunswick's government accepted the pleas of discouraged CPF supporters, approved a levy on the province's counties and municipalities, and invited the local-provincial Fund executive to set the amount to be paid quarterly to the CPF's national treasurer in Ottawa.[83]

The third Maritime province, Prince Edward Island, was small, agricultural, and insular in more than geography. Its few hundred men at Valcartier represented a higher share of the province's population than its mainland neighbours. When PEI's lieutenant governor launched the Island's Patriotic Fund on 21 September, 1,000 of Charlottetown's 11,000 people attended. With Chief Justice Sir William Sullivan as president and Maj. A.A. Bartlett as secretary, the usual executive committee and committee of ladies emerged: the men to find the money and the women to investigate the beneficiaries. A seven-member finance committee quickly collected $4,000 and a seven-member relief committee cautiously prepared to spend it. Living costs were lower in PEI than anywhere in Canada and by December 1914, the Fund needed only $384 to meet reported needs.[84] The island province continued to pay its needy families significantly less than any other region in Canada while continuing to collect impressive amounts of their savings in individual trust funds, an achievement credited to an effective Ladies Auxiliary.[85] By

1916 the provincial government contributed about half the Fund's income and the Island was more than self-sufficient. In his official history of the CPF, Morris conceded that "the record of Prince Edward Island in its relationship with the Fund, compares favourably with the records of the other Maritime Provinces."[86]

Although Newfoundland was not a part of Canada in 1914, some Newfoundlanders joined the CEF. Many more joined the "blue puttees," Newfoundland's own battalion-sized contribution to the Empire's war effort. Its members were paid at British rates, though the Dominion's cost of living approximated Canada's, particularly after wartime prosperity sent profits and prices soaring. Inspired by Lady Davidson, wife of the governor, 700 women met in St. John's on 31 August 1914 to create a Patriotic Association of the Women of Newfoundland, better known as the WPA. For once, an island organization transcended the usual denominational, urban-rural, and occupational barriers of Newfoundland society, and by 1915 it boasted 151 branches devoted to knitting, sewing, preparing bandages, and raising funds through concerts, bazaars, and an art calendar featuring "a young lady sewing bandages for the wounded heroes at the front." The WPA provided comforts for Newfoundland troops overseas, visited their families, and equipped and funded Waterford Hall as the Naval and Military Convalescent Hospital in St. John's. A significant contributor to the war effort and to raising the consciousness of Newfoundland women, the WPA was not a solution for the financial needs of soldiers' dependants.[87]

A couple of days before the WPA's founding meeting, on 29 August 1914, a Newfoundland Patriotic Association was privately constituted to assist disabled soldiers and to supplement the incomes of soldiers' families. Like its Canadian counterparts, it was buoyed by huge enthusiasm and collected $88,000 within its first seven months. By the end of 1914 it had paid out $11,716, more than most comparable Canadian Patriotic Fund branches, but the gap between living costs and soldiers' incomes was very much greater than in Canada. In its 1915 session, the Newfoundland Assembly heard the grievances of dependants of the Newfoundland Regiment and passed legislation for an official Newfoundland Patriotic Association to pay out funds for dependent relatives of soldiers (with no mention of "need") and "afterwards to such other objects connected therewith as may be deemed desirable." In the absence of other programs, these came to include disabled veterans and cases with "a moral claim upon the generosity of the public."[88]

Like other institutions, the Newfoundland Patriotic Association worked better in St. John's than in the outports. Lacking a system of branches, it depended on merchants, clergy, and visiting government officials to report need. As in Canada, the Association's officers strenuously denied that they were managing a charity, but its historian records that "Families were to be no better off on ... the Patriotic fund than they would have been with the breadwinner present and contributing his pre-1914 income."[89] Its benefits came by generosity, not right. A poor region even amidst temporary prosperity, Newfoundland's patriotic fund collected only about $0.40 per family at a time when the CPF's average was closer to $4.00. Newfoundland's government added to the burden of families and the fund by refusing to make pay assignments compulsory. By the summer of 1917, over 500 soldiers had cancelled them. The government also delayed until September 1917, just before a crucial election, to introduce a $20 separation allowance.[90]

Meanwhile, the Canadian Patriotic Fund accepted responsibility for families of Newfoundlanders in the CEF. Since this was an extraterritorial commitment, it required the first amendment to the Canadian Patriotic Fund Act, approved without significant discussion early in the 1915 session of Parliament.[91] By January 1916 the CPF supported fifteen Newfoundland families at a cost of only $183 per month.[92]

While Ames faced special problems in almost every province, none equalled those in his own Quebec. As he would have appreciated better than most Conservatives, enthusiasm for the European war was fleeting and localized. The near-instinctive homeland loyalty of many Canadians of British ancestry was not echoed for France among most French Canadians. The connection had ended badly in 1760 and a sense of betrayal after the Peace of Paris in 1763 had been reinforced by alienation after the French Revolution. Intellectuals might have been moved by the visit of the French frigate *Capricieuse* in 1855, but for other *Canadiens*, the ship's name said it all. The anticlericalism of the more recent governments of the Third Republic had been denounced in Quebec Catholic pulpits, sometimes by clergy who had emigrated from France rather than suffer the curtailment of their function as leaders and teachers of the nation, and who denounced the Third Republic to their classes and congregations as *la gueuse*, or "the beggar woman."

Initially, the plight of France and Belgium, invaded by Teutonic hordes, had inspired sympathy, and there was approval that Great Britain had met its obligations as an ally. That Canada should send volunteers to Britain's aid met only a few of the objections raised at the time of the South African War in 1899. The leading opponent at that time, Henri Bourassa, was visiting Alsace when the war broke out in August 1914, and only narrowly escaped internment in Germany. Instead, he travelled through a rapidly mobilizing France, impressed by the *Union sacrée* that united a bitterly divided people in a shared crusade. Could a similar mood sweep Canada, ending the vicious discrimination against French and Catholic education in Ontario and across the prairies? If so, engagement in a short war might be advantageous, and his young newspaper, *Le Devoir*, spread the message.

Of course, the small, somewhat ideological daily hardly even pretended to persuade young men to enlist. Nor did larger media. The Royal Montreal Regiment, an amalgam of some of Montreal's oldest militia units, included a French-speaking company from the 65th Carabiniers de Mont-Royal. If every French-speaking volunteer in Valcartier had been collected in one unit, they might have formed a single undersized infantry battalion among the seventeen Sam Hughes organized. That was, in fact, the Canadian tradition, but Sam Hughes ignored it. Only in October was French Canada allowed its representative unit, Le 22e bataillon canadien-français. The 22nd Battalion struggled to fill its ranks, and was finally moved to Amherst to stem the tide of desertion. Its successor, the 41st Battalion, turned into one of the worst units ever organized for the CEF. With a corrupt colonel and a drunken chaplain, it soon became a refuge for the unemployed and the unemployable. Other battalions followed, along with sometimes ingenious attempts to alter public sentiment and to reverse the initial errors, indifference, and neglect.[93]

Across Canada, Ames's model of a Patriotic Fund could at least count on patriotism, however defined. The thought of men leaving their families to risk their lives for a mother country inspired powerful sympathy. Local pride inspired communities to do their best to meet the full costs of family support, even if, objectively, it was almost impossible for them to do so. Pride even moderated the expectations of the claimants. However, those were not reasonable working assumptions in Quebec outside Montreal and scattered English-speaking communities in the Eastern Townships, the Gaspé, or the Ottawa valley. At Rimouski, St-Hyacinthe, or Chicoutimi, local notables were not likely to come forward to summon meetings and collect donations. If local *curés* were inspired to encourage a *collecte* at the church door on a Sunday, it was more likely for the *blessés de l'Ontario,* the victims of Ontario's Regulation 17 against French-language schools, and even those donations tended to be frugal.

Elsewhere, premiers and lieutenant governors gave the Patriotic Fund all the support they could. In Quebec, at least until 1917, Sir Lomer Gouin, the Liberal premier, made no secret of his conviction that supporting soldiers' families was the direct and appropriate responsibility of the federal government, and not a burden to be dropped on his province or its people. Lacking persuasive francophone voices of its own, the CPF seemed unable to answer even the malicious allegations cited by its own historian: "'The Patriotic Fund ... serves to assist the families of men who come over from England and enlist in this country to get better pay and better conditions for their wives and families' was a familiar canard."[94] Without rebuttal, such charges simply entered public consciousness.

Ames appreciated that Quebec needed the fundamentally redistributive policy of the national CPF more than any other province. In Montreal a conscientious effort, backed by a "day's pay" collection scheme, allowed the fund to argue that at least three-quarters of its contributors were francophones.[95] Sherbrooke in the Eastern Townships, heavily influenced, like Montreal, by its English-speaking elite, developed one of the earliest branches anywhere, on 27 August 1914. By the end of 1914 Sherbrooke had sent $10,595 to Ottawa. In Stanstead County, south of Sherbrooke, a local man, E.W. Hay, managed the fund for an area extending to Magog, Beebe, and Coaticook, and distributed $9,375 to a total of twenty-nine families. A largely anglophone county council subscribed $7,000 to the national Fund. More surprising was Trois-Rivières, with its overwhelmingly francophone population. The community collected $30,460.64 and requisitioned only $18,314.80. Local leadership under the Hon. J.A. Tessier probably made the difference.

Quebec City, too, ignored language and political divisions under the leadership of the Hon. Cyrille F. Delage as president, Col. B.A. Scott as vice-president, and the Hon. Philippe Paradis as honorary secretary. The Hon. L.-A. Taschereau, a future Liberal premier, served as chair of the relief committee. The city branch spread rapidly after organizing attempts in neighbouring counties and districts failed, and ultimately the branch's activities extended as far as Lac St-Jean, the Magdalen Islands, Gaspé, and Mégantic.[96] Elsewhere, small local committees, often headed by a local mayor, distributed funds and sent in any contributions. Joliette in the Saguenay was more generous than most. From the branch's organization in July 1916, Mayor J.A. Guilbault sent in $730.70 and requisitioned $2,902.99 for local families. At L'Annonciation, Mayor Alfred Robidoux collected $50.00 and required $2,322.00, while Dr. J-M. Longtin at Laprairie needed $702.79 while his community subscribed only $1.29.[97] By the summer of 1916, Ames could claim forty-seven branches in Quebec, but elsewhere, he confessed, "scattered families ... requiring to be helped, receive such assistance by direct remittance from the Head Office."[98] From Ottawa, the Fund did all that it could to encourage formation of local branches, but with more emphasis on the investigation of claims and organizing practical assistance to families than on collecting funds. When appeals came from unorganized regions, as they did with some frequency, Fund officials dealt with them as well as they could from a distance.

With about a third of Canada's population, Ontario's three military districts sent 7,380 infantry in the first rush to Valcartier, and ultimately enlisted close to half the members of the Canadian Expeditionary Force. Ethnically and ideologically, Ontario was the region of Canada most easily mobilized for a war inspired by loyalty to the British Empire. But Ontario was not so easily organized to fit Herbert Ames's blueprint for the Canadian Patriotic Fund. No Ontario branch was formed to provide organizing direction to the province's towns, cities, and counties. The national office in Ottawa dealt directly with those of the province's communities that affiliated, and the lieutenant governor played a smaller role in the Fund and its local structure than in other provinces. Though Conservatives were in power at Queen's Park as in Ottawa, Ontario's government jealously guarded its autonomy. Its provincial Soldiers' Aid Commission, primarily designed to re-establish returning soldiers, filled at least some of the family-support roles that the CPF came to play elsewhere. At the same time, the province offered encouragement, authorized municipalities to subscribe tax funds to the Fund, and eventually made substantial contributions to the CPF and to its campaign expenses.

Like Montreal, Toronto and its surrounding county of York had organized themselves in advance of the national organization. So had similar funds in Kingston, Ottawa, London, and Belleville, and organizations in Welland and Bruce counties emerged almost simultaneously with the action of Parliament. Twenty-four branches took shape in September 1914, including Sault Ste-Marie, Kitchener, Guelph, and Elgin, and Frontenac, Lambton, Stormont, Dundas, and Glengarry counties. Twelve more appeared in October, including in the major cities of Hamilton, Brantford, Oshawa, Port Arthur, and Galt. By the first anniversary of the war, Ontario had 100 branches of the CPF, including twenty-seven that covered whole counties. As elsewhere, but perhaps a little more so, some funds saw no need to affiliate with the national body. Halton and Lincoln counties and Paris, Preston, Sarnia, and Windsor retained their independence throughout the war, though Morris would gratefully note in his history that Windsor and Halton County also made generous gifts to the national Fund. "In the other places, local needs only were met."[99] By the time the CPF summoned a conference of eastern Canadian branches in Toronto in May 1916, Ontario had organized close to 150 branches, each as distinct as Nova Scotia or Saskatchewan. The Fund attempted to rank them by size, from largest to smallest number of beneficiaries, to regulate the number of permissible paid employees. The smallest branches were expected to function purely with volunteers.[100]

Ontario's strong tradition of county governments provided the Fund with a robust administrative and financial framework in rural areas of the province. Faced with the practical problems of collecting contributions from scattered farms and small businesses, almost every rural council decided to levy a rate. The importance of county councils became apparent when six of the twelve areas of Ontario that proved unable to finance their own needs turned out to be unorganized administrative districts on the edges of settlement and without authority to levy an assessment: Rainy River, Thunder Bay, Timiskaming, Nipissing, Parry Sound, and Muskoka.

More typically, Peel County Council met on 3 September, reflected on the likely needs, and boosted its taxes by one mill for patriotic purposes in time to catch the deadline for the local papers.[101] The annual yield, $14,650, turned out to be sufficient to meet the county's financial need. Raising local taxes was by no means Peel's only response. By the summer of 1915, the Women's Patriotic League of Cooksville had raised over $1,000 for several wartime charities. Erindale women organized themselves as prodigious knitters, delivering boxes of mitts, scarves, and wrist protectors for the use of soldiers. In Lorne Park, a colony of Toronto cottagers, L.A. Hamilton organized the County of Peel War Auxiliary, whose members took responsibility for visiting soldiers' families. It soon spread northward through the county and, in December 1915, affiliated with the national CPF. "Few counties," acknowledged Philip Morris, "were better organized than Peel."[102]

Others would doubtless have claimed to be just as good. Bruce County's CPF branch began in Walkerton in 1914 and soon covered the whole county, with the distinct exception of Port Elgin where E. Roy Sayles, publisher of the local paper, held sway. Like Peel, Bruce levied a rate and the county warden, Walkerton lawyer Alex McNab, took charge of the branch. Bruce supported about 350 families and contributed about $127,000 to the national Fund.[103] Frontenac County was a rock-lined, hardscrabble southern extension of the Precambrian shield, and its wartime burdens grew rapidly when its core city, Kingston, soon became a major centre for mobilization and training. Soldiers summoned their families, and local farmers eagerly made them paying guests as an added revenue source. Frontenac developed both a city and a county branch. The former, organized on 27 August, affiliated in September with the national CPF and proceeded as soon as it could to fundraising. During the third week of September, Kingston contributed $51,000. Meanwhile the county council granted $2,000 for the needs of soldiers' dependants and invited its warden, J.A. Kennedy, and the county clerk, J.R. Bradshaw, to cooperate with local reeves in its distribution.[104]

Oxford County in western Ontario was a much more prosperous region. Its Patriotic Association was launched early in the war with the optimistic intention of insuring all the men of the county who went to the war. This was far beyond the objects of the national Fund, and Oxford remained proudly independent until December 1915, with a large and broadly representative executive and $80,000 raised by public subscription. When the county finally joined the central body, it had first to arrange to meet the liabilities it had contracted to pay premiums for its insurance policies. By this time, however, enthusiasm for fundraising had long since declined and the county council had agreed to imitate its neighbours and levy a rate. The county's two towns, Woodstock and Ingersoll, agreed to a pro rata contribution. The Oxford Patriotic Association continued, though its primary focus, with Ontario's Soldiers' Aid Commission, was finding work for returning veterans and assisting them in their relations with hospital and pension officials.[105]

Outside Toronto, Hamilton was Ontario's chief industrial city, with a long record of community activity to sustain its self-chosen slogan as "the ambitious city." As in Montreal, a Hamilton Boer War Fund had survived intact, and it provided emergency grants worth more than $4,000 before its balance of $13,494.92 was folded into the new fund. While a visit by Ames provided the occasion, the dynamo behind the old fund and the new was Lt.-Col. Sir John Hendrie, a wealthy local businessman, militia officer, racing enthusiast, and promoter of causes. A former Hamilton mayor and minister in the provincial government, Hendrie soon departed to become Ontario's lieutenant governor, but he left behind a strong and ambitious executive. Cyrus Birge, president of the Mercantile Trust, replaced Hendrie as chairman; Robert Hobson, president of the Steel Company of Canada, chaired the finance committee, and W.H. Lovering, the local deputy registrar of deeds, gave virtually his full time to running the relief committee. The Hendrie family provided free office space to house a staff of four that soon grew to eighteen paid and five volunteer members. Hamilton's branch soon extended to cover all of Wentworth County, including the town of Dundas.[106]

In Sault Ste-Marie, the small industrial city that had grown up at the juncture of Lake Superior and Lake Huron, the initiative for a patriotic fund came from the local collector of customs, Harry Plummer. He began collecting support in early August, but it was 18 September before he had enough backers to call a meeting. Plummer was everyone's choice for president, and the local county court judge was chosen to chair the relief committee. The steel industry that was the core of the region's prosperity had experienced hard times with the collapse of Canada's latest railway boom, and the Sault's leading citizens were not confident of their ability to raise much money. The patriotic generosity of a significantly non-British workforce also seemed doubtful. The answer, earlier than elsewhere, was a "day's pay" scheme, in which workers signed away one day's pay per month, which the employer transmitted to the fund. The corporation thus got much of the credit, and its employees had the option of explaining why they did *not* choose to make a modest contribution to the needs of soldiers' wives. In the tight job market of 1914, refusal might be an act of wage-ending courage.

Across the vast region that the province still called "New Ontario," from Cobalt to Kenora, similar Patriotic Fund branches developed in most of the cities, sometimes extending to a neighbourhood town or township. True to their relentless rivalry, Port Arthur affiliated with the national Fund while its neighbour, Fort William, proudly kept its independence. Only one other point in the vast Thunder Bay district, Schreiber, contributed to the Fund. In contrast, twenty-two tiny communities in the Algoma District contributed funds to the CPF in Ottawa.[107] Families left behind by a soldier son or husband sometimes also sent their appeals to

Ottawa, only to have them returned for investigation to the nearest available branch. On the whole, they were more likely to depend on their neighbours for help or to suffer alone.

While the Patriotic Fund might have welcomed a seamless national organization, the independence of some towns and cities and of Manitoba had the advantage of permitting comparisons. Different policies, too generous or too restrictive, created critics, particularly as the CPF's rates and policies became better known. However, Morris confessed, when soldiers complained, "It was unsatisfactory to have to explain that their wives were living in towns over which the national executive had no authority or influence."[108] It was more than embarrassing when a family moved into such an independent district and was denied benefits. But creating a nationwide organization in a country as large and diverse as Canada could not be managed in a day or a year, or perhaps ever if no one could agree on how long it would be needed. The European war was not over by Christmas, and no one knew how much longer it would last.

Patriotic Fundraising

The Patriotic Fund and its branches needed money, and the purpose of the organization would vanish if most of that money was not found from local and individual generosity. Herbert Ames had used his experience and Montreal's example as a guide to creating and organizing CPF branches across Canada. His city's rich experience in charitable fundraising was its next contribution to liberating more Canadian breadwinners to fight.

Soon after its creation on 17 August, the Montreal branch's Finance Committee began planning a week-long "Whirlwind Campaign" to raise $1 million. Such campaigns were common in the life of any large city, though Montreal's cultural and linguistic divide created significant differences. Under cover of a committee of prominent names, chaired by Herbert Holt of Montreal Light, Heat and Power, William Birks, John Ross, and Arthur R. Doble of Royal Securities got busy. Ross handed over a 3,000-name prospect list prepared for a Montreal General Hospital campaign. Ames convinced the Duke of Connaught, as president of the CPF, to launch the campaign in Canada's largest city. The Canadian Club delivered teams of canvassers and provided its regular September luncheon as a platform for the Duke. J. Murray Gibbon, publicist for the Canadian Pacific Railway (CPR), organized banners, "clocks to show progress," and $29,000 in free newspaper space. His artists delivered suitably draped wives, children, and Union Jacks, and his copywriters asked "Shall we let them starve?" and concluded, a little mendaciously: "This is not a charity!"[109]

Ross organized the canvassers in twenty-three teams, eight reserved for French Canadians, one each for Jews, Belgians, and the Irish, and the rest for Montreal's English community. A "Trouble Committee" would resolve difficulties between rival team captains and their members. The committee also had to reassure competing winter relief campaigns: "When the Montreal committee is of the opinion that it has pledges and sets aside a sufficient amount to cover its own cases and a fair contribution toward the general needs throughout Canada," Ames explained a little ponderously, "the committee desires to consider itself empowered to transfer the surplus, if any, to other similar organizations with like objects."[110]

The Duke of Connaught reached Montreal on the morning of 11 September. While his duchess visited the new Red Cross headquarters, he inspected the new statue of his older brother, King Edward VII, in Phillips Square. By the time he reached the Windsor Hotel, it was packed with Montreal dignitaries – the archbishop, Mayor Martin, business leaders, and colonels – backed by 600 cheering supporters. Patriotic women applauded from the gallery. The duke's speech, delivered without notes, took two minutes.[111] In reply, Rodolphe Lemieux, Sir Wilfrid Laurier's Montreal lieutenant, urged French Canadians to imitate the loyalty of Irish Home Ruler John Redmond and former Boer general and South African prime minister, Louis Botha: "We who live in Canada under the British regime may imagine that it is also the happy fate of other humans to live under foreign domination. Unhappily, it is not so. The current war is a living proof that even in countries that are called civilized, people still live in slavery."[112]

Campaign organizers were deluged by patriotic proposals. A firm printed a thousand cardboard collection boxes for stores and banks. The Salvation Army staffed fifty kettles to collect small change on the day after canvassing ended. Archbishop Bruchési directed that his special parish collection for winter relief be shared with soldiers' families.[113] Notman & Son printed a hundred group photos from Valcartier, to be sold for a dollar each.[114] Merchants contributed bags of potatoes, cords of wood, and $4,300 in bread tickets. The Dorval Jockey Club offered a day's receipts – though the committee rejected the gift after reports of questionable ticket sellers. Indeed, many of the gifts caused more pain than gain. Collection boxes proved "hard to locate and collect," and experience showed most money-raising schemes "to be failures or frauds, and yielding little to the fund."[115]

The main campaign, however, was a success. Though one francophone canvassing team collapsed, the other twenty-two met daily for lunch at the Windsor Hotel to hear speeches and present reports. On Monday, 14 September, the CPR's Sir Thomas Shaughnessy took the chair and Archbishop Bruchési spoke. With most big donations known, the campaign was already halfway to its target. Investment dealer and top YMCA fundraiser John Wilson McConnell's team took an early lead, followed by Percy Molson, and then David Friedman's Jewish team. Tuesday's speaker was Bishop Farthing and on Wednesday it was the turn of Herbert Holt and a Presbyterian, the Rev. James Barclay, chairman of the Protestant School Commissioners. On Thursday, Mortimer Davis of Imperial Tobacco introduced Rabbi Nathan Gordon. "Great Britain has been all that she could be to the Jews," declared Gordon, "and now the Jews will be all they can be to her."[116] Friday's lunch was carefully bilingual, with Chief Justice Sir Alexandre Lacoste in the chair and the popular Methodist preacher, Dr. C.A. Williams, ready to congratulate the triumphant canvassers.

And triumphant they were. Final team reports brought the Montreal total to $1,490,494. While some donations had been strategically delayed, others needed last-minute work. On Thursday, economist Édouard Montpetit denounced allegations by "certain newspapers" that French Canadians had been stingy; the fact was, Raoul Dandurand later recalled, French-speaking Montrealers were much poorer than their English-speaking neighbours.[117] He and Col. Labelle prodded their teams into new efforts.

On the 18th, real estate broker Ucal-H. Dandurand's team placed third with $114,853, behind McConnell's with $224,817 and Molson's with $142,059.[118] Lacoste rejoiced in "the bonds that unite French Canadians and English Canadians" and *La Presse* repeated Williams's boast that "all our difference, all the racial conflicts ... have given way to an 'entente cordiale.'"[119] Ucal Dandurand collected an ivory mirror for "his unfailing good humour," and Percy Molson received white kid gloves for causing the trouble committee no trouble, and the Friday lunch turned into a patriotic auction. A ring, donated through Sir Thomas Shaughnessy by an anonymous woman who identified herself as "A Daughter of Loyalists," cost Salim Boosamra $1,000. A member of Montreal's Lebanese community, he explained: "I came to this country about twenty years ago without a cent, and I am making money here, and am glad to help this good cause."[120]

Montreal's Whirlwind Campaign ultimately collected $1,613,726, mostly in monthly pledges, with $145,500 from the city's banks, $175,330 from municipalities, led by Montreal's $150,000, and $100,000 from the CPR. The seven French-speaking teams averaged $42,506; Friedman's team raised $59,190 and the English-speaking teams averaged $87,064.[121] In a separate effort, John W. McConnell persuaded employers to convince workers to give a day's pay each quarter.[122] Participating firms ranged from Imperial Tobacco, with 7,000 workers, to Westmount Heating and Plumbing, where half a day's pay netted $150 to the Fund.[123] A group calling itself "Protestant servants of houses at St-Bruno" handed in $57.[124] Expenses for the Whirlwind Campaign were small: $537.75 for clerical assistance, $347.98 for printing, $250.00 for advertising. Canvassing teams and committee members paid for their own lunches. With a little exaggeration, Montrealers boasted that they had raised $2 million, double the Toronto total and six times the amount claimed by third-place Winnipeg.[125]

Similar campaigns had been repeated at varying volumes in Toronto, Winnipeg, Vancouver, Halifax, Hamilton, and cities, towns, and villages across Canada. On the far side of the country, Hedley did its best to match Montreal's week-long effort. Townspeople were summoned to the Fraternity Hall on the evening of Friday, 23 September. The Hedley Brass Band provided the music and local notables apparently offered a minimum of rhetoric. As the *Hedley Gazette and Similkameen Advertiser* reported: "The meeting was unique of its kind. There was no flamboyant oratory, no flag-waving, no jingoism of any kind – and one would have said no enthusiasm until the call for subscriptions came." People came forward quietly and pulled out anything from $1 to $5 until the night brought a total of $300. Their names were published for posterity. Six donors gave between $20 and $25, fourteen committed to $10, and forty gave $5. The *Gazette's* editor approved: "Probably never in the history of Hedley has there been a public meeting with less outward demonstration of loyalty than that of Friday evening, and perhaps never one at which more genuine loyalty was shown. To us there was something refreshing in the simple, direct methods adopted by the committee that they did not bait the hook with a concert, a dance or a bazaar; and be it said to the eternal honour of the contributors that they gave of their means according to the measure of their ability, without having the hook so baited."[126]

In ensuing weeks, another forty-five residents gave amounts ranging from $1 to $10, for a further $267. Among them were all four of Hedley's Chinese residents. As a further contribution, Hedley's women organized a show called "Lady Masons," a farce presumably based on the presumed antics of the Masonic Lodge. Admission on 6 October was set at $0.50.[127]

Internment and Families

That fall, not only soldiers' families faced enormous difficulties as a result of Canada's response to the European war. Prewar Canada had welcomed a large tide of immigrants. During the Laurier years of prosperity, Clifford Sifton had vigorously marketed Canada's prairies as "The Last, Best West," and his agents had carried the message deep into central Europe, where soil and climate offered an excellent preparation for the challenges of prairie farming. Thousands of Ukrainians and Poles saw Canada as an alternative to grinding poverty, military service, and inferior status in the Hapsburg provinces of Galicia and Ruthenia. Most German-speaking Canadians traced their roots back to the American Revolution or to disbanded mercenary regiments in the British service, but several thousands had brought their professional skills and education to Canada before the war. Suddenly, they became enemy aliens, viewed with resentful suspicion by their Canadian neighbours. International law entitled a belligerent to intern enemy subjects of military age, and Great Britain had detained at Harwich a trainload of young Germans, mostly players in the small brass bands that enlivened English cities. Germany responded in kind, and many Canadian students and travellers behind German lines, including Ernest Macmillan, the future conductor of the Toronto Symphony, and Dr. Henri Béland, MP for the Beauce and a former Liberal postmaster general, became prisoners in Berlin.

In Canada, the government had too many other concerns in the early weeks of the war to worry about internment, and any loyal German or Hapsburg subject eager to do his patriotic duty had plenty of time to slip over the border to the neutral United States. However, faced with the British example and advice and growing public pressure, Canada soon found itself burdened with hundreds and then thousands of German and Austrian civilian prisoners. After allegations of German atrocities during the invasion of Belgium and the sinking of the *Lusitania* in April 1915, public demands for vengeance were met by expanded internment. At its height, internment was the fate of over 6,000 Canadian residents. By 1916 labour shortages had encouraged the release of most of the Ukrainians who, by the common consent of all but hysterical bigots, had never posed a security threat. A few thousand prisoners, mostly Germans, remained concentrated at Vernon, Kapuskasing, and in an old factory at Amherst, where, for a few months in 1917, they were joined by Leon Trotsky. By 1920 shipping had been found to send them home to a shattered and turbulent postwar Germany.[128]

Like military regulations, international conventions made no provision for families. What happened to the wife and children of a German-born city engineer confined to a cell at Kingston's damp old Fort Henry, or in a log cabin at Spirit Lake in backwoods Quebec? At Vernon, an internment camp in the British Columbia interior, families shared confinement with their interned breadwinner, but this was exceptional and far from pleasant.[129] Instead, internees' families could look forward to penurious living allowances paid out by internment authorities, amidst increasingly hostile neighbours.

Largely immune to the public hysteria that propelled internment, Ottawa recognized that the war would end, and that people who had emigrated to Canada might well still be needed. There was obviously no prospect that Vienna or Berlin would provide relief funds, nor would donors to the Patriotic Fund. Robert Dexter, secretary of Montreal's Charity Organization Society, confessed in 1917 that the burden of internees' families had fallen on his association, with discreet funding from Ottawa. Eager, as we shall see, to demonstrate the superiority of profession-alism in social work, Dexter embraced the challenge. As he explained to his American counterparts at the outset of their own war effort:

> Governments are not equipped for such work, and cannot easily adapt themselves to it in war time. The care of alien enemies by their own people for obvious reasons is not wise. There is no better opportunity for disloyal activities. Even when those in charge are absolutely reliable, the danger of misconstruction by the public is too great to be encountered. In this connection may I suggest that if any charitable organiza-tion takes over this sort of work it would be ill advised to employ agents or district secretaries of German extraction or even of German name? The public is very quick to seize on anything of this sort.[130]

The Canadian Patriotic Fund was an early application of a now-popular device called a government-organized nongovernmental organization or GONGO. Ottawa had no machinery or precedent for the costly and controversial burden of supporting soldiers' families across nine provincial jurisdictions and scattered across the world's second-largest country. Thousands of controversial and sensitive deci-sions about benefits and who would receive them were therefore handed off to an ostensibly independent and nonpolitical body that would be influenced by its own constituents and especially by its more influential donors. Rather than ministers and officials, the Patriotic Fund would decide how well Mrs. Private Smith or Madame Untel would live.

4
Choices and Responsibilities

While the Patriotic Fund certainly aimed to encourage recruiting among family men and to save the federal government much of the cost of providing its soldiers with an adequate "family wage," Ames and his associates could draw on the powerful maternalist beliefs developed across Canada before 1914 to claim support for wives and children. Surely soldiers' families deserved the best from their community. Canadians might be ambivalent about whether wives should work, but most of them had both a sound and a sentimental commitment to motherhood and to the welfare of children. Writing in 1917, the American social worker Paul Kellogg saw the maternalist core of CPF policy: "In all cases, the theory of the fund has been neither to see women bearing the double responsibilities of mother and father, forced to go out and earn a living while the man fights overseas; nor on the other hand to see the grant go as a surplus to women who, from choice or fortune, gain an ample income elsewhere."[1]

While Ames and his closest colleagues may have envisaged a scheme of social reform, a core function of the Patriotic Fund was to absorb some of the responsibilities of loyal husbands and devoted sons. Once widespread recruiting was under way in 1915, the CPF provided recruiting officers with a card to be distributed to any applicants, answering such obvious questions as what would they be paid – a dollar a day and ten cents of field allowance – and how long they were expected to serve: "Until the end of the war, and six months after if required." Other questions included:

> What will my wife receive during my absence? Every month there will be paid her a separation allowance of $20.00 (also a part of your pay) and if this not be enough to comfortably maintain your family, the Canadian Patriotic Fund will further assist them.

> What will be done for my wife and children if I die while on active service? The Government will provide an adequate pension, that will enable the family to live comfortably, until the children are old enough to look after themselves. The widowed mother of a single man, if the son be her sole support, is treated in the same way as a wife.

If you wish further information, ask the secretary of the branch of the Canadian Patriotic Fund in your town.[2]

The government, as Ames constantly insisted, could not discriminate. Once it had determined that a private soldier would be paid $1.10 a day and that his wife could receive his separation allowance of $20 a month, it had done its duty. Because of rank or qualification, soldiers could earn more pay, but only according to the official scale set by their grade or qualification. As a nongovernmental organization, financed by generosity, not taxes, the Patriotic Fund was expected to differentiate among different levels of need. If a soldier's wife received $15 because she had three children, her childless neighbour would have to be satisfied with $5. Indeed, she might well have to be satisfied with nothing at all, since her separation allowance added to her husband's pay assignment of $15 should have been sufficient for a woman quietly living alone.

The right to discriminate presented managers of the Patriotic Fund at the national and local level with some specific dilemmas. The claims of a wife and children might be obvious, but had a soldier's mother ever really depended on him for support? Perhaps soldiering was his first paying job. If she was a penniless widow with a single son, the case was made, but would CPF donors tolerate support for a widow left in wealthy circumstances or with a number of civilian sons easily able to support her? Which soldiers' families were in genuine need and what was the appropriate level of support?

Complexities were everywhere. In a large country burdened with the logistics of long-haul transportation, the cost of living varied substantially, generally rising from east to west and south to north. Farm families lived more cheaply than families in small towns, and the higher costs of rent, fuel, and groceries in cities were recorded in the monthly issues of the government's *Labour Gazette.* Twenty dollars, Ames reminded the Special Committee on Pensions in 1916, "will do a great deal more in Prince Edward Island than it will do in the Yukon." In consequence, the CPF supplement in 1916 averaged $10.00 in Prince Edward Island, $15.23 in eastern Ontario, and $20.61 in Vancouver.[3] Still, could a national association largely dependent on local branches to raise its funds appear to discriminate, even on the basis of the statistics published by the Department of Labour and its barely fledged experts?[4] Could it ignore the redistributive resentment if some of its branches were too generous with other people's donations?

Canada's sparse military experience provided few precedents for the issues faced by the CPF. Peacetime militia pay had usually been a $7.00 bonus for a farmer or his son to spend a couple of weeks at a summer camp, with a tent and rations "all found." In a city battalion, $0.50 for a training parade was ample reward for an evening out with the "boys." Men who volunteered for the Permanent Force entered a low-status occupation, often one step ahead of hunger or the sheriff. That perception changed in wartime when soldiers became, at least briefly, national heroes, ideally drawn from every class and income level. Some members of the CEF were unskilled labourers and many more were skilled workers. Fewer than one in five claimed to have come directly from a farm. One in ten was a clerical worker, and 15,000 of the 619,000 CEF members had been students on the verge of a professional career.[5] Rumour placed an occasional eccentric millionaire in the ranks; needle-sorting of attestation papers for the CEF's official history found plenty of educated professionals, skilled artisans, and even a former vice-president of the Royal Bank of Canada (Table A4, p. 245). Experience revealed a leavening of the sick, lame, and lazy, such as the alcoholic, violent, and brain-damaged Pte. J.A. Couche, five times enrolled in Montreal and just as often discharged.[6] A few families probably found themselves better off on a $20 separation allowance and $15 from assigned pay than before the war, when a drunken husband might have appropriated the entire family income to support his habit.[7] Many more saw soldiering as a short interval of patriotic self-denial.

Satisfying Need

In devising appropriate "objects" for the Fund, Ames had insisted on a requirement of "need." How much money did a soldier's wife and children really need for an adequate standard of living? While Ames and CPF officials soon agreed that branches would have to set their own local rates, the national officers wanted to design central guidelines to establish maximum allowances. Was there a standard level of benefit, Ames wondered, that "would not demoralize the poorer class, nor impose too many restrictions on the customs of those who had lived at a higher standard"?[8] Ames soon persuaded his national executive that a woman needed at least $30 a month to live in an eastern city and $40 in the west. She needed an additional monthly allowance of $3.00 for a child under five, $4.50 for a child aged five to ten, and $7.50 for a child aged ten to fifteen. Older children presumably ate more and wore more expensive clothing. After the age of fifteen, soldiers' children, like other working-class youth, could be expected to earn their own living. Fortunately for the Fund's donors, most soldiers were young and their dependants therefore turned out to be fewer than Ames had expected, averaging a woman and two children.[9]

The east-west distinction was potentially touchy, since Ames expected the bulk of CPF donations to come from Montreal and Toronto. He also recognized that the cost of living in a big city was too large for most small towns. "Whether the maximum scale was to be adopted in any particular city or district was left to the discretion of the local committee," Philip Morris recorded later. "It was intimated, however, that in the smaller towns and rural communities a reduction of at least 20 percent might well be put into force."[10] Trust in the inherent frugality of local committees proved to be a safe bet, but variations in benefits, particularly among Ontario's many autonomous local branches, created significant ill feeling when a soldier's family moved from place to place. In May 1916, reported Morris, the average allowance was $18.07 in Owen Sound and $15.82 in Peterborough, but any justification for the difference was not apparent to the national office.[11] Nor did the gap between Hamilton's $20.09 and Ottawa's $16.63 or Port Arthur's $14.65 seem reasonable. On a national scale, the ranges were larger and perhaps more defensible. By May 1915 the average payment to families in heavily rural Prince Edward Island was $9.70; in New Brunswick it was $15.27, and in Quebec and Ontario it was $16.85. Despite the west coast's high cost of living, British Columbia paid an average of $16.52, but Alberta and Saskatchewan paid out $24.10 and $24.71 respectively. Undoubtedly the national office was alarmed at prairie generosity, but nationwide equalization at, say, $24.00 a month would have added at least $1 million a year to CPF expenditure, not to mention fostering the "demoralization" due to overly generous support that perennially alarmed CPF officials and some of its donors.[12]

A country that depended on charitable impulses for a wide variety of social benefits, from hospital construction to winter clothing for the destitute, knew the limits of generosity, and how easily it curdled at even a faint suggestion that donors were supporting the undeserving. As soon as they understood the CEF's pay procedures, CPF committees had argued that pay assignments must be made compulsory for soldiers with dependants. Surely the ultimate responsibility of a husband and father was to support his family as well as he could. Even if the mechanisms of pay assignment were initially undependable, the principle was widely publicized and generally known. Sending home at least $0.50 a day might not keep a private's wife and children in great comfort but, added to separation allowance, it guaranteed an income of at least $35.00 a month. Making such an arrangement voluntary was inequitable among married soldiers; worse, the Fund's donors might soon recognize the cost of keeping a feckless soldier's family in decent circumstances was falling disproportionately on them and rebel.[13] Whatever its definition of "need," the burden on the CPF would be significantly smaller if assigned pay was compulsory.

Prodded by resolutions from Montreal and other branches, on 13 October 1914 the CPF's national executive committee discussed compelling a married soldier to hand over three-quarters of his pay to his wife as a condition for a Fund grant. Members were urged to reflect on the resulting strong disincentive for married men to enlist and discussion was deferred. Col. Hughes was not inclined to interfere with his soldiers' freedom to spend their pay. Neither was the Department of Justice. Its advisors reported that the Militia Department had no legal authority to interfere with a man's right to dispose of his earnings. Surely a husband was the best judge of his family's circumstances, insisted the government's lawyers.[14]

Leaders of the Patriotic Fund saw the issue differently. Soldiers who spent all their pay and left their families to depend entirely on separation allowance and the CPF burdened the Fund far more than those who accepted their "manly responsibility" to send home all they could. Meanwhile, so long as assignments were voluntary, the Fund could not count them as a wife's income without giving husbands a reason to cut them off. Nor, for the same reason, could they consider the postenlistment wages received from private employers as an entitlement.[15] When it met in November, the CPF's national committee was armed with the British regulations that required married soldiers to assign half their pay. The British example was authority enough to demand a 50 percent pay assignment from married members of the CEF. From England, Co. Ward added his support as paymaster general. Not only had "a large number of men never ... made any effort at all to provide for their families," overpaid Canadian soldiers were making a nuisance of themselves: "The main trouble is due to the excessive amount of money the men are receiving. I may say that Lord Kitchener is quite annoyed to think that our men are getting 4/6 a day and separation allowance for their families as against the fighting 'Thomas Atkins' who is willing to serve his country in the new Army for 1/ a day."[16]

After a brief campaign concerted by the newly knighted Sir Herbert Ames, the Patriotic Fund view prevailed. On 23 January 1915 Borden's cabinet approved an order-in-council ruling that, barring special circumstances argued by the soldier, half the pay of noncommissioned ranks in receipt of separation allowance must be assigned to their dependant as of 1 April 1915.[17] For its part, the CPF agreed not to consider assigned pay in assessing the allowance levels for soldiers' dependants. The fiction that the assignment was a soldier's personal choice would be sustained and the extra money would be available to pay down debts or develop a postwar nest egg. However, the CPF's consciousness that a private's wife could now count on her assigned pay demonstrates that the principle was a fiction for the Fund too.

Indeed, after assigned pay became obligatory, the Patriotic Fund was soon criticized for excluding AP from its calculations of dependants' income. Though Ames had pressed for compulsory pay assignments, he was unapologetic about this policy. Yet once a federal order-in-council made assigned pay a prerequisite for a separation allowance, many private's wives now automatically received $35 a month, more than Ames himself believed that they really needed. In a public accounting of the Fund's policies in 1915, Ames offered his justification: "Bill Smith's wife and her children may have had a trying time for several winters, and her husband may not have been regarded as one of the foremost citizens of the town in which they live; but when he enlists ... and does his duty faithfully by the King and country, Mrs. William Smith's position in life advances accordingly, and she is entitled to live in reasonable comfort."[18]

In *Our National Benefaction*, written to promote CPF fundraising in 1915 and 1916, Ames insisted that the Fund was not a charity and denounced those who treated soldiers' wives like down-and-outs, handing out clothes, groceries, and coal.[19] Ames believed in removing low-income families from the reach of this concept of charity. Allowing a soldier's wife $15 that she could use as savings served Ames's larger social purpose in developing the Patriotic Fund. More than most members of his class, he had encountered the Canadian poor, and he had come to recognize both the benefit of systematic thrift and the practical difficulties of exercising it. In a more nuanced argument than that of enhancing Mrs. Smith's economic status, he revealed the Patriotic Fund's social engineering project:

> Many men enlist whose families are in debt, and it is thought wise that the assigned pay should at first go to wipe out these obligations. Then, during the long, hard Canadian winter, an ill-furnished home could hardly be improved or an ill-clad family adequately clothed out of the allowance paid by the Canadian Patriotic Fund, so the soldier's wife is advised to use the assigned pay to furnish the house and clothe the children. Latterly our committees have been preaching the doctrine of saving against the day of the soldier's return ... It does not follow that a frugal soldier's wife, who by denying herself can lay something against her husband's return, is being too generously treated by the Patriotic Fund.[20]

As he visited branches, Ames insisted that Fund visitors must stress virtues of thrift and prompt payment of bills to their charges. Thanks to the extra $15 of assigned pay, most soldiers' wives, he insisted, had never been better off.

In 1916, after Parliament belatedly agreed to review Canada's badly outdated military pension provisions, Ames insisted on appearing before the Special Committee to argue that soldiers' widows would need a smaller pension than the CPF had judged necessary for their comfort, because the Fund's generosity would have raised them out of a state of debt and destitution. "Nearly all of these families have reached the level of decent subsistence if they have been in any way careful of the amount that was given them," Ames told the Special Committee, "so that by the time the Government gives these families a pension, the woman is outfitted in conformity with her situation in life."[21] An added benefit of the CPF policy became apparent later. In 1914 living costs in a depression-ridden Canada were stable or shrinking, a trend that continued for the first year of the war. An ideal growing season and bumper crops in 1915 replaced the serious drought and widespread crop failures experienced the previous year. Industrial production, though fuelled by munitions and supply contracts, took two years to revive, and the full impact of financing Canada's war effort by debt only began to inflate prices in 1916. By 1918 wartime inflation had expanded Canadian living costs by about 55 percent.[22] The surplus that some soldiers' families had gained in the first years of the war soon evaporated. However, when the government increased a private's separation allowance to $25 just before the 1917 election, the CPF felt little need to revise its allowance levels except in parts of western Canada.[23]

Acute inflation continued after the war, while the CPF found that an unexpectedly early armistice had left it with an unexpectedly large surplus. Faced with rising criticism, the national office felt obliged to raise its family maximum from $30 in the east and $40 in the west to a Canada-wide $50. For families with over seven children, even that maximum was breached. The *Labour Gazette* calculated that the budget for a working-class family of five in early 1919 required $23.49 a week.[24] With $15 in assigned pay, a separation allowance raised by postwar increases to $30, and an average allowance of $25 from the CPF, a wife and three children could count on $70 a month. With fathers, representing a notional third of family expenditure, still overseas, the CPF could congratulate itself that its typical family was still, if barely, in the black.[25]

Despite repeated public denials, the Patriotic Fund behaved like a charity, and many working-class families resolutely refused in principle to seek its aid. To some, as F.H. Kidd warned the prime minister, the humiliation of accepting Patriotic Fund charity for their families was a solid deterrent to enlisting: "The recipient of a share of that fund will, upon opening the package, no matter how splendid the covering, find 'Charity' inside every time."[26] Others saw a resource to be tapped. "Don't be a bit backward about going after the Patriotic & get all you can," Pte. Ernest Hamilton urged his wife. A fellow soldier with two children had claimed to Hamilton that he had done better than Hamilton's family with the Toronto and York Patriotic.[27]

Although the Patriotic Fund had set its income levels so that every private's wife at least could have been a beneficiary, only about three-quarters of the 60,000 recipients of separation allowance in 1916 (and ultimately only a third of 150,000

wives of the CEF) received assistance from the CPF. The remainder, Ames concluded, had sufficient income. Some had higher-ranking, better-paid soldier-
husbands; others had private incomes from farms, businesses, their families, or
their husband's peacetime employer.[28] Like other working-class women, many soldiers' wives had taken in boarders or their neighbour's laundry, or they sewed or
cleaned houses for better-off women of the community. Many continued to do so
once their husbands enlisted.

Others, as a Toronto CPF volunteer complained, did not. "Many women with
children, who at first were putting in three or four days a week at patriotic work are
now forced to remain at home doing their own housework," complained Katherine
O'Brien, "I think it is a disgrace ... that some women whose brains would be valuable in patriotic work are compelled to give it up because we are fostering a spirit of
extravagance and wastefulness among the lower class of women."[29] Both the *Labour
Gazette* and *Women's Century* reported that the Toronto and York branch of the
CPF tried to respond to O'Brien's complaint by reassuring soldiers' wives that personal earnings from domestic service would not affect their "Patriotic" allowances.[30]

Once children found part-time jobs or helped with a neighbours' chores, they
became a source of family income. Grown offspring were routinely expected to
contribute their income to the family. In January 1916 the Fund had 28,435 families
to look after with 77,042 persons (fewer than three per family). Of course there
were families with eight and even ten children, Ames reported, and CPF pamphlets routinely illustrated its generosity to a wife with three children, but "generally speaking, we consider our average family to consist of a woman, a child running
about, and a baby."[31]

Should a childless wife have a claim on the Patriotic Fund? Initially, the CPF saw
no distinction, but the contradictory opinions of donors forced choices. In better-
off working-class families, marriage was the end of a woman's outside earning; in
others, she continued earning until pregnancy.[32] In Britain, Herbert Asquith's government argued that it would be unfair to other working women to subsidize a
soldier's childless wife, thereby allowing her to accept work at lower wages.[33] CPF
branches split on whether to encourage women to leave the workforce or to appear
to be compelling a soldier's wife to work. The compromise was to recommend to
branches that a childless wife receive a nominal $5 monthly allowance while ig-
noring her earnings in any calculation of her needs.[34] When Canada faced an acute
labour shortage in 1917, the Fund decided to ignore all women's waged earnings in
assessing need.[35] Bert McCreath, president of the Toronto CPF's 50,000 Club of
small donors, reported that workers at a Queen Street factory refused to contribute when they discovered that a fellow worker, a soldier's wife, was collecting $5 a
month of "their" money. Meanwhile, a King Street factory threatened to cut off its

donations unless a soldier's wife among its workers received her CPF due. "It is just such cases as these which show what discrimination and tact is necessary in administering the Fund," McCreath concluded.[36]

Allocating support to a soldier's mother was often more complicated than providing support for a wife and children. Not only was the soldier's father expected to provide for his wife; the soldier's brothers were equally expected to share the burden. Had a soldier actually supported his mother before he enlisted or was the army his first employer? Was the mother really "deserving"? When Mrs. Robson of Cobourg complained to the prime minister that, despite losing her only son to the CEF, the Patriotic Fund had denied her help, the local branch had to explain that Mr. Robson, "a first-class carpenter and well able to work," had gone on a drunk and lost his job, and the Robsons' two married daughters were "in good circumstances." Putting Mrs. Robson "on the fund" would merely encourage the undeserving.[37]

Was Shelburne's CPF being racist when it complained that Bertha Love and Louisa Farmer were unmarried mothers who had supported their sons before they enlisted in Nova Scotia's 2nd (Coloured) Construction Battalion, not the reverse, and were therefore not entitled to any support from the CPF or the Militia Department? Philip Morris replied that their separation allowance (SA) came on the advice of a local lawyer, John Hood, and the Rev. W.B. Hill. The Nova Scotia secretary, Arthur Barnstead, reported that the Shelburne committee was surprised at Hood and assumed that, since Hill was "a coloured man, a painter by trade ... it is not thought that his recommendation would be without prejudice under the circumstances."[38] A year later, Shelburne's local chairman, Robert Irwin, was so furious that his taxes supported Mrs. Farmer that he refused to bother with requests to investigate cases. What was the point of making investigations if a bastard could direct public money to his illegitimate mother? It was "an example which does not go much towards encouraging private citizens toward thrift, economy or conservation. It is cases like this that disgust sensible people with the administration of branches like you [sic]."[39] "I find Mr. Irwin's attitude very irritating," commented Philip Morris, "Me thinks he doth protest too much."[40]

Prejudice may not have been limited to black beneficiaries. The Belgian consul raised the case of Marie Évard of Stellarton, cut off by the Pictou CPF. Approached by Barnstead, local officials responded with both indignation and some vagueness: "The character and manner of life of this woman has been such that the committee felt that they could no longer continue to grant her any allowance from the Fund." She had been cut off before and reinstated on promise of reform but without effect. The case, the Pictou secretary claimed, "has seriously effected [sic] the contributions from Stellarton."[41]

Another Nova Scotia case revealed further complexities of family support and more forbearance. Austen Evans had worked for the Fisheries Department, earning $70 a year. He also worked as a barber in Chester to support his wife and nine children, and when he enlisted, he was assumed to qualify for separation allowance and CPF. After seven months, it was ruled that, as a government employee, even if part-time, he did not qualify for SA, and his wife, now sick, had to repay half the $140 overpayment. A Halifax contributor raised the sad case and Philip Morris in Ottawa confirmed the facts. After the Lunenburg branch reported that Mrs. Evans's income of $55 a month, including $10 from the Fund, was enough for her "to live comfortably in Chester." Barnstead suggested that a six-month "compassionate allowance" would be fair.[42]

Although the Patriotic Fund had been instituted to meet the needs of low-income working-class families, its terms of reference included officers as well as other ranks. Like private soldiers, some officers had left their families encumbered by private school fees, extensive life insurance premiums, and old debts. Many Canadians accepted British commissions and then discovered that their pay was devoured by the aristocratic expectations, expensive uniforms, and mess bills of a British regimental officer. Maintaining a gentlemanly lifestyle, even in time of war, sometimes left too little to meet a married junior officer's domestic responsibilities. Moreover, the British Army did not extend separation allowance to officers' families.

Needy officers and their families were an embarrassment to the Patriotic Fund. A populist segment of donors and MPs would have denied them any help at all. By 1916 Ames had transferred 909 such cases to an officers' subcommittee of the national executive in Ottawa, managed by Charles Magrath, former Tory MP for Medicine Hat and chairman of the International Joint Commission, and by J.M. Courtney, a former deputy minister under Laurier and treasurer of the South African War-era CPF Association. The committee met privately, examined claims, and distributed a total of $204,847 in allowances that were substantially higher than for lower-rank families, without sharing gossip with CPF branches or potential critics.[43] Their inquiries, Magrath privately explained, depended on information discreetly shared with him by the presidents of "two of our Banks."[44] In his history of the CPF, Morris insisted that no CEF officer over the rank of captain got any help from the fund and concluded, a little defensively, that "the officers' subcommittee would have been quite justified in giving considerably larger allowances to the families of commissioned officers than were actually paid."[45]

If a soldier was killed or died on active service, the 1915 amendments to the Canadian Patriotic Fund Act permitted the allowance paid to his family to continue until a pension was either granted or denied. Equally, the allowance continued if a sick or disabled soldier was hospitalized, but not after he was sent home with full pay and the CEF's subsistence allowance. Once a soldier was discharged, or if he deserted the CEF, his pay ceased and so did any CPF allowance. If a soldier was sentenced to six months or more of imprisonment, his pay, benefits, and CPF allowance also ceased. His family's resulting destitution became part of his punishment. Arrested after deserting the army, Trooper G.A. Flint was sentenced to two years in prison. "Desertion comes under the Civil Code," the Frontenac County CPF representative bluntly informed Annie Flint, "Therefore you are not entitled to patriotic Allowance."[46] Mrs. Perry's husband was sent home for four days to look after his sick wife, overstayed his leave by one day, and was docked five days' pay. "That is why they cannot get men as they think that all the Col[onel]s are the same," warned Mrs. Perry.[47]

Excluding the Undeserving

Claims investigations soon involved the Fund in the complexities of family circumstances. Did a deserted wife have a legitimate claim to her husband's support? Fund officials generally handled that problem by considering themselves the agents of the soldier, not of his family. If the man had abandoned his wife, so, generally, would the Fund. Indeed, in February 1917 its national executive rejected the proposal from an advisory committee that a deserted legal wife should be urged to seek alimony through the Militia Department.[48] When a son who was supporting his mother, a deserted wife, decided to enlist, the woman had to establish her claim as his mother at a lower rate of support than if she had been a wife.

Controversy continued to swirl around "unmarried wives." The CEF inherited the British Army's tolerance of common-law and bigamous connections.[49] After the national CPF executive in Ottawa accepted that any two-year-old relationship would be treated as a marriage, Montreal's Helen Reid was particularly indignant: in her view, the policy countenanced "bigamy, non-support and desertion," imperilled the family, and turned Canada into "a happy hunting ground" for "any Britisher or foreigner, who is tired of his own domestic responsibilities."[50] Appealing against an order-in-council that legitimated SA and AP for unmarried or bigamous Canadian wives, Reid's feminist fury exploded:

> We spend millions yearly selecting and breeding pigs, horses, cattle, etc. What kind of men and women of the future will Canada have, if some thought is not given to the conservation of family life and the maintenance of the laws of decency governing the same in Canada.
>
> That the Order in Council deliberately penalizes decent married women with their children, while freeing the renegade husband not only from the punishment due his

crime, but places them in a less favourable position socially than that accorded women in polygamous countries. In the Turkish harem all wives and children are provided for. In Canada, only the last light o' love with whom the soldier has lived for two years, may claim maintenance.[51]

When two claims for SA and AP were presented for the same soldier, the Montreal auxiliary wanted the legal wife always to have precedence, provided no claim of "unworthiness or misconduct" could be proven against her. But the Fund also faced the imperfections of its own clients. When women became pregnant when their husbands were in Europe, Reid's branch automatically lowered the mother's allotment "because of her conduct." "Thoroughly respectable soldiers' wives," Reid explained, "angrily resent the reflection on their own character which such episodes are bound to induce."[52] Other branches were sometimes more tolerant, seeking repentance and a change of companions.

Sensitive to community morality, the militia's Pay Department responded to reports of misconduct by asking the local CPF to investigate and, if the allegation had a foundation, cancelling separation allowance or transferring it to the CPF to make financial arrangements for any children. As a member of the House of Commons Special Committee on Returned Soldiers in 1917, Calgary millionaire bachelor, CPF branch president, and Tory MP Richard Bedford Bennett was outraged to discover that his government acted as a moral censor. Herbert Ames disagreed: "When the soldier goes to the front, he leaves his wife and family, usually, in trust to the Government and the Patriotic Fund. Now if the woman becomes immoral and forgets the care of her children and becomes a drunkard, and those children are likely to starve or run wild, the country owes an obligation to the children as well as the wife."[53]

In practice, the Fund's view was usually a little more charitable. When they could, CPF officials tried to resolve quarrels and reconcile husbands and wives, even after cases of infidelity. "To visit the sins of the parent upon the children was no part of the Fund's policy," Morris commented a little archly. "No matter how much the woman may have erred, the Fund's duty to the soldier required that it look after his children." Generally, this meant seeking foster care in a local orphanage. However, Morris claimed, the local branch recognized that losing her children was "a sore punishment" and "the chance of a reunion seldom failed to act as a spur towards better things." In his history of the Fund, Morris recalled a little complacently, "Many women, especially those who had escaped the more unfortunate consequences of their indiscretion, were enabled with the Fund's assistance, to rehabilitate themselves, while in cases where the husband had become aware of the state of affairs the Fund has not infrequently induced him to take a tolerant view."[54]

A lesser but sometimes troublesome issue was the Fund dependant who failed to pay her debts. Local merchants were likely to be influential contributors to the CPF. After appropriate investigation of the case and of the wisdom of the merchant in extending credit, branches were encouraged to transfer a portion of her allowance to a woman's creditor. "Needless to say," Morris boasted, "firms that sold musical instruments &c., to soldiers' dependants on the instalment plan were given no consideration."[55]

The Fund easily accepted the claims of a soldier's immediate family and, somewhat less generously, his mother. If the son could prove that he was her sole support, a mother might expect up to $10 a month. Otherwise, responsibility for a mother fell strictly on her husband and on a soldier's siblings, if they were old enough to earn.[56] What about a soldier's sisters? The question was asked in 1914 on behalf of an unmarried Permanent Force major, accustomed in peacetime to supporting his three unmarried sisters. He got little sympathy. In 1917 the Hamilton branch raised the case of Bugler John McQueen. His mother had died earlier that year, and then one of his sisters, an Eaton's employee, had been hospitalized. Another sister earned $8 a week in a dry goods store and a third stayed home and kept house for the family. McQueen and his brothers sent home $47 a month but since both separation allowances and the CPF contribution ceased on the mother's death, the family could not support a $2,900 mortgage, $60 a year in taxes, and over $100 in medical bills. Could anyone help? Until the CPF helped secure an order-in-council to allow dependent sisters to claim separation allowance, the short answer was no.[57]

An even commoner problem, and a frequent cause of destitution among elderly members of the working class, was the man who switched his support from aging parents or from the children of a previous marriage to his new wife. An ideal son would wait until his parents had died to create his own family, but the CEF contributed to temptation by moving a soldier far from his family roof and home community. Working-class incomes were usually too small to support two sets of dependants, and separation allowance was designed for a single set of beneficiaries. Ultimately, the Fund ruled that branches could pay up to $30 a month to mothers and to motherless children until a soldier returned and put all his dependants under a single roof.[58]

The CPF always recognized that its budgets did not normally allow for the emergencies that routinely shattered the economies of poor families. Fires, floods, sickness, pregnancy, and death were met with special compassionate allowances, ranging from $10 for home nursing care to $250 for a major operation. In a number of communities, the local CPF branch arranged with doctors and hospitals to give care at reduced rates or at no cost. Mount Sinai, Quebec's only free sanatorium, "though primarily for Hebrew patients," agreed to provide free care for soldiers' families.[59] Lawyers could also be persuaded to reduce or waive their fees for soldiers' families.

Like the government and most prudent parents, the CPF was strongly averse to wartime marriages, and directed its branches to ignore claims from wives who had married after their husbands had enlisted. Even before an order-in-council denied separation allowance to any soldier marrying after September 1914, the Patriotic Fund had disallowed claims by postenlistment wives.[60] The Fund's support for "preventing Tom, Dick, Harry etc. of taking advantage of the Government and marrying any woman who came along" was eventually modified by both the CEF and the CPF for couples who could prove a pre-enlistment engagement.[61] The rule was bent again in the summer of 1916, by which time a number of postenlistment wives were pregnant. Since maternalist priorities mattered to the Fund, the national executive ruled that once a child was born, the wife and her infant were to be treated like any other mother and child; meanwhile, during her pregnancy, she would receive the same $5 allowance as any other childless wife.[62] Another delicate problem confronted both the Militia Department and the Fund when a soldier finally married his common-law wife, as Colour-Sergeant Sharpe of the 3rd Battalion did early in 1916. As an unmarried wife, Alma Freed had been eligible for support; as a postenlistment wife, she was not.[63] Common sense prevailed.

Also like the government, the Patriotic Fund worried a lot about being the victim of fraud. Relief committees were repeatedly reminded to visit all applicants and to investigate their circumstances before approving allowances. Chasing offenders could be complicated. Mrs. Elizabeth Laycock of Montreal received separation allowance from her son and alleged sole support, Pte. George Laycock of the 148th Battalion. But G.W. Elliott of the Montreal branch accused her of also receiving money from a husband in England and therefore defrauding the government. Helen Reid, closer to Montreal's beneficiaries, reported that Mrs. Laycock was a woman of seventy-two, her stepson George had earned $50 a month before the war, a twenty-one-year-old daughter was confined to a TB sanatorium, and a son, age eleven, was at school. Faced with more details, Elliott had to confess that he had confused Elizabeth Laycock with Elizabeth Thyn, also a widow, whose son had been invalided home. Both women had used only their first names as signatures.[64]

In 1915 Mme Florida Mercier took the CPF to court in Montreal. The local branch had cut her payment because it found that she was receiving separation allowances from each of her two sons in uniform. She lost, Mr. Justice Maclennan explained, "because she was receiving what she had always received." No one, he added, had an enforceable claim on the CPF.[65] The Fund announced a clear legal victory. For all the CPF's official auspices, intimate links with the Militia Department, and nationwide responsibilities, the Mercier judgment established that the Patriotic Fund was a private charity, whose specific judgments could not be successfully appealed to the courts.

Protecting donors' interests could annoy the Fund's beneficiaries, but public outcry damaged everyone. In October 1915 the Montreal branch asked the local press, French and English, to forward any signed letters of complaint to the committee before publication "to give us an opportunity to reply thereto."[66] Some wives resented visits by better-off women with intrusive questionnaires and a sometimes patronizing air. An angry article in the scandal-mongering *Beck's Weekly* drew a pained and lengthy response from Herbert Ames. Visitors, he insisted, were devoted volunteers who had been carefully instructed that allowances from the Fund were a right – at least to those who deserved them. Questions about the husband or son were wholly legitimate; ascertaining the name of a woman's clergyman was valuable for records in the event of a husband's death or a family bereavement. As for checking up on fraud, he reminded donors, "Many canvassers will remember when they were soliciting subscriptions, how they were repeatedly assured that the Fund would be imposed upon and the money enjoyed by the undeserving. The very precautions, which case after case of imposture have taught the Relief Committee are absolutely necessary, are now criticised as offensive to the recipient."[67]

Keeping Track

By 1916 the Patriotic Fund had achieved impressive national coverage. Manitoba remained autonomous but it shared its information and benefited from CPF guidelines, as did some of the dwindling number of autonomous local funds. Quebec, as in other aspects of the war, remained a troubling exception. Outside Montreal, Quebec City, and the Eastern Townships, little CPF organization could be found in Quebec until a special organizing drive in 1917. Some business was done informally, sometimes directly by the deputy minister of militia and defence, Sir Eugène Fiset, a former medical officer in the South African War. The mayor of St-Moïse and Father J.V. Beaulieu united to persuade Fiset to compel Pte. Belliveau to support his widowed mother. The widow, Précille Chartrand, complained that she had never seen the $45 a month her son had been promised on her behalf when he joined the 22nd Battalion. Fiset personally sent her a card for her curé to sign. Lt.-Col. Émile Rioux asked "mon cher Fiset" to send him the cheque he had negotiated for Mme Amédée Gagnon for otherwise he would never be paid for his services. She lived in the country and could come in and collect. Fiset obliged.[68]

Though both the prime minister and Ames deplored patronage politics and struggled to eliminate it from wartime policy and the CPF, the traditional assumption that benefits bought favours died very hard. On 29 January 1917, Nova Scotia MP George Kyte insisted that all manner of military decisions, from officers' commissions to granting separation allowance to soldiers' mothers, were issues of party patronage in his province: "The mother of the young Liberal recruit will have grave difficulty getting her separation allowance, whereas the mother of the young Conservative recruit, notwithstanding the fact that her husband is living and supporting her, will get separation allowance without any difficulty." All Ames could say in response was to insist that Arthur Barnstead, the CPF's chief official in the province, was "a Liberal of the Liberals" but "fair to every person regardless of the party to which he or she belongs."[69]

When the Hon. Albert Edward Kemp, MP for Toronto-East, replaced Hughes as minister of militia in November 1916, he accepted the back-channel influence of A.H. Birmingham, Liberal-Conservative organizer for Ontario. True, Mrs. Ellen Johnston had received SA from two of her soldier-sons when a son still at home could support her, but she had sent three boys to the front, Birmingham argued, and she was a faithful member of the Loyal Orange Lodge, as were all her sons. Similar consideration was owed to the widow of a veteran employee of Kemp's old firm, the Sheet Metal Company.[70]

In Ottawa the national CPF maintained comprehensive records of beneficiaries and entitlements, fed by systematic reports from the Militia Department and from branches across Canada. A staff of clerks updated cards and checked, for example, that no wife could make simultaneous claims in two adjacent branches. No system dependent on pens, cards, and human error was perfect. Lost, confused, and incomplete records victimized families.

The CPF soon discovered that militia records could not always be relied upon to keep track of significant numbers of deserters and deadbeats. Nor could military discipline. Pte. Thomas Brown of the 129th Battalion was a widower who left his four children in the care of the Hamilton-Wentworth branch of the Fund. What happened to them after he deserted?[71] The Fund's policy was to cut off the families of such men until they had actually embarked. If the man had a conscience, the children's plight would presumably restore him to his duty.

The secretary of the Brantford branch of the CPF complained that Pte. Walter Jackson, a local soldier with a large family and a sick wife, had not only boasted that he could avoid going overseas by switching battalions, but that he had managed three such transfers already. After much correspondence, the Fund cut Jackson off until he actually went overseas, though the branch secretary suggested that he be released from the army. Unless he was forced to assist his family, "it is going to be very hard for them to get through this winter."[72] Fund officials believed that there were lots of men like Jackson, and they urged that separation allowance not be paid until a soldier had definitively left Canada. On 24 January 1916 the Militia Department agreed. Agnes Georgeson was one of the early victims, and she left a memorable cry of pain: "What really is the matter that I ain't getting my money from the army the way I ought to. I have been to the Pat[riotic] fund and they will do nothing not even give me groceries. They have been awful nasty to me, wont [sic] listen to me at all, just turn me right down. I wonder how they expect me and my 3 children to exist. I have had nothing from Ottawa. There must be something wrong. I have got to have money soon or I must have my husband home to see if he can't get a job, as we are practically starving."[73]

In fact, Daniel Georgeson had wanted to switch battalions and taken bad advice, accepting a discharge before joining the other unit. Immediately, under the CPF's rule, his family lost all support until Georgeson's new unit left Canada, leaving Agnes Georgeson and her three children to live on air. Since unemployment had driven her husband to enlist, she had no savings. "I can't rest I am just worried to death thinking about the whole business," she told her husband's colonel, "For pity's sake try and help us someway out of the difficulty."[74] It took three months and a host of letters, all acknowledging her urgent need, before Mrs. Georgeson escaped her difficulty.

Bureaucrats were cheerfully abused in a society that generally believed that most rules were meant to be bent. Was the CEF responsible that Bella Wood failed to receive separation allowance? Her husband had neglected to show that he was married.[75] Florence Harding and her child had to turn to public charity because her soldier-husband sent her only a few dollars, refused to assign pay, and therefore, under the rule the CPF national executive had demanded, denied her both separation allowance and CPF assistance.[76] Dora Horwood was one of the Manitoba Patriotic Fund's more troubled beneficiaries, but her experience reveals some of the linkage between the Patriotic Fund rules and the military bureaucracy. Her husband Fred, a pastry cook, had married her in England. Three months later, she gave birth to a child that was plainly not his. They emigrated to Winnipeg shortly before the war, and he soon added three more children of his own to their family, but it was not a happy marriage. The story of his original cuckolding spread through his home town in England; the putative father emigrated to Canada and, Horwood claimed, resumed relations with Dora. Mrs. Horwood, her husband complained, would "enter the Bake shop ... and creep behind me while I was working, and kick me several times without me saying or doing anything and the propreator [sic] had to tell her he would send for the Police."[77]

When Fred Horwood joined Lord Strathcona's Horse, escape as well as patriotism may have been a motive. After receiving six months of benefits from the Manitoba Patriotic Fund (MPF), Mrs. Horwood lost her allowance because her husband had not volunteered for the CEF but for Home Service in a Permanent Force regiment.[78] A desperate Dora Horwood explained that she spent $18 a month on rent and gas, $4 for electricity, and $5 on instalments for her sewing machine. Her newest baby was sickly and needed special food and a nurse. More generous than the CPF, the MPF had allowed her $21, which still left her short of money. She could not work, she explained to the lieutenant governor, because her children were too small.[79]

By summer, the Horwood family was also sick and Fred was overseas: "I want justice anyway," she warned the MPF's Charles Roland, "for I would rather be starved than half-starved."[80] The MPF turned to military channels to pressure her husband to send home more than the $40 a month he provided in SA and AP. Instead, a resentful Pte. Horwood attempted to cancel all allowances. "He alleges immorality prior to marriage," reported Col. Ingall, "and states that owing to cruelty he was forced to leave her."[81] When the MPF summoned Mrs. Horwood to their downtown Winnipeg office to discuss this delicate matter, she refused: "Had the streets not been so busy I would have tried to manage the children, but the eldest is not yet 6 & the baby is only 2 & the others 4 so you will see it is not possible." Still, whatever her faults, the MPF found no basis for Fred's complaints or for dropping his support.[82] But Mrs. Horwood's problems did not cease. She remained short of money and by the summer of 1918 her landlord was dunning the MPF for Mrs. Horwood's unpaid rent.[83]

Extraterritoriality

The families of French, Belgian, and British reservists had given the Patriotic Fund its first impetus. Unlike Canada's policy, the British separation allowance took account of family size. The British also insisted that soldiers make pay assignments, but while a Canadian private could assign $15, the best a British private could manage was about $5. If his wife had one child, she could count on an additional $16.68 per month from Britain. French families received even more minute amounts from France, while the Belgian government, exiled from all but a few square miles of its territory, could afford nothing at all. The Canadian Patriotic Fund made up the difference. A 1915 amendment to the CPF Act had extended the

Fund's territorial limits to the Dominion of Newfoundland, a benefit to Newfoundlanders who enlisted in the CEF rather than accepting the British rates paid to the Newfoundland Regiment.

When Italy entered the war as an ally early in 1915, the Fund took a hard look at Italians in Canada. Most, Ames explained to a parliamentary committee in 1916, were "sojourners," living together in boarding houses and intending to return to Italy once they had earned some money. "Where the Italians go to some big Italian boarding house where they largely live in a communal way," Ames reported, "we do not help such families." Families living in houses and, as E.W. Nesbitt, Oxford North's Liberal MP, explained, committed to becoming "good Canadians" were considered for CPF allowance, though at a much lower rate than British, French, or Belgian families.[84] While the wife and child of a British reservist could count on $35.82 from the Fund for a monthly income of $57.50, an identical Italian family collected $6.00 from Italy and $17.00 from the CPF, or $23.00 per month. The Fund saw no need to hide or even explain its discrimination. It was perhaps fortunate that few Italian families depended on the Fund's meagre generosity.[85]

Some soldiers' wives, recently emigrated from Britain, turned to the CPF to ask for their return fare. Fund managers generally approved. Seventy percent of the soldiers in the First Contingent were British-born. Even by the end of the war, that was still true of half the members of the CEF. Many British-born soldiers had developed strong family roots in Canada but others were recent arrivals. British wives had good reason to return to their parents and to the more familiar surroundings and lower living costs of their homeland. Once in Britain, a wife might also see her husband during his annual two-week leave from the front or as a convalescent in hospital. A husband's Canadian pay and separation allowance went a lot further in the British Isles than in Canada, and until the last, hungry and inflationary years of the war, wives in the UK were probably better off. Though undermining the federal government's goal of populating Canada with largely British stock, the CPF recognized that it was lightening its own burden. Branches also demanded written assurances that the beneficiaries of a free passage "home" would not become a burden on the British or Canadian authorities.[86]

After 1916 passage from Canada to Britain was approved for wives and families only in dire, life-threatening cases. But the repatriation policy ended entirely in 1917 after Germany announced its new policy of unrestricted submarine warfare on ships heading to Britain. The resulting food shortage in Britain persuaded Canada's high commissioner, Sir George Perley, to urge Canadian wives to return to Canada. Among those who came out to Canada were women a later generation would know as "war brides." Since these were the result of postenlistment marriages, the CPF could well have ignored them. However, by 1918 the national executive had recognized their plight: "These women are not conversant with Canadian customs and experience great difficulty in finding employment for some time after their arrival." Local committees, the executive ruled, were authorized to assist such women at the usual rates. The CPF could bear some of the cost of reducing Britain's hungry population.[87]

Once in England, wives of Canadian soldiers were beyond assistance from the Canadian Patriotic Fund. In difficult cases, Sir George Perley turned to the National Relief Fund, one of several CPF counterparts in Britain, with the obvious argument that the Canadian fund supported needy British families in Canada. Other soldiers in the CEF had left families and relatives in the United States. Many Canadians living in the United States sent contributions to the Patriotic Fund, often with promises of other assistance. Ames took advantage of these promises to create auxiliaries in Boston, Chicago, Detroit, Pittsburgh, New York, San Francisco, and other American cities, and donations from American residents were funnelled back to the American branches until the United States entered the war in 1917. The American Red Cross soon filled the role of the CPF and the British National Relief Fund.[88]

Home Defence Families

As we have seen, the CPF's definition of "active service" excluded those who stood guard only in Canada. Thousands of militia were called out at the outset of the war to protect seaports, railway bridges, and even the Welland Canal, but got no more pay than if they had gone to a summer training camp or turned out for "strike duty." Once Germany's Far East squadron had been sunk in the Battle of the Falklands and its commerce raiders had been driven from the sea, any direct threat to Canada's safety seemed to dissolve. However, deployed garrison troops, and the contractors who benefited from supplying them, had become local assets. Only a little ingenuity was needed to persuade local military authorities and politicians that hidden but deadly dangers persisted, and that soldiers had to be deployed domestically. The hysteria that confined thousands of newcomers from central Europe to barbed-wire enclosures guarded by militia seemed cruelly absurd even a generation later, but in 1915-16 it reflected a passionate public will.

The realization that home defence was safe work was small comfort to the 9,000 soldiers doing sentry duty in all phases of the Canadian climate, in defended areas from Halifax to Esquimalt or at internment camps from Amherst to Nanaimo.[89] Soldiers on duty in Canada received the same rates of pay as in the CEF, but, even if they lived apart from their wife and family, they had no right either to separation allowance or, despite assurances in 1914 from the prime minister and the minister of public works, to any benefits provided by the CPF.[90] Subsidizing soldiers who stayed safely at home to defend Canada was not Herbert Ames's intention nor, he believed, was it acceptable to CPF contributors. If the guardians of Partridge Island or the Welland Canal wanted more money for their families, they should transfer to the CEF and go overseas.

This was easier for some parts of the country to accept than others. While many CPF branches heard from families of men employed as Home Defence soldiers or internment camp guards, the issue was more intense for branches in Nova Scotia and British Columbia and in parts of Ontario where such troops were stationed. "My husband's home and children are just as dear to him and worth as much as any other man's," complained Mrs. S.H. Raun, who claimed that her husband had been promised CPF aid before he enlisted. Now that her husband was kept in Canada to serve in the Welland Canal Protective Force, she had only $35 a month to keep herself and two children, "which in these hard times it takes all one can get to live on."[91] Mrs. Raun got no satisfaction from either the government or the CPF.

As wartime inflation sent prices soaring, military pay grew steadily less adequate, whether the man earning it was posted at Arras or Esquimalt. Meanwhile, the Patriotic Fund seemed to grow steadily more exclusive. From St. Catharines, Mrs. H.M. Humly complained in January 1917 that $1.00 was now worth only $0.65 and dropping. Anne Failes, whose husband also served on the Welland Canal Protective Force, reported that she paid $10.00 per month for rent, $10.00 for groceries, $5.00 for gas and fuel, $3.50 for clothes and boots, $2.50 for meat, and $2.00 each for milk, schoolbooks, and an allowance to her aged parents, leaving nothing for a doctor or medicine if any of her four children got sick. Neither her advocacy nor that of her local district officer commanding, Maj.-Gen. Logie, made any difference.[92] Pte. W.R. Duke, who guarded German internees at the remote northern Ontario settlement of Kapuskasing, might as well have been in France so far as his family in New Liskeard was concerned. He received $300 a year less than a CEF soldier, and his wife had had to leave their three children and go to Haileybury to find work. "Now is it fair," she asked the prime minister, "that a Government should place parents in such a position that both had to be away from their home and family and no one to train the children for proper citizens of Canada?"[93] A desperate Katie Dickinson, with five sick children and mounting medical debts, pleaded that her husband be sent overseas: he "could fill a needy corner at the 'Front' if he only had the chance, & then his family could be placed out of reach of want." She got her wish.[94]

Should families of soldiers who had returned from overseas but remained on duty be allowed to turn to the CPF? By 1917 thousands of disabled and convalescent soldiers had returned to Canada from England.[95] A 1915 amendment legitimated CPF allowances for returned soldiers' families while they remained in hospital. How-ever, CEF members fit enough to serve in Canada were transferred to Special Serv-ice companies, holding units that increasingly replaced Militia units as guards, garrisons, and duties as miscellaneous as stoking the furnaces in the Toronto ar-mouries or enforcing discipline in convalescent homes run by the Military Hospi-tals Commission. Was it fair to cut off CPF allowances to families that had received them for months and years? Branches were divided. One solution was for the CPF to urge the Militia Department to release soldiers with two or more children or who received more than $20 a month from the Fund, so that they could benefit from rising civilian wages.[96] Assuming that it would do so, the CPF could argue that the married men who remained were both exceptional and essential and could continue to receive allowances, though at a reduced rate. Support from the CPF for families of members of the Canadian Military Police, expanded rapidly in 1918 to pursue conscription dodgers, depended on whether the soldier had been trans-ferred from the CEF or had enlisted directly. The latter were still excluded.[97]

Elizabeth Kerr's soldier-husband had returned from Europe with a hernia. Stirred by his brother-in-law's death overseas, he re-enlisted, though he was now unfit to go overseas. Mrs. Kerr therefore could not count on the CPF. With the winter approaching, she explained to Maj.-Gen. Logie, that, on $40 per month, she could not even afford to lay in her coal supply: "Now sir don't you think that if a man is willing to give his time to the army, that they should look after his wife and family, either that or discharge him and let him go so that he can work and earn enough. I cannot go to work myself as I am not very strong and I have two small children to look after."[98] Faced with the refusal of the Toronto and York Patriotic Society to alter its policies, Maj.-Gen. Logie could only tell Mrs. Kerr that he was sorry. "This is a civilian association run by a civilian committee," he assured her, and she must make her own approach, perhaps through the Toronto and York County Patriotic Fund Association.[99] Ultimately, the CPF agreed that members of Special Service companies qualified for allowances. This was not wholly popular and, as Morris recorded, at least one Ontario branch defied the ruling.[100]

Montreal's Relief Committee

Once its 1914 Whirlwind Campaign to raise money was completed, the Montreal branch's relief committee took over centre stage from the finance committee. While Clarence Smith was an active chairman, the *Montreal Daily Star* identified Miss Helen Reid as "General-Director" and "commanding officer of this regiment which is defending the families of soldiers from want and hardship."[101] Equally, the paper assured its readers, Reid defended donors. A blacklist recorded those "who were doubtful or who had made false representations."[102] The key to her system, adapted from Rufus Smith's Charity Organization Society, was volunteer visitations. Visitors were organized by city ward, with French, English, Catholics, and Protestants treated separately. By November 1915 Reid was seeking "Hebrew" volunteers to visit Jewish families. Visitors' vigilance expanded the "Black and Doubtful List" to 100 families, some of them imposters and others who had failed to report a husband's return from Valcartier.

By mid-October 1914, 1,158 Montreal families had applied for aid and $55,962 had been paid out. Operating separately, the Franco-Belgian office registered 404 families and paid out $12,300.[103] The Fund lightened its lists by returning 108 women and children to England, while the Franco-Belgian office dispatched 19 families, 43 persons in all. By August 1915 the Montreal branch had seen 5,742 applicants, of whom 4,746 were approved. Of the recipients, 1,046 were French Canadian, 720 "British Canadian," 2,117 hailed from the British Isles, and 27 were Jewish. The Franco-Belgian Committee had 562 French and 112 Belgian recipients. By 1917 the branch reported 9,227 applicants, of whom 6,573 were wives, 1,866 were dependent mothers, 198 were dependent fathers, and 584 were "others" – presumably orphaned children. Of the Fund's charges, 202 adults, 85 children, and 312 infants had died.[104] By war's end the branch claimed to have dealt with 15,000 families.

Who qualified for assistance? According to CPF statute, the branch rejected the claims of the family of a Montrealer interned in Germany, of a partially blinded Calgary soldier in Montreal's Royal Victoria Hospital, and a wife abandoned before her husband enlisted. As for "stay-at-home soldiers," militia called out for sentry duty, the Montreal branch tried to compromise. Pressed hard by the Soldiers' Wives League, which was dominated by militia officers' wives, the Montreal branch decided that a man and wife could get along on militia pay, "but if there were children, an allowance was granted them at the rates given for the children of those serving abroad."[105] Later in 1915, worried about its income and discontent among donors, the CPF's national executive insisted that all branches eliminate assistance to families of Home Service soldiers.[106] This was hard for some Montreal families. In 1918 Mrs. J.T. Ainsworth wrote to the prime minister to explain that her husband, a musician, had joined the band of the 215th Battalion, but when ill health forced him to transfer to a Home Service unit, she and her son lost her benefits. "I would not care if I could get something for the boy," she pleaded with Borden, "as you know sir what a lot a young boy can eat besides clothes."[107]

In April 1915, 2,263 English-speaking Montreal families averaged $16.93 monthly and 467 Franco-Belgian families averaged $23.36.[108] Maternity benefits, curtailed and then eliminated in the Fund's second year, constituted a significant saving. Nevertheless, in August 1916 the Montreal branch's monthly relief payment rose to

$56,456 for the Drummond Street office and $11,585 for the Franco-Belgian Committee. Except in the early winter months of 1917 and 1918, when families got advances to help with winter fuel bills, it never again reached as high.[109] When conscription replaced volunteers, only single men were taken.

In the contemporary spirit of "efficient" social service, Reid launched her visitors on a vigorous pursuit of imposture and fraud. Families on the Fund were "carefully investigated, re-investigated and visited." No system was perfect: "We have found that the most experienced investigators can be misled by unscrupulous women who are trying to make all they can from employers, Government and Fund." But without the Fund, "many a worthy, grateful wife and mother would be in sore distress."[110] Sensible women, Reid insisted, were not offended by searching questions, though some "of an oversensitive nature" became indignant: "In several suspicious circumstances it has been found that the women who have applied cannot produce their marriage certificates and are unworthy applicants ... Women have applied under assumed names posing as wives of soldiers when they have husbands alive and not in the service. Others have signed on as widows when a husband has been in the immediate background, while others have hastily adopted one or two children in order to draw increased allowances."[111]

Effective policing depended on good records, a major problem for the CEF's amateur paymasters and makeshift administration. Eager recruiters often exaggerated what volunteers could expect from the Fund. The challenge to enroll French-Canadian volunteers led to lowered standards and then to mass desertion and discharges. In October 1915 Clarence Smith reported that he had sent a branch official to Valcartier with 218 names from two French-speaking Montreal battalions, only to find that 65 had already deserted or been discharged. A month later, 158 of 184 married men from the notorious 41st Battalion and 96 of 121 family heads from the 57th Battalion had absented themselves without leave, an unjustified drain of $4,064 a month for the Montreal branch (and three times as much for the Militia Department).[112]

The national executive endorsed Smith's proposal that such families get no money until their man was safely overseas.[113] Not all women accepted their fate. If her husband had deserted, one woman complained, "It is ... the carelessness of the officers or leaders of his regiment who are responsible and not I. When I signed my consent to let him enlist, I did it with the understanding I should have the support of your Committee as well as that of the Government, and if your Committee refuse to meet its engagements I will bring the matter to the Court."[114]

Montreal's relief committee wrestled with decisions large and small. Distributing free bread tickets from a patriotic baker, it concluded, was unfair to other bakers. After two months, the Fund stopped helping with water rates. Would the committee pay two employees for a separate Franco-Belgian office? For the sake of peace, reluctantly, yes. A wife deserted by her soldier-husband before his enlistment had no claim for SA or CPF assistance, but if her son enlisted and sought a separation allowance for her, the CPF could assist her. And of course, a soldier's mother could only claim support if she had been supported by her unmarried son before his enlistment.

Should soldiers' wives be encouraged to work? Contemporary convention dictated that a wife, and certainly a mother, stayed home, but reality had compelled many mothers to leave their children with relatives or neighbours and earn what they could – as middle-class women might have realized from the lives of their own charwomen. As the husband's surrogate, should the CPF encourage or even permit a woman to work? If it discouraged work, did the CPF aggravate the "servant problem," a concern close to the hearts of its lady volunteers and the wives of major donors? Helen Reid was indignant to discover that the Hamilton branch encouraged childless wives to work by continuing working women's allowances – giving the woman more than she needed. To Ames she explained Montreal policy: "We make no difference in a woman's budget provided she does only casual work, charring, washing etc., for not more than three days a week. If she is in a regular position, factory, shop, service, or work every day, we lower her allowance, and we encourage our women with young children who have sufficient income from separation allowance, assigned pay and the Fund to stop at home, and take care of their children. This evidently is not the attitude in Hamilton and perhaps not elsewhere."[115]

Fiscal rigour extended to the Fund's paid staff and volunteers. The wife of the branch's paid manager, G.W. Elliott, complained that her husband was pushed to exhaustion and the edge of ill-health by the demands of his board.[116] The Montreal branch treasurer, John W. Ross, arranged for CPF finances to be audited at no cost by a group of junior accountants and later by Cushing & Hodgson and George A. Touche & Co. Interest payments on its deposits at the Bank of Montreal more than covered the Montreal branch's entire administrative costs, a common CPF experience. The interest encouraged Ross to keep branch receipts in Montreal, rather than transferring them to Ottawa, as Patriotic Fund rules dictated.[117]

Montreal, claimed Clarence Smith, kept 650 women volunteers busy or waiting: 150 took turns in the office and 400 served as visitors. Others joined a waiting list.[118] Volunteers and ten paid staff kept branch offices open five days a week, sent 300 letters a day, and interviewed hundreds of clients. The work, claimed Ames, was far harder than volunteers were accustomed to do, and the few amenities were cheap. "Several times a week a member of the Ladies Auxiliary brings her own maid and dispenses tea at her own expense and a few moments of rest is provided out of a busy day."[119] Helen Reid expected a visitor to call on ten families, to keep a "businesslike record of her families," to attend ward meetings monthly, and provide written reports every two months. Special four-to-six-week courses were available, though, she confessed, few women found time to take them.[120]

Robert Dexter, an American professional social worker who had taken over Montreal's Charity Organization Society from Rufus Smith, praised Reid but had little faith in her untrained volunteers. In 1917 he advised a newly belligerent United States to use trained professional social workers if they imitated the CPF. Soldiers' families presented plenty of problems, he warned, from indolence and extravagance to immorality; only first-class social work would control costs. In Montreal, Dexter complained,

> Reliance on volunteer service has made the Fund undemocratic and less efficient. Its visitors are necessarily of the leisure class, most of whom have never worked before. One reason for this has been the administrative expense bogy. An attempt is constantly being made to cut down the expense of administration without intelligent consideration of the interest of the families. They deserve the best social service, just as they deserve the best medical service that the community can provide, and it is unfair to turn loose on them hundreds of more or less efficient volunteers, many of whom have had no trained leadership and cannot be given it now. It is not only unfair to the families of the soldiers but it is unfair to the volunteers themselves. Without sufficiently helpful oversight, they often get unfortunate reactions from their experiences. I have talked with many of the volunteers who affirm that all poor people are liars; that they are all immoral; or, on the other hand, that they are all exploited.[121]

Dexter's professional pride was no concern of Herbert Ames, with the whole of Canada to organize. Knighted in the spring of 1915 for his energetic leadership of the CPF, Ames combined both the guiding vision and the energy and shrewdness needed to create a coast-to-coast organization. Part of his shrewdness was to insist that control of the Fund lay with the donors. Like any political leader interpreting the desires of an amorphous mass citizenry, Ames felt free to embody the collective will, even when he found himself at odds with loudly expressed opinions. Like his prime minister, Ames was powerfully influenced by the Progressive movement in the United States. Repelled by the waste and corruption inherent in democratic vote buying, and shocked by the selfish greed of corporate monopoly, Progressives sought to bring business efficiency to government with a minimum of democratic interference. Often this was achieved through assigning public responsibilities to appointed commissions, such as the Hydro Electric Power Commission created by Ontario in 1906 to manage the province's electricity supply, or through municipal

Boards of Control, elected by all the city's voters and absorbing powers exercised by ward-based aldermen. "The Fund," as Philip Morris reported, "always meant business."[122]

"To the uninitiated, to the more or less superficial observer," Morris confessed, "it appeared sound and logical that the support of soldiers' dependants should be borne entirely by the Federal Government." Such views Ames and his officials dismissed as wrong. So long as it depended exclusively on private generosity, the Fund could make distinctions. Separation allowance was characteristic of what the state had to do – a one-size-fits-all payment that ignored family size and circumstances. One of Ames's favourite illustrations was the possibility that "Mr. Millionaire" and his coachman both enlisted as privates. "Mrs. Millionaire and Mrs. Coachman each get \$20. It is of little account to Mrs. Millionaire, but it is not enough for Mrs. Coachman if she has four or five children."[123]

In April 1916, when Ames spoke to the House of Commons Special Committee on Pensions, he estimated that the Militia Department was paying between 50,000 and 60,000 separation allowances and that the CPF, exclusive of Manitoba, issued about 35,000 monthly cheques, leaving about 15,000 families that did not need CPF help.[124] Six months later, after Canada had been scraped for CEF volunteers, 150,000 soldiers collected separation allowance for their dependants, while the Fund offered an average of \$192 a year to 60,000 of those families. The added cost of raising everyone's allowance by that amount would have been at least \$8,640,000, all of it unnecessary in the eyes of the CPF's managers. Since the money would have been borrowed, Ames warned, the debt would have been borne by future generations of Canadians, including veterans and their families.[125] Instead, the Fund collected from those who had stayed out of the firing line. Its volunteer visitors could assess specific family needs and circumstances and, within broad guidelines, relief committees answerable to wealthy branch executives tailored allowances to need, subject only to the satisfaction of the donors.

The Fund was not in fact wholly dependent on private donors. From the outset, some branches in rural counties and townships were funded by local taxes. Several cities and provinces pledged major gifts to the Fund over several years and funded CPF administration. In Parliament Ames insisted that he always tried to persuade county councils to vote unanimously: "On one occasion, when a discussion arose in a county council as to the amount to be granted, and it was apparent that there would be a division, and that the result of the division would be a more generous amount for the fund, I told them that we would prefer to have a smaller amount unanimously voted."[126] In time, some provinces replaced voluntary donations with a tax-funded contribution to cover the CPF's local costs. However, Ames insisted, if Ottawa had supplanted the Fund with its own tax dollars, other levels of government would promptly have withdrawn their support, at a time when the federal government's borrowing power was already badly strained.

If relieving soldiers' dependants was the Patriotic Fund's first great responsibility, it could do so only if it met a second responsibility: to find the funds. Within a week of the governor general's first appeal, the duke had received four cheques for $25,000 each. Within a month the CPF had deposited $285,000 in donations. By the end of 1914 its bank balance exceeded $2 million, and the interest alone was sufficient to pay the Fund's national administrative costs. Another $4 million had been pledged by donors across Canada. In a 1916 speech in the House of Commons, Ames rejoiced that social pressure had effectively forced all but a small minority to contribute to the Fund: "Our slogan has always been 'Fight or pay.' We call upon the people to enlist or help others to enlist. We sometimes say: 'If you cannot put the "I" into fight, put the "pay" into patriotism,' and that serves as a slogan on any platform. We have no conscription in Canada, and probably never shall have."[127]

Indeed, at a time when conscription was being debated by prominent Canadians, Ames argued that contributions to the Patriotic Fund accentuated a subconscious pressure for voluntary enlistment:

> The sacrifices that the people of this Dominion are making, from the richest to the poorest, that every class in every community is making ... all go into one common purse, and all represent self-sacrifice on the part of our people; and that self-sacrifice serves as a tonic, because we find that a community which gives in money is always willing to give in men. It would be a genuine deprivation and the taking away of an uplifting influence from the people of Canada if opportunities for voluntary subscription were removed or were replaced by compulsory taxation for purposes such as these.[128]

At Christmas 1914 the prospect of war stretched at least a year into the future. Like everyone else, the CPF had to settle in for a long struggle. During 1915 the Canadian Expeditionary Force tripled from 59,144 to 158,859 men and women.[129] In each successive month, demands on the Fund increased, particularly in the second half of 1915, after Sir Robert Borden set a target of 250,000 soldiers, Sir Sam Hughes had authorized scores of new battalions, and the pace of recruiting quickened. Between June and October, the Fund spent $700,000 more on allowances than it received, and the Fund's national executive struggled to cut expenses, forbidding any aid to families of Home Service soldiers, and directing that families must empty their savings before seeking compassionate assistance.[130] A major new national fundraising effort was needed.[131]

In October 1915 Ames published *How Much Shall We Give?*, a statistical account of the Fund's income and expenditure by province, with a detailed description of the CPF's good works. The pamphlet also set a national target of $7.5 million for 1916, and provincial quotas based on the 1911 census: $0.61 per capita for the Maritimes, $0.60 for Quebec, $0.92 for Ontario, $2.00 for Alberta, $1.00 for Saskatchewan, and $1.37 or a total of $650,000 from British Columbia. Manitoba, still independent, was expected to raise $1 million for its own needs, or $1.90 per person.[132]

On New Year's Day 1916, almost all Canadian newspapers reported Sir Robert Borden's pledge that Canada would raise half a million soldiers. The press also carried a personal appeal from the Duke of Connaught that was read from most church pulpits. In it, the governor general appealed for a day's wages from each Canadian for the Patriotic Fund. To respond to the prime minister's initiative, the national office raised its target to $8 million and revised the provincial and regional quotas proposed in October: $4,500,000 for Ontario or $1.50 per person, $1,500,000 from Quebec, $700,000 from the three Maritime provinces, and $500,000 each from the three western provinces associated with the national fund.[133] Targets were divided among cities, towns, and counties. Alberta split its share equally between North and South. All were urged to "give until it hurts." Posters, buttons, newspaper advertisements, and plentiful professional advice fuelled local campaigns.[134]

Campaigns began across Canada in late January. In Ontario, Guelph was the winner when its citizens contributed a total of $90,000. In Ottawa, poorly paid federal civil servants were set a target of $100,000, a quarter of the city's objective. Spurred on by departmental rivalry, they came up with $145,000. Across the Ottawa River in Hull, a largely francophone community produced $30,000. Emulation, guilt, and employer pressure helped push donations far above quotas in many places.

In tiny Hedley, the 1916 campaign began when Fred Nation, organizing secretary for the British Columbia branch, brought his message to the community in late December 1915. The local newspaper gave higher billing to the governor general: "Probably the most democratic member of the royal family of the most democratic kingdom in the World. A soldier from the ground up. With an independent income, absolutely above the suspicion of graft, petty or grand, whose every thought is for the people of Canada, and of whom Canadians have been justly proud." Conscious of its stay-at-home readership, the *Hedley Gazette and Similkameen Advertiser* reminded them how to fight the war: "The Patriotic Fund is the ammunition of the stay-at-homes. In a large sense, it is the sinews of war as far as Canada is concerned. It is the means best adapted for the man with responsibilities and dependants to do 'his bit.'" Donors were listed on the paper's front page. When M.C. Hill reported that his poor hearing had barred him from the CEF, his contribution rose from $3 to $6. Headed by $200 from the Hedley Gold Mining Company and including $6 from the town's four Chinese, the community's January contribution was $597. Word that a meeting in South Vancouver had urged the government to pay for the Fund inspired the editor to declare that the locals must have been captured "by the Kaiser and his band of cut-throats."[135]

Almost half the CPF's 1916 collection came from the rival cities of Montreal and Toronto. Both cities tried to broaden their donor base. Toronto's "50,000 Club" was designed to collect 50,000 dollar-a-month contributors. A special committee claimed that it had found 85,000 members, with the added benefit that most of them would keep on contributing for the duration of the war. The work of collecting the enormous number of tiny contributions was staggering, and organizers were on the verge of paying the house-to-house canvassers when Mrs. H.P. Plumptre offered her women's committee. In perseverance and thoroughness, claimed Bert McCreath, the women "are so far ahead of any male persons in the same capacity that they should not be mentioned together."[136] As volunteers, moreover, women cost nothing. Toronto's schoolchildren, an obvious target for eager patriots, contributed over $15,000, much of it doubtless channelled from their parents.

Across the country, newspapers backed the campaign with selected stories about farmers giving the proceeds of a "patriotic acre," or a lighthouse keeper near Vancouver who contributed $1,000 earned selling flowers to passing tourists. An elderly Nova Scotia couple, Ames reported, had given him the money they had been saving for a trip to Halifax to see off their soldier-son, "perhaps for ever."[137] Chikchagalook, an Inuit of remote Herschel Island in the Beaufort Sea, encountered brief celebrity because of his gift of $20. Even better known was Moo-che-we-in-es, a Cree from the Onion Lake reserve in Saskatchewan, who sent $150 late in 1915, via Duncan Campbell Scott, deputy superintendent of Indian affairs. "Looking for every human story we can find," Ames asked Scott to press Moo-che-we-in-es for details and was provided with a letter in Cree that the Fund used for one of its posters: "I heard there was a big war going on over there; I feel like I want to help you some way and the best I can do it to send a little money for I can't go myself as I am nearly blind." "You and your Indians give us a continuing succession of splendid news items," a delighted Ames responded to Scott: "We scatter them broadcast with the intimation that if an Indian can see his duty in such a fashion, there is no excuse for a white man in falling down in his."[138] The condescension was wholly unconscious.

Montreal's 1916 campaign illustrated both the techniques recommended by the national office and the strains developing between French and English as the war continued. As early as June 1915 the Montreal branch had reluctantly recognized the need for another major fundraising campaign.[139] Outside the major cities and Quebec's English-speaking communities, the province had shown little interest. Senator Dandurand had led a delegation to Quebec City to persuade Premier Sir Lomer Gouin to contribute from Quebec's provincial coffers and utterly failed.[140] Passionate pro-British patriotism aroused few echoes in French-speaking Quebec, and Henri Bourassa's *Le Devoir* had inspired a more congenial crusade against *les Boches de l'Ontario,* presenting Ontario's Regulation 17 as an assault on the education rights of the French minority. Whatever their sympathy for the French and Belgians, French Canadians were reluctant to enlist in an English-speaking army in a war that seemed utterly remote from their interests. Instead, as depression changed to an economic boom, pressures to enlist were replaced by opportunities for well-paid jobs in Quebec's factories.[141]

Montreal's CPF branch accepted the whole of Quebec's 1916 target of $1,500,000. Learning from their 1914 experience, the finance committee proposed larger teams, each with a French and English captain to avoid the undertone of unpleasant linguistic rivalry that had developed in the previous campaign. Most of the veterans of the 1914 campaign returned, and the Windsor Hotel contributed committee rooms and a daily lunch. The Canadian Pacific Railway's publicity department produced the advertising, this time displaying Canada's Red Ensign more conspicuously than the Union Jack. The most frequent advertisement featured a mother and children staring into a bleak winter: "Some women are giving their men. Some men are giving their lives. What are you giving?" A leaflet entitled "How Much Should One Give to the Patriotic Fund?" claimed that $16 a month was the average payment to the family of a married soldier.[142]

Nationwide friction between French and English affected the campaign. Late in 1915, when CPF stalwart Ucal Dandurand asked the city of Maisonneuve to renew its $5,000 contribution, aldermen complained that "French-Canadian families had great difficulty in obtaining what was due to them by the Fund while English-speaking families had no difficulty at all." Despite Dandurand's insistence that French and English shared equally in managing the Fund, Maisonneuve's council tabled the issue.[143] George Gibbons promptly drafted a letter for the Fund executive, explaining that each ward had a French as well as an English head, and that seventy-two of the Fund's lady visitors were French Canadians. "Besides this," the statement reported, "everything that could be done for the education of the French speaking mothers in hygiene, domestic economy etc. has been at their disposal in their own language. In each district, French-Canadian doctors have during the past summer, given addresses to the mothers on the best hygienic methods of raising babies etc."[144]

The committee got another unpleasant surprise on 16 January when it invited Montreal's city council to double its 1914 gift of $150,000. Aldermen Ménard and Lapointe reminded their visitors that the council had been blamed by English newspapers for borrowing to meet city expenses. Montreal was too poor to pay. "It's not our war," added Alderman Pauzé. And how dare the Patriotic Fund, in a report written by Helen Reid, criticize Quebec's lack of compulsory schooling? How could anyone condemn the province, asked Alderman St-Pierre, and then look to Quebec for money? The blame, added Ménard, lay not just with the English Canadians but with French Canadians like Ucal Dandurand, for allowing insults to be published. What about a special tax on behalf of soldiers' families? "Don't try to load the blame for a tax on the Patriotic Fund," responded Dandurand, pointing out that the council had itself to blame for a $2 million deficit.[145]

On 22 January, as canvassing began, Ottawa's French-speaking Catholic clergy publicly rejected the Patriotic Fund. To resist tyranny and conserve their language and schools, they were "obliged today to concentrate all their energies and all their financial resources to the bilingual question."[146]

Gamely, the Duke of Connaught came to Montreal on 21 January to open the campaign, praising "the men in the large businesses like the C.P.R. and other railways, in many large factories and munition works in this city, who are giving so generously and who have responded so well, giving one day's pay a quarter to the Fund."[147] A press statement insisted that "a valuable feature of the Patriotic Fund in the Province of Quebec is the effect it has had in unifying the French and English elements."[148] Instead of seven French-speaking teams out of twenty-three, as in 1914, the eighteen teams included an average of eleven French- and eighteen English-speaking members.[149] In fact, the 1916 campaign went better than anyone in Montreal could have expected. When he spoke at the first campaign lunch, Monseigneur Bruchési ingeniously linked the voluntarism of the CEF and of the Patriotic Fund, and condemned a dispute that undermined Canada's war effort: "What is at the root of the dispute? Two hundred thousand men, glorying in the name of British subjects, loyal to their king and country, making it a point of honour to speak English, ask simply to speak the language of their ancestors, the sweet and beautiful French language, and to teach it freely to their children. That is all, and the answer lies with men of good will."[150]

As in 1914, money poured in: $856,585 by the third day, $2,379,854 by the final day, and $2,510,287 when the final pledges were added. The day's pay scheme, still managed by J.W. McConnell, produced close to $500,000 in pledges from Montreal employees. Still, the success had a sour note. McConnell gave companies the credit although the cash came from workers, leading Henri Bourassa's *Le Nationaliste* to complain of the unfair pressure that might potentially be brought to bear on employees who refused: "They put themselves potentially in disgrace with their bosses. As a result, they run the risk of receiving no pay raises and of being laid off if the occasion arises. There has been flagrant injustice."[151] *La Presse*, Montreal's biggest daily, gave editorial support, but without the flamboyant coverage it had given the previous campaign. Montreal's tiny and impoverished Lebanese community, with 181 contributions from 181 approaches totalling $2,244.03, set a patriotic example, but it was small compensation for Montreal's deeper divisions.[152]

Few in the rest of the country probably noticed. Instead, the Patriotic Fund managers focused on their successes. British Columbia, still in the economic doldrums, raised almost $1 million, close to double its target. While Saskatchewan and New Brunswick had struggled, Nova Scotia and Prince Edward Island exceeded their quotas. Instead of the $8 million the CPF had set as a nationwide target, the total received in cash and pledges was $11,573,344.66, almost 50 percent more than planned. Meanwhile, the demands had also grown. Choosing New Year's Day to give an example of earnestness to his British senior allies, Borden had set Canada's target at one man in eight. This could only be achieved, Ames recognized, if even more men with family responsibilities enlisted. In January 1916 CPF branches paid out $565,000 in allowances across Canada; in July, total disbursement for the first time exceeded six digits – $1,065,074.55 – and subsequent months came close to that figure for the rest of the year. Fundraising, the Patriotic Fund's second responsibility, would be even heavier in 1917.

A Third Responsibility

In almost every community, local executives appointed finance and relief committees to manage the Fund's two statutory responsibilities. The work was not equal: fundraising campaigns required months of planning and a frenzied week of collecting; relief went on throughout the year and required committee members to attend few meetings but to visit families monthly. In Kingston, Hugh C. Nickle, chairman of the relief committee, personally signed each of the hundreds of cheques mailed out monthly to branch beneficiaries, and claimed to have collected $15,000 in initial separation allowance cheques for soldiers' families in his city. R.M. Anderson, chairman of the Elgin County branch, wrote 600 letters to the government in 1916 for his military families, and 700 in 1917.[153]

But aside from collecting funds and distributing relief, the Patriotic Fund also developed what its sponsors termed a "Third Responsibility." In taking charge of the Fund, Ames's motive had been neither to raise nor to spend money but to prove his conviction that helpful advice and systematic oversight could wean the poor from habits of life that kept them poor. While by no means all soldiers or their families were poor, the CPF's mandate excluded those Ames had defined as "Mrs. Millionaire" and focused on "Mrs. Coachman." Montreal's Helen Reid mobilized her 600 volunteers largely for this social service work. No one did more to exercise or to publicize the CPF's third responsibility.

Support from the Fund depended on home visits, initially by male members of the branch donations committee, then increasingly by their wives and daughters and their friends. Visiting began with the task of verification. One of the earliest issues of the CPF *Bulletin* underlined the results of investigations – a mother collecting from the CPF when two other breadwinners already gave her an income of $126.50 a month, and another improper beneficiary who had received $50.00 a month from her husband's peacetime employer.[154] Visitors reported moral turpitude, neglected children, and extravagance, conducting an informal means test when they reported signs of recipients living above their humble station.[155] Was a telephone evidence that a woman was a spendthrift? CPF officials were inclined to think so. Certainly any sign of extravagance would exasperate donors, especially the local businesses that provided much of the local leadership and donations. In his speech to an audience of recipients at Galt (now Cambridge), Ames urged the women to report mistaken payments and "improper" use of fund by others. Above all, he reminded them: "We expect of you that you establish and encourage a high standard of living in your neighbourhood. To do this, all care should be directed to payment of just debts, careful spending, proper housing, regular attendance at church, the children's school attendance, and a careful choice of friends and company."[156]

Nellie McClung, one of Canada's best-known authors, offered a characteristically uplifting account of a CPF recipient in a short story published in 1917. "Surprises" describes a childless wife busy squandering her $5 CPF allowance: "Mrs. Elizabeth Tweed, wife of Pte. William Tweed, was giving trouble to the Patriotic society. It was bad enough for her to go out evenings with an officer, and dance in the afternoon at the hotel *dansant* in a perfect outburst of gay garments; but there was no excuse for her coming home in a taxi-cab, after a shopping expedition in broad daylight, and to the scandal of the whole street, who watched her from behind lace curtains." Patriotic Fund contributions fall off in the neighbourhood, but Tweed's IODE visitor is "told to go to a region which is never mentioned in polite society except in theological discussions." Mrs. Kent, the local head of the Red Cross, gets better results. An ensuing exchange with Mrs. Tweed's latest boyfriend, who blames her qualms on women getting the vote, leads the soldier's wife to a radical lifestyle change. She cancels her CPF grant, finds work as a waitress, banks her separation allowance and makes it clear to predatory males that she is a faithful wife. To both McClung and the CPF, this was an admirably instructive ending.[157]

Handling local inquiries and investigations for the separation allowance administrators of the Militia Department was a logical extension of a local committee's oversight of its largely female charges. Fund representatives investigated reports of adultery, drunkenness, child abuse and neglect, and their advice was sufficient to suspend or cancel Militia Department separation allowances, though it was left to the soldier, after receiving the reports, to decide whether to alter his pay assignment.[158]

In Helen Reid, Ames had found an almost ideal co-adjutor. Part of Reid's view of her third responsibility was found in her "black book" of wives who had disgraced their calling. One was Margaret Curran, who left Montreal for Toronto owing rent and without informing the branch. Since Mrs. Curran seemed "a very respectable looking woman," Martha E. Fennix, Reid's Toronto counterpart, demanded more details. "Our further investigation," Reid reported, "shows that she left Montreal in the night, owing money to her Landlord, Grocer, Sewing Machine agent, and Gas Company, and in fact to nearly everyone she had had anything to do with." Even Curran's German mother, who had showed up in Montreal, was astonished by her flit. "Mrs. Curran cannot be believed," Reid concluded, "and should be kept under the most strict supervision, not only on account of her German origin, but on account of her character."[159]

Another of Reid's cases, Mrs. Wineas Zwingli, was left by her husband with $40 in assigned pay and allowances, plus a small tobacco and candy store. The CPF added $24 for her and four small children, but cut off her allowance after police alleged that the store was a "blind pig" and the woman was pregnant. The Militia Department followed the CPF example and cut off her separation allowance. Though a lawyer took up Mrs. Zwingli's case, the chair of the Montreal relief committee, Clarence Smith, firmly responded that the Fund was answerable only to its executive.[160] The Mercier case in 1915 was his confirmation. As Helen Reid later confessed to an American audience, she had been dismayed to find women selling liquor without a permit but with the collusion of the police, and "soldiers' wives actually being kept by policemen while their husbands were at the front." Such women immediately forfeited their SA, AP, and CPF, she reported, and they were both exceptional and the fault of governments "who have failed to give us prohibition in wartime": "Our women as a whole are a fine, splendid lot of patriotic souls, not only giving their men, but maintaining a special standard of justifiable pride and good conduct in their different neighbourhoods."[161]

Assistance to families, Reid insisted, could not be limited to money: "advice, instruction and sympathy increase our service manifold."[162] Battling child mortality was a logical priority in a city with Montreal's notorious sanitary problems: "A married soldier at the Front has a far greater chance to live facing German bullets than has his baby born here in the city at the present time."[163] Printed brochures on nutrition, domestic sanitation, and personal hygiene accompanied the monthly cheque. Recipients learned how to complain to City Hall about windowless rooms and building defects. During the summers of 1915 and 1916, Reid organized displays by volunteer doctors and nurses. In 1914 the relief committee authorized a special $5 maternity grant at birth and an extra dollar a week for two weeks before and six weeks after the event. The local IODE offered "a baby trousseau if needed."[164] Convinced that there was a connection between child deaths and employment, Reid encouraged mothers to stay home unless a Fund visitor argued special circumstances. Poverty, illness, indifference, and a proliferation of saloons, Reid argued, contributed to juvenile delinquency and child neglect. So did "moving picture shows" and Quebec's lax school attendance laws.[165] Reid's local leaders promoted school attendance with twenty prizes for children with the best record of attendance, conduct and progress.[166]

Reid's lady visitors encouraged lonely wives to come together. At Red Cross Clubs, wives met for tea and completed 62,000 items of sewing in a year, from pneumonia jackets to pillow slips.[167] Montreal's Archbishop Bruchési soon sponsored a separate club for 1,500 Catholic wives, with speakers, moving pictures, and music. Reid hired nurses to lecture on infant care and a domestic science teacher to instruct wives how to cook, manage a household, and economize. The Fund advised local hospitals on how much soldiers' wives could afford for treatment and childbirth, identified sympathetic doctors and lawyers, and encouraged tuberculosis sufferers to seek treatment at Mount Sinai Sanatorium.[168] One ward organization arranged for young women to visit a country home as an escape from the city. The Brewery Mission Camp and Murray Bay House welcomed soldiers' families "who needed a change and proved worthy of a holiday."[169] French and English lawyers cooperated in over 200 cases requiring legal aid, and the Fund buried 132 women and children who had no relatives or means.

Most volunteers continued until the war's end, though Reid admitted that she preferred "a greater number of cases with fewer willing Visitors who do the work well" rather than carrying more but less dependable volunteers.[170] A 1918 article celebrating Montreal's CPF ladies' auxiliary boasted that it was "the core and centre of the 'Entente Cordiale' between races and religions in Montreal." However cordial the entente, Catholics visited Catholics and Protestants, Protestants.

The women who had started in 1914, claimed the CPF *Bulletin,* were still at their posts, "weary, yes, but bigger, broader, finer and braver women than when they started."[171]

Montreal visitors came face to face with the realities of working-class urban life: "Unemployment, immorality, desertion, eviction by hard-hearted landlords, land lots to be forfeited, piano to be sacrificed, furniture not paid up, child lost, boy drowned in cellar, street car accidents, infantile paralysis, delay in receipt of Government Allowances, mother died and children to be placed, transportation needed; all these and other sad tales have to be considered and disposed of."[172] Reid was proud of her volunteers and defensive about their lack of training. She was scornful of other women who, sometimes on behalf of their husbands' CEF battalions, dared to invade her territory and who constituted, in her view, "a menace."

> The fact that 25 or 30 women are wives of officers of a battalion does not in itself qualify them for the difficult and important matter of visiting and befriending the families of the soldiers ... A battalion visitor will perhaps walk miles to visit one of her own families, but, limited in her interest to her own battalion, she does not call next door on the wife of another battalion's soldier, nor does she usually enquire what help is being given by the Fund and the Fund visitor to her own families, whom she visits more or less regularly, and often drops if she goes overseas to join her husband. These difficulties will always be hard to overcome, but education and demonstrations of mistakes as well as cordial invitations to participate in some possibly important committee capacity, will often bring an errant patriotic worker into line with socialized work.[173]

Other CPF branches addressed their third responsibility, if only by passing on advice from the national office, but only Hamilton-Wentworth came close to Montreal in letting its good works be known. Like Montreal, the Hamilton branch provided a children's clinic, free medical consultations, a subsidized coal supply, temporary lodging for widows, and deduction plans to help beneficiaries buy war savings certificates. While the branch hired a few visitors to check on its families, it put more of the burden on local clergy, inviting them to report cases of overpayment and to instill "the doctrine of 'save and serve.'" A national crisis was the Spanish influenza epidemic of 1918-19. While other branches provided home nursing, housekeepers, and even pall bearers and burial plots, the Hamilton branch opened its own makeshift hospital in the mansion of a wealthy but deceased Hamilton citizen. The premises were occupied on 16 October 1918, opened on 19 October and kept open until 21 December at a cost of $12,000. The hospital treated ninety-six dependants and six staff, with four deaths in 1,215 patient-days. The local militia supplied most of the beds and promised three military nurses if needed, but the branch found its own volunteers.[174]

Across the country, Fund visitors, paid or volunteer, befriended lonely wives, provided advice for problems that may have seemed insuperable, and drew the local branch's attention to cases of need, but their employer was always the Fund, and their primary duty was to protect its donors from fraud and waste. When Mrs. E. Morris, the wife of an Ottawa soldier, complained to the prime minister that the Fund had ignored her problems, R.A. Hurdman, secretary of the Ottawa branch, reported that she and her three children had received about $22 a month since her husband joined in 1916, plus occasional advances and help with her fuel. Mrs. Morris's visitor had noticed that "she does not know the value of money or how to spend or rather save it."[175] Daisy Justice also complained to the prime minister that the Fund had suspended her. The Toronto and York branch replied that Mrs. Justice's visitor had called a city nurse to confirm that the Justice children were badly neglected and inadequately clothed, though their mother left early in the morning and returned late at night, "always very well dressed herself." After her visitor was satisfied that Mrs. Justice was doing better, her allowance was restored.[176]

Ames had little trouble persuading colleagues on the national executive that they had a role in ending poverty. By December 1914 Montreal's relief committee was considering how to "foster habits of thrift amongst the families visited." The city's CPF executive urged Ottawa to bank half a soldier's pay until he returned.[177] In the name of the third responsibility, G.W. Elliott, the branch's senior paid official, spent hours persuading wives to maintain their husband's life insurance. In a single month, he claimed, he had saved 102 policies from lapsing. "Our experiences are frequently amusing," he reported, "and illustrate the strange perverseness of human nature. We have argued with a woman for an hour over the relative value of a new skirt and a policy on the life of her husband at that time actually dodging German souvenirs in Flanders. Another woman would allow her husband's policy to lapse rather than take the premium out of the Savings Bank."[178]

Worried that many of its charges had more money to spend than ever in their lives, the Fund drafted *A Message to the Canadian Soldier's Wife*, a pamphlet warning of the effects of extravagance on donors, and exhorting all to save for the time when their husbands would come home from the war.[179] Visitors often had to counsel wives who had been left to cope with creditors and landlords owed months of back rent. Leaflets enclosed with the monthly Patriotic Fund cheque urged "Don't Forget your Savings Bank Account." Toronto and Montreal summoned recipients to public meetings to underline the message. In Galt, Ames lectured soldiers' wives about the wisdom of "starting a Savings Account in case of sickness and trouble and for when the soldier returns."[180] The Galt branch criticized its families for such extravagances as buying oranges rather than apples. The local treasurer, F.S. Jarvis, added a little disingenuously, "We have been told that some wives object to our mentioning the subject of saving so often, but we might say that we only write these letters in a general way and for those who are not interested in the question of saving, it need not apply."[181]

In Nova Scotia, Arthur Barnstead dealt with enraged donors complaining that CPF beneficiaries left their accounts unpaid and boycotted merchants who dunned them, even when they were CPF contributors. Montreal also had to assure contributors that its clients would pay their bills. While the badly indebted got help, the branch reported in 1915 that "the Fund families are encouraged and urged in every way to meet their just obligations."[182]

In the West, many young farm families had been buying their land on the instalment plan. Provincial legislatures passed debt moratorium legislation on behalf of soldiers, but some land was patently worthless. Patriotic Fund advisors could work out payment plans for overdue debt, often with free advice from sympathetic lawyers, but "in advising the soldier's wife to discontinue payments and forfeit the amount already paid, a committee ran the risk of incurring the soldier's displeasure."[183] In 1914-18, it was a man's world. The Saskatchewan branch, with the most generous allowances in the country, devised a unique solution. Once assigned pay became compulsory in early 1915, it instituted compulsory trust savings accounts for each of its beneficiaries, deducting $16 a month from CPF allowances to hold in trust. In an emergency, instead of providing special funding, Saskatchewan let beneficiaries draw from their account: frugal and fortunate women could welcome their homecoming husband with anything from $300 to $600 in savings.[184] This plan was enthusiastically described in the CPF *Bulletins* of October and November 1915. A few branches followed suit; in August 1915 the Huron County branch arbitrarily held back half its monthly allowance as a form of compulsory savings, paying it out only when the committee concurred.[185]

Other branches promoted the Victory Bonds and War Savings Certificates, instruments the government used to extend its wartime borrowing to average citizens. The CPF branch in the Ontario town of Hespeler boasted of selling $18,000 in Victory Bonds to its frugal recipients. Thirteen of its families saved enough to buy their own homes.[186] The CPF's advisory committee proposed withholding money from soldiers' wives so that they could buy War Savings Certificates, but Nova Scotia's Arthur Barnstead demurred. Donors would be indignant that the Fund paid beneficiaries so much they could afford to save. Besides, his families'

CPF cheques averaged only $12 a month.[187] In England, Pte. Ernest Hamilton responded to War Bond advertising by suggesting a $50 investment for each of their two children, leaving the decision up to Sara in Toronto: "Do you need a new hat or dress? I hope it is not necessary for you to stint yourself to buy the clothes necessary for yourself & the babies. It must take some management for you to get along on the money you receive but do not be backward about using our bank accounts if you need it."[188]

The 1916 Eastern Conference

Like other Canadian institutions, the CPF was essentially both local and central. Nothing happened in the name of the Fund, from collecting contributions to distributing relief to visiting soldiers' families, without local effort and initiative. Yet every penny collected in the CPF's name was vested in the National Committee and distributed according to the policies adopted, sometimes after months of debate, by its thirty-four-member national executive. The strains were predictable and, by the spring of 1916, sufficient to persuade Ames to encourage Toronto's bid for a national meeting. The meeting, held on 16-18 May, attracted 197 participants, overwhelmingly from Ontario's 150 local and county branches, with a handful of visitors from other eastern provinces.[189] Fewer than 10 percent of participants were women.

Ames and Morris lectured the gathering on the workings of the central organization and its immense bureaucratic load. F.H. Dobbin of Peterborough offered practical advice on building and managing a small branch. For the relief or distribution committee, he warned, "Do not seek those who are termed your best citizens." In Peterborough, he reported, one of the most useful members was the local bill poster; another was adjutant of the Salvation Army Corps.[190] Judge Livingstone of Welland County talked of district organization and Hamilton's relief chairman, W.H. Lovering, a member of the national executive, expanded on his branch's tough-minded approach to relief. Clarence Smith came from Montreal to promote the third responsibility and the achievements of Helen Reid and her ladies' auxiliary. To conclude, Ames returned to share his view of "trusteeship": "We feel that when the man went to the Front, he passed over his wife and children to the Patriotic Fund to hold for him in trust. We wouldn't be doing our whole duty toward the man if we didn't do everything we could to make that home a better home, to make the woman a better woman, and the children a better and healthier class of children than when he left."

Helen Reid herself came to a later session of the conference to report her achievements and to promote them in other branches:

We can exert a tremendous influence in the home of almost every soldier who has gone to the Front. Anything that can be done without impertinence, without intrusion, without making the women in the home feel that you are enquiring into things that are not your business at all, I think can be undertaken by our branches and in the year that is coming our branches will give that line of work more consideration than before. Think what it means to make a better home than it was when the man went away, think what it means to him to come home to find his home cleaner and sweeter. Think what it means to him when the woman says to him: I have been gradually learning to live up to a scale I have not had before; I want to live up to that scale in the future.[191]

As often happened at CPF gatherings, the impact of the Fund on domestic servants was raised. Why pay anything to a childless wife when her separation allowance and assigned pay should be quite sufficient? She should be encouraged to work, given that the CPF's volunteers often carried an unwanted load of their own housework. "Such women were wasting too much of their time at moving picture shows or in the streets," complained Katherine O'Brien, and "as a result the domestic servant problem had become acute." The mostly male delegates disagreed, and Hugh Nickle, head of Kingston's relief committee, set the tone: "He did not understand why, when a husband enlisted, his wife should be expected to become a charwoman." Provided the marriage predated the husband's enlistment, and a wife met all the Fund's requirements, most delegates agreed that a $5 a month allowance was reasonable for a childless wife.[192]

Ames urged Arthur Barnstead to organize a similar conference for the Maritime provinces, but a pending Nova Scotia election was too much of a distraction. It was also apparent that the other provinces wanted their own conferences. Instead, both men saved a few weeks for a summer tour and Ames came in September to shore up branches that, Barnstead believed, had fallen down on their fundraising.[193]

A provincial convention for the Saskatchewan branch in Regina on Tuesday, 27 June 1916 gave a pretext for a western interprovincial conference on the ensuing two days, with representation from British Columbia and Alberta branches and ten delegates from Manitoba's independent organization. Sixty-four men and six women met. Although this may be an artifact of the reporting, they heard more outspoken discussion and displayed more competitive pride in funds collected, branches organized, and relief prudently administered than did the Toronto conference. Ames repeated his stress on uniformity, but delegates agreed that a uniform provincial relief rate would be unworkable. Ames also repeated his claims for the uplift possible through the Fund's third responsibility, though with less answering enthusiasm than in Toronto.[194]

Ames and the delegates also got a thorough briefing from J.A. Calder, provincial treasurer of Saskatchewan's Liberal government, on the province's new Patriotic Purposes Tax. Set at one mill on rateable property, the tax was intended to support Belgian, Polish, and Serbian relief, the Red Cross, and hospitals and convalescent homes as well as the CPF.[195] Was taxation the right way to fund the CPF? In Regina, Ames kept discreetly mum, though he confessed that bank interest was no longer sufficient to meet the Fund's administrative costs.[196] However, by the end of July, Ames had recovered his optimism. The Fund, he announced, had no intention of approaching the Dominion government for money and never had intended to do so: "What the Provinces and municipalities may do is another matter."[197]

Letting Its Good Works Be Known

Some communities faced special crises. The explosion of the French steamer *Mont Blanc* in Halifax harbour on 6 December 1917 devastated the city's working class districts and directly affected 111 soldiers' families. Forty-seven of the families lost their homes and twenty-seven dependants died. Most disasters had only one or two human faces. For instance, a British reservist left a wife and four children. His wife charred for $2 a week and a daughter, fifteen, earned $5 a week. A CPF visitor found the rest of the children sick, hungry, and ill clothed, and the furniture sold for food. The CPF visitor arranged school for an eleven-year-old girl and medical treatment for a six-year-old. It paid old bills, arranged for a warmer house, and delivered Christmas presents and a food hamper. When the mother took in a boarder, sleeping the rest of her family on one bed and a sofa, the visitor persuaded the boarder to move out. After two attempts, the Fund got the woman home to Scotland. The visitor recorded thirty-eight visits in six months.

Family crises were fertile ground for bureaucratic confusion. When Cpl. W.H. Norton's wife was dying in the winter of 1917, he persuaded his friend Harry Sykes and his wife to take on four-year-old Bessie Norton. Meanwhile, the dying Mrs. Norton arranged with Jane House, a widow, to care for the child. The Oxford Patriotic Association (OPA) agreed to pay Mrs. House $4.50 a month plus Bessie's allowances. On 10 February, Cpl. Norton heard of his wife's death and asked the Sykeses to intervene. Mrs. Sykes appeared at the OPA with Cpl. Norton's written instructions to give her his assigned pay, but Norton had already written to thank Mrs. House, and the OPA officials much preferred her to the new claimant from out of town.[198] Brantford's CPF had a similar experience: a local soldier appealed to the branch that his wife was sick with pneumonia, he was about to embark for Europe, and a newborn child would be left unattended. His wife died before he left Halifax, and the branch persuaded authorities to grant the soldier compassionate leave and persuaded several wealthy local people to pay for a nurse to care for the child. Until the man could return to Brantford, the branch also fended off other family members. As the CPF *Bulletin* reminded its readers, the Fund looked after "the interests of the *soldier*."[199]

Like most charities, the CPF needed to publicize its good works. Some of the stories were harrowing. An unemployed bricklayer joined up, leaving his wife pregnant with their fourth child. The Fund's visitor got their rent lowered, and arranged for the eldest daughter to go to hospital. Then the mother and second child caught measles and the baby was also hospitalized. Next the mother came down with rheumatism, the second child with mumps, and the baby with pneumonia. The baby died and was buried at CPF expense, and in October 1915 the family finally sailed home to England. The Fund's visitor recorded forty visits, plus others by doctors, nurses, and a home helper.[200] Another wife lost her allowance after she showed up at the Patriotic Fund office drunk and with another man. Relatives would do nothing, nor would she join her husband's parents in England. The woman was eventually hospitalized for alcoholism, and a CPF volunteer visited her daily until she died. Then the Fund arranged a funeral "for the woman nobody wanted!"[201] At the end of the war, Hamilton's branch found the money to publish an attractive pamphlet signalling its good works, together with pages of anonymous case histories. It was a shrewd investment for posterity.[202]

The Fund's perspective on its work was not, of course, shared by all. Middle-class visitors held obvious power over the Fund's needy clients, and back-alley gossip was not always as positive as CPF volunteers felt they deserved. The direct evidence that historians seek is almost wholly missing. A woman's letters to her son or husband had no chance of survival when their recipient was reduced to the barest necessities and "sleeping rough" in a muddy trench. Would most women have shared their discontents and anxieties with a man who seemed to have much heavier anxieties to bear? Would they have reported affairs and entanglements he must never discover? Interviewed in Toronto by a students' oral history project sixty years after the war, Frank Bell recalled boarding with a Montreal woman whose husband was overseas. She and her two daughters lived a lonely and frugal life, with $20 from her husband and $20 from the Fund. "This was administered by a group of rich men's wives, and if they found that a wife was running around, or that she was living beyond her means (they thought) or something, they would cut her off."[203]

For military historians, the opening of the Somme offensive on 1 July 1916 marked a great turning point in the war. Romantic voluntarism perished with the 60,000 British casualties on that awful day. For Canadians, too, 1916 marked a turning point. Voluntary recruiting, which continued at a considerable pace during the winter, slowed to a crawl as spring approached. Canada's munitions industry, reorganized by Sir Joseph Flavelle and the Imperial Munitions Board, now offered employment to almost anyone, male or female, who wanted it. Women began appearing as streetcar conductors, bank tellers, and in other traditionally male jobs. By the autumn, price inflation had become perceptible in most parts of Canada. Employers had to start considering whether patriotic arguments could delay wage and salary increases without costing them their work force.

As Ames and his colleagues contemplated a fresh round of fundraising for 1917, they had to wonder whether price increases would curb patriotic generosity, not to mention eroding the financial margin that enabled the Fund to teach its clients habits of thrift. In outlining what he called "the proposition of 1917," his fundraising target, to the eastern conference in 1916, Ames recognized a tendency to turn to taxation rather than donations to support soldiers' families. New Brunswick had led the way, Saskatchewan and Manitoba had followed, and Ontario's treasurer had warned that he was considering the trend.[204] CPF activists at the eastern conference split on voluntarism or taxation, and the tax supporters in turn divided on whether Ottawa, the provinces, or municipalities were the most appropriate tax source. Certainly they anticipated that government taxation of business and corporation profits, starting in 1917, would cut heavily into big-city corporate contributions. Ames's proposition of 1917 was even more apparent in the West. For Ames, tax-based funding would spell the end of the Patriotic Fund as a charity he could guide and even control.

Naturally, change did not come everywhere or at once. To an editor in Hedley, deep in the mountains of British Columbia, the people in Vancouver South who condemned the Patriotic Fund and demanded that the federal government take it over might seem like stooges of "the Kaiser," but two years of war had already raised the question of whether a private charity could appropriately exercise all the responsibilities that the Canadian Patriotic Fund had assumed.[205]

5
Homecomings

Armies begin to dissolve as soon as they are formed. Although 600,000 soldiers joined the CEF during the war, it never mustered more than about 120,000 soldiers in the Canadian Corps to fight the Germans. The rest were coming, going, training, sick, or stuck in some task often far from the front line. At the end of the war, barely 250,000 Canadians remained to be brought home across the Atlantic.

Some family reunions began soon after the CEF formed in Valcartier. For example, it is easy to imagine but impossible to document the homecomings of the men expelled from the CEF for lack of a wife's permission to enlist. Nor, in its inexperience, did the CEF prepare for its own casualties. Princess Patricia's Canadian Light Infantry (PPCLI), composed primarily of British Army reservists, entered the line in December 1914, three months before the rest of the CEF, and soon suffered its first casualties. Wounded in France with the PPCLI and still partially paralyzed, Harry Jennings returned with a draft of Canadian "undesirables," some of them insane. At Halifax, he was stripped of his British uniform, given civilian "slops" and sent by day-coach to Calgary. W.A.R. Holmes à Court complained from Battleford that his draft of thirteen sick and eight "undesirables" was confined in a Liverpool lodging house before being shipped steerage class to Quebec City. For his triumphal return to Battleford he, too, was stripped of his khaki uniform and provided with a $7.50 civilian suit, without shirt, socks, or underwear. Public opinion expressed an appropriate indignation.[1]

Canadian officials in England responded predictably that the complaints were "exaggerated to the extreme" but immediately ordered segregation of the unfit from the misfits. In Ottawa, a board of officers met in April 1915 and proposed that newly arrived convalescents be held in a tented camp at Valcartier. The officers proposed that the St. John's Ambulance Society might be invited to manage the makeshift hospital and to escort convalescents to homes for invalids across Canada.[2]

Compassionate Leave

By no means all soldiers who came home were sick, wounded, or undesirable. In exceptional circumstances, a soldier's family could claim compassionate grounds for his return. The mortal illness of a wife or mother would not usually suffice, but if no other family members could be found to care for potential orphans, their father might return. Another consideration could be a business or farm in crisis, such as through the death of a partner, or facing imminent but avoidable ruin.[3]

CEF officers could usually claim leave to cross the Atlantic more easily than soldiers in the ranks. Indeed, until 1918 a commissioned officer was considered a gentleman who had offered his services to the king, and His Majesty was too much of a gentleman to hold an officer against his will and to his personal detriment. An officer also paid his own way home and back.[4] A soldier, in contrast, had signed away his freedom when he enlisted, and could not be expected to pay his way. Nor could he be trusted to make a claim for compassion without investigation, normally by the local Patriotic Fund branch or by some other agency that was not going to be "imposed upon."

A privilege as rare and as desperately sought as home leave was jealously regarded, and it was all too easy to allege favouritism or prejudice when a claim was granted or denied. In France, only Army or Corps commanders could approve a month's special leave; in Canada the Militia Department tried to decentralize the key decisions on compassionate leave to the military districts. A soldier might explain his circumstances within his own unit but sooner or later a request to investigate would pass through Ottawa to one of the thirteen districts. Requests originating from civilians in Canada were sometimes complicated by family ignorance of a soldier's regimental number, unit, or branch. Conditions for leave or discharge varied until Maj.-Gen. Sidney Mewburn, minister of militia in Borden's Union government, set out to systematize them at the height of the overseas manpower crisis in 1918. He ended distinctions between soldiers and officers below the rank of lieutenant-colonel, and set out three criteria and a variety of practical tests:

> It is useless to submit any case that does not show that some serious change has occurred in the situation since appointment or enlistment, creating severe hardship and calling for *immediate* remedy.
>
> In the second place, a real necessity for the discharge must be shown on other than sentimental grounds; that is to say it must appear that he would be able to accomplish some real and material good in the alleviation of the situation of distress which has arisen or was imminent.
>
> Third it must be shown that the state of affairs on which the application is based could not be adequately attended to by anyone else acting under Power of Attorney or otherwise, such as a solicitor, relative or friend, or cannot be satisfied by the issue of separation allowance, assigned pay, or allowance from the Canadian Patriotic Fund, or other Fund.[5]

The ban on "sentimental grounds" meant that fatal illness or death, long service, or being an only son were never enough unless a soldier could bring some specific, material benefit by his presence. One of the commonest appeals was for the soldier's labour on a family farm. Anyone making the case had to prove that the soldier had put in at least a year's farm labour before enlisting and that absolutely no other labour was available. Soldiers with domestic troubles had to prove that there was no relative or friend who could help. Also insufficient was a wife's difficulty in controlling children "by reason of their growing older or of her ill health."[6]

Learning that his wife was fatally ill, one soldier applied to return in August 1917. The application was denied and he was still overseas when his wife finally died in December 1918. His mother had taken over his child, but his wife's long illness had left his house and furniture at the centre of a legal dispute. Only with the war over did he finally get his discharge. When another soldier's wife died in 1915, his grandmother took on his two children; when she died in 1918, the aged grandfather, unable to cope, placed the children in a boarding house. Only after three months of investigation was the father granted his discharge.[7] Gunner J.B. Saul, in France for a year, asked leave to help his invalid wife cope with three children and an $800 mortgage on their $1,800 house. Sgt. H.L. Broadbent, twenty-seven months in France, was needed because his mother had died intestate, leaving his two young siblings to cope. Bdr. John Miller had left Canada in 1916 with no idea that the war could last so long. The man hired to run his farm had quit, and it was the sole support for his wife and two children. Saul, Broadbent, and Miller all made acceptable cases, fully vouched for, but all three claims were cancelled on 24 April 1918 because of the major German offensive.[8]

After the Armistice, the rules changed. Financial distress ceased to be a factor; serious illness or death, confirmed by medical certificate, became all that mattered, with the hope that a soldier could return to see his relative before death.[9] During the demobilization period, the Militia Department recorded 4,046 applications for compassionate discharge, of which 1,344 were granted.[10]

Coping with Military Convalescents

Instead of accepting Sam Hughes's makeshift arrangements for a convalescent hospital at Valcartier, the prime minister stripped the overburdened Militia Department and its Army Medical Corps of the responsibility for invalided soldiers and on 30 June 1915 appointed a Military Hospitals Commission (MHC) under his Senate leader, Sir James Lougheed. The MHC was one of several new semiprivatized bureaucracies designed to manage Canada's war effort. The Commission was directed to "deal with the provision of hospital accommodation and convalescent homes for officers and men of the Canadian Expeditionary Force who return invalided from the Front."[11] Among the ten original MHC members was Clarence Smith, relief chairman of the Montreal CPF. The brains of the new Commission was its permanent secretary, Ernest Henry Scammell. The son of a prominent English Baptist minister who had done much for British veterans of the South African War, the younger Scammell had worked as secretary of the Canadian Peace Centenary Commission, and the MHC inherited the CPCC's office and furniture.[12] Scammell brought his father's experience, some idealism, and considerable passion to his new work.

The MHC created its first convalescent homes in large houses made available by their wealthy owners, and in disused school or hospital buildings like Toronto's abandoned General Hospital and the former Knox College, and in Montreal's Loyola College and Grey Nuns convent. The owner of Winnipeg's unprofitable Deer Lodge Hotel generously made it available at cost. Scores of local struggles developed over inappropriate accommodation, opportunistic proprietors, and possessive local volunteers, such as Winnipeg's IODE, who stoutly denied that their "home" was a poorly heated firetrap.

The MHC soon recognized that its immediate medical burden was not wounded returnees but thousands of ailing CEF recruits. A particular concern was how to treat hundreds of tuberculosis sufferers, enlisted in the absence of proper techniques for detection and diagnosis. Each tubercular patient insisted that he must have contracted the disease while in uniform, and medical knowledge of the disease was still too shaky to refute the claim. The MHC became a major client for the country's scattered and undercapitalized TB sanatoria.[13] Another crisis occurred when, late in the autumn of 1915, the CEF staff in England decided to empty its overseas hospitals. Over 600 invalids were loaded on the *Metagama* and dispatched to Quebec City in November 1915. Given barely a week's notice, the MHC realized that it only had a single small convalescent home at Quebec. With regular trains crowded and rolling stock conscripted for troop traffic, railway companies could supply only worn-out colonist cars to meet the ship and distribute the unexpected influx. As unhappy invalids spread across Canada, complaints reverberated back to the MHC offices in Ottawa.

One result of the *Metagama* affair was closer liaison with the Militia Department, larger institutions, and bigger plans. Samuel Armstrong, an Ontario civil servant responsible for the institution building of the expansive Whitney years, joined the Military Hospitals Commission to enlarge its facilities. His first choice fell on the prison and the mental hospital he had helped to build in Guelph and Whitby, Ontario. At Halifax, where space could not be found, Armstrong embraced experimental construction methods and threw up Camp Hill Hospital in record time. The *Metagama* incident also helped endow the MHC with a frosty view of soldiers and their supporters. Military invalids soon lost their heroic aura to those who had to handle them, while those who espoused their cause easily became nuisances. "These women – and sometimes it is a case of men –" complained Scammell, "will ... hold meetings and issue reports from which it appears that the Government is utterly callous and is doing nothing to meet the situation. These busybodies do a great deal of harm."[14] "Business principles" rapidly displaced patriotic voluntarism, as they had in the Patriotic Fund. As Sir Herbert Ames scoffed, the assumption that "kindly individuals would donate their homes and make everything lovely for a few soldiers" faded fast.[15]

As a nonmilitary agency, the MHC initially intended to treat veterans as civilians. Chief among the problems it soon encountered was discipline. Before antibiotics were deployed to kill infection, convalescents often spent months, even years, in hospital beds recovering from their wounds. Radical debridement (scraping away all affected flesh) was the only approved treatment for the multiple infections a bullet took into a soldier's body, and it turned the bullet's narrow path into a cavity as big as a man's fist.[16] Months of convalescence made patients impatient and hard to control, while liquor, women, and other temptations lay just beyond the doors of hospitals and convalescent homes. Medical and nursing staff had little authority over rowdy patients and even less tolerance for them. Consequently invalids remained in uniform under the authority of a special MHC Command, exercised by either Home Service or convalescent officers, sergeants, and military police. Afflicted by prostitutes and bootleggers who brought their services to its door, the Grey Nuns Convalescent Hospital in downtown Montreal was a constant source of trouble for its authorities. According to Warrant Officer Napoléon Marion, the MHC did not take the trouble to recruit French-speaking staff.[17] Instead, a new commanding officer built cells in the hospital basement for his more unruly patients.

Ideally, once he returned to Canada, an invalided soldier had recovered sufficiently to be discharged from the CEF, receive a disability pension for any permanent injury, find civilian employment, and resume supporting his family. Relapses were common, however, and the government and its agencies would have looked hard-hearted if discharged veterans had been abandoned to care for their own disabilities. Once readmitted to the MHC's institutions, civilian patients were both free of military discipline and lacking in means to support themselves or their families. The easiest solution was to reattest them so that they could resume their former rank and pay.

No one prepared soldiers' families for the challenge of welcoming home a man whose afflictions might range from a slightly stiff knee to full-blown insanity.

Despite the familiar stereotypes of war wounded, by the spring of 1917, the MHC had received only nine blinded soldiers and 177 major amputees. The majority of the disabled were victims of disease, not battlefield wounds. The same disproportion of sick and wounded was apparent among pensionable disabilities. A generalized public sympathy for suffering heroes rapidly gave way to suspicions of malingering, self-indulgence, hypochondria, and self-pity.

Wives, mothers, and children were as trapped as any veteran by the contrasting public moods of generosity and criticism, since their welfare now depended on the soldier's success in winning a pension, not to mention the family burden of coming to terms with the pain, frustrations, and humiliations of a disabled husband, son, or father.[18] Ten months after he enlisted, at the end of October 1916, Robert Anderson, thirty-six, returned to his wife and children in Woodstock with shrapnel in his left temple, severe headaches, deafness, and a mental condition officially described as "dull," possibly from the opiates prescribed for his pain. Nothing more could be done for him medically. Since he had been assigned only a fourth-class pension of $16 a month, he tried to return to his job as an iron moulder at Stuart's Stove Works. It was too much for him and by the summer of 1917 the Andersons were "practically destitute."[19] Letitia Lamer's husband Joseph, a shoemaker, came home on two canes and claimed to be paralyzed after being blown up by an artillery shell. Medical authorities found no functional evidence of injury and denied him a pension.[20] Another Woodstock soldier, F.H. Hudleston, was a former piano polisher at Hay & Co. He returned with feet so deformed from rheumatism that he could only sit down to work. Local authorities found him a clerical job at the post office at $700 a year – until he failed the civil service exam.[21] These families had no alternative to destitution.

What was the role of the Patriotic Fund? On 9 October 1914, one of the few Canadians to anticipate the problems of returning soldiers, Mrs. Florence Cole of the Soldiers' Wives League, had tackled Herbert Ames on the issue. Armed with her South African War experience, she asked what the CPF would do about "men who may return from active service abroad out of health and with no employment." The answer from Ames was blunt. The Fund had extended its mandate to cover British and Allied reservists; it could do no more.[22] As soon as a soldier returned to Canada, whatever his condition, CPF allowances stopped. Families promptly noted the distinct drop in their income, even when a convalescent soldier was able to furnish separation allowance and a pay assignment, and their complaints made trouble for the CPF. After all, these were not Home Defence soldiers serving safely on the Welland Canal; they and their families were victims of a cruel war. What did the Patriotic Fund mean by scorning them? In its first set of amendments to its founding act, the Patriotic Fund hurriedly gave itself authority to extend its help to the disabled or, more precisely, to:

a. Officers and men who return to Canada incapacitated by wounds, injuries or disease received or contracted while on active service.

b. Residents of Canada, who are widows, children or dependent relatives of officers or men resident of Canada, who are incapacitated by wounds, injuries or diseases received or contracted on such active service.[23]

CPF assistance was restricted to six months and ended whenever the beneficiary received a gratuity, pension, or allowance from any of His Majesty's governments or any foreign government "in consequence of incapacity or death occurring as aforesaid."[24] Beyond any kindly but informal concern of Fund visitors, widows and their children then ceased to be CPF responsibilities. To alleviate its own burden and to avoid obvious public indignation, the CPF also helped persuade the government to continue both separation allowance and pay assignments to widows and children until a pension had been assigned.[25]

Retaining a convalescent veteran in the CEF allowed a soldier in hospital to provide for himself and his family. Very few soldiers or dependants in 1916 were eager to start living on the Canadian military pension of $40 a month for a totally disabled rank-and-file soldier.[26] Remaining in uniform, however, delayed a process that Scammell recognized as almost more important than physical rehabilitation: the reconversion of a soldier into a civilian. A recurrent theme among Hospital Commission administrators was the suspicion that military service, for all its purported demands and discipline, left veterans work-shy and purposeless.[27] Scammell's father's work with South African War veterans had convinced his son that the prime challenge in restoring a disabled veteran to civil life was fitting him for peacetime employment. This idea was bold and controversial: at a time when vocational training in Canada was primitive, preparing the disabled to fill skilled and well-paid jobs seemed an idealistic experiment.[28] Would employers accept workers with severe disabilities as other than appropriately paid charity cases? Could a soldier with limited education and work experience as a farm hand or bush worker be transformed into a skilled tradesman? Yet as CEF casualties mounted the alternatives were limited. Paying adequate pensions could bankrupt a country accustomed to finding most of its revenue from tariffs and excises. And what would happen to voluntary recruiting if crippled soldiers and their families were left to beg or starve?

As with most innovations, effective implementation of Scammell's idea of vocational training proved to be a difficult process. Provinces controlled education and training. Ontario, the leader in the vocational field, saw no need to adapt its schools or teachers to the special needs or expectations of disabled adult learners. Nor would its professional teachers yield their authority to part-time instructors, even if they were veterans who had the sympathy of other ex-soldiers. Other provinces followed Ontario's example.

After a frustrating year, MHC administrators finally found Walter E. Segsworth, a Toronto mining engineer who insisted that the right place for industrial training was in industry. Segsworth took over the MHC's vocational training on 1 August 1916. Instead of letting men choose their new trades, Segsworth insisted on firm guidance and sharp cost control. A former carpenter already had some of the woodworking skills to make himself a cabinetmaker. A railway brakeman with a missing leg had much of the experience needed to become a station agent or a telegrapher. Segsworth tackled the consequences of long months of convalescent idleness. Soon, even the bedridden laboured at handicrafts taught by specially recruited "ward aides." Once ambulatory, patients were assigned to "curative workshops" or to tending their hospital's gardens, crops, or poultry. Only on release did occupational training begin, sometimes at existing trade schools, most often on the job.[29]

Unaware of the wrath across the road at Queen's Park, where Ontario's Department of Education fumed at the invasion of its training monopoly, Dean Frederick Haultain of the University of Toronto's School of Mining Engineering made his faculty and his own considerable energy and ingenuity available to Segsworth to help retrain veterans. Hart House, the latest gift of the Massey family to the university, became a training centre where, for example, young women learned to teach vocational skills and David McDougall, blinded with the PPCLI, taught other blinded soldiers the techniques of massage.[30]

Part of Segsworth's task was to convince disabled veterans to persist with learning a skill instead of grabbing wartime wages in a short-term job. An elaborate MHC publicity campaign, complete with pamphlets and magic lantern slides, assured any Canadians who could be lured into lecture halls that the MHC was doing much for returned men, but that most would have to be done by the men themselves. The MHC poster boy was a fictional "Private Pat," an amputee who scorned handouts and yearned for the outdoor life: "Lend us a hand to get our legs again, real or artificial, and you'll see if we don't keep our end up and make our own living like the rest of you."[31]

Even the spirited Private Pat felt entitled to a pension for "his old leg." How could his claim best be met? The clearest answers were eventually formulated by Maj. John Launcelot Todd. A Victoria-born tropical medicine specialist and McGill University professor, he had married Marjory Clouston, daughter of the general manager of the Bank of Montreal.[32] Having joined the Army Medical Corps in 1914, he went to England and, for lack of more suitable employment, was assigned to Sir Montague Allan's Pension Board. Todd promptly persuaded himself that pensions represented a crucial policy problem that he was well fitted to tackle. Equally obviously, the rest of his board were pompous fools. His African experience was no help. "It's handling negroes and boys who do or are done at the word," he complained to his wife, "that makes me so clumsy in managing thoroughbred horses and silly white men."[33] Still, Todd read all he could, visited the British at Chelsea and, in 1916, spent months in France to see how the French coped with hundreds of thousands of invalids.

Everywhere he found schools training the disabled in vocational skills and especially in bookkeeping and accounting. "Some of them have never known how to read or write," he reported, "and the primary classes for illiterates without arms or legs sometimes are very pathetic." French pensions, he reported, were meagre but rational. Unlike the British, who had succumbed to Asquith's desire to match pensions to prewar earnings, French pensions did not shrink if an ex-soldier earned more than he had before enlistment.[34] The most useful British contribution, thought Todd, was a single, unsentimental definition of disability. However educated, skilled, or well paid he might be, an ordinary soldier brought no more than "a healthy mind and body to the public service," and "the market for healthy bodies is said to be the 'general market for untrained labour.'"[35]

Like Scammell, Todd insisted that, if a veteran was not to become a hopeless burden on himself, his family and, especially, the state, he must become self-supporting. Appropriate training would fit a disabled man for a carefully selected occupation; agents would locate appropriate employment; the veteran and his family would receive training allowances to support them during the transition. The rest was up to the man himself. A positive role for the soldier's family was not an explicit part of Todd's plan.[36]

The prolonged war had created a rare moment when such an experiment might succeed and carry over to a postwar world. Labour shortages in Canada reinforced patriotic pressures on employers to hire returned soldiers. The results might not be ideal, but in wartime, disabled ex-soldiers got the benefit of the doubt. If the disabled could be trained and inured to serious work, rehabilitation would succeed, and an otherwise inevitable pressure for more and higher pensions would be alleviated. Indeed, swept up by the faith of converts, some vocational training enthusiasts predicted that the newly skilled disabled would soon earn more than they could have hoped to do had they returned to their former jobs in prewar Canada.[37]

Returned Disabled

Inevitably, some soldiers would never come home and others would never be whole. Death and injury were expected in any army, though the expectation by families of compensation for such losses was relatively new in 1914. Pensions for both widows and disabled soldiers mattered enormously during the First World War because not only was it the most murderous in human history, it was also the most regenerative. Never had so many soldiers, and so many of the sick and maimed, survived their suffering. In the first five months of war, France lost 300,000 dead, but twice as many survived terrible wounds. Nor, since armies were enlisted from a cross-section of the population, could the disabled and their families be condemned to the customary beggary of old soldiers. Transformative thinking was urgently needed everywhere. In Canada, remote from the war, with a tradition of meagre public revenues and a patronage-ridden public service, and exposed to questionable British and American models, the challenge was great.

Accidents during summer training camps had given the Canadian militia some precedents. Under the provisions of King's Regulations and the small red handbook of *Regulations and Orders for the Canadian Militia,* a board of officers was summoned, met to review the circumstances, and reported its recommendations, to be reviewed by "higher authority." In anticipation of casualties, the minister of militia had authorized a special Pensions and Claims Board in England, under the chairmanship of Col. Sir Montague Allan, scion of the wealthy Montreal shipping family, to review cases before they returned to Canada. Allan and his board read case files and recommended how much of the maximum disability pension of $264 a year a soldier deserved. Anyone less than totally disabled would, of course, receive less than the maximum. The widow of a private soldier killed in action could also expect $264, plus $37 for a family of three or more offspring.

Soldiering, as we have seen, had never been a generous or a democratic trade. Common soldiers took their chances. Among the deductions that shrivelled the British soldier's famous shilling a day was a ha'penny a week for his postdischarge pension. Ideally he spent it in the magnificent Royal Hospital, Chelsea, established, tradition insists, after pleading by King Charles II's good-hearted mistress, Nell Gwynne. Most old soldiers lived less comfortably as "out-pensioners." Canada had plenty of experience with them, since veteran pensioners seemed to be ideal for British garrisons along the US frontier. If they succumbed to the temptation to desert, they left their pension behind. Few thought the benefits were worth the exertion or the risks. Military pensioners garrisoned Fort Garry in the late 1840s and filled the ranks of the Royal Canadian Rifles, Britain's North American garrison regiment until 1871. Most stayed behind when the British Army withdrew, and a British official remained to pay their pensions, and those of the short-service "reservists" who emigrated to Canada.

British military pension practices, with their mixture of aristocratic and poor house presumptions, were easy fodder for Canadian critics of Empire, though Canada's arrangements were no better. Several UK military charities served the interests of disabled veterans and their families, but their boards were stiff with titled and superannuated admirals and generals, and the benefits were frugally distributed.[38] Visitors to London reported that bemedalled amputees peddling pencils at street corners were a common sight in the prewar Imperial capital. Since Canada took no financial responsibility for its South African War soldiers after they landed in South Africa, the 1900 version of the Patriotic Fund Association could only enhance the British pensions provided for disabled Canadian veterans and their widows. The Association was as officer-dominated and as frugal as its British exemplars.

The democratic practices south of the border were not always preferable. Civil War veterans had been welcomed as heroes, cheered, banqueted, and then ignored in a society that soon forgot them. Only after they organized into the Grand Army of the Republic, linked up with claims agents, pension attorneys, and the Republican Party, and invaded Washington to help defeat President Cleveland in 1888 did American veterans begin to collect. By 1914 spending on veterans absorbed a fifth of the US federal budget, and righteous critics listed "the pension evil" along with elected judges, Tammany Hall, and lynchings as hallmarks of the excesses of American democracy.[39]

Canada was too close to the United States to be wholly immune to American example. In 1871 the US Congress had granted service pensions to aged survivors of the War of 1812; Alexander Mackenzie's cash-poor Liberal government reluctantly followed suit in 1875. Persuaded that no more than 600 veterans would apply, Mackenzie was astonished to find that more than 1,800 old men qualified for their allocation of $20 a year. Mackenzie refused to extend the benefit to widows; Washington was less prudent. The last American veteran of the War of 1812 died in 1907, but Esther Ann Hill Morgan was still collecting her pension during the Korean War. By contracting a deathbed marriage for the sake of a tiny lifetime income, Mrs. Morgan typified another "pension evil," the so-called pension widow. Mackenzie's successor in 1896, Sir Wilfrid Laurier, stood fast against recognition of veterans of the Fenian Raids, but Robert Borden's Conservatives came through with $100 each for about 6,000 venerable New Brunswickers, Quebeckers, and Ontarians – and 11,160 Nova Scotians, whose service in 1866 had been nominal, obligatory, and completely risk-free. As the money poured into the prime minister's home province, the opposition cried foul.[40]

In the confusion of battle, even the fact of death was not always easy to establish. At Ypres in April 1915, where the raw Canadian division suffered its first mass casualties, much of the battleground, along with most of the corpses, had to be abandoned to the Germans; elsewhere, men whose bodies had been buried by an exploded mine or a crushed dugout or dissolved in a shell burst were registered as missing until death could be confirmed. No one wanted the awful responsibility of reporting a living comrade to be dead. Indeed, official responsibility devolved on the Militia Department's director of records to sign the typical telegram that informed a Toronto wife on 16 September 1917 that she was now a widow: "Deeply regret inform you six seven eight one nought nine Pte. James Joseph Dowling, infantry officially reported killed in action september ninth nineteen seventeen." A formal letter of condolence followed from the minister of militia a week later, all too obviously a form letter with the words "husband, No. 678109 Pte. James Joseph Downing" inserted in their own line. The letter continued with stubborn righteousness, "The heavy loss which you and the Nation have sustained would indeed be depressing were it not redeemed by the knowledge that the brave comrade for whom we mourn performed his duties fearlessly and well as became a good soldier, and gave his life for the great cause of Human Liberty and the Defence of the Empire. Again extending to you in your bereavement my condolence and heartfelt sympathy." During the war close to 60,000 such letters were sent to Canadian homes.

Pensions for Widows

In 1914 a Canadian military widow could hope for a pension of three-tenths of her husband's pay plus one-tenth each for up to two children, or a maximum of $200.50 a year for a private's family.[41] Vaguely aware that 1885-era pension policies would not fit the CEF or the new war, the federal government passed a series of orders-in-council to meet special problems. In April 1915 the battle at Ypres had cost the CEF over 6,000 dead and wounded, half its infantry strength. In the wake of the awful news, the cabinet approved pension increases for the lower ranks and adapted militia regulations to the CEF. A private's widow could now count on $22 a month and $5 for each child; a lieutenant-colonel's wife could expect $75 a month and $10 for each of her children.[42] In July the government extended the CEF's rules to Canada's tiny navy; in September it allowed CEF officers to claim the pensions for their acting wartime rank rather than their previous militia rank.[43] By mid-February 1916, Canada had granted pensions to 586 widows and 863 children, and 2,179 pensions to disabled soldiers and their families, almost all of them temporary.

The inadequacies and inconsistencies of pension administration pushed the government into allowing a special parliamentary committee on pensions under the Hon. J.D. Hazen, the somewhat underemployed minister for Canada's navy. The committee met from 14 March to 10 May 1916, at a time when most MPs and media were preoccupied with the wartime "Shell Scandal."[44] An obvious concern for the committee was the meagre level of Canadian pensions: although a British private's widow received only $126 a year, New Zealand paid $316 to Canada's $264. Senior officers were less well treated. A British lieutenant-colonel's widow could expect $900 and a New Zealander, $768, while the comparable Canadian widow received $720. While the 1916 committee removed the needs test for a widow's pension, they were strong enough in demanding good behaviour to provoke a plea from Mrs. Adam Shortt of the National Council of Women, conveyed by Ernest Scammell, that "no widow shall lose her pension except after due warning that she runs a risk of forfeiting it; followed by a conviction for some serious offence."[45] This appeal did not form part of the committee's recommendations. Would widows' pensions be accorded to soldiers' "unmarried wives"? Hazen's committee cushioned political sensitivities in elaborate verbiage:

> That in the event of an application being made for a pension on behalf of a woman who has, without being married to a member of such Force, lived with him as his wife, or on behalf of the child or children of any such man or woman, the Commission be authorized to grant the customary pension for a wife or for a child or children, on being satisfied that the circumstances were such as to warrant the conclusion that the woman had at the time of enlistment and for a reasonable time previously thereto, publicly been represented as the wife of said member of such Force, or if the Commission is satisfied that justice would be done by the recognition of such woman, for the purpose of pension, as the wife of such member.[46]

While widows were an obvious concern, the committee directed more attention to the disabled and their families, and the destitution they faced from current pay and pension scales and policies. A prominent Toronto architect, Frank Darling, acted as a spokesman for his city's veterans. Pensions, he insisted, were not charity but a national obligation: "It is therefore necessary to state with emphasis that the duty of supporting the disabled men should, and must be undertaken solely by the Government, and that whatever is necessary for this purpose must be paid out of the revenue of the country."[47]

To the government and many of its supporters, this was more warning than inspiration; it made advice from both Ernest Scammell and John Todd on how to avoid a crushing pension burden all the more welcome. Supporting men and their families while they learned an appropriate trade might be a radical innovation, but what if, as Scammell claimed, it would save the treasury from relentless pension demands later on? The hope led the government into new legislation.[48] Todd's proposal to place pension administration in the hands of scientific experts, immune from political pressure, fitted the temper of the times and conformed closely to the "progressive" vision of good government Sir Robert Borden had presented years earlier in his 1907 Halifax program. Seldom has a parliamentary committee seen faster implementation of its somewhat complex desires.

On 3 June 1916, an order-in-council established a three-member Board of Pension Commissioners (BPC) with exclusive jurisdiction over naval and military pensions. The Board's decisions would be final and without appeal, though applicants might appear before the Board in person or through counsel.[49] Ten-year terms and generous salaries were intended to render pension commissioners immune from political advice or pressure.[50] The three new commissioners were certainly as immune as any Canadians could be from the temptations of bribery and extravagance. The chair was given to John Kenneth Leveson Ross, the young Montreal millionaire better known for offering $500,000 to build a Dreadnought battleship, and for contributing his yacht *Albacore* to Canada's wartime navy.[51] The second member, Col. R.H. Labatt, was a member of the brewing family and a keen part-time soldier whose ulcer and heart problems had ended a more active career in command of the CEF's 4th Battalion. Convinced that he had devised the machinery to save Canada from an American-style "pension evil," Maj. Todd was the most junior of the three commissioners.

Since Ross seldom came from Montreal and Labatt's health problems soon earned him a total disability pension, Todd had a free hand to shape the BPC according to his principles.[52] As Todd had proposed, the commissioners would determine disability pensions solely on the basis of evidence provided by medical examiners. The Board originally inherited the six categories of the previous pension regime but soon began appraising disability in percentages derived from a "Table of Incapacities." Borrowed from the French, the table closely resembled the "meat charts" adopted by the new workmen's compensation boards in some American states and the province of Ontario.[53] The hundred different levels of disability were divided into twenty categories, each representing a 5 percent pension increment. The Board announced that most disability pensions would be reviewed annually to see whether entitlement had changed, but no consideration would be given to other earnings. If a pensioner had been, or managed to become rich, that was entirely his business. Since weaning the disabled from pensioner status was one of Todd's goals, small pensions could be compounded into a single gratuity. Under Todd's system, most disability pensions would be small. By 1920, Canada would ultimately have the most generous pensions in the world, but barely 7 percent of the disabled would ever earn them, while 71 percent would collect less than a 20 percent pension.[54]

The government continued the 1916 rates for dependant and disability pensions until the outburst of inflation and a new special parliamentary committee in 1917 encouraged significant increases. By the fall of 1917 a soldier's widow was allowed a pension of $480 a year, plus $96 for each child up to sixteen for a boy and seventeen for a girl. If a soldier left no widow or child, he could leave $480 a year to his dependent mother or father, and $96 to a dependent brother or sister. A totally disabled private soldier could count on $600 a year, plus $96 for his wife and each of his children. At the other end of the BPC's disability scale, a private judged to have only a 5 percent disability would receive a pension of only $30.00 a year plus $4.80 for his wife and $6.00 for each child.[55] The 1916-17 increases created new discrimination: until 1916 pensions for a widow and a disabled soldier had been identical. MPs agreed with a familiar CPF argument: a widow could support her family on 20 percent less money because she was spared the cost of providing for her husband.[56] CPF policy also encouraged an age maximum for a pensioners' children.

Inevitably, the merits of Todd's principles were more obvious to him than they were to pensioners, their dependants, and even to examining physicians, particularly after the BPC showed no inhibitions about challenging the judgment of medical professionals who had actually seen and examined patients. Todd's rebuttal was as simple as it was infuriating: if the Board ignored doctors' advice, it was because the professionals had failed to describe symptoms as objectively and scientifically as the Board required. The Board also held more complete medical records for CEF members than local examiners. It could, for example, recognize symptoms of venereal disease, an unacknowledged but epidemic medical problem that a soldier might not have shared with his examining physician. In a ruthless little sneer, Todd hinted at secrets best not disturbed: "There are very few among us," Todd observed, "who have not had an acquaintance who has died of locomotor ataxia and whom we never thought of as syphilitic."[57] Since the Board of Pension Commissioners acted with scientific objectivity, Todd insisted, it was deplorable even to consider any appeal from its rulings. If the diagnosis provided to the Board was inaccurate, the Board would cheerfully pay for a correction, but it could hardly be expected to waste public money to secure a repetition of a diagnosis.

One question that Todd's science could not easily answer was summed up in the polysyllabic word "attributability." Did a soldier's illness or injury have to be strictly attributable to military service to qualify for a pension, or was wearing a uniform blanket insurance for any medical mishap? The financial consequences of this question for a soldier and his dependants were enormous. Should Curly Christian, one of the rare black soldiers in the CEF and its sole quadrilateral amputee, have qualified for a pension? There was some evidence and much suspicion that he had been drunk when he lay down on the railway tracks where a passing train severed his four limbs. Mike Pearson, a flight cadet and future prime minister, was hit by a London bus in a blackout. Was that an attributable injury? Another future prime minister, John Diefenbaker, fell backwards into a trench in England and was invalided home. Would an investigation have discovered carelessness or horseplay?[58]

Battlefield wounds, illnesses arising from trench conditions, injuries on a dark night in France, and even training accidents might seem sufficiently "attributable" to army service, but what about the dozen decrepit recruits Sir Montague Allan encountered at Shorncliffe (an historic British army camp just south of Dover that became a Canadian base), including one with a missing right arm, another with "claw feet," and seventy-nine-year-old Pte. W.J. Clements from Guelph with arteriosclerosis and "arteries very hard and brittle."[59] All had been accepted as fit for active service by CEF recruiters and approved by one or more medical officers. All were now utterly unfit. Was their condition in any way "attributable to service"? The majority of cases coming before the BPC in 1916-17 presented medical disabilities, such as tuberculosis or cardiac dysfunction, that only incompetent or collusive, and certainly inadequate, medical screening had allowed into the CEF. If it adopted the "insurance principle," the BPC might well load Canadian taxpayers with a significant share of the costs of prewar poor health.

Todd, of course, had a preference. "My opinion," he told the 1917 parliamentary Special Committee on Returned Soldiers, "is that Canadian military pensions should be Canadian military pensions ... My conception of a military pension is one that compensates an individual for any personal detriment – I don't care when it comes on – resulting from service." If that was not Parliament's intention, if it wished "to insure our soldiers and sailors against all the risks of existence during the time they are in the Canadian Expeditionary Force," then let it be said plainly.[60] In practice, with appropriate misgivings and a determined lack of clarity, that seemed to be more or less precisely what Parliament had wished in 1916. Faced with the controversies inevitably attending his stricter approach, Todd acquiesced. Moreover, even if tuberculosis sufferers had brought their disease with them into the CEF, he favoured compulsory treatment. "If, through the desirability of providing properly for tubercular soldiers," Todd suggested to the 1917 committee, "sound machinery for dealing with tubercular citizens were established, much good would result from a great evil."[61]

A tougher question for both the pension system and the Patriotic Fund was what to do about British and foreign reservists whose families had been heavily subsidized by the Fund while the men fought. By Canadian standards, British and foreign pensions for widows, orphans, and the disabled were as meagre as their pay. While confident that Canadian widows could manage on a little less than the CPF had guaranteed them, Ames was passionate that the reservists and their families must share a Canadian standard of pension income. To suspicious and even hostile MPs, Ames laid out the argument: "You have in the same town two families: the two men have gone to the front; one is fighting in an Imperial regiment, and the other in a Canadian regiment; both are bona fide residents of the town, both men intended to remain there; both intended to bring up their four or five children there. And yet the widow whose husband was in a Canadian regiment will receive an adequate pension to live upon decently, and the other, because her husband went in an Imperial regiment, cannot live on her pension in Canada."[62]

Ames would ultimately win the argument. Allied reservists who had settled in Canada and ultimately even those who emigrated would share in the Canadian pension and re-establishment system. It was harder for the government or the Fund to reconcile another problem with the pension legislation. All widows were entitled to a widow's pension, whether or not they had received separation allowance. Therefore the dead soldier's dependent mother, who may well have received his separation allowance rather than the wife he married after enlistment, found her income terminated. Dependent sisters, fathers, and any other beneficiaries of a soldier's assigned pay were similarly cut off for the sake of a woman they might never have met. A more generous posterity might argue that all should have pensions, but legislators in 1916 and 1917 saw such generosity with public funds as profligacy. Much as he could transmit only a single separation allowance, a Canadian soldier could leave only one pension.

Disabled soldiers who returned to Canada presented even more complex concerns. If a soldier was discharged to civilian life, his pay and allowances ceased, but would his employment income support him and his family before his gratuity, normally three months' pay, ran out? Why would his wife promptly inform the local CPF of her husband's return and cut off her only remaining source of income? What if her husband was too disabled ever to work at his old trade? Even with Scammell and Segsworth, retraining was only a contingent possibility, not a universal program. If a disabled soldier remained in uniform while in an MHC convalescent home or hospital, he was no longer overseas. Therefore his family was no longer entitled to a Patriotic Fund allowance, either immediately or, from 1915, six months after his return. That period might easily be exhausted before a convalescent's treatment was complete. In 1916, after the homeward flow of soldiers became significant, Ames posted a CPF official to the CEF discharge depots at Quebec City or at Halifax with orders to notify the branches of any of their soldiers who had returned to Canada.

The Patriotic Fund representative at Quebec City, W.S. Morris, dreamed up the idea of issuing a discharge button to returning soldiers. An act of generosity initially funded by an $800 donation from Mrs. Eden G. Warner, the badge included an enamelled Union Jack surrounded by a scroll proclaiming "For Service at the Front" and surmounted by the letters CPF. The bronze buttons gave men an added incentive to check in with the CPF representative, and they promised a man welcome immunity from being harassed on his hometown main street by recruiters or women bearing white feathers. The initial funds provided 6,000 buttons; thereafter, more money was contributed by the Hon. Wallace Nesbitt, MP for Oxford and honorary president of the St. John's Ambulance Society. In May 1917 the Militia Department took on the cost of producing buttons, and in August it took over full responsibility. The letters CEF replaced CPF, and the back henceforth included a serial number and a minatory inscription: "Penalty for misuse 500 dollars or six months imprisonment."[63]

The Stress of War

One issue linked the crucial questions of family entitlement and attributability, and it was virtually invisible: mental health. Generations later, a high-profile case of a general driven to madness by his inability to prevent mass murder in Rwanda forced Canadians to recognize post-traumatic stress disorder (PTSD) in soldiers compelled to witness horrors and endure great dangers during their peacekeeping duties.[64] Such cases were increasingly recognized in the Canadian Forces during the 1990s, and there was a slower but similar awareness that soldiers' wives and families often bore the brunt of the behaviours associated with PTSD and had a corresponding role in a member's rehabilitation. PTSD counselling became a major responsibility for Military Family Resource Centres, particularly on bases with frequent operational deployments.[65] It also became apparent that stress-related disabilities could also result from overwork, heavy responsibilities, and accidents or mishaps encountered in daily life. In the Second World War, huge losses were incurred by a phenomenon generally described as "battle exhaustion" and diagnosed as the psychological consequence of exposures to quite widely varied periods of battlefield danger.[66]

In the First World War, most of this awareness was far in the future. Certainly medical officers encountered front-line soldiers suffering from mutism, paralysis, uncontrollable crying, and kindred symptoms. Determined to find a physical explanation for every condition, they initially labelled such cases as "shell shock," an analogy to those found dead after a major explosion without a mark on them to justify decease.[67] The futility of such a diagnosis for a growing number of invisibly disabled casualties led the British medical authorities to direct them to be labelled "NYD-N" or "not yet diagnosed – nervous." Such cases were then divided into "neurasthenia" or nervous exhaustion, largely found among officers and treated with rest, recreation, and a prolonged escape from the front, or "hysterical," a condition more common among lower-ranked soldiers and, in peacetime, found among poor women in British workhouses who presented with paralysis or mutism as a reason not to work.[68]

The diagnosis suggested the cure. Dr. Lewis Yealland, who had returned to London's Queen's Square mental hospital after several years at McGill University, claimed to cure every such case that came to his "Black Chamber." "The sting of a whip, no matter how vigorously applied," he cheerfully reported, was "almost nothing compared with the sudden severe shock of a faridic current." Since Yealland claimed conversation and sympathy only aggravated the problem, he strapped his patients to a table and applied his wire brushes with a will. Sometimes, he confessed, it took a few hours to get a complete cure; others yielded at the sight of the instruments.[69] The pain, explained Lt.-Col. Colin Russell, commanding the CEF's special hospital for "nervous" cases at Ramsgate, "gives the man an excuse to tell his comrades he had received some powerful treatment. He can thus save his face."[70]

Victims of battlefield stress had little reputation to save. Conscious of hysteria's widely believed link to impoverished women, the official Canadian medical historian, Sir Andrew Macphail, defined shell shock as a "manifestation of childishness and femininity" in a soldier.[71] When Sir Edward Kemp, as militia minister, sought advice on Canada's military-medical problems, his panel of doctors was generally optimistic but viewed mental defectives as worse than hopeless: "individuals of constitutionally inferior type will form a class of tramps, ne'er do wells and criminals that history shows has always followed a war. If at large and allowed to procreate, they will beget their kind."[72] Their families, presumably would share their fate, becoming equally useless members of society.

The whole business of cowardice and its psychological underpinnings was both incomprehensible and embarrassing and, therefore, excised so far as possible from official records and avoided in public or private discussion. Sir Arthur Currie spelled off battle-exhausted brigadiers by giving them a turn running a training camp in England. Brig.-Gen. W.A. Griesbach ordered company commanders in his 1st Brigade to know their men well enough to get rid of known cowards and weaklings before they fell foul of military law.[73] About one such soldier, Pte. Fraser recalled that when threats and ridicule failed, the man was sent down the line to join "Canada's large army of misfits."[74] A small platoon of that army, twenty-five soldiers, was shot by firing squad, almost all of them for offences linked to a loss of the courage Canadians took for granted in their soldiers.[75] The rest came home, unknowingly bringing with them to families and future loved ones the consequences of stress and trauma that their society could not treat, understand, or even recognize.

At the time, it was enough, surely, that a man had returned unharmed from a terrible war. If a wife or children suffered, surely widows and orphans had fared worse. No one at all would come home to them. If a veteran was unusually morose or ill-tempered or seemingly inert, perhaps these qualities were the evolution of prewar qualities, or they would wear away with affection, patience, and the familiar sights of home. If many ex-soldiers drank too much or whiled away too many hours with old comrades, a wise wife or mother made allowances. Wasn't that the way most men were? Marriage in 1919 was for better or worse, motherhood was long-suffering, insanity was a taboo, and family embarrassments were kept private. If complaints were aired, the Pension Board could strip away even physical disability benefits for "the man's own good" when it suspected a psychological root to a veteran's inability to earn.[76]

Pensions and Applied Bureaucracy

How did all the plans, principles, and practices of re-establishment affect Canadian soldiers and their families? Like many schemes, they worked best for those who did not really need them. Ottawa, most provinces, and several large cities had kept civil service positions open for employees who joined the CEF. So had some large corporations. Lance-Cpl. Louis Lallicheur returned to New Brunswick on crutches with a pension of $8 a month. As a federal preventive officer, he earned a salary of $800, although when pain from his wounds kept him from working, he earned nothing. Another New Brunswicker, Pte. W.J. Cahole, had a better job as a landing waiter for the Customs Department, at $850 a year. He also had a pension of $8 a month, which hardly seemed generous for a man who had lost all his teeth and his lower jaw. Still, by Dr. Todd's calculations, he could still work.

Both men were better off than Pte. Fred Hyatt of Saint John, who had earned $75 a month before the war to support his wife and three children. He came home with progressive motor ataxia to a gratuity of $100, no pension, and no job. Pte. George Henderson, also of the 55th Battalion, had lost part of his cranium and was partially paralyzed. He was confined to the Saint John Asylum, leaving his wife and children as a public charge on the city's flinty charities. Both suffered from a BPC conclusion that their disabilities might be aggravated by a pension or that they had come into the war with them. Was it reasonable, veterans demanded, that men who had been medically examined at enlistment and afterwards and passed as fit, suddenly lost their pensions because their severe disabilities were blamed on pre-enlistment conditions?

A Toronto veteran and former boxing champion, Bill Turley, returned from France in December 1915 with acute synovitis of the right knee. He was awarded a third-class pension and given three months of treatment without pay. Since he was pensioned, the Patriotic Fund cut off allowances to his family, and Turley supported himself, he confessed, by appealing to friends and borrowing. With help from his MP and the Military Hospitals Commission, he finally won a modest pension of $270 in May 1916. As a representative veteran, Turley told the 1916 parliamentary special committee that all returned soldiers suffered delays in being paid. Pte. William Childs suffered fainting spells and a stiff right elbow. The pension commissioners cut his pension from 20 to 10 percent after Childs confessed that his fainting spells only came every six to seven weeks and cost him only about 2 percent of his working time. This, the Board ruled, was not "a great disability." Cpl. James McRae from Montreal's 14th Battalion suffered corneal opacity which, according to a medical board in England, had been aggravated by shell shock. He came home, was discharged and was going blind when the BPC telegram arrived announcing that his pension was cancelled because the medical finding made no scientific sense. By coincidence, his wife had just been admitted to hospital.[77]

Wartime Winnipeg was a beacon of patriotic commitment but it was not invariably generous. The president of a local veteran's club, A.C. Hay, was a former accountant with a wife and three children. He returned from the war suffering from poison gas and injured feet. His employer, explained Hay, "does not feel very kindly towards this war," and offered Hay $10 less than his 1914 salary, though there was nothing wrong with his head. Veterans also denounced Winnipeg's assistant postmaster. Veterans who got their Post Office jobs back claimed that he gave them the dirty work of sorting mailbags. A German bullet through his wrist ended Sgt.-Maj. Whitton's career as a gymnastic instructor at Appleby College, a private boys school near Toronto. He had to make do with work in a munitions plant. While the plant did not discriminate against wounded men, the war had cost him a proud professional role. Another man with little to show for his suffering was Sgt.-Maj. Langtry. A prewar Toronto policeman, he had spent nine months at the front, succumbed to trench fever, and was released as unfit for further service – with only a $50 gratuity and little prospect of future police work.

Todd's procedures were based on objective medical analysis of the facts – such as they seemed to a professional practitioner – with a minimum of sentiment. They made sense to him and to most MPs, but soldiers saw them differently. "You just walk in there stiff and rigid and you are under military discipline," explained a former sergeant and prewar lawyer, E.R.R. Mills; "it is a private speaking to a colonel ... When you go before a medical board, you are treated as a malingerer if you are a private."[78] Defined himself as "functionally disabled," a euphemism for shell shock, Mills helped Ottawa veterans prepare their cases. One of them, Herbert White, claimed he had lost an eye in the army but the BPC insisted it was a pre-enlistment disability. "I would have tried to get a pension while in the army," he explained to Mills, "but cannot talk very plain and was afraid of them laughing at me."[79] Another veteran and veterans' spokesman, Norman Knight, explained a common pitfall for a soldier facing a board: "No man, unless he is playing a game, wants to make himself out worse than he is, consequently when they come before one of these boards, and the doctor asks them how they are, they say: 'I'm feeling pretty fine to-day.'"[80] That often became the medical judgment, too. Faced with bureaucracy and delay, what did veterans do? "It is a temperamental matter," the Toronto veteran W.E. Turley told the special committee: "If you feel like writing, you will write. If you are a little stoical, you will pray and that is about all you can do. You are in the lap of the gods as it were."[81]

Faced with bureaucratic authority, soldiers and their families lacked the leverage to get results. Pte. John Carolan had earned $8 a day before the war as an inspector at the Dodge car factory in Detroit. A shell left a cavity in his skull big enough for three fingers, and the pain drove him to plead either for a silver plate or death. Silver plates, said an MHC doctor, were old-fashioned, and he was fitted instead with an aluminum cap. Carolan found it too hot and too tight and he was not wearing it at his automotive job when a small steel fragment hit his wounded head and left him unconscious for days. He recovered sufficiently to go to Ann Arbor to have a silver plate inserted at his own expense.[82] Was this any concern of the Canadian government?

Sometimes even officials felt helpless. Calgary MP R.B. Bennett demanded of a Toronto paymaster why there were such delays in the pay system. "The system wants more electricity," he proclaimed.[83] Precisely. Since the paymaster was required to send his queries by mail, not by telegram, the waiting could be endless, but the delay affected only the ill-paid soldiers.[84] Regulations, however ingenious, often failed to anticipate the complexities and misfortunes of life. Pte. Harding, forty-six, had worked for twenty-two years in England's Woolwich Arsenal. He joined the CEF, fell sick of tuberculosis, was released on a third-class pension, and was advised to move to Regina for its dry climate. To support their ten children, his wife was compelled to find work. Harding was run over by a Regina streetcar and killed, in a tragedy that no government policy could remedy.[85]

In 1918 Norman Knight raised the case of Pte. Richardson, whose wife had died while he was in France. Her sister quit her job to raise the soldier's three children. Then Richardson himself was killed in action. If his wife had lived, she would have had a widow's pension as well as the allowance for each child. But her sister had no claim to any pension beyond the money due to the children. Of course, she could send them to an orphanage or offer them for adoption and they would get the higher allowance allowed to orphans but, if that happened, Knight insisted, "Those children will never know, when they grow up, who their father was."[86]

Veterans Get Organized

Veterans needed advocates to help them through the bureaucracy that awaited them, and often they turned to their fellows. In his plan for returned soldiers, Ernest Scammell had argued the need for veterans' clubs, where men could meet others with the same experience, share experiences and grievances, and get a response from "proper authorities."[87] John Todd agreed. Otherwise, he warned, "The soldiers will become banded together in Associations serving their particular interests, as distinguished from those of the nation."[88] There was no lack of agencies eager to help entertain ex-soldiers. Halifax's Reception Committee, backed by the Red Cross, Knights of Columbus, and the YMCA, welcomed soldiers returning through Pier 2. Ottawa's IODE chapters provided cheap meals and a reading room. Several provincial governments established organizations to assist veterans to find suitable work or to rehabilitate an abandoned farm or business. Ontario's Soldiers' Aid Commission established branches across the province to help returned soldiers find work. Saskatchewan's Returned Soldiers' Employment Commission sponsored 400 branches of a Welcome and Aid League. In Montreal, Arthur Doble's Khaki League was originally organized to provide a recreation room for a new CEF battalion. Backed by Molsons, Marlers, Cloustons, and other wealthy families, the League soon established a convalescent home and provided beds and meals for transient ex-soldiers. By 1916 it had branches in Quebec City, Halifax, and Saint John. Mrs. Denholm Molson, the Khaki League's "Mother Molson," became a frequently cited expert on veterans.

Victoria's Legion of Frontiersmen, a patriotic men's club that distributed military ranks and dress uniforms to its members, decided to organize and represent veterans. With an MHC subsidy, Vancouver's Canadian Club established a Returned Soldiers' Club in a disused school. Worried by potential militancy, Winnipeg's Mayor P.D. Waugh sponsored a Returned Soldiers' Association to help veterans find work and suitable comradeship. It was funded with membership fees and books of stamps marked "Be a Sticker." The Association was not a voice for veterans unless, as returned soldier Angus Hay was told, he paid $5 – two weeks' pension for him – to buy a vote.[89]

Nor did it help William Laidlaw, who had left most of his left leg in France. The BPC had allowed him a second-class pension of $192, and the Manitoba Returned Soldiers' Commission found him a job learning to make toys, but his limb maker said his stump was too short to fit a prosthesis. Laidlaw thought it was because the man was German-born. When his wound suppurated, he returned to hospital, his retraining income ceased, and his family was left with his $16 monthly pension. Laidlaw's luck changed only after T.S. Ewart, a pertinacious Liberal lawyer, took up his case. His pension promptly rose to $50 a month, with an extra $26 as a training allowance for a renewed course.[90]

In 1916 Winnipeg veterans organized their own meeting to publicize the plight of soldiers' wives, whose monthly income had dropped from an average of $52.50 to a meagre $22.00 because of their husbands' partial disability pensions. To add prestige, they invited the venerable Sir Charles Tupper. The old political warhorse dutifully came, but his comments defined the returned soldiers as greedy troublemakers. A struggling Canada, "with her cup running over," would, he insisted, meet its obligations. This was not quite the message the veterans had wanted.[91]

"Pension attorneys" and "claims agents" were a throwback to the American "pension evil"; so was pressure from veterans and their political allies. Toronto mayor Tommy Church, a Tory populist, had denounced Sir Sam Hughes for warning Canadians not to pamper returned soldiers. "Under our Militia Department," retorted Church, "everybody in sight was pampered but the soldiers on active service." He wanted veterans to have free telephones, electricity, and admission to baseball games. Perhaps conscious of how useful an ally the Grand Army of the Republic had become to the Republican Party, Church wanted a GAR for Canada. Montreal lawyer, poet, and civic reformer W.D. Lighthall insisted he was not starting a Canadian version of the GAR when he wrote to its Washington headquarters for a copy of the regulations and Robert Beath's history of the organization. After an early meeting of the Canadian Association of Returned Soldiers (CARS), Lighthall wrote to the Sydney *Bulletin* to propose that Australians share in "a Grand Army of the Empire."[92] Despite warnings from the deputy minister of militia, surgeon general Eugène Fiset, who considered it "inadvisable,"[93] an Ottawa branch of CARS was chartered. A public meeting in Montreal on 6 November 1916, in the presence of the local district officer commanding, Maj.-Gen. E.W. Wilson, chose an executive of returned soldiers and laid the groundwork for a national organization. Members of CARS promptly excluded all but "overseas men" from their organization, and Lighthall was obliged to watch his creation from the sidelines.

From Halifax to Victoria, a score of returned-soldier organizations took shape in 1916, often in a climate of resentment at officially sponsored clubs. When Parliament summoned representative veterans to meet its Special Committee on Returned Men in Toronto in 1917, the occasion allowed a preparatory meeting on 17 March to plan a national organization. In turn, the meeting helped persuade railway companies to allow delegates to travel to Winnipeg at half-fare to create a national association on 1 April 1917. Adopting the name that Winnipeg veterans had chosen for their own club, the convention proclaimed itself a Great War Veterans' Association or GWVA, elected officers, and passed a succession of fiery resolutions. Delegates demanded a flat $1,200 pension for the totally disabled, regardless of rank. If the pension commissioners changed local recommendations, there must be an appeal to a higher body. Veterans demanded a civilian Department of Demobilization "conducted along strictly nonpartisan and business lines." Made aware of the Last Post Fund, a Montreal charity that provided burials for penniless local veterans, the GWVA demanded that the government "meet the cost of a decent interment" for all ex-soldiers. Western veterans demanded a 320-acre land grant and a minimum $2,000 loan to any soldier who went overseas and to each war widow, "provided always that the title of the land be entrusted to a responsible trustee." Further, as trustees for men still in the fight, they demanded conscription of men and wealth and of enemy aliens, a furlough for "Old Originals" of the First Contingent and a still higher head-tax on Chinese immigrants. Amidst much egalitarian talk and use of the word "Comrade" to address members, Maj. Willard Purney, a Halifax lawyer, emerged as the GWVA's first president. Five of the twelve-member executive were former commissioned officers in the CEF.[94]

The GWVA reflected a discovery almost every soldier made almost as soon as he was back in Canada – or Germany or Great Britain. Trench soldiers had become distinct. No one could share what they had experienced overseas; attempts to do so usually seemed patronizing and exasperating. The GWVA, most of its founding members insisted, had to be limited to men who shared that experience. Since 1885 Winnipeg had been home to the Army and Navy Veterans, an association of former sailors and soldiers that had welcomed hundreds of British veterans to the West. Now it expected to lend the new organization its experience and connections. Instead, after an angry debate, a majority of delegates restricted GWVA membership to those who had crossed the ocean in the current war. When the majority refused to make concessions, the Army and Navy Veterans walked out.[95]

Besides their transforming overseas experience, Canada's returned soldiers shared another condition: poverty. Except in the higher ranks, CEF pay barely matched the wages of unskilled labour, and its value had shrunk significantly as inflation spread across Canada. In the excitement of enlistment, few had expected their loss of income to be more than a temporary inconvenience, but the pensions for widows and the seriously disabled promised to trap them and their families in permanent poverty. And whatever the GWVA might become when the war ended and the entire CEF came home, in 1917 it was primarily an organization of disabled pensioners from the ranks.

The GWVA was also capable of exploiting wartime idealism. Summoned to one of the final meetings of the 1917 parliamentary committee, GWVA leaders had an opportunity to establish their credibility with politicians on the eve of a crucial general election. Elected national secretary of the GWVA at Winnipeg, Norman Knight mustered all his eloquence to inspire the committee: "We see no reason why our own country, this fair Canada, should not take the lead and by so doing, point the world to a happier way of settling differences, broader and more generous, vindicating her absolute faith and perfect confidence in the men who counted it joy to serve in her hour of need, suffering, enduring and dying, when the hearts of loved ones, mothers, wives and children, breaking at home, preferred rather a nation's honour than the love of son, husband, and father."[96]

Poverty was an old, familiar reality in Canada, easily marginalized by the affluent, and possible to escape with the aid of a skill and a steady run of employment. However, disabled veterans, war widows, and orphans had an advantage other poor Canadians had always lacked: a public claim to entitlement. Their poverty could not be blamed on bad character or self-indulgence: it was the clear consequence of a public sacrifice to the common good. Whether they had defended the Empire, fought Prussian militarism, or upheld Canadian pride, soldiers and their families had begun to pay a price that all had promised to share. In 1917 that price was still being exacted.

That spring, Canadians debated another way of paying that price, through age-based conscription of young men, regulated by a Military Service Act. Meanwhile, the latest special committee of Parliament had set out to review what was being done for the newly organized and militant returned men. The prime minister had turned to Sir Herbert Ames to chair the 1917 committee, confident that the honorary secretary of the Patriotic Fund would be a well-informed and prudent guide to what Canadians were learning to call "re-establishment." His co-chairman, R.B. Bennett, was Senator Lougheed's Calgary law partner. Many of the members of the 1916 committee returned. So did their witnesses.

As a witness, Todd felt fully in control. The Board of Pension Commissioners was working well. For example, Pte. Edward James had led his three sons into the CEF in 1914. Discharged in 1916, James claimed that asthma, caused by poison gas, left him helpless. Was this fair? Board records showed that James had lied about his age and offered no medical basis for his claim. He had no claim to a pension.[97]

Pte. Poirier had a 40 percent pension for the eye he had lost in action, but he lost his Post Office job after his other eye began to fail. Since he could write only in French, Poirier had felt silenced by the anglophone military bureaucracy until fellow veterans came to his aid. Nevertheless, Board records showed no evidence that the state of the other eye was a military responsibility.[98] Surely, an MP expostulated, it was not government policy to offer as little as it could. "That," Ames rejoined, "is the policy of any and every Government, and always will be."[99]

Ill at ease and poorly briefed, veterans often made unsympathetic witnesses. One elderly soldier made few friends when he complained that the pension system favoured professionals and those in sedentary occupations, a fair summary of the members of the committee. G.H. Herbert, a PPCLI veteran from Saskatchewan, argued that a private who lost his leg suffered more than a similarly disabled captain, who could easily return to his law practice. The lawyers on the committee resented this suggestion. Was he a socialist when it came to returned men, Ames demanded? "Yes, sir," said Herbert, "I am."[100] Sgt.-Maj. E.W. Guilfoyle from Calgary complained that insane soldiers were entitled to something better than placement in provincial asylums with ordinary lunatics. Like other veterans, he also wanted all aliens disfranchised. "Once a German, always a German," he explained, "and I believe these men will vote in a way detrimental to the interests of the returned soldiers."[101]

Compared to those of the preceding committee, the 1917 committee's recommendations were modest. The Pension Act should be made permanent. And since inflation had devoured the improvements in 1916, pensions should be increased, which, as we have seen, they were. Late in the session, Purney and the new GWVA executive were granted a hearing, much of it devoted to diluting any apparent impression of radicalism at Winnipeg. Capt. Kenneth Macpherson of the Ottawa branch used considerable ingenuity in shrinking the GWVA demand for a flat $1,200 pension to a mere $840. Other executive members confessed that, if men were conscripted, the veterans would sacrifice "the extras." What the GWVA needed, its secretary confessed, was formal recognition for its intermediary role: "We really think that the powers now are really trying to do for the returned soldier all they possibly can do, but we do not want the returned men to go about telling other people all their grievances. Let them come to us and we will take the matter up with the proper authorities."[102] What more could Ames, Todd, or Scammell wish?

Moreover, if the GWVA membership was inclined to extremes, a more conservative alternative soon appeared. Shocked at GWVA radicalism and annoyed that it had narrowly agreed to establish its headquarters in Ottawa, some leading Winnipeg citizens hurriedly secured a charter for the Army and Navy Veterans.[103] Sixty-three delegates, representing 8,337 veterans, met in Winnipeg from 11 to 15

May 1918, and chose Maj. W.J. Tupper, grandson of the former Tory prime minister, as their president. ANV membership was open to any veteran with at least six years' service in His Majesty's forces, or who had served in France, but not to those who had stayed in England "unless they could prove it was through no fault of their own." The GWVs, sniffed a delegate, "take a man if he has been in the army five minutes and had the clothes on." The ANV headquarters naturally remained in Winnipeg.[104]

At their April convention, GWVA officials had claimed to speak for 10,000 returned soldiers though the organization could only count twenty-seven branches with 3,884 members, none of them with cash to spare. To finance an organization, the GWVA needed the charity it deplored; to collect money, it needed a charter that Sir James Lougheed, chairman of the Military Hospitals Commission, proved distinctly reluctant to approve. Without it, branches and provincial commands only gradually took shape. British Columbia veterans had come together even before the Winnipeg convention; Ontario followed in May, and Saskatchewan in November. Provincial delegates concocted militant programs, demanded money for pensions, disabled pay, and re-establishment, denounced aliens and safety-first officers, and frequently condemned the Patriotic Fund for operating like a charity. Local branches echoed their demands. In Ontario's tobacco-growing Oxford County, returned soldiers denounced "the practice of various cranks throughout the country in condemning the Red Cross and other societies for sending cigarettes to soldiers in the trenches."[105] All ardently endorsed conscription. By the end of 1917, the GWVA claimed eighty branches with 30,000 members, though the truth was probably closer to 15,000.

The GWVA insisted that it was nonpartisan, but veterans in 1917 could hardly back Laurier and his anticonscriptionists. Borden's October-born Union government apparently met the GWVA criteria. Though its words promised nothing new, the Unionist program spoke unctuously of a generous future: "The men by whose sacrifice and endurance the free institutions of Canada will be preserved must be re-educated where necessary and re-established on the land or in such pursuits or vocations as they may desire to follow. The maimed and the broken will be protected, the widow and the orphan will be helped and cherished. Duty and decency demand that those who are saving democracy shall not find democracy a house of privilege, or a school of poverty and hardship."[106]

For the 1917 election, the Unionists gained a full-scale commitment from the GWVA. Promoted to colonel, Willard Purney left for overseas to administer the Military Voters Act in Britain and Flanders.[107] GWVA branches endorsed a variety of soldier candidates, and veterans guided democracy by breaking up anticonscription meetings in Ottawa, Winnipeg, Toronto, and Vancouver. Twenty officers stood as Union candidates; sixteen of them won, and Maj. G.W. Andrews, running in Winnipeg Centre, won the biggest majority in the election.[108] Norman Knight, the GWVA's national secretary, modestly claimed the reward: "It has been urged by many," he reminded the prime minister in March 1918, "that the returned soldier and his loyal connexion, our brave women folk, had quite as much to do with the return of the Union Government as any other force in Canada. All we ask in return is a little consideration."[109]

"Not the Man I Was"

Soldiers who returned during the war had changed much more than the months or years of absence, or even the coarsening effect of men living among men, might have warranted. Front-line soldiers gained an experience other Canadian soldiers, even many who were overseas, had escaped. In the trenches, soldiers shared cold and mud and squalor, and they had also lived in prolonged and acute danger from shelling, snipers and machine-gun fire. They had watched comrades torn to shreds and they had waited for men to die in agony from the effects of poison gas, always knowing that it could next be their fate. Some had consciously killed enemies, with a grenade, a sniper's rifle, or even, very occasionally, with a bayonet. Artillery bombardments had reduced men to a helpless terror as the death-dealing explosions came steadily closer. Letters home might claim that a dead comrade "never felt a thing"; veterans knew the truth: horribly wounded men often lived for hours in indescribable agony when no medical help could reach them. Many soldiers had faced the need to launch their bodies out of a trench into a seemingly suicidal attack across No Man's Land.

Soldiers wondered whether wives back in Canada could ever understand the awful imperatives that compelled them to risk their lives. Writing from his drab barrack room in England, Ernest Hamilton had to explain how, with a wife and children he loved, he could volunteer to transfer to a CEF battalion at the front:

> It is not because I desire to kill or be killed but that I thot it my duty to do my bit after being in the army two years & this war will go down in history as the greatest the world ever took part in & it is for the benefit of our children that I want to take part in it & they may realize some day why Dad would leave them & their mother to take part in this awful war but believe me sweet heart it hurt me more than you know to leave you & the babes & it is still hurting but we can only hope & pray that we will live to enjoy a few more years of happiness.[110]

Mixed with the battlefield casualties were men whose fate had been determined by strong British beer and diseased English prostitutes. In Britain, Canadian soldiers had challenged the Australians for the venereal disease championship and won, with a 16 percent rate of infection. Only then had Canadian authorities ignored moralizing chaplains and joined their allies in establishing "Blue Light depots" for disinfection and preventive education. But the damage had already been done, both to soldiers and to their families in Canada.[111]

Some families never reunited. An ocean and years away from home, some soldiers had forgotten their families in favour of fresh relationships in Great Britain. The long absence had also led some wives into infidelity. In the little city of Woodstock, Ontario, Bert Lynn's wife Mary lost their two neglected children to the Children's Aid Society for moving in with another man. She moved to Toronto, reported the local Patriotic Association, "where her parents have undertaken to attempt her reform."[112] Martha Campbell also lost her child for a similar offence, but apparently it was only "an adopted child" whom she had borrowed from the local shelter for the added income.[113]

In May 1918, *Toronto Saturday Night* echoed Kingston MP William F. Nickle's claim that the "matrimonial complications" arising from the war were an argument for easier and cheaper divorce. Parliament was not persuaded, though divorces in Canada, which had averaged forty annually in the ten prewar years, averaged five hundred annually in the years 1920-4.[114] Since divorce was both scandalous and hugely expensive, some returning soldiers chose "the poor man's decree nisi" and simply abandoned their families to start a new life elsewhere. Others faced up to an appalling situation, like the soldier who could not afford to divorce the wife who had deposited their children in the local poor house and abandoned them.[115]

In a country far removed from war and its social consequences, returning veterans were imperfect heroes. It was not only MHC officials who complained that invalided soldiers lacked the purpose and self-discipline that their honoured status demanded. Unable or reluctant to link battle experience to psychological disability, civilians blamed the veterans' behaviour on the alleged traditional fecklessness of soldiers. Perhaps men who could count on the army for a roof, blankets, and meals, whether or not they did a day's work, had suffered a weakening of moral fibre. The best cure was an uncompromising dose of independence. When Sir Robert Borden promised "full re-establishment" to the soldiers he addressed before their historic attack on Vimy Ridge, perhaps that was what he meant.

Among the sufferers from both the putative disease and the approved cure were soldiers' families. Widows, whose husbands were gone forever, might envy wives whose husbands returned, even on crutches or with invisible psychological wounds, but a wife's burden was not necessarily lighter than a widow's. Left to manage with the help or meddling of Patriotic Fund visitors, wives had grown into many responsibilities, making decisions that often reminded a husband that he had vacated his accustomed role as head of the family, disciplinarian, and financial guardian. Wives and children bore the brunt of the men's adjustment and, for the most part, they bore it silently. All the symptoms of post-traumatic stress, from uncontrollable garrulousness to long periods of angry withdrawal, were now shared by a family on a significantly reduced income. The inexplicable restlessness that most veterans described as their dominant postwar response disrupted family life.

Living with Shell Shock

Worst off among the war-disabled were those defined as "functional," "neurasthenic," or shell-shock cases. Such men, claimed Lt.-Col. Colin Russell, the CEF's chief specialist in shell shock, had consciously willed themselves into their state to escape their military responsibilities. To grant them pensions was to reward them. "You have thrown away the four aces," he warned, and Todd's Board had respected his scientific advice.[116] When the new government proposed yet another special committee on pensions and returned soldiers for the new Unionist-dominated Parliament in 1918, Todd was content to have another chance to present his case.

This time, many of the members were new and the chairman, Newton Rowell, was the former Ontario Liberal leader whose change of allegiance had made Unionism possible. Another member was the independent-minded Tory and Patriotic Fund activist from Kingston, William Nickle. The veterans, too, were better prepared and, whatever the ideological rivalries between their organizations, Norman Knight of the GWVA and Sgt. Herbert Jarvis of the ANV worked closely together.

Todd and the BPC staff ran into trouble with the new special committee very soon. Surely, the BPC insisted, Pte. Childs with fainting fits that cost him only 2 percent of his working time was well treated with a 10 percent pension. Nickle exploded: "I think we are getting entirely too scientific in estimating the degree of disability these men are suffering." A bitter issue for veterans was the unequal treatment of officers that continued, with rank-based pensions and treatment pay, into civilian life. "In a democratic country such as this," declared the ANV's Sgt. Jarvis, "I do not think we should have this class distinction amongst the civilian population."[117] "The man in the ranks," claimed Knight, "feels that his service was just as self-sacrificing as that of any of the officers ... There is no reason why an officer should get more pension than any other man."[118] The committee listened attentively. When the war ended, men in the ranks would have more votes than ex-officers.

MPs and veterans soon targeted Todd's colleague, Col. Labatt, as proof that officers were far better treated than soldiers. Sgt.-Maj. Arthur Tooke from Barrie, a member of Labatt's 4th Battalion, had been buried alive by German shells and suffered a nervous breakdown. Sent home in the *Metagama* and discharged in 1916, Tooke received a 5 percent pension of a mere $2.66 a week to support a family of three. Only a good-hearted employer kept the Tookes from starvation by giving the veteran a job in his foundry in Chatham. Meanwhile, Tooke's former commanding officer collected a disability pension of $2,160 a year for himself and two teenaged children, not to mention his $5,000 salary as a pension commissioner. Harry H. Stevens, a Vancouver Tory with a keen nose for scandal, did his best to make Labatt nationally known. Since Labatt could not be a pension commissioner *and* totally disabled, Stevens argued, his pension was either due to misrepresentation or undue influence.[119] Stevens did not raise the possibilities that Labatt might want to be useful and that he brought front-line experience to the Board.[120]

That winter, Ross and Todd had left Labatt in charge of the BPC and gone to England to wind up Sir Montague Allan's Pensions and Claims Board and to reduce dependant pensions for widows of Canadians in England to the more meagre British rates. Ross came home eager to meet the parliamentary committee, to denounce the Civil Service Commission for trying to make him hire ex-farmers and railway brakemen as staff and for forcing the Board to abide by civil service summer hours of 9 to 4. Instead, the special committee demanded to know why Ross worked part-time for a full-time salary. Why did pension commissioners use a rubber signature stamp to approve pensions? Unlike "attributability" or "functional cases," Labatt's pension and Ross's absenteeism were issues the public could understand. Todd and the Board solicitor were left to improvise a defence, yielding on some points and wielding the evil American example when they could. In the United States, regional boards competed with each other to be generous. Canada could not afford such behaviour. Perhaps, they conceded, a soldier who got as far as France or Flanders could be considered to have no prior disabilities.

Labatt, whose sense of duty had brought him back to Ottawa, was an obvious sacrifice. Maj.-Gen. Sidney Mewburn, the new Unionist minister of militia, defended his fellow Hamiltonian; other ministers were silent. Labatt was arguably an example of Parliament's 1916 policy that earnings must not affect a pension, but that did not trouble his parliamentary critics. When the special committee reported on 20 May, it lectured the commissioners on their duty and insisted that each pension order must be signed by hand. It urged Board medical examiners to confer with a local medical board if they disagreed with its recommendation, and refused to grant the more generous Canadian pension rates to British and Allied reservists who returned to Canada. To equalize pensions across the ranks, as the

GWVA demanded, Rowell explained, would be a breach of contract with the officers. Labatt resigned at once, and was dead within a year, leaving his family too poor to own his mountainside mansion in Hamilton.[121]

For all their organizing, the GWVA and ANV had little to show for their 1918 efforts. Though wartime inflation was well on its way to halving the value of a 1914 dollar, the government got through the 1918 session without increasing soldiers' pay or pensions for widows and the disabled. Conscription, not cash, would now pressure Canadian men to fill the ranks of the CEF. Still, the veterans had established the right to be consulted, and they outlasted Todd and his colleagues. In 1918 one of Ross's horses won the Triple Crown of racing and $1 million. Suddenly the racetrack seemed infinitely more attractive to him than battles with the Civil Service Commission or MPs. Exasperated at the prospect of scribbling his name on thousands of pension awards, Todd also got ready to retire. It was time, he told his mother, for "a general with a wooden leg and lots of medal ribbons."[122]

Establishing Civil Re-Establishment

Meanwhile, Canada's disabled soldiers had to endure a major turf war. Creation of the Military Hospitals Commission in 1915 had been a mixed blessing, but it certainly rescued sick and injured soldiers from a Militia Department hard-pressed even to provide medical services overseas, much less across Canada. Employing its own nurses, orderlies, and administrators, and hiring part-time civilian practitioners, MHC staff had developed an extensive network of convalescent hospitals and homes for the sick and wounded, as well as sanatoria for its many tuberculosis sufferers. More were on stream. Fed up with his talkative commissioners, Sir James Lougheed simply stopped summoning them, leaving officials to make decisions and assign resources. With its innovative ideas on vocational training and an active publicity machine, the Hospitals Commission defined itself as a wartime success story. After the United States entered the war in April 1917, and Americans looked briefly to Canada for advice and example in coping with modern war, the MHC had much to share: its advances in vocational training, curative workshops, cafeteria service, hospital dieticians, and the "quick-build" Camp Hill hospital in Halifax.

The MHC had a strained relationship with the Militia Department, however, and particularly the Canadian Army Medical Corps (CAMC), which saw the MHC as an upstart body whose medical expertise was represented by its medical director, Dr. Alfred E. Thompson, brewer, hardware merchant and Conservative MP for the Yukon.[123] Voters, raised on the legend of Florence Nightingale, were sensitive to allegations that wounded heroes had been mistreated. Relations with the

CAMC were aggravated by a midwar shortage of medical personnel and the MHC's tendency to appoint junior military officers, not senior doctors, to run its establishments. At about the time that Col. Herbert Bruce of Toronto's Wellesley Hospital was composing his blistering and biased report on the CAMC in Britain, Lt.-Col. Frederick Marlow, a popular Toronto gynecologist, was doing the same to the MHC. Both reports were secret yet widely leaked, and both spelled trouble for both their authors and their intended victims.[124]

Marlow wanted the CAMC to regain control of MHC hospitals, and complained that professional medical priorities had been ignored too long. Fed up with a lack of official response, he resigned, gave his reasons, and provoked a brief uproar just as his boss, Minister of Militia Sir Edward Kemp, believed that he had secured a compromise favourable to the CAMC. Instead, the bureaucratic struggle continued through 1917, while the government and most Canadians had more important issues on their minds than whether Toronto doctors should have to journey out to Guelph or Whitby to see their military patients, or what role Senator Lougheed could play if he didn't head the MHC.

Among the collateral benefits of forming a Union government was a solution to a fundamentally silly display of professional self-importance. In the turmoil of fitting Liberals into the Cabinet, adding a new department was easy. In 1917 the GWVA had proposed a Department of Demobilization.[125] Since the British had already created a Ministry of Pensions, why not create a Canadian counterpart under Senator Lougheed? He could control the vocational training assets created by the Military Hospitals Commission, the Board of Pension Commissioners, the MHC's prosthetics factory in Toronto, a Soldier Settlement Board to meet the hopes of prairie veterans for land and loans, and whatever else was necessary for postwar reconstruction. The Militia Department would be welcome to take over the MHC's military hospitals, which, when the war ended, would rapidly become a wasting asset.

After three weeks of dickering and delay, three orders-in-council were signed on 21 February 1918. One created a Department of Soldiers' Civil Re-establishment (DSCR) for Lougheed, the second an Invalided Soldiers Commission (ISC) for the remaining MHC functions, and the third transferred some MHC hospitals to the Militia Department. Soon, some 1,359 beds, a quarter of them still under construction, passed to CAMC control, while 5,575 beds, mostly in sanatoria, remained under the ISC for postdischarge cases.[126] Who had won? As with many noisy struggles, the aftermath was anticlimactic. In Toronto, Gertrude Vankoughnet, honorary superintendent of soldiers' comforts for the MHC, complained that four automobiles, donated for the benefit of patients, had been seized by army officers. She got no satisfaction. The head of the MHC Command reassured subordinates that "things will carry on pretty much as they are now" and he was right.[127] In his history of the CAMC, Sir Andrew Macphail complained about the misery of CAMC doctors working in Canada under close civilian scrutiny: "The grumbler, the malingerer, and the neurotic never failed to find an audience equally neurotic and ready to lend an ear to murmurings and complaint."[128]

The military takeover was barely complete in the summer of 1918 when Allied hopes for victory suddenly took a turn for the better. As the tide turned and the Canadian Corps experienced both its greatest victories and its heaviest casualties of the war, the dreaded Spanish flu suddenly spread across Canada. That the elderly and ailing should die in the epidemic was predictable; that the toll also fell on fit, young soldiers found a familiar explanation: military incompetence. Toronto's base hospital, located in the city's disused general hospital, admitted 2,100 influenza cases; 270 developed pneumonia and 90 died. This was hardly abnormal before antibiotics, but Mayor Tommy Church turned the tragedy into a scandal; a grand jury denounced negligence and poor accommodation, and the CAMC, not the MHC, took the abuse. While Toronto's politicians and journalists enjoyed their righteous indignation, the tragedy left families, the CAMC's own historian suggested, "to suffer severely and unnecessarily with the thought of their relatives dying for lack of care."[129]

Meanwhile, MHC officials created the new DSCR. Samuel Armstrong, the Ontario civil servant who had created thousands of beds for the MHC, became deputy minister; Ernest Scammell became assistant deputy minister, and Walter Segsworth continued as director of vocational training. Lt.-Col. Frederick McKelvey Bell, an Ottawa doctor who had won acclaim for the MHC's Halifax operations during and after the terrible 6 December explosion, became medical director. Far from a defeat, shedding hospitals turned out to be an advantage for an agency that badly needed time to prepare for its greatest test.

A Time of Turmoil

Meanwhile, its clients and chief critics made their peace with a war-weary but strangely innocent homeland. The last two years of the war were probably the hardest period of the twentieth century for Canadians. The blithe, optimistic patriotism that had carried much of the country through the first two years of the war had been exhausted by the setbacks of 1916. The failure of voluntary recruiting had set old against young, women against men, English-speaking Canada against French-speaking Quebec, and both against newer Canadians from central Europe. The debate was conducted with an almost unrestrained fanaticism of language and action. Wartime shortages had been largely resolved by inflation, leaving the poor unable to afford food, fuel, and clothing. Since soldiers and their families had been consigned by public policy to be among the poor, returning veterans saw the injustice. Conscious of their own sacrifices and caught up in their own diverse varieties of indignation, better-off Canadians barely noticed.

Canada's labour revolutionaries, active and eager before the war, had largely been silenced in the climate of the early war years. Their resolutions for a general strike against war had been mocked by the near-universal patriotic enthusiasm in English-speaking communities, and by the thousands of unionists who abandoned jobs – or unemployment – to enlist. Inspired by the revolution in Russia, the anger over conscription, and the aching desire for an end to the war, in 1918 radicals took heart, particularly in western Canada. Veterans might also rage at profiteering, immigration, and the assumed privileges of their officer class, but they had no common cause with those who called them dupes and stooges of capitalism. Overwhelmingly, returned men were the allies and agents of comrades who continued fighting the war in Europe. After Albert Goodwin, vice-president of the British Columbia Federation of Labour, was shot fleeing arrest under the Military Service Act, his comrades called a general strike. BC veterans responded by smashing their way into the Vancouver Labour Temple, trashing the premises and forcing the Labour Council secretary, Victor Midgley, to kiss the Union Jack.[130] When veterans met, they shouted their hostility to "slackers," enemy aliens, and any who challenged their patriotic and pro-Imperial orthodoxy.

When the GWVA met in Toronto at the end of July 1918 for its second convention, delegates were in a fighting mood. Leaders of the Ontario command were bent on getting involved in politics. Accordingly they wanted to open the ranks of the GWVA to anyone who had served, however briefly, in the CEF.[131] To carry their views, they had bullied the executive to get extra delegates. Other veterans were furiously opposed, and it took frantic, all-night diplomacy to keep the association from exploding. Discussing richer pensions and denouncing aliens brought the veterans together again. Delegates agreed unanimously that "O Canada" should have precedence, as a national anthem, over "God Save the King." However, when they were invited to sing, there was an embarrassed silence: no one remembered the words.[132]

That night, 2 August, midsummer heat sent crowds into Toronto's downtown streets. Suddenly, rumours flashed through the crowd that Greek waiters at the White City Café on Yonge Street had roughed up a disabled veteran. A crowd of veterans raced up the street and, as bystanders cheered, demolished the restaurant. Veterans destroyed ten more restaurants despite the efforts of a few police. Then they commandeered cars and wrecked another Greek restaurant in the West End. Next morning, Mayor Church denied any liability and blamed military authorities for failing to control soldiers. On the night of 3 August, angry, baton-swinging Toronto police cleared Yonge Street, pausing to bludgeon a drunken legless veteran named Mason Button and an angry but sober GWVA activist, Lt.-Col. A.T. Hunter.[133]

By the following morning, Toronto editors had decided, regardless of evidence, that the GWVA was responsible for the Greek restaurant riots. Indeed, Col. Purney and his executive had hurriedly drafted a resolution blaming "some returned soldiers" for undermining the GWVA and disgracing its cause.[134] Perhaps more unconsciously revealing was the response of David Loughnan, an Ulster-born British Columbian who had survived his unit's destruction at Ypres in 1915 by crawling half a mile with his intestines protruding through a gaping wound. Single-handedly he had created *The Veteran*, which he made the largest-circulation Canadian magazine of its era. In the wake of the riot, he summed up his own angry frustrations: "Without attempting to justify the conduct of the rioters in Toronto, we would draw the attention of the Canadian people to the fact that many returned men do sincerely feel that the Government and people of Canada have failed to implement the gracious promises of special treatment and consideration made to them ere they sailed overseas. Neglect to control profiteering, to work out a sane land settlement and land policy, and to regulate the alien problem, have all combined as irritants upon men whose nerves have not been improved by their trials in the trenches."[135]

Loughnan's readers were not the only Canadians who entered the year of victory with a growing sense of grievance. Improvised policies that left soldiers' families to experience poverty, charity, and amateur social engineering had worked for a while, but Canada had changed too much in the wartime years for the ideas of 1914 to work. Much of that change had worked in the minds of men who had already returned from the wars to Canada to discover that sense of entitlement that would distinguish veterans from other claimants for public attention. By volunteering to defend their country, they had earned its recognition and so had their families. They had no intention of being shoved back among the undeserving. In the army, soldiers had learned that grumbling was their only right. Once discharged, they found that they and their wives and families had much to grumble about.

6
Grumbling and Complaining

Caught up in the 1914-18 war, Canadians had as little experience of a prolonged nationwide crisis as their descendants at the beginning of this century. True, they were far more familiar with death, starting with appalling rates of infant mortality, continuing with a childbirth mortality toll that, by itself, gave women a significantly shorter life expectancy than men, and ending with early death from diseases we now cure with a few pills. Most families lived without even the shreds of a social safety net to alleviate the economic misfortunes that afflict any free market economy. If the Laurier years had been a period of unusual growth and prosperity for most Canadians, good fortune had never been universal. The later Laurier years had seen inflation and the beginnings of the economic instability associated with Robert Borden's early years in office.

Still, the Great War imposed a far heavier burden than most families had ever experienced, and its continuation month after month, defied comparison with anything but the American Civil War of the 1860s or the Napoleonic wars a full century earlier. Wars had happened in most people's lifetime, of course, and any literate child had learned about them through romantic tales of gallant soldiers, prancing horses, and booming cannon. Victory might be deferred a few months by political mismanagement or military misjudgments, as it had been in the Crimean War of 1854-5 or the South African War of 1899-1902. Hence, it was not entirely unexpected, despite the European precedents, that the war did not end by Christmas 1914, or even that it would take all of 1915 to create an Allied war machine capable of teaching the Prussian militarists a lesson. Hence the mingled enthusiasm and optimism of most Canadians in 1915 as they went about creating their share of the most formidable army the British Empire had ever mobilized.

Although victory might take as long as 1916, surely then it was assured. The British Army's khaki-clad soldiers, every one of them a volunteer, came from every corner and social class of Britain and its self-governing Dominions, proportionately more from New Zealand and Australia than from Canada, but all of them convinced that their free-spirited courage must overwhelm the kaiser's overdisciplined armies. That confidence was shared and even amplified behind the front and among the soldiers' families. Even in the foul mud and stench of the front-line trenches, soldiers lived out the romantic myth of courage, sacrifice, and triumph that had shaped the history and literature they read in school, in the daily press, in magazines, and in novels, and which was repeated in public speeches and private conversations. The myth of divinely guided and righteous invincibility equally sustained mothers, wives, and children.

Instead, at a cost so appalling it could scarcely be admitted, the great Allied offensive of 1916 almost immediately bogged down on the Somme. Early on 1 July, the Empire's new armies had pushed forward; in a few horrible hours, 60,000 men had fallen, and the carnage continued in the ensuing days. In September, when the Canadian Corps finally came down from Flanders to join the offensive, 24,000 dead and wounded Canadians were soon added to the toll. Today, we may know why. The commanders of the great offensive at the Somme certainly lacked inspirational genius, but they also lacked junior officers and soldiers sufficiently trained to manoeuvre around enemy defences, artillery shells powerful and reliable enough to destroy enemy wire entanglements, dugouts, and artillery, and the mobility to reinforce success faster than the weary legs of soldiers plodding through deep mud could travel.[1]

What was obvious at the time was that casualties had been enormous while gains, when translated to a map of reasonable scale, had been trivial. All the confidence and all the sacrifices had not sufficed for victory. The heroic legends had to be rewritten. Somehow, both leaders and led would have to steel themselves for further struggle and fresh sacrifices; they could never again do so with the heedless optimism that was the casualty of Verdun for the Germans and French and of the Somme for the British Empire.

In an age before opinion polls and kindred gauges of the public mood, demoralization is difficult to demonstrate and impossible to prove. Defeatism was a private response, resolutely hidden from public view. "We are not interested in the possibilities of defeat," Queen Victoria had told Arthur Balfour in 1899 when he brought her news of "Black Week" disasters early in the South African War.[2] The response of their ancient Queen was a model for all her subjects. From the prime minister to the youngest soldier's bride, the only acceptable response was renewed dedication plus a sharp eye for the "slackers" who had somehow managed to undermine the national effort. In Britain, Lord Lansdowne, the Anglo-Irish aristocrat and former governor general of Canada, argued for a negotiated peace with Germany as an alternative to the destruction of his country and, even more certainly, his own class. He was denounced and reviled by almost all who discovered his activity.[3] In Canada, the Bonne Entente movement, which had struggled to arouse a shared patriotism between English- and French-speaking Canadians, withered into resentment and anger against those who had spurned their invitation to sacrifice.[4] The CEF certainly needed more men than voluntarism produced after the spring of 1916, but the emotional fuel that fed the conscription crusade emerged from the war news in the summer and fall of 1916.

Like most movements of opinion, none of this happened at once or to everyone in Canada. As early as September 1915, Sir Robert Borden had been disillusioned by Imperial leadership when he visited England and found that, as usual at that season, many cabinet ministers had deserted London for the grouse moors.[5] Only the minister of munitions, David Lloyd George, had remained staunchly at his post. Even Borden's closest associates had barely a suspicion of his mood, but he rejoiced when a parliamentary coup d'état at the end of 1916, partly engineered by Canadian-born multimillionaire and newspaper proprietor Sir Max Aitken, substituted David Lloyd George for Herbert Asquith as prime minister. At last, Borden believed, the Empire's war effort would be conducted by the only dedicated minister he had encountered during his 1915 visit, and Canadian views would be heard.[6] Insulated from such experiences, most Canadians kept their faith in Britain's leadership and despised only their own prime minister. Others masked their doubts in more fervid commitment. Still others put their heads down and survived, or even prospered.[7]

The Somme had cost the CEF more than a third of its front-line soldiers, a third of them dead. That would have been a heavy price for an Allied victory, and it guaranteed that the war would continue. How could anyone in a democracy admit that such a sacrifice had been in vain? For soldiers' wives, the long, lonely wait for the war to end and their husbands to return was prolonged into 1917 and almost certainly beyond. Few of them shared their lonely misery with their men. What could a mere soldier do about the trench stalemate except get himself killed or maimed? Though the primary breadwinner, an early twentieth-century father had much more to contribute to the family than his paycheque. The chores of parenting in most working-class families were not equally shared; fathers were missed not because they prepared an occasional meal, changed diapers, or made the beds but because a father shared in the education and especially the discipline of his growing children. The women who inherited these responsibilities did so with the added burden of social illegitimacy. Acting outside her conventional role, a lonely wife easily imagined that her husband could more easily have crushed youthful rebellion or adolescent defiance.

On 6 April 1917, when the United States entered the war, Canadians gained a rare opportunity to compare their military experience with that of their neighbours and an even rarer chance to offer Americans advice. Maj. Todd made himself available to preach his views on pensions, well aware that a different American example would soon undermine his model. Other advisors to the Military Hospitals

Commission as well as Helen Reid of the CPF eagerly publicized their experience at American conferences.[8] Herbert Wolfe, an American actuary who visited Ottawa in the spring of 1917 to check on Canadian benefits for dependants, reported that wives received a minimum of fifteen and a maximum of twenty days' pay per month from enlisted men, plus a separation allowance that ranged from $20 for privates to $60 for lieutenant-colonels. Some municipalities, notably in Ontario, provided life insurance, and any soldier who lived within the Toronto city limits was insured for a $1,000 death benefit until six months after discharge. The Patriotic Fund paid a private's wife with three children anything from $10 to $25 extra in a large city. Pensions for dependants of the dead ranged from $480 for a private's widow to $2,700 for a brigadier-general's. Pensions for the disabled depended on the disability, but if the disability was over 50 percent, child allowance could be claimed at rates from $6 for former ranks up to lieutenant, and $10 for a lieutenant-colonel. For soldiers in hospital, the Military Hospitals Commission provided $8 a month for maintenance and $1 a day if at home, plus an allowance based on family size of up to $55 a month. With spending money and maintenance, a convalescent with a wife and six children could spend up to $93 a month.[9]

When the American Red Cross took on the CPF's family relief role for the United States, it had to define a benefit scale. By discreetly adding assigned pay to its own scale, ignoring its earlier promise not to do so, the CPF persuaded its supporters that American families would fare worse than Canadians – only $30 for a childless American wife compared to $45 in Canada; $45 for a US wife with two children compared to $57 in Canada; and $51 for a US family with four children compared to the CPF income total of $63.[10] Under pressure from Saskatchewan, the national executive had reluctantly raised the maximum allowance in the West to $45 in 1917, but that was still too little help for a woman with a large, hungry family.

Money was not a family's only need. British Columbia historian Charles Humphries describes the plight of an officer's wife, Ina Burdett-Burgess, trying to manage her husband's farm, finance their expensive house in Vancouver, and educate a wilful son at a private school. Only occasional cash from family and friends in England kept her solvent, but who, outside her immediate circle, could appreciate her stress?[11] With the best will in the world, the Patriotic Fund visitor was no substitute for a devoted or even a wayward husband. By her own standards and those of her censorious neighbours, there was often no legitimate alternative source of companionship. The months passed, turned into a year, and dragged into a second and a third. Each in her own way, soldiers' wives grew lonely. The letters came, but each day brought the fear that a final, chilling telegram would come from Ottawa: "Deeply regret inform you ..."

In 1914 and 1915 voluntary recruiting had depended, in significant part, on winning support from families. The separation allowance had been a significant gesture to win over the wives of potential recruits. Thanks to $20 a month, husbands could do both their patriotic and their manly duty. When mothers were recognized as a restraining influence on recruiting, separation allowance was cautiously extended to them. However, when Sir Robert Borden returned from Britain in April 1917, bent on conscription to fill the ranks of the CEF, costly incentives to voluntarism lapsed. Instead, as the government contemplated a prolonged war, the financial implications suggested renewed prudence and restraint.

Voluntarism in Montreal, 1917

The winter of 1916-17 marked a last desperate phase of patriotic voluntarism in Canada. At the start of 1916, after the prime minister pledged to put half a million Canadians in uniform, recruiting totals had soared, only to fizzle as warm weather approached. Few of the new battalions authorized that year filled their ranks unless they recruited older men for the Canadian Forestry Corps or the Canadian Railway Troops. Plenty of Canadians had decided to resist recruiting appeals, but French-Canadian resistance, highlighted by Henri Bourassa and his newspaper, *Le Devoir*, became a sufficient explanation to many British Canadians for any shortage of military manpower. The failings of Canada's resolutely unilingual militia organization were unknown or irrelevant to the majority of Canadians. So were arguments that Quebeckers were better employed growing food or manufacturing shells in Montreal's burgeoning munitions factories. Certainly a host of well-paid jobs in munitions and manufacturing was an effective check on recruiting, particularly in a population unmoved by appeals to Imperial patriotism.[12]

At the start of 1917, the national CPF announced its Canada-wide goal as the $12.5 million needed to support 50,000 families and 150,000 individuals.[13] On 12 January 1917, Montreal's Patriotic Fund anxiously unveiled a new campaign for mid-February. Balances were positive but, as Herbert Ames had confessed to Borden in 1915, "Lord knows what 1917 will bring." It would not bring peace, and inflation would increase the burden on the Fund's families. A larger Expeditionary Force would require larger transfers to poorer provinces. Moreover, the mood in Quebec might soon be very much worse. Conscription, only a vague threat in 1916, was approaching, possibly heralded by the National Registration cards Ottawa distributed in January. The clinching argument for the CPF drive was an imminent campaign for the Red Cross. Negotiations led to a joint campaign, with the Patriotic Fund taking five-sixths of the proceeds and the Red Cross accepting the balance.

In Montreal, fundraising mechanics were now a ritual. The branch treasurer, John W. Ross, prepared canvassing records and warned the Windsor Hotel. Acutely aware of its francophone deficiencies, the finance committee added Tancrède Bienvenu, general manager of the Banque Provinciale, and O.S. Perrault, treasurer of Imperial Tobacco. Other positions were opened to Red Cross representatives. Ames lined up the new governor general, the Duke of Devonshire, for an opening speech. The Bell Telephone Co. offered free service and Cadillac Motors provided cars "for use at the discretion of the executive." An outdoor advertising firm printed half the 10,000 posters and painted nine large signs free of charge.[14] The key tactical question was how to organize canvassers to collect a target of $1,750,000. This time, there would be fourteen English teams and "as nearly as possible an equal number of French," which, as in 1914, would work separately.[15] To equalize results, the teams – French or English – would be paired between rich and poor areas.[16] Jews, approached through Mortimer Davis, replied through David Friedman that they refused to be "segregated as a separate team" as in 1914 or ignored as in 1916, but would join existing teams.[17] J.R. Genin's Belgian team now included Italians, and, claimed the *Daily Star,* "probably" Chinese and "Syrians." For the first time a "Ladies' team" appeared, jointly headed by Mrs. Huntly R. Drummond and Mme Rosaire Thibaudeau.[18] They were assigned a target of $50,000. Ucal Dandurand and Brig.-Gen. A.E. Labelle organized the French-Canadian volunteers. In 1914 about 75 French Canadians had joined canvassing teams, and in 1916, about 180. This time, according to the *Gazette,* there were "251 men, representing every sphere of French-Canadian activity."[19]

Other changes reflected greater French influence and a desperate attempt to sustain "bonne ententism." When the Duke of Devonshire came on the evening of 9 February, French-speaking volunteers would welcome him to the Monument National.[20] J. Murray Gibbon's advertising combined the Union Jack with the tricolour of France. English readers were given the choice of supporting the Red Cross or the Iron Cross, while *La Presse* gave the alternatives as "La Croix-de-Fer ou la Croix-Rouge." Readers of *Le Devoir* escaped such sterile patriotism: their message began with a modest invitation to "ceux qui veulent s'inscrire" (those who wish to subscribe). Montreal's press, bullied into donating space, boasted that the city would surpass the $3,260,000 raised with paid ads in Toronto. J.W. McConnell's day's pay campaign became the Fund's main showpiece for French-Canadian participation, particularly after team captain Joseph Versailles pointedly insisted that French-Canadian workers, not their English-speaking employers and managers, made up the bulk of the contributors and deserved the credit. When John Best, a Conservative MP from Ontario, sneered at French-Canadian indifference to the Patriotic

Fund, it was the Ontario-born McConnell who replied, by way of the Opposition leader, Sir Wilfrid Laurier. Not only had half the $500,000 raised from workers in 1916 come from "French-Canadian workingmen and women," English and French were also working to raise another $2.5 million.[21] As the campaign approached, McConnell emphasized to the press that "over forty-five thousand French-speaking individuals have contributed, many of whom represent whole families." In his "bonne entente team," he welcomed "the readiness with which the foremen and superintendents of factories, both French and English," backed the Fund.[22]

Bonne ententism paved the way for a new visit to City Hall. Again headed by Ucal Dandurand, with former mayors Laporte and Guerin in attendance, the Patriotic Fund and Red Cross delegation presented its most French face. Flanked by controllers and aldermen, Mayor Médéric Martin could not have been more charming. "There has been mention of what Toronto has done," he declared, "of what French-Canadians should do, but that is not the question. We are all, whether French, English, Irish or any other nationality, we are all Canadians in Canada, and as such must all work hand in hand for this great undertaking."[23] A delighted deputation departed with a pledge of $1 million.

At the Monument National on 9 February, the Duke of Devonshire found the mayor, the archbishop, Senators Raoul Dandurand and T. Chase Casgrain, Judge Lafontaine, and Dr. Lachapelle on the platform. Introduced with impeccable patriotism by Victor Morin, president of the Société St-Jean-Baptiste, the duke responded in careful French. Archbishop Bruchési and Senator Dandurand were eclipsed by the rhetoric of Laval university economist Édouard Montpetit. Recalling the four draped figures around the statue of Edward VII in Phillips Square, representing Canada's four founding nations, he noted that only France was seated: "First among them, she had seized the land; she was at home ... Above, the royal arms and the Peacemaker-King, Edward VII, robed in royal dignity, extends to the crown a protective hand that the nations have learned to respect."[24] The observation drew thunderous and prolonged applause. It was a message from which both English imperialists and French-Canadian nationalists could and did draw comfort.[25]

The ensuing week was a triumph. By the second day canvassers recorded $2.1 million in cash and pledges, and in midweek McConnell won headlines in French papers by declaring that French Canadians had contributed fully half of the day's pay commitments so far. By the final banquet on Friday, their share had bounded to 62.5 percent of a total estimated at $851,393.13. Only the results of the Ladies' Team, claimed the *Gazette* ($167,980, eighth among the joint reports), were received with more enthusiasm. The final campaign total was $4,316,563. There was, William Birks proclaimed, "neither Liberal nor Conservative, French nor English,

Jew nor Gentile." To celebrate the city's official gift of $1 million, Ucal Dandurand chimed in. "When one thought of the comradeship of the English and the French soldiers," the *Daily Star* quoted him, "one wondered how anything but good comradeship could exist in this bilingual city."[26]

In light of the Ontario school crisis, barely fading in February 1917, and the looming Conscription crisis, the bonne ententism of the Patriotic Fund's third campaign had an air of the unexpected or the much-denied. For Montreal's English-speaking leaders, it was an unaccustomed but necessary recognition of a majority they normally took for granted. It had been easier, in two previous campaigns, to consider contributions from the Angus Shops or Mortimer Davis's factories as the generosity of the CPR or Imperial Tobacco, but to get the funds, McConnell had finally acknowledged the men and women at the pay wickets. Ames, Ross, and Birks had handed over a new governor general to French Montreal. Even *Le Devoir* contributed $1,828.00 in space and *La Presse* $11,073.15, second only to the *Daily Star*. From the mayor to *Le Monde Ouvrier,* there was willing participation in the campaign. Why did Mayor Martin and Premier Gouin become forthcoming? Why had French-Canadian leaders lent such energy to the campaign? There was no single reason. Adding the humanitarian Red Cross to the Patriotic Fund improved the campaign's appeal. So did the beneficiaries, lonely victims of a struggle they had not started and could not stop. Among the French-speaking leaders who spoke for the Fund, however, there was a common theme: Quebec had voluntarily done its duty and would continue to do it – voluntarily.

Across Canada, that message was ignored. Simultaneous campaigns in every city in Canada meant that each community had its own preoccupations, with no more than an occasional jealous glimpse at Canada's biggest city. Toronto boasted that it put Montreal to shame with a target of $2.5 million and pledges worth $3,258,972, or $10 for each man, woman, and child. To match McConnell's day's pay scheme, Toronto offered Bert McCreath's 50,000 Club, with each member paying a dollar a month and hundreds of tireless women volunteers to track them down.[27] Meanwhile, in their own local campaigns, Hamilton and Wentworth raised $670,000, Ottawa and Carleton, $400,000, and Quebec City, $250,000. St. Catharines's $100,000 was hardly notable but represented $12 per citizen. That was outdone by Camrose, a coal-mining town in Alberta, which raised $22 a head.

In Montreal and across Quebec, the good will of February faded fast. In April, when the postmaster general, Pierre-Édouard Blondin, and Maj.-Gen. François Lessard threw their prestige into recruiting a 258th Battalion across Quebec, they found, by a generous calculation, only eighty-seven volunteers.[28] When the Military Service Bill was announced in May, the city of Montreal defaulted on $875,000 of its pledge.[29] It was not the Fund's only unpaid pledge – Ross confessed to $953,353 in outstanding pledges by the end of the war – but it was the largest. Soon Sir Hugh Graham's *Montreal Daily Star* would editorialize that the members of the CPF's finance committee were the men to "clean out City Hall."[30] During the summer of 1917, anti-recruiting riots and disturbances spread across Montreal. Conscription in the form of the Military Service Act received royal assent on 29 August, a hot night. Five hundred young men smashed the windows at the *Gazette* and would have done the same to the *Star* if leaders had not drawn them off to the Champs de Mars for a night of fervid oratory. At midnight, police broke up the crowd and sent it home.[31]

That summer, CPF publicists boasted that "The Fund is regarded as the core and centre of the 'Entente Cordiale' between races and religions in Montreal. French and English, Roman Catholic, Protestant and Hebrew – all work together in perfect amity, both in the Office and in the District."[32] Canadians, like Montrealers, had to learn to conduct their affairs across deep chasms of difference. Across the country, CPF organizers found disturbing signs that volunteering was close to its limits in fundraising as well as recruiting. Hundreds of organizations now competed for patriotic dollars. Some were fraudulent, many were inefficient, all of them exhausted and bewildered potential donors. In Britain a War Charities Act had tried to regulate the problem by registration. After a poor woman tried to sell shoelaces to an Ontario MP on behalf of soldiers at the front, the finance minister, Sir Thomas White, followed suit in the autumn of 1917, promising an exemption for the CPF "as a matter of course."[33] By 1919 the War Charities Branch had registered 742 societies, from the Ontario Women's Christian Temperance Union to the White School Patriotic Fund of Southampton, Ontario; 455 of the organizations were IODE chapters. At least 641 of them were run by women. As of the Branch's final report on 1 April 1919, Canadian war charities apart from the CPF had raised $14 million.[34]

The Impact of Inflation

In 1915 it had been reasonable to suggest that, with income from separation allowance, assigned pay, and the CPF, many soldiers' wives were better off than they had been before the war. While the typical member of the Canadian Expeditionary Force was more likely to be a mature skilled urban tradesman than the farmer or rancher depicted by Sir Max Aitken's brilliant overseas propaganda machine, the prewar depression had cut average earnings and sometimes cancelled them altogether.[35] The depression had also curbed the price increases most Canadians had begun to notice after 1907. Indeed, the cost of living was a little lower in 1915 than it had been in 1914. If the Allied war effort had ended in triumph in the summer of

1916, as many had fondly expected, Canada would have escaped the war with little economic or political disruption, and a justified sense of having done reasonably well by its soldiers and their families. The failure of the Somme offensives wrote a very different chapter.

From the outset of the war, Ottawa had assumed that the financial burden of the war would fall on the future beneficiaries of a struggle for peace and freedom, the generations as yet unborn. The government promptly suspended the convertibility of its currency and abandoned the gold standard. Apart from additional luxury taxes and excises, Sir Robert Borden and his colleagues agreed that the costs of the war would largely be financed by borrowing. If Canada was to retain its attraction for immigrants, the minister of finance explained, it could not be allowed to become a high-tax country. After European money markets were closed to outsiders, Ottawa turned to New York – Wall Street was already the chief source of capital for France, Russia, and Great Britain – and, with considerable misgivings, to Canadian citizens. A weak bond market responded readily to a safe and potentially wealthy buyer. By 1915 Ottawa was spending more on its military institutions ($173 million) than its entire public expenditure in 1912 ($143 million).[36] Tax revenue rose from $126 million in 1913 to $197 million in 1917 and $234 million in 1918, largely because of a rapid increase in customs revenue and a new excess profits tax that yielded $13 million in 1916 and $33 million in 1918.[37]

While the CEF absorbed more than a third of a million men into its ranks, a Shell Committee, transformed into the Imperial Munitions Board (IMB) under Toronto meat-packing executive Joseph Flavelle, grew Canada's artillery shell capacity from a single government-run factory producing 340 shells a week for the annual militia artillery practice into the largest industry in Canada. Its 365 factories in 110 cities and towns employed 350,000 men and women, and exported almost 24 million shells in 1917. The IMB then branched into shipbuilding, aircraft manufacturing, chemical production, and a host of related industries.[38] Like Canada's army, munitions production was financed by debt.

As any conventional economist would recognize, this was a situation tailor-made for inflation.[39] In *Northern Enterprise,* his history of Canadian business, Michael Bliss describes the war years as "the worst roller coaster of price changes" Canadians had ever seen.[40] The roll began quite imperceptibly in the first two years of the war. *Labour Gazette* national price indexes, based on surveys in sixty cities, showed small drops in the price of several food commodities such as milk, eggs, and potatoes, plus fuel, light, and rent, between 1914 and 1915.[41] Industrial inflation caught up to consumer prices in 1916. With some regional differences but no exceptions, food prices rose that year by about 10 percent over 1914, with growing momentum in the later months. In 1917, as the author of the *Canadian Annual Review* claimed, the cost of living suddenly became "a Great War problem."[42] That year, the overall increase was about 34 percent over 1914. By 1918 the 1914 food dollar was worth about $0.65. The dozen eggs that cost $0.34 in 1914 cost $0.536 and a five-pound bag of rolled oats had risen from $0.225 to $0.40. Fuel and light that cost a family $1.90 a week in 1914 cost $2.85 in 1918. Only rents were relatively stable, rising from $4.65 to $4.89, but averages were particularly misleading when an influx of munition workers or a disaster like the Halifax Explosion transformed local housing markets. Any family forced to move faced a dramatic increase. By the end of 1917, many soldiers' families were hurting.

Challenged by a report in the *Labour Gazette* arguing that the necessary income for a family in Canada was $10 to $12 more than any soldier's family currently received from official sources, the CPF *Bulletin* responded that the numbers ignored the absent adult male member in "its" families. In fact, it claimed, the CPF allowances were "almost scientifically accurate" in measuring what was necessary. The *Bulletin* admitted the allowances were not generous: "If the Labour Department's figures are correct, it means that to enjoy luxuries a soldier's wife must forfeit what are almost necessities." Though the Fund had initially agreed to ignore a husband's $15 pay assignment as a source of family income, assigned pay suddenly became part of its calculations.[43]

Most urban Canadians heated their homes by coal, much of it imported from the notorious cartel that dominated the Pennsylvania and West Virginia mines. In the winter of 1916-17, prices soared as high as $20 a ton in Montreal. After the United States entered the war in April and launched its own industrial mobilization, prices threatened to climb even faster. Foreseeing the problem, the Montreal CPF branch negotiated a wholesale price of $10 a ton, with a $0.50 charge for bagging, and offered supplies to their clients at cost. More than 1,900 Montreal families took advantage of the deal, and even more in 1918.[44] Hamilton, Winnipeg, and some other cities followed Montreal's example.

The rising cost of living persuaded Canadians to raise their incomes. With booming times, most entrepreneurs could afford to hold back a little more for themselves and their families. Thanks to the CEF and the Imperial Munitions Board, Canadian labour was scarce and getting scarcer. Unionized workers found that even a threat of a strike would often win concessions. Union membership grew rapidly in 1917, and so did wages, as prudent employers pre-empted the temptation to organize by a timely pay hike. Meanwhile, those whose pay was set publicly, from members of parliament and cabinet ministers to members of the judiciary, were compelled to set an example of austerity. That example extended to soldiers, who of course were not organized; any concerted attempt to improve soldiers' pay would have constituted mutiny. The government could have increased military pay or raised the separation allowance, but after the Military Service Act, the main pressure point – recruitment – was gone. Overseas members of the CEF in France or Britain were largely untouched by inflation in any case. Even in Canada, soldiers generally depended on the government for their rations and accommodation. It was their families, still living on 1914 incomes, who were exposed.

Soldiers' families were not bound by military discipline, but they were not bound by much else, either. At a time when women's organizations proliferated as never before in Canada, an assertive national or even local organization for military dependants might have seemed a logical outgrowth of shared problems and common loneliness. Indeed, Helen Reid's "third responsibility" in Montreal included efforts to gather soldiers' wives by ward and district to discuss common problems and approved solutions. Montreal Catholics saw the possibilities – or the threat – of such gatherings and responded with meetings of their own. However, women did not find it easy to criticize the organization that brought them together and whose financial support might so easily be withdrawn.

Montreal's Soldiers' Wives League, with branches in Ottawa, Saint John, and Kingston, might have been an alternative and, indeed, it has been so portrayed by historian Nancy Christie.[45] The SWL's Florence Cole certainly took grievances to senior officials of the Militia Department and got results, but it may have been difficult for those officials to distinguish between the polite but assertive Mrs. Cole and her husband, Lt.-Col. Minden Cole, prominent insurance executive and former commanding officer of the Montreal Garrison Artillery.[46] Cole's predecessor as SWL president, June Busteed, was married to a leading Montreal corporation lawyer and colonel of the 3rd Victoria Rifles.[47] Formed primarily by militia officers' wives as early as 1894, the League's branches had administered much the same kind of relief program during the South African War that the Patriotic Fund did in 1914. Concerned with Serbian relief, prohibition of liquor in Quebec, and organizing an interdenominational service in 1918, the Soldiers' Wives League was not a trade union for military dependants.[48]

Eventually, however, some soldiers' wives overcame their poverty, isolation, and sense of dependence and began to organize. The 1917-18 yearbook of the National Council of Women of Canada (NCWC) reported a "large and flourishing" Soldiers' Wives Club at Cobalt that survived into the 1918-19 yearbook with hopes for "better results with their [garden] plots."[49] Another Soldiers' Wives Club affiliated to the NCWC was reported in Red Deer, Alberta.[50] A more ambitious and militant organization reported by the Brantford Local Council of Women in 1918 was the Soldiers' Associated Kith and Kin. Described as "an exceedingly large and active organization" with a Junior Association, the Kith and Kin "safeguards the welfare of our soldiers at home and abroad"[51] More precisely targeted at soldiers' dependants was the Soldiers' Wives and Mothers League, with branches in Prince Albert and Saskatoon, where the founding mother was Mrs. Walter C. Murray, wife of the president of the University of Saskatchewan.[52]

The Great War Next of Kin Association (NOKA), with branches in Winnipeg, Calgary, and Edmonton in 1916 and 1917, and in some smaller cities in 1918, was a specific response to inadequate pay and allowances. Historian Linda Kealey has found that branches in Winnipeg and Calgary were primarily organized by privates' wives, with backing from local labour and socialist women, and were soon caught up in the militant mood that would lead to the Winnipeg general strikes of 1918 and 1919, and the One Big Union. The Calgary founder was Jean McWilliams, a prewar immigrant from Scotland who had worked as a cleaning woman and police matron to support herself and her two children in her husband's absence. She bought a boarding house, and learned her socialism from talking with her boarders.[53] According to the Winnipeg labour newspaper, the *Voice,* Calgary's NOKA demanded equal pensions for privates and officers, free vocational training for soldiers' children, price controls, higher taxes on the rich, and disfranchisement for enemy aliens, as well as increased pensions and allowances for soldiers' wives, widows, and other dependants.[54] "Make the pay of the private soldier at least equal to that of the civilian," argued Mrs. Adam Shortt. "Inaugurate, in short, a truly democratic method of carrying on the war, and there will be no slackers."[55]

The Calgary women spread their organization to Medicine Hat, Lethbridge, and MacLeod, but the Edmonton NOKA stole a march by seeking incorporation through Alberta's first woman MLA, Roberta McAdams, a military nurse elected by overseas soldiers in 1917.[56] Fearful of losing their name, the Calgary leaders demanded an audience with Premier Arthur Sifton and his cabinet, denounced the Edmonton women as mere officers' wives intent on social and charitable activities, and claimed the NOKA title on the basis of age, class, and size. Despite, and possibly because of, their backing from Alberta's new Non-Partisan League, Sifton did nothing. Talks between the rival organizations failed, and both survived amid bad feeling.[57] As Kealey acknowledges, most next-of-kin organizations resembled Edmonton's service-oriented club, not Calgary's militantly pro-labour and socialist association.

When soldiers' wives and mothers met, their common goal was to win the war and bring home their men. Vancouver's Local Council of Women reported to the NCWC in 1917 that it had endorsed a resolution from the South Vancouver Soldiers' and Sailors' Wives and Mothers Association "requesting the Government to enforce conscription and so help our boys to end this war."[58] The Association was not mentioned a year later though, as we shall see, it was certainly active. An Ontario-centred association that was soon closely chaperoned by wealthy benefactors was the Associated Kin of the CEF. Started in London in 1917 by Gordon Wright, whose wife had been a leading prewar peace activist, the Toronto branch was formed with lawyer J. Hamilton Cassels as president and prominent financier Aemilius Jarvis as treasurer. Its goals included securing recruits, protecting the home interests of absent men, and recognizing mothers who had lost sons overseas. It was, commented the *Canadian Annual Review,* "neither so effective nor so strong as the G.W.V.A."[59]

More affluent women thought that women who lacked money could follow Jean McWilliams' example and earn some. That was the anti-inflation strategy eventually espoused by the Patriotic Fund, at least for childless wives. From the outset, as we have seen, branches had debated and then supported the supply of charwomen and domestic servants by ignoring a wife's personal earnings in assessing her need. That policy became even more patriotic and overt with the expansion of the wartime munitions industry and the call from the Imperial Munitions Board for thousands of women to enter the grimy, noisy, dangerous, and wholly unfamiliar world of metal manufacturing.[60]

Contemporary feminism urged the rights of women to be all that they could be; however, its powerful maternal strain condemned anything that separated a mother from her children. On few subjects did Miss Reid and other women of the Patriotic Fund speak with more categorical assurance than the necessity of the maternal presence in the child's home. Their own mothers may have abandoned them to a succession of nurses, nannies, maids, and governesses, but the scientific study of motherhood had led them to the axiom that the child abandoned was the child who died. Maternal responsibility had been the unspoken argument for a separation allowance and for the supplementary contribution of the Patriotic Fund. In a nation that now faced the loss of more thousands of its bravest and best young men, motherhood was also a patriotic cause. However, it did not seem to provide Fund officials with a sufficient argument for matching the rising cost of living with more generous income. After all, donors were hurting too. As for the government, it tackled the cost of living problem by appointing W.F. O'Connor, the Halifax lawyer who had drafted the 1914 War Measures Act, as cost of living commissioner and ordering him to report on the problem. Within weeks, he had begun to stalk his quarry.

Back in Canada after an emotional tour of the death and devastation his munitions had helped to wreak, Joseph Flavelle was honoured with a baronetcy in 1917 for turning Canada into a major munitions producer. Henceforth Flavelle and his male heirs would bear the title "Sir." When he summoned a meeting of Imperial Munitions Board subcontractors, he found in them little of his elevated patriotic mood. Instead, they grumbled about their production difficulties, delays, the demands of labour, and their own shrinking profit margins. An indignant Flavelle answered their whining with an intensely emotional description of the courage and sacrifice he had seen in the front lines in France. Out of many lively phrases, one stuck in his audience's minds and in historical memory: "Profits?" cried Sir Joseph in answer to a complaining contractor. "Send profits to the hell where they belong."[61] Some in Flavelle's audience wondered whether Sir Joseph had lost his mind; others outside the room believed that the devout Toronto financier had laid his expert finger on the cost-of-living problem. Prices rose because rich and powerful people wanted to get richer and exploited wartime scarcity. The soaring cost of living was due to profiteering. Sir Joseph's phrase was so satisfying to ordinary Canadians that he might well have deserved further honours.

Unfortunately, only weeks later, Flavelle himself was fingered by W.F. O'Connor. His meat-packing firm, William Davies, had made a five-cent profit on each of the millions of pounds of Canadian bacon sold to the British Army. Worse, had the company pumped the bacon full of water to increase the weight? Flavelle's hypocritical distinction between the profits of other men and his own fed the bitter, suspicious, and egalitarian mood of Canada in 1917.[62] The specific charges were false or grossly exaggerated, but there was no doubt that the managerial skills Sir Joseph patriotically contributed to munitions production had given him a hugely profitable wartime bacon business. As "His Lardship" and "the Baron of Bacon," Flavelle became the symbol for a crusade against hereditary titles for Canadians carried to a triumphant conclusion in 1919 by Kingston MP and future CPF national secretary William F. Nickle.

Buoyed by fundraising results in 1917 that had far exceeded past results and even new targets, the Fund executive cautiously allowed branches to increase their payments by raising the maximum permissible allowance.[63] Originally set at $30 in the east and $40 in the western provinces, the Fund's executive increased the maximum in April 1917 to $45 and, by the end of 1918, to $50 anywhere in Canada. Some branches conformed and raised rates; others held the line. In January 1919 the Fund ruled that a family with more than seven children could go over the $50 limit with an extra $3 per extra child.[64] It was hardly luxury.

When Helen Reid spoke to American audiences in 1917, one of her concerns was that the United States would undermine the CPF by funding family support through the government. To an audience of social workers, she warned that the cost of administration and of providing needlessly generous grants would be enormous. She warned her audience of social workers in Philadelphia that their role would vanish: "None of the personal interest and friendly help which we of the Fund have found so precious and so real in cementing and binding together all classes, races and religions of our community, could or would be given by an impersonal, soulless Government. Our soldiers' families are entitled to something more than money, which by itself can never replace the father or son absent at the front. To the loneliness and helplessness of the families are also added dangers and temptations which no Government Department can guard against."[65]

In Canada's Parliament, opposition criticism of the Patriotic Fund had begun slowly. After all, prominent Liberals had been involved in its creation and the Liberal governments that had won most provinces by 1917 were as much involved in the Fund as were Conservatives. Leaving a key role in compensating soldiers to a private corporation hardly answerable to Parliament was beginning to seem questionable when the pay scales were patently inadequate. Still, when Frank Oliver, Liberal MP for Edmonton and publisher of the Edmonton *Bulletin,* opened his attack on the Fund on 20 January 1916, he stood virtually alone. The Fund, he charged, was unfair to soldiers' families by leaving them to the mercy of its discretion, and it was unfair to contributors because of the wide variation in what people in similar communities actually gave. People in Barrie, Ontario, had averaged $0.28, in Collingwood, $1.12, and in the Windsor suburb of Walkerville, $11.18. The reason was no mystery to Oliver; local employers had summoned their men and compelled a donation: "Of course they do not have to contribute but they can lose their positions if they do not contribute."[66]

When George Graham, a Liberal from Guelph, followed Oliver's theme on 1 February, he worried sympathetically about waste and confusion in CPF fundraising and recalled that he and a cabinet minister had been enlisted to speak for rival patriotic organizations. More serious was the feeling that the Patriotic Fund was distributed in an aura of charity: "I know families who are proud in spirit, and entitled to be proud in spirit, for they are among nature's noble men and noble women though in ordinary circumstances. Ladies with the best intentions, with a heart bubbling over to do something, would visit these homes, and without knowing it, would leave the impression that they were peddling out a charitable pittance to some person who for some fault of their own was on the municipality, or the Government."[67]

When Parliament began debating conscription in July 1917, the possibility that the Patriotic Fund was a disincentive to recruiting got a brief workout from a New Brunswick Liberal, A.B. Copp. In a diversionary motion, he proposed that the Military Service Act be deferred "until such adequate provision has been made for the dependants of soldiers enlisted for overseas as will remove the necessity of raising money by public subscription for their support." This invited fellow Liberal and Patriotic Fund critic Frank Oliver to table a CPF pamphlet instructing soldiers' wives on how to spend their allowance. Copp's motion was defeated by 115 votes to 36, but even the Fund's official historian acknowledged that the pamphlet's wording was "simple."[68]

From being above reproach, at least among the country's opinion leaders, by 1917 the Patriotic Fund had become controversial. The Fund's seeming indifference to the plight of families caught in a cost-of-living spiral reflected its class bias at a time when the unexpectedly added sacrifices of a prolonged war had to be equal sacrifices. Three years into the war, was it fair that soldiers' families depended on a charity for their daily bread? Why not increase pay and separation allowance, at least for lower-ranking soldiers, and abandon the Patriotic Fund? If that meant taxing the incomes of wealthy profiteers, so much the better. Conscription of manpower should be accompanied by conscription of wealth. Instead of raising funds from charity, the CPF should be funded by a tax on Canadian incomes.

Almost from the outset of the war, several Ontario counties had met their Patriotic Fund obligations by levying a rate on property owners.[69] Alberta, Saskatchewan, and British Columbia assumed the administrative costs of the Fund. Recognizing that most counties of the province could not be organized for the Patriotic Fund, the New Brunswick government provided almost $250,000 in 1915. In 1916 it debated organizing a compulsory assessment of municipalities, and in 1917 it did so. The provincial executive of the CPF was assigned the responsibility for apportioning a levy that ranged from $150,000 for the city of Saint John to $484 for the town of Sunny Brae. "This method of financing the Fund in New Brunswick," reported Morris, "was regarded by the provincial executive as so satisfactory that a similar course was pursued in 1918."[70]

Embarrassed that its provincial branch of the CPF had failed to be self-supporting in 1914 and 1915, the Saskatchewan government came up with a monthly contribution of just over $55,000 for the balance of the war. Not everyone approved. When Saskatchewan's Provincial Equal Franchise Board met in Regina on 4 September 1917, it bluntly resolved that "the rates of pay given to Canadian privates and the separation allowance [be] raised so that there will be no necessity for a patriotic fund."[71]

After three successive CPF campaigns, each struggling to meet higher targets, Albertans were weary and exasperated. Organizing in rural areas was particularly difficult, and war-weariness led campaigners to focus less on donors than on those who refused. The 1917 executive meeting of the South Alberta CPF on 2 August produced an unexpected consensus in favour of taxation, with the main debate being whether the money should come from Ottawa or the province. The majority preferred Ottawa, but when the CPF's national executive insisted on continuing voluntary campaigns, both Alberta branches looked to their provincial legislature. The result was Alberta's Patriotic Tax Act, allowing municipalities, at their discretion, to levy a special rate to be paid to the Patriotic Fund in Alberta.[72] The provincial government itself promised $800,000 for 1918, paid equally to the North and South Alberta branches on a monthly basis. Donations then notably fell off.

Turbulence across the Mountains

In no province did the Patriotic Fund become more contentious than in British Columbia. Perhaps that was because the ideological polarization of west coast politics had begun early: in 1902 the province was the first part of the British Empire to elect two avowed Socialists to its legislature. The prewar depression had gone deepest in BC, and lasted longest. For a full year prior to the outbreak of war in 1914, much of the province's militia had been stationed at Nanaimo to overawe coal miners whose strike had turned violent when, as usual, the owners had introduced strikebreakers. When war came, miners had joined up, in part to feed their families. They had paused only to ensure that "enemy aliens," some of them hired as strikebreakers, were securely interned. By switching more of Canada's trade to Britain and Europe, the war only deepened the economic depression in the province and heightened the general misery.[73]

At the same time, the provincewide depression did little to cut the highest cost of living in Canada. Elsewhere the CPF might claim to be a little more generous than absolutely necessary, but no such claim was justified in BC. Because conditions had already reduced many families to accepting relief, there may have been more of the hard edge of charity among the Patriotic Fund's relief committees. An anonymous soldier's wife, cited by the Federation of Labour's *British Columbia Federationist,* complained of worrying from month to month "as to whether her 'patriotic', as it is generally termed, would be reduced" or being summoned to the office "at a stated time to be subjected to a 'gruelling' [sic] and prying into her private affairs which is sometimes the prelude to a reduction." She had money in the bank when she applied, and therefore was kept waiting for three weeks. The CPF allowance, she insisted, was part of her husband's income, and investigators had no more right to pry into how she spent her money than she had to inquire into their spending:

> No decent-minded woman likes to think of having to take charity and that's what we are made to feel it is very often. Our men are working 24 hours a day, 7 days a week. Are we not entitled to a comfortable living when they are doing this? We know they are fighting for their country, but what constitutes "their country"? – their wives and

kiddies and homes – that is what they are fighting for deep down in their hearts. And while they are fighting for their own homes, they are also doing it for the other fellow who has not gone. And this includes the committee of the Patriotic Fund.[74]

Hard times had helped British Columbia generate the highest proportion of voluntary enlistment to population of any Canadian province. Out of just under 400,000 residents in the 1911 census (probably closer to 450,000 by 1914), the province dispatched a total of 50,000 men to the CEF plus 2,000 British reservists. Until 1917 the province sustained six battalions in the Canadian Corps, four of them from Vancouver.[75] In return, economically battered British Columbia was one province the national CPF was sure it would have to help. Instead, the province's competing Patriotic Fund organizations raised $3,352,257 and remained self-sufficient until the end of 1915. In September 1915 Ames himself went to Victoria to meet the provincial executive and assure them that, provided British Columbians made an adequate effort, "The position of soldiers' dependants in the province would be in no way prejudiced or affected if the subscriptions fell short of the requirements."[76] There was more than flattery in Ames's message. Isolated amid their mountains into three major rival CPF organizations and over 200 small ones, British Columbians were united only in their suspicion that nothing good would ever reach them from Ottawa, while Ames was persuaded that the local organization was far from efficient. Through diplomacy, he managed to win a salaried appointment for Fred Nation, an energetic full-time paid provincial fundraiser who just happened to be a local director of Ames-Holden.[77] The results were rapid. At the end of 1915, British Columbia accepted a fundraising target of $600,000, $475,000 of it from Vancouver. By the end of 1916 the CPF had raised $1,059,249, more than half of it – $542,650 – outside the two major cities. Ames recognized that Nation deserved the credit, but the BC organization credited the province's mining companies for borrowing Montreal's day's pay scheme and applying it implacably to their miners. A day's pay once a month allowed Trail's 4,000 people to contribute $99,440.23, or almost $25.00 per capita, while Silverton, with only 800 citizens, surpassed all others at $43.00 per person. For once Vancouver and Victoria were quite overshadowed.[78]

Among thousands of employees committed to day's pay schemes across Canada were provincial government employees. They were an easy target: though poorly paid, they owed their jobs to political patronage. Their work was seldom onerous but, as "servants of the Queen," they had no rights. Their fellow citizens alternately envied and scorned them. British Columbia's deputy game wardens were typical. They had been signed up for a day's pay a month in December 1915. Ralph Smith, a former labour leader who now served as provincial treasurer in a new Liberal government, solemnly reminded all provincial employees of their duty. Giving up a day's pay might seem impossible in some cases, Smith acknowledged, but the sacrifice had to be measured against "the right of those fighting for our liberties at the front to the knowledge that their dependants are at least free from the cares of want."[79]

Collecting from deputy game wardens seemed to raise few problems. As local leaders in their small communities, some wardens were already involved in the fund. Their chief concern was to get local recognition for their contributions. At Nicola, Geoffrey Lodwick gave $5 a month to the Merritt branch and his wife was president of the local Red Cross.[80] At Elko, C.J. Lewis strongly favoured the check-off but he needed "documentary proof" to show CPF collectors in Fernie that he was a "bona fide subscriber." T.L. Thacker in Hope was willing to give more – even $10 a month – if it was credited in Hope.[81] Such requests seemed easy to grant, but the policy was administered by clerks in Victoria who wanted no complications or extra paperwork. Nor, like other employers, did the provincial government want to dilute its appearance of generosity.

For some game wardens, with large families and inflation already biting in the province with Canada's highest cost of living, a full day's pay was indeed a burden. A.A. Ward had promised a dollar a month but, he complained, living costs in Cranbrook were already 20 to 40 percent higher than on the coast, and he was going deeper into debt monthly. "I expect further heavy family expense this year," he explained to his superior, "but won't bother you with my problems as you likely have enough of your own unless you would like an accounting of my financial standing."[82] H.B Dawley at Courtney was resigned but, he confessed, he could not afford it. "I think its the same elsewhere as hear [sic]," he offered in a familiar lament, "but what I was going to say is this a person is called on two or three times every week to give some money to one of these funds and then they have all kinds of red cross entertainments or something of that kind and ladys come to you to buy Tickets so you see it all costs something besides the cost of living."[83] Facing termination, the deputy warden at Lillooet tried to save his last paycheque intact. He was too late.[84]

The convenience of a monthly check-off was unquestionable. It caught every worker on the payroll but taxed them according to their income. It was voluntary because individuals were free to approach their employer and ask to be exempted for a period or permanently. Of course, as Ward hinted, a man might be reluctant to share the secrets of his family's finances with others, least of all an employer. But given the state of the BC economy, a worker might be even more reluctant to draw an employer's negative attention, particularly if he was an immigrant from central Europe or Asia. In wartime, local nativism had switched targets from Asians to "enemy aliens," and the victims of local suspicions were often hurried to internment camps from Nanaimo to the Crowsnest Pass.

Unlike provincial civil servants, BC miners, loggers, and construction workers had unions eager to remedy and even to exploit grievances. Lacking any of the structures or procedures for collective bargaining they would gain in the Second World War, labour organizations survived on the political cunning, economic opportunism, and, when all else failed, the ideology of their leaders. In British Columbia, they faced some of the most powerful and arrogant employers in the country, but on one issue, Asian immigration, unions shared common ground with the majority of the province's European and even Aboriginal population. Where the employers stood on the issue was no secret: they wanted cheap labour to counter the high costs of extracting the wealth of a rich but remote region. Laden as it was with racial bigotry, the immigration question embarrassed later generations of labour apologists, who struggled to find other issues. To contemporaries, however, immigration created a class issue that pitted the bosses against the masses of British Columbia. If the bosses favoured the Patriotic Fund, the CPF, ineluctably, become part of class politics.

It had not been that way in 1914. Formed in 1889 as a by-product of the local Nine Hours movement, the Vancouver Trades and Labour Council (VTLC) had achieved more respectability than some of its more militant members liked.[85] On 11 August 1914, when Vancouver's mayor convened the Board of Trade, Red Cross Society, IODE, Local Council of Women, and the Conservative and Liberal clubs to organize the Vancouver Citizen's War Fund, the president of the VTLC was present. J.H. McVety, a Canadian-born machinist, veteran socialist, and long-term labour politician, solemnly reported back to his members on the Patriotic Fund, Vancouver's Home Guard, and the civic War Relief Committee.[86]

Labour's view was that relief funds must apply to all in distress, whether or not they were relatives of men who had gone to war. Relief was certainly needed. After two years of mass unemployment, claimed McVety, relief workers had found appalling misery in the city and its South Vancouver suburbs. Some who canvassed for funds discovered circumstances that led them to dig into their own pockets.[87] The VTLC's Helena Gutteridge reported on unemployed women, many of them penniless and hungry. She persuaded the Local Council of Women to create a Women's Employment League.[88] Some soldiers' families were so desperately poor, McVety reported, that fourteen wives had applied for relief funds before their husband's signature was dry on the enlistment roll. Clearly men were willing to risk a soldier's death to feed their families and wives were desperate enough to agree.[89]

Generally, Vancouver and BC labour seem to have found little to criticize in the Patriotic Fund or the treatment of soldiers' families during the first years of the war. The relief crisis among its own members and among Vancouver's working poor was sufficient preoccupation. One way to find jobs for unemployed workers was to send them to Britain to take wartime jobs in munitions factories, and some 1,700 men eventually crossed the Atlantic. No doubt there was a British demand for labour, but Canadian newspapers significantly exaggerated the wages a man could expect to earn.[90] The British had agreed to pay five shillings a week until a man found work, leaving him perhaps a shilling a week to send home. Once employed, rates for new workers were about two pounds a week, leaving about $3 for families left behind in Canada. When the Canadians learned that British workers, forced to live too far from home to commute, easily got an extra half-crown a day, they were furious.

It took months before the British Board of Trade, the UK Ministry of Munitions, and Canada's Department of Labour agreed to pay Canadian dependants a weekly allowance of seventeen shillings and six pence, or $4.25. Meanwhile, like soldiers, the "mechanics" were accused of failing to make proper provision for their families. This set the Labour Council in motion, with McVety and Gutteridge pressuring Ottawa for action and trying to interest local patriotic societies in the women's plight.[91] Though a separation allowance for Canadian munition workers was approved in November 1915, the VTLC was still pleading the case of munition workers' families a year later.[92]

Much had changed by 1917. The rising cost of living was hardly a new problem, particularly on the west coast, but suddenly it had become "an issue." That coincided with the return of prosperity to British Columbia. As Vancouver historian Alan Morley argues, the best proof of a boom was a series of major and successful strikes in the spring and summer, from BC Sugar Refineries in April to BC Electric for a month in June and July 1917. Meanwhile, in Vancouver rents allegedly rose by 20 percent.[93]

On 23 February 1917 the *Federationist* launched a campaign against the CPF. If the ruling classes could deal with soldiers' dependants on the basis of charity in time of war, what would stop them from leaving workers' families to charity in time of peace? "And the most impudent and insulting part of the whole precious scheme lies in the fact that at least a large portion of this delectable fund is wrung from poorly paid wage workers themselves and by a process that savors strongly of blackmail," the paper wrote. If men and women could not hold even poorly paid jobs "unless they come through at periodical intervals for the 'fund,'" what else could it be called? The answer was for the government to pay adequate wages: "At a time when millions of dollars are being wrestled from the government by big and little grafters of all types, it is rather unseemly that soldiers' dependants should have to suffer the humiliation of a miniature inquisition in order to receive what should be theirs by rights."[94]

The *Federationist* headlined an even more forceful complaint from Frank Edwards, an ex-longshoreman and recently wounded returned soldier. Edwards was outraged that his wife, "Lilooet Jane," had been cut off the Fund, apparently because she had saved money and put it in the bank. Where was that fact on the blotter the CPF had issued him as "Facts for the Canadian Soldier to Know"? "Please don't weary us with recitations of possible misconduct of my wife," said Edwards. "Remember you are running a Patriotic Fund, not a Scandal shop."[95]

Demonstrating that the money was turned into charity doled out haphazardly by heartless officials to helpless women and children ennobled a cause that might otherwise seem unpatriotic or even selfish. When the CPF insisted that its grants were allotted like any other pay, the *Federationist* answered it was simply not true: "And the difference is the crux of the whole trouble. Neither the Separation allowance nor the assigned Pay is subject to the whim of nose-poking investigators, glorified private detectives, society-lady supervisors or the 'interpretations' and 'decisions' of a coterie of citizens however well intentioned."[96]

By March 1917 the Labour Council had found a specific stick to beat the Patriotic Fund with. In January C.H. Bonnor, secretary of the Vancouver CPF, had warned a recipient, Mrs. Elizabeth "R," that to receive her cheque, she had to show up monthly with proof she had paid $10 on her mortgage with the Dow Fraser Trust Company. Was the Patriotic Fund acting as a collection agency for a rapacious trust company? Never, responded Bonnor: "The National Executive takes the view, and rightly so, that a woman must not live off her landlord, and the Canadian Patriotic Fund also." Either Mrs. R should pay the equivalent of a fair rent, or be considered the full owner and rich enough not to need a full grant. In fact, the VTLC insisted, the mortgagee had died in California and the Dow Fraser firm wanted the property. The woman was being harassed while her only advisor "was thousands of miles away in his country's service." A husband might have reminded her that she benefited from war relief acts for the protection of a soldier's property. Instead, pressured by the CPF's Bonnor, Mrs. R had gone to Dow Fraser. Given the alternative of abandoning her winter fuel supply, she had signed a quit claim. With a desirable property in hand, Dow Fraser generously allowed her to stay until the end of the war for only $5 a month. Based on an eight-week investigation of the case, a March meeting of the VTLC voted fifty-one to two to limit its support for the CPF to four months, pending a federal investigation, "and we further instruct our membership that on or after 1 December 1917, to refuse further support to the Patriotic Fund."[97]

In March Vancouver newspapers announced a meeting on 2 April to form a "Soldiers' and Sailors' Wives and Mothers' Association" with, in addition to general welfare, the unexpectedly practical purpose "that those desiring to do so may secure employment as fruit pickers during the coming season." Local fruit growers, lacking harvest labour, had appalled BC public opinion by petitioning for the right to import Chinese workers to save their crop. Mobilized by the IODE, the YWCA, and Mrs. Janet Kemp, patriotic young women willing to spend nine-hour days toiling in local orchards were an alternative. Soldiers' wives were one source; university co-eds were another. One result was an organization with an even bigger mouthful of a name, the Canadian Association of Soldiers' and Sailors' Mothers and Wives League of the British Army and Navy, with Mrs. Kemp as president.[98] In addition to recruiting harvesters, the Mothers and Wives sent the prime minister a resolution urging him to double soldiers' pay to $2.50 a day and to raise officers "on actual service to whatever amount deemed wise."[99]

Two weeks later on 16 April, the VTLC organized its "mass meeting" of soldiers' wives and dependants to denounce the administration of the CPF and to demand that Ottawa pay the money as wages. The *British Columbia Federationist* reported the women at its meeting as "thoroughly disgusted with the professional 'charity' methods of the Canadian Patriotic Fund committee," but most of the speakers were men. R. Parm Pettipiece urged women to fight for a principle: high enough wages for soldiers to make proper family support possible. Munition workers were well paid; why not soldiers? Getting to the point that bothered labour, he pointed to workers at the Britannia Mine who had to contribute to the CPF or quit. Under the guidance of the Rev. Dr. Charles Cameron, the women organized themselves as a "Soldiers' Wives and Dependants Protective League."

By September the labour council's league had quarrelled with Mrs. Kemp's league, and Janet Kemp was denounced in the press and among wives for recruiting fruit pickers for her own orchard. In the midst of a turbulent meeting, Mrs. Kemp refused to resign and abruptly closed proceedings by falling in a faint.[100] Her organization survived to be registered with the NCWC under the proud title of "Wives, Mothers and Widows of Great Britain's Heroes," under the presidency of Mrs. J.C. Kemp at 23 Broadway West.[101] The VTLC organization under Mrs. Jean K. Macken survived a schism led by a Mrs. M. Fink because, according to a reporter, Mrs. Fink "did not offer the suggestion politely."[102]

The actions by the Vancouver Trades and Labour Council and exposure of the "Mrs. R" case were no doubt embarrassing to the local CPF but, considering the real sources of Fund financing, labour resentment in the rest of British Columbia was more disturbing. At Nanaimo a prominent activist, Joe Naylor, spent May Day regaling miners and their families with descriptions of their employers as "Kaisers of the Cumberland" with their Prussian methods.[103] In August miners in Sandon met to warn that any deduction for the Patriotic Fund without the donor's signed consent would be considered "unfair." Frank Botha, financial secretary of the Sandon local, added a warning that any discrimination by the employer would be fought to the bitter end. When they opened their August pay packets and saw the deduction, the night shift at the Slocan Star mine walked out. Many miners, reported the *Federationist,* were of Austrian and Italian origin.[104] A prompt and predictable response, published in the Victoria *Colonist* and echoed by sheaves of venomous letters in police files, warned "Gentlemen of foreign extraction" that they should not be lulled by the "foolish, easygoing way in which they have been looked after in this country":

> It is obvious that if the authorities would take every able bodied white man of a certain age and draft them into the army for fighting purposes, and that is a square deal, then there is nothing unfair about drafting each bohunk into a sort of industrial army and making them subservient to some sort of military law, which would justify a poke in the slats with a bayonet unless the said bohunks worked for a soldier's wage, but in the comparative safety of our different mines or industries or such work where they would be the most useful.[105]

At Trail, Consolidated Mining and Smelting produced twenty to fifty tons of zinc a day, mostly sold to the Imperial Munitions Board. The local manager, Selwyn Blaylock, faced Ginger Goodwin, the local secretary of the Western Federation of Miners. Blaylock gave way on the CPF check-off: contributions were personal, and smeltermen could make their intentions known at the bank. Next payday, as eighty-five men lined up, both Blaylock and Goodwin were on hand. The manager proceeded to explain how economically and efficiently the Fund was managed. Then Blaylock addressed Goodwin: "He was there to hear any man say otherwise," a reporter recorded, "and would proceed to knock him down."[106] A few months later, Goodwin was shot dead as a fugitive from the Military Service Act and, his biographer claims, as a victim of Blaylock's hostility. At Greenwood, militant miners intended to follow Sandon's example and walk out, but they were persuaded to follow the VTLC and give the government until the end of the year:

> In their opinion the collection and administration of the fund was entirely wrong, that the man who was willing but can ill afford, may continue to pay, while the

unwilling one, though perhaps well able, has a clear option. That the only way to have a fund adequate and satisfactory to all, is for it to be handled on a compulsory taxation basis, which will not discriminate; that the proper office for such a fund is either the Dominion or the provincial house, that we notify you of our intention to cease contributing on 1 January 1918, therefore giving you some time to inaugurate some other method, and prevent the possible hardship from being imposed upon the recipients of the fund.[107]

Such wording, courageous sounding yet reasonable, was widely echoed in BC mining communities and by the end of the year had even been endorsed by Victoria's moderate Capital City Labour Council.

Criticism of the Patriotic Fund was not limited to labour activists. In February 1916 the reeve of working-class South Vancouver had urged the prime minister to support soldiers' families by taxation, not by public generosity.[108] The *Vancouver Daily World* reported "hearty applause" from the Rev. Richmond Craig's Presbyterian congregation when he suggested in early May 1917 that the CPF be nationalized and managed by a government commission.[109] At a Win-the-War rally held in South Vancouver in October, a Mrs. Gardiner was a platform speaker on behalf of soldiers' wives and dependants. If Herbert Ames was right that only a quarter of the CPF's funds came from the rich, then the poor had given $15 million, which was unfair. That was the cue for a Mrs. Robinson to demand that soldiers get enough pay that their families would not need to seek charity.[110]

Once it was organized, the Great War Veterans' Association also joined the critics. At its 1918 BC convention in New Westminster, the local GWVA demanded that Ottawa raise the money to rescue soldiers' dependants from "the taint of charity." Delegates from Fernie and Victoria disagreed, but Sgt.-Maj. Jimmy Robinson brought the convention around with a speech demanding equal pay and benefits for all, "for Canada's army is a citizen army drawn from all ranks of the community."[111]

The Fund's defenders, on the other hand, were headed by British Columbia's lieutenant governor, Frank Barnard. Even with a new War Income Tax, introduced as a form of "conscripting wealth," 90 percent of Canadians were untouched by federal taxation. The tax fell on individuals with an annual income over $1,500 and on families earning more than $3,000 a year. The Patriotic Fund, Barnard claimed, involved everyone: "The Government is not undertaking this work. Therefore, the people must."[112] Potentially, the Fund's best argument might have been that it could bypass the bureaucratic rules that tied governments in knots. Take the plight of Mrs. Busst, a Vancouver woman who had raised four children after her husband deserted her. Two sons joined up and sent her their assigned pay, but when she fell sick, that was not enough to support her and the two remaining children. Could she have separation allowance? Yes, said the Militia Department, if she had proof of her husband's death. The regulations were clear, but the demand was impossible. How could she know where her husband had gone? Only "the Patriotic" was free to help her, if it chose to do so.[113] Of course, Mrs. Busst's case and many others were not public property, and those who complained of their treatment by the Fund were not always compelled to tell the whole story.

The "Patriotic" under Attack

Meanwhile in the summer of 1917 in Ottawa, the government was in the throes of trying to organize its survival in the face of punishing casualties on the Western Front, Quebec's outrage at the Military Service Act, and the quietly throbbing problem of imminent railway bankruptcy. With help from a Military Voters Act enfranchising soldiers and a Wartime Elections Act that replaced votes for citizens from enemy countries naturalized since 1903 with votes for soldiers' wives and female relatives, Borden found it easier to form a Union government with pro-conscription Liberals. Partly as a gesture to newly enfranchised women and also for administrative convenience, separation allowance for privates was increased to $25 a month.[114] The Patriotic Fund would simply have to manage. By the autumn, the prospects for further fundraising across Quebec and even in Montreal were bleak, and at the CPF offices, the word from British Columbia was exasperating.

Labour militancy and criticism of the Patriotic Fund was not restricted to British Columbia. As early as 1915 Alberta farm activists had called for a tax-supported CPF. In November 1916 a mass meeting at the Bijou Theatre in Edmonton had reflected resentment of the Patriotic Fund and its "semi-forced contributions" of 5 percent from stenographers earning $15 a week or men supporting families on less than $90 a month.[115] Edmonton's *Nutcracker* denounced the Patriotic Fund as "a relic of barbarism ... It reminds me of the old scheme, in the backwoods days, when a wagon went around among the neighbours picking up odds and ends for a family which had had the misfortune to get burned out. Here is a nation fighting for its life, and the support of the widows and orphans of the men who gave their lives – their all – is left to the cold and careless hand of charity."[116]

Alberta's Non-Partisan League took early aim at the wealthy. J.C. Knight returned to Drumheller as a wounded veteran, his socialism intensified by the war. It was no mystery to him why the head of the Ames-Holden boot and shoe company also headed the Patriotic Fund. "The connection between the Fund and the Manufacturers' Association is quite apparent," he advised the *Alberta Non-*

Partisan: "I have held, and the conviction remains, that the organization of the Patriotic Fund was only a move by the manufacturers to side-step an income tax."[117]

Calgary radicals did not have to create a suitable next-of-kin association; it existed, if it could protect its name from the officers' wives in Edmonton, and its platform extended to widows and orphans as well as wives and children. "The rights of small nations are paralleled in Canada by the rights of war-orphaned children," explained the *Nutcracker*, "and the mothers are going to fight for these rights at home: unequal pensions for equal service, and charity instead of hard-earned remuneration are not considered to be good for democracy – for the Next-of-Kin will seek to rectify these."[118] Launching a fight with the officers' wives who led the Edmonton Next-of-Kin may have been an ill-advised start to their campaign, but others argued that the class war always started close to home.

With conscription, class war was not necessarily a far-fetched criticism of Canada's war effort. If the state could take a man's body for the army, why not his fortune to support that army? If the state compelled a man to serve, then it was "the duty of the State to make full and ample provision for the widows, orphans and dependants of the soldier, rather than make them 'dependants' on charity."[119] Ames's best argument, that the CPF could adjust its allowances to such grounds of need as family size, struck his labour critics as irrelevant. As an employer, did Ames pay his workers according to the size of their family?

By 1917 the pensions administered by the new Board of Pension Commissioners took account of the number of children in a soldier's family; so could a federally administered allowance board. By the end of that year calling for an end to the Patriotic Fund had become a commonplace of labour rallies across Canada, from lumber workers in The Pas, Manitoba, to Toronto dressmakers. Concern and even animosity over the private management of soldiers' families was apparent in letters to the prime minister from mayors, businessmen, farmers, and even Sir Lomer Gouin, the Liberal but quite conservative premier of Quebec.[120]

The response of the Canadian Patriotic Fund to the sudden thunder of criticism was that of a good soldier under fire: lie low, keep calm, and remember that enemies do what enemies must. The Patriotic would, sooner or later, be attacked by the unpatriotic. The righteous would be condemned by the unrighteous. Writing after the war but in full memory of the hostile response, Philip Morris recalled the "marked hostility" suddenly manifested by BC miners to "the voluntary method" of contributing to the Fund: "To what extent this hostility among the men themselves was earnest is not known, nor can the sincerity of their demands for taxation be verified. As a poll tax had already been imposed by the provincial Government that avenue was practically closed and it was doubtless quite apparent to the more intelligent of the miners that no other system of taxation was likely to fall upon them and their fellows. The miners were largely of foreign nationality, while their unions were generally officered by men of alien birth or of pronounced socialistic tendencies."[121]

Although Fund officials insisted that the Military Service Act would add to their burdens, conscription was at least initially reserved for unmarried men. Some conscripts did support their families, but mothers and the rare dependent father or sister had never offered the potential political problem of wives and dependent children.[122] Meanwhile each shipload of convalescent soldiers quietly reduced the CPF burden, though the return of Canadian families from Britain, in response to the German blockade, meant that some inevitably needed CPF assistance. Whatever their weariness and resentment of criticism, CPF officials were confident that the Fund was a success. Collections in 1917 exceeded expectations and, outside Quebec and the hinterland labour communities of the Canadian West, the results in 1918 could be as good or better. Everyone was weary of the war and, if the weak-willed fell to complaining, it was up to their betters to set a good example.

One of several promises made when the 1917 election contest suddenly seemed frighteningly tight was that vigorous implementation of conscription would allow furloughs to Canada for soldiers who had been a very long time overseas. Unfortunately for homesick soldiers and their lonely wives, conscription was not implemented vigorously. The Military Service Act was a proceduralist's delight: months were consumed as reluctant conscripts passed through three layers of appeals that led to 221,949 exemptions, not to mention 24,139 defaulters.[123]

With Russia completely out of the war after signing the Treaty of Brest-Litovsk on 3 March 1918, and German armies free to mass on the Western Front, the Corps commander, Sir Arthur Currie, agreed to release no more than the married "Old Original" survivors of the First Contingent for a three-month furlough to Canada. But only 838 soldiers, a mere 230 of them from the 1st Division, reached Canada.[124] On 8 March 1918 the German offensive fell on the Allied line. Within weeks the British Fifth Army had ceased to exist, and other parts of the Allied line reeled back. The Canadian Corps, occupying familiar ground at Vimy, seemed almost magically immune, but a badly frightened Borden government, already steeled to defy election promises and cancel MSA exemptions, ignored sentimental arguments that Old Originals on furlough had done enough and should be released. While almost two-thirds of them found ways, legitimate or otherwise, of resisting the call, 39 percent returned to duty in France or England. They rejoined the Corps in time for its Hundred Days campaign from August to October 1918, and shared its heaviest losses of the war.

If mothers and wives had voted for the Union government in hope of seeing their loved ones on leave soon, only a few got their wish. The rest lived on through the dreariest year of the home-front war, with shortages added to rising prices, and the weary resentments of 1917 turning darker. If the dream of early victory had faded in the summer and fall of 1916, now those who followed the war felt the chill fear of defeat. So often had German armies been defeated and their soldiers annihilated that official, morale-building propaganda was increasingly dismissed as a lie, devised by politicians, abetted by business, and marketed through the prestige of many of the authors the Edwardian age had most admired.[125]

When would the war be over? What would remain of the virtues for which fighting had once seemed worthwhile? These were questions that war leaders left for their retirement years. In the face of savage attacks on his honour and integrity, Sir Joseph Flavelle had not resigned his functions at the Imperial Munitions Board. Helen Reid had not quit because the Patriotic Fund had approved support for "unmarried wives," and Sir Herbert Ames felt no need to listen to impractical demands that soldiers' pay be raised sufficiently to relieve their families from patriotic charity. Victory, both Marshal Ferdinand Foch and Field Marshal Sir Douglas Haig believed, was the reward for the general with the toughest, most enduring will. Most Canadian leaders had been taught in the same school.

Still, as the war dragged on towards a fifth year, the Fund had to recognize its critics and its own difficulties. Even in 1916, Ames had worried about how voluntary fundraising would be affected by a war-induced federal Excess Profits Tax and a new income tax, not to mention the government's vigorous hawking of War Savings Bonds. Small donations are always important but, as any experienced fundraiser knows, large contributions are crucial to meeting a significant target. When the CPF focused on millionaires and large corporations in its annual campaigns, publicized big donations, and listened attentively to the opinions of the very rich, it was respecting fundraising experience. Why, asked the CPF *Bulletin*, did the Patriotic Fund have the policy, deplored by organized labour, of investigating every application? Because of "the utter unreliability of the statements made not only by some of the applicants themselves, but by those apparently responsible citizens who vouch for them."[126] The rich felt safer entrusting their money to hard-headed cynics.

In Parliament, Ames rose on 30 April 1918 to report that the Patriotic Fund was paying out about $1 million a month to support more than 50,000 families. Over its history, the Fund had received upwards of $50 million in patriotic giving, but the government's efforts to raise revenue through taxes and war savings bonds were now encroaching on CPF income. Volunteers who had worn out themselves and their friends selling war bonds were now too exhausted to take up a Patriotic Fund campaign. The answer, Ames knew, had already been found in rural parts of the country, with a small levy on property. Money was not needed in 1918 but Ames now expected the government, having encroached on the CPF's revenues, to come to the aid of the Patriotic Fund from 1 April 1919.[127]

Ames got prompt backing from Sir Rodolphe Lemieux, the Montreal financier and Liberal MP who had been involved in the CPF from its outset: "I know that many people in very ordinary circumstances have hesitated to subscribe because they thought their subscription was too modest, while the names of large subscribers were being paraded before the public." Since the CPF's main contributors now paid most of the taxes, "I think the levy of a special tax of one mill on the dollar, for instance, would be received with pleasure by the whole people of Canada."[128] Despite a brief riposte by fellow Liberal J.G. Turriff that "the poor people of Canada have given more largely in proportion to what they have than the wealthy people," the two men agreed on the tax.[129]

Confident that the government would accept its added responsibility, Ames assured the *Victoria Daily Times* during a September visit that if donors would continue their generosity until March 1919, they would afterwards get no more calls from the Patriotic Fund. As for increased rates of allowance, he would promise only to meet "reasonable demands" and he reminded the reporter that "it was absolutely necessary to take cognizance of the change in the middle west sections where living costs had risen more in proportion as compared with sections nearer to the Pacific coast."[130] Prices were now higher in Alberta and Saskatchewan than in BC. Was the government taking over the administration of the Fund, asked the *Times,* as Vancouver papers had claimed? "Sir Herbert said he was obviously misquoted. He stated that the Government is not taking over the administration of the fund and consequently our appeal goes to the volunteer committees to continue their patriotic labours."[131] The critics had been heard. Four years of fundraising had been enough. In 1919 the Patriotic Fund and perhaps the Great War would enter a new era.

7
Victory for Whom?

Devout forecasters recognize a severe limitation on their craft: only God really knows the future, and She isn't telling. Still, a desperate desire to know what will happen tomorrow or next month governs us all. So does the expectation that we must prepare for what might be called the "prophetic consensus." In the spring of 1917, it had appeared that voluntary recruiting would not keep the four Canadian divisions on the Western Front up to strength at a time when the Allies believed that Germany would profit from its victory in Russia faster than the United States could create an army and send it to Europe. So guided, in 1917 the Borden government tore up its old promises and subjected Canada to a bitterly divisive debate on conscription. Sir Robert Borden's solemn dedication to the Empire's victory left him little choice. Eight months later, to win the election on 17 December, Sir Robert's Unionist government believed it had to grant widespread exemptions from the Military Service Act to please farmers, serving soldiers, and the women it had enfranchised for their patriotism. Then, after dramatic German victories in March and April 1918, Borden refused to allow his election promises to jeopardize the Allied cause. He cancelled the exemptions.

Because Borden made an error in prediction, this response has been damned by generations of historians. In the end, Canada's "MSA men" were not really needed. The Allied line fell back but somehow it never broke. Though the Canadian Corps was severely extended and temporarily dissolved to plug gaps in the Allied line, pure chance spared it from heavy casualties between March and July 1918. Military experts should have noted Borden's more serious miscalculation. Even if tens of thousands of exempted MSA men could have been caught, trained, and delivered to Canadian divisions in France within a mere four months, they would still have arrived too late for even the last German offensive in 1918.[1] Experts, of course, play little role in historical or political debates.

Not all the expectations for 1918 were unfulfilled. For Canadians and most other belligerents, it was the hardest, meanest year of the war. During 1917 Canadians had had to come to terms with a war that was not to be won on schedule. They had grumbled and complained and finally agreed, by a decisive majority in the 17 December election, to carry on. In 1918 most hardships grew harder. Prices and scarcity increased. So did casualties, particularly in the second half of the year.

Cancelling exemptions meant that farmers' sons disappeared into the CEF, or into the woods, and their labour was not really replaced by bank clerks, teachers, or schoolboys pretending to be "Soldiers of the Soil." Farmers complained that amateur labour damaged crops and reduced harvest yields. More than ever, Canadians scapegoated and victimized the foreign-born, tried to ban their newspapers, and expanded the federal police forces into a nationwide organization to track down draft dodgers and alleged "subversives." Waves of regulations under the 1914 War Measures Act banned hoarding and strikes. An "anti-loafing" law, much admired by Sir Robert Borden, compelled all males to perform, or pretend to perform, "useful" work.[2]

Soldiers' families entered a third or fourth year of loneliness and increasing privation. No one told Mrs. J.L. Smith that the CPF had refused to pay its allowances to soldiers in the Forestry Corps or the Canadian Railway Troops, though her husband had told her to expect the money when he persuaded her to go to Canada. She even had to pay full fare for herself and her three children. "Is this what they call Canadian fair play?" she demanded.[3] Sybella Potts of Grenfell, Saskatchewan, thirty years a widow, had sent both her sons to the war, and both had returned unable to support her. One wounded son had a wife and three children; the other "had never been able for much since he got the crash in the Flying machine and got all the Bons [sic] in his feet & legs Broken." At age sixty-five, she had tried to make a living by nursing but now she was too sick. After she had "lived on moulded bread and cold water for 7 days," she was desperate enough to share her story with King George V if necessary.[4] Homesickness affected soldiers, too. "I think the Canadian soldier's worst trial is the fact that he is unable to go home to see his wife & family occasionally as the French & English can do," wrote Ernest Hamilton after less than a year apart from Sara, "& I think it would be the best treat of my life if I could see you & my children for a short time each year."[5]

In the bitter mood of 1918, Patriotic Fund supporters focused on a continuing complaint: how to force noncontributors to give. Even members of the Victoria Board of Trade agreed that the answer was a federal government tax, though some suggested doubling the province's new flat-rate head tax, at least for the duration of the war.[6] When even business leaders looked to taxes to support the Patriotic Fund, the future of voluntary funding looked gloomy indeed.

The actual results of fundraising sent an even grimmer message. In November 1917 Toronto, the country's most whole-heartedly patriotic big city, had almost missed its $75 million Victory Bond target, even with the full backing of city leaders and newspapers.[7] What would happen to the annual Patriotic Fund appeal in January? Toronto's CPF subscriptions had risen each year by about $1 million, from $1,014,482 in 1914 to $3,205,292 in 1917. Local organizers invited Sir Sam Hughes to open the 1918 campaign at Massey Hall before an enthusiastic audience. All newspapers contributed free full-page advertisements for the duration of the three-day campaign. Mrs. H.P. Plumptre of the CPF Women's Committee sent 2,500 women to canvass door-to-door for contributions. Men, explained Bert McCreath of the 50,000 Club, might not have had the time to do a tiresome job so conscientiously.[8] An auction offered such prizes as a Stoney Lake cottage and four acres of bush land, or the Bible that had accompanied Sgt. Matt Wayman to Vimy Ridge. The city's public and separate schools collected $27,000 from teachers and pupils, and a mother docked a penny from her children each time they uttered a slang word. Yet the city fell short of its 1917 total and needed a fourth day to reach its 1918 target. Torontonians surpassed the previous CPF total by a mere $3,089, and only because the city council doubled the ratepayers' compulsory contribution to $1 million.[9] Across Ontario, CPF donations fell by $440,000 from the 1917 high of $7,687,109.[10]

As for the home of Canada's wealthiest patriots, beyond encouraging its regular contributors and urging subscribers to day's pay schemes to continue their generosity, the Montreal branch did not even dare launch a 1918 fundraising campaign in a city so bitterly resentful of conscription. After the $2,839,833 the branch had forwarded to the national treasurer in 1917, Montreal's 1918 contribution was only $638,878.[11] Even volunteers for Helen Reid's organization were harder to keep. "The roll of volunteer workers has passed the 1,400 mark," Reid reported to an American audience, "but many of these women are now over in England and France. Others have drifted off to easier work, others to the long rest from which they will not return."[12] Almost everywhere, CPF volunteers were harder to find as the war brought women more interesting opportunities for service.

On the eve of Toronto's 1918 campaign, Mr. Justice Mulock confirmed a rumour when he announced that he would be launching the CPF's final appeal, and offered the Fund's latest explanation of so fundamental a change: "The growth of opinion in favour of the Dominion Government assuming responsibility for the Fund is due I need hardly say not to any dissatisfaction with its administration but rather to a feeling that the burdens of maintaining it should be as some think more equally distributed. Those who believe that the Government should provide the funds believe also that the present system of administration should be continued."[13]

Canadian Families in Britain

Not only soldiers but many of their wives spent the war across the Atlantic. Lacking the financial constraints of lower-rank families, many Canadian officers' wives had joined their husbands in England in the early days of the war.[14] Sometimes British themselves, and more often close to British upper- and middle-class lifestyles in their upbringing, such women felt at home in Great Britain. Their husbands' service with the Canadian Corps was often interspersed with periods of training, staff employment, and convalescence in England. British and CEF policy allowed officers on the Western Front four week-long leaves away from the trenches each year, a privilege that added to the attraction of England for many of their wives.[15] Soldiers in the ranks were permitted only a single annual two-week escape from the front, which obviously gave their Canadian families no opportunity to see them.

Since 1914 the Patriotic Fund had offered some practical and financial encouragement to families of lower-ranking soldiers moving "home" to England to be closer to a British reservist or a CEF member. Once in Britain, such women were no longer a charge on the CPF. Much as the CPF dealt with families of British reservists, British patriotic charities such as the Soldiers' and Sailors' Families Association (SSFA) were expected to meet the special needs of CEF families in the United Kingdom. Their needs were real. Pte. Irwin's wife arrived in Liverpool with six children, one of them born during the voyage, and was admitted to the local infirmary "without a ha'penny to her name."[16] When Mrs. S.M. Cooke arrived in London from Sydney, Cape Breton, she was very sick, all four of her children had measles, her severely wounded husband was in hospital, and the British charitable authorities were soon fed up with them all. By reporting Mrs. Cooke's desperate circumstances, Jean Ives of the Canadian Red Cross in London prevailed on the Nova Scotia CPF to provide a little extra help.[17]

R.B. Barron, treasurer of the City of London branch of the SSFA, took on the problems of families from the Dominions. He arranged with Queen Charlotte's Lying-In Hospital to accept maternity cases and with another hospital for venereal disease. "It is well within the knowledge of all who had experience of social work in this country," Barron explained to Sir Richard Turner, commanding Canada's Overseas Forces, "that before the War, when men migrated to Canada and left their wives here, they frequently lost interest in their families." To his satisfaction, if not necessarily that of the men's spouses in Canada, Barron reported that he had managed several reconciliations.[18]

A common problem for Canadian families in England occurred when their soldier died or was evacuated back to Canada and discharged. Few had the means to pay for their family's return passage to Canada. Pte. W.F. Workman, wounded at Ypres, had already left for Canada when Mrs. Workman appeared at the High Commission, eager to rejoin him in Calgary. She had only seven pounds sterling, far short of her fare.[19] Officials at the Quebec docks sometimes assured soldiers

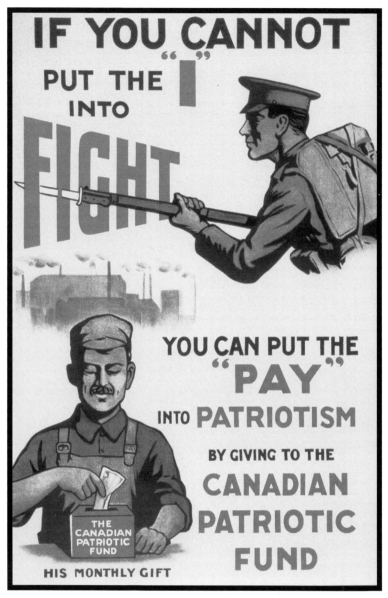

"Fight or pay" was a slogan for the Canadian Patriotic Fund, rendered in every imaginable variety as its managers pressured rich and poor alike. As with voluntary enlistment, the alternative was state intervention. When voluntarism failed to find enough soldiers, the Fund would turn to governments and taxation, particularly after a war income tax and an excess profits tax threatened the Fund's wealthiest backers.

French reservists in St. Boniface, 11 August 1914. Europe's huge conscript armies depended on millions of reservists returning to fill the ranks on mobilization. The call reached half way around the world to these loyal French reservists in St. Boniface, Manitoba. The disruption for families and employers was enormous but modern wars lasted only a few weeks, didn't they?

Italian reservists in Toronto, 1915. With Toronto's Mayor Tommy Church prominent among them, Italian reservists joined their British, Belgian, and French counterparts when Italy entered the war. Considered "sojourners," not real immigrants, Italians and their families suffered discrimination from the Patriotic Fund. Of course, as Ames boasted, a charity had every right to discriminate, while a government had to treat all equally.

After over four years away in England, France, and North Russia, Sergeant François-Xavier (Frank) Maheux proudly rejoins his "poor Angeline" and their children in 1919, confident that he will now give them the better life he had promised in his wartime letters home. It would not be easy.

Proudly wearing their brand new uniforms and stiff-peaked caps, two soldiers escort a wife and child at Toronto Exhibition Park. As a mother with a child, the woman was guaranteed Patriotic Fund support and in 1915 could even find herself better off with a soldier-husband than if he had stuck to the average civilian job. That would change, of course, especially if he was killed or wounded and she and her child depended on a pension.

A Canadian soldier in France with a railway crossing guard. While soldiering was an intensely male experience, soldiers in France did not inhabit a monastery. At the end of the war, many Canadian soldiers returned with British war brides but only a small handful married in France or Belgium. Language, local values, and strong official discouragement of post-enlistment marriage provided a sufficient barrier.

Lily Fields Mackinnon, wife and soon widow of a corporal in the PPCLI, and her two children, Archie and Annie. Lily Fields and Ron Mackinnon were married in 1911 and their marriage ended with his death in 1917. A Toronto printer and peacetime militia volunteer, Ron was killed with the Patricias at Vimy Ridge. Annie would die during the influenza epidemic of 1919. Archie served in the Second World War.

Women volunteers collecting soldiers' comforts, Toronto. Comforts ranged from cigarettes, chocolate, and home baking to products of knitting and needlework that reminded a cold, lonely, and homesick soldier of the pleasures of home and family. Since a soldier had to carry everything he owned, parcels were quickly shared and consumed by comrades but knitted socks or a flannel "cholera belt" worn around the stomach, were more personal.

Women holding a bazaar for war aid. Sewing, knitting, and rolling bandages were obvious and traditional female contributions to the war effort. The Patriotic Fund involved hundreds of women in a new activity that would soon become a new profession called social work. Visiting soldiers' families to determine that they were entitled to aid was more demanding for most Canadian women than knitting woollen socks or hemming a bandage.

One of the first woman graduates of McGill University, Helen Reid was the Montreal manager of Ames's experiment. Volunteer supervisor of social work for St. John's Ambulance, she became convenor of the women's auxiliary of the Montreal Patriotic Fund and guiding spirit in dispensing "the alms of good advice" to the Fund's clients.

Montreal's wealthiest voters trusted Sir Herbert Ames to represent them in Parliament. Heir to the city's biggest boot and shoe factory, Ames believed that poverty could be cured by education and example. The war gave him the opportunity to prove his claim in a Canada-wide social experiment on the families of Canada's soldiers.

Facing page, bottom: "Christmas, 1917" suggests the temptations of class warfare for the badly battered opposition. The soldier's family, too poor to provide some of the common staples in a working-class kitchen is contrasted with businessmen, enjoying the benefits of their greed. The automobile was a wartime symbol of conspicuous consumption.

A knitting circle for soldiers' wives and mothers, Toronto. Part of the Patriotic Fund's Third Responsibility was to bring lonely wives together to share problems under the Fund's guidance and supervision and to keep them busy, as if mothers were not busy enough. By the end of the war, wives in western provinces had created a few associations with radical agendas, but the widespread influenza epidemic stopped such movements from meeting and perhaps growing.

As honorary secretary-treasurer for the Victoria Patriotic Aid Society, Mrs. W.E. Oliver was caricatured on the eve of her retirement as she was and as she might have been in the eyes of her clients and of a sympathetic colleague. Whatever her attitude, she exercised powerful authority over wives, who had no appeal against her rulings.

With food production lagging for lack of labour and exemption from conscription for farmers' sons cancelled in April 1918, Ottawa mobilized high school boys as Soldiers of the Soil. Farmers complained that the boys, as well as older adults sent to do similar work, were too inexperienced and physically weak to do a good day's work and many did more harm than harvesting. This advertisement was really designed to sell clothes.

"Moo-che-we-in-es" advertisement for the CPF. When an elderly Cree from Saskatchewan's Onion Lake band contributed $150 to the Patriotic Fund, Herbert Ames demanded details. His explanation was all that the Fund or the Superintendent-General of Indian Affairs, Duncan Campbell Scott, could have wished or devised: "I heard there was a big war going on over there; I feel like I want to help you some way and the best I can do it to send a little money for I can't go myself as I am nearly blind."

"Time for a Hog-Killing!" When inflation began to undermine family economies and Ames's experiment in social reform, economists might have blamed excessive reliance on debt to fund the war effort, but most Canadians condemned profiteering, aided by a government official who fingered the huge wartime profits collected by Sir Joseph Flavelle's bacon-processing business. Sir Joseph's product and his advice to fellow magnates to "send profits to hell where they belong" was irresistible, even if the allegation was almost baseless.

Facing page, bottom: Boy Scouts in front of Patriotic Fund Headquarters, Toronto. Launched in 1914, the Patriotic Fund was the fourth venture in funding part of a war effort from private enthusiasm. Aware of the stigma, the Patriotic Fund denied that it was a charity but the difference became hard to see when the prejudices of donors took priority over the interests of the beneficiaries. As one of the newest patriotic organizations in Canada, Boy Scouts were on hand to set an example of helpfulness.

Children were part of the war effort. To prepare the young for their vast conscript armies, European countries had embraced free primary education, strict public health measures, and industrial safety. Wartime Canada followed suit. A series of patriotic booklets kept Ontario school children in touch with the official version of the war and supplied teachers with quizzes and patriotic activities such as collecting scrap and tending a victory garden.

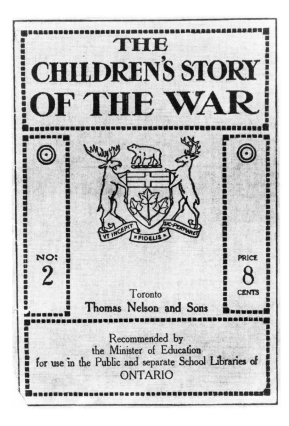

THE
CHILDREN'S STORY
OF THE WAR

NO: 2

PRICE 8 CENTS

Toronto
Thomas Nelson and Sons

Recommended by
the Minister of Education
for use in the Public and separate School Libraries of
ONTARIO

Many wartime products depended on the recycling of scarce materials but organizers of wartime salvage campaigns afterwards confessed that their real purpose was to give people at home a sense that they were actively engaged in the war effort. Keeping people busy also discouraged moping and negative thinking.

While Canada did not ration consumers during the First World War as it would in the later war, it tried to discourage hoarding of scarce products, enforced by fines and by neighbourhood informers whose "patriotic duty" was to tattle on those suspected of owning more coal or flour or sugar than they really needed.

"If you cannot join him, you should help her." The Patriotic Fund's theme of "fight or pay" suggested an equivalence between risking one's life in uniform and giving one's money to support soldiers' families that hardly bears examination but would have been comforting to wealthy Canadians eager to appear patriotic without the inconvenience of actual soldiering.

By 1914, a primary responsibility for any decent man was to provide for his mother or his wife and family. By common consent, even a Canadian soldier's $1.10 a day could not stretch that far. Hence the Patriotic Fund's vital role in recruiting a volunteer army. An honourable man could enlist with a clear conscience. Would he feel deceived?

G.P.

MINISTER'S OFFICE

OTTAWA. September 26, 1917.

Personal.

Dear Mrs. Dowling,

   I desire to express to you my very sincere sympathy in the recent decease of your husband, No. 678109 Pte. James Joseph Dowling, who in sacrificing his life at the front in action with the enemy, has rendered the highest services of a worthy citizen.

   The heavy loss which you and the Nation have sustained would indeed be depressing were it not redeemed by the knowledge that the brave comrade for whom we mourn performed his duties fearlessly and well as became a good soldier, and gave his life for the great cause of Human Liberty and the Defence of the Empire.

   Again extending to you in your bereavement my condolence and heartfelt sympathy.

   I am,

   Your faithfully,

A.E. Kemp.

   Minister of Militia and Defence
         for Canada.

Mrs. I.M. Dowling,
  504 Parliament St.,
    Toronto, Ont.

Letter of condolence from the Hon. A.E. Kemp, Minister of Militia and Defence to Mrs. I.M. Dowling. Such letters were carefully drafted to embody all the appropriate sentiments, to avoid any imaginable offence, and to apply to as many families as possible without alteration. While despised by the sophisticated, such letters told many ordinary people that their sacrifice had mattered.

"These four mothers gave to their country 28 brave sons." Maternal feminists had claimed that war depended on mothers to produce the sons who did the fighting. Honour and support was due to women who helped fill the ranks of the Canadian Expeditionary Force. Patriotic applause had to be accompanied by patriotic dollars since those brave mothers' sons were also their parents' old-age security.

A military amputee in an invalid chair with his daughter. When a soldier returned disabled, his family faced a lifetime of meagre pension income, regularly reviewed by a remote and arbitrary Board of Pension Commissioners, and the pain and awkwardness of the disability itself. If the disability resulted from the stress of battle, even an admission could imperil a soldier's pension. Veteran and family suffered in silence.

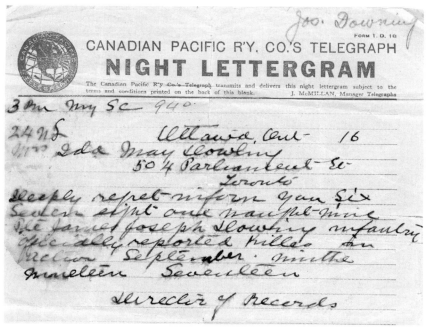

Death notice from the Director of Records to Ida May Dowling, 1917. This was the message that every soldier's wife or mother dreaded to receive. Often it came at night. Lacking telephones, telegraph boys delivered them by bicycle, sometimes pausing because newspapers commissioned them to collect a photograph of the dead soldier from his grieving family. James Dowling was a casualty of fighting near Lens in September 1917.

that the CPF would pay the cost of returning their families. After all, hadn't the Fund helped them to go to England? "This is not true," groaned the CPF's Philip Morris. It was even less true "of wives that may have been acquired since the soldiers' arrival in England."[20] J.W. Borden, accountant general of the Militia Department, explained that many such wives and families were quietly shipped home on government transports at no cost. However, he provided a more orderly solution by providing the high commissioner with a fund of $15,000 to assist cash-strapped CEF dependants.[21]

In 1917 Germany had gambled that an unrestricted submarine blockade of the United Kingdom would starve the British into surrender before the Americans could make a difference in the war. Aided by the reluctance of both the Admiralty and British ship owners to introduce a convoy system, the Germans sank millions of tons of shipping and came close to success.[22] Dependent on imports for their food supply, the British were soon hungry. Removing surplus population was an obvious response. Canada dutifully banned women and children under twelve from travelling to the war zone, enforced by a fine or prison term for any ship's master, manager, or agent who ignored the order. This was soon modified for special cases – to allow a major's wife to visit her dying spouse, and an English visitor to go home to her seriously ill husband.[23] Meanwhile, between April 1917 and the Armistice in 1918, Canada's Department of Immigration claimed to have brought 22,000 dependants to Canada at their own expense, leaving about 35,000 Canadian military dependants in Britain at the end of the war.[24] Wartime marriages in England had contributed about 15,000 dependants to the total.

Less than three weeks after Ames's announcement to Parliament about future CPF funding, on 18 May 1918 Parliament accepted a modest amendment to the CPF Act, clarifying that its beneficiaries had to be residents of Canada.[25] Now that taxpayers were soon to finance the benefits, MPs on both sides felt entitled to criticize. Hugh Morphy, a lawyer from Listowel and the Tory member for Perth North, was appalled, if a little belatedly, to learn that the CPF provided for families of French, Russian, Italian, Portuguese, and Russian reservists. "Are we to provide for every indigent of Europe," he demanded, "simply because of the fact that a soldier's wife happens to have come here, probably sent here by the country in which she lives, to get rid of her?"[26] A Liberal from Assiniboia, J.G. Turriff, agreed. Belgian and French reservists' families were acceptable, "But why should we burden ourselves with the responsibility of looking after the relatives of Italians who join their army in their own country?"[27] In fact, as the minister of justice, C.J. Doherty, explained, the amendment would deny support to all but families living in Canada. Rodolphe Lemieux reminded fellow MPs that the Fund prevented abuse: "When a request is made by a family for aid, the Patriotic Fund at once sends a committee of two or three ladies to inquire into the circumstances of that family, and in many cases, for good reason, aid is refused or delayed."[28] Neither Morphy nor Turriff was appeased. What about the Japanese? What had they or the Italians done for Canadians stranded in their countries?

Even though Ames had given the government notice that the CPF expected taxpayers to take over its expenses in 1919, the Patriotic Fund worried about its income and held the line on benefits.[29] Still, dependants returning from England had to be absorbed if "in need." So must the brides Canadian soldiers had married in England, regardless of regulations. Local committees were authorized to help both categories of returning wife and to grant $30 to a widowed mother who lost her benefits when her son married overseas.[30]

Militancy and the "'Flu"

During 1918 the militancy visible among some soldiers' wives in Vancouver and Calgary spread to other major cities, largely encouraged by the growth of veterans' organizations under the lead of the Great War Veterans' Association. Frank Giolma, a veteran from Victoria and newly elected member of the BC legislature, attended the riot-plagued GWVA convention in Toronto in August 1918, but his main report to the *Victoria Times* on his return was the "growing discontent" among soldiers' wives in Winnipeg and Toronto about the Patriotic Fund, and plans for a "Poverty Parade" to press demands for support of $100 a month at a minimum.[31] Meanwhile, Vancouver unionists had found an eloquent soldier's wife to lead their campaign. Mrs. John Lorimer confessed that she would never have accepted a cent from the "Patriotic" if she had not been convinced "it was rightly mine." Then she discovered that the money was "dragged from our store girls who have not enough to live on themselves, and also from our poor men employed by companies and corporations."[32] By 1918 the *British Columbia Federationist* boasted that Mrs. Lorimer had "proven her ability at all times to think clearly and act wisely" and she was chairing meetings in the fight "for the home against the Huns at home."[33]

Vancouver's veterans soon found themselves torn between attacking the labour movement's antiwar radicalism and supporting its condemnation of the Patriotic Fund and government neglect of soldiers' families. In September Charles Gale, Vancouver's new mayor, summoned an evening meeting at city hall amidst talk of direct action on "the bitter complaint of the soldiers' dependants as to the inadequacy of the provision made for their maintenance by the government." He was soon outflanked by Mrs. Lorimer and by Mrs. Macken of the Wives and Mothers, who spoke of "silent women going about day after day, trying to buy shoes for our children." Mrs. Borland, her voice hoarse from previous speeches, claimed she could see, under the white crosses in France and at Mountain View Sanatorium near Vancouver, broken-hearted men crying, "Would to god I had never gone."[34] The mayor's proposal that a petition for a minimum of $100 a month be sent to the influential Board of Trade for its endorsement provoked catcalls from the crowd. Mrs. Lorimer insisted that $2,100 was now the minimum acceptable annual allowance. Ernest Winch, the current president of the VTLC, scorned the idea of "petitioning" people they had just elected. Instead, his word "demand" was substituted for "petition," only to be displaced by "command." Should they seek allies from the Rotary Club and others who might bring weight to bear on the government? "Put the resolution right here and now," shouted Mrs. Borland. "Their children are not hungry and going without shoes."[35]

Within days of the Vancouver meeting, a far worse threat to families began to pass across Canada. Spanish influenza allegedly entered Canada in mid-September with men attending a training camp for a new Polish Army at Niagara-on-the-Lake near St. Catharines. Other vectors included soldiers, dependants, and visitors returning from England and the United States. Troopships carrying conscripts took it back to England. The virus spread fast, hitting thousands by early October. Ultimately one in six Canadians suffered the disease. Remote communities suffered most. A third of the population of Labrador died, and half the Inuit. The horror of the Spanish flu was that, like the war itself, it seemed especially fatal to the young and healthy. While the influenza virus crippled its victims, the accompanying pneumonia was often the killer, and in 1918 there was very little in medical knowledge to help a patient resist.

In cities and towns hospitals were soon jammed. Since nurses had little effective protection, they shared in the toll. Everywhere, women found themselves in the front line, tending the sick, fighting dirt, and trying to protect their families by whatever remedies, sound or foolish, were recommended by the usual array of experts and quacks. Schools were closed and some were turned into emergency hospitals. To prevent contagion, all gatherings, even church services, were curtailed. Alberta commanded its population to wear gauze masks; many others did so voluntarily. People avoided each other whenever they could. The eventual toll of the Spanish flu was close to 50,000 Canadian dead, not many fewer than the 61,000 Canadians who died in the accompanying Great War.[36]

In Hamilton, as we have seen, and in other communities, CPF branches invoked their "third responsibility" to provide makeshift nursing homes for soldiers' families. Soon, local branches accepted the tragic burden of coping with surviving orphans after their mothers had died. Meanwhile, the kind of meetings that might have spread or amplified the message of the mayor's rally in

Vancouver had become unthinkable. In the face of a contagious epidemic, avoiding mass meetings was obvious advice.[37]

Family tragedy had always provided an argument for compassionate home leave for serving soldiers. Mrs. Ezra Snow of Lynn, Massachusetts, pleaded with the minister of justice that her husband be allowed leave from the Canadian Engineers depot at St-Jean-sur-Richelieu because she was sick, as well as his mother and their two-month-old baby.[38] So was Mrs. Belcher of Kelliher, Saskatchewan, along with her eldest boy. Their house also badly needed fixing against the coming prairie winter.[39] Perhaps the most striking influenza-related appeal came from Mary Wray of Montreal, whose son had enlisted with the 79th Battery twenty months earlier and who "wanted to get a few Huns before he came home." Now, as a trained embalmer, he was badly needed by the family funeral home to cope with the victims of the epidemic. His only brother had barely recovered after two weeks in hospital, but he had to carry the whole burden. "It is a gruesome business to be in," confessed Mrs. Wray, "but if brought up in it you get accustomed to it."[40] Without her soldier-son, the family firm was steadily losing customers.

Victory and Demobilization

Even as the Allied line fell back, Germany's last chance for victory in the Great War rapidly faded. At Doullens, the British finally yielded overall command of their armies to Ferdinand Foch, a French general as unmoved by defeat as their own Sir Douglas Haig. Using France's remarkable railway network to move reinforcements faster than the Germans could march, Foch stopped his exhausted enemy each time the Germans seemed on the verge of a breakthrough. Now that the Germans had been drawn beyond their well-designed defences, Foch could launch a series of devastating attacks on their improvised trenches. One such assault, on 8 August at Amiens, gave the Canadian and Australian army corps their only joint action of the war. Each corps advanced eight to nine miles, displaying the contrasting techniques that each young nation's army had mastered in 1917.[41] When he heard that even battleworthy German units had given way at Amiens without serious resistance, their general, Erich von Ludendorff, called 8 August "the Black Day of the German Army."

In the ensuing hundred days of fighting, the Canadian Corps suffered its heaviest casualties of the war. At Drocourt-Quéant, the Canal du Nord, Cambrai, and finally at Valenciennes, the Corps repeatedly cracked strong German positions. The 120,000-member Canadian Corps absorbed more than 30,000 casualties between August and November, twice the losses at Passchendaele, three times the cost of Vimy Ridge. Thanks to Borden's conscripts, the Corps ended the war as the strongest formation of its kind on the Western Front, with four full battalions per brigade. Only in the final stages of the war were any significant number of conscripts needed to fill the Canadian ranks. Most of the so-called MSA men never actually experienced battle.

Perhaps if Borden had known what was going to happen, Canada, like Australia, might have escaped conscription. The Corps might not have won the ensuing military victories, which, in any case, present-day Canadians have almost forgotten, and the war might have continued until 1920, as Borden and most Allied leaders grimly expected. Canada would have found itself even more deeply enmeshed in a struggle to overthrow the Bolshevik revolution and restore Russia to the war with Germany. The catastrophic Spanish flu, which ended the worst year of the war, would have made 1919 even more stressful and agonizing. As the sole major belligerent with reserve strength, the United States might have become the world's sole superpower in 1920 rather than seventy years later.

"Might have beens" are almost as irresistible for historians as second-guessing is for political scientists, but reality is fascinating enough. On 8 August, Foch and Haig planned to do little more than drive the Germans back from Amiens, a key railway junction. Instead, a limited attack turned into the first of a wave of assaults that led to the collapse of the Austrian and German monarchy and a German appeal for an Armistice at 11 a.m. on 11 November 1918. Because victory was the outcome, few recognized the costs. Only the British media recognized Canada's "Hundred Days" contribution, to the unconcealed resentment of Britain's own hardpressed army. Bitterness at the cocky Canadians contributed to the bad feelings that underlay some of the demobilization riots in Britain in the spring of 1919.[42]

Mrs. Wray, who insisted that her son was no slacker, could offer the excuse that, by the time she wrote, the war was now over and so were her son's chances of killing "Huns." In reality the war was not over. On 11 November in the Forest of Compiègne Marshal Foch and German plenipotentiaries had signed no more than an armistice. The German armies were withdrawing to an uninvaded Germany, while the Allies occupied the crossings of the Rhine. From Mons in Belgium, where the four divisions of the Canadian Corps had ended the war, two divisions marched on to the Rhine; the rest bivouacked to await events. The war was interrupted but it could easily resume. No, it could not. The war was over. For the victorious but exhausted Allies and their beaten but unconquered enemies, more fighting was unthinkable. Formally, the war ended at Versailles outside Paris on 28 June 1919, by which time the armies of both sides had dissolved. If the Germans had lost the strength to resume the war, the Allies had long since lost the means to impose their peace. The same populations that had demanded that the German lemon be squeezed "until the pips squeaked" had cried even more insistently for demobilization.[43]

Exasperated by the discipline of a collective war effort, populations seemed a little out of control. Warned by premature rejoicing over a "false armistice" proclaimed from New York on 7 November, Ottawa had proposed that Armistice celebrations be delayed until 1 December, when the influenza contagion might have died away or been killed by the cold. No one paid the slightest attention. In Ottawa and most major cities, excited crowds tore off their gauze masks, jammed the streets, and celebrated. For Canadians, the war was over.

Mrs. Wray was not alone in asking for her son. Floods of similar letters from soldiers' families deluged Militia Headquarters. The minister, Maj.-Gen. Sidney Mewburn, let it be known that he could not possibly read them all. Since no wife or mother wrote without her unique personal claim, that was no disincentive at all. From Lac St-Jean, Lude Doucet's disabled husband and their two remaining sons, sixteen and fourteen, could no longer work their 400 acres. Without their twenty-two-year-old, who had dutifully reported for the MSA, they insisted that they would have to sell out. "But we are willing to keep on farming and produce more in order to accumulate food for the allies," she concluded diplomatically, if only she could have her son.[44] This was the common theme in letters from all agricultural regions.

Elsewhere, widows pleaded with Mewburn or his staff for sons to support them now that their husbands were gone. Many writers were poor and desperate. All four of Mrs. Jane Hill's sons had joined up from Montreal's slum-ridden St-Henri district: one was overseas, one was in hospital, and two had been killed. "As soon as our boys were dead," she complained, "there pay was stopd. And we have been struglin on ever since with paying rent and buying wood to burn it is impossible to get enough to eat much less clothes to wear."[45] Some families were simply desperately lonely. Mrs. Zarsky of New York had been rather proud that her son had joined the Canadians, but the war was over, she had not seen him for three years, "and my heart yearns for him."[46]

The end of the war brought little relief to those who mourned the missing. Hope could never entirely be extinguished and neither could lives be entirely resumed. Gordon Parker was engaged to marry the widow of a British Army reservist who farmed near him in Saskatchewan, but the man had only been reported "missing, believed killed." Two years later, in August 1919, Parker still needed definite proof before he could be married.[47] A year later, the Rev. Roy Frid of Brantford posed the same question on behalf of a widow whose husband had been missing since June 1916. A certificate of "presumed death" had been issued for "official purposes" in March 1917, but a Militia Department lawyer had to warn Frid that the widow might be liable for prosecution for bigamy if she remarried and her first husband showed up.[48]

For two years the GWVA campaigned for a pension for the wife and sons of Company Quartermaster Sergeant Ball, who had been sent to Marseilles in 1919 and disappeared with a substantial sum of money to rent films for his unit. Comrades assumed that he had been knocked on the head, robbed, and drowned, but they failed to persuade the Board of Pension Commissioners. At the end of 1921, Ball showed up in Saint John with an epic tale of amnesia and adventure. He had indeed been knocked on the head at Marseilles and robbed. Next he was shanghaied to New Orleans and then to Morocco, where he was forced to serve in the Spanish Foreign Legion. He deserted but was recaptured, and the British consul rescued him from a Spanish firing squad at the last moment![49]

Bringing Them Home

The needs of a continuing war faded fast from Canadian consciousness, even in Ottawa. Families wanted their soldiers back, and every soldier wanted to come home at once. Demobilization planners had wrestled for months before the Armistice with calculations of how much shipping would survive the U-Boat campaign, the damage the 1917 explosion in Halifax did to the port facilities, and the frail capacity of Canada's bankrupt, worn-out railways. The British set an example of elaborate postwar manpower planning, identifying "demobilizers" and "pivotal men" among its soldiers to be selected for early release and a strategic role in reviving the postwar economy. Canada, too, needed specially skilled workers to convert factories and relaunch peacetime industries. In both countries, such men tended to be conscripts or late-joined volunteers, while the survivors of 1914 had the smallest role in meeting postwar commercial needs. Yet, surely, the "Old Originals" were the men with the highest moral claim to early release?[50]

Into this conundrum came demands that married men should be released first. Family reunion must be a priority, plus it would result in savings on separation allowance and the potential $16 million burden of taking over the Patriotic Fund. Sadly, planners reported, it was not possible. Soldiers would come home as soon as could be managed, but the army could not simply be torn apart or it would lose the capacity to feed, manage, and even demobilize itself. Indeed, compassionate special cases must be treated as they had been during the fighting, through proper military channels and with no special favours. Otherwise, morale and discipline might plummet.[51] Nor could soldiers allegedly "doing nothing" in Canada necessarily be released early. Those who could be spared would go, with priority for those earning separation allowance, but most had a vital role in the demobilization of soldiers returning from overseas.[52]

Word of postwar mutinies in Canadian Corps units in France and Belgium frightened a government that had accepted post-Armistice occupation duties in Germany.[53] Troops landing from the steamer *Northland* at Halifax on Boxing Day raged about bad food, cramped quarters, and thieving stewards. Public opinion demanded a royal commission, which, within a month, called for far higher shipping standards for returning troops than when they had gone overseas.[54] As the main voice of veterans, the GWVA urged the government to leave soldiers overseas until spring, when there would be more jobs and opportunities for them. Meanwhile, the Corps commander, Sir Arthur Currie, insisted that his men come home in formed units, to preserve discipline and to parade their achievements before their fellow Canadians. Faced with more months in a damp, cold, expensive, and unwelcoming Britain or Belgium, soldiers, like their families at home, conspicuously felt otherwise, and rioted violently to demand a swift homecoming.

The repatriation to Canada was ultimately faster than most experts had foreseen. After all, the St. Lawrence was closed by ice, which limited troopships to two winter ports. After consultation with the railways, Ottawa imposed a limit of 20,000 men a month along the Intercolonial Railway from Halifax, which, after the explosion, utterly lacked any facilities to billet soldiers in winter, and 10,000 on the Canadian Pacific Railway line from Saint John, New Brunswick, through the United States. Wounded would return on hospital ships to Portland, Maine, and along the Grand Trunk Railway to Montreal. The *Northland* decision made it even harder to compete with the Americans for suitable ships. The cancellation of two ships that did not meet the new standards also led straight to the Kinmel mutiny of 5-6 March 1919 in North Wales, resulting in five dead and twenty-three wounded soldiers.[55] Shocked by the carnage at Kinmel, the British were persuaded to lend a "monster ship," the *Olympic,* sister ship to the *Titanic,* to transfer over 5,000 Canadians to Halifax in a single voyage.[56] A few more riots later in the spring, including one near Windsor in which a British police sergeant died, continued to accelerate repatriation. By the end of June 1919, two months ahead of General Mewburn's expectations, the great majority of Canadian soldiers were home from the war.

So were their British-based families. At the Armistice, the Canadian High Commission had estimated 50,000 to 60,000 Canadian dependants living in Britain, by no means all of whom intended to return to Canada. Encouraged by Canada's London-based immigration and colonization commissioner, Lt.-Col. Obed Smith, the Ministry of the Overseas Military Forces of Canada established a special program to repatriate wives and any children under eighteen years of age. The plan routed a married soldier and his family to a common base at a former convalescent depot at Buxton, near Manchester, within easy distance of the port at Liverpool.

There they would sail together on special "family ships" destined for Saint John.

The problems of moving dependants were soon highlighted by the voyage of the *Scandinavian,* a family ship that left Liverpool on 28 December 1918 with 1,175 passengers, 282 of them children and 174 of them under twelve. Two weeks earlier, in London, passengers had spent all day in a queue, waiting for their tickets. At noon, the staff simply closed up and left for lunch. The sailing had then been delayed for the two weeks over Christmas, leaving families to cope, and mothers and children were utterly exhausted and querulous when they boarded the ship at Liverpool. Military authorities still did not know whether the government would refund the dependants' passage and they ordered staff to say nothing. As the ship toiled through the worst of a North Atlantic winter crossing, conditions in the overcrowded third-class quarters were nightmarish: screaming children, seasick mothers, plugged toilets, and vomit everywhere. A YWCA worker and two nursing sisters did their best, but the medical officer, a major in the Canadian Army Medical Corps, allegedly stayed drunk and abusive through the voyage. The stewards were dirty, unhelpful, and corrupt. Four first-class passengers surrendered their cabins to sick mothers, but the captain did not consider it his duty to encourage further volunteers. By the time the *Scandinavian* docked in Saint John, two soldiers and two mothers had died, leaving four new orphans.[57] Unlike the *Northland,* officials suppressed any inquiry, referred complaints to the ship's owners, Montreal's Allan Line, and persuaded the government to move swiftly on some issues the high commissioner, Sir George Perley, and Lt.-Col. Smith had been urging for months.

By order-in-council on 29 January 1919, the cabinet agreed to imitate Britain, Australia, New Zealand, and South Africa, and provide free third-class passage to returning soldiers' dependants, without distinction between those who had originally come from Canada and those who were emigrating for the first time. Soldiers and certainly officers who wished to pay more for better accommodation were welcome to do so. With a nod to the *Scandinavian,* those who had travelled since 11 November (and eventually, those who had crossed before that date) would have retroactive reimbursement. Though the costs would come from the War Appropriation, henceforth the work would be undertaken by the Department of Immigration and Colonization, not by the Ministry of Overseas Military Forces. Immigration restrictions for any dependants who had never been in Canada were waived.[58] Two months later, a second order-in-council denied free passage for those who had gone to Europe since the Armistice.

Despite military protests about the difficulties of maintaining discipline, soldiers and their dependants bunked separately but met on board ship and, in some vessels, took their meals together. Regularly faced with angry soldiers protesting ship conditions and their wives' treatment, the conducting officers in charge of military passengers pleaded for separation but, insisted Albert Carman, the historian of demobilization, this was impractical "because of the human and political factors of the situation."[59] Third class in an immigrant ship was an ordeal for any traveller and, in order to squeeze in more bodies, troopships in wartime had been stripped of amenities even immigrants expected. Apart from their own passage to Britain, few soldiers and even fewer wives can have had prior experience of the conditions in steerage. Even some who had paid extra for better accommodation found themselves relegated to the crowded, stinking bowels of their ship and to the limited deck space reserved for the poorest passengers. The continuing ravages of influenza added to the misery and the death toll.

The *Scandinavian* experience led to improved food, better medical care, and alleviation of some of the absurdities of military discipline. This relieved some shipboard hardships, though not nearly as much as pleasanter weather. The YMCA staff on dependant ships organized activities, ran "Baby Shows" and, Carman noted, rescued some wives from third class by persuading ailing officers' wives in first-class cabins to employ them as nurses.[60] Lt.-Col. Obed Smith had seen it all before: "Just so long as the ocean gets rough in bad weather, and people suffer from mal de mer and many travel third class who never travelled that way before," he explained, "these complaints will continue."[61]

At Saint John, family reception had to be improvised in the overcrowded CPR immigration shed by a committee grouping sixteen to twenty organizations. Halifax volunteers, who had managed similar reception duties during the war, had expected to continue in 1919.[62] Haligonians were annoyed and skeptical, but Saint John pride and energy overcame most difficulties.[63] Local women organized a rest room, sick bay, crèche, and kitchen for "the tired women, nerve-racked and weary with the discontents of steerage accommodation on an ocean liner during the winter."[64] Immigration doctors vaccinated the new arrivals. The local Patriotic Fund secretary, F.S. West, negotiated hospital accommodation for sick mothers and organized burials for those who had not survived the journey. Since ships rarely arrived without ten to twelve patients in need of care, local military authorities reopened one of their own hospitals. Mrs. Gordon Holder of the Saint John branch of the CPF accepted the burden of notifying relatives in England and advising any husband who had lost his wife: "Saddest of all was the task of comforting little children that were sometimes left motherless and whose fathers were still in Europe."[65]

In April, when the St. Lawrence opened for navigation, the reception centre at Saint John closed and the women of Quebec City, French and English, took over the responsibility for receiving families. The local YWCA paid for another set of restrooms, and the CPF paid for a canteen to be run by the IODE. The Montreal

CPF branch sent Frances Hains to do what F.S. West had done at Saint John.[66] Immigration regulations required an adult newcomer to Canada to have at least $25 to pay their onward costs. Even if their passage had been paid, few wives had much money left after the voyage, and sometimes purses or tickets had been lost or stolen. Apart from the ticket, the balance of the travel costs to their Canadian destination was a family responsibility. Ordinary immigrants without means were sent to immigration limbo; soldiers' dependants were referred to the CPF. A reciprocal arrangement with the American Red Cross covered dependants who returned via United States ports.[67]

The railway companies met the dependants' ships with the same colonist cars that had carried millions of immigrants across the country before the war. Wooden bunks, a stack of well-worn mattresses, pillows, and blankets, and a couple of wood-burning stoves greeted passengers arriving at Saint John or Quebec City. Soldiers were issued dining car meal tickets for the journey across Canada, but their families were urged to save the cost and buy the "Food Package" on sale for $1.50 at the Discharge Depot.[68] Travel by rail, even to southern Ontario, consumed a couple of days from Saint John, while a journey to British Columbia could take a week. Women who had lived all their lives in England could hardly imagine Canada's vast distances. "It was remarkable," commented Morris, "how many women thought they could travel to Western Canada with two or three children, at an expenditure for meals and incidentals of three or four dollars." With whatever misgivings, CPF officials laid out the money. "There were occasional cases," Morris added, "in which a woman had only colonist transportation for the train, but was not physically fit to endure the relative discomforts of that method of travel." When it judged necessary, the Fund paid for better accommodation.[69] "As human nature is," Carman observed, "there were applications for funds made in cases where the need did not exist."[70]

At each major station along the railway lines across Canada, CPF branches organized information, emergency accommodation, and support for the travellers. At Montreal, Helen Reid's auxiliary provided a committee to meet each trainload of dependants. Toronto women opened a special hostel for the "war brides," and Patriotic Fund branches in Winnipeg, Regina, Calgary, and Vancouver followed suit. While most families were accompanied by the husband and were met, eventually, by his family, some faced a strange new land alone. Many discovered that their Canadian husband had exaggerated the comfort and sophistication of his homeland and of his own home. Some war brides found themselves pegged as a conniving interloper who had robbed aged parents of the son who would otherwise have supported them, or as the wicked witch in a small-town wartime romance gone sour with time and distance.[71]

Between the Armistice and the end of 1919, 267,813 Canadian soldiers and 37,748 dependants crossed the Atlantic.[72] As minister of Overseas Military Forces of Canada, Sir Edward Kemp believed that most Canadians would fail to make a success of living in England. His officials made it as hard as possible for Canadian soldiers to take their release in the United Kingdom, but 15,182 CEF members signed away their right to be repatriated, joining another 7,136 discharged during the war. They were outnumbered by 24,753 "Imperials" from Britain and other dominions who pinned their hopes on emigrating to Canada. Soon, only a handful of Canadian convicts in British prisons remained as vestiges of the enterprise that had begun at Plymouth on 13 October 1914.[73]

While the great majority of Canadians overseas had spent the Great War in Britain, France, or Belgium, a few were scattered around the world, wherever the Allies served. Their relatives were easily persuaded that they would be left behind. Anna Sims, the Toronto mother of a Royal Air Force cadet, feared that Canada had forgotten all about her son and his friends training in Shorncliffe, Kent: "just one ship would bring all of them."[74]

Some Canadians were indeed beyond reach in 1919. Conscripts were included in the Canadian brigade Sir Robert Borden volunteered for Vladivostok, to help a force of former Czech prisoners of war escape from Bolshevik-controlled Russia. Canadian volunteers had also joined British-led expeditions to Archangel and Murmansk. Among them was Sgt. Frank Maheux. Posted to a training unit in England after his bout with VD, he was soon utterly bored with military routine. Going to North Russia, he wrote to his "poor wife, Angeline," would get him closer to Canada. What he could not confess to her was that his case of gonorrhoea in London in 1917 doomed him to a full year of quarantine on the wrong side of the Atlantic.[75] Maheux injured his foot on the ship going to North Russia and spent his first few months in hospital and convalescing. Hardly had he settled in for the Russian winter than news came of the Armistice. As a small comfort, he assured Angeline that if he had gone to France he might have been wiped out with the rest of his 21st Battalion breaching the Drocourt-Quéant line.

The poverty and squalor Maheux found in North Russia were as familiar to an Ottawa Valley lumberjack as the snow and cold, but he found the people different. Billeted on a Russian family, he was embarrassed when the woman of the house offered him all she had, two hard chunks of black bread. "Just to show you the kind of people they are, the poor woman she undress herself in front of all of us, also the little girl put on night clothes," he wrote. The woman next offered her unsought guests all her blankets and quilts but once she thought Maheux was asleep, she grabbed two of them back. Acutely embarrassed to be found wearing only his shirt, Maheux confessed to Angeline that he feigned sleep. By winter's end, Maheux and just about every other Allied soldier was satisfied, as he said, to "let the bloody Russians settle their business themselves."[76]

Ottawa emphatically agreed, and allowed the British only a couple of weeks delay before releasing the Canadians. Maheux sailed from Murmansk in late April. His release came in May. By 15 June he was in Ottawa, a civilian with a transport warrant to Maniwaki, $35 for a new suit of civilian clothes, and $750 to his credit as a War Service Gratuity for a sergeant who had served since December 1914. Throughout the war, Maheux had promised his wife that their hard times were over. They would live in a house; he would learn to farm; they would never again be separated. Instead, during the 1920s, Maheux found work building forest ranger towers in Quebec. In 1929 veterans' preference got him a job in the Ottawa post office. Lacking supporting evidence in his medical records, a skeptical Pension Commission refused Maheux's claim for a double hernia. In 1940 Maheux was fit enough to volunteer for the Veterans' Guard of Canada, but a few months of guarding German prisoners broke down his health and he went back to his old job. In 1951, at age seventy, he retired and died a year later, a veteran, like his wife, of the stresses of a great war.[77]

Coming Home Again

No single veteran or veteran's family is typical, but Frank and Angeline Maheux illustrate several patterns. As wife of a CEF soldier, she received separation allowance. Grudgingly and under compulsion, he assigned her half his pay before he left Canada in May 1915, and, though the Patriotic Fund was not organized in Maniwaki, its Ottawa office mailed her an allowance cheque for herself and her three children. She was hard up, initially because her husband had left many debts, and later because of the rising cost of living, but probably the war years were far from her worst years economically. She and her husband corresponded extensively and emotionally, and if he was not wholly faithful to her, the stress of four years of separation were not easy to bear for a man who made no secret of his physical desires.

After the war, the Maheuxs were not alone in hoping that they would live better than they had before. The government may have hoped that they would, too, but apart from the War Service Gratuity, Ottawa felt too financially burdened to make any serious offer to veterans. Maheux's thoughts of becoming a farmer never came to fruition because he had neither land nor experience, and vocational training was reserved for disabled soldiers considered likely to benefit from it. A veterans' preference clause allowed easier access to entry-level positions in the public service of Canada and its counterparts in most provinces and cities. This clause ultimately helped give Maheux a steady job and income in the Post Office, plus retirement benefits, at an age when his physical limitations would have interfered with his employability in the woods. For those who could take advantage of it and had modest horizons, veterans' preference meant an improved life.

It is a common experience that a long-awaited delight loses much in the realization. Not all those who had yearned for home and family, and not all who awaited them, were fulfilled by the meeting. Three or four years is a long time in the life of a marriage and of young children. The father who had left in 1914 or 1915, and whose photograph had filled a central place in the home, looked very different when he returned in 1919. So did his wife and his children, and so did life. Currie had insisted that the CEF return in formed battalions for the sake of discipline, but this was a near-run thing. Most units managed to stay together just long enough to march through hometown streets to a civic reception. Then, as the speeches began, the ranks dissolved into hundreds of family reunions. Next day, soldiers reluctantly lined up for the last time to hand in weapons and kit and collect back pay, a discharge certificate, their service lapel badge, part of their War Service Gratuity, a $35 civilian clothing allowance and, if they needed it, a warrant for whatever travel was required to take them to their final destination. When they left, they were civilians, free to pass a gauntlet of religious and charitable organizations offering their services on the way to the street.

From his dismal barrack room in England, Pte. Ernest Hamilton had promised his wife that, when he returned, they could have a second honeymoon. This time he would not lose the key to their trunk, and she had better get used to seeing the ceiling for a very long time.[78] Did their marriage resume like that? His family cannot remember and probably was never told. They do know that Hamilton did not return to his pre-enlistment job as a prison guard. He had trouble finding other durable employment until, like Frank Maheux, he found a job in the Post Office. In 1920 his adored and beautiful Sara suffered a stroke that left her lame for the rest of her short life. Another stroke in 1934 left her bedridden until she died in 1936. Ernest Hamilton followed her in 1946, soon after his retirement.

Veterans of the First World War and their families recall an almost uncontrollable restlessness and impatience among the returned men. Soldiers could never really share their experiences with civilians, even in their own family, nor could they respect the stress and sacrifice of those who had stayed in Canada. Describing the impact of the world wars on his home community of Dorchester, New Brunswick, Douglas How recalled, "In the village, in a sense, the war became a sort of no man's land, which people usually did not enter. The returned men did not talk about it because they had been there, and others did not talk about it because they hadn't, and lads found that what patrols they sent into no man's land came back to report the trenches empty and their curiosity unfulfilled."[79] Even soldiers themselves were deeply divided among those who had experienced the trenches and the larger number who had "soldiered" in England or Canada, or in "safety first" jobs behind the lines. Nor could the front-line soldiers recapture the dense comradeship of their old battalion, platoon, or section. What family could ever be as close as the few men with whom you had shared the bowel-loosening terror of imminent death as the explosions came steadily closer down the trench line?[80]

Canada's late-war boom and inflation soared into 1920 and collapsed in 1921. Many of the jobs created for veterans, and especially for their disabled comrades, promptly vanished. Most Canadians then moved on. Life was struggle enough for most people to spare much sympathy for veterans and families the government had apparently treated with sufficient, if not excessive, generosity. In a Canada still enmeshed in a wartime crusade for virtue, abstinence, and righteousness, many ex-soldiers defiantly drank, smoked, swore, gambled, and drifted from job to job. A prominent former army medical officer wondered publicly whether soldiering was a kind of disease. "They have become accustomed to having everything done for them," explained Col. Alexander Primrose, first postwar president of the Toronto Academy of Medicine: "they lose all ambition and have no desire to help themselves."[81]

Brig.-Gen. J.A. Gunn, a staff officer, warned that the war had transformed each soldier: "His training had been to think of nothing but killing the Boche. Every other thought had as far as possible been excluded from his mind ... To a very great extent, he has been relieved from instituting things, and above all that self-interest which is essential to success in civil life has been suppressed."[82] Given the extraordinary diversity of soldiers and military experiences, any specific advice about soldiers was largely absurd, but it touched a common core of experience and anxiety. Returned soldiers were never quite as they were expected to be. Given time and a kindly but firm hand, the knowing agreed, veterans would settle down again. Meanwhile, their wives must live their lives as well as they could with a husband who was sometimes penniless, unemployable, and emotionally disturbed.

Dora Horwood's troubles, which had preoccupied officials of the Manitoba Patriotic Fund in 1916-17 (see Chapter 4), did not end when her husband came home with Lord Strathcona's Horse in 1919. Fred Horwood came back to Winnipeg on 2 June, gave Dora $25, and disappeared. She tried to intercept her half of his War Service Gratuity and pleaded with the Manitoba Patriotic Fund to find her a lawyer. "I should be so glad of some advice," she wrote, "as I don't know what to do."[83] According to Fred, the father of their first child had appeared from England and Dora wanted Fred out of the way: "I could never look or do anything right and I had to leave because I was getting run down and I was in very poor health through her nagging at me, which was everlasting," claimed Fred, "and I am a total ab-stainer, and I have never tasted liquir in my life althou my wife used to tell every-body where we stayed when I was with her that she had to nag me because I was always drunk."[84] False or true, Fred was gone, and Dora and their four children became a postwar burden for the MPF as long as her children were of school age: "We allow $50.00 per month," her case worker explained, "and Mrs. Horwood goes out nursing to supplement this."[85]

Manitobans had been pioneers in mothers' allowance and their Patriotic Fund had remained under provincial control.[86] Like the national CPF, though with fewer constraints, the Manitoba Fund applied its surplus to deserted mothers under the guardianship of Helen Reid's local counterpart, Edith Rogers. Most of her clients, like Mrs. Horwood, had anticipated their plight long before the war ended. Olive Bell's husband, Will, had been commissioned from the Permanent Force in 1916 but she needed the Patriotic Fund from the beginning. When her husband was discharged in 1919 and did not come home, the MPF sent money, but they ex-pected Mrs. Bell's elderly father to pursue the man. From a distance, Will Bell pleaded for patience as he pursued one futile business proposition after another. Finally Mrs. Bell became Case 686. After repeated threats to cut off desertion cases, Manitoba finally ended its financial support to solders' wives in March 1928. By then Mrs. Bell's children were close to leaving school and she was left at almost age fifty to support herself. Edith Bonus presented a more complex case. Pte. Bonus was her second husband and, after two of her daughters alleged to him that she was having an affair, he suspected he might not be the last. MPF investigators reported that her neighbours and doctor upheld Edith's good name; Mrs. Bonus, in turn, was perhaps forgivably vengeful towards her daughters, and furious at her husband. Needless to say, Pte. Bonus did not return to the nest.

Elizabeth Douglas had a sadder tale. She and her three children came back from Scotland in 1919 after her husband had already returned to Canada. She discov-ered that he had failed to make payments on their shack in Transcona, and her young family was homeless. Meanwhile, Douglas had deserted her for a Mrs. Sneesly. Rather than go home to Scotland, Mrs. Douglas stayed in Winnipeg and found work cleaning the GWVA club rooms; the veterans took up her cause, the MPF made her an allowance, and she rented a small cottage that she furnished with proceeds of damages after her youngest daughter was hit by a streetcar. Mrs. Douglas received some MPF support at least until 1928.

Making a Surplus Disappear

Because the war had ended blessedly early, the Patriotic Fund could afford to support Dora Horwood and other abandoned wives and mothers; it could care for the families of soldiers struck down by the Spanish flu; it could even help transport English wives to their Canadian homes. For an organization that had denied its families relief from record wartime price increases, the CPF had ended the war in November 1918 with an embarrassingly large surplus. As of 31 March 1919, the Canadian Patriotic Fund had collected, from all sources, including bank interest and foreign contributions, $47,153,819.35. It had spent $38,452,000.91, leaving a balance of $8,701,818.44.[87]

The gap between the amount Montrealers had contributed and what their soldiers' families had received was far larger. After John W. Ross completed his post-Armistice accounts, he reported $8,333,544 in branch receipts (including Montreal's default and $270,795 in accumulated bank interest). The Montreal CPF had spent only $3,158,528 on relief in its own community and $105,926 on administration. Ross had forwarded $2,020,528 to Ottawa for redistribution, leaving an unspent balance of more than $3 million. Ross and Reid might be proud of their frugal management but, as Reid herself acknowledged, "many subscribers might retire if they knew that the bulk of money subscribed in Montreal was still untouched by Montreal and was being used for National purposes."[88]

When Nova Scotia's New Glasgow branch proposed a $5 Christmas bonus for all its CPF beneficiaries at the end of 1918, Arthur Barnstead sought Ottawa's approval. It was "irregular" to spend $15,000 in such a way, he confessed, but at an average of $12 per family, Nova Scotia paid well below the national average and had a large balance in hand. Instead of the normal grudging reply, Morris responded effusively that there would be "no objection whatsoever ... we are glad to have an opportunity of heartily endorsing the same."[89]

The Fund had to consider further needs it might meet with its wartime reserves.[90] At the end of 1918 the CPF ended its discrimination against large families by removing the upper limit on its allowances. It declared all postenlistment wives, negligent mothers, and even immoral wives eligible, provided they showed a proper humility. Even the families of soldiers imprisoned in England and of uncaptured overseas deserters could have up to six months of benefits unless the man came home. Since no one in the CEF could now go overseas, a husband on Home Service was no longer a bar to support.

When a wife in 1914 gave permission for her husband to enlist, she might have foreseen the risk of death or disablement, but, as Philip Morris recalled, these were not the only threats: "She ran the further risk of his infidelity, with its possible consequences of desertion."[91] The CPF could not do much to restore missing husbands, but it could support deserted wives. Or should it? In its final form, as of May 1921, the CPF's policy displays the symptoms of a bitter wrangle in the national executive. Assistance to deserted wives would be limited to those who were "completely and apparently permanently physically or mentally incapacitated."[92] The generosity of the Manitoba Fund appears to have been less discriminatory.

The Fund also showed an overdue concern for aged parents thrown on their own resources by a son who, "with time on his hands, money in his pocket, and the King's uniform on his back, found courtship pleasant and marriage easy.". To the government and most people, Morris wrote, such a marriage was insignificant, but "to the aged people or the aged parent, it more nearly approaches the tragic." Other tragedies occurred when a veteran returned safe and sound, only to be crippled within a few months by a chronic illness or to die from influenza, or to have his wife suffer or die. Morris conceded, "In such a predicament, it is not surprising if he sometimes wonders whether his services to his country in her hour of need do not justify a further helping hand in his own trouble."[93]

There were limits. A Belgian count complained to the prime minister about an elderly former Belgian living near Lac St-Jean, whose son had been ordered by a Belgian court to pay him a pension. During the war, the son enlisted and could not send money even if he had earned it. The CPF had supported the old man but he claimed that, when he was the only proconscription voter in 1917, he was cut off by the local committee. A patriotic Belgian family in the neighbourhood had taken him in, but they were now going home to Belgium. He asked, "Is this the way the Canadian authorities treat the dependants of allied soldiers when they speak the French language and profess the catholic faith"?[94] Postwar generosity to wartime allies had curdled; there was no reply.

On 17 June 1919, after an all-night sitting, an exhausted Parliament was invited to cancel the 1915 amendment that had limited the CPF's life to six months after the war, and authorized it to help soldiers' families until its money was gone. Confused by the bill, J.A. Calder invited Ames to explain, and the architect of the Patriotic Fund made his last speech on its behalf.[95] Sir Herbert Ames's interest and involvement in the Fund had diminished as staff took over and its functions grew more routine. In September 1919 he found a fresh opportunity for his idealism and experience as financial director in the secretariat of the new League of Nations in Geneva.[96] His successor, former Kingston MP William F. Nickle, was related to the tireless relief committee chairman of the Kingston branch and, since 1916, had been a member of the national executive. Best known for his prickly independence and his legislation banning hereditary titles for Canadians, Nickle had resigned his seat in Parliament and was eager to serve. Sir Henry Drayton, who had succeeded the exhausted Sir Thomas White as Sir Robert Borden's minister of finance, also inherited his post as the CPF's honorary treasurer.

Under new leadership, the staff proposed, the Fund could continue to play a useful short-term postwar role: "How long the Fund will be able to mitigate the sufferings of these people cannot definitely be stated," Morris warned his readers in 1920. "It is hoped, however, that the money available will last for several years, and that when its resources are exhausted, the need of assistance will no longer exist."[97] To celebrate the CPF's prolonged life and new roles, Sir Henry Egan, seconded by Ames, proposed that the Pension Board imitate the Fund's systematic home visits to its pensioners and their families "to the end that these be encouraged and helped to make the best use of the Governmental grants."[98] After four years of wartime visiting, the "alms of good advice" still seemed well worth distributing.

Ottawa now turned to the Fund as a mechanism for some reluctant spending of its own. With a quarter-million soldiers home from overseas, discharged and looking for work, seasonal unemployment in the coming winter of 1919-20 seemed to be heading for an alarming record. Winter relief was strictly a municipal responsibility, but an emergency seemed to be brewing and Ottawa had become accustomed to tackling, and being seen to tackle, war-related emergencies. Nervous about potentially turbulent veterans, Parliament belatedly voted $40 million as a Federal Emergency Appropriation for their benefit.[99] Normally Ottawa had no means of disbursing money to the needy, but the CPF organization offered a solution. With branches everywhere and a record of detailed investigation, frugality, honesty, and systematic cost control, the Fund was invited to deliver the government's one-time Federal Emergency Relief Allocation, or FERA. Reluctantly, the national executive agreed. When the branches proved even more reluctant, the national office set up a large parallel organization, mainly staffed by returned officers and commanded by Nickle's fellow Kingstonian, Brig.-Gen. A.E. Ross of the CAMC.

CPF branches learned of the latest call on their patriotism as Christmas approached. On 17 December 1919 Gen. Ross of the new Federal Emergency Appropriation Department met the Montreal executive and found them in a surly mood. Their war was over, their volunteers had other lives to lead, and jobless veterans were not the sort of clients the Patriotic had grown used to. Finally Helen Reid and Clarence Smith set out their terms: the Montreal branch would cooperate, but it was "absolutely necessary to have a separate staff and organization."[100] From the local board, Brig.-Gen. A.E. Labelle chose Lt.-Col. Léo LaFlèche, a wounded 22nd Battalion veteran, to head a special committee of former officers. The branch treasurer, John W. Ross, became a conduit for money he did not want, to people he did not entirely trust.

Benefits under the Emergency Appropriation were reserved for those who had been living in Canada before the war and who had served overseas. Included were men who had found work at pay so poor that they could not support their family. A single man could collect up to $50; a man and wife, $75 plus $12 for a first child, $10 for the second, and a family maximum of $100. Since the local organizations only got going after the start of 1920, officials were authorized to make payments retroactive to November 1919.[101]

Col. LaFlèche and his director, Maj. A. Gauvreau, struggled to satisfy indigent veterans, a resentful and disapproving Montreal branch, and CPF officials in Ottawa.[102] Though LaFlèche was told to expect 800 returned soldiers, his staff dealt with 8,566 applicants. Between 23 December 1919 and 20 February 1920, they distributed $236,360 to 4,694 men. For weeks his clerks struggled without forms or records. LaFlèche had estimated a staff of sixteen; eventually he employed almost 200 men, including eighty investigators. Most were picked from the relief lines, among them six former CEF medical officers who collected relief in return for treating men not sick enough for hospital.[103] While many applicants found work, others used every trick to get benefits. Meanwhile, William Nickle demanded every precaution – and then condemned LaFlèche for the extravagance of hiring auditors.[104] A worse explosion followed when LaFlèche granted his employees two weeks' leave with pay after they had wound up their work. The hapless Ross was commanded to recover the money. "He cannot sacrifice consistency for the price of popularity," wrote Nickle's deputy.[105] It was language designed to provoke the eminent branch treasurer to rage.

While others in her branch fumed at the postwar burdens, Helen Reid launched a fresh initiative with a CPF Health Clinic, opened in early November 1919 for families of ex-soldiers. It also provided a base for a study of the health "defects" of a thousand soldiers' children, ranging from adenitis to warts, from lice to decayed teeth. The results were worse than comparable studies in the United States and England: only two children were "defect-free," one sad waif was burdened with fifteen of them, and the average was six per child. Reid blamed parental poverty, ignorance, and selfishness and insisted that the only cure lay with visiting nurses dedicated to training mothers. The clinic closed after a year and Reid was left to publish her study at her own expense.[106]

Nova Scotia, whose CPF records survived, in part, in the provincial archives, was almost as reluctant as Montreal to share the work of the Federal Emergency Appropriation.[107] Some individuals and some local branches accepted the burden only after personal appeals from Arthur Barnstead, the provincial secretary. Travelling in midwinter to reorganize branches and to find substitutes was an added ordeal that Nickle, Gen. Ross, and other CPF officials in Ottawa were loath to acknowledge. As in Montreal, forms were a problem. Some arrived late in December, others were lost in the mail, and who in the branches would receive them? At the end of January 1920, Barnstead could report to Gen. Ross that only Halifax and Yarmouth had so far managed to distribute money.[108] Meanwhile Philip Morris pestered him for details for his CPF history. Barnstead replied, "You have piled so much work on us down here and I do not know when I can possibly get it done and in any event the work of the Patriotic Fund is not completed until we get through with this Emergency Appropriation."[109]

At the other end of the country, British Columbia branches appear to have been less reluctant to get involved, but delays in getting information, stationery, and forms were greater. As wives had found during the war, the number of branches was an incentive to applicants to register in a number of places, notably in both Vancouver and Victoria, in the hope of collecting benefits from both. Maj. Christie of the Victoria office assured the *Daily Times* that, after scrupulous investigation by CPF workers, he had assisted over 1,500 veterans to collect monthly benefits ranging from $50 for a single man to a maximum of $100 for a family, with more from the CPF if a family could not make ends meet.[110]

After several brief extensions in the spring of 1920, the CPF wound up its unemployment relief on 24 April, having spent, Morris reported, a mere $5 to $6 million on its clients, though "it was only kept at such a low figure by the most careful investigation of all claims."[111]

With peace, voluntarism faded. Helen Reid continued her work but, as the caseload dwindled, the number of paid visitors, investigators, and office staff grew. In the summer of 1920, the CPF's national office complained, Montreal needed thirty paid staff at $3,282.12 a month to distribute $14,854.00 in relief to 167 permanent cases, while Toronto managed three times the case load with twenty staff. Montreal, explained Clarence Smith, had always been more active in social service. More to the point, Smith concluded, Miss Reid (added late in 1918 as the sole woman member of the CPF national executive) "would not be satisfied with a third-rate office."[112] After April 1922 no new applicants were accepted, and in its final year, 1922-3, the Montreal branch spent $256,173 on 468 families.[113]

The Montreal branch's social work ended in April 1923. At a reception on 16 March, Bishop Farthing presented Clarence Smith with an engraved silver urn, and his wife with a bouquet of roses and sweet peas. There had been no thought of race or creed, Smith said: "If other societies would obey the same lines, they would progress farther."[114] In Montreal, explained Helen Reid, only 165 cases could count on continuing help. The rest of the Fund's 300 mothers would "be left to their own resources, and have to bring up their families the best way they can." Most other provinces, she pointed out, had mothers' allowances: in 1923 Quebec remained one of four exceptions.[115]

Bonuses and Farms

In February 1919, bored, freezing veterans and their friends had crowded into Calgary's Allen Theatre to get warm and have some fun. George Waistell, former British merchant skipper and CEF veteran, had an engaging idea. While other Canadians had been staying home and getting rich, soldiers had been dying for just $1.10 a day and, as returned men soon discovered, their families had been left in poverty. Simple justice demanded restitution. Veterans, claimed Waistell, were entitled to a bonus of $1,000 if they had served in Canada, $1,500 if they had reached England, and a full $2,000 if they had gone to France. Promptly endorsed by some Tory and populist politicians, sympathetic women's organizations, a scattering of unions, and businessmen who saw it as an alternative to even more costly government paternalism, the Calgary bonus resolution soon joined the tangle of policies, platforms, tactics, and demands that helped make 1919 one of the most turbulent years in Canada's history.[116]

The bonus was *not* the policy of Col. Willard Purney or of the GWVA's new secretary-treasurer, C. Grant MacNeil, or of other men who had taken the lead in the Great War Veterans' Association. On the contrary, they saw it as a mad idea, likely to absorb and even more likely to dispel the national generosity towards Canada's defenders, which they had been working hard to focus on the war's permanent victims: widows, orphans, and the war-disabled. These were the vulnerable people who would be trampled in a stampede by able-bodied veterans for $2 billion in spending money.

Nevertheless, by summer the bonus campaign had enough power to capture the backing of the national Liberal leadership convention in Ottawa that elected William Lyon Mackenzie King.[117] A rival to the GWVA, the Grand Army of Canada, intent on mobilizing the veteran vote as a political force, found the bonus an ideal plank. So did some Ontario Tories. One of them, Toronto's Mayor Tommy Church, had been hunting for ways to nail returned soldiers to his brand of populist Conservatism. The bonus also suited J. Harry Flynn, a plump American demagogue who had come over the border in 1917 to join the Canadian Army Medical Corps. Flynn summoned a throng of veterans to Toronto's Queen's Park on Sunday, 7 September 1919. "Let us put a peaceful demand," he cried, "and if it is not answered, I say let us take it by force."[118] The crowd roared approval, and made him president of a Returned Soldiers' Gratuity League. When Bill Turley, the disabled ex-boxer who headed the GWVA in Ontario, tried to argue with Flynn, the crowd of ex-soldiers howled him down and threatened to beat him up.

During the summer, Sir Robert Borden's government had already said no to the bonus. The War Service Gratuity had cost $130 million, and soldier settlement would cost at least as much more. Pensions that year would add an annual burden of $35 to $40 million. At $2 billion, the proposed bonuses would double the national debt and, once the money was spent, Borden suspected that the veterans would be back for more. By November, when the issue came to a parliamentary vote, almost every MP, including the Liberals, agreed with the government. A few maverick Toronto Tories, Mayor Church, W.F. McLean of the *Toronto World,* and Col. J.A. Currie, MP for Simcoe-North, stayed with the bonus until the end.[119]

Throughout 1919, the GWVA had annoyed potential members by opposing their $2,000 bonus while campaigning for its more vulnerable constituents. In the aftermath of the bonus's defeat, the GWVA lost thousands of members, many to Flynn's new "Grand Army of United Veterans," some to the Army and Navy Veterans and most to come to personal and private terms with their own re-establishment. Borden's government was left with an unfair reputation for ignoring the veterans, and the substantial pension reforms that were instituted in 1919 were largely overlooked.

Far from ignoring the need to re-establish returned soldiers, the government had poured much energy and money into the traditional Canadian dream of turning men into prosperous, self-sufficient farmers. The Soldiers' Settlement Act of 1918 bore a slightly misleading resemblance to another veteran of Canada's wars: the tradition of paying off old soldiers with land grants. As early as the Régiment Carignan-Salières in the 1660s and as recently as the South African War, veterans had regularly been rewarded with the one resource most Canadians considered limitless and free: land. Ottawa had learned from history that land grants to veterans usually fell into the hands of speculators, adding substantially to the cost and inefficiency of genuine land development. By 1917 the government also realized that it had nothing like enough suitable land to turn even 100,000 veterans into settlers. Instead, the government designed the Soldiers' Settlement Act as a hard-headed colonization scheme, with low-cost loans and favourable terms reserved strictly for veterans who could persuade a board that they had the experience, connections, and physical strength to make a commercial success of farming.[120]

Part of the heat that fuelled the Calgary resolution came from anger that the minority of veterans selected as soldier settlers had gained a form of bounty denied to others. But soldier settlers were not envied very long. Thousands of unqualified veterans had felt encouraged to apply and, while many were rejected, too many were accepted by soft-hearted selection boards. Having exposed their families to the miseries of the war years, thousands of ex-soldiers next led their wives and children into the hardships, frustrations, and ultimate failure of establishing a farm during some of the most difficult years Canadian agriculture has experienced. They bought land, equipment, and livestock when prices were at their postwar high, repaid their loans after farm prices had collapsed, and struggled with the

sharp practices of professed patriots who had unloaded bad land with the collusion of complacent local committees. Some who have examined their experience
in the context of other colonization schemes have concluded that, on the whole,
Soldier Settlement was no worse and in some ways much better than other contemporary plans. Though more than half the veterans had failed by 1929, the rest
had managed to own and to farm their own land.[121] It was successful enough to
justify a more generous Veterans' Land Act as part of the 1945 Veterans' Charter
after the Second World War.

Wives and Widows As Pensioners

During the war years, most returned soldiers in Canada had suffered from some
disability. Veterans' organizations like the GWVA or the ANV reflected their concerns. The organizations acted as trustees for all soldiers, but they were best qualified as a lobby for the CEF's sick and wounded. In 1919, it had been the turn of
250,000 able-bodied veterans to return to their homes and families. Another 60,000
men would never return, of whom about 10,000 left widows and children and
another 5,000 left dependent parents, sisters, or brothers. Over time, veterans would
be killed by their disabilities as certainly as if they had perished on the battlefield,
leaving widows and children equally eligible for pensions.[122] As Canada's pension
liability rose, from $7.27 million in the last year of the war to over $25 million by
1920, wealthy and influential Canadians wondered whether the country could sustain the burden.

The public was sufficiently conscious of soldiers' widows and mothers that the
government instituted a small Silver Cross of Sacrifice as a reward for the loss of a
son or husband.[123] However, twice as many wives and nine times as many children –
over 100,000 Canadians – depended on a soldier's disability pension as well as on
his ability to earn a postwar living.[124] The long, intense struggle over pension administration, and the annual attempts to change the rules, often successful in the
House of Commons, only to be reversed at the last minute by the Senate, affected
next of kin as well as veterans until R.B. Bennett's pension restructuring in 1933.[125]

Continuing a routine begun in 1916, Parliament annually appointed a special
committee to review the current agenda of veterans' issues, from pension levels to
the need to finance Returned Soldiers' Insurance.[126] In 1918 the advice of a parliamentary committee persuaded Ottawa to added a $96 bonus to a private or cor-
poral's widow's $480 pension, and $66 to the $510 paid a staff sergeant's widow.[127]
In 1919 a committee headed by Liberal-Unionist Newton Rowell successfully recommended that the government level up all lower-rank pensions to the $720 it
paid a lieutenant's widow. The following year Ottawa increased the pensions further

so that a soldier's widow could count on at least $900 a year, plus allowances for her children. Pensions for widows of higher-ranking soldiers remained unchanged. A lieutenant-colonel's widow could count on $1,248, about as much as Mrs. A.T.H. Williams had received from Parliament after her husband died in the North-West campaign of 1885.[128] Though even Ontario's lieutenant governor, Col. Sir John Hendrie, with two sons in the CEF, publicly advocated an end to the distinctions between officers and men, the Borden government could not quite accept the demand for pension equalization, though it obviously recognized that privates and their wives had more political influence than colonels' wives.[129] Children were now pensioned equally, whatever their father's rank, at $180 for the first, $144 for the second, and $120 for the third and subsequent children, doubled in the event that they were orphans.[130]

In 1921 the postwar boom ended. By then the maximum disability pension for a CEF veteran ranking between private and lieutenant was the same as a widow's, $900: including a cost-of-living bonus that was soon rendered permanent. Children brought in additional allowances, and a wife with a totally helpless man on her hands could still claim an extra $300. When the Americans raised their pension to $1,200, Ottawa hurriedly pointed out that a Canadian veteran with a wife and two children received $1,380, while the British maximum was $728 and the Australians, once the leaders, could now afford only $696 a year.[131] But most disability pensions remained far below the maximum. In 1919, 38,098 privates, collecting $6,528,494 in disability pensions, averaged about $171 each for themselves and their families, about a 20 percent pension.[132]

Despite Todd's search for simple, universal principles, reality always proves more imaginative than theory. A widow's pension reflected the government's inheritance of a responsibility that her husband, had he not died, was legally bound to fulfill. What about a deceased soldier's responsibility for his parents? As both the Patriotic Fund and the Separation Allowance Board had agreed during the war, a man had a duty to his widowed mother, and to both parents if they were penniless. Quebec's civil code enforced such obligations, even to a second generation. In December 1916, when Pte. Camille Belliveau's widowed mother was left old, sick, and unable to work, Mayor Morin, backed by Father Beaulieu, could command the soldier to claim his separation allowance and to make a pay assignment.[133] Elsewhere in Canada the principle lived through the vagaries of the common law and custom.

The Board of Pension Commissioners decided to assume the role of a dutiful son and brother, but only after applying a rigid means test. The elderly widows of two prewar brigadier-generals discovered that the meagre $500 pensions left them by their husbands made them too well off for any pension support from the sons they had lost in the war. Remedying their plight, an official explained, would be "class legislation."[134] The BPC also adopted a postwar rule of thumb that any living son must be worth at least $10 a month to his mother. Maj. C.G. Power, a Liberal MP from Quebec City, advocated that a mother's pension be as unconditional as a widow's, but without success. As London's Hume Cronyn, chairman of the 1920 Pensions Committee, demanded, who would grant a pension to a woman with "three or four strapping sons"?[135]

Under its postwar chairman, Col. John Thompson, the BPC soon proved both tireless and cunning in protecting the treasury by reducing the "pension burden."[136] Not all MPs liked the consequences. There was "nothing more nauseating to the widowed mother of a fallen soldier," complained George Nicholson, a member of Parliament, "than to have these inspectors coming around to see whether the small amount of pension on which they can hardly live is being augmented in any way."[137] Like the CPF, the BPC preferred the term "visitors."

A soldier's widow was spared a means test, but she had to establish her marital status with the Board. At the 1919 parliamentary committee, an MP professed astonishment that pensions might be paid to "unmarried wives." Another MP demanded whether the phrase was a "Yankeeism." "It is not a Yankeeism," responded Sir Rodolphe Lemieux, "it is paganism."[138] This exchange triggered two days of intermittent righteousness and realism that wound up when the chair, Newton Rowell, pointed out that Sir Rodolphe had been a member of the 1916 committee that endorsed the pension rights of an "unmarried wife." The offending phrase was replaced by the ingenious circumlocution "a woman awarded a pension under subsection 3 of section 32 of this Act."[139] In the Senate, Raoul Dandurand coyly asked the government leader, Sir James Lougheed, "Does this payment to the concubine of the soldier do any violence to my hon. friend's sense of propriety?" Apparently it did not.[140]

A Canadian wife in an innocently bigamous relationship was usually favoured over her wronged British predecessor, but Mary Knight lost her widow's pension when the Board discovered that a previous husband who had deserted her in 1903 was still alive.[141] When a soldier, insanely convinced that he was married to Lady Astor, broke from his escort and successfully fled, his real wife and three children lost their disability pension.[142] The dependants of an insane deserter had no claim to any benefit.

For the Pension Board, marriage was a lifelong contract: if a widow remarried or strayed from widowly chastity, she lost her pension. However, the BPC encouraged remarriage by offering a final year of pension as a lump sum "dowry." Even more than the Patriotic Fund in wartime, BPC visitors pursued whispers of immorality or criminality. Even a charge of bootlegging could cost an offender her pension without notice or appeal.[143] Like the Patriotic Fund, the Board believed that a mother should stay home with her children. When Brig.-Gen. H.H. MacLean, the MP for Saint John, suggested that such women could earn a living, a shocked official rejoined: "Why should the widow of a man who laid down his life for his country be expected to work?" MacLean promptly aggravated his offence by adding that, after all, "privates' wives came from the servant class," words that helped end his political career.[144]

Widows and mothers were the Board's most frequent dependent pensioners, but the BPC also served as parent and guardian to soldiers' children, at least until the age of sixteen for boys and seventeen for girls. They could be supported until they were twenty-one if suffering "physical or mental infirmity" or if "making satisfactory progress in a course of instruction approved by the Commission." The Pension Commission confessed that such permission was seldom given since it encouraged youngsters to seek "inferior clerical positions."[145]

One kind of woman was firmly denied a pension: anyone who had married a veteran after his disability had appeared. Even so-called unmarried wives found their pensions cancelled if a BPC visitor discovered that they had formalized their union. When the GWVA's Grant MacNeil and Thomas Caldwell, a New Brunswick Progressive MP, urged such cases in the 1920s they were invariably reminded of "pension widows," the conniving American harpies who lived on the avails of deathbed marriages to veterans. The wiser kingdom to the north would avoid such symbols of the "pension evil" and the perversion of human nature. After all, warned Mrs. Warmington, a major's widow, "Every woman would want to get married if she thought she was going to be maintained."[146] MacNeil's cases included a woman whose spouse had subsequently been healthy enough to win a Military Cross for gallantry, and another whose husband had then been fit enough to be accepted in the Permanent Force before he died. Other women who had kept their prewar engagement to marry were dismissed as authors of their own misfortune. Only in 1930, with an election pending, did the federal government finally concede the point and modify the law.[147]

Cutting the Pension Burden

At the end of the war, the Board of Pension Commissioners had issued 10,488 dependant pensions worth $4,168 million and 15,335 disability pensions worth $3,105,000. In 1921, when pensions reached their first postwar peak, 19,209 dependants collected a total of $12,954,000 while 51,453 disabled pensioners shared $18,231,000.[148] The mounting number of disabled soldiers particularly troubled conservative Canadians. Surely soldiers who had returned able-bodied from the war were inventing ailments and injuries to continue at the public trough and to off-load on to taxpayers their manly responsibility to support themselves and their families. In fact, many soldiers had suffered from sickness and wounds during their service, recovered, and signed away any claim at their discharge rather than risk spending more time in uniform. However, the "insurance" principle Maj. Todd had warned Parliament about still covered them for the consequences of "ailments and injuries" recorded in their military medical records. It might be long after when sudden pain, fever, or debilitating weakness, or perhaps only a comrade's pension bonanza, revived a claim for a disability "attributable" to military service.

After a year in office, Col. Thompson had some serious ideas about how to re-duce the pension burden. Commuting minor pensions made sense because either they would last the longest or else the small disability would grow with age into a larger claim. The temptation of laying their hands on $300 or $700 instead of tiny monthly pension cheques was too much for most veterans and, despite their deep misgivings, GWVA officials had to heed their members. Next, Thompson and his officials set out to remove "six little words" from section 11 of the Pension Act, insist-ing that it would merely bring the law "into line with the general law of other coun-tries." The 1920 special committee on veterans was so full of self-congratulation for granting a pre-election 50 percent pension bonus, it barely noticed that it had eliminated the so-called insurance principle that had allowed veterans to claim for any medical problem encountered during their service, directly attributable or not. Not even the GWVA saw the significance.[149]

After the longest campaign in Canadian history, the 6 December 1921 election delivered a shaky new Liberal government, Canada's first parliament of minori-ties, and an opposition divided on almost every issue but cost-cutting. Mackenzie King chose Maj. Herbert Marler, a right-wing Montreal Liberal, to head the 1922 parliamentary committee on re-establishment. The MPs agreed to continue the pension bonus, to add a year of access to Returned Soldiers' Insurance, and to repatriate CEF veterans who had failed to find work in England. On the other hand, Marler frustrated any attempt to restore the insurance principle and ap-proved Col. Thompson's policies, insisting that an appeal tribunal for pension claimants would simply have nothing to do. Resentful physicians persuaded him to recommend a medical advisory board to hear appeals strictly on medical grounds.[150]

That year, the GWVA decided to match an American Legion-inspired "Clean-Up" campaign to deal with war-related claims by demanding a Canadian "Clean Sweep." As he reviewed its progress, the GWVA's Grant MacNeil noted a pattern. Men whose wartime wounds had flared into a new disability learned that there was "a missing link" in their claim. Women whose pensioner-husbands died of their disabilities learned that they now had no claim to a widow's pension. Ailing veterans, for whom Returned Soldiers' Insurance was invented and extended, had their applications rejected.[151] An anonymous brown envelope gave MacNeil a peek at BPC internal decision making and Thompson's machinations with the insurance principle. Just as Marler tried to wind up his committee, he faced a furious MacNeil. He sent the GWVA official to Col. Thompson. The BPC chair was blunt: he didn't give a damn about MacNeil's complaints; he enforced the law just as Parliament wrote it.[152] MacNeil could give up or fight. On 15 June, reporters grabbed copies of the telegram MacNeil sent Marler's committee: "Following recent disclosures surrounding Parliamentary inquiry, we openly charge Pensions Board with contemptible and cold-blooded conspiracy to deprive ex-service men of rights previously granted by Parliament. There has been deliberate concealment, secret regulations, pensions and insurance, in direct violation intention of Parliament and deliberate attempt to disguise facts before present Parliamentary Committee. This is culmination unsympathetic policy of increasing severity during recent months."[153]

MacNeil's message delighted the media, exasperated Marler, and confused the opposition. It allowed a new prime minister to hand over the alleged misdeeds of a previous government's appointees to a royal commission headed by a Nova Scotia Liberal, Lt.-Col. J.L. Ralston. Rapidly realizing that MacNeil's charges implicated lazy members of Parliament more than Col. Thompson, Ralston swiftly dismissed them. A different commission, such as the one proposed by Department of Soldiers' Civil Re-establishment (DSCR) officials, might then have congratulated Col. Thompson for saving taxpayers from a Returned Soldiers' Insurance scheme bankrupted by deathbed applications, or for dating the "Declaration of Peace" on 1 January 1920, not the actual date of 1 September 1921, to cut off more claims.[154] Instead, Ralston and his colleagues complained that the BPC had seen its sole duty as a trustee of public funds: "This function was, after all, secondary to the duty of the Pensions Board as a Trustee of the rights and benefits which Canada intended for ex-service men and their dependants."[155] Instead of denouncing the GWVA secretary, Ralston recruited him to organize the commission's hearings so that he could really find out how pensions and re-establishment had worked. For his part, MacNeil selected and briefed "human documents" among the pensioners to illustrate how DSCR and Pension Board decisions operated.

In January 1923 Ralston and his colleagues set out across Canada, starting at the Camp Hill veterans' hospital at Halifax, crossing the continent to Vancouver and returning in thirty-eight days. Since contented veterans had no reason to appear, the commission heard a lot of complaints. Toronto veterans complained of millions of dollars wasted on relief when they wanted jobs. TB sufferers at Montreal shared their grim alternatives: demoralization during years in a sanatorium or hunger and relapse at home on an overly meagre pension. At Halifax, Regina, and Toronto, witnesses complained of the harassment of war widows by BPC investigators. After Mrs. Lesten, an elderly war widow in Winnipeg, took in a disabled friend of her late husband as a boarder, a "lady visitor" listened to malicious gossip and reported that Mrs. Lesten was "ill advised," which cost her her pension. Mrs. Bland in Toronto also lost hers, despite support from the DSCR.[156] MacNeil's "human documents" gave sympathetic reporters lots to write about.

Col. Ralston decided to break the cornerstone of Todd's pension system by recommending three-member local appeal boards and an Ottawa-based federal appeal board with ultimate jurisdiction. While veterans could hire their own counsel, official "soldiers' advisors" would prepare and submit cases at no expense.[157] Near the end of the 1923 session, the House of Commons quickly agreed; the Senate did not. Predominantly Tory-appointed, resentful of GWVA lobbying, and professing devotion to the country's finances, the Senate gutted Ralston's proposals, leaving dissatisfied pension claimants with no more than a seven-member travelling Federal Appeal Board armed with virtually no grounds to change BPC rulings. Only a little government backbone forced senators to agree to restore the "insurance principle" to the notorious Section 11.[158]

Ralston submitted four reports, each a little more cautious than its predecessor. Even though many veterans had good reason to regret their commutations, he refused to reverse them. Nor would he add to the mounting costs of Soldier Settlement by approving wholesale revaluation. Despite learning the sad plight of so-called pension widows, all that Ralston would say for women who had married a disabled veteran was that a pension might be justified if the marriage had occurred within a year of the pensioner's discharge.[159] For women who lost their pensions on remarriage and then lost their second husband, his solution was a frugal compromise: if a woman was widowed within five years and left destitute, she might be restored to her former pension with the "dowry" deducted.[160] Though obviously exasperated by the veterans' insatiable demands, Ralston's main target remained the BPC. At least half the allegations against pensioned widows, he reported, were malicious and untrue: "All, however, are investigated with a thoroughness that is undaunted ... Enquiries are frequently made as to whether any man lives in the house, how many beds there are, and where placed. Young children, even those of the widow herself, have been questioned on these and other suggestive subjects."[161]

In 1924 the House of Commons came to the latest batch of Ralston recommendations so late in the session that Parliament was about to be prorogued when

Senator Dandurand brought the MPs' amendments to the Senate. "A wink is as good as a nod to a blind horse," declared Conservative Brig.-Gen. W.A. Griesbach. Then he and his fellow senators slashed away at "the other place's" amendments with such abandon that MPs briefly considered postponing their break.[162] Instead, they settled for the prime minister's pledge to reform the Senate.[163] Nothing, of course, happened.

By 1930, when pension reform returned to the national agenda on the eve of another election, much had changed. MacNeil and the GWVA were both gone, victims of a scandal cunningly engineered by the DSCR's Ernest Scammell, seconded by Senator Griesbach.[164] A veterans' unity campaign, led by the British wartime commander-in-chief, Earl Haig, led in 1925 to creation at Winnipeg of the Canadian Legion. This time, senior Canadian officers followed Haig's example and got involved. A prewar chief of general staff and British wartime commander in Mesopotamia, Sir Percy Lake, was the Legion's first president. Sir Arthur Currie succeeded to the post in 1928-29. Among the major Canadian veterans' organizations, only the Army and Navy Veterans, with Senator Griesbach as president, stayed out. By 1930 the Canadian Legion claimed 70,000 paid memberships.[165]

The Legion was also exasperated by the pension process. Despite a popular image of youthfulness, the average age of CEF members had been close to thirty, and veterans in their forties felt a lot older than their years. Lacking the energy to perform heavy or sustained work, returned men spoke of suffering "burn out."[166] For all its ingenuity in avoiding claims, the BPC had been compelled to add 10,000 disability pensioners between 1925 and 1930, and if 20,000 had not commuted their tiny pensions in 1921, there would have been many more. The Pensions Appeal Board, grudgingly forced through the Senate, had managed to hear only 15,075 of the appeals lodged by the end of 1928, and had allowed 1,341 of them.[167] Sir Arthur Currie typified veterans better than he knew. A robust commander of the Canadian Corps in 1919, by 1930 the principal of McGill University was a stooped, white-haired old man of fifty-four, so plagued by ill health that he could not attend meetings of the Canadian Legion he headed. At Regina, Col. Léo LaFlèche read the president's speech, in which Currie proclaimed himself "not only amazed but ashamed that eleven years after the war it is necessary not only to plead but to fight for justice." The Pension Act must be overhauled, he announced, and the BPC regulations "redrafted from beginning to end."[168] The delegates roared their delight, not only at the sentiments but at the influence Sir Arthur Currie surely represented.

When Parliament met in a pre-election session in 1930, veterans' concerns matched the growing armies of unemployed as core political issues. For the first time, all veterans' organizations, even the ANV, appeared behind Currie's leadership to face a joint committee of unusually respectful senators and MPs. Not since 1919 had the atmosphere been so cooperative. Behind the scenes, the committee chair, Maj. C.G. Power, drafted legislative recommendations. From the veterans' side, Col. LaFlèche acknowledged that ex-soldiers could be undeserving and that pension claims deserved "a fair and reasonable measure of proof."[169] MPs and senators were even more obliging. Pensions commuted a decade earlier would be restored. Returned Soldiers' Insurance, closed in 1923, would be reopened for three more years. Even the "pension widows" were accepted: a woman who had married a pensioner before January 1930 would have as good a claim to a widow's pension as if she had been married in 1914.[170]

Todd's all-powerful Pension Board would henceforth determine only routine cases. Others would be judged by a nine-member travelling pension tribunal. Instead of the untrained and sometimes inept official soldier advisors, a veterans' bureau with qualified "veterans' advocates" would prepare cases, and the BPC would have a chief commission counsel, with a small staff, to present the other side. A three-member Pension Appeal Court with a presiding judge, as Ralston had proposed in 1922, would be final arbiter. Veterans would even have the benefit of the doubt: "the body adjudicating on the claim shall be entitled to draw and shall draw ... all reasonable inference in favour of the applicants."[171]

There was even more. Of 24,708 original soldier settlers, 11,912 were still struggling to pay off their loans. At the end of May 1930 the government wrote off $11.3 million in soldier-settler indebtedness.[172] For the burnt-out cases, the Liberals' new, means-tested old-age pensions would come too late, at age seventy. Instead, impoverished veterans aged sixty or more, and those who were younger but unemployable for physical or mental reasons, could apply for a War Veterans Allowance of $240 a year for a single man and $480 for a married couple.[173] Beguiled into the earlier bipartisan spirit for veterans' legislation, R.B. Bennett's Conservatives suddenly reared back in political horror. The allowance, cried Bennett, was "the worst piece of political legislation any parliament has had to consider on the eve of an election."[174] Confident that the votes of veterans and their families had already been successfully won, Mackenzie King left implementation of the allowances and the new pension organization until after the election.

By now, there was very little left on the Legion's agenda, and a contented Sir Arthur Currie assured Mackenzie King: "It is my opinion that you will hear very little more of this matter for many years to come." Voters saw to that on 28 July 1930 by giving R.B. Bennett's Conservatives a substantial victory. However, veterans found little comfort in the Tory victory. Under Walter Woods, a veteran and a soldier settlement official whom Bennett knew from Calgary, the War Veterans Allowance turned into the least troublesome of veterans programs, but pension procedures soon bogged down deeper than ever. Bennett chose an Alberta judge, J.D. Hyndman, to head the Pension Appeal Court and let the veterans nominate the new tribunal. The new structure inherited a backlog of 6,000 cases and soon had thousands more.[175] Filing a claim cost a veteran nothing, the deepening Depression provided ample motive, and a change of government and pension system revived hopes. The tribunal, with its veteran-selected members, occasionally tended to display generosity, but when the BPC chief commission counsel challenged its sympathetic judgments before the Pension Appeal Court with crisp arguments and statements of fact, Hyndman and his colleagues gave most claimants short shrift.[176]

By the end of 1931 more than 13,000 pension applications had piled up. By the summer of 1932, 3,000 claimants had reached the tribunal; only 650 had won anything, and half these favourable verdicts were reversed on appeal.[177] Frustrated claimants denounced the Canadian Legion, and the Toronto and District Command even refused to send in its dues.[178] Sir Arthur Currie blamed the Pension Board for "throwing sand in the works."[179] The *Canadian Veteran*, a short-lived Depression-era paper, blamed the prime minister: the pension machinery was working perfectly, it claimed, to allow R.B. Bennett to deprive returned men of their rights.[180]

The Bennett government met the crisis characteristically by making it politically worse. First, it ignored or misinterpreted advice and offended friends. The prime minister recognized the folly of having two bodies to approve pensions, and amalgamated the BPC and the tribunal in a new eight-member Canadian Pension Commission, leaving the Veterans' Bureau and the Pension Appeal Court. However, he then fired the veterans' appointees and named as chair none other than the arrogant Col. John Thompson. The veterans were so furious that Bennett finally began to hear their message. Thompson turned out to be an ideal appointee as the franchise commissioner required by the 1934 Election Act, and the chairman of the short-lived Dominion Veterans' Alliance, Mr. Justice Fawcett Taylor of the Manitoba Court of King's Bench, took his place on the new Pension Commission. The institutional turmoil ebbed away, and Bennett's 1933 pension structure survived both the Second World War and a Cold War until the Mulroney Conservatives came to power in the 1980s.

Only a minority of veterans were themselves directly affected by pension administration, but pensioners' families shared all the consequences. Their standard of living was often determined by remote judgments of a son's, husband's, or father's disability. Would the next review of a veteran's leg or lungs end even his meagre pension income? Families shared the benefits when the government belatedly offered compensation for the fact that prostheses seldom fitted comfortably and often tore the wearer's clothes; families were the victims when commutation turned out to be an unlucky gamble. Whatever the regime for administering them, the number of disability pensions, and their cost, grew significantly, from 42,932 pensions worth $7,470,000 in 1919 to 56,996 pensions worth $27,059,000 in 1930 and 80,194 pensions worth $30,094,000 on the eve of another world war in 1939. Meanwhile death, remarriage, and maturity had reduced the number of dependent pensioners to 17,896 and their total pensions to $10,318,000.[181]

8
Never Again

As a memorial for the Fund and a gift for its volunteers, the national executive of the CPF commissioned Philip Morris to write a report on the Great War edition of the Fund. Copies still appear occasionally in rural book sales and small town antique shops, often inscribed with the name of a dedicated but long-forgotten volunteer. Values have changed so much that it is hard now to romanticize the Fund or any other aspect of the Great War. It was created because there was a need to be met, and resources could best be found by asking people who had more than enough to pay.

In 1914 prevailing ideas reflected a society in which most people were poor, and scarcity, greed, and selfishness were taken for granted. If soldiers would enlist for $1.10 a day, why pay more? If some needed more to provide for their families, why hand money to others who would waste it? Let the community choose between fighting and paying. A patriotic fund let a time-honoured technique provide the money and distributed it to those who needed it. If donors were intently concerned about how their money was subsequently spent, that was an asset, not a liability, unless the promoters of the cause were careless or dishonest. An employer expected his employees to contribute to a cause he endorsed: surely they owed him that much after he had given them work and wages. Why set a good example if it is not to be followed?

These were conventional thoughts, shared by the men and women who organized the Patriotic Fund across Canada in the autumn of 1914 and the winter of 1915 and by those who agreed to contribute. They fitted, sometimes a little awkwardly, with less familiar thoughts about the central role of motherhood in the family and the nation, and the importance of adequate income in making motherhood effective. Should a mother leave her children to earn a livelihood for them? Conventional answers would have varied from never, to only in the last extremity. This might seem paradoxical, since wealthy women routinely employed nurses, nannies, and other servants to bear the burdens of child rearing. But in their own minds, affluent mothers were present and in full control.

Reading about soldiers' families ninety years ago, we are easily reminded how little psychological considerations mattered to them or their minders.[1] Innumerable unconnected anecdotes record enough of the mental and social state of individual veterans to suggest that, if post-traumatic stress disorder is now a widespread diagnosis among Canadian service members, it must have, *a fortiori,* been present among front-line veterans of the CEF. Families recollect a father or a favourite uncle who was never the same after the War. My colleague Donald Creighton attributed his reluctance to serve in the Second World War to the inexplicable mental transformation of a cherished family friend by his experiences during the First World War. Yet, as so often in this narrative, it is easier to explain why the obvious evidence is missing than it is to fill in the blanks. And as so often in my historical explorations, I have concluded one task with more than enough *terra incognita* for the next one.

On 10 September 1939 Canada was at war again. Seventeen years after Montreal's CPF branch had finally closed its office, no one thought seriously about reopening it for the Second World War. The services of Herbert Ames, John W. Ross, and Helen Reid were not summoned to advise on a new Patriotic Fund. After her work for the Montreal branch, Reid had continued her career of promoting social work and extending her interest in the world. Out of her experience and that of the men and women who worked with her, McGill University was persuaded to create a school of social work under T. Howard Falk. Herbert Ames devoted first his talents and then his sympathies to the League of Nations, though R.B. Bennett was not persuaded to make him Canada's representative at Geneva. John W. Ross remained a respected Montreal accountant and a devoted servant of a widening range of local and national charitable causes. After an interwar career as a soldier, veteran, and bureaucrat, Maj.-Gen. Léo LaFlèche was needed. As minister of war services in the wartime Liberal government, he oversaw many of the benevolent family services the Patriotic Fund had provided in the earlier war. By then only a few Canadians protested that it was none of the government's business.

Having disposed of the Canadian Patriotic Fund, Canadians would not revive it. The First World War had persuaded Canadians to look to their government for more than their ancestors had imagined possible. By 1918 there was a widespread feeling, even in Quebec, that the days of patriotic charity were over. During the war years, the CPF had shown how a form of mothers' allowance could work; by 1920 all but Quebec and the Maritime provinces had adopted their own version. In 1939 all mothers could turn to their province in times of desperate need and, if the answering gesture was reluctant, miserly, and brutally judgmental, at least it was not the hand of charity but of legally defined entitlement.

In the Second World War the Canadian government sought to profit from First World War experience. Most politicians, officials, and military commanders had lived through the earlier war and reflected on its lessons. A population of 11 million Canadians entered the war reluctantly, eager to avoid the sacrifices of the earlier conflict. A brush with disaster in 1940 transformed the war effort until a tenth of the population wore uniform. Those who did not fight paid enough taxes almost to finance Canada's actual war effort, though not the loans the Dominion made to Britain and other allies.

In 1939 army rates of pay were higher than in 1914-18, $1.30 a day for the lowest ranks, rising after six months to $1.50 and to $1.60 for a lance-corporal. The Royal Canadian Air Force paid its members more generously. Trades pay, ranging from $0.25 to $0.75 according to level of skill, replaced working pay. Members of the Canadian Women's Army Corps were initially paid three-quarters of the men's rate, a proportion raised to four-fifths in 1943.[2]

The government directed in 1939 that recruiters favour unmarried men, and some units took the instructions literally. Dependants' allowance replaced both separation allowance and family support from the Patriotic Fund. The allowance was paid at a flat monthly rate of $35 for a wife and $12 each for the first two children. Initially, those were the only children recognized, but recruiting pressure loosened the restrictions. In 1941 dependants' allowance was extended by $10 for a third and $8 for a fourth child, and on 1 January 1943, all ranks could draw children's allowance for up to six children and for one dependent parent. Cost of living bonuses compensated for wartime inflation, but after a surge in 1940-41, effective price and wage controls kept prices largely stable. The children's allowance was cut off at sixteen for boys and seventeen for girls, but might be extended to nineteen for a student making satisfactory progress towards completing junior matriculation or an approved course of instruction. To qualify for the dependant's allowance, a soldier was compelled to assign half his pay to the dependant.

The Marsh Report in 1943 suggested that a family with three children needed $128.85 to make ends meet in wartime Canada.[3] At the time, a soldier's wife with three children received $94.60 but, as the CPF had noted a quarter-century earlier, she did not have to feed or clothe her husband. To provide the emergency assistance that the Patriotic Fund had also been intended to provide, a Dependants' Allowance Board was established early in 1942, with local advisory committees relying on existing social work agencies, usually the Red Cross, for case investigations.[4]

After the war, a Canada vastly more affluent than in 1919 could afford benefits for ex-service members and their dependants that were unimaginable after the earlier war. The Canadian Pension Commission was free to apply the insurance principle to compensate death and disability without recourse to the constraint of attributability. In addition to their war service gratuity and special allowances, returning service members could claim as many years and months of education as they had spent in uniform or a rehabilitation grant of comparable value. Although the Second World War also left its tragic permanent casualties and the families fated to care for them, Canadians could boast that they had provided their veterans with the most generous demobilization benefits in the world. The greatest of these was undoubtedly the longest unbroken era of affluence in Canada's history.

Among the architects of Canada's Second World War policies were men and women who had suffered and survived the earlier Great War and who had learned from that experience to have faith in generosity, foresight, and the long-term benefits of sharing. In a modern age characterized by me-first selfishness, orchestrated contempt for democratic government and community, and deepening extremes of wealth and poverty, impotence and power, Canadians have lessons to learn from their ancestors in two world wars. They might begin by remembering the wartime sacrifices shared by wives and mothers and children of those who served and suffered in warfare.

Appendix

Table A1

Rates of pay, Canadian Expeditionary Force, 1914-18

Rank or appointment	Pay ($ per diem)	Field allowance ($ per diem)	Separation allowance ($ per month)
Major-general	20.00	4.00	60.00
General staff officer – 1st grade	10.00	3.00	60.00
General staff officer – 2nd grade	8.00	3.00	60.00
Assistant director of medical services	8.00	3.00	60.00
Chief paymaster	8.00	3.00	60.00
General staff officer – 3rd grade	5.00	3.00	60.00
Divisional paymaster	5.00	3.00	60.00
ADC to commander	3.00	3.00	40.00
Brigade commander	9.00	3.00	60.00
Brigade major	6.00	3.00	60.00
Colonel	6.00	1.50	60.00
Lieutenant-colonel	5.00	1.25	60.00
Major	4.00	1.00	50.00
Captain	3.00	0.75	40.00
Lieutenant	2.00	0.60	30.00
Paymaster	3.00	0.75	40.00
Quartermaster	3.00	0.75	40.00
Warrant officer	2.00	0.30	30.00
Quartermaster sergeant	1.80	0.20	25.00
Orderly room clerk	1.50	0.20	25.00
Squadron, battery, company sergeant-major	1.60	0.20	25.00
Squadron, battery, company quartermaster-sergeant	1.50	0.20	25.00
Colour sergeant or staff sergeant	1.60	0.20	25.00
Sergeant	1.35	0.15	25.00
Corporal	1.10	0.10	20.00
Bombardier or 2nd corporal	1.05	0.10	20.00
Trumpeter, bugler, drummer	1.00	0.10	20.00
Private, gunner, driver, sapper, batman, cook	1.00	0.10	20.00

Source: PC 2264, approved 3 September 1914, cited in Col. A. Fortescue Duguid, *Official History of the Canadian Forces in the Great War, 1914-19,* General Series, vol. 1, *Chronicle, August 1914-September 1915* (Ottawa: King's Printer, 1938), appendix 91, 61-2.

Table A2

Rates of support for families of privates, 1918

| | Canada | | | Great | | United |
| | SA | CPF | Total | Britain | Australia | States |
Dependants	($)	($)	($)	($)	($)	($)
Wife	25	5	30	9	10	15.00
Wife, 1 child	25	15	40	16	13	25.00
Wife, 2 children	25	18	43	21	16	32.50
Wife, 3 children	25	22	47	24	19	37.50
1 child	25	–	25	7	–	5.00
4 children	25	5	30	25	–	30.00
Widowed mother	25	10	35	9	10	10.00

Source: Special Committee on Pensions, 1918, *Report,* 185.

Table A3

Marital condition of the Canadian Expeditionary Force, 1914-19

	Married	Single	Widow(er)	Total
Serving outside Canada				
Officers	7,375	15,353	118	22,846
Nursing sisters	42	2,354	15	2,411
Other ranks	80,930	314,762	3,643	399,335
Total	88,347	332,469	3,776	424,592
Serving in Canada				
Officers	1,718	1,590	15	3,323
Nursing sisters	5	436	2	443
Other ranks	36,000	153,280	2,001	191,281
Total	37,723	155,306	2,018	195,047
Total in CEF				
Officers	9,093	16,940	133	26,166
Nursing sisters	47	2,790	17	2,854
Other ranks	116,930	468,042	5,644	590,616
Total	126,070	487,772	5,794	619,636

Source: NAC, MG 30, Duguid Papers, "C.E.F. Statistics," Marital condition.

Table A4

Civil occupations of members of the Canadian Expeditionary Force, 1914-19

Agriculture	122,050
Building trades	57,259
Civil and municipal	6,057
Clerical	52,755
Domestic and personal services	31,109
Engineers, firemen	11,454
Forestry	11,571
Hunting and fishing	4,086
Labourers	75,546
Manufacturing	77,626
Mechanics	6,597
Mercantile	23,012
Mining	14,130
Printers, engravers	6,431
Professional	29,540
Students	15,023
Transportation	58,336
Ill defined	8,886
Not stated	4,702
Total	616,170

Source: NAC, MG 30, Duguid Papers, "C.E.F. Statistics," Occupations.

Table A5

Cost of living and the CPF-SA benefits, 1915

Province	Family[1] ($)	Adjusted[2] ($)	CPF + SA[3] ($)	Difference ($)
Prince Edward Island	47.06	35.81	31.20	−4.61
Nova Scotia	50.94	38.44	35.00	−3.44
New Brunswick	51.86	38.51	35.32	−3.19
Quebec	51.20	37.00	36.30	−0.70
Ontario	46.97	37.92	37.22	−0.70
Manitoba	58.15	48.15	43.60	−4.55
Saskatchewan	63.04	51.34	42.73	−8.61
Alberta, south	61.76	45.26	37.30	−7.96
Alberta, north	61.76	43.61	45.51	+1.90
British Columbia	63.00	53.45	39.79	−13.66

1 Cost of living figures for food, fuel, and rent for a family of five.
2 Adjusted for missing father.
3 SA of $20.00 plus CPF assistance for a family of five.
Source: Cost of living surveys from *Labour Gazette*, 1914-19.

Notes

Preface

1 Sandra Gwyn, *Tapestry of War: A Private View of Canadians in the Great War* (Toronto: Harper Perennial, 2004), 92.
2 Queen's University Archives, title 9, Frontenac County Records, 1916-17, investigation slip, 3 March 1916.
3 Margaret McCallum, "The Canadian Patriotic Fund and the Care of Soldiers' Families, 1914-1918," unpublished paper in the author's possession (March 1982), 12.
4 William Raynsford and Jeannette Raynsford, *Silent Casualties* (Madoc, ON: Merribrae Press, 1986), 37-40.

Chapter 1: War and Families

1 In most European countries, young men served in their national army for two years as conscripts (three years in France) and then joined the reserves, with an obligation to serve until they reached old age.
2 Clarence de Sola was better known in Montreal as a prominent leader of the city's Jewish community. See Gerald Tulchinsky, *Taking Root: The Origins of the Canadian Jewish Community* (North York, ON: Stoddart, 1997), 263-8. Quotation from *La Presse*, 2 August 1914, 1.
3 *Le Devoir*, 4 August 1914.
4 "La guerre n'est pas une excursion à Saint-Irénée, c'est un fléau." *La Presse*, 6 August 1914.
5 *Le Devoir*, 3 August 1914.
6 *La Presse*, 4 August 1914. Raoul Dandurand remembered thinking that Britain's entry equalized France's struggle against German might. See Marcel Hamelin, ed., *Les mémoires de Raoul Dandurand* (Quebec: Presses de l'université Laval, 1967), 187.
7 Cited by John H. Thompson, *The Harvests of War: The Prairie West, 1914-1918* (Toronto: McClelland and Stewart, 1978), 111.
8 See G.W.L. Nicholson, *Canada's Nursing Sisters* (Toronto: Samuel, Stevens and Hakkert, 1976).
9 "Dans les circonstances présentes où c'est l'existence même de la patrie qui est en jeu, il n'y a pas de doute que chaque Français ne fasse tout son devoir." *La Presse*, 2 August 1914.
10 *La Presse*, 21 August 1914.
11 On reservists, see Col. A. Fortescue Duguid, *Official History of the Canadian Forces in the Great War, 1914-19*, General Series, vol. 1, *Chronicle, August 1914-September 1915* (Ottawa: King's Printer, 1938), 61-2. When the Russians objected, nationals enlisted in Canada's Second Contingent were released, but a special decree from the czar rescinded the disability in June 1915. Britain established a camp at Trois-Rivières for Montenegrin reservists, almost all from the United States. Some 2,500 were embarked for the Mediterranean by September 1915.
12 On Cardwell's reforms, see Herman Gaston de Watteville, *The British Soldier: His Daily Life from Tudor to Modern Times* (London: J.C. Dent, 1954), 163-8; on previous "long service" enlistment, 53-8. For criticism, see John Fortescue, *The Empire and the Army* (London and Toronto: Cassell, 1928), 275-6.
13 A.J.P. Taylor, *English History 1914-1945* (Oxford: Oxford University Press, 1965), 53-6.

14 See Desmond Morton, "The Cadet Movement in the Moment of Canadian Militarism, 1909-1914," *Journal of Canadian Studies* 13, 2 (1978).

15 James Gildea, *Historical Record of the Soldiers' and Sailors' Families Association, 1885-1916* (London, 1916), 254.

16 Richard Glover, *Peninsular Preparation: The Reform of the British Army, 1795-1806* (Cambridge: Cambridge University Press, 1963), 221. The formula was later adopted by units of the United States Army dispatched for frontier service.

17 De Watteville, *British Soldier,* 125, 133.

18 Glover, *Peninsular Preparation,* 222.

19 De Watteville, *British Soldier,* 124.

20 On British soldiers and their wives see ibid. ch. 9; Glover, *Peninsular Preparation.* A well-informed, if fictional, depiction of British military family life in Wellington's era may be found in Thomas Hardy's *The Dynasts: An Epic Drama* (London: Macmillan, 1913). See Part Third, Act 1, Scene 2; Act 2, Scene 1; and Act 7, Scene 5, the Women's Camp near Mont St-Jean.

21 De Watteville, *British Soldier,* 130.

22 Ibid., 134.

23 Ibid., 188.

24 Ibid., 190-1.

25 Graham Wootton, *The Politics of Influence: British Ex-Servicemen, Cabinet Decisions, and Cultural Change (1917-1957)* (London: Routledge and Kegan Paul, 1963), 18.

26 Unfortunately the money to cover the cost vanished in transit. See R.C. Brown and Desmond Morton, "The Embarrassing Apotheosis of a 'Great Canadian': Sir Arthur Currie's Personal Crisis in 1917," *Canadian Historical Review* 60, 1 (March 1979).

27 *King's Regulations and Orders for the Canadian Militia, 1910* (Ottawa: King's Printer, 1910), s. 830(2).

28 Ibid., s. 832.

29 Ibid., s. 844.

30 Desmond Morton, *A Military History of Canada* (Toronto: McClelland and Stewart, 1999), 127.

31 *Queen's Regulations and Orders for the Canadian Militia, 1887* (Ottawa, 1887), s. 712.

32 See Charles G. Roland, "War Amputations in Upper Canada," *Archivaria* 10, 2 (1980), 81-2.

33 Canada, *Sessional Papers,* 1890, no. 3A, 38.

34 Report of the Committee of the Privy Council, 8 July 1885, *Canada Gazette;* Canada, *Sessional Papers,* 1886, no. 80e; *Militia General Orders,* no. 14, 9 July 1885, in *Canada Gazette,* 11 July 1885.

35 See Canada, House of Commons, *Debates,* 28 February 1890, 1268, 1272.

36 Ibid., 1274-9, 1268.

37 Desmond Morton and Glenn Wright, *Winning the Second Battle: Canadian Veterans and the Return to Civilian Life, 1915-1930* (Toronto: University of Toronto Press, 1987), 11; National Archives of Canada (NAC), RG 9, II A 1, vol. 185, A3744; NAC, MG 27ID3, Caron Papers, vol. 98, f. 56380, Lt.-Col. H.G. Grasett to Sir Adolphe Caron, 17 April 1888, and throughout. The pension regulations required that a widow's pension be discontinued "should she subsequently prove unworthy of it or attain to wealthy circumstances" and "it shall not be conferred if the applicant be left in wealthy circumstances." *Militia General Orders,* no. 14, 9 July 1885, s. 995, in *Canada Gazette,* 11 July 1885; Canada, *Sessional Papers,* 1886, no. 80e.

38 Cartwright raised the issue at the end of the 1886 session and returned to it in 1887. By then the minister, Sir Adolphe Caron, had forgotten the matter, and Swinford's name was recalled as Swinburne. See Canada, House of Commons, *Debates,* 2 June 1886; 3 June 1887, 746-7; 22 June 1887, 1268.

39 Williams had launched the unauthorized and bloody charge that ended the Métis resistance at Batoche on 12 May 1885, and the commander of the force, Maj.-Gen. Fred Middleton, seems to have been distinctly rude to him in the aftermath. Williams died of fever some weeks later. See Desmond Morton, *The Last War Drum: The North West Campaign of 1885* (Toronto: Hakkert, 1972), 90-2, 141-2, 151; *Militia General Orders*, no. 14, 9 July 1885, in *Canada Gazette*, 11 July 1885; "Arthur Trefusis Heneage Williams," *Dictionary of Canadian Biography*.

40 On Mrs. French, see NAC, RG 9, series II-A-1, vol. 185, f. A3744; on Mrs. Ryan, see Canada, House of Commons, *Debates*, 28 February 1890, 1268; on both, see Canada, *Sessional Papers, 1889*, vol. 3, Report of the Auditor General, C-184; 1904, vol. 1, on militia widow pensioners.

41 See Morton and Wright, *Winning the Second Battle*, 10-11.

42 A. Norman Jaffares and Martin Gray, eds., *Collins Dictionary of Quotations* (Glasgow: HarperCollins, 1995), 722 [letter to Sir Theodore Martin, 1870].

43 Cynthia Comacchio, *Nations Are Built of Babies: Saving Ontario's Mothers and Children, 1900-1940* (Montreal and Kingston: McGill-Queen's University Press, 1993), 3-4.

44 Helen MacMurchy, *Infant Mortality: First Special Report* (Toronto: L.K. Cameron, 1910); and Comacchio, *Babies*, 36.

45 C.A. Hodgetts, "Infant Mortality in Canada," *Canadian Medical Association Journal* 1, 8 (1911): 273.

46 Helen MacMurchy, *Infant Mortality: Third Special Report* (Toronto: L.K. Cameron, 1912), 117.

47 "Infant Mortality," editorial, *Canadian Public Health Journal* 6, 10 (1915): 510.

48 Pasteurization in Ontario waited another twenty years for Mitchell F. Hepburn's Liberal government. It was imposed in 1938 over furious rural resistance and was remembered by Hepburn and his biographer as his one unquestionably good deed. See Neil McKenty, *Mitch Hepburn* (Toronto: McClelland and Stewart, 1967), 167; John T. Saywell, *"Just Call Me Mitch": The Life of Mitchell F. Hepburn* (Toronto: University of Toronto Press, 1991), 374. On pasteurization, see also Comacchio, *Babies*, 44-7.

49 Comacchio, *Babies*, 52, quoting C.A. Hodgetts, "Statistics and Publicity in Child Welfare Work," *Canadian Public Health Journal* 12, 3 (1921): 111.

50 Mrs. Arthur (Emily) Murphy, "What Twelve Canadian Women Hope to See As the Outcome of the War," *Everywoman's World*, April 1915, 6.

51 Helen Merrill, in ibid., 33.

52 Lucy Maud Montgomery, in ibid., 7. On her views, see Owen Dudley Edwards and Jennifer H. Litster, "The End of Canadian Innocence: L.M. Montgomery and the First World War," in *L.M. Montgomery and Canadian Culture*, ed. Irene Gammwel and Elizabeth Epperly (Toronto: University of Toronto Press, 1999), 31-2 and throughout.

53 Millicent Fawcett, "What Twelve Canadian Women Hope to See As the Outcome of the War," *Everywoman's World*, April 1915, 30. A pioneering British suffragist, Fawcett exercised some of her influence through her husband, Henry, a blind Cambridge professor, MP, and Liberal cabinet minister in the Gladstone era.

54 The magistrates in the rural county of Berkshire met in a tavern at Speenhamland to discuss how to relieve starvation among rural labourers and their families, and decided on a minimum income financed by local property taxes.

55 One of the three reforming Poor Law commissioners was Sir Francis Bond-Head, later lieutenant governor of Upper Canada in 1837 and sometimes blamed for provoking William Lyon Mackenzie to rebel.

56 For an account of the Charity Organization movement in Britain and the United States, see Kathleen Woodroofe, *From Charity to Social Work in England and the United States* (London: Routledge and Kegan Paul, 1968).

57 Veronica Strong-Boag, "'Wages for Housework': Mothers' Allowances and the Beginnings of Social Security in Canada," *Journal of Canadian Studies* 14, 1 (1979): 25-6.

58 See Nancy Christie, *Engendering the State: Family, Work, and Welfare in Canada* (Toronto: University of Toronto Press, 2000), 55, 57.

59 Paul Kellogg, an American commentator on social policy, strongly favoured a nongovernmental Patriotic Fund as a bulwark against overpayment and "demoralization" of the poor. See ibid., 55.

60 Ontario Mothers' Allowances Commission, *Annual Report*, 1920-21, 27, cited in Strong-Boag, "Wages for Housework," 27.

61 "Les sanglots d'une mère et de ses enfants qui voyaient partir leur être le plus cher." *La Presse*, 19 August 1914.

62 NAC, MG 28, I 5, vol. 1, CPF *Circular* no. 2, [October 1915].

63 Dandurand was a director of Montreal Trust, Montreal Cottons, Sun Life Insurance, the City & District Savings Bank, the Dominion Coal Co., *La Patrie*, and the Grand Trunk Pacific Railway, and was former president of the Montreal Citizens' Association. See Henry J. Morgan, *Canadian Men and Women of the Time*, 2nd ed. (Toronto, 1912), 294-5. On Dr. Lachapelle, the great crusader for public health in Montreal, see ibid., 684, and J.T. Copp, *The Anatomy of Poverty: The Condition of the Working Class in Montreal, 1897-1929* (Toronto: McClelland and Stewart, 1974), 92.

64 "Il faut que nos compatriotes qui quittent le Canada pour aller remplir leur devoir de soldat partent sans inquiétude sur le sort de leurs familles, qu'ils aient la certitude que ceux qu'ils laissent ici seront entourés de la plus grande solicitude." *Le Devoir*, 10 August 1914.

65 Ibid., and *La Presse*, 7 and 10 August 1914.

66 Founded in Montreal in 1900 by Margaret Polson Murray, the IODE was dedicated to promoting British imperialism largely through scholarships and prizes through Canada's schools. The war provided a fresh avenue for promoting imperial causes.

67 Philip H. Morris, *The Canadian Patriotic Fund: A Record of Its Activities from 1914 to 1919* (Ottawa: s.n., [1920?]), 107.

68 Col. A. Fortescue Duguid, *Official History of the Canadian Forces in the Great War*, General Series vol. 1, *Chronicle, August 1914-September* 1915 (Ottawa: King's Printer 1938), 72. The original battalion included representatives of every British regiment but one. Most were "time expired" men who no longer had a reservist's obligation.

69 For the importance of the precedent for Canada see NAC, MG 30E82, C.A. McGrath Papers, vol. 2, CPF *Circular* no. 4, 4.

70 Identified by the archbishop of Canterbury as "that rather strange phrase," the term "unmarried wives" recognized a reality of industrial working-class family life but horrified much respectable opinion. Faced with the need to investigate claims, the British accepted that two years of cohabitation constituted a family union.

71 Wootton, *Politics of Influence*, 18.

72 On benefits to reservists' families, see NAC, MG 28, I 5, vol. 1, CPF *Bulletin* [no. 1, October 1914].

73 Pay scales for the Canadian Expeditionary Force were set out in PC 2264, 3 September 1914, published in Duguid, *Official History of the Canadian Forces in the Great War*, vol. 1, *Chronicle*, appendix 91. See also NAC, RG 2 A1a, box 1098. Australia was the most generous paymaster in the First World War, paying its private soldiers $1.46 a day. Germany exceeded France at $0.105, while Hapsburg privates could count on $0.025.

74 In lieu of survey data, the Department of Labour's *Labour Gazette* asked its local correspondents to survey available unions that kept tabs on whether members were employed. In 1914 unions in Canada represented only 166,000 predominantly skilled workers out of a

labour force of about 2,935,000 men and women. *Historical Statistics of Canada,* 2nd ed. (Ottawa: Statistics Canada, 1983), D-86, E-125.

75 MPs spent only part of a morning discussing a War Appropriation Act which, by 1919, had virtually quintupled the national debt. See Canada, House of Commons, *Debates,* 21 August 1914, 52-60.

Chapter 2: Pay and Allowances

1 Hughes was not alone. See Desmond Morton, "The Cadet Movement in the Moment of Canadian Militarism, 1909-1914," *Journal of Canadian Studies* 13, 2 (1978). James Laughlin Hughes was superintendent of Toronto's schools, a devoted Conservative, Orangeman, and proponent of cadet training for both genders who also believed in equal pay for women teachers, votes for women, teaching art and music, and public kindergartens for Toronto toddlers.

2 Ron Haycock, *Sam Hughes: The Public Career of a Controversial Canadian, 1885-1916* (Waterloo: Wilfrid Laurier University Press, 1986), 177-82. A livelier, eyewitness account is C.F. Winter, *The Hon. Sir Sam Hughes: Canada's War Minister, 1911-1916* (Toronto: Macmillan, 1931), 74-8.

3 Even in 1914, the enemy was often defined as "Fenian." Luke Dillon, captured after a bungled Fenian attack on the Welland Canal in 1898, was released from penitentiary just before the war broke out.

4 Montreal *Gazette,* 15 August 1914.

5 Adjutant general to administrative staff, 17 August 1914, Militia Orders no. 372, "Mobilization for Service Overseas," cited in Col. A. Fortescue Duguid, *Official History of the Canadian Forces in the Great War, 1914-19,* General Series, vol. 1, *Chronicle, August 1914-September 1915* (Ottawa: King's Printer, 1938), Appendices, 43-4.

6 PC 2102, 11 August 1914, NAC, RG 2 A1a, box 1096. (PC 2182, 21 August 1914, and PC 2405, 19 September 1914, ibid., boxes 1096, 1097, 1100, extended this privilege to civil servants returning to the French, Belgian, or Russian armies. The privilege was later modified and, on 1 July 1918, discontinued with a guarantee of the former positions "if still capable of filling them." Duguid, *Official History of the Canadian Forces,* vol. 1, *Chronicle,* 59.

7 See *Handbook of the Land Forces of British Dominions* (London: His Majesty's Stationery Office, 1911), 126.

8 In the British Army, medical, supply, pay, and other administrative services were referred to as "departments"; hence the Canadian terminology. Like other professions, soldiers revel in language that deliberately or accidentally confuses outsiders.

9 Canada, *Militia List,* August 1914, 119.

10 On the mobilization at Valcartier, see G.W.L. Nicholson, *Official History of the Canadian Army in the First World War: Canadian Expeditionary Force, 1914-1919* (Ottawa: Queen's Printer, 1962), and Duguid, *Official History of the Canadian Forces,* vol. 1, *Chronicle,* ch. 1, 46-93.

11 See PC 2254, 3 September 1914, in Duguid, *Official History of the Canadian Forces,* vol. 1, *Chronicle,* appendix 91, 61-2 and NAC, RG 2 A1a, box 1098. For CEF pay scales, see Table A1, p. 243.

12 On separation allowance and assignments, see Duguid, *Official History of the Canadian Forces,* vol. 1, *Chronicle,* 57 and appendix 92, 62.

13 National Archives of Canada (NAC), RG 24, box 820, HQ 54-21-10-1, Mrs. Paul Poisson to the Hon. Sam Hughes, 20 August 1914.

14 Ibid., Mrs. H. Geddes to minister, [received 26 August 1914].

15 NAC, RG 24, box 820, HQ 53-21-10-1, Mary Elizabeth Agnew to minister of militia, 24 August 1914, 358.

16 NAC, RG 24, box 820, HW 54-21-10-1, Mrs. Thomas Humphreys to Col. Sam Hughes, n.d., 136.

17 NAC, RG 24, vol. 520, HW 54-21-10-1, Mrs. R.H. Murray to the minister, 21 September 1914.

18 Ibid., Mrs. F.H. Dayton to the Hon. Col. Sam Hughes, 21 August 1914.

19 Ibid., Mrs. A.E. Hall to the minister, 21 August 1914 and 25 August 1914. The former adjutant of the Governor General's Bodyguard had been accepted by Lt.-Col. J.A. Currie, MP, of the 48th until an anonymous letter revealed his adulterous affair. Currie dropped him. Mrs. Hall denied she had written the letter and wanted her husband overseas, provided she gained financial support.

20 NAC, RG 24, box 820, HQ 54-21-10-1, Mrs. Marion Presnail to minister of militia, n.d., 877.

21 Ibid., W.J. Thompson, South Leeds L.O.L. to Col. Hughes, 19 August 1914.

22 Ibid., O'Meara to Governor General, 18 September 1914, referred to Hughes.

23 Ibid., Mrs. Boyling to Minister, [20 August 1914].

24 Duguid, *Official History of the Canadian Forces,* vol. 1, *Chronicle,* appendix 94, 62. Soldiers sent home at the request of a family member were the second-largest category, after the five officers and 2,159 other ranks sent home for medical reasons and ahead of the thirteen officers and 269 other ranks who asked to be released.

25 Col. W.R. Ward, the CEF's chief paymaster, suggested that the large number of subsequent claims for separation allowance grew out of concealment of marriage. Ward also noted that this entailed great hardship on many soldiers' families. NAC, RG 24, vol. 1271, HQ 593-2-35, Ward to J.W. Borden, accountant and paymaster general, 4 November 1914.

26 NAC, RG 24, vol. 820, HQ 54-21-10-1, Mrs. S. Donaldson to Department of Militia and Defence, 8 September 1914.

27 NAC, RG 24, vol. 1271, HQ 893-2-35, f. 2, 137, Mrs. Wharton to Militia Department, 5 December 1914.

28 NAC, RG 24, vol. 4656, f 99-88, vol. 1, Henry T. Denison to Col. A. LeRoy, 12 September 1914, and note on memo from OC, 6th Field Company, CE; Charles W. Humphries, "Keeping the Home Fires Burning: British Columbia Women and the First World War," paper presented to Canadian Historical Association, Charlottetown, PEI, 31 May 1992, 7.

29 NAC, RG 24, box 526, HQ 54-21-10-1, George Boyle to minister, [received 2 October 1914].

30 NAC, RG 24, vol. 914, HQ 54-21-23-8, Sgt. Sydney A. Hart to minister of militia, 28 September 1914.

31 Ibid., H.T. Eggleton to minister of militia, 29 September 1914.

32 The federal government, most provinces, and some municipalities continued to pay civil servants who enlisted. So did the major railways and some other large employers. This was the clearest proof that business and political leaders believed in a short war and a need to retain experienced but patriotic employees.

33 Some historians have theorized about the social significance of separation allowance and related family policies. See Nancy Christie, *Engendering the State: Family, Work, and Welfare in Canada* (Toronto: University of Toronto Press, 2000), 46-93 throughout.

34 Report of 27 August 1914 to PC 2266, 4 September 1914, NAC, RG 2 A1a, box 1098.

35 In the British Army, assigning pay was a prerequisite for separation allowance; in Canada, Sam Hughes initially refused this condition. He believed it would be discriminatory and officious to tell a married soldier how to spend his pay, whatever Patriotic Fund officials might argue.

36 A. Fortescue Duguid, *Official History of the Canadian Forces in the Great War, 1914-19,* General Series, vol. 1, *Chronicle, August 1914-September 1915* (Ottawa: King's Printer, 1938), appendix 230, 163.

37 NAC, RG 24, vol. 1271, HQ 593-2-35, Ward to J.M. Borden, accountant and paymaster general, 4 November 1914.

38 Ibid. See also Duguid, *Official History of the Canadian Forces,* vol. 1, *Chronicle,* appendix 230, 163.

39 NAC, RG 24, vol. 1271, HQ 593-2-35, chief paymaster to accountant and paymaster general, 4 November 1914.

40 Maj. C.M. Ingalls testimony, Special Committee Appointed to Consider, Inquire into, and Report upon the Reception, Treatment, Care, Training the Re-Education of the Wounded, Disabled and Convalescent who have served in the Canadian Expeditionary Force, *Proceedings, Evidence and Reports* (Ottawa: King's Printer, 1917), 1125 (hereafter Committee on Returned Men, 1917).

41 Duguid, *Official History of the Canadian Forces*, vol. 1, *Chronicle*, appendix 124, 164.

42 NAC, RG 24, vol. 1343, HQ 593-3-22, Memorandum, n.d.

43 Among the complaints was one from the adjutant of the 24th Battalion on behalf of Mrs. J.A. Gunn, the wife of his commanding officer. See NAC, RG 24, vol. 1343, HQ 593-3-22, Capt. Gerald Furlong to A&PMG, 26 December 1914.

44 NAC, RG 24, vol. 1271, HQ 593-1-35, vol. 3, Borden to Ward, 4 January 1915. See also the Stalker case: NAC, RG 24, vol. 1234, HQ 593-1-12, Fiset to British consul general at San Francisco, 26 March 1918.

45 NAC, RG 24, box 914, HQ 54-21-23-8, vol. 2, Maj. A.O. Lambert to Mrs. W. Edwards, 8 December 1914.

46 Albert Carman, *The Return of the Troops: A Plain Account of the Demobilization of the Canadian Expeditionary Force* (Ottawa: Government Printing Bureau, 1920), 114; No author, *Financial Instructions and Allowances* (Ottawa: Government Printing Bureau, 1916), art. 226.

47 Maj. C.M. Ingalls testimony, Committee on Returned Men, 1917, 1163-9.

48 *Haileyburian*, 30 March 1915, extract cited in NAC, RG 24, vol. 1235, HQ 593-1-13.

49 NAC, RG 24, vol. 1235, HQ 593-1-12, "Memorandum re John C. Douglas."

50 Desmond Morton and Cheryl Smith, "Fuel for the Home Fires: Taking Care of the Women They Left Behind" *Beaver* 75, 4 (1995): 13.

51 The Board was constituted under PC 447, 16 February 1917, NAC, RG 2 A1a, box 1162, to include a major and a captain, both returned unfit from the front, and a Patriotic Fund representative.

52 J.W. Margeson testimony, Special Committee Appointed to Consider and Report upon the Pension Board, the Pension Regulations, and the Sufficiency of Otherwise of the Relief Afforded Thereunder ... *Proceedings, Evidence and Reports* (Ottawa: King's Printer, May 1918), 1812 (hereafter Committee on Pensions, 1918).

53 Duguid, *Official History of the Canadian Forces*, vol. 1, *Chronicle*, 164.

54 On internment during the First World War, see Desmond Morton, "Sir William Otter and Internment Operations in Canada during the First World War," *Canadian Historical Review* 55, 1 (1974); Desmond Morton, *Silent Battle: Canadian Prisoners of War in Germany, 1914-1919* (Toronto: Lester Publishing, 1992); Bohdan S. Kordan and Peter Melnycky, *In the Shadow of the Rockies: Diary of the Castle Mountain Internment Camp, 1915-1917* (Edmonton: Canadian Institute of Ukrainian Studies Press, 1991); Lubomyr Luciuk, *A Time for Atonement: Canada's First National Internment Operations and the Ukrainian-Canadians, 1914-1920* (Kingston, ON: Limestone Press, 1988); and Lubomyr Luciuk, *Ukrainians and Internment Operations in Ontario during the First World War* (Toronto: Multicultural Historical Society of Ontario, 1988).

55 See NAC, MG 24, box 919, HQ 54-21-23-8, vol. 15, f. 202 ff., Colin Mackintosh, secretary Carleton Place CPF, to secretary, the Militia Council, 12 August 1916, about families of soldiers transferred to Renfrew for duty and required to pay $0.60 a day in board. With six children to support, Mrs. H. Turner pleaded for her husband's subsistence money when he came home on furlough to Toronto from Kapuskasing where he was an internment camp guard. Nothing could be done for her. Ibid., vol. 18., Mrs. H. Turner to minister of militia [received 20 January 1917].

56 NAC, RG 24, vol. 921, HQ 54-21-23-8, Mrs. F.H.J. Taylor to paymaster general, 9 September 1917.

57 NAC, RG 24, box 919, HQ 54-21-23-8, vol. 18, no. 347, Mrs. Clarence Macgregor to minister of militia, 6 February 1917. Her husband had been rejected for the First Contingent for medical reasons and enlisted as orderly sergeant for the Khaki Home. He was then reduced to private because the establishment was reduced, paid as a single man, denied separation allowance, and eventually raised to corporal without additional pay.

58 NAC, RG 24, vol. 1252, HQ 593-1-82, no. 141, Gwatkin to accountant and paymaster general, 26 October 1917, with enclosure. (The member appears to have been Hector McInnes, chairman of the Halifax CPF relief committee.)

59 Report of 7 October 1914 to PC 2553, 10 October 1914, NAC, RG 2 A1a, box 1101.

60 Duguid, *Official History of the Canadian Forces,* vol. 1, *Chronicle,* 59-60; PC 2597, 17 October 1914 and PC 1043, 8 May 1915, NAC, RG 2 A1a, boxes 1101 and 1114.

61 See NAC, RG 24, box 510, HQ 54-21-10-1, Mrs. J. Hunter to Hughes, 2 September 1914, on behalf of her son, a Saskatchewan homesteader: "Some say it will be taken from him, but when he was called to fight for his country I don't think it would be fair."

62 Wording from PC 2615, NAC, RG 24, box 1252, HQ 593-1-82, 112. See also NAC, RG 2 A1a, box 1154.

63 See J.W. Margeson testimony, Committee on Pensions, 1918.

64 PC 2266, 4 September 1914, NAC, RG 2 A1a, box 1098, set out the initial terms and rates for separation allowance in a single page. For comparison by 1917, the forty-four sections of regulations filled five columns of the *Canada Gazette* and needed a Separation Allowance Board to interpret them. PC 2370, 25 September 1917, *Canada Gazette,* 51, 11 (5 September 1917). See also NAC, RG 2 A1a, box 1178.

65 NAC, RG 24, box 824, HQ 54-21-10-1, Evelyn Moor to minister of militia, 2 September 1921, and chief clerk's minute.

66 Morris, *Patriotic Fund,* 36.

67 NAC, RG 24, box 822, HQ 54-21-10-1, Mrs. A. Clymer to minister of militia, 5 May 1915. Col. W.E. Hodgins explained to Mrs. Clymer that she would need at least $15 and perhaps as much as $24 if her husband had been a year in uniform. Even then "the decision rests entirely with the Officer Commanding the Unit to which he belongs."

68 NAC, RG 24, vol. 947, HQ 54-21-23-25, vol. 16, Viola Young to paymaster, Halifax, 7 February 1917; and ibid., G.B. Brackenbury to Sergeant Disher, on telephone conversation, n.d.

69 NAC, RG 9, III, vol. 178, 6-M-377, Carson to Hughes, 8 June 1916.

70 PC 193, 28 January 1915, NAC, RG 2 A1a, box 1107.

71 NAC, RG 24, vol. 1252, HQ 593-1-86, Charles S. Green to Sir R.L. Borden, 9 May 1917. In 1918, at its annual meeting, Fund delegates proposed to end the pre- and postenlistment distinction, but the national executive only concurred on 9 January 1919, once the war was safely over.

72 NAC, RG 24, vol. 1252, HQ 593-1-82, draft order-in-council, 27 June 1917, 261-2.

73 This is a family story.

74 On SSFA, see Graham Wootton, *The Politics of Influence: British Ex-Servicemen, Cabinet Decisions, and Cultural Change (1917-1957)* (London: Routledge and Kegan Paul, 1963), 18-19.

75 Carman, *Return of the Troops,* 158, reports that 37,748 dependants returned to Canada under official arrangements at the end of the war. Others helped persuade 22,308 soldiers to remain in Britain, somewhat to the dismay of the Canadian authorities who predicted (correctly) that despite signing waivers some would demand belated repatriation at government expense. Desmond Morton and Glenn Wright, *Winning the Second Battle: Canadian Veterans and the Return to Civilian Life, 1915-1930* (Toronto: University of Toronto Press, 1987), 112.

76 PC 2605, 26 November 1915, amending PC 2266, 27 August 1915, cited in Morton and Smith, "Fuel for the Home Fires," 15. See NAC, RG 2 A1a, boxes 1127 and 1122.

77 NAC, RG 24, box 825 HQ 54-21-10, f. 124, George Robinson to Sir Sam Hughes, 8 October 1915.
78 NAC, RG 24, vol. 1234, HQ 593-1-12, J.W. Borden minute to Treasury Board to General Fiset, 10 August 1915. The order was passed, and in January 1916 James Stevens, paralyzed from the waist down, expressed his gratitude for $120 in SA. NAC, Kemp Papers, vol. 34, f. 1198, Stevens to Edward Kemp, 12 January 1916.
79 Canada, House of Commons, *Debates,* 24 February 1915, cited in *Canadian Annual Review,* 1915, 188.
80 NAC, RG 24, vol. 823, HQ 54-32-10-1, vol. 11, Col. L.W. Shannon to secretary, Militia Council, 17 May 1915, p. 46.
81 Ibid., Lt.-Col. E.I. Leonard to AAG, 1 Division Area, 14 May 1915, p. 45.
82 NAC, RG 24, box 824, HQ 54-21-10-1, Mrs. Nora Howl to Gen. Sam Hughes, 2 July 1915, and J.S.S. to Mrs. Howl, 13 July 1915; NAC, RG 24, box 826, HQ 54-21-19-1, Mrs. Emma Everley to Maj.-Gen. Sam Hughes [sic], n.d., 75.
83 Sandra Gwyn, *Tapestry of War: A Private View of Canadians in the Great War* (Toronto: Harper Perennial, 2004), 142.
84 NAC, RG 24, box 827, HQ 54-21-10-1, Mrs. Frank Harvey to Hughes, 4 February 1916.
85 *Canadian Annual Review,* 1915, 185-6.
86 See Charles Stewart, *"Overseas": The Lineages and Insignia of the Canadian Expeditionary Force, 1914-1919* (Toronto: Little and Stewart, [1971]). Hughes's boasting ignored the painful problem that generals called "wastage." Replacing casualties in the Canadian Corps required about 20,000 fresh soldiers a year for each of its divisions in the line. By the autumn of 1916, the Corps had four divisions and needed 80,000 men a year.
87 It was a promise soon broken. The Canadian Corps needed only 48 of the 258 battalions raised for it, and few recruits after early 1915 served with the unit they first joined. Leslie M. Frost, *Fighting Men* (Toronto: Clarke-Irwin, 1967), 88-94, describes the angry disillusionment of members of a battalion raised in Orillia, Ontario. An admirer of Sam Hughes, the future premier of Ontario blamed the generals for his hero's policy.
88 NAC, RG 24, vol. 918, HQ 54-21-23-8, vol. 17, Mrs. H. Plume to the minister, 1 December 1916, 131.
89 Ibid., HQ 54-21-23-1 and 593-1-12, Alice Watts to J.W. Borden, 22 October 1916; and vol. 16, Report of Capt. B. Thompson, chief inspector, Pay Accounts and Records.
90 Maj. C.M. Ingalls testimony, Committee on Returned Men, 1917, 1164.
91 Helen Reid, "War Relief in Canada," *Proceedings of the Annual Conference on Social Work* (Philadelphia: N.p., 1917), 134-5.
92 E.M. MacDonald, House of Commons, *Debates,* 1 February 1917, 383.
93 Herbert Ames, House of Commons, *Debates,* 1 February 1917, 383-4.
94 NAC, RG 24, vol. 4285, 34-1-10, vol. 2, John D. Adams, Toronto and York Patriotic Fund Association, to OC, Military Police, Exhibition Park, 21 November 1914; ibid., S.P. Shantz to Maj.-Gen. F.L. Lessard, 25 November 1914.
95 See NAC, RG 24, vol. 960, HQ 54-21-23-53862019, AMATO, Frank.
96 Queen's University Archives, title 9, Frontenac County Records, Visitors' Record Cards, 1915-1919, Bradshaw to T.S. Munro, 2 April 1917, cited in David Laurier Bernard, "Philanthropy vs. the Welfare State: Great Britain's and Canada's Response to Military Dependants in the Great War" (MA thesis., University of Guelph, 1992), 66.
97 In early 1917 Helen Reid reported that 11,000 Montreal families had applied for CPF assistance out of 37,000 men who had enlisted. Of the 11,000 families, 4,000 had qualified for regular CPF allowances. "Most of those not now on the Fund," she claimed, "are dependants of soldiers who have become casualties and are either discharged, killed in action, or have been invalided home and pensioned, etc." Reid, "War Relief in Canada," 132-3.

98 The army took the view that venereal disease was a "self-inflicted wound." On venereal disease, see Sir Andrew Macphail, *Official History of the Canadian Forces in the Great War, 1914-1919: The Medical Services* (Ottawa: King's Printer, 1925), 179.

99 NAC, RG 24, vol. 4664, f. 99-1, vol. 2, Frank Beard to district officer commanding, MD 11, 28 November 1916; Capt. the Rev. J.H. Hooper to officer commanding 6 Field Company, CE, 9 December 1916.

100 NAC, RG 24, vol. 4285, 34-1-10, vol. 1, Blanche Cushman to Col. W.A. Logie, 14 May 1915.

101 NAC, RG 24, vol. 1252, HQ 593-1-82, petition from Mrs. A.W. Matsell and six other wives of members of 14 Company, CASC, MT Section.

102 See Table A2 for comparable rates of family support among the Allies. J.W. Borden estimated that 85 percent of SA recipients were privates' relatives and that 100,000 conscripts would have 5,000 widowed mothers. NAC, RG 24, vol. 1253, HQ 593-1-82, accountant and paymaster general to minister of militia, 17 November 1917.

103 See Maj. J.W. Margeson testimony, Committee on Pensions, 1918, *Proceedings*, 180.

104 Committee on Returned Men, 1917, *Report*, 1183, exhibit 1.

105 Ibid., 1161. See also 1158-60.

106 Committee on Pensions, 1918, *Proceedings*, 131.

107 PC 447, 16 February 1917.

108 Nova Scotia Archives and Records Management, CPF records, vol. 497, f. 5, Barnstead to Morris, 12 December 1917.

109 NAC, RG 24, vol. 1234, HQ 293-1-12, W.S. Edwards to secretary, Militia Council, 2 April 1918, 778, 831.

110 NAC, RG 24 vol. 4286, HQ 34-1-10, vol. 3, May B. Morris to assistant adjutant-general MD 2, 29 November 1918.

Chapter 3: The Patriotic Fund

1 Philip H. Morris, *The Canadian Patriotic Fund: A Record of Its Activities from 1914 to 1919* (Ottawa: s.n., [1920?]), 61.

2 *Canada Year Book*, 1915, 567-8.

3 Only 23.2 percent of Montreal children went beyond the most elementary stages of education in 1916, compared with 33 percent in Toronto and 44 percent in New York. Between the first and fourth levels, Protestant enrolment dropped by 25 percent, while Catholic enrolment fell by 75 percent. See *Canada Year Book*, 1914, 101-4; *Canada Year Book*, 1915, 123-7; and J.T. Copp, *The Anatomy of Poverty: The Condition of the Working Class in Montreal, 1897-1929* (Toronto: McClelland and Stewart, 1974), 60-1. On education generally, see pp. 60-9 of the last.

4 See Paul-André Linteau, *Histoire de Montréal depuis la Confédération* (Montreal: Boréal, 1991), 210-11.

5 In 1921 Arthur St-Pierre estimated the average at 1.4 persons per room. See Copp, *Anatomy of Poverty*, 71.

6 Linteau, *Histoire de Montréal*, 228-9.

7 Herbert B. Ames, *The City below the Hill: A Sociological Study of a Portion of the City of Montreal, Canada* (1897; reprinted with an introduction by P.F.W. Rutherford, Toronto: University of Toronto Press, 1972), 68.

8 McCord Museum of Canadian History, P217-C/7, J.W. Ross Papers (hereafter Ross Papers), *Annual Report of the Charity Organization Society of Montreal, 1901*, 5. On the COS, see 114-20.

9 Linteau, *Histoire de Montréal*, 218. See 219-24, throughout.

10 *Montreal Daily Star*, 13 August 1914.

11 On pre-1914 municipal reform in Montreal, see John Irwin Cooper, *Montreal: A Brief History* (Montreal: McGill-Queen's University Press, 1967), 133-5; Linteau, *Histoire de Montréal*, 254-61.

12   Linteau, *Histoire de Montréal*, 259-62; Cooper, *Montreal*, 138-44.
13   *Le Devoir*, 4 August 1914; *La Presse*, 16 September 1914.
14   Desmond Morton and Glenn Wright, *Winning the Second Battle: Canadian Veterans and the Return to Civilian Life, 1915-1930* (Toronto: University of Toronto Press, 1987), 5-6.
15   Morris, *Patriotic Fund*, 8-9.
16   Ibid. Quotation from NAC, RG 24, vol. 23, f. 49-5-1, Norman Macdonald to Sir Frederick Borden, 10 August 1904. On Mulloy see NAC, RG 7 G-21, vols. 365, 2425; RG 38, vol. 69, f. 175; Morton and Wright, *Winning the Second Battle*, 11-12, 31; Jack Schecter, "The Achievements of Trooper Mulloy," *Canadian Military History* 11, 1 (2002): 71-9.
17   On Ames and the Patriotic Fund see Morris, *Patriotic Fund*, 7-14; and Margaret McCallum, "Assistance to Veterans and Their Dependants: Steps on the Way to the Administrative State, 1914-1929," in *Canadian Perspectives on Law and Society: Issues in Legal History*, ed. W. Wesley Pue and Barry Wright (Ottawa: Carleton University Press, 1988), 157 ff.
18   *Montreal Daily Star*, 11 August 1914.
19   Ibid.
20   Ross Papers, box 1, Montreal Patriotic Fund minute books (hereafter "minute books"), general committee, 12 August 1914, 70-4.
21   *Montreal Daily Star*, 11 August 1914.
22   Ibid., 13 August 1914.
23   Minute books, executive committee, 88-90. Both Mrs. Busteed and Mrs. Cole were the wives of socially prominent militia colonels.
24   Minute books, general committee, 14 August 1914, 85.
25   Ibid., 80-4.
26   Minute books, executive committee, 17 August 1914, 88-90.
27   National Archives of Canada (NAC), C.A. Magrath Papers, MG 30, E 82, f. HY, Magrath to Ames, 9 September 1914.
28   Ian Miller, *Our Glory and Our Grief: Torontonians and the Great War* (Toronto: University of Toronto Press, 2001), 21; Morris, *Patriotic Fund*, 51, 69, 99.
29   Morris, *Patriotic Fund*, 224.
30   *Toronto Daily Star*, 17 August 1914, 6.
31   Toronto *Mail and Empire*, 25 August 1914, 4; *Toronto World*, 25 April 1914, 1. See also Adrian P.N. Lomaga, "For King and Country: The Workers of the Toronto and York Branch of the Canadian Patriotic Fund," research paper for the author, 26 July 2002, 1-3; Miller, *Glory and Grief*, 25-6.
32   Morris, *Patriotic Fund*, 9.
33   Ibid.
34   NAC, MG 28, I, 5, vol. 1, CPF national executive minutes, 18 August 1914.
35   In 1899 the Laurier government had accepted only the cost of raising and transporting Canadian contingents to the South African War. Their expenses in South Africa, including pay, allowances, and pensions, were left to the British taxpayer. The 1914 War Appropriation Act committed $50 million for "defence and security, naval and military operations," for war insurance, and "any measure deemed necessary by the Governor in Council." A. Fortescue Duguid, *Official History of the Canadian Forces in the Great War, 1914-19*, General Series, vol. 1, *Chronicle, August 1914-September 1915* (Ottawa: King's Printer, 1938), 42.
36   Bill No. 7, "A Bill to Incorporate the Canadian Patriotic Fund," Special Session, 21 August 1914, s. 3; see also Morris, *Patriotic Fund*, 9.
37   Canada, House of Commons, *Debates*, 22 August 1914, 87.
38   Ibid., 88, 97.
39   Ibid., 89.
40   Ibid., 90.

41 Ibid. 91-2.

42 Ibid., 92. See debate, 87-92.

43 The point was underlined when Ames spoke to the first interprovincial conference of CPF branches in Toronto on 16 May 1916. See CPF, *Reports of the Proceedings of a Conference of Representatives of Branches of the Canadian Patriotic Fund in Eastern Cities, 16, 17, 18 May 1916*. (Ottawa: CPF, 1916), 8-9.

44 NAC, RG 24, vol. 4649, f. 99-26. sub-vol. 1, C.H. Bonnor to officer commanding, MD 11, 31 May 1916, cited in Charles W. Humphries, "Keeping the Home Fires Burning: British Columbia Women and the First World War," paper presented to Canadian Historical Association, Charlottetown, PEI, 31 May 1992, 8.

45 See Bill no. 7, "A Bill to Incorporate the Canadian Patriotic Fund," Special Session, 21 August 1914.

46 Cited in Morris, *Patriotic Fund*, 15.

47 The office procedures were described by Morris to the Conference of Branch Representatives for Eastern Canada on 16 May 1916. See CPF, *Conference of Representatives*, 8-11.

48 The July 1914 issue of the *Labour Gazette* indicated that a six-room worker's dwelling with a convenience rented monthly for $6-8 in Charlottetown, $15-20 in Halifax, $14-18 in Montreal, $30 in Winnipeg, and $20-25 in Vancouver. Edmonton at $35 was the high-rent capital, though Toronto at $23-27 was highest in the East. A house without a convenience cost $2-5 less. A bushel and a half of potatoes varied from a low of $0.90 in Moncton and $1.40 in Toronto to a high of $2.40 in Brandon. British Columbia, which imported its potatoes in hundred-pound sacks from California, was hard to compare. *Labour Gazette* 16, 1 (1914), 110-14.

49 See Desmond Morton and Cheryl Smith, "Fuel for the Home Fires: Taking Care of the Women They Left Behind," *Beaver* 75, 4 (1995): 11-13.

50 In 1917 Philip Morris confessed that support without CEF allowances or pay usually included "a certain measure of hardship." NAC, RG 24, vol. 1252, HQ 593-1-86, Philip J. Morris to J.W. Borden, 19 June 1917.

51 Morris, *Patriotic Fund*, 15.

52 Canon Rénaud replaced Archbishop Bruchési, as he would for the remaining meetings, and Senator Fred Béique, another wealthy French Canadian, joined Dandurand. *La Presse* and *Montreal Daily Star*, 24 August 1914; minute books, executive committee, 24 August 1914, 94.

53 Minute books, executive committee, 26 August 1914, 104. As we shall see, Montreal found this an impossible rule to follow to the letter and, as Canada's wealthiest CPF branch, did not. Manitoba refused to comply and remained out of the CPF, as did funds in several Ontario and western cities.

54 Smith had been president of the McCready Shoe Company before it merged with Ames-Holden shortly before the war.

55 *Montreal Herald*, 8 January 1916. See *Everywoman's World*, November 1914.

56 Minute books, executive committee, 4 September 1914, 110-11.

57 Morris, *Patriotic Fund*, 255-6; Saskatchewan Archives, *Report of the Saskatchewan Branch of the CPF as of 30 June 1916*, Regina branch, 3-4.

58 Morris, *Patriotic Fund*, 259.

59 Ibid., 109.

60 Ibid., 110, 122.

61 Ibid., 52.

62 Ibid., 58-9.

63 Among them were J.E. Stauffer, who was killed overseas, Lt.-Col. Nelson Spencer of Medicine Hat, and Dr. J.S. Stewart of Lethbridge, later brigadier-general and commander of the 3rd Division's artillery. See Morris, *Patriotic Fund*, 68-9; and G.W.L. Nicholson, *Official*

History of the Canadian Army in the First World War: Canadian Expeditionary Force, 1914-1919 (Ottawa: Queen's Printer, 1962), 542.

64 Morris, *Patriotic Fund,* 71.
65 On the strike and the Militia's role, see Maj. T.V. Scudamore, "Aid to the Civil Power," *Canadian Defence Quarterly* 9, 2 (1932).
66 Helen Reid, "War Relief in Canada," *Proceedings of the Annual Conference on Social Work* (Philadelphia: N.p., 1917), 130.
67 Henry J. Morgan, *Canadian Men and Women of the Time,* 2nd ed. (Toronto, 1912), 60-61, 885; Morris, *Patriotic Fund,* 89-90.
68 *Hedley Gazette and Similkameen Advertiser,* 10, 36 (21 September 1914).
69 *Vancouver Daily Province,* 28 August 1914, cited by Patricia Roy, *Vancouver: An Illustrated History* (Toronto: James Lorimer, 1980), 87.
70 W.J. Bowser, Sir Richard McBride's sudden successor in 1915, appointed Flumerfelt his provincial treasurer. Flumerfelt's defeat in the ensuing by-election in Victoria was an early warning of the coming Conservative debacle. See Margaret Ormsby, *British Columbia: A History* (Toronto: Macmillan, 1964), 392.
71 Morris, *Patriotic Fund,* 90. Morris (p. 100) explains that, of disbursements of $1,265,329, the Victoria branch spent only $5,178 on other forms of relief.
72 Ibid., 99.
73 Ibid., 104.
74 Ibid., 269.
75 Instead of making Canada's only full-time infantry regiment part of the First Contingent, Sam Hughes offered it as a garrison for Bermuda, relieving a British Army battalion to serve in France. The regiment reached France in 1916, being replaced by the 38th CEF Battalion from Ottawa, and then by the 163rd Battalion from Montreal.
76 The Maritime provinces, particularly Nova Scotia, resented the fact that the CPF misreported their contributions and lumped their three provincial branches together. The CPF excuse was that the Militia Department reported Maritime enlistments as a group, and that contributions and enlistments had to be compared on a regional basis. Nova Scotia Archives and Records Management (NSARM), MG 20, CPF Nova Scotia branch, vol. 498, f. 1, Nova Scotia secretary to Ames, 5 January 1916, and Ames to Nova Scotia secretary, 12 January 1916.
77 On Barnstead, see Halifax *Maritime Merchant,* 17 October 1907, 23.
78 By May 1916 Nova Scotia had twenty-three local organizations. See Ames's report in CPF, *Conference of Representatives,* 10.
79 Morris, *Patriotic Fund,* 135.
80 NSARM, MG 20, CPF Nova Scotia branch, executive minutes, 25 September 1914.
81 Ibid., 16 September 1914.
82 Morris, *Patriotic Fund,* 123, 127-8, 129.
83 Ibid., 124-5; New Brunswick, *Statutes,* An Act to assist in carrying out the objects of the Canadian Patriotic Fund, 1916, 6 Geo. V, c. 8, pp. 49-53.
84 In Morris's *Patriotic Fund,* the Island takes up less than three pages (231-3).
85 Ibid., 231-2. Prince Edward Island was a pioneer in retaining allowances as a form of forced savings for its allowance receivers, and Morris credited the PEI Ladies' Auxiliary for pressuring wives to take this course.
86 Ibid., 233. Over the course of the war, PEI's net contribution to the national CPF was $29,000.
87 Gale Warren, "The Patriotic Association of the Women of Newfoundland, 1914-1918," (BA honours thesis, Department of History, Memorial University of Newfoundland (MUN), 1996), 12; Teresa Bishop Stirling, "Newfoundland's Struggle for the Women's Franchise" (BA honours thesis, Department of History, MUN, 1982), 5-7; Patricia O'Brien, "Women's Move-

ment," in *Encyclopedia of Newfoundland and Labrador*, ed. Joseph R. Smallwood, vol. 5, 609; *Distaff*, 1916-17.

88 Newfoundland Patriotic Association, "Report of the Trustees," *Appendices, Journal of the Newfoundland House of Assembly*, 1919, 315. See also Patricia O'Brien, "The Newfoundland Patriotic Associations: The Administration of the War Effort, 1914-1918" (MA thesis, MUN, 1981), 201-2; Stirling, "Women's Franchise," ch. 4.

89 O'Brien, "Newfoundland Patriotic Associations," 205.

90 Ibid., 203-9.

91 Canadian Patriotic Fund Act, *Statutes of Canada*, 1915, 5 Geo. V, c. 2, s. 2. Other sections made provision for payments to disabled soldiers who had returned to Canada, a flow that had begun early in 1915, and to their dependants.

92 "Comparative Statement of Disbursements of Branches in the Various Provinces," tabled for the Special Committee Appointed to Consider and Report on the Rates of Pensions to be Paid to Disabled Soldiers and the Establishment of a Permanent Pensions Board, Canada, *Sessional Papers*, 1916, appendix 4, *Proceedings*, 162.

93 See Desmond Morton, "The Short Unhappy Life of the 41st Battalion, C.E.F.," *Queen's Quarterly* 81, 1 (1974): 70-9. See also Desmond Morton, "Le Canada français et la milice canadienne (1868-1914)," in *Le Canada Français et la guerre*, ed. Jean-Yves Gravel (Montreal: Editions du Boréal-Express, 1974), 23-46; Desmond Morton, "French Canada and War, 1868-1917" in *Society and War in North America*, ed. J.L. Granatstein and R.D. Cuff (Toronto: Thomas Nelson, 1971), 84-103; Desmond Morton, "The Limits of Loyalty: French-Canadian Officers in the First World War," in *The Limits of Loyalty*, ed. Edgar Denton III (Waterloo: Wilfrid Laurier University Press, 1980), 81-97; and Jean-Pierre Gagnon, *Le 22e bataillon (canadien-français), 1914-1919, Une étude socio-militaire* (Quebec: Presses de l'université Laval, 1986).

94 Morris, *Patriotic Fund*, 236.

95 Ibid., 235.

96 Ibid., 248-9.

97 Ibid., 242.

98 CPF, *Conference of Representatives*, 9.

99 Morris, *Patriotic Fund*, 142.

100 CPF, *Conference of Representatives*, 9.

101 *Streetsville Review and Port Credit Herald*, 3 September 1914.

102 Morris, *Patriotic Fund*, 197; *Streetsville Review and Port Credit Herald*, 7 October 1915; Desmond Morton, "What Did Peel County Do in the Great War?" *History and Social Science Teacher* 23, 1 (1987): 25-30.

103 Allan Bartley, *Heroes in Waiting: The 160th Bruce Battalion in the Great War* (Walkerton: Brucedale Press, 1996), 155-6.

104 See Morris, *Patriotic Fund*, 158-9. Since Frontenac County's records have been deposited with the Queen's University Archives, researchers into the Patriotic Fund have an exceptional opportunity to see how Bradshaw in particular handled his responsibilities. See Christie, *Engendering the State*, 61-77 passim.

105 Oxford County Archives, Norwich, Records of the Oxford Patriotic Association.

106 Morris, *Patriotic Fund*, 220-1.

107 Ibid., 145. On Sault Ste-Marie, see pp. 145-6; on Port Arthur and Fort William, pp. 208-9.

108 Ibid., 18.

109 Ross Papers, box 1, clippings.

110 Ross Papers, box 2, "The 1914 Whirlwind Campaign."

111 *Montreal Daily Star*, 12 September 1914; see also Montreal *Gazette*, 12 September 1914.

112 "Nous qui vivons au Canada sous le régime britannique, nous pourrions nous imaginer que c'est aussi l'heureux sort d'autres humains qui vivent sous une domination étrangère.

Malheureusement, il n'est pas ainsi. Le guerre actuelle est une preuve vivante que dans les pays que l'on dit civilisés le peuple vit encore en servitude." *La Presse,* 12 September 1914.

113   Minute books, executive committee, 4 December 1914. The parish collection yielded a total of only $9,400, half for the Fund.

114   Ibid., 4 September 1914, 107.

115   Ibid., Report of the Finance Executive Committee, 4 September 1914, 107. Among the least profitable and most troublesome donations was a $1,000 bond for Hillcrest Collieries, handed over by a financially troubled Montrealer who wanted $500 to go to the Fund, $200 for the McGill College Canadian Officers Training Corps contingent, and $300 "for another good purpose." The bond stayed around until 1921, accompanied by querulous letters from the donor. Whatever the CPF gained, W.F. Angus, treasurer for the McGill COTC, claimed that it had yielded his fund only $6.25. Ross Papers, vol. 2, C.P. Hill to J. Ross, 14 January 1915 and following.

116   Montreal *Gazette,* 17 September 1914.

117   *Le Devoir,* 18 September 1914. Montpetit claimed that a quarter of the $1 million target would come from French-Canadian pockets. There is no evident statistical basis for this or any other such claim outside the list of contributors in the Ross Papers, which were not broken down by national origin. Dandurand had set out to raise $100,000 from a hundred patriotic "citoyens à l'aise" and learned how scarce they were. See Marcel Hamelin, ed., *Les mémoires de Raoul Dandurand* (Quebec: Presses de l'université Laval, 1967), 188.

118   See also minute books, finance committee, 9 September 1914, 2. On Ucal Dandurand, see Morgan, *Canadian Men and Women,* 295.

119   Lacoste said, "les liens qui unissent les canadiens-français et les canadiens-anglais." Williams said, "Toutes les différences, tous les conflits de race ... ont fait place à une 'entente cordiale.'" *La Presse,* 19 September 1914.

120   *Montreal Daily Star* and Montreal *Gazette,* 19 September 1914.

121   For results see Appendix B of Desmond Morton, "Entente cordiale? La section Montréalaise du Fonds patriotique canadien, 1914-1923: Le Bénévolat de guerre à Montréal," *Revue d'histoire de LAmérique française* 8, 2 (199); and Ross Papers, Montreal branch statements, August 1914 to 30 June 1918. See also Montreal *Gazette,* 19 September 1914. Montreal's $150,000 gift was split between Ucal Dandurand's team and Alderman O'Connell's.

122   On McConnell, see Morgan, *Canadian Men and Women,* 754.

123   Montreal *Gazette,* 12 September 1914.

124   See Montreal *Gazette, Montreal Daily Star, La Presse,* and *La Patrie,* 12-19 September 1914; Ross Papers, vol. 2, "Report on Whirlwind Campaign, 1914."

125   Ross Papers, box 3, "First Montreal Canadian Patriotic Fund Campaign, September 14-18, 1914," loose-leaf folder.

126   *Hedley Gazette and Similkameen Advertiser,* 10, 37 (1 October 1914).

127   Ibid., 10, 38 (8 October 1914).

128   On internment, see Chapter 2, n. 54.

129   On Vernon, see Desmond Morton, *The Canadian General: Sir William Otter* (Toronto: Hakkert, 1974), 333, 336, 339, 344, 349.

130   Robert C. Dexter, "War Relief and Charity Organization," *Charity Organization Bulletin* 8 (1916-17): 52-3.

Chapter 4: Choices and Responsibilities

1   Cited by Nancy Christie, *Engendering the State: Family, Work, and Welfare in Canada* (Toronto: University of Toronto Press, 2000), 55-6.

2   Cited in the Victoria *Colonist,* 4 September 1915. On 4 December, the *Colonist* explained the procedure of the local branch after the soldier filled out the CPF form, with investigation,

verification, record keeping locally and in Ottawa, and approval by three trustees that "prevent any laxity or extravagance" to reassure donors.

3 Special Committee Appointed to Consider and Report upon the Rates of Pensions to be paid to Disabled Soldiers and the Establishment of a Permanent Pensions Board, *Reports and Proceedings* (Ottawa: King's Printer, May 1916), 152 (hereafter Committee on Pensions, 1916).

4 See Chapter 3, n. 48.

5 National Archives of Canada (NAC), A.F. Duguid Papers, "CEF Statistics." A list of the first forty-nine beneficiaries of the Montreal branch to die in the war was presented by Helen Reid to the House of Commons Committee on Pensions in 1916. Prewar monthly incomes ranged from $32 for a young man who left his mother and four young siblings, to $120 for a man who left a wife and three children, and averaged $61. The median family size was two children, but six of the twenty-eight who left wives also left five or six children. Committee on Pensions, 1916, *Proceedings*, 176.

6 Desmond Morton and Glenn Wright, *Winning the Second Battle: Canadian Veterans and the Return to Civilian Life, 1915-1930* (Toronto: University of Toronto Press, 1987), 25, n. 34; NAC, RG 9, III A 1 ser. 8, vol. 37, f. 8-2-10, Reid to Carson, 5 June 1916; Carson to Hughes, 7 June 1916.

7 NAC, R.L. Borden Papers (hereafter Borden Papers), OC 331, CPF, *Reports of the Proceedings of a Conference of Representatives of Branches of the Canadian Patriotic Fund in Eastern Cities, 16, 17, 18 May 1916.* (Ottawa: CPF, 1916), 19-20.

8 Philip H. Morris, *The Canadian Patriotic Fund: A Record of Its Activities from 1914 to 1919* (Ottawa: s.n., [1920?]), 29.

9 Herbert Ames testimony, Committee on Pensions, 1916, *Proceedings*, 5 April 1916, 161-2.

10 Morris, *Patriotic Fund*, 30.

11 At the Eastern Canada conference of CPF representatives that month, Ames chose Peterborough's F.H. Dobbin to report on branch administration. He confessed that his branch had ignored the national guidelines but insisted that local married men were enlisting enthusiastically, and local opinion considered the payments generous: "Judicious, thoughtful and considerate pruning may save a branch an expenditure of hundreds of dollars per month." Borden Papers, OC 331, CPF, *Reports of the Proceedings of a Conference of Representatives*, 18.

12 Ibid., 31-2.

13 NAC, RG 24, vol. 1271, HQ 593-2-35, Ames to Hughes, 18 November 1914; ibid., Hughes to Ames, 4 December 1914; NAC, MG 28, I 5, vol. 1, CPF Circular no. 2, "Separation Allowance & Assigned Pay" [October 1915].

14 NAC, RG 24, vol. 1271, HQ 593-1-35, E.L. Newcombe to Eugène Fiset, 5 December 1914 and Fiset to Newcombe, 8 December, 1914, citing Article 986 of the Royal Warrant, ss. 144, 145, The Militia Act.

15 NAC, MG 28, I 5, vol. 1, CPF Circular no. 2, "Separation Allowance & Assigned Pay," [October 1915]; NAC, MG 28, I, 5, vol. 1, CPF national executive minutes, 13 October 1914.

16 NAC, RG 24, vol. 1271, HQ 593-2-35, Ward to Fiset, January 1915.

17 Report of 18 January 1915, reflecting British and Patriotic Fund pressure, and PC 1148, 23 January 1915.

18 Herbert Ames, *Our National Benefaction* (Ottawa: CPF, 1915) 12.

19 Ibid., 14-15. See also Barbara Wilson, *Ontario and the First World War, 1914-1918* (Toronto: University of Toronto Press, 1977), lx, 48-9; House of Commons, *Debates*, 23 June 1923, 3479-80.

20 Herbert Ames, *The Second Year of the War: What It Means to the Canadian Patriotic Fund* (Ottawa: CPF, 1915), 8.

21 Committee on Pensions, 1916, *Proceedings*, 153.

22 Dr. Alice W. Turner, "Sequences of Economic Events in Canada, 1914-1923," Report to the Advisory Committee on Reconstruction, n.d. (Metropolitan Toronto Reference Library, cited

by Margaret McCallum, "The Canadian Patriotic Fund and the Care of Soldiers' Families, 1914-1918," unpublished paper, March 1982, 4, n. 18.

23 Morris, *Patriotic Fund*, 32.

24 *Labour Gazette* 19, 3 (1919): 343-8.

25 Morris, *Patriotic Fund*, 32-3.

26 Borden Papers, C-4309, F.H. Kidd CI to Borden, 28 October 1916, 30544-5.

27 Private collection, Ernest Hamilton letters, Ernest to Sara Hamilton, 30 October 1917.

28 McCallum, "Canadian Patriotic Fund," 4, suggests that in 1915 the ratio was closer to half the separation allowance recipients. See Ames testimony, Committee on Pensions, 1916, *Proceedings*, 150.

29 *Toronto Daily News*, 17 May 1916, cited by Margaret McCallum, "Assistance to Veterans and Their Dependants: Steps on the Way to the Administrative State, 1914-1929," in *Canadian Perspectives on Law and Society: Issues in Legal History*, ed. W. Wesley Pue and Barry Wright (Ottawa: Carleton University Press, 1988), 159. Sensitive to the charge that the Patriotic Fund had reduced the supply of charwomen to its wealthy subscribers, Philip Morris questioned whether a mere $5 a month would persuade a woman to remain idle.

30 *Labour Gazette* 16, 6 (1916): 1279; *Women's Century* 4, 2 (1916). See also NAC, MG 28, I, 5, vol. 1, N.F. Davidson to the national executive committee, 16 September 1916, insisting that the Toronto and York Branch "sees itself in no way responsible" for any shortage of female labour.

31 Committee on Pensions, 1916, *Proceedings*, 151.

32 Morris, *Patriotic Fund*, 256-7.

33 Great Britain, House of Commons, *Debates*, 11 November 1914, 31.

34 Mrs. H. Collinson twice asked the Calgary branch for assistance. Belatedly the branch secretary acknowledged that her earnings of $30 a month as a waitress should not have denied her assistance. Borden Papers, C-4308, secretary, Calgary branch, to Ames, 20 November 1915.

35 Morris, *Patriotic Fund*, 36.

36 NAC, RG 24, vol. 4286, 34-1-10, vol. 3, *Toronto & York Annual Report, 1 January 1918*, "Report of the 50,000 Club."

37 Borden Papers, C-4309, OC 267, Ben Ewing to Philip Morris, 4 February 1916, 30239.

38 Nova Scotia Archives and Records Management (NSARM), MG 20, CPF Nova Scotia branch, vol. 497, fld. 5, Barnstead to Morris, 15 and 27 March 1917; Morris to Barnstead, 21 and 31 March 1917.

39 Ibid., fld. 3, Robert Irwin to director of Separation Allowance and Assigned Pay Board, 27 August and 11 September 1918; SA&AP Board to Irwin, 5 and 24 September 1918.

40 Ibid., Morris to Barnstead, 24 September 1918.

41 Ibid., fld. 2, consul of Belgium to Nova Scotia secretary, 18 May 1917; copy of reply to Philip Morris, 23 May 1917.

42 Ibid., Barnstead to H.H. MacIntosh, 17 May 1917; Morris to Nova Scotia secretary, 31 May 1917; Barnstead to MacIntosh, 8 June 1917.

43 Ames's report to the Special Committee on Pensions in April 1916 indicated that forty-six officers' families (out of a total of 28,279 families) received an average of $22.07 a month (as compared to an average of $20.22 for Vancouver families or $15.23 for families in Ontario). See Canada, *Sessional Papers*, 1916, appendix 4, *Proceedings*, 161.

44 NAC, C.A. Magrath Papers, vol. 2, file no. 4, CPF, cited by David Laurier Bernard, "Philanthropy vs. the Welfare State: Great Britain's and Canada's Response to Military Dependants in the Great War" (MA thesis, University of Guelph, 1992), 77, n. 67.

45 See Morris, *Patriotic Fund*, 39.

46 Queen's University Archives, Frontenac County Records, 1919, title 9, J.W. Bradshaw to Annie Flint, 30 April 1919. See also Canadian Patriotic Fund Act, *Statutes of Canada*, 1915, 5 Geo. V,

c. 2, ss. 3a, 3b; Morris, *Patriotic Fund*, 340, 341-2. In military law, "desertion" was distinguished from "absence without leave" by a soldier's apparent intent never to return to his duty.

47 NAC, RG 24, vol. 916, HQ 54-21-23-8, Mrs. E. Perry to commanding officer, 1 January 1916.

48 NAC, MG 28, I, 5, vol. 1, CPF national executive meeting, 20 February 1917.

49 Some were common-law wives, others were bigamous wives of British immigrants who had left a family in England. As the minister of militia conceded, "Quite a large number of cases of soldiers having two wives have come to light." See PC 2615, 28 October 1916, NAC, RG 2 A1a, box 1125.

50 Reid encountered 184 such cases in the files of the Montreal branch alone. McCallum, "Canadian Patriotic Fund," 165.

51 NAC, RG 24, vol. 1252, HQ 595-1-82, Helen Reid, "Protest against P.C. 2615," 114.

52 Cited by McCallum, "Canadian Patriotic Fund," 161.

53 Special Committee Appointed to Consider, Inquire into, and Report upon the Reception, Treatment, Care, Training and Re-Education of the Wounded, Disabled and Convalescent who have served in the Canadian Expeditionary Forces, *Proceedings, Evidence and Reports* (Ottawa: King's Printer, 1917) (hereafter Committee on Returned Men, 1917); McCallum, "Canadian Patriotic Fund"; CPF *Bulletin*, no. 37 (July 1918): 3.

54 Morris, *Patriotic Fund*, 37. See also Hamilton and Wentworth Branch, CPF, *Five Years of Service, 1914-1919* (N.p.: N.d.), 31-4, on how the Hamilton branch had managed an errant wife.

55 Morris, *Patriotic Fund*, 37.

56 CPF *Bulletin*, May 1918.

57 NAC, RG 24, vol. 1252, HQ 593-1-82, W.H. Lovering to Philip Morris, 31 March 1917; Morris to Maj. Everett Bristol, 2 April 1917. The change was helped by the fact that PC 3192, 30 December 1916, the SA regulations for the Royal Canadian Navy, were slightly less restrictive than those for the CEF, allowing "the cases of other persons, concerning whom clear proof of actual dependency can be produced" to be judged on their individual merits. See NAC, RG 2 A1a, box 1158. Since it was anomalous that a sailor's sister could be helped and a soldier's sister could not, the change was made. See NAC, RG 24, vol. 1252, HQ 593-1-86, Philip J. Morris to J.W. Borden, 19 June 1917.

58 CPF *Bulletin*, June 1918.

59 CPF, Montreal Branch, *Report of the Montreal Branch, Canadian Patriotic Fund, 1914-1917* (Montreal, 1917), 37; Morris, *Patriotic Fund*, 42.

60 NAC, MG 28, I, 5, vol. 1, CPF national executive minutes, 13 January 1915; PC 193, 28 January 1915.

61 NAC, RG 24, vol. 1235, HQ 593-1-12, L.S. Fraser to Lt.-Col. C.S. McInnis, 22 August 1916.

62 Morris, *Patriotic Fund*, 256-7.

63 Sharpe, who would return as an officer in the 116th Battalion, had supported Alma Freed since Valcartier in September 1914. However, Freed's employer, Toronto's Board of Control, demanded that she marry or lose her job. Later, a neighbour complained that Mrs. Sharpe was "carrying on intrigues since [Sharpe] went back to his battalion last month and otherwise acting in an extravagant manner on her separation money." See NAC, RG 24, vol. 1235, HQ 593-1-12, L.S. Fraser to Lt.-Col. C.S. McInnis, 22 August 1916.

64 NAC, RG 24, vol. 1234, HQ 593-1-12, R.P. Brown to deputy minister, 19 December 1916, 580; Reid reports, 8 November 1916; Elliott to Brown, 19 December 1916. The confusion was embarrassing to the Montrealers since they had come to Ottawa to complain of Pay Department inefficiency.

65 Borden Papers, C-4308, CPF *Bulletin*, October 1915.

66 McCord Museum of Canadian History, P217-C/7, J.W. Ross Papers (hereafter Ross Papers), box 1, Montreal Patriotic Fund minute books (hereafter "minute books"), executive

committee, 9 October 1914, 129. Only the *Montreal Herald* agreed; see minute books, executive committee, 6 November 1914, 141.

67 Cited in Desmond Morton, "Entente cordiale? La section Montréalaise du Fonds patriotique canadien, 1914-1923: Le Bénévolat de guerre à Montréal," *Revue d'histoire de LAmérique française* 8, 2 (199): 225; McCord Museum of Canadian History, Montreal branch, SPC, minute books, October 1914, 80; criticisms in *Beck's Weekly*, 24, 31, October 1914.

68 NAC, RG 24, vol. 1234, HQ 593-1-12, Mayor Morin and Fr. J.V. Beaulieu to Fiset, 2 December 1916; la veuve Victorin Lussier to Fiset, 24 November 1916; Fiset to Lussier, 29 December 1916; Émile Rioux to Fiset, 15 May 1916. Mme Gagnon had written directly to the prime minister from her home in D'Israeli, claiming that she and her six children were starving. See NAC, RG 24, vol. 943, 21-23-25, vol. 5, Mme Alphonse Gaudet to "mons. borden," [May 1916].

69 House of Commons, *Debates*, 29 January 1917, 202-3.

70 NAC, MG 27IID9, Kemp Papers, vol. 34, f. 1198, Birmingham to Kemp, 7 November 1916; Kemp to AA & PMG, 13 October 1916.

71 Ibid., D.G. Almond to Col. S.C. Mewburn, 6 September 1916.

72 NAC, RG 24, vol. 4286, 34-1-10, vol. 2, H.T. Wall to Maj.-Gen. Logie, 30 September 1916.

73 NAC, RG 24, vol. 4656, f. 990-88, vol. 3, Agnes Georgeson to Lt.-Col. J.W. Warden, 102nd Battalion, 17 March 1916, cited by Charles W. Humphries, "Keeping the Home Fires Burning: British Columbia Women and the First World War," paper presented to Canadian Historical Association, Charlottetown, PEI, 31 May 1992, 4-6.

74 Ibid., C.H. Bonnor, CPF Vancouver, to Capt. H.B. Scharschmidt, 18 March 1916; Warden to district officer commanding, MD 11, 19 March 1916; district staff adjutant, MD 11 to Hon. Secretary, CPF, 4 April 1916; cited in Humphries, "Keeping the Home Fires Burning," 4-5.

75 Ibid., Maj. Charles Clarke, 30th BC Horse, to district staff adjutant, MD 11, 23 August 1915.

76 Ibid., George D. Ireland (relief officer, Vancouver) to Maj. J.R. Tite, 23rd Battalion, 26 August 1916.

77 Archives of Manitoba, Manitoba Patriotic Fund, case file 4243, Mrs. Horwood. Mrs. Horwood had a different version. Fred said he was a teetotaller, Dora claimed he was a drunk. When she visited him at work to plead with him to come home, she had two twin babes in her arms and the proprietor had promised to persuade him to rejoin his family. Ibid., secretary, MPF, to SA & AP Branch, 25 August 1919.

78 Ibid., secretary, MPF, to Mrs. Horwood, 12 January 1916, in response to Horwood to Roland, 20 August 1915. Though Lord Strathcona's Horse had a regiment overseas in the Canadian Cavalry Brigade, it still maintained depots in Winnipeg and Calgary.

79 Ibid., Mrs. Horwood to Sir Douglas Cameron, 13 January 1916, and to Charles Roland, 16 January 1916.

80 Ibid., Mrs. Horwood to MPF, 7 July 1916.

81 Ibid., secretary, MPF, to SA & AP Branch, 22 June 1917; Lt.-Col. C.M. Ingalls to secretary, MPF, Winnipeg, 17 October 1917.

82 Ibid., Mrs. Horwood to Mr. Hooper, 21 October and 13 November 1917. On the investigation, see MPF to SA & AP Branch, 16 November 1917.

83 Ibid., Mrs. Horwood to MPF, 14 August and 4 September 1917; C. Buffet, Trustee Company of Winnipeg, to secretary, MPF, 3 August 1918. Since the firm claimed to be patriotically managing properties for enlisted men it expected the MPF's backing.

84 Committee on Pensions, 1916, *Proceedings*, 160.

85 An Italian private earned $0.20 a day, and a French private only $0.055 a day, compared to $1.10 for a Canadian, $1.46 for an Australian, and $0.105 for a German.

86 Morris, *Patriotic Fund*, 33, 45.

87 NAC, MG 28, I, 5, vol. 1, CPF national executive minutes, resolution of 4 April 1918.

88 Morris, *Patriotic Fund*, 37-8.

89 NAC, RG 24, vol. 922, 54-21-23-11, memorandum to A.E. Blount (R.L. Borden's secretary), 13 October 1914, claimed that a married soldier doing garrison duty at Halifax usually lived at home and received $1.10 a day plus $0.75 for subsistence, which was "very nearly equivalent" to what men at the front received. "As wages go, these men are very well paid. To compare their services or their hardships with those who have to face the Germans is an absurdity."

90 As Hughes explained in June 1916, CEF and Permanent Force rates of pay were the same, but CEF members could direct $20 to their families while soldiers in Canada could only claim the difference between $0.75 a day and the cost of their daily rations, or about $6.50 a month. See NAC, RG 24, vol. 1229, HQ 583-1-11, minister of militia to governor general in council, 6 June 1916.

91 NAC, RG 4, vol. 4286, 34-1-10 vol. 2, Mrs. S.H. Raun to Maj.-Gen. Logie, 16 August 1916.

92 NAC, RG 24, vol. 1252, HQ 593-1-82, Mrs. E.J. Failes to Gen. Logie, 5 June 1917, and memorandum, general officer commanding, MD 2, to Militia Council, 28 June 1917; Mrs. H.M. Humly to minister of militia, 31 January 1917. Gen. Logie was district officer commanding Military District No. 2, covering Toronto and central Ontario.

93 NAC, RG 24, vol. 922, HQ 54-21-23-8, Mrs. W.R. Duke to Borden [October 1917].

94 NAC, RG 24, vol. 4652, f. 99-36, vol. 1, Katie F. Dickinson to Col. J.H. Duff Stewart, 16 July 1916. See also Humphries, "Home Fires," 8.

95 On their conditions, see Morton and Wright, *Winning the Second Battle*, 19-43.

96 Nova Scotia reported 108 such families, with 45 of them collecting assistance and three families receiving over $20 a month, all in Cape Breton mining communities where the cost of living was high. Morris asked the Nova Scotia secretary to ask the local military authorities to have the three heads of families discharged. NAC, RG 8, vol. 497, f. 2, Morris to Barnstead, 17 March 1917, and throughout.

97 Morris, *Patriotic Fund*, appendix A, 342-3.

98 NAC, RG 24, vol. 4286, 34-1-10, vol. 2, Mrs. Kerr to Maj.-Gen. Logie, [August 1917]; A.A.G. to Toronto & York Patriotic Fund, 25 July and 13 August 1917.

99 Ibid., Logie to Kerr, 21 August 1917.

100 Morris, *Patriotic Fund*, 34.

101 *Montreal Daily Star*, 12 September 1914. See also *Everywoman's World*, November 1914.

102 By November 1914 Reid reported a hundred such cases, some of them families whose man had returned from Valcartier, others "imposters with no rightful claim whatever on the Fund." Minute books, executive committee, 6 November 1914, 138.

103 The Franco-Belgian office continued to operate separately with its own staff and volunteers until the final months of 1919, spending a fifth to a quarter of the Montreal branch's relief funds. Ross Papers, vol. 1, Financial Statements, September 1914 to June 1918; July 1918 to 31 December 1919.

104 See McCord Museum of Canadian History, CPF, Montreal Branch, *First Annual Report*, appendix C.

105 Soldiers serving in Canada earned $1.10 a day plus $0.75 for subsistence. The Montreal committee proposed an allowance of from $0.10 to $0.25 a day for children depending on their age. See minute books, executive committee, 9 October 1914, 127; 23 October 1914, 133; *Montreal Daily Star*, 17 and 21 October 1914.

106 See Dandurand-Nichols motion, CPF national executive committee, 6 October 1915, in Borden Papers, OC 267.

107 Borden Papers, OC 267, C-4304, Mrs. J.T. Ainsworth to Borden, [1918], 30745.

108 Minute books, executive committee, 15 January 1915, 159.

109 Ross Papers, vol. 1, Montreal branch audited statements to 30 November 1918. See also Morton, "Entente cordiale," 246, appendix C.

110 CPF, Montreal Branch, *First Annual Report*, 13.

111 Ibid., 23.
112 Borden Papers, OC 267, Clarence Smith to Philip Morris, 29 October 1915.
113 NAC, MG 28, I, 5, vol. 1, CPF national executive minutes, 4 November 1915 (on Smith's letter to Morris), 26.
114 NAC, RG 24, vol. 943, 54-21-23-25, vol. 4, Madame Aimé Smith to Montreal CPF, 8 December 1915.
115 Ibid. NAC, MG 28, I, 5, vol. 1, CPF national executive minutes, Reid to Ames, 22 September 1916. See also Ross Papers, vol. 2, Reid to W.H. Lovering, 22 September 1916.
116 See, for example, Ross Papers, vol. 2, Elliott to Ross, 3 November 1915 and reply; Cora Elliott to Ross, 2 May 1917.
117 Ross Papers, box 2, E.L. Brittain to Ross, 16 September 1916, and Ross to Brittain, 13 October 1916.
118 Borden Papers, OC 331, CPF, *Reports of the Proceedings of a Conference of Representatives*, 38.
119 *Beck's Weekly*, 31 October 1914; also [Helen Reid], *Report of the Montreal CPF, 1914-1917* (Montreal: CPF, 1917), 37-9.
120 CPF, Montreal Branch, *First Annual Report*, 40-1.
121 Robert C. Dexter, "War Relief and Charity Organization," *Charity Organization Bulletin* 8 (1916-17): 55-6.
122 Morris, *Patriotic Fund*, 16.
123 Ames testimony, Committee on Pensions, 1916, *Proceedings*, 151. The same image appears in House of Commons, *Debates*, 29 February 1916, 1255 ff.; and CPF *Bulletin*, September 1916.
124 Committee on Pensions, 1916, *Proceedings*, 5 April 1916, 150.
125 See, for example, Victoria *Colonist*, 5 October 1916.
126 House of Commons, *Debates*, 29 February 1916, 1257.
127 Ibid., 1257.
128 Ibid., 1258.
129 G.W.L. Nicholson, *Official History of the Canadian Army in the First World War: Canadian Expeditionary Force, 1914-1919* (Ottawa: Queen's Printer, 1962), appendix C, 546.
130 NAC, MG 28, I, 5, vol. 1, CPF national executive minutes, 6 October 1915.
131 Morris, *Patriotic Fund*, 21.
132 CPF, *How Much Shall We Give? Receipts and Expenditures of the Canadian Patriotic Fund during the First Year of the War: The Needs of the Future* (Ottawa: CPF, 1 October 1915).
133 Provinces had helped negotiate their quotas and sometimes challenged the figures in Ames's original pamphlet, See, for example, correspondence between Ames and Arthur S. Barnstead, the Nova Scotia provincial secretary, January-March 1916. NAC RG 10, vol. 497, fld. 1.
134 Morris, *Patriotic Fund*, 21-2; McCallum, "Canadian Patriotic Fund," 159.
135 *Hedley Gazette and Similkameen Advertiser* 12, 8 and 15 January 1916.
136 NAC, RG 24, vol. 4286, 34-1-10, vol. 3, *Report of the Toronto and York Branch, Canadian Patriotic Fund*, 1 January 1918, 50,000 Club Report.
137 Morris, *Patriotic Fund*, 27.
138 NAC, RG 10, vol. 6762, file 455-2-2, Ames to Scott, February 1917. See also ibid., Moo-chew-in-es to Scott, December 1916; Morris, *Patriotic Fund*, 23.
139 "It was the consensus of the meeting," the secretary recorded in June, "that Montreal had contributed its full share towards the fund ... and that it would be inexpedient to take steps looking to a further canvass, in any case before the month of December." Minute books, executive committee, 25 June 1915.
140 Ibid., 8 October and 19 November 1915. Rural Ontario had also lagged in the CPF and other aspects of the war effort, but an organizer raised contributions in the non-urban counties to about $0.90 a head. The comparable Quebec figure was $0.09. See Borden Papers, OC 267, Ames to T.C. Casgrain, 13 January 1916. On Quebec see Morris, *Patriotic Fund*, 235 ff.

141 On French Canada and the war, see Elizabeth Armstrong, *The Crisis of Quebec* (New York: Ams Press, 1937).

142 Campaign material may be found in Ross Papers, box B/1, scrapbook for the 1916 campaign.

143 Montreal *Gazette*, 23 December 1915.

144 Minute books, executive committee, 23 December 1915, 2; Montreal *Evening News*, 24 December 1915. CPF, Montreal Branch, *First Annual Report*, 7, lists twenty-seven districts, all with English-speaking heads, twenty with French-Canadian joint heads and one, St. Lawrence, with a Jewish joint head. One of the French-Canadian heads covered more than one ward.

145 "N'essayez-pas de charger le comité du Fonds patriotique de la responsabilité d'une taxe," said Dandurand. See *Montreal Daily Star* and *Montreal Herald*, 17 January 1916; Ross Papers, B/1, scrapbook for the 1916 campaign, p. 217; Montreal *Gazette*, 18 January 1916. Cynics noted that Controller Côté proposed to find the money for the CPF from the public works budget.

146 See *Montreal Daily Star*, 22 January 1916; *La Patrie*, 22 January 1916.

147 *Addresses Delivered before the Canadian Club of Montreal, 1915-1916* (Montreal, 1916), 103.

148 Montreal *Gazette*, 21 January 1916.

149 The separate Irish, Jewish, and Belgian teams of 1914 were not reconstituted. Indeed, without Friedman's team, Jewish participation almost vanished. From the lists of team members, only a handful of Jewish names can be identified, including Alderman Rubinstein and clothier Morris Ogulnik. See Ross Papers, box B/1, scrapbook for the 1916 campaign.

150 "Qu'y a-t-il donc au fond? Deux cent milles hommes glorieux de leur titre de sujets britanniques fidèles à leur roi et à leur patrie, se faisant un point d'honneur de parler l'anglais, demandent simplement à parler aussi la langue de leurs ancêtres, la belle et douce langue française, et à l'enseigner librement à leurs enfants. C'est tout, la réponse appartient aux hommes de bonne volonté." *La Patrie*, 24 January 1916.

151 "Ils se mettaient virtuellement en disgrace auprès de leurs chefs. Ils courraient par la suite le risque, ou de n'avoir pas d'augmentation de traitement, ou d'être éconduits dès que l'occasion s'en présentera. Il y a eu dans celà un abus flagrant." *Le Nationaliste*, 30 January 1916.

152 Morton, "Entente cordiale," 233-4; *Montreal Daily Star*, 29 January 1916. The paper referred to the Lebanese community as "Syrian": "Team No. 6 reported the contributions from the Syrian Colony of Montreal. The Syrian Colony has a number of very poor members, and those who could not possibly contribute were not asked ... 181 Syrians were asked, and 181 Syrians donated. All of this money was paid to the captain in hard cash."

153 Morris, *Patriotic Fund*, 154.

154 Borden Papers, RLB Misc., C4308 30065, CPF *Bulletin* no. 4 (September 1915).

155 Desmond Morton and Cheryl Smith, "Fuel for the Home Fires: Taking Care of the Women They Left Behind," *Beaver* 75, 4 (1995): 17; Morton, "Entente cordiale," 224-9.

156 CPF *Bulletin*, November 1916.

157 Nellie McClung, "Surprise," in *The Next of Kin: Those Who Wait and Wonder* (Toronto: Thomas Allen, 1917), 73-7.

158 Maj. C.M. Ingalls testimony, Committee on Returned Men, 1917, *Proceedings*, 1162.

159 NAC, RG 24, vol. 4285, 34-1-10, vol. 1, Helen Reid to Martha E. Fennix, 27 November 1915.

160 Borden Papers, C-4308, Henry Tucker to R.L. Borden, 5 February 1918, and following.

161 All quotations from Helen Reid, "War Relief in Canada," *Proceedings of the Annual Conference on Social Work* (Philadelphia: N.p., 1917), 136.

162 CPF *Bulletin*, August 1915.

163 Reid reported the Montreal rate in 1914 as 182 deaths per 1,000 infants under one year (Morris, *Patriotic Fund*, 41). Comparable figures were 100 in the United States, 91 in Great Britain, and 53 in New Zealand. Official figures may be found in Montreal Board of Health, *Annual Report* (Montreal, 1916), 46. See also J.T. Copp, *The Anatomy of Poverty: The Condition of the*

Working Class in Montreal, 1897-1929 (Toronto: McClelland and Stewart, 1974), 93-4. Of 619,636 members enlisted in the CEF during the war, 59,544 died while in their service, or 96 per thousand. See Nicholson, *Canadian Expeditionary Force,* appendix C, 546-8, tables 1-4.

164   CPF, Montreal Branch, *First Annual Report,* 36.

165   Ibid., 38. The Fund claimed a 41 percent increase in delinquency by boys and 43 percent for girls in the third year of the war.

166   Morris, *Patriotic Fund,* 246; Morton, "Entente cordiale," 228-9.

167   CPF, Montreal Branch, *Report, 1914-1917,* 34-5.

168   Ibid., 37; Morris, *Patriotic Fund,* 42.

169   Morris, *Patriotic Fund,* 35; CPF *Bulletin,* July 1918.

170   Cited in Morris, *Patriotic Fund,* 34.

171   Cited ibid., 43.

172   CPF, Montreal Branch, *Report, 1914-1917,* 22.

173   Reid, "War Relief in Canada," 134.

174   Morris, *Patriotic Fund,* 222-32.

175   Borden Papers, OC 267, George Yates to Mrs. E. Morris, 8 April 1918, and R.A. Hurdman to Philip Morris, 10 April 1918. Hurdman also claimed that a Mrs. Smith had lost her position as a government office cleaner "owing to inefficiency."

176   Ibid., J.A. McElroy, Toronto & York Patriotic Association, to George Yates, 15 October 1918.

177   Minute books, executive committee, 4 December 1914, 146-9; 18 December 1914, 152.

178   CPF *Bulletin,* December 1916, cited in Morris, *Patriotic Fund,* 43.

179   Morris, *Patriotic Fund,* 42; CPF, *A Message to the Canadian Soldier's Wife* (Ottawa, 1915).

180   The speech was published in the CPF *Bulletin,* November 1916, in a special issue on thrift.

181   Letter from F.S. Jarvis in the CPF *Bulletin,* March 1917.

182   CPF, Montreal Branch, *First Annual Report,* 37.

183   Morris, *Patriotic Fund,* 45.

184   CPF *Bulletin,* October 1915. Because the highest allowance levels in the country were tied to thrift, they were impossible for Ames to criticize, even in a province that lagged in contributions.

185   CPF *Bulletin,* October 1915, November 1916.

186   Morris, *Patriotic Fund,* 42, 43, 148, 185, 215, 246, 256-7; McCallum, "Canadian Patriotic Fund," 10-11.

187   NSARM, MG 20, CPF Nova Scotia branch, vol. 497, fld. 4, Morris to Barnstead, 9 January 1917, and Barnstead to Morris, 17 February 1917.

188   Private collection, Ernest Hamilton letters, Ernest to Sara Hamilton, 28 November 1917.

189   In Nova Scotia, Arthur Barnstead excitedly proposed to send a representative from each county branch. That was too expensive, said Morris, and a single Nova Scotia representative would do. Barnstead did not come. See PANS, MG 20, CPF Nova Scotia branch, vol. 497, fld. 1, Barnstead to Morris, 25 April 1916 and following.

190   Borden Papers, OC 331, CPF, *Conference of Representatives,* 16.

191   Ibid., 42.

192   Ibid., 23.

193   NSARM, MG 20, CPF Nova Scotia branch, vol. 498, fld. 1; Ames to Barnstead, 5 May, June 8, and September 14 1916; Barnstead to Ames, 11 May, 2 June, 13 June, 3 August, and 24 August 1916; fld. 4, Barnstead to Morris, 29 May 1917.

194   Saskatchewan Archives, Regina branch, Western Interprovincial Conference, published with CPF, Saskatchewan Branch, *Report,* 1916, 27-46.

195   An Act to Raise Pensions for Patriotic Purposes, Saskatchewan, *Statutes of Saskatchewan, 1916,* 6 Geo. V, c. 6, 43-6. In 1917 an amendment act imposed an 8 percent penalty for overdue

payments and added a $2 poll tax on all males over twenty-one not in uniform (*Statutes of Saskatchewan, 1917,* 7 Geo. V, c. 2, 10-11).

196 At Regina Ames admitted that 0.6 percent of income was being absorbed in administration, a tiny share, but a contradiction of one of the Fund's most popular boasts.

197 Statement on 31 July 1916, cited in Victoria *Daily Colonist,* 1 August 1916.

198 Oxford County Archives, Oxford Patriotic Association, f. 43; Cpl. Norton to John White, president, OPA, [received 19 March 1918]; chairman relief committee, OPA, to director, SA & AP Branch, 22 February and 11 March 1918. In 1921 the Oxford Patriotic Association recalled that it held $377.56 in trust for Bessie Norton. Did the money belong to her or to her father, who was planning to marry again? If he used it to buy a house, would it be a real investment in the child's welfare? The question is not answered in the records. See Oxford Patriotic Association, f. 43, G.R. Pattullo to Lt.-Col. McMullen, 15 February 1921.

199 CPF *Bulletin,* December 1916.

200 CPF, Montreal Branch, *First Annual Report,* 25-6.

201 Ibid., 29.

202 CPF, Hamilton Branch, *Five Years of Service: The Canadian Patriotic Fund, Hamilton and Wentworth Branch* (Hamilton: n.p. [1920]).

203 Cited in Daphne Read, ed. *The Great War and Canadian Society: An Oral History* (Toronto: New Hogtown Press, 1978), 189.

204 Borden Papers, OC 331, CPF, *Conference of Representatives,* 59-60.

205 *Hedley Gazette and Similkameen Advertiser* 12, 8 (9 March 1916), 3.

Chapter 5: Homecomings

1 Desmond Morton and Glenn Wright, *Winning the Second Battle: Canadian Veterans and the Return to Civilian Life, 1915-1930* (Toronto: University of Toronto Press, 1987), 6-7.

2 Ibid., 7.

3 In 1917, the 2nd Canadian Division listed four conditions for special leave: (1) "urgent private affairs which necessitate presence and did not admit of delays," (2) dangerous illness of a wife, parent or child, or (3) their death, or (4) "Misconduct of wife or other circumstances requiring arrangements for custody of children." National Archives of Canada (NAC), RG 9, III, vol. 4888, fld. 17, f. 1.

4 In 1918 Lt.-Col. Leonard Ibbotson, who had spent the war overseas, asked to go home to sort out the family business. His brother had been killed, and his father, seventy, was foolishly trying to switch from munitions making to tractor building and had had two severe illnesses. University of Western Ontario Archives, Leonard Ibbotson scrapbook, 7 October 1918.

5 Cited in Albert Carman, *The Return of the Troops: A Plain Account of the Demobilization of the Canadian Expeditionary Force* (Ottawa: Government Printing Bureau, 1920), 123-4.

6 Ibid., 125.

7 Carman, *Return of the Troops,* 128-9. When the second soldier finally got his discharge, he was already absent without leave.

8 NAC, RG 9, III, vol. 4626, fld. 9, f. 6, 2nd Division Artillery.

9 NAC, RG 24, vol. 436, HQ 54-21-1-88, "Memorandum Respecting Return of Soldiers from Overseas," 29 January 1919.

10 Carman, *Return of the Troops,* 130.

11 Formation of Military Hospitals Commission by PC 1540, 30 June 1915, cited in *Canadian Annual Review,* 1915, 263 and found in NAC, RG 2 A1a, box 1118.

12 On Scammell, see NAC, RG 32, c-2, vol. 232, f. 862, C.F. Hamilton to William Foran, 6 November 1918; ibid., "Memorandum re Services and Activities of Ernest Henry Scammell," 7 July 1935.

13 On the MHC, see Morton and Wright, *Winning the Second Battle*, 19-24; Katherine McCuaig, "From Social Reform to Social Service: The Changing Role of Volunteers: The Anti-Tuberculosis Campaign, 1900-1930," *Canadian Historical Review* 61, 4 (1980); H.D. Chadwick and A.S. Pope, *The Modern Attack on Tuberculosis* (New York: Commonwealth Fund, 1946).

14 NAC, RG 38, vol. 198, f. 6091, Scammell to Lt.-Col. D.W. Rowley (MHC member) 5 April 1916.

15 Ames testimony, Special Committee Appointed to Consider, Inquire into, and Report upon the Reception, Treatment, Care, Training and Re-Education of the Wounded, Disabled and Convalescent who have served in the Canadian Expeditionary Forces, *Proceedings, Evidence and Reports* (Ottawa: King's Printer, 1917), 232 (hereafter Committee on Returned Men, 1917).

16 On medical treatment, see Desmond Morton, "Military Medicine and State Medicine: Historical Notes on the Canadian Army Medical Corps in the First World War, 1914-1919," in *Canadian Health Care and the State: A Century of Evolution*, ed. C. David Naylor (Montreal and Kingston: McGill-Queen's University Press, 1992), 38-66.

17 Committee on Returned Men, 1917, *Proceedings*, 62.

18 See Morton and Wright, *Winning the Second Battle*, 24-31.

19 Oxford County Archives, Oxford Patriotic Association, reel 3, series 12, E, f. 2; L.E. Lowman to secretary, Soldiers' Aid Commission, 13 July 1917, J.B. Jupp MD, medical examination, 17 August 1917; E.W. Nesbitt MP to Board of Pension Commissioners, 18 August 1917. Under the original military pension regulations adopted in April 1915, Canadian military disability pensions were awarded according to four classes that depended on the degree of disability and the circumstances in which it was incurred. The first degree (full pension of $264 a year for a private) was reserved for soldiers "totally incapacitated" as a result of wounds, injury, or illness incurred in action or in the face of the enemy. Second degree pensions ($192 a year) went to a private totally incapacitated during drill, training, or other duties, or "materially incapacitated" in action or in the face of the enemy. Third degree pensions went to those "materially incapacitated during drill or training, etc." or "in a small degree incapacitated in action." A fourth degree pension was for those "in a small degree incapacitated" during training. A widow could claim $22 a month and the wife of a disabled soldier might be granted half the rate for a widow until her man died. A child was worth $5 a month. This was set out in an order-in-council after the Second Battle of Ypres. See PC 289, 29 April 1915, in *Canada Gazette* 48, 44 (1 May 1915): 416-17 and NAC, RG 2 A1a, box 1113.

One of Todd's achievements was to eliminate the distinction between battle and action-related and training-related disabilities and to move to five and eventually twenty different classes of disability, based on percentages.

20 Ontario's Soldiers' Aid Commission tried repeatedly to get Lamer a 35 percent pension for his disability while the Board, just as firmly, refused because of the "functional" nature of the disability. Losing patience when Lamer failed to repay its loans, the Solders' Aid finally refused to lend him money to buy shoemaking tools for his trade. Oxford Patriotic Assocation, f. 37, précis of Lamer Case.

21 Oxford County Archives, Oxford Patriotic Association, reel 3, series 12, E, f. 32. Hudleston to Lowman, 20 February 1917; R.M. Stewart to Lowman, 13 November 1918; Hudleston to Charles Foran, 2 February 1919.

22 NAC, MG 28, I, vol. 1, CPF Records, Florence Cole to Ames, 9 October 1914, 15 January 1915; CPF to Cole, 21 January 1915; See Philip H. Morris, *The Canadian Patriotic Fund: A Record of Its Activities from 1914 to 1919* (Ottawa: s.n., [1920?]), 9.

23 Canadian Patriotic Fund Act, *Statutes of Canada*, 1915, 5 Geo. V, c. 2.

24 Ibid.

25 NAC, RG 24, vol. 1252, HQ 593-1-82, J.W. Borden to Col. Ward, 8 May 1917. Dropping from full pay to a pension could still be a blow. Sir George Perley cited one senior officer whose

widow had been assigned almost all his pay. Her income would drop from $240 to a maximum pension of $104 a month. Ibid., Perley to Kemp, 1 June 1917.

26 Canadian pension rates for 1914-16 are reported in the *Canada Year Book*, 1915, table 24, 650. SA continued for three months after a soldier's death and pension officials asked for a further three months if they were not ready to decide.

27 By the end of the twentieth century, commentators might recognize the symptoms of post-traumatic stress disorder, but at the time of the First World War any diagnosis that hinted at psychological injury was either insanity or self-indulgence.

28 On Scammell's ideas, see Morton and Wright, *Winning the Second Battle*, 16-18; NAC, RG 38, vol. 137, f. 7-12, Scammell to Lougheed, 19 July 1915. See also F.H. Sexton, "The Training of Disabled Soldiers for Suitable Occupations," *Halifax Morning Chronicle*, 27 October 1915; Ernest Scammell, "Canadian Practice in Dealing with Crippled Soldiers," *American Journal of Care for Cripples* 5, 2 (1917).

29 On Segsworth's plans and operations, see Walter E. Segsworth, *Retraining Canada's Disabled Soldiers* (Ottawa: N.p., 1920).

30 On retraining see Segsworth, *Retraining*, 24; NAC, RG 38, vol. 138, f. 8638, Department of Soldiers' Civil Re-establishment, *Invalided Soldiers' Commission* (Ottawa, 1919), 24-5. Aided by his remarkable wife, McDougall continued at the university as a crusty but effective professor of history.

31 Invalided Soldiers' Commission, *The Soldier's Return: How the Canadian Soldier Is Being Refitted for Industry* (Ottawa, 1919), 44; See also J.S. McLennan, *What the Military Hospitals Commission Is Doing* (Ottawa: King's Printer, 1918); and Morton and Wright, *Winning the Second Battle*, 39-43.

32 On Todd, see Henry J. Morgan, *Canadian Men and Women of the Time*, 2nd ed. (Toronto, 1912), 1104.

33 J.L. Todd to Marjory Todd, 6 October 1915, in Bridget Fialkowski, ed., *John L. Todd, 1876-1949: Letters* (Senneville, QC: privately published, 1977).

34 See J.L. Todd, "The French System of Return to Civil Life of Cripples and Discharged Soldiers," *American Journal of Care for Cripples* 5, 1 (1917).

35 Cited in Morton and Wright, *Winning the Second Battle*, 50. See also NAC, RG 9, II B 2, vol. 3583, f. 22-4-23, "Recommendations of the Pensions and Claims Board, CEF as to Pensions and Other Matters," s. 7; and Canada, *Sessional Papers*, 1916, no. 185, 49.

36 On Todd's ideas, see Major, CAMC, "Returned Soldiers and the Medical Profession," *Canadian Medical Association Journal* 7, 4 (1917).

37 See J.L. Todd and Thomas B. Kidner, "The Re-training of Disabled Men," *American Medicine* (Spring 1917).

38 Morton and Wright, *Winning the Second Battle*, 12-13; and NAC, Borden Papers, OC 323, (1) (a) vol. 71, A.F. Messervey to Borden, 17 March 1915, f. 36548. The Royal Patriotic Fund Corporation supported the widows of soldiers and sailors; the Soldiers' and Sailors' Families Association supported wives and other dependants left destitute by an absent service member, and the Soldiers' and Sailors' Help Society, under the patronage of Lord Roberts, sought to assist disabled veterans to become self-supporting. By 1916 Britain boasted over 6,000 county, corps, regimental, and other associations, private trusts, and appeals devoted to the welfare of soldiers and providing influence and some gratification to the country's governing class. See Graham Wootton, *The Politics of Influence: British Ex-Servicemen, Cabinet Decisions and Cultural Change, 1917-57* (London: Routledge and Kegan Paul, 1963), 16-37.

39 On the "pension evil" see James Bryce, *The American Commonwealth*, 2nd ed. (New York: Macmillan, 1910), vol. 1, 180; Mary R. Dearing, *Veterans in Politics: The Story of the Grand Army of the Republic* (Westport, CT: Greenwood Press, 1974); Gustavus Weber and Laurence F. Schmeckbier, *The Veterans' Administration: Its History, Activities and Organization*

(Washington: Brookings Institution, 1934); Willard Waller, *The Veteran Comes Back* (New York: Dryden Press, 1944), 97-9; Dixon Wecter, *When Johnny Comes Marching Home* (Boston: Houghton-Mifflin, 1944), 211 ff. For Canadian comments, see NAC, Borden Papers, OC 327, vol. 73, J.G. Adami, "Memorandum upon the Civil War Pension Evil in the United States"; Lt.-Col. J.S. Dennis, "Provision for Crippled Soldiers by the Military Hospitals Commission of Canada," *American Journal of Care for Cripples* 5, 1 (1917): 177 ff.

40 On the Fenian Raid bounty, see NAC, RG 9, II A 4, vol. 28, especially *Report of the Board of Inquiry relating to Claims of Applicants for Fenian Raid Volunteer Bounty in ... Nova Scotia, 1914*; House of Commons, *Debates*, 28 March 1913, 6677 ff. Unlike the volunteer militia in other British North American provinces, militia service in Nova Scotia was still universal and obligatory in the 1860s and the provincial militia had been mobilized against the Fenian threat.

41 Col. A. Fortescue Duguid, *Official History of the Canadian Forces in the Great War, 1914-19*, General Series, vol. 1, *Chronicle, August 1914-September 1915* (Ottawa: King's Printer, 1938), 57-8.

42 PC 887, 29 April, 1915, NAC, RG 2 A1a, box 1113.

43 See PC 289 and 887, 29 April 1915; PC 1712, 21 July 1915; and PC 2312, 30 September 1915, NAC, RG 2 A1a, boxes 1113, 1119, and 1124. Some officers had advanced far beyond their militia rank and it would be painful for a woman who believed she was a colonel's widow to be pensioned as though he had been still a captain or lieutenant.

44 The Shell Scandal reflected the chaotic management of shell production in Canada by the Hughes-appointed Shell Committee. By 1916, large contracts had been let, little had been shipped, and poor-quality shells and lack of shells bedevilled the British and Canadian forces. Among the few solid allegations was one involving Hon. Lt.-Col. J. Wesley Alison, a promoter and Hughes crony who had done shady business with some crooked American businessmen. The Shell Scandal seemed to promise the Liberals a victory if the election had been called. Shades of the 2004 Sponsorship Scandal. See Michael Bliss, *The Canadian Millionaire: The Life and Business Times of Sir Jospeh Flavelle, Bart, 1858-1939* (Toronto: Macmillan, 1978).

45 Special Committee Appointed to Consider and Report upon the Rates of Pensions to be Paid to Disabled Soldiers and the Establishment of a Permanent Pensions Board, *Report and Proceedings* (Ottawa: King's Printer, May 1916) (hereafter Committee on Pensions, 1916), *Proceedings*, 59.

46 Committee on Pensions, 1916, *Report*, paragraph 17, 5-6.

47 Canada, *Sessional Papers*, 1916, no. 185, 60.

48 Committee on Pensions, 1916, *Proceedings*. Recommendations were embodied in PC 1334, 3 June 1916, NAC, RG 2 A1a, box 1124.

49 PC 1334, 3 June 1916.

50 Political "pull" had been a bipartisan concern in the special committee. Hazen had insisted that a Board decision must be final so that "no impression can be allowed to get abroad in the country that a man's claim to a pension can be influenced in the slightest degree by pull or influence of any kind." (House of Commons, *Debates*, 18 May 1916). E.M. Macdonald, the Cape Breton Liberal, had also worried about the American example of pensions for "every one who has gone across" and pressures to increase pension liability (ibid., 4137-8).

51 Ross is described in James Bannerman, "The Biggest Spender We Ever Had," in *Maclean's Canada: Portrait of a Country*, ed. L.F. Hannon (Toronto: McClelland and Stewart, 1960), 225-30, and Morgan, *Canadian Men and Women*, 973-4.

52 Morton and Wright, *Winning the Second Battle*, 54-6.

53 The six categories related to degrees of disability, not, as previously, to the circumstances in which disability had been suffered. The highest category, 100 percent, might be awarded for loss of both eyes or both legs, or incurable tuberculosis. Loss of both feet or one hand and a

foot would represent an 80 percent disability. Loss of a hand, one leg at the knee, a tongue, or a nose would constitute 60 percent; losing one eye, one foot, or both thumbs, or total deafness meant 40 percent, while loss of one thumb or an ankylosed elbow, knee, or shoulder earned a 20 percent pension. An ear or an index finger represented less than a 20 percent loss. Pension Regulations, 12 December 1916, Committee on Returned Men, 1917, 133-7.

54 Morton and Wright, *Winning the Second Battle,* 237.

55 See *Canada Year Book,* 1916-17, table 25, 644; table 26, 645.

56 On pension rates, see *Canadian Annual Review,* 1920, 456.

57 Committee on Returned Men, 1917, *Proceedings,* 1053. On venereal disease in the CEF, see Janice Dickin McGinnis, "From Salvarsan to Penicillin: Medical Science and VD Control in Canada" in *Essays in the History of Canadian Medicine,* ed. Wendy Mitchinson and Janice Dickin McGinnis (Toronto: McClelland and Stewart, 1988), 126 ff.; Jay Cassel, *The Secret Plague: Venereal Disease in Canada, 1838-1939* (Toronto: University of Toronto Press, 1987), 122-44; Sir Andrew Macphail, *Official History of the Canadian Forces in the Great War, 1914-1919: The Medical Services* (Ottawa: King's Printer, 1925), 29, 279.

58 On Pearson, see John English, *Shadow of Heaven: The Life of Lester Pearson,* vol. 1, *1897-1948* (Toronto: Lester and Orpen Dennys, 1989), 44. While Pearson claimed that his accident occurred at Hendon, where he was training to become a pilot, it happened when a bus hit him during the blackout when he had been technically absent without leave in London.

Diefenbaker's autobiography claimed that he was in the bottom of a seven-foot trench at Crowboruh when, at the end of a day's training, someone dropped an entrenching tool on him, hurting his back. Internal bleeding and spinal damage ended his career as an officer but, while recalling his early membership in both the GWVA and the Canadian Legion, he makes no reference to seeking a pension. Lore has it that when Diefenbaker became prime minister he summoned his War Service Record from the National Personnel Records Centre in Tunney's Pasture and it was never returned, making all claims about his war record ultimately unverifiable. See John G. Diefenbaker, *One Canada: Memoirs of the Right Honourable John G. Diefenbaker. The Crusading Years, 1895-1956* (Toronto: Macmillan, 1975), 89-90.

Was either injury pensionable? Under the insurance principle, yes, to the degree that they caused continuing disability. Did they result in pensions? I believe not. Most injuries did not qualify as continuing.

59 NAC, RG 9, III, vol. 54, HQ 54-10-12-15, Lt.-Col. Sir Montague Allan to HQ Canadian Training Division, Shorncliffe, 6 July 1916. On unfit soldiers see NAC, RG 9, III, vol. 90, 10-12-15, Major Kemp to the Adjutant-General, C.E.F., 31 October 1916; and RG 24, vol. 1144, HQ 54-21-51, C.O.C. Canadians to secretary, Militia Council, 16 July 1916. Recruiting unfit men with the connivance of medical officers became a serious problem for the Militia Department in 1916. The 118th battalion, recruited in Waterloo County and notorious for the trouble it caused German-speaking residents, reported 725 recruits but after a summer of training only 251 were found fit to serve. See testimony of Col. F.W. Marlow, Committee on Returned Men, 1917, *Proceedings,* 205-8.

60 Todd testimony, Committee on Returned Men, 1917, *Proceedings,* 1053-4.

61 Ibid.

62 Committee on Pensions, 1916, *Proceedings,* 154.

63 On the buttons, see Morris, *Patriotic Fund,* 45; *Industrial Canada,* January 1916, 962; John Robbie, *Canadian War Service Badges, 1914-1954* (Surrey, BC: John Books, 1995), 17.

64 See Lt.-Gen. Roméo Dallaire, *Shake Hands with the Devil: The Failure of Humanity in Rwanda* (Toronto: Random House, 2003); and Carol Off, *The Lion, the Fox and the Eagle* (Toronto: Vintage Canada, 2001).

65 See *Proceedings of a Conference on the Military Family in Canada* (Montreal: McGill University, 2002).

66 See, in particular, Terry Copp and Bill McAndrew, *Battle Exhaustion: Soldiers and Psychiatrists in the Canadian Army, 1939-1945* (Montreal and Kingston: McGill-Queen's University Press, 1990).

67 For a description of such casualties by a young Canadian medical officer and future health minister, see R.J. Manion, *A Surgeon in Arms* (New York: Doran, 1918), 163-4.

68 On the handling and treatment of the problem, see Thomas E. Brown, "Shell Shock in the Canadian Expeditionary Force, 1914-1918: Canadian Psychiatry in the Great War," in *Health, Disease and Medicine: Essays in Canadian History*, ed. C.G. Roland (Hamilton: Hannah Foundation, 1984).

69 Lewis R. Yealland, *Hysterical Diseases of Warfare* (London: Macmillan, 1918), 3, 8-23, and throughout.

70 Lt.-Col. Colin K. Russell, "The Nature of War Neuroses," *Canadian Medical Association Journal* 61 (1939): 550, and earlier testimony at Committee on Returned Men, 1917, *Proceedings*, 134-53.

71 Macphail, *Medical Services*, 278.

72 NAC, Borden Papers, vol. 53, OC 238, 25800, Lt.-Col. John McComb and Maj. John Russell, "Report on the Care and Rehabilitation or the Disabled Soldier in Canada."

73 NAC, RG 9, III, vol. 3042, fld. 216, vol. 7, Griesbach training memorandum, 1918.

74 R.H. Roy, ed., *The Journal of Private Fraser, 1914-1918: Canadian Expeditionary Force* (Victoria: Sono Nis Press, 1985), 94.

75 See Desmond Morton, "The Supreme Penalty: Canadian Deaths by Firing Squad in the First World War," *Queen's Quarterly* 79, 3 (1972).

76 The subject of insanity and mental imbalance in veterans is dealt with in Morton and Wright, *Winning the Second Battle*, 27, 39, 55, 75, 77, 79, 90, 95-7, 131-3, 169.

77 Committee on Returned Men, 1917, *Proceedings*, 770, 780, 811, 2052.

78 Special Committee Appointed to Consider and Report upon the Pension Board, the Pension Regulations, and the Sufficiency or Otherwise of the Relief Afforded Thereunder, *Proceedings, Evidence and Reports* (Ottawa: King's Printer, 1918), 21, 68 (hereafter Committee on Pensions, 1918), 68.

79 Ibid., *Proceedings*, 95.

80 Norman Knight testimony, Committee on Returned Men, 1917, *Proceedings*, 1252.

81 W.E. Turley testimony, Committee on Returned Men, 1917, *Proceedings*, 774.

82 Ibid., 1108-9.

83 Ibid., 849.

84 Lieut. Chadwick testimony, Committee on Returned Men, 1917, *Proceedings*, 587.

85 Ernest Scammell testimony, Committee on Returned Men, 1917, *Proceedings*, 1123.

86 Committee on Pensions, 1918, *Report*, 19.

87 Ernest Scammell, *The Provision of Employment for Members of the Canadian Expeditionary Force on Their Return to Canada ...* (Ottawa: King's Printer, 1916), 10.

88 NAC, RG 38, vol. 200, f. 8-67, pt. 1, Todd to Scammell, 27 December 1916.

89 Committee on Returned Men, 1917, *Proceedings*, 851.

90 Ibid., 1174-7.

91 Cited by H.W. Hart in the *Veteran*, September 1921, 6.

92 Sydney (Australia) *Bulletin*, 23 February 1916.

93 Thomas Mulvey, undersecretary of state, referred the question to Fiset. His objections were overruled by Minister of Justice Charles J. Doherty, who saw no reason to interfere with the liberty of returned soldiers.

94 *Manitoba Free Press*, 13 April 1917; Committee on Returned Men, 1917, *Proceedings*, 1198-9, 1212.

95 *Manitoba Free Press*, 10-12 April 1917; NAC, Records of the Royal Canadian Legion, minute book of the Great War Veterans' Association, 1-8.

96 Committee on Returned Men, 1917, *Proceedings,* 1199.
97 Ibid., 1250-1.
98 Ibid., 1249-50.
99 Ibid., 1252.
100 Ibid., 887.
101 Committee on Pensions, 1918, *Proceedings,* 909.
102 Morton and Wright, *Winning the Second Battle,* 72.
103 The GWVA took note that in the Senate, the Army and Navy Veterans charter had the full support of Sir James Lougheed, who had delayed and resisted the larger organization's bid for legal recognition.
104 *Proceedings of the First Convention of the Army and Navy Veterans of Canada* (Winnipeg, 1918); *Manitoba Free Press,* 11-16 May 1918.
105 Oxford County Archives, Oxford Patriotic Association minute books, 9 July 1917.
106 Owen Carrigan, *Canadian Party Platforms* (Toronto: Copp Clark, 1968), 77.
107 See Desmond Morton, "Polling the Soldier Vote: The Overseas Campaign in the 1917 General Election," *Journal of Canadian Studies* 10, 4 (1975): 44 ff.
108 *Canadian Annual Review 1917,* 636-7.
109 NAC, Borden Papers, vol. 241, f. RLB 2504, Knight to Borden, 8 March 1918, 134909.
110 Private collection, Ernest Hamilton letters, Ernest to Sara Hamilton, 24 May 1918. Sara Hamilton had not long to worry. Her husband was shot through the shoulder at Amiens on 8 August 1918. It was the "Blighty" most soldiers wanted, a wound sufficient to get him repatriated to England without leaving a major permanent disability. See ibid., 11 August and following.
111 See Desmond Morton, *When Your Number's Up: The Canadian Soldier in the First World War* (Toronto: Random House, 1993), 199-203; Cassel, *Secret Plague,* 127-9; Macphail, *Medical Services,* 179, 292-3.
112 Oxford County Archives, Oxford Patriotic Association, f. 41, vice-chairman, relief committee, to Separation Allowance and Assigned Pay Board, 7 November 1917. Allowances for the children were transferred to the Children's Aid Society.
113 Ibid., reel 3, E, f. 13, chairman of the relief committee, OPA, to director, SA & AP, 11 September 1918; chief constable of Tillsonburg, report, 22 July 1918.
114 In the ten years before 1914, Canada experienced 399 divorces; during the six years 1914-19, there were 369, and in 1920-1924 there were 2,569. See *Canada Year Book,* 1925, 963. The *Year Book* attributed the increase to the unsettling psychological climate and the long separations between men on active service and their wives.
115 NAC, RG 38, vol. 168, f. 571, Scammell report, 11 May 1920.
116 Committee on Pensions, 1918, *Proceedings,* 134-53; Recommendation re the Final Disposal of Cases of Neurasthenia and So-Called Shell Shock, ibid., 156-7.
117 Ibid., 30.
118 Ibid., 23.
119 House of Commons, *Debates,* 15 May 1918, 1981.
120 Another allegedly favoured officer was G.R. Bradbury, an 1885 veteran and Manitoba MP who took the 108th Battalion overseas but was returned to Canada and released for angina pectoris. Veterans argued that he had been sick for ten of his twenty years in Parliament and would collect a military pension of $760 a year for a mere two weeks overseas. Bradbury also thought his pension was unjust, and appealed for more money. Committee on Returned Men, 1917, *Proceedings.*
121 At $1,200, Lt.-Col. Labatt's pension was no larger than the pension Lt.-Col. A.T.H. Williams had left his family in 1885. Lower rank pensions improved significantly during the war and until 1920, but officers' pensions remained unchanged except for flat-rate inflation bonuses.

By 1920 a totally disabled private received the same $900 pension as a similarly situated lieutenant, with identical allowances for their wives ($300) and children ($180 for the first, $144 for the second, and $120 for others). *Canada Year Book* 1920, table 26, 680.

122 Todd to Rosanna Todd, 24 February 1919, in Fialkowski, *Todd*, 348-9.

123 On Thompson, see Committee on Returned Men, 1917, *Proceedings*, 991. Only two members of the MHC were physicians, and their average age was seventy-one. Col. Thompson was fifty-seven.

124 On Marlow's report, see ibid., 166-80, 182-230, 805-7; *Canadian Annual Review*, 1916, 381, and 1917, 533. On his charges, see comments by Fred Pardee, MP, Committee on Returned Men, 1917, *Proceedings*, 58-9; Morton and Wright, *Winning the Second Battle*, 84-9. For Bruce's report, see Herbert A. Bruce, *Report on the Canadian Army Medical Services* (London: N.p., 1916); Herbert A. Bruce, *Politics and the C.A.M.C.* (Toronto: William Briggs, 1919); Herbert A. Bruce, *Varied Operations* (Toronto: Longman Green, 1958); Desmond Morton, *A Peculiar Kind of Politics: Canada's Overseas Ministry in the First World War* (Toronto: University of Toronto Press, 1982).

125 Committee on Returned Men, 1917, *Proceedings*, 1199. Norman Knight claimed, for the GWVA, that just as experts had made men into soldiers, "It is going to take experts, men of broad knowledge and big hearts, who know Canada well, to accomplish this greatest project (with one exception perhaps – the winning of the war) before the people of Canada to-day." Ibid.

126 Morton and Wright, *Winning the Second Battle*, 90-1; See PC 432, 433, and 434, 21 February 1918, NAC, RG 2 A1a, box 1189; NAC, Borden Papers, vol. 98, f. OC 493, Lougheed to Borden, 14 February 1918, 52659; NAC, Kemp Papers, vol. 107, f. 1, Mewburn to Borden, 19 February 1918.

127 NAC, RG 38, vol. 162, f. 1847, Lt.-Col. J.J. Sharples to Lt.-Col. R.S. Wilson, 9 March 1918; ibid., vol. 163, f. 1832, Mrs. G. Vankoughnet to Samuel Armstrong, n.d.

128 Macphail, *Medical Services*, 322.

129 NAC, Adami Records, RG 9, III B 2, vol. 3754, Maj. C.V. Currie, "History of the CAMC in MD 2," 5; *Canadian Annual Review*, 1918, 560.

130 *British Columbia Federationist*, 2 and 9 August 1918; Martin Robin, *Radical Politics and Canadian Labour, 1880-1930* (Kingston: Queen's University Centre for Industrial Relations, 1968), 152.

131 To critics and supporters alike, part of the strength of the Grand Army of the Republic was that it accepted the membership of more or less anyone who had worn the blue uniform of the Union side, however brief their service, and demanded pensions for anyone who had served as little as ninety days. While it made organizational sense to maximize membership, the GAR lost a little credibility by including among its heroic veterans men who had not really risked much by standing guard for ninety days outside Cincinnati.

132 *Toronto Daily Star*, 31 July-3 August 1918.

133 Morton and Wright, *Winning the Second Battle*, 82; "Report of the Investigation into the August Riots," Toronto *Telegram*, 10 October 1918; Ontario Archives, R.L. Church Papers; *Canadian Annual Review*, 1918, 586.

134 See *Toronto Daily Star*, Toronto *Globe*, and Toronto *Mail and Empire*, 2-4 August 1918; Archives of Ontario, T.L. Church Papers, "Report of the Investigation into the August Riots"; Toronto *Evening Telegram*, 10 October 1918; *Canadian Annual Review*, 1918, 586.

135 *Veteran* 1, 10 (1918): 13.

Chapter 6: Grumbling and Complaining

1 On Canadian tactics and technology at the Somme, see Bill Rawling, *Surviving Trench Warfare: Technology and the Canadian Corps, 1914-1918* (Toronto: University of Toronto Press, 1992), 67-86.

2 Cited by Lady Gwendolyn Cecil, *Life of Robert, Marquis of Salisbury* (London: Cassell, 1931), and A. Norman Jaffares and Martin Gray, eds., *Dictionary of Quotations* (London: Collins, 1995), 722.

3 On Lansdowne's "Peace Letter" see Thomas W. Newton, *Lord Lansdowne: A Biography* (London: Macmillan, 1929), 463-83.

4 Led by prominent Toronto lawyer John M. Godfrey and the blinded Lorne Mulloy, the Bonne Entente movement had attempted to bring together French- and English-speaking business and community leaders to rally a country divided by Ontario's Regulation 17 and by the Bourassa-led opposition to British influence. A few dinners, several warm toasts, and much talk left "bonne ententeism" as a symbol of futile good will. See Mason Wade, *The French Canadians, 1760-1945* (Toronto: Macmillan, 1956), 720-2.

5 See R.L. Borden, *Memoirs* (Toronto: Macmillan, 1938), vol. 1, 507-9; R. Craig Brown, *Robert Laird Borden: A Biography*, vol. 2, *1914-1937* (Toronto: Macmillan, 1980), 30-1.

6 Brown, *Robert Laird Borden*, 67 ff.; Borden, *Memoirs*, vol. 2, 620-6. A pro-Boer in 1899, the leading architect of the early British welfare state, and a populist orator of notable fervour, ultra-Liberal David Lloyd George was almost everything Borden was not, but the British politician's dedication to the war effort provided common ground enough.

7 Contemporaries would soon scapegoat "profiteers" as the principal cause of inflation, but John Thompson found that prewar immigrants from central Europe, despised and abused by their Anglo-Saxon neighbours, did well out of dependable markets and high wartime prices while menfolk from neighbouring English-speaking farms missed out because they were serving in the CEF. See John S. Thompson, *The Harvests of War: The Prairie West, 1914-1918* (Toronto: McClelland and Stewart, 1978), 85-6.

8 See J.L. Todd, "The French System of Return to Civil Life of Crippled and Discharged Soldiers," *American Journal of Care for Cripples* 5, 1 (1917); J.L. Todd, "The Duty of the War Pension," *North American Review* 210 (October 1919); J.L. Todd, "The Meaning of Rehabilitation," *Annals of the American Academy of Political and Social Science* 80 (November 1918); J.L. Todd and Thomas B. Kidner, "The Re-Training of Disabled Men," *American Medicine* (Spring 1917); and Helen Reid, "War Relief in Canada," *Annual Conference on Social Work* (Philadelphia, 1917), 126-39.

9 Herbert Wolfe, "Care of Dependents of Canadian Soldiers," report to the Children's Bureau of the United States Department of Labour in *Labour Gazette* 17, 7 (1917): 567-8. Wolfe also noted a life insurance of $1,000 provided to officers and soldiers by the City of Toronto, using a Municipal Insurance Bureau when private carriers refused the burden.

10 Philip H. Morris, *The Canadian Patriotic Fund: A Record of Its Activities from 1914 to 1919* (Ottawa: s.n., [1920?]), 31. The Canadian figure includes separation allowance and assigned pay as well as the Patriotic Fund grant. The American figure includes the Red Cross grant only.

11 Charles W. Humphries, "Keeping the Home Fires Burning: British Columbia Women and the First World War," paper presented to Canadian Historical Association, Charlottetown, PEI, 31 May 1992, 9-11.

12 A small part of the prosperity was sucked away by wartime charities. As well as the Patriotic Fund's $2,510,287, the YMCA's Red Triangle Huts netted $96,629, the Soldiers' Wives League gathered $35,000, and the Khaki League received $100,000 for its soldiers' homes. Belgian Relief received $200,000, the McGill COTC had been worth $100,000, and British Seamen's Relief, $300,000. McCord Museum of Canadian History, P217-C/7, J.W. Ross Papers (hereafter "Ross Papers"), box 1, Notes, Montreal Wartime Charity Campaigns.

13 *Canadian Annual Review*, 1917, 451.

14 Ross Papers, box 1, Montreal Patriotic Fund minute books (hereafter "minute books"), finance committee, 12 January 1917; finance executive committee, 26 January 1917, 8 February 1917.

15 Minute books, finance committee, 12 January 1917, 2. See also draft speech to CPF workers, [1917].
16 *La Presse*, 12 February 1917.
17 Minute books, finance committee, 16 January 1917; 26 January 1917, 1.
18 See Marcel Hamelin, ed., *Les mémoires de Raoul Dandurand* (Quebec: Presses de l'université Laval, 1967), 195.
19 Montreal *Gazette*, 9 February 1917.
20 Minute books, finance committee, 26 January 1917, 1; 2 February 1917, 1-2.
21 House of Commons, *Debates*, 1917, vol. 1, 1918.
22 Montreal *Gazette*, 2 February 1917.
23 Montreal *Evening News*, 12 February 1917. See Ross Papers, box B/2, scrapbook for the 1917 campaign.
24 "La première, elle s'est emparée du sol, elle est chez elle ... Plus haut, le manteau royal et le roi pacifique Edouard VII, revêtu des attributs royaux, étend sur la couronne une main protectrice que les nations avaient appris à respecter," *La Presse*, 10 February 1917.
25 See Omer Héroux, "Elle est chez-elle," *Le Devoir*, 12 February 1917; *Montreal Daily Star*, 10 February 1917.
26 *Montreal Daily Star*, 17 February 1917.
27 See *Toronto World*, Toronto *Globe*, and *Toronto Daily Star*, 23-6 January 1917; Ian Miller, *Our Glory and Our Grief: Torontonians and the Great War* (Toronto: University of Toronto Press, 2002), 60-2; National Archives of Canada (NAC), RG 24, vol. 4286, 34-1-10, vol. 3, President's Report, Toronto and York Canadian Patriotic Fund, 1917. Toronto also confessed to stealing a march on Montreal by persuading parents of US-owned branch plants to send CPF contributions to Toronto rather than Montreal. See Paul Kellogg, *The Patriotic Fund of Canada* (New York: American National Red Cross, Department of Civilian Relief, 10 April 1917), 54.
28 Jean-Pierre Gagnon, *Le 22e bataillon (canadien-français), 1914-1919, Une étude socio-militaire* (Quebec: Presses de l'université Laval, 1986), 206-12.
29 The deed not only outraged Fund leaders but had to be kept deadly secret if the money was ever to be retrieved. Ross Papers, vol. 2, Ross to Sir Herbert Holt, 7 October 1918; Holt to Ross, 7 October 1918.
30 Montreal *Daily Star*, 5 March 1917.
31 Kathleen Jenkins, *Montreal: Island City of the St. Lawrence* (New York: Doubleday, 1966), 455-6.
32 CPF, Montreal Branch, *Report of the Montreal Branch, Canadian Patriotic Fund, 1914-1917* (Montreal, 1917), 39.
33 War Charities Act, 20 September 1917, *Statutes of Canada*, 1917, 7-8 Geo. V, c. 38. See David Laurier Bernard, "Philanthropy vs. the Welfare State: Great Britain's and Canada's Response to Military Dependants in the Great War" (MA thesis, University of Guelph, 1992).
34 The CPF ($47,268,812) and the Red Cross ($8,971,989) were exempt from the act. Canada, "Report of the War Charities Branch of the Department of Secretary of State," *Sessional Papers*, 1919, no. 29, 155-81.
35 Tim Cook, "Documenting War and Forging Reputations: Sir Max Aitken and the Canadian War Records Office in the First World War," *War in History* 10, 3 (2003) describes Aitken's mastery of the images needed to give Canadians prominence in British and American coverage of the war.
36 *Historical Statistics of Canada*, 2nd ed. (Ottawa: Statistics Canada, 1983), H19, H34.
37 Ibid., H1, H3, H9, H11, H18.
38 See David Carnegie, *The History of Munition Supply in Canada* (London: Longmans, Green, 1925), xix-xxvii. When the war ended, Sir Joseph Flavelle laid off 289,000 workers virtually overnight. In his chapter on the IMB workforce, Carnegie carefully avoids giving a size for the Board's workforce beyond 35,000 women (p. 254).

39 Conventional economists were less in evidence in 1917 than today. J. Castell Hopkins, editor of the *Canadian Annual Review*, considered inflation an inevitable consequence of war, aggravated by profiteering, inefficiency, spoilage, and people enjoying enough prosperity to bid up the price of the better cuts of meat. See *Canadian Annual Review*, 1917, 442 ff. Conservative MP A.K. Maclean demanded more controls on prices and even the closing of wheat exchanges. Ibid., 443-4.

40 Michael Bliss, *Northern Enterprise: Five Centuries of Canadian Business* (Toronto: McClelland and Stewart, 1987), 383.

41 "Retail Prices of Staple Articles of Consumption in Canada in the Middle of June," *Labour Gazette* 17, 1 (July 1915): 104-7; see also *Historical Statistics of Canada*, "Cost of Living," series K1 to K4.

42 *Canadian Annual Review*, 1917, 439; "Retail Prices of Staple Articles of Consumption in Canada in the Middle of June," *Labour Gazette* 18, 7 (July 1917): 552-5; 19, 7 (July 1918): 542-5.

43 Claims in the May 1916 *Labour Gazette* were rebutted by the CPF *Bulletin* in July 1916 with an eye to the donors: "There would therefore appear to be not even slight ground for the charge frequently made that the allowances from the Patriotic Fund are too generous."

44 Morris, *Patriotic Fund*, 43, 247.

45 Nancy Christie, *Engendering the State: Family, Work, and Welfare in Canada* (Toronto: University of Toronto Press, 2000), 62, describes Soldiers' Wives Leagues as "the mutual protection leagues founded by working-class women," citing Kellogg, *Patriotic Fund*, 37; Herbert Ames, *Fight or Pay*, pamphlet (N.p.: N.d.), 858; Minute book, 1899-1915, 57.

46 NAC, RG 24, vol. 4107, HQ 54-21-1-29, vol. 1, Mrs. Cole to Col. Ward, 10 March 1916, f. 142, on Mrs. Hishon: "She rang me up to tell me that she had received her Sep. All. cheque and that 'it was the first lucky thing that had happened to her for years.'"

47 Henry J. Morgan, *Canadian Men and Women of the Time*, 2nd ed. (Toronto, 1912), 150, 249. The president of the Kingston SWL, Mrs. T.D.R. Hemming, was married to a Permanent Force colonel.

48 Much of the information about the Soldiers' Wives Leagues comes from annual reports of the National Council of the Women of Canada (NCWC) and its Local Councils. See Montreal Local Council of Women, *22nd Annual Report*, 1915-16, 27; *23rd Annual Report*, 1916-17; and *24th Annual Report*, 1917-18, 13, 17-18, 28.

49 *Yearbook of the NCWC*, 1917-18 (Toronto: Bryant Press, 1918), 153; *Yearbook of the NCWC*, 1918-19 (Toronto: Bryant Press, 1919), 266. The plots presumably were gardens.

50 *Yearbook of the NCWC*, 1917-18, 199; *Yearbook of the NCWC*, 1918-19, 256.

51 *Yearbook of the NCWC*, 1918-19, 138.

52 Ibid., 262.

53 On McWilliams, see Glenbow Museum, M 724, f7; *Calgary Herald*, 25 July 1981; Linda Kealey, *Enlisting Women for the Cause: Women, Labour and the Left in Canada, 1890-1920* (Toronto: University of Toronto Press, 1998), 205, n. 30.

54 Rachel Coutts in Winnipeg *Voice*, 7 September 1917. Postwar resolutions reported by Coutts included the eight-hour day, income tax, government control of the liquor business, a general strike to win conscription of wealth, replacement of jails by houses of correction and, of course, more for soldiers' dependants. Kealey, *Enlisting Women*, 206.

55 Edmonton *Nutcracker*, 17 August 1917, 13.

56 McAdams was a niece of a prominent Ontario Conservative, W.B. Hanna.

57 Kealey, *Enlisting Women*, 206-7; *Calgary Daily Herald*, 4, 5, and 8 March 1918; Edmonton *Nutcracker*, 10 May 1917; Winnipeg *Voice*, 18 May 1917; Pat Turner, "Amelia Turner and Calgary Labour Women, 1919-1935," in *Beyond the Vote: Canadian Women in Politics*, ed. Linda Kealey and Joan Sangster (Toronto: University of Toronto Press, 1989), 112, n. 26. See also *Alberta Non-Partisan*, 15 March 1918, 6; 10 May 1918, 5.

58 *Yearbook of the NCWC*, 1917-18, 158. See also Margaret Laning Hastin and Lorraine Ellenwood, *Blue Bows and the Golden Rule: Provincial Council of Women of BC: An Historical Account* (Cloverdale, BC: Provincial Council of Women of BC, 1984), 29.

59 *Canadian Annual Review*, 1917, 339.

60 Carnegie, *Munition Supply*, 254-5.

61 Bliss, *Northern Enterprise*, 378.

62 See Michael Bliss, *A Canadian Millionaire: The Life and Business Times of Sir Joseph Flavelle, Bart., 1858-1939* (Toronto: Macmillan, 1978), 329-62. For a contemporary and sympathetic view, see *Canadian Annual Review*, 1917, 444-5, 447-51.

63 In January 1917 Toronto set an objective of $2.5 million and raised $3.3 million; Montreal's campaign, as we saw, had the same target but raised $4.29 million. Quebec City raised $250,000, Halifax, $200,000, Vancouver, $400,000, Calgary, $175,000, Ottawa, $400,000, and Hamilton, $675,000. *Canadian Annual Review*, 1917, 452.

64 *Canadian Annual Review*, 1919, 32-3.

65 Reid, "War Relief in Canada," 131.

66 House of Commons, *Debates*, 20 January 1916, 111.

67 Ibid., 1 February 1916, 501.

68 Morris, *Patriotic Fund*, 42. See House of Commons, *Debates*, 5 July 1917, 3077-83.

69 One such county was Peel, next to Toronto. See Desmond Morton, "What Did Peel County Do in the Great War?" *History and Social Science Teacher* 23, 1 (1987): 26; Morris, *Patriotic Fund*, 197. When the Ontario city of London proposed a two-mill rate to fund the Patriotic Fund, the local labour council was vehemently opposed. It was up to the federal government to provide for soldiers' families, said the chairman of the LTLC's legislation committee. *Labour World*, 26 March 1916.

70 Morris, *Patriotic Fund*, 125-6. New Brunswick, *Statutes*, The New Brunswick legislation is 5 Geo. V 1915, c. 3, An Act re Contributions to the Canadian Patriotic Fund, passed 29 April 1915, 203-4; amended by 6 Geo. V, c. 4, passed 7 April 1916, An Act to Confirm a Grant in Aid to the Canadian Patriotic Fund, 43-53; amended by 8 Geo. V, c. 29, passed 22 June 1917, An Act to Confirm Arrangements Made for the Canadian Patriotic Fund, 98-101; amended by 8 Geo. V, c. 27, passed 26 April 1918, An Act to Amend and Assist in Carrying out the Objects of the Canadian Patriotic Fund, 165-8.

71 Cited in *Women's Century*, October 1917, 15 col. 1, 20 col. 3. On 14 March 1916 the Saskatchewan Legislature adopted 6 Geo. V, c. 6, An Act to Raise Pensions for Patriotic Purposes, 43-6; amended on 10 March 1917 by 7 Geo. V, c. 2, An Act to Amend the Patriotic Revenues Act, 10-11. Manitoba's corresponding legislation, approved on 10 March 1916, was 6 Geo. V, c. 111, the Patriotic Levy Act on petition from the Union of Manitoba Municipalities. It was amended twice, on 9 March 1917 by 7 Geo. V, c. 17, and on 6 March 1917, by c. 59, Patriotic Levy Amendment Acts.

72 Alberta's Patriotic Tax Act, adopted on 5 April 1917, was 7 Geo. V, c. 17; amended on 13 April 1918 by 8 Geo. V, c. 12.

73 Patricia Roy, *Vancouver: An Illustrated History* (Toronto: James Lorimer, 1980), 87.

74 *British Columbia Federationist*, 30 March 1917, 5.

75 Not even with the Military Service Act could such strength be sustained, and two British Columbia battalions were withdrawn and replaced by units from Nova Scotia and Ontario. See G.W.L. Nicholson, *Official History of the Canadian Army in the First World War: Canadian Expeditionary Force, 1914-1919* (Ottawa: Queen's Printer, 1962), 225-7.

76 Morris, *Patriotic Fund*, 89-90.

77 Though Nation dramatically increased the income of the CPF in British Columbia, his salary ($3,000) and his commercial connection with Ames made him a target for critics of the Fund. See Henry Pearce in Victoria *Colonist*, 7 July 1916; *Victoria Daily Times*, 3 November 1916, 7.

78 Morris, *Patriotic Fund,* 91-2; Victoria *Colonist,* 10 September 1916.

79 British Columbia Archives, GR 0446, BC Provincial Game Warden Originals, 1905-1922, box 70, file 8, Ralph Smith to "Employees of the Government of British Columbia," 18 December 1916.

80 Ibid., Geoffrey Lodwick to Williams, 5 January 1916. R.T. Richardson, deputy warden at Fort Steele, had organized the Fort Steele Patriotic Fund.

81 See ibid., correspondence with Lewis, Thacker, and S.S. Boyd in Clinton.

82 Ibid., A.A. Ward to Williams, 8 January 1916.

83 Ibid., Dawley to Williams, 1 January 1916, and reply, 5 January 1916.

84 Ibid., H.J. Blurton to Williams, 16 March 1916, and reply, 20 March 1916.

85 Certainly its most recent historian has deplored its cautious "labourist" tendencies. See Mark Leier, *Red Flags and Red Tape: The Making of a Labour Bureaucracy* (Toronto: University of Toronto Press, 1995). See also Paul Phillips, *No Power Greater: A Century of Labour in British Columbia* (Vancouver: BCFL and Boag Foundation, 1967), 18-19, 49-51, 63-4.

86 UBC Special Collections, Vancouver and District Labour Council (VTLC) minutes of regular meetings, 3 September 1914. On McVety, see Leier, *Red Flags and Red Tape,* 67-8, 159-60, 171-4; and Mark Leier, *Where the Fraser River Flows: The Industrial Workers of the World in British Columbia* (Vancouver: New Star Books, 1990), 70-7.

87 UBC Special Collections, VTLC minutes of regular meetings, 17 September 1914, 193.

88 Ibid., 1 October 1914, 201; 19 November and 3 December 1914. On Gutteridge, see Irene Howard, *The Struggle for Social Justice in British Columbia: Helena Gutteridge, the Unknown Reformer* (Vancouver: UBC Press, 1992). Apart from marrying a veteran (very unhappily), Gutteridge seems to have had little contact with soldiers' wives.

89 UBC Special Collections, VTLC minutes of regular meetings, 5 December 1914, 222.

90 Men believed they would earn at least three pounds a week in England (Toronto *Globe,* 3 June 1915), and the Calgary *Morning Albertan* (18 June 1915) indicated "in some cases" rates of six to seven pounds a week. The Victoria *Colonist* (15 June 1915) cited a recruiter who declared that the average rate would run from $20 to $25 per week.

91 Vancouver and District Labour Council, Executive Minutes, 15 November 1915, 441; 2 December 1915, 443.

92 UBC Special Collections, VTLC minutes, executive committee, 2 December 1916, 443. On the munition workers' families, see Humphries, "Home Fires," 12-15. Workers began to leave British Columbia for the United Kingdom in June 1915 (Humphries, "Home Fires," 3).

93 Alan Morley, *Vancouver: From Milltown to Metropolis* (Vancouver: Mitchell Press, 1961), 148-9.

94 *British Columbia Federationist,* 23 February 1917, 1.

95 Ibid., 27 April 1917, 1. Since Edwards was a returned soldier, his wife had presumably lost her claim to the Patriotic Fund when he landed at Quebec.

96 Ibid., 30 March 1917, 5.

97 Ibid., 31 August 1917, 6, summarizes the case and decisions.

98 *Vancouver Daily World,* 22 March 1917, 8. Mrs. Kemp was a well-known Vancouver club woman, active in the National and Local Council of Women, the IODE, and the King's Daughters, and a pioneer in self-insurance for women family members. See *Vancouver Sun,* 23 March 1917, 5, and 18 March 1947, 10; *Vancouver Province,* 28 January 1960, 15. On women as fruit pickers, see *Victoria Daily Times,* 10 May 1917, 11; 16 June 1917, 7; 12 July 1917, 11. Thanks to Jennie Clayton for drawing my attention to this research.

99 NAC, Borden Papers, C-4404, Canadian Association of Mothers and Wives of Soldiers & Sailors of Greater Vancouver and Burnaby to Borden, 15 June 1917, 142308-9.

100 *British Columbia Federationist,* 14 September 1917, 1. For additional reports see *Vancouver Daily World,* 13 September 1917, 14, and 25 October 1917, 9.

101 *Yearbook of the NCWC,* 1918-19, 273.

102 *Vancouver Daily World,* 25 October 1917, 9.
103 Susan Mayse, *Ginger: The Life and Death of Albert Goodwin* (Madeira Park, BC: Harbour Publishing, 1990), 113.
104 *British Columbia Federationist,* 7 September 1917, 8; Victoria *Colonist,* 4 September 1917.
105 "Mining in British Columbia," Victoria *Colonist,* 4 September 1917, citing the Kaslo *Kootenaian,* 4, 30 August 1917.
106 Mayse, *Ginger,* 122-3.
107 *British Columbia Federationist,* 19 October 1917, 1.
108 NAC, Borden Papers, OC 267, James B. Springforth to Borden, 2 February 1916.
109 *Vancouver Daily World,* 7 May 1917, 16. The *Federationist* reported on 21 May 1917 that the BC Methodist Conference had urged that the CPF be made into a purely government institution. The national moderator, the Rev. Albert Moore, had inveighed against raffles as a means of raising patriotic funds.
110 *Vancouver Daily World,* 24 October 1917.
111 *British Columbia Federationist,* 10 May 1918, 4.
112 *Victoria Daily Colonist,* 21 November 1917, 7.
113 Humphries, "Home Fires," 5-6. See Naomi Griffiths, *The Splendid Vision: A Centennial History of the National Council of Women of Canada, 1893-1994* (Ottawa: Carleton University Press, 1993), 129.
114 The argument, as we saw in Chapter 2, was that sergeants were entitled to $25 separation allowances, and that news of promotions and demotions took so long to reach Ottawa that wives were often owed or owing for a significant number of months.
115 NAC, Borden Papers, C-4309, 30555.
116 Edmonton *Nutcracker,* 25 December 1916, 12.
117 *Alberta Non-Partisan,* 23 November 1917. As an Old Original of 1914, Knight nursed the further suspicion that Ames was responsible for the CEF's "Sham Shoes," the cardboard-lined light boots originally issued to Canadian troops in 1914 until they dissolved in the English mud. See A. Fortescue Duguid, *Official History of the Canadian Forces in the Great War, 1914-19,* General Series, vol. 1, *Chronicle, August 1914-September 1915* (Ottawa: King's Printer, 1938), 78, 145, 147, 170 and appendices 204 and 223; House of Commons, *Debates,* 1914, 2372-479; "Report of Special Parliamentary Committee on Boot Inquiry ...," House of Commons, *Journals,* 1915, vol. 51, part 3.
118 Edmonton *Nutcracker,* 10 May 1917, 7.
119 Christie, *Engendering the State,* 61.
120 Ibid., 60-1 and notes.
121 Morris, *Patriotic Fund,* 96-7.
122 Some conscripts married to avoid conscription, but too late. Pte. Albert Matta married a girl with three children. When that failed to exempt him, he deserted, was caught at Detroit and sent overseas. As a prisoner, he received neither pay nor separation allowance, and Mrs. Matta badly needed work. The family, wrote Woodstock's L.E. Lowman, was "in pitiful circumstances." Oxford County Archives, Oxford Patriotic Association, f. 42, Pattullo to P.H. Morris, 9 December 1919.
123 G.W.L. Nicholson, *Official History of the Canadian Army in the First World War: Canadian Expeditionary Force, 1914-1919* (Ottawa: Queen's Printer, 1962), 353.
124 NAC, RG 9, III, vol. 4839, AA & QMG, 1st Division.
125 See Jeffrey Keshen, *Propaganda and Censorship during Canada's Great War* (Edmonton: University of Alberta Press, 1996) and Peter Buitenhuis, *The Great War of Words: British, American and Canadian Propaganda and Fiction, 1914-1933* (Vancouver: UBC Press, 1987).
126 CPF *Bulletin,* October 1917, n.p.
127 House of Commons, *Debates,* 30 April 1918, 1292.
128 Ibid., 18 May 1918, 2199.

129 Ibid., 2199-201.
130 *Victoria Daily Times,* 4 September 1918, 15.
131 Ibid.

Chapter 7: Victory for Whom?

1 CEF volunteers in 1915 and 1916 normally spent up to a year in Canada before embarking for England, and their serious training began only after their arrival in Britain. See Desmond Morton, *When Your Number's Up: The Canadian Soldier in the First World War* (Toronto: Random House, 1993), 71-93.

2 Desmond Morton and J.L. Granatstein, *Marching to Armageddon: Canadians and the Great War, 1914-1919* (Toronto: Lester, Orpen and Dennys, 1989), 191.

3 National Archives of Canada (NAC), R.L. Borden Papers, OC 267, C 4304, Mrs. J.L. Smith to the prime minister, 30 May 1918. The Fund worried that donors would complain that railway builders and tree choppers were not really putting their lives in danger at the front, though some Canadian Railway Troop units, caught in the 1918 offensives, had to fight. As a sergeant's wife, Mrs. Smith was not likely to be in need. Above all, the CPF law had to be changed to end restrictions on domicile.

4 NAC, RG 24, vol. 922, 54-21-23-8, vol. 26, 148, Sybella Potts to Militia Department, 30 October 1918.

5 Private collection, Ernest Hamilton letters, Ernest to Sara Hamilton, 12 June 1918.

6 *Victoria Daily Times,* 9 April 1918, 13; 10 April 1918, 1.

7 The campaign included an actual tank in the streets, "its quick-firing guns peeping wickedly from the various embrasures and whirling around in response to the human touch within its armoured interior." A final effort moved the Toronto total from $63 million to $76 million from 101,467 residents. See *Toronto Daily Star,* 4 December 1917, 1; Ian Miller, *Our Glory and Our Grief: Torontonians and the Great War* (Toronto: University of Toronto Press, 2001), 151-2.

8 NAC, RG 24, vol. 4286, 34-1-10, vol. 3, *Report of the Toronto and York Branch, Canadian Patriotic Fund,* 1 April 1918, 50,000 Club Report.

9 Philip H. Morris, *The Canadian Patriotic Fund: A Record of Its Activities from 1914 to 1919* (Ottawa: s.n., [1920?]), 225-6; Miller, *Glory and Grief,* 163-4; *Toronto Daily Star,* Toronto *Globe,* and Toronto *Mail and Empire,* 22-6 January 1918. Targets were measured by funds subscribed, not paid. Of $3,208,381 subscribed to the Toronto and York branch, only $2,485,305 was paid by 1920. Toronto City Council's decision to cut its grant when the war ended in November contributed $300,000 to this shortfall (Morris, *Patriotic Fund,* 225). Outrage at the imposition of conscription had led Montreal's council to cancel the balance of its contribution in 1917, though this was kept a deadly secret. See McCord Museum of Canadian History, P217-C/7, J.W. Ross Papers (hereafter "Ross Papers"), vol. 2, Ross to Sir Herbert Holt, 7 October 1918; Holt to Ross, 7 October 1918.

10 Morris, *Patriotic Fund,* 393.

11 Ibid., 310.

12 Helen Reid, "The Third Responsibility," CPF *Bulletin,* July 1918.

13 NAC, RG 24, vol. 4286, 34-1-10, vol. 3, Toronto and York Annual Report, 1918, 10 October 1918.

14 Lt.-Col. J.J. Creelman, an outspoken Montreal gunner, found the wives "very much in the way." He felt they kept their husbands' minds off their profession and made night training difficult, writing, "The noblest duty of a wife is to stay at home." NAC, MG 30, E 8, Creelman Papers, Journals, 28 October, 9-10 December, 11 December.

15 On leave, see Morton, *When Your Number's Up,* 106, 133-5.

16 NAC, RG 24, vol. 736, HQ 54-21-6-50, Col. W.E. Ward to the Canadian high commissioner, 18 October 1915.

17 Nova Scotia Archives and Records Management (NSARM), MG 20, CPF Nova Scotia branch, vol. 497, fld. 3, Jean D. Ives, Canadian Red Cross, to secretary, NS CPF, 9 July 1915. The British limit was five pounds, which Mrs. Cooke had received. Arthur Barnstead of the CPF had paid $98 to get Mrs. Cooke to England, and added $25 because "some special consideration on compassionate account must be shown," n.p.

18 NAC, R.E.W. Turner Papers, vol. 12, f. 86. R.B. Barron, treasurer, City of London SSFA, to investigator, Separation Allowances Branch, OMFC, 28 September 1918, 8008.

19 NAC, RG 24, vol. 736, HQ 54-21-6-50, Col. W.R. Ward to the Canadian high commissioner, 18 October 1915.

20 NAC, RG 24, vol. 736, HQ 54-21-6-50, Philip Morris to adjutant general, [December 1915]; assistant adjutant general to Morris, 4 December 1915.

21 PC 760, 1 April 1916, NAC, RG 2 A1a, box 1138.

22 During the Great War there was no effective way to detect a submerged submarine. The Germans had attempted unrestricted submarine warfare in 1915, but US outrage when Americans drowned in the torpedoed British liner *Lusitania* led the Germans to cancel the technique until desperation drove them to brave the threat that the Americans would join the war. Convoys exploited the submarine's poor ability to find targets and had produced great results off European coasts, but the Admiralty stubbornly believed that they were obsolete and ship owners feared losing a competitive edge when all ships were delayed to form a convoy and then arrived at their destination at the same time.

23 PC 494, 29 February 1917, and PC 9405, 5 April 1917, NAC, RG 2 A1a, boxes 1163 and 1167.

24 Wartime conditions cost the Immigration Department its cheap transatlantic rate. The high commissioner's fund helped but soldiers' dependants were expected to pay their own way. If they could not, money was stopped from the husband's pay. The third-class rate was seven pounds ten shillings for adults, half that for children, and ten shillings for infants. The cabin rate was thirteen pounds for adults, half that for children and thirty shillings for infants. See NAC, RG 24, vol. 744, HQ 54-21-6-85, superintendent of immigration to minister's private secretary, 30 March 1918.

25 Canadian Patriotic Fund Amendment Act, *Statutes of Canada*, 1918, 7-8 Geo. V, c. 35.

26 House of Commons, *Debates*, 18 May 1918, 2200.

27 Ibid., 2201.

28 Ibid., 2199.

29 Would the government act? When Doherty was asked on 18 May, the minister of justice gave a political veteran's answer: he was not in a position to say but members "may rest assured that so far as I am concerned the suggestion shall have earnest consideration with a view to settling on a course of action." Ibid., 2209.

30 MG 28, I D 5, vol. 1, CPF national executive minutes, 4 April 1918.

31 *Victoria Daily Times*, 14 August 1918.

32 *British Columbia Federationist*, 23 February 1917, 1.

33 *British Columbia Federationist*, 20 September 1918, 4.

34 Ibid., 1.

35 Ibid.

36 On the epidemic, see Eileen Pettigrew, *The Silent Enemy: Canada and the Deadly Flu of 1918* (Saskatoon: Western Producer, 1983).

37 Vancouver's next mass meeting of wives and mothers occurred at the Orpheum Theatre in December, with women predominating, and unanimous resolutions for substantial increases in the payments to widows and orphans. *Victoria Daily Times*, 9 December 1918, 3.

38 NAC, RG 24, vol. 436, HQ 54-21-1-88, Mrs. Ezra Snow to minister of justice, 5 November 1918, 32-3.

39 Ibid., Mrs. E.L. Belcher to Gen. S.C. Mewburn, 13 November 1918.

40 Ibid., Mrs. Mary Wray to Militia Headquarters, 19 November 1918.

41 Canadian tactics featured set-piece precision in the use of artillery support and infantry fire and movement; Australians infiltrated the enemy's front lines before the offensive began, and encouraged low-level initiative. See Desmond Morton, "Changing Operational Doctrine in the Canadian Corps, 1916-17," *Army Doctrine and Training Bulletin* 2, 4 (1999): 35-9.

42 Desmond Morton, "Kicking and Complaining: Demobilization Riots in the Canadian Expeditionary Force, 1918-1919," *Canadian Historical Review* 61, 3 (1980): 334-60.

43 Among the demands for German reparations was repayment of the $80,000 levied on taxpayers in New Brunswick's Northumberland County. If Germany did not pay the money back, taxpayers were being punished. NAC, R.L. Borden Papers, G. Williston, secretary-treasurer Northumberland County, to the prime minister, 19 February 1919, 30817.

44 NAC, RG 24, vol. 436, HQ 54-21-1-88, Mme Lude Doucet to minister, 11 December 1918, author's translation.

45 NAC, RG 24, vol. 436, HQ 54-21-1-88, vol. 4, Mrs. J. Hill, St-Henri, to Mewburn, 26 December 1918.

46 Ibid., Mrs. Zarsky to Militia Department, [after 7 April 1919].

47 NAC, RG 24, vol. 445, HQ 5421-1-182, Gordon Parker to minister of militia, 30 July 1919.

48 Ibid., Roy W. Frid to War Records Office, Ottawa, 15 July 1920; Judge Advocate General Branch to Frid, 20 July 1920.

49 See *Veteran*, 18 February and October 1921.

50 On Canadian demobilization planning see Morton, "Kicking and Complaining"; Morton, *When Your Number's Up*, 265-6.

51 See NAC, RG 24, vol. 436, HQ 54-21-1-88, "Memorandum Respecting Return of Soldiers from Overseas," 29 January 1919; ibid., Capt. Mills to George Weathereld, 1 March 1919. Lacking the confidential knowledge that underlay a compassionate claim, it was feared that jealous comrades would see early release as a consequence of "political pull." In fact, processing of compassionate claims during the months of demobilization dragged inordinately on both sides of the Atlantic, despite official pressure. The procedure involved military district headquarters in Canada as well as a complex and changing bureaucracy in Britain, Belgium, and Germany. See ibid., Maj. W.R. Creighton (Mewburn's secretary) to adjutant general, 24 February 1919.

52 Ibid., "Memorandum Respecting Discharge of Soldiers in Canada," 29 January 1919.

53 On the Nivelles mutiny, see NAC, RG 9 III, vol. 93, f. 10-12-50, vol. I and vol. 2232, D-6-29 D 9. See also NAC, MG 27, II D, 9, Kemp Papers, vol. 155.

54 *Report of the Royal Commission to Inquire into ... the Treatment of the men of the Canadian Expeditionary Force while on board the Transport Northland* (Ottawa, 1919). The miserable conditions were standard for steerage passengers and so were the peculations by the stewards. Leaving the ship tied up under the lights of Halifax because Canadian officials would not work on Christmas Day was a major factor in the discontent; so were reporters, still eager in December 1918 to meet returning troopships and to listen to grievances.

55 While the conditions in a large, poorly disciplined transit camp on a bleak, rain-swept Welsh hillside contributed to trouble, the cancellation of two ships slated to carry men from Kinmel was the precipitating incident. See Morton, "Kicking and Complaining," 344-5.

56 Relying on its local reporter, the London *Times* portrayed Kinmel as a Bolshevik revolution manqué, with canteen girls raped, a Victoria-Cross-winning major trampled to death by his men, and British troops with machine guns holding the Canadians at bay. The *Olympic*, hitherto too valuable for the New York run to be risked in Halifax, was the solution to an unexpected crisis. Ibid.

57 On the *Scandinavian*, see Desmond Morton and Glenn Wright, *Winning the Second Battle: Canadian Veterans and the Return to Civilian Life, 1915-1930* (Toronto: University of Toronto Press, 1987), 110; NAC, Kemp Papers, vol. 135, f. c-3, Mewburn to Kemp, 25 January 1919; Hogarth to Kemp, 17 February 1919; report of Mrs. Yeman, n.d.

58 PC 179, 29 January 1919, NAC, RG 2 A1a, box 1216. See Albert Carman, *The Return of the Troops: A Plain Account of the Demobilization of the Canadian Expeditionary Force* (Ottawa: Government Printing Bureau, 1920), 131-2; NAC, Turner Papers, vol. 12, f. 91, Mewburn to Kemp, 9 January 1919.

59 Carman, *Return of the Troops,* 134.

60 Ibid., 138.

61 NAC, R.E.W. Turner Papers, vol. 12, f. 91, Lt.-Col. J.O. Smith to Maj. Macdonald, 11 March 1919.

62 This had been Ames's expectation, and he had discussed arrangements, authorized part-time paid staff in the person of E.W. Bremner, and resisted British plans to send families to New York. NSARM, MG 20, CPF Nova Scotia branch, vol. 498, fld. 2, Ames to Barnstead, 15 May and 6 June 1918; Barnstead to Ames, 20 June, 1918; Morris to Barnstead, 20 May 1918.

63 In May 1918 Morris had warned the Halifax and Montreal CPF to prepare for shiploads of dependants, but the policy of sending only soldiers to Halifax meant that few families arrived. NSARM, MG 20, CPF Nova Scotia branch, vol. 497, f. 3, Morris to Barnstead, 2 May 1918; Barnstead to Morris, 31 December 1918; Morris, *Patriotic Fund,* 47.

64 Carman, *Return of the Troops,* 67.

65 Morris, *Patriotic Fund,* 48. See also pp. 46-7 and 128, and Carman, *Return of the Troops,* ch. 6 and ch. 14.

66 Morris, *Patriotic Fund,* 48.

67 Carman, *Return of the Troops,* 140.

68 Ibid. At $1.50, a box with a loaf of bread, a couple of tins of meat, jars of jam and peanut butter, and a packet of soda biscuits, plus a can opener and a bottle opener, was intended to keep two people for two days. Ibid., 71; *Back to Mufti* 1, 1 (February 1919).

69 Morris, *Patriotic Fund,* 47.

70 Carman, *Return of the Troops,* 138.

71 See Frances C. Harris, "Why I Married My Canadian Husband," *Everywoman's World,* June 1919, 18, for witty advice on how the 60,000 Canadian women rendered spinsters by English war brides should respond: "We may have to be old maids but it does not necessarily follow that we are going to lead the aimless existence which custom prescribed for our early Victorian great grand-aunts."

72 Carman, *Return of the Troops,* 154.

73 Ibid., 24-5, 153; NAC, Sir James McBrien Papers, 1, f-1, Kemp to McBrien, 14 November 1919. By the end of 1919, 500 destitute Canadian veterans had asked for return passage to Canada. Some "Imperials" were Canadians serving with British regiments, the Royal Air Force, or the Inland Water Transport in Mesopotamia.

74 NAC, RG 24, col. 436, HQ 55-21-1-88, f. 34, Anna L. Sims to minister of militia, [May 1919], 182. Sir Eugène Fiset, Mewburn's deputy, assured her in classic bureaucratic prose "that arrangements have been made by which all Canadians serving as Cadets in the R.A.F. and whose services can be spared are to be returned to Canada at the earliest possible date." Ibid., 185.

75 Quarantine was an alternative to establishing an infection camp somewhere in Canada and publicizing a scandal most Canadian authorities preferred to hush. On venereal disease, see Jay Cassel, *The Secret Plague: Venereal Disease in Canada, 1839-1939* (Toronto: University of Toronto Press, 1987); Janice Dickin McGinnis, "From Salvarsan to Penicillin: Venereal Disease Control in Canada, 1919-1965," in *Essays in the History of Canadian Medicine,* ed. Wendy Mitchinson and Janice Dickin McGinnis (Toronto: McClelland and Stewart, 1988).

76 Desmond Morton, "A Canadian Soldier in the Great War: The Experiences of Frank Maheux," *Canadian Military History* 1, 1-2 (1992): 87.

77 In 1972 Maheux's daughter persuaded Angeline to contribute all that remained of her husband to the National Archives of Canada. On their life, see Morton, "A Canadian Soldier."

78 Private collection, Ernest Hamilton letters, Ernest to Sara Hamilton, 17 July 1918.

79 Douglas How, *One Village, One War: 1914-1945* (Hantsport, NS: Lancelot Press, 1995), 89-90.

80 Morton and Wright, *Winning the Second Battle*, 112-19. For a chilling account of the effects of bombardment in creating terror, see Charles Harrison, *Generals Die in Bed* (New York: Morrow, 1930).

81 Alexander Primrose, "Presidential Address," *Canadian Medical Association Journal* 9, 1 (1919): 8-9.

82 *Toronto Daily Star*, 7 February 1919.

83 Archives of Manitoba, Manitoba Patriotic Fund, case file 4243, Mrs. Horwood, Mrs. Horwood to Solandt, 22 July 1919.

84 Ibid., Horwood to Capt. Shipwood, War Service Gratuity branch, 15 July 1919. On her response, see Secretary, MPF to SA & AP Branch, 25 August 1919.

85 Ibid., Horwood Case, February 1922.

86 The Manitoba Fund's records have partially survived, including a few case files for deserted mother-led families. See Archives of Manitoba, Manitoba Patriotic Fund, P 189, f. 3, Edith Rogers Papers, F-6, from which the following stories are taken.

87 Comparative Statement of Receipts and Disbursements from 1 September 1914 to 31 March 1919, in Morris, *Patriotic Fund*, 273-4.

88 Ibid., 244-5; Ross Papers, box 2, Helen Reid to Ross, 30 January 1918. See also Ross to Reid, 5 January 1918, 2 and 13 February 1918.

89 NSARM, MG 20, CPF Nova Scotia branch, vol. 497, f. 3, Nova Scotia secretary to Morris, 27 December 1918; Morris to Barnstead, 31 December 1918.

90 *Canadian Annual Review*, 1919, 60.

91 Morris, *Patriotic Fund*, 333.

92 NAC, MG 28, I, 5, vol. 1, CPF national executive minutes, 30 May 1919, 20 May 1920, 5 May 1921.

93 Morris, *Patriotic Fund*, 333.

94 NAC, Borden Papers, OC 367, C4304, Baron J. de Fallon to prime minister, 28 June 1919, 30846-7.

95 See House of Commons, *Debates*, 9 June 1919, 3240; 17 June 1919, 3738-40; Canadian Patriotic Fund Amendment Act, 7 July 1919, *Statutes of Canada*, 1919, 9-10 Geo. V, c. 44.

96 Toronto *Globe*, 13 September 1919; Morris, *Patriotic Fund*, 334.

97 Morris, *Patriotic Fund*, 334.

98 NAC, MG 28, I, 5, vol. 1, CPF national executive minutes, 27 June 1919.

99 Canada, *Sessional Papers*, no. 14, *Report of the Department of Soldiers' Civil Re-Establishment for 1921*, 93-4. See also *Canadian Annual Review*, 1919, 598 and 1920, 452.

100 Ross Papers, box 1, Montreal Patriotic Fund minute books, executive committee, 17 December 1919, 173-4.

101 CPF, *Federal Emergency Appropriation Department Regulations* (Ottawa: CPF, 1919), 3-8; Morris, *Patriotic Fund*, 334-6.

102 On the attitude of the Montreal branch, see NAC, MG 30, Calder Papers, Brig.-Gen. A.E. Ross to the Hon. J.A. Calder, 22 January 1920.

103 Ross Papers, box 2, "Report of the Federal Emergency Appropriation in Montreal, 20 February 1920."

104 Ross Papers, box 2, Nickle to Ross, 28 February 1920. The auditor, Col. W.F. Dowie, had been auditor at the Overseas Military Forces of Canada headquarters in London.

105 Ibid., Brittain to Ross, 4 June 1920.

106 Helen R.Y. Reid, *A Social Study along Health Lines of the First Thousand Children Examined in the Health Clinic of the Canadian Patriotic Fund, Montreal Branch* (Montreal: N.p., 1920) [CIHM 77705].

107 NSARM, MG 20, CPF Nova Scotia branch, Federal Emergency Appropriation, vols. 497-8.

108 Ibid., Barnstead to Ross, 24 January 1920.
109 Ibid., Barnstead to Morris, 28 January 1920.
110 *Victoria Daily Times,* 21 January 1919.
111 Morris, *Patriotic Fund,* 336.
112 Ross Papers, vol. 2, Correspondence, June-July 1920, Smith to Ross, 10 August 1920; see also Morris to Ross, 22 July 1920.
113 See *Summary of a Survey of the Protestant and Non-Sectarian Relief Organizations of Montreal by Miss E. Francis O'Neill at the Request of the Financial Federation of the Montreal Council of Social Agencies* [February 1924].
114 *Montreal Daily Star,* 17 March 1923.
115 Montreal *Gazette,* 5 April 1923. On the experience of mothers' allowance in Ontario, see Margaret Jane Hillyard Little, *No Car, No Radio, No Liquor Permit: The Moral Regulation of Single Mothers in Ontario, 1920-1997* (Don Mills, ON: Oxford University Press, 1998).
116 Desmond Morton and Glenn Wright, "The Bonus Campaign, 1919-21: Veterans and the Campaign for Re-establishment," *Canadian Historical Review* 64, 2 (1983); Morton and Wright, *Winning the Second Battle,* 122; *Calgary Daily Herald,* 24 February 1919; James Eayrs, *In Defence of Canada: From the Great War to the Great Depression* (Toronto: University of Toronto Press, 1964).
117 *Toronto Daily Star,* 7 August 1919; for the resolution, see Owen Carrigan, *Canadian Party Programs* (Toronto: Holt, Rinehart, 1968).
118 Toronto *Evening Telegram,* 8 September 1919; *Toronto Daily Star,* 8 September 1919.
119 On the outcome, see Morton and Wright, "Bonus Campaign," 162-7.
120 Nurses and both of Canada's two female soldiers were barred from Soldier Settlement, as were disabled veterans, on the argument that only "bona fide" farmers were welcome. Unfortunately, the prospect of farming had been held out to the disabled veteran in "Private Pat," the government's most popular pamphlet on the disabled, and some of the applicants accepted for Soldier Settlement made "bona fide" look like a general blessing.
121 On Soldier Settlement, see Morton and Wright, *Winning the Second Battle,* 142-54, 207-9. The author accepts Arthur Meighen's view that Soldier Settlement was neither a gratuity nor a bonus, and the terms of the act make that clear. Those who pretended otherwise did themselves and the veterans no favour.
122 In 1919 the government reported 10,405 widows' pensions, 3,620 for dependent mothers, 827 for dependent fathers, and 30 for grandparents. War-related pensions supported 16,594 children, 741 orphans, and 126 dependent brothers and sisters. *Canada Year Book,* 1919, table 27, 610.
123 Jean Blewett imagined that the name and design was so appropriate that "it must have been conceived by a sister woman." *Everywoman's World,* May 1919.
124 A decade after the war, the government reported 54,520 disability pensioners supporting 40,160 wives, 69,267 children, and 1,304 "others." *Canada Year Book,* 1930.
125 Pension administration was a major theme in post-1919 veterans' policy in Canada. See Morton and Wright, *Winning the Second Battle,* 155-77, 202-13.
126 Since returned men, particularly those who had been disabled, found it impossible to purchase life insurance for their dependants at affordable rates, the government provided Returned Soldiers' Insurance. Devised by G.D. Finlayson, the Dominion superintendent of insurance, and Thomas Bradshaw, who had managed Toronto's wartime insurance, RSI offered a simple term life policy of up to $5,000 with no medical exam. See Morton and Wright, *Winning the Second Battle,* 137-8 and throughout.
127 *Canada Year Book,* 1919, 606-7.
128 See ch. 1, n. 37.

129 "With the same sacrifice, and very often – the private soldier having given up a good deal more than the officer – many times the case, with so democratized an army as that which has covered Canadian arms with glory, the Lieutenant Governor declared himself to have long been a convert to the idea of equalization." *Victoria Daily Times,* 14 August 1918, 9.

130 *Canada Year Book,* 1920, table 25, 679.

131 See Ernest Scammell, *Summary of Activities of the Government of Canada in Connection with the Demobilization and Re-Establishment of Members of the Canadian Expeditionary Force to 31st December, 1923* (Ottawa: King's Printer, 1924), 40-1; *Canada Year Book,* 1920, 680-1; *Canadian Annual Review,* 1920, 40-1.

132 *Canada Year Book,* 1920, table 26, 680-1.

133 NAC, RG 24, vol. 1234, HQ 593-1-12, Mayor Morin to Sir Eugène Fiset, 2 December 1916, 482.

134 House of Commons, *Debates,* 25 June 1919, 4031; Special Committee Appointed to Consider the Questions of Pensions and Pension Regulations and All Matters Pertaining Thereto and to Prepare a Bill Dealing with Pensions for the Consideration of the House, 7 May 1919, *Proceedings, Evidence and Reports* (Ottawa, 1919), 178-81, 236 (hereafter Committee on Pensions, 1919).

135 House of Commons, *Debates,* 23 June 1920, 4042-3; Special Committee Appointed by Resolution of the House of Commons to Consider the Question of Continuing the War Bonus of Pensioners, and any Amendments to the Pension Law Which May Be Proposed, *Proceedings, Evidence and Reports,* 18 June 1920 (Ottawa, 1920), *Proceedings,* 57-67 (hereafter Committee on Pensions, 1920); Morton and Wright, *Winning the Second Battle,* 160.

136 Thompson was a capable Ottawa lawyer who had raised a battalion for the CEF. An austerely conservative bachelor, he was the son of Canada's first Roman Catholic prime minister. See Morton and Wright, *Winning the Second Battle,* 161.

137 House of Commons, *Debates,* 23 June 1920, 4042.

138 Ibid., 28 June 1919, 4209. The issue returned on 30 June 1919, 4277-83. Members had bypassed the earlier reference at section 32 of the Pension Act, *Statutes of Canada,* 1919, 9-10 Geo. V, c. 43 and were debating section 42.

139 House of Commons, *Debates,* 30 June 1919, 4290. Section 32(3) of the Pension Act continued to use the offending phrase, a British, not an American, creation.

140 Senate, *Debates,* 3 July 1919, 871.

141 See Special Committee Appointed by Resolution of the House of Commons on the 10th of March, 1921, to Consider Questions Relating to the Pensions, Insurance and Re-establishment of Returned Soldiers ... May 26th, 1921, *Report* (Ottawa, 1921), 243, 461. By taking a case to court, the BPC had confirmed that a man could not be convicted of bigamy if the second marriage occurred outside the country.

142 Nancy Astor was Britain's first woman member of Parliament.

143 Pension Act, 1919, s. 40; House of Commons, *Debates,* 5 May 1925, 2855-61; Ralston testimony, Royal Commission on Pensions and Re-Establishment, *Final Report* (Ottawa, 1924), 100-1.

144 Committee on Pensions, 1920, *Report,* 343, 348-63; *Manitoba Free Press* and *Toronto Daily Star,* 7 May 1920.

145 Pension Act, 1919, s. 22. See also Special Committee on Pensions and Returned Soldiers' Problems, 1928, *Reports, Proceedings and Evidence* (Ottawa, 1928), 409.

146 Committee on Pensions, 1919, 44.

147 On pension widows, see Morton and Wright, *Winning the Second Battle,* 205, 208, 210, 220; *Veteran* 6, 10 February 1923. On the US example, see Archibald testimony, Committee on Pensions, 1919, *Proceedings,* 56-7; House of Commons, *Debates,* 25 June 1919, 4176, and 22 June 1922, 3447; Senate, *Debates,* 26 June 1922, 674-5.

148 See *Canada Year Book,* 1931, table on 1044.

149 The words promised pensions for death or disability "attributable" to military service. On the techniques used by Thompson and his officials, see Morton and Wright, *Winning the Second Battle,* 161-2.

150 On the Special Committee, see *Toronto Daily Star,* 17-22 June 1922; House of Commons, *Debates,* 22 June 1919, 3344-9, and Ladner amendment, 23 June 1922, 3453-5; *Veteran* 7, 20 May and 24 June 1922.

151 See *Veteran* 7, 4 March and 22 May 1922.

152 Morton and Wright, *Winning the Second Battle,* 164.

153 Royal Commission on Pensions and Re-establishment, *Report on the First Part of the Investigation* (Ottawa, 1923), 5.

154 Ibid., 44-6, 80-91, 107-9.

155 Ibid., 129.

156 *Veteran* 8, 21 August and 1 September 1923.

157 Royal Commission on Pensions and Re-establishment, *First Interim Report on the Second Part of Investigation* (Ottawa, 1923), 12, 14-15, 23-6.

158 Senate, *Debates,* 29 June 1923, 1258 ff., 1275-8.

159 Royal Commission on Pensions and Re-establishment, *Final Report,* 23-31; *Veteran* 8, 31 March 1923.

160 Royal Commission on Pensions and Re-establishment, *Second Interim Report on Second Part of Investigation* (Ottawa, 1924), 6-7.

161 Royal Commission on Pensions and Re-establishment, *Final Report,* 101.

162 Senate, *Debates,* 18 July 1924, 890.

163 House of Commons, *Debates,* 18-19 July 1924, 4860-9.

164 Morton and Wright, *Winning the Second Battle,* 191-6.

165 Ibid., 178-201.

166 In 1935 the Hyndman Committee estimated the average age of veterans as forty-seven and of disabled pensioned at forty-one. On "burn-out" see Robert England, *Discharged: A Commentary on Civil Re-establishment of Veterans in Canada* (Toronto: Macmillan, 1943), 29; A.G. Butler, *Australian Army Medical Services in the War of 1914-1918,* vol. 3, *Special Problems and Services* (Canberra: Australian War Memorial, 1943), 816, attributed the term to Canada.

167 A.J. Hunter, "Cruel Nonsense in Pension Procedure," *Saturday Night,* 29 March 1930; NAC, RG 38, vol. 231, f. 8622, Scammell to minister, 15 June 1930. On numbers of appeals, see *Canada Year Book,* 1931, 1044, 1046.

168 NAC, Currie Papers, vol. 26, "President's Message," 26 November 1928; *Legionary* 3, 7 (1928).

169 Special Committee on Pensions and Returned Soldiers' Problems, Comprising Amendments to the Pension Act, Soldiers' Insurance Act, Land Settlement Act, the Establishment of a Pension Tribunal and a Pension Appeal Court for War Veterans, 23 May 1930, *Reports, Proceedings and Evidence* (Ottawa, 1931), *Proceedings,* 11 (hereafter Committee on Pensions, 1930). On LaFlèche, see *Legionary* 4, 8 (1930).

170 Committee on Pensions, 1930, *Proceedings,* xii-xiii.

171 Ibid., xvii, 20-1.

172 Ibid., 55, 498; *Canadian Annual Review,* 1928-9, 178.

173 NAC, RG 38, vol. 195, f. 7261, "Pensions and Other Postwar Benefits," 19; for details see Senator Laird, Senate, *Debates,* 15 May 1930, 210-11; *Canada Year Book,* 1932, 1056-7.

174 House of Commons, *Debates,* 267, 270.

175 On the aftermath of the 1930 reforms, see Morton and Wright, *Winning the Second Battle,* 208-12.

176 Most of the cases reaching the tribunal were not new to the Board of Pension Commissioners. As a reader of many veterans' appeals in the period, I was struck that many pages of letters and testimonials to character and suffering were followed by a concluding one-page

BPC report, invariably neatly typed, full of precise dates and presumed facts that left little doubt that the previous claims had included at least a measure of *supressio veri*. Only someone with a strong, instinctive distaste for the BPC could entirely ignore its advice.

177 *Canadian Veteran,* 1 November 1932. On appeals, see NAC, Ralston Papers, vol. 153, Scammell to Reg Bowler, 10 January 1934.

178 NAC, MG 28, I 298, vol. 1, f. 4, Canadian Legion minute books, book 2, 200, 226.

179 Currie to Maj. J.S. Roper, 28 May 1931, cited by *Legionary* 6 (July 1931). See NAC, R.B. Bennett Papers, reel M-1261, R.B. Bennett to Currie, 31 December 1931, 322039.

180 *Canadian Veteran,* 1 November 1932.

181 *Canada Year Book,* 1940, 1066.

Chapter 8: Never Again

1 In her history of social work in Great Britain and the United States, Kathleen Woodroofe reserves the 1920s for the Freudian revolution in American thinking, while its impact on Britain was far more muted. Canada in those years was shaped by both American and British influences, but Freudian psychology, with its emphasis on the individual's role and responsibility, soon comfortably dominated professional practice wherever social work rejected any kinship with socialism. See Woodroofe, *From Charity to Social Work in England and the United States* (London: Routledge and Kegan Paul, 1968), 118 ff.

2 C.P. Stacey, *The Official History of the Canadian Army in the Second World War,* vol. 1, *Six Years of War* (Ottawa: Queen's Printer, 1955), 52, 126.

3 Serge Durflinger, "Verdun during the Second World War," (PhD diss., McGill University, 1997), 311. Robert England commented that a small family would have trouble supporting itself on the dependants' allowance in a large city. See England, *Discharged: A Commentary on Civil Re-establishment of Veterans in Canada* (Toronto: Macmillan, 1943), 152.

4 England, *Discharged,* 151-2.

Bibliography

Archives and Libraries

ARCHIVES OF ONTARIO
T.L. Church Papers

ARCHIVES OF MANITOBA
Manitoba Patriotic Fund Records
Edith Rogers Papers F 6 SCWF
Winnipeg Industrial Bureau, *9th Annual Report,* December 31 1915, MG 10, A2, box 36

BRITISH COLUMBIA ARCHIVES
BC Provincial Game Warden Originals, 1905-1922
Cominco Papers, MS 15, box 29, file 3, West Kootenay Power & Light Co., papers on Patriotic
    Fund
Oliver, William Edgar, 1867-1920 lawyer, box 4, personal papers, Mrs. W.E. Oliver, file 12
    (scrapbook) and file 13, correspondence re 1915-19

CATHOLIC ARCHIVAL CENTRE, ST. JOHN'S, NF
Most Rev E.P. Roche papers, vol. 2 1915-1950, Armed Forces, 1915-1945

McCORD MUSEUM OF CANADIAN HISTORY
J.W. Ross Papers, P217-D/12

METROPOLITAN TORONTO REFERENCE LIBRARY
Turner, Dr. Alice W. "Sequences of Economic Events in Canada, 1914-1923." Report to the
    Advisory Committee on Reconstruction, n.d.

NATIONAL ARCHIVES OF CANADA (NAC)
R.B. Bennett Papers
Sir Robert L. Borden Papers
J.A. Calder Papers
Canadian Patriotic Fund National Minutes and Bulletins
Sir Adolphe Caron Papers
J.J. Creelman Papers
Sir Arthur Currie Papers
Department of Militia and Defence Records
Department of National Defence Records
A.F. Duguid Papers
Sir Edward Albert Kemp Papers
Sir James McBrien Papers
C.A. McGrath Papers
François-Xavier Maheux Papers

Privy Council Office
J.L. Ralston Papers
Records of the Royal Canadian Legion
Sir R.E.W. Turner Papers
Toronto and York CPF Annual Report, 1 January 1918, "Report of the 50,000 Club"

Nova Scotia Archives and Records Management (NSARM)
Canadian Patriotic Fund, Nova Scotia Branch

Oxford County Archives, Norwich
Records of the Oxford Patriotic Association

Private collection
Letters of Pte. Ernest Hamilton

Provincial Archives of Alberta
CPF Minute Book, North Alberta Branch

Queen's University Archives
Frontenac County Records, 1916-19

Saskatchewan Archives
Reports and Documents of the Saskatchewan Branch of the CPF

University of British Columbia Special Collections
Vancouver Trades and Labour Council Minutes of Regular Meetings

University of Western Ontario Archives
Leonard Ibbotson Papers

Government Publications

Canada
Alberta. *Statutes,* 5 April 1917, 7 Geo. V, c. 17. Patriotic Tax Act. Amended 13 April 1918 by 8 Geo. V, c. 12.
Board of Pension Commissioners. *Instructions and a Table of Incapacities for the Guidance of Physicians and Surgeons Making Medical Examinations for Pension Purposes.* Ottawa, 1917.
Canada. Auditor General's Report on Appropriations. *Sessional Papers,* 1889, vol. 3.
–. *Militia List,* August 1914.
–. National Accounts. *Sessional Papers,* 1890, no. 3A.
–. Pensions Granted to Members of the CEF to 16 February 1916. *Sessional Papers,* 1916, no. 185.
–. Regulations as to Pensions and Gratuities. *Sessional Papers,* 1886, no. 80e.
–. "Report of the War Charities Branch of the Department of Secretary of State." *Sessional Papers,* 1919, no. 29.
–. *Sessional Papers,* 1904, vol. 1, no. 17.
Canadian Patriotic Fund Act. *Statutes of Canada.* 1915, 5 Geo. V, c. 2.
Canadian Patriotic Fund Amendment Act. *Statutes of Canada.* 1918, 7-8 Geo. V, c. 35.
Canadian Patriotic Fund Amendment Act. *Statutes of Canada.* 1919, 9-10 Geo. V, c. 44.
Department of Militia and Defence. *Regulations and Orders for the Militia of Canada, 1883, 1887, 1906.* Ottawa, 1883, 1887, 1906.

–. *Militia General Orders, 1868-1918.*
–. *Queen's Regulations and Orders for the Canadian Militia, 1887.* Ottawa, 1887.
Department of Pensions and National Health. *Annual Reports, 1928-1930.*
Department of Soldiers' Civil Re-establishment. *Annual Reports, 1919-1927.*
–. *Back to Mufti.* Ottawa, 1919.
– [W.E. Segsworth]. *Canada's Work for Disabled Soldiers.* Ottawa, 1919.
–. *The Care and Employment of the Tuberculous Ex-Service Man after Discharge from the Sanatorium.* Ottawa, 1920.
–. *Handbook for the Information of Former Members of the Canadian and British Forces Resident in the United States of America.* Ottawa, 1920.
–. *Invalided Soldiers' Commission.* Ottawa, 1919.
–. *Reconstruction Bulletin.* Ottawa, 1917-1918.
–. *Report of the Work of the Invalided Soldiers' Commission.* Ottawa, 1918.
–. *Returned Soldiers' Hand Book.* Ottawa, 1919.
Historical Statistics of Canada. 2nd ed. Ottawa: Statistics Canada, 1983.
House of Commons. *Debates and Journals,* 1914-1930.
Invalided Soldiers' Commission. *The Soldier's Return: A Cheerful Chat with Private Pat/Le Soldat revient: une causerie avec Poil-aux-Pattes.* Ottawa: King's Printer, 1919.
–. *The Soldier's Return: How the Canadian Soldier Is Being Refitted for Industry.* Ottawa: King's Printer, 1919.
–. *Some Facts about Occupational Therapy and Curative Workshops.* Toronto, 1919.
King's Regulations and Orders for the Canadian Militia, 1910. Ottawa: King's Printer, 1910.
Manitoba. *Statutes,* 10 March 1916, 6 Geo. V, c. 111. Patriotic Levy Act. Amended 9 March 1917 by 7 Geo. V, c. 17.
Military Hospitals Commission. *The Soldier's Return: From "Down and Out" to "Up and In Again": A Little Chat with Private Pat.* Ottawa, 1917.
New Brunswick. *Statutes,* 29 April 1915, 5 Geo. V, c. 3. An Act re Contributions to the Canadian Patriotic Fund, 203-4. Amended by 6 Geo. V, c. 4, An Act to Confirm a Grant in Aid to the Canadian Patriotic Fund, 7 April 1916, 43-53. Amended by 8 Geo. V, c. 29, An Act to Confirm Arrangements Made for the Canadian Patriotic Fund, 22 June 1917, 98-101. Amended by 8 Geo. V, c. 27, An Act to Amend and Assist in Carrying out the Objects of the Canadian Patriotic Fund, 26 April 1918, 165-8.
Newfoundland. "Annual Report of Pensions and Disabilities Board." *Journals of House of Assembly,* appendix, 366-7. 1917.
–. "Report of the Trustees." *Journal of the Newfoundland House of Assembly, Appendices,* 1919.
Overseas Military Forces of Canada. *Report, 1918.* London: n.p., 1919.
Pension Act. *Statutes of Canada.* 1919, 9-10 Geo. V, c. 43.
Repatriation Committee. *War to Peace: The programme of the Canadian Government Regarding the Returned Soldiers and Readjustment to Industrial Conditions.* Ottawa, 1919.
Royal Commission on Pensions and Re-establishment. *Report on the First Part of the Investigation.* Ottawa, 1923.
–. *First Interim Report on Second Part of Investigation.* Ottawa, 1923.
–. *Second Interim Report on Second Part of Investigation.* Ottawa, 1924.
–. *Final Report.* Ottawa, 1924.
Royal Commission to Inquire into and Report as to the Treatment of the Men of the Canadian Expeditionary Force While on Board the Transport *Northland* on Her Voyage from Liverpool to Halifax. *Report.* Ottawa, 1919.
Saskatchewan. *Statutes of Saskatchewan,* 14 March 1916, 6 Geo V, c. 6. An Act to Raise Pensions for Patriotic Purposes.
–. 10 March 1917, 7 Geo. V, c. 2. An Act to Amend the Patriotic Revenues Act.

Senate. *Debates and Journals,* 1914-30.

Special Committee Appointed by Resolution of the House of Commons of Canada on 30 March 1922 to Consider Questions Relating to Pensions, Insurance and Re-establishment of Returned Soldiers ... *Proceedings and Reports.* Ottawa, 1922.

Special Committee Appointed by Resolution of the House of Commons on the 10th of March, 1921, to Consider Questions Relating to the Pensions, Insurance and Re-establishment of Returned Soldiers ... May 26th, 1921. *Proceedings, Evidence and Reports.* Ottawa, 1921.

Special Committee Appointed by Resolution of the House of Commons to Consider the Question of Continuing the War Bonus of Pensioners, and any Amendments to the Pension Law Which May Be Proposed ... 18 June 1920. *Proceedings, Evidence and Reports.* Ottawa, 1920.

Special Committee Appointed by the Resolution of the House of Commons on the 18th of September, 1919, and to Whom Was Referred Bill No. 10, An Act to Amend the Department of Soldiers' Civil Re-establishment Act, 21 October, 1919. *Proceedings and Reports.* Ottawa, 1919.

Special Committee Appointed to Consider and Report upon the Pension Board, the Pension Regulations, and the Sufficiency or Otherwise of the Relief Afforded Thereunder ... 20 May 1918. *Proceedings, Evidence and Reports.* Ottawa, 1918.

Special Committee Appointed to Consider and Report upon the Rates of Pensions to be paid to Disabled Soldiers and the Establishment of a Permanent Pensions Board. *Report and Proceedings.* Ottawa, May 1916.

Special Committee Appointed to Consider, Inquire into, and Report upon the Reception, Treatment, Care, Training and Re-Education of the Wounded, Disabled and Convalescents who have served in the Canadian Expeditionary Forces ... *Proceedings, Evidence and Reports.* Ottawa: King's Printer, 1917.

Special Committee Appointed to Consider Questions Relating to the Pensions, Insurance and Re-establishment of Returned Soldiers, 1924. *Proceedings, Evidence and Reports.* Ottawa, 1924.

Special Committee Appointed to Consider the Questions of Pensions and Pension Regulations and All Matters Pertaining Thereto and to Prepare a Bill Dealing with Pensions for the Consideration of the House, 7 May 1919. *Proceedings, Evidence and Reports.* Ottawa, 1919.

Special Committee on Pensions and Returned Soldiers' Problems, 1928. *Reports, Proceedings and Evidence.* Ottawa, 1928.

Special Committee on Pensions and Returned Soldiers' Problems, Comprising Amendments to the Pension Act, Soldiers' Insurance Act, Land Settlement Act, the Establishment of a Pension Tribunal and a Pension Appeal Court for War Veterans, 23 May 1930. *Reports, Proceedings and Evidence.* Ottawa, 1931.

Special Committee on Pensions and Returned Soldiers' Problems, *Report.* Ottawa, 1933.

Special Committee on the Boot Inquiry, 1915. *Journals of The House of Commons,* Session 1915, vol. 51, appendix no. 4, Report of the Special Committee on the Boot Inquiry Respecting Army Boots Supplied to the Department of Militia and Defence for the Canadian Expeditionary Force. *Report,* 5-27. *Testimony,* 27-1213.

War Charities Act. *Statutes of Canada.* 1917, 7-8 Geo. V, c. 38.

War Charities Branch, Department of the Secretary of State. *Report, 1919.* Canada, *Sessional Papers,* 1 April 1919, no. 29.

GREAT BRITAIN

Handbook of the Land Forces of British Dominions. London: His Majesty's Stationery Office, 1911.

House of Commons. *Debates,* 1914-1916.

Ministry of Pensions. *Comparative Tables Showing the Weekly Rates of War Pensions and Allowances*. London, 1919.

War Office. *Funds, Associations, Societies etc. for the Assisting of Serving and Ex-Service Officers, Men, Women and Their Dependents*. London, 1920.

OTHER PUBLICATIONS

Addresses Delivered before the Canadian Club of Montreal, 1915-1916. Montreal, 1916.

Ames, Herbert B. *The City below the Hill: A Sociological Study of a Portion of the City of Montreal, Canada*. 1897. Reprinted with an introduction by P.F.W. Rutherford, Toronto: University of Toronto Press, 1972.

–. *Our National Benefaction*. Ottawa: CPF, 1915.

–. *The Second Year of the War: What It Means to the Canadian Patriotic Fund*. Ottawa: CPF, 1915.

Armstrong, Elizabeth. *The Crisis of Quebec*. New York: Ams Press, 1937.

Army and Navy Veterans. *Proceedings of the First Convention of the Army and Navy Veterans in Canada*. Winnipeg, 1918.

Bannerman, James. "The Biggest Spender We Ever Had." In *Maclean's Canada: Portrait of a Country*, ed. L.F. Hannon. Toronto: McClelland and Stewart, 1960.

Bartley, Allan. *Heroes in Waiting: The 160th Bruce Battalion in the Great War*. Walkerton: Brucedale Press, 1996.

Beckett, Ian F.W., and Keith Simpson, eds. *A Nation in Arms: A Social Study of the British Army in the First World War*. Manchester: University of Manchester Press, 1985.

Béland, Henri. *The Returned Soldier*. Ottawa: King's Printer, [1920].

"Benefits for Families." *Labour Gazette* 17, 7 (1917).

Bernard, David Laurier. "Philanthropy vs. the Welfare State: Great Britain's and Canada's Response to Military Dependants in the Great War." MA thesis, University of Guelph, 1992.

Bishop, C.W. *The Canadian YMCA in the Great War*. Toronto: YMCA, 1924.

Bland, Lucy. "Guardians of the Race." In *The Changing Experience of Women*, ed. E. Whitelegg et al. Oxford: Martin Robinson, 1982.

–. "Purity, Motherhood, Pleasure or Threat: Definitions of Female Sexuality, 1900-1970." In *Sex and Love*, ed. S. Cartledge and J. Ryan. London: Women's Press, 1983.

Bliss, Michael. *A Canadian Millionaire: The Life and Business Times of Sir Joseph Flavelle, Bart., 1858-1939*. Toronto: Macmillan, 1978.

–. *Northern Enterprise: Five Centuries of Canadian Business*. Toronto: McClelland and Stewart, 1987.

Borden, Henry, ed. *Letters to Limbo*. Toronto: University of Toronto Press, 1971.

Borden, R.L. *Memoirs*. 2 vols. Toronto: Macmillan, 1938.

Brereton, J.M. *The British Soldier: A Social History from 1661 to the Present Day*. London: Bodley Head, 1986.

Brown, R. Craig. *Robert Laird Borden: A Biography*. Vol. 2, *1914-1937*. Toronto: Macmillan, 1980.

Brown, R. Craig, and Desmond Morton. "The Embarrassing Apotheosis of a 'Great Canadian': Sir Arthur Currie's Personal Crisis in 1917." *Canadian Historical Review* 60, 1 (1979).

Brown, Thomas E. "Shell Shock in the Canadian Expeditionary Force, 1914-1918: Canadian Psychiatry in the Great War." In *Health, Disease and Medicine: Essays in Canadian History*, ed. C.G. Roland. Hamilton: Hannah Foundation, 1984.

Bruce, Herbert A. *Politics and the C.A.M.C.* Toronto: William Briggs, 1919.

–. *Report on the Canadian Army Medical Services*. London: N.p., 1916.

–. *Varied Operations*. Toronto: Longman Green, 1958.

Bryce, James. *The American Commonwealth*. 2nd ed. New York: Macmillan, 1910.

Buckley, Suzann, and Janice Dickin McGinnis. "The Failure to Resolve the Problem of VD among the Troops during World War I." In *War and Society,* ed. Brian Bond and I. Roy. London: Croom Helm, 1977.

–. "Venereal Disease and Public Health Reform in Canada." *Canadian Historical Review* 63, 3 (1982).

Buitenhuis, Peter. *The Great War of Words: British, American and Canadian Propaganda and Fiction, 1914-1933.* Vancouver: UBC Press, 1987.

Butler, A.G. *Australian Army Medical Services in the War of 1914-1918.* Vol. 3, *Special Problems and Services.* Canberra: Australian War Memorial, 1943.

Cairns, Alex, and A.H. Yetman. *The History of the Veteran Movement, 1916 to 1925 and of the Canadian Legion, 1926 to 1935.* 2 vols. Winnipeg: Manitoba Veteran, [1961].

Canadian Bank of Commerce. *Letters from the Front, 1914-1919.* Toronto: Canadian Bank of Commerce, 1919.

Carman, Albert. *The Return of the Troops: A Plain Account of the Demobilization of the Canadian Expeditionary Force.* Ottawa: Government Printing Bureau, 1920.

Carnegie, David. *The History of Munition Supply in Canada.* London: Longmans, Green, 1925.

Carrigan, Owen. *Canadian Party Platforms.* Toronto: Copp Clark, 1968.

Cassel, Jay. *The Secret Plague: Venereal Disease in Canada, 1839-1939.* Toronto: University of Toronto Press, 1987.

Cecil, Lady Gwendolyn. *Life of Robert, Marquis of Salisbury.* London: Cassell, 1931.

Chadwick, H.D., and A.S. Pope. *The Modern Attack on Tuberculosis.* New York: Commonwealth Fund, 1946.

Christie, Nancy. *Engendering the State: Family, Work, and Welfare in Canada.* Toronto: University of Toronto Press, 2000.

"Civil Re-establishment." *Encyclopedia of Newfoundland and Labrador,* ed. Joseph R. Smallwood, vol. 5, 446-7. St. John's, NF: Newfoundland Book Publishers, 1981.

Comacchio, Cynthia. *Nations Are Built of Babies: Saving Ontario's Mothers and Children, 1900-1940.* Montreal and Kingston: McGill-Queen's University Press, 1993.

Cook, Tim. "Documenting War and Forging Reputations: Sir Max Aitken and the Canadian War Records Office in the First World War." *War in History* 10, 3 (2003).

Cooper, John Irwin. *Montreal: A Brief History.* Montreal: McGill-Queen's University Press, 1967.

Copp, J.T. *The Anatomy of Poverty: The Condition of the Working Class in Montreal, 1897-1929.* Toronto: McClelland and Stewart, 1974.

Copp, Terry, and Bill McAndrew. *Battle Exhaustion: Soldiers and Psychiatrists in the Canadian Army, 1939-1945.* Montreal and Kingston: McGill-Queen's University Press, 1990.

CPF (Canadian Patriotic Fund). *Federal Emergency Appropriation Department Regulations.* Ottawa: CPF, 1919.

–. *How Much Shall We Give? Receipts and Expenditures of the Canadian Patriotic Fund during the First Year of the War: The Needs of the Future.* Ottawa: CPF, 1 October 1915.

–. *A Message to the Canadian Soldier's Wife.* Ottawa, 1915.

–. *Proceedings of the Western Interprovincial Conference of the CPF Organization, Regina, Wed and Thu, 28-29 June 1916.* Regina, 1916.

–. *Reports of the Proceedings of a Conference of Representatives of Branches of the Canadian Patriotic Fund in Eastern Cities, Toronto, 16-18 May 1916.* Ottawa: CPF, 1916.

–. *The Second Year of the War: What It Means to the Canadian Patriotic Fund.* Ottawa: CPF, 1915.

CPF, Hamilton Branch. *Five Years of Service: The Canadian Patriotic Fund, Hamilton and Wentworth Branch.* Hamilton: n.p., 1920.

–. *Report of the Canadian Patriotic Fund, Hamilton and Wentworth Branch.* Hamilton, [1920?].

CPF, Montreal Branch. *Annual Report of the Relief Committee.* Montreal, 1915-17.

–. *Report of the Montreal Branch, Canadian Patriotic Fund, 1914-1917.* Montreal, 1917.

CPF, Montreal Branch, Relief Committee. *Report of the Work of the Canadian Patriotic Fund, August 1914 to August 1917.* Montreal, 1917.

Craig, Grace Morris. *But It Is Our War.* Toronto: University of Toronto Press, 1981.

Creighton, Louise. *The Social Disease and How to Fight It.* London: Longman's, Green, 1914.

Dallaire, Lt.-Gen. Roméo. *Shake Hands with the Devil: The Failure of Humanity in Rwanda.* Toronto: Random House, 2003.

Dearing, Mary R. *Veterans in Politics: The Story of the Grand Army of the Republic.* Westport, CT: Greenwood Press, 1974.

Dempsey, James. *Warriors of the King: Prairie Indians in World War I.* Regina: Plains Research Center, 1999.

Dennis, Lt.-Col. J.S. "Provision for Crippled Soldiers by the Military Hospitals Commission of Canada." *American Journal of Care for Cripples* 5, 1 (1917).

de Watteville, Herman Gaston. *The British Soldier: His Daily Life from Tudor to Modern Times.* London: J.C. Dent, 1954.

Dexter, Robert C. "War Relief and Charity Organization." *Charity Organization Bulletin* 8 (1916-17).

Diefenbaker, John G. *One Canada: Memoirs of the Right Honourable John G. Diefenbaker. The Crusading Years, 1895-1956.* Toronto: Macmillan, 1975.

Diltz, Bert. *Stranger Than Fiction.* Toronto: McClelland and Stewart, 1969.

Dionne, Raoul. "Journal d'un aumônier de la guerre 1914." *Cahiers de la Société historique acadienne* 17, 2 (1986).

Duguid, A. Fortescue. *Official History of the Canadian Forces in the Great War, 1914-19.* General Series. Vol. 1, *Chronicle, August 1914-September 1915.* Ottawa: King's Printer, 1938.

Durflinger, Serge. "Verdun in the Second World War." PhD diss., McGill University, 1997.

Durkin, Douglas. *The Magpie.* Toronto: University of Toronto Press, 1974.

Dyhouse, Catherine. *Girls Growing up in Late Victorian and Edwardian England.* London: Routledge and Kegan Paul, 1981.

Eayrs, James. *In Defence of Canada: From the Great War to the Great Depression.* Toronto: University of Toronto Press, 1964.

Edwards, Owen Dudley, and Jennifer H. Litster. "The End of Canadian Innocence: L.M. Montgomery and the First World War." In *L.M. Montgomery and Canadian Culture,* ed. Irene Gammwel and Elizabeth Epperly. Toronto: University of Toronto Press, 1999.

England, Robert. *Discharged: A Commentary on Civil Re-establishment of Veterans in Canada.* Toronto: Macmillan, 1943.

–. *Living, Learning, Remembering: Memoirs of Robert England.* Vancouver: University of British Columbia Centre for Continuing Education, 1980.

English, John. *Shadow of Heaven: The Life of Lester Pearson.* Vol. 1, *1897-1948.* Toronto: Lester and Orpen Dennys, 1989.

Fialkowski, Bridget, ed. *John L. Todd, 1876-1949: Letters.* Senneville, QC: privately published, 1977.

Fortescue, John. *The Empire and the Army.* London and Toronto: Cassell, 1928.

Frost, Leslie M. *Fighting Men.* Toronto: Clarke-Irwin, 1967.

Frost, Stanley Bryce. *McGill University: For the Advancement of Learning.* Vol. 2, *1895-1971.* Montreal and Kingston: McGill-Queen's University Press, 1984.

Gaffen, Fred. *Forgotten Soldiers.* Penticton, BC: Theytus Books, 1985.

Gagnon, Jean-Pierre. *Le 22e bataillon (canadien-français), 1914-1919, Une étude socio-militaire.* Quebec: Presses de l'université Laval, 1986.

Gildea, James. *Historical Record of the Soldiers' and Sailors' Families Association, 1885-1916.* London: N.p., 1916.

Glover, Richard. *Peninsular Preparation: The Reform of the British Army, 1795-1806*. Cambridge: Cambridge University Press, 1963.

Godley, Hugh, ed. *The Manual of Military Law*. 6th ed. London: HMSO, 1914.

Granatstein, J.L., and J.M. Hitsman. *Broken Promises: A History of Conscription in Canada*. Toronto: Oxford, 1977. Reprinted Toronto: Copp Clark Pitman, 1985.

Great War Veterans' Association. *Report of the First Convention, Winnipeg, Manitoba*. Winnipeg: GWVA, 1917.

Griffiths, Naomi. *The Splendid Vision: A Centennial History of the National Council of Women of Canada, 1893-1994*. Ottawa: Carleton University Press, 1993.

Hamelin, Marcel, ed. *Les mémoires de Raoul Dandurand*. Quebec: Presses de l'université Laval, 1967.

Hardy, Thomas. *The Dynasts: An Epic Drama*. London: Macmillan, 1913.

Harris, Frances C. "Why I Married My Canadian Husband." *Everywoman's World*, June 1919.

Harris, Garrard. *The Redemption of the Disabled: A Study of Programmes of Rehabilitation for the Disabled of War and Industry*. Toronto: McClelland and Stewart, 1919.

Harrison, Charles. *Generals Die in Bed*. New York: Morrow, 1930.

Hastin, Margaret Laning, and Lorraine Ellenwood. *Blue Bows and the Golden Rule: Provincial Council of Women of BC: An Historical Account*. Cloverdale, BC: Provincial Council of Women of BC, 1984.

Haycock, Ron. *Sam Hughes: The Public Career of a Controversial Canadian, 1885-1916*. Waterloo: Wilfrid Laurier University Press, 1986.

Henderson, Rose. *Women and War*. Montreal: n.p., 1924.

Hodgetts, C.A. "Infant Mortality in Canada." *Canadian Medical Association Journal* 1, 8 (1911).

–. "Statistics and Publicity in Child Welfare Work." *Canadian Public Health Journal* 12, 3 (1921).

Hopkins, J. Castell. *The Province of Ontario in the War*. Toronto: Warwick Bros. and Rutter, 1919.

How, Douglas. *One Village, One War: 1914-1945*. Hantsport, NS: Lancelot Press, 1995.

Howard, Irene. *The Struggle for Social Justice in British Columbia: Helena Gutteridge, the Unknown Reformer*. Vancouver: UBC Press, 1992.

Humphries, Charles W. "Keeping the Home Fires Burning: British Columbia Women and the First World War." Paper presented to Canadian Historical Association, Charlottetown, PEI, 31 May 1992.

Hunt, M. Stuart. *Nova Scotia's Part in the Great War*. Halifax: Nova Scotia Veteran Publishing, 1920.

Hunter, A.J. "Cruel Nonsense in Pension Procedure." *Saturday Night*, 29 March 1930.

"Infant Mortality." Editorial. *Canadian Public Health Journal* 6, 10 (1915).

Jaffares, Norman, and Martin Gray, eds. *Dictionary of Quotations*. London: Collins, 1995.

Jenkins, Kathleen. *Montreal: Island City of the St. Lawrence*. New York: Doubleday, 1966.

Johnson, J.K., ed. *The Canadian Directory of Parliament*. Ottawa: Public Archives of Canada, 1968.

Johnson, Paul B. *Land Fit for Heroes: The Planning of British Reconstruction, 1916-1919*. Chicago: University of Chicago Press, 1968.

Kealey, Linda. *Enlisting Women for the Cause: Women, Labour and the Left in Canada, 1890-1920*. Toronto: University of Toronto Press, 1998.

Kealey, Linda, and Joan Sangster, eds. *Beyond the Vote: Canadian Women in Politics*. Toronto: University of Toronto Press, 1989.

Kearney, Kathryn. "Canadian Women and the First World War." *Women's Studies/Cahiers de la femme* 3, 1 (1981).

Kellogg, Paul. *The Patriotic Fund of Canada*. Pamphlet. New York: American National Red Cross, Department of Civilian Relief, 10 April 1917.

Keshen, Jeffrey. *Propaganda and Censorship during Canada's Great War*. Edmonton: University of Alberta Press, 1996.

Kidner, Thomas B. "Vocational Re-education of Disabled Soldiers." National Education Association, *Addresses and Proceedings* (1918).

Kordan, Bohdan S., and Peter Melnycky. *In the Shadow of the Rockies: Diary of the Castle Mountain Internment Camp, 1915-1917*. Edmonton: Canadian Institute of Ukrainian Studies Press, 1991.

Lang, W.R. *The Organization, Administration and Equipment of His Majesty's Land Forces in Peace and War*. Toronto: Copp Clark, 1916.

Leier, Mark. *Red Flags and Red Tape: The Making of a Labour Bureaucracy*. Toronto: University of Toronto Press, 1995.

–. *Where the Fraser River Flows: The Industrial Workers of the World in British Columbia*. Vancouver: New Star Books, 1990.

Lind, Mayo. *Letters of Mayo Lind*. St. John's: Robinson, 1919.

Linteau, Paul-André. *Histoire de Montréal depuis la Confédération*. Montreal: Boréal, 1991.

Little, Margaret Jane Hillyard. *No Car, No Radio, No Liquor Permit: The Moral Regulation of Single Mothers in Ontario, 1920-1997*. Don Mills, ON: Oxford University Press, 1998.

Lomaga, Adrian P.N. "For King and Country: The Workers of the Toronto and York Branch of the Canadian Patriotic Fund." Research paper for the author, 26 July 2002.

Luciuk, Lubomyr. *A Time for Atonement: Canada's First National Internment Operations and the Ukrainian-Canadians, 1914-1920*. Kingston, ON: Limestone Press, 1988.

–. *Ukrainians and Internment Operations in Ontario during the First World War*. Toronto: Multicultural Historical Society of Ontario, 1988.

McCallum, Margaret. "Assistance to Veterans and Their Dependants: Steps on the Way to the Administrative State, 1914-1929." In *Canadian Perspectives on Law and Society: Issues in Legal History*, ed. W. Wesley Pue and Barry Wright. Ottawa: Carleton University Press, 1988.

–. "The Canadian Patriotic Fund and the Care of Soldiers' Families, 1914-1918." Unpublished paper, March 1982.

McClung, Nellie. "Surprise," *The Next of Kin: Those Who Wait and Wonder*. Toronto: Thomas Allen, 1917.

McCuaig, Katherine. "From Social Reform to Social Science: The Changing Role of Volunteers: The Anti-Tuberculosis Campaign, 1900-1930." *Canadian Historical Review* 61, 4 (1980).

Macfie, John. "Letters Home." *Beaver* 69, 5 (1989).

–, ed. *Letters Home*. Meaford, ON: Oliver Graphics, 1990.

McGinnis, Janice Dickin. "From Salvarsan to Penicillin: Medical Science and VD Control in Canada." In *Essays in the History of Canadian Medicine*, ed. Wendy Mitchinson and Janice Dickin McGinnis. Toronto: McClelland and Stewart, 1988.

–. "The Impact of the Epidemic Influenza, Canada, 1918-1919." *Historical Papers/Communications historiques* (1977): 120-41.

McGrath, P.T. "Pensions and the Care of Disabled Soldiers." Address to Patriotic Association, 10 Oct. 1916. St. John's *Evening Herald*, 1917.

McKenty, Neil. *Mitch Hepburn*. Toronto: McClelland and Stewart, 1967.

McLennan, J.S. *What the Military Hospitals Commission Is Doing*. Ottawa: King's Printer, 1918.

MacMurchy, Helen. *Infant Mortality: First Special Report*. Toronto: 1910.

–. *Infant Mortality: Third Special Report*. Toronto: L.K. Cameron, 1912.

Macphail, Sir Andrew. *Official History of the Canadian Forces in the Great War, 1914-1919: The Medical Services*. Ottawa: King's Printer, 1925.

Major, CAMC. "Returned Soldiers and the Medical Profession." *Canadian Medical Association Journal* 7, 4 (1917).

Manion, R.J. *A Surgeon in Arms.* New York: Doran, 1918.

Mathieson, William B. *My Grandfather's War: Canadians Remember the First World War.* Toronto: Macmillan, 1977.

Mayse, Susan. *Ginger: The Life and Death of Albert Goodwin.* Madeira Park, BC: Harbour Publishing, 1990.

Mee, Arthur. *The Fiddlers.* London, 1916.

Miller, Ian. *Our Glory and Our Grief: Torontonians and the Great War.* Toronto: University of Toronto Press, 2002.

Montreal Board of Health. *Annual Report.* Montreal, 1916.

Morgan, Henry J. *Canadian Men and Women of the Time.* 2nd ed. Toronto: William Briggs, 1912.

Morley, Alan. *Vancouver: From Milltown to Metropolis.* Vancouver: Mitchell Press, 1961.

Morris, Philip H. *The Canadian Patriotic Fund: A Record of Its Activities from 1914 to 1919.* Ottawa: s.n., [1920?].

Morton, Desmond. "The Cadet Movement in the Moment of Canadian Militarism, 1909-1914." *Journal of Canadian Studies* 13, 2 (1978).

–. "Le Canada français et la milice canadienne (1868-1914)." In *Le Canada Français et la guerre,* ed. Jean-Yves Gravel. Montreal: Editions du Boréal-Express, 1974.

–. *The Canadian General: Sir William Otter.* Toronto: Hakkert, 1974.

–. "A Canadian Soldier in the Great War: The Experiences of Frank Maheux." *Canadian Military History* 1, 1-2 (1992).

–. "Changing Operational Doctrine in the Canadian Corps, 1916-17." *Army Doctrine and Training Bulletin* 2, 4 (1999).

–. "Entente cordiale? La section Montréalaise du Fonds patriotique canadien, 1914-1923: Le Bénévolat de guerre à Montréal." *Revue d'histoire de l'Amérique française* 53, 2 (1999).

–. "French Canada and War, 1868-1917." In *Society and War in North America,* ed. J.L. Granatstein and R.D. Cuff. Toronto: Thomas Nelson, 1971.

–. "Kicking and Complaining: Demobilization Riots in the Canadian Expeditionary Force, 1918-1919." *Canadian Historical Review* 61, 3 (1980): 334-60.

–. *The Last War Drum: The North West Campaign of 1885.* Toronto: Hakkert, 1972.

–. "The Limits of Loyalty: French-Canadian Officers in the First World War." In *The Limits of Loyalty,* ed. Edgar Denton III. Waterloo: Wilfrid Laurier University Press, 1980.

–. "Military Medicine and State Medicine: Historical Notes on the Canadian Army Medical Corps in the First World War, 1914-1919." In *Canadian Health Care and the State: A Century of Evolution,* ed. C. David Naylor. Montreal and Kingston: McGill-Queen's University Press, 1992.

–. "Noblest and Best: Retraining Canada's War Disabled." *Journal of Canadian Studies* 16, 34 (1981).

–. *A Peculiar Kind of Politics: Canada's Overseas Ministry in the First World War.* Toronto: University of Toronto Press, 1982.

–. "Polling the Soldier Vote: The Overseas Campaign in the 1917 General Election." *Journal of Canadian Studies* 10, 4 (1975).

–. "Resisting the Pension Evil: Bureaucracy, Democracy and Canada's Board of Pension Commissioners, 1916-1933." *Canadian Historical Review* 58, 2 (1987): 199-224.

–. "The Short Unhappy Life of the 41st Battalion, C.E.F." *Queen's Quarterly* 81, 1 (1974).

–. *Silent Battle: Canadian Prisoners of War in Germany, 1914-1919.* Toronto: Lester Publishing, 1992.

–. "Sir William Otter and Internment Operations in Canada during the First World War." *Canadian Historical Review* 55, 1 (1974).

–. "The Supreme Penalty: Canadian Deaths by Firing Squad in the First World War." *Queen's Quarterly* 79, 3 (1972).

–. "What Did Peel County Do in the Great War?" *History and Social Science Teacher* 23, 1 (1987).

–. *When Your Number's Up: The Canadian Soldier in the First World War.* Toronto: Random House, 1993.

Morton, Desmond, and J.L. Granatstein. *Marching to Armageddon: Canadians and the Great War, 1914-1919.* Toronto: Lester, Orpen and Dennys, 1989.

Morton, Desmond, and Cheryl Smith. "Fuel for the Home Fires: Taking Care of the Women They Left Behind." *Beaver* 75, 4 (1995): 12-19.

Morton, Desmond, with Glenn Wright. "The Bonus Campaign, 1919-21: Veterans and the Campaign for Reestablishment." *Canadian Historical Review* 64, 2 (June 1983).

–. *Winning the Second Battle: Canadian Veterans and the Return to Civilian Life, 1915-1930.* Toronto: University of Toronto Press, 1987.

Neary, Peter. "How Newfoundland Veterans Became Canadian Veterans: A Study in Bureaucracy and Benefits." In *Twentieth Century Newfoundland Explorations,* ed. James Hiller and Peter Neary. St. John's, NF: Breakwater Books, 1994.

Nevitt, Joyce. *White Caps and Black Bands: Nursing in Newfoundland to 1934.* St. John's, NF: Jesperson Press, 1978.

Newton, Thomas W. *Lord Lansdowne: A Biography.* London: Macmillan, 1929.

Nicholson, G.W.L. *Canada's Nursing Sisters.* Toronto: Samuel, Stevens and Hakkert, 1976.

–. *The Fighting Newfoundlander: A History of the Royal Newfoundland Regiment.* Ottawa: Government of Newfoundland, 1964.

–. *Official History of the Canadian Army in the First World War: Canadian Expeditionary Force, 1914-1919.* Ottawa: Queen's Printer, 1962.

Noel, S.J.R. *Politics in Newfoundland.* Toronto: University of Toronto Press, 1971.

O'Brien, Patricia. "The Newfoundland Patriotic Associations: The Administration of the War Effort, 1914-1918." MA thesis, Memorial University of Newfoundland, 1981.

–. "Women's Movement." In *Encyclopedia of Newfoundland and Labrador,* ed. Joseph R. Smallwood, vol. 5, 609. St. John's, NF: Newfoundland Book Publishers, 1981.

–. "World War I." In *Encyclopedia of Newfoundland and Labrador,* ed. Joseph R. Smallwood, vol. 5. St. John's, NF: Newfoundland Book Publishers, 1981.

Off, Carol. *The Lion, the Fox and the Eagle.* Toronto: Vintage Canada, 2001.

Ogburn, William F. "Marriages, Births and Divorces: American Family in World War II." *Annals of the American Academy of Political and Social Science,* September 1943.

Ontario Mothers' Allowances Commission. *Annual Report,* 1920-21.

Ormsby, Margaret. *British Columbia: A History.* Toronto: Macmillan, 1964.

Overton, James. "Self-Help, Charity and Individual Responsibility." In *Twentieth Century Newfoundland Explorations,* ed. James Hiller and Peter Neary. St. John's: Breakwater Books, 1994.

Patriotic Association of the Women of Newfoundland. *Annual Report.* St. John's: PAWN, 1916, 1917.

Pedley, J.H. *Only This: A War Retrospect.* Ottawa: Graphic Publishers, [1927].

Perry, J. Harvey. *Taxes, Tariffs and Subsidies: A History of Canadian Fiscal Development.* Vol. 1. Toronto: University of Toronto Press, 1955.

Pettigrew, Eileen. *The Silent Enemy: Canada and the Deadly Flu of 1918.* Saskatoon: Western Producer, 1983.

Phillips, Paul. *No Power Greater: A Century of Labour in British Columbia*. Vancouver: BCFL and Boag Foundation, 1967.

Prentice, Alison, Paula Bourne, Gail Cuthbert Brandt, Beth Light, Wendy Mitchineson, and Naomi Black, eds. *Canadian Women: A History*. Toronto: Harcourt Brace Jovanovich, 1988.

Primrose, Alexander. "Presidential Address." *Canadian Medical Association Journal* 9, 1 (1919).

Proceedings of the First Convention of the Army and Navy Veterans of Canada. Winnipeg, 1918.

Rathbone, Eleanor. *The Disinherited Family*. London: George Allen and Unwin, 1927.

Rawling, Bill. *Surviving Trench Warfare: Technology and the Canadian Corps, 1914-1918*. Toronto: University of Toronto Press, 1992.

Rawlinson, James H. *Through St. Dunstan's to Light*. Toronto: Thos. Allen, 1919.

Raynsford, William, and Jeannette Raynsford. *Silent Casualties*. Madoc, ON: Merribrae Press, 1986.

Read, Daphne, ed. *The Great War and Canadian Society: An Oral History*. Toronto: New Hogtown Press, 1978.

Reid, Gordon, ed. *Poor Bloody Murder: Personal Memoirs of the First World War*. Oakville, ON: Mosaic Press, 1980.

Reid, Helen. *A Social Study along Health Lines of the First Thousand Children Examined in the Health Class of the Canadian Patriotic Fund, Montreal Branch*. Montreal: N.p., 1929.

–. "War Relief in Canada." *Proceedings of the Annual Conference on Social Work*. Philadelphia: N.p., 1917.

Research Group on International Security. *Proceedings of a Conference on the Military Family in Canada*. Montreal: McGill University, 2002.

Robbie, John. *Canadian War Service Badges, 1914-1954*. Surrey, BC: John Books, 1995.

Robin, Martin. *Radical Politics and Canadian Labour, 1880-1930*. Kingston: Queen's University Centre for Industrial Relations, 1968.

Robinson, Catherine Beverly. *Soldier Citizens*. Toronto: N.p., 1918.

Roland, Charles G. "War Amputations in Upper Canada." *Archivaria* 10, 2 (1980).

Roy, Patricia. *Vancouver: An Illustrated History*. Toronto: James Lorimer, 1980.

Roy, R.H., ed. *The Journal of Private Fraser, 1914-1918, Canadian Expeditionary Force*. Victoria: Sono Nis Press, 1985.

Russell, Lt.-Col. Colin K. "The Nature of War Neuroses." *Canadian Medical Association Journal* 61 (1939).

St. Louis, E. "Memorandum on Canadian Indians in the Two World Wars." Report of the Department of Indian Affairs. Ottawa, 1950.

Saywell, John T. *"Just Call Me Mitch": The Life of Mitchell F. Hepburn*. Toronto: University of Toronto Press, 1991.

Scammell, Ernest. "Canadian Practice in Dealing with Crippled Soldiers." *American Journal of Care for Cripples* 5, 2 (1917).

–. *The Provision of Employment for Members of the Canadian Expeditionary Force on Their Return to Canada and the Re-education of Those Who Are Unlikely to Follow Their Previous Occupations Because of Disability*. Ottawa: King's Printer, 1916.

–. *Summary of Activities of the Government of Canada in Connection with the Demobilization and Re-Establishment of Members of the Canadian Expeditionary Force to 31st December, 1923*. Ottawa: King's Printer, 1924.

Schecter, Jack. "The Achievements of Trooper Mulloy." *Canadian Military History* 11, 1 (2002): 71-9.

Scudamore, Maj. T.V. "Aid to the Civil Power." *Canadian Defence Quarterly* 9, 2 (1932).

Segsworth, Walter E. *Retraining Canada's Disabled Soldiers*. Military Hospitals Commission pamphlet. Ottawa, 1920.

Shamgar-Handelman, Lea. *Israeli War Widows: Beyond the Glory of Heroism*. South Hadley, MA: Bergin and Garvey Publisher, 1986.

Sharpe, Christopher. "The Race of Honour: An Analysis of Enlistments and Casualties in the Armed Forces of Newfoundland, 1914-1918." *Newfoundland Studies* 4, 1 (1988): 27-55.

Skocpol, Theda. *Protecting Soldiers and Mothers: The Political Origins of Social Policy in the United States*. Cambridge and London: Belknap Press of Harvard University Press, 1992.

Socknat, Thomas. *Witness against War: Pacifism in Canada, 1900-1945*. Toronto: University of Toronto Press, 1987.

Stacey, C.P. *The Official History of the Canadian Army in the Second World War*. Vol. 1, *Six Years of War*. Ottawa: Queen's Printer, 1955.

Steinhart, Allan L. *Civil Censorship in Canada during World War I*. Toronto: Unitrade Press, 1986.

Stetson, D. *A Women's Issue: The Politics of Family Reform in England*. London: Greenwood Press, 1982.

Stewart, Charles. *"Overseas": The Lineages and Insignia of the Canadian Expeditionary Force, 1914-1919*. Toronto: Little and Stewart, [1971].

Stirling, Teresa Bishop. "Newfoundland's Struggle for the Women's Franchise." BA honours thesis, Department of History, Memorial University of Newfoundland, 1982.

Strong-Boag, Veronica. *The Parliament of Women: The National Council of the Women of Canada, 1893-1929*. Mercury Series, no. 18. Ottawa: National Museum of Man, 1976.

–. "'Wages for Housework': Mothers' Allowances and the Beginnings of Social Security in Canada." *Journal of Canadian Studies* 14, 1 (1979).

Summary of a Survey of the Protestant and Non-Sectarian Relief Organizations of Montreal by Miss E. Francis O'Neill at the Request of the Financial Federation of the Montreal Council of Social Agencies. [February 1924].

Thompson, John H. *The Harvests of War: The Prairie West, 1914-1918*. Toronto: McClelland and Stewart, 1978.

Todd, J.L. "The Duty of the War Pension." *North American Review* 210 (October 1919): 767.

–. "The French System of Return to Civil Life of Cripples and Discharged Soldiers." *American Journal of Care for Cripples* 5, 1 (1917).

–. "The Meaning of Rehabilitation." *Annals of the American Academy of Political and Social Science* 80 (November 1918).

Todd, J.L., and Thomas B. Kidner. "The Re-training of Disabled Men." *American Medicine* (Spring 1917).

Tulchinsky, Gerald. *Taking Root: The Origins of the Canadian Jewish Community*. North York, ON: Stoddart, 1997.

Turner, Pat. "Amelia Turner and Calgary Labour Women, 1919-1935." In *Beyond the Vote*, ed. Linda Kealey and Joan Sangster. Toronto: University of Toronto Press, 1989.

Wade, Mason. *The French Canadians, 1760-1945*. Toronto: Macmillan, 1956.

Walker, James St. G. "Race and Recruitment in World War I: Enlistment of Visible Minorities in the Canadian Expeditionary Force." *Canadian Historical Review* 70, 1 (March 1989).

Waller, Willard. *The Veteran Comes Back*. New York: Dryden Press, 1944.

Warren, Gale. "The Patriotic Association of the Women of Newfoundland, 1914-1918." BA honours thesis, Department of History, Memorial University of Newfoundland, 1996.

Weber, Gustavus, and Laurence F. Schmeckbier. *The Veterans' Administration: Its History, Activities and Organization*. Washington: Brookings Institution, 1934.

Wecter, Dixon. *When Johnny Comes Marching Home*. Boston: Houghton-Mifflin, 1944.

Whitton, Charlotte. "Helen Richmond Young Reid." *Canadian Welfare* 17, 3 (1 July 1941).

–. "John Howard Toynbee Falk." *Canadian Welfare* 26, 1 (April 1951).

Wilson, Barbara. *Ontario and the First World War, 1914-1918.* Toronto: University of Toronto Press, 1977.

Winter, C.F. *The Hon. Sir Sam Hughes: Canada's War Minister, 1911-1916.* Toronto: Macmillan, 1931.

Woodroofe, Kathleen. *From Charity to Social Work in England and the United States.* London: Routledge and Kegan Paul, 1968.

Woods, Walter F. *Rehabilitation: A Combined Operation.* Ottawa: Queen's Printer, 1953.

Wootton, Graham. *The Politics of Influence: British Ex-Servicemen, Cabinet Decisions and Cultural Change (1917-1957).* London: Routledge and Kegan Paul, 1963.

Yealland, Lewis R. *Hysterical Diseases of Warfare.* London: Macmillan, 1918.

Young, W.R. "Conscription, Rural Depopulation and the Farms of Ontario, 1917-1919." *Canadian Historical Review* 53, 3 (1972).

Index

accidents, in summer training camps, 142
active service: definition of, 61, 108;
   disabilities resulting from, 148
Agnew, Mary Elizabeth, 30
Ainsworth, Mrs. J.T., 111
Aitken, Sir Max, 172, 178
Albert, King, 2
Alberta: average CPF payments in, 92; civil
   servants' contributions, 67-8; CPF in,
   67-70; government funding of CPF,
   186-7; Non-Partisan League, 182, 196;
   opposition to CPF, 196-7; Patriotic Tax
   Act, 187; per capita quota, 117; prices in,
   200; university staff contributions to
   CPF, 68
Alderson, Edmund, 35
alien disenfranchisement, 159
Allan, Sir Montague, 141, 142, 148, 164
Allan Line, 7, 213
Amato, Angeline, 47
Amato, Frank and Mary, 47
Ames, Herbert Brown: advice to Nova
   Scotia branch, 74; background, 51; on
   children of immoral mothers, 100; on
   county councils, 115; on CPF and
   voluntary enlistment, 116; on CPF
   disbursements, 199-200; on CPF not
   being a charity, 94; creation of CPF, 54,
   55-7; on discrimination, government vs
   CPF, 90; on discrimination among levels
   of need, 90; in Edmonton, 68-9; on
   finances of CPF, 117; on habits of the
   poor, 121-2; on Home Service, 109; on
   home visits, 94, 103; on Home vs overseas service, 64-5; on Indian donations,
   118; insistence on requirement of need,
   91; on Italians in Canada, 107; knight-
   hood, 114; last speech of, 222; leadership
   of CPF, 114; in League of Nations, 240; in
   Montreal City Hall, 52; on Montreal's
   working-class districts, 51; on notifica-
   tion of discharged soldiers, 150; and

patronage politics, 104; on pay errors, 47;
   on pensions for reservists, 149; Progressive Movement and, 114; on Quebec
   branches, 79; on returning soldiers, 138;
   on role in ending poverty, 126; at
   Saskatchewan conference, 129-30; on
   savings accounts, 126-7; on soldiers' pay
   rises, 198; and start of CPF, 59-60; use
   of Montreal as model for other CPF
   branches, 83; in Victoria, 188, 200; on
   widows' pensions, 94-5; on wives' use
   of assigned pay, 94
Amherst (NS): internment camp in, 87
Amiens, 208, 209
Anderson, R.M., 121
Anderson, Robert, 138
Andrews, G.W., 161
antibiotics, 137, 167
Appleby College, 153
Archangel, 216
armies: in 18th-19th centuries, 3-5; mass, 5;
   reserve formations, 4
Armistice, 209-10
Armstrong, Samuel, 136-7, 167
Army and Navy Veterans (ANV), 227, 228,
   235
Army Medical Corps, 27, 135
Army Service Corps, 27-8
Ashdown, J.H., 67
Asquith, Herbert, 22, 27, 39, 44, 96, 141, 172
Australia: and conscription, 209; disability
   pensions in, 229; free passage for
   returning soldiers' dependants, 213;
   universal military training, 8; venereal
   diseases in, 162; volunteers from, 170
Austria, 1
Austrians, internment of, 87

Balfour, Arthur, 171
Ball, Sgt., 211
Bank of Montreal, 53, 64, 65
Barclay, James, 85

Barnard, Frank, 71, 195
Barnstead, Arthur S., 73, 97, 98, 104, 127-8,
  129, 221, 224, 225
Barrie (ON): Fund contributions in, 185
Barron, R.B., 204
Bartlett, A.A., 75
Batoche, 13
battalions: bataillon canadien-français,
  22e, 78; Construction, 2nd, 97; 41st, 78,
  112; 57th, 112; new, 43-5, 116; Railway
  Construction, 257th, 45-6; 229th, 45;
  256th, 46; 258th, 177
battle exhaustion, 150-1
BC Electric, 191
BC Sugar Refineries, 191
Beath, Robert, 156
Beaulieu, J.V., 103, 229
Beck's Weekly, 103
Bee, Thomas M., 66
Béland, Henri, 87
Belcher, Mrs., 208
Belgian Relief, 74
Belgium, 1, 2; families in, 106
Bell, Frank, 131
Bell, Frederick McKelvey, 167
Bell, Olive and Will, 220
Bell Telephone Co., 175
Belleville (ON), 57
Belliveau, Camille, 229
Bennett, R.B., 69, 100, 154, 158, 236, 237, 240
Bermuda, 73, 74
Berthiaume, Trefflé, 20
Best, John, 175-6
Bienvenu, Tancrède, 175
bigamy, 99-100, 210, 230
Birge, Cyrus, 82
Birks, William M., 57, 83, 176-7
Birmingham, A.H., 104
birth rate, and military strength, 16
Bisaillon, Pierre-H., 2
Black Watch, 11
Bland, Mrs., 234
Blaylock, Selwyn, 194
Bliss, Michael, 179
Blondin, Pierre-Édouard, 177
Blue, John, 68
Board of Pension Commissioners (BPC),
  158-9, 211, 229-30; disbursements of,
  231-2; and family size, 197; founding of,
  146-7; as guardian to children, 231; home

visits, 223; MacNeil's accusations, 233;
  and marriage/remarriage, 230; royal
  commission on, 233-6; and shell
  shock, 163
Boards of Control, 115
Boer War. *See* South African War
Bonnor, C.H., 61-2, 192
Bonus, Edith, 220
Boosamra, Salim, 85
Booth, Charles, 51
Borden, J.W., 34, 43, 205
Borden, Sir Fred, 27
Borden, Sir Robert L.: assigning of family
  policy to CPF, 24; on conscription, 201;
  Conservative victory in 1911, 52; economic stability in early years of office,
  170; enlistment targets, 44-5, 116, 174; and
  exemptions from military service, 201;
  on financing of war, 179; and GWVA,
  160-1; and launching of CPF, 59; and
  next-of-kin association, 48; at outbreak
  of war, 1; and patronage politics, 104;
  and pay assignment, 93; progressive
  vision of good government, 146;
  raises separation allowance, 48; on re-
  establishment, 162; regarding dependants, 61; selection of Hughes as minister
  of militia, 25; and separation allowances,
  41, 54-5; Union government formed, 196;
  on veterans' bonus, 226-7; and veterans
  of Fenian Raids, 143; visit to Britain, 172,
  174; visit to Britain and France, 44-5;
  winning 1911 election, 23
Borland, Mrs., 207
Botha, Frank, 194
Botha, Louis, 83
Bourassa, Henri, 52, 77, 119, 120, 174
Boyle family, 31
Boyling, Garfield, 31
Bradshaw, J.R., 81
Brantford: CPF, 104-5, 130-1; Local Council
  of Women, 181
Brewery Mission Camp, 124
Brisset des Nos, M. and Mme Paul, 20
Britain. *See* Great Britain
Britannia Mine, 193
British Army, 170; compulsory pay
  assignment in, 93; families in barracks,
  10; Fifth Army, 198; married quarters, 10;
  as model for Canadian Militia, 10-11;

preparedness for war, 22; recruiting bounties, 8; recruitment of soldiers, 7-8; reservists, 8; sale of commissions/ promotions, 8; separation allowances, 10, 22, 98; size of, 8; soldiers' wives, 9-10; veterans' pensions, 142-3; volunteer nature, 7

British Columbia: average CPF payments in, 92; benefits to veterans, 225; cost of living in, 187, 191; CPF in, 61-2, 71-2, 187-8; day's pay scheme in, 188-90; deputy game wardens in, 188-9; and Federal Emergency Appropriation, 225; Federation of Labour, 168, 187, 191-2; fundraising in, 121, 188; government funding of CPF administrative costs, 186; head tax, 202; Home Service in, 109; labour movement, 190-5, 206; per capita quota, 117; poverty in, 70-1; prewar depression in, 70, 187; prosperity return in, 191; relief committees, 187; strikes in, 191; unemployment in, 70; voluntary enlistment from, 70, 188

British Columbia Federationist, 187, 191-2, 193, 194, 206

Brittain, E.L., 62

Broadbent, H.L., 134

Brown, George William, 66

Brown, J.R., 71

Brown, Thomas, 104

Bruce, Herbert, 166

Bruce County (ON): CPF in, 81

Bruchési, Paul-Napoléon, 55, 56, 84, 120, 124, 176

Budka, Nicholas, 6

Bulman, W.J., 66

Bulyea, George H., 68, 69, 70

Burdett-Burgess, Ina, 173

Busst, Mrs., 195-6

Busteed, June, 56, 57, 65, 181

Button, Mason, 169

Cadillac Motors, 175

Cahole, W.J., 152

Calder, J.A., 130, 222

Caldwell, Thomas, 231

Calgary: Allen Theatre, 226; CPF in, 69; IODE in, 57; Next of Kin Association, 182, 197; prewar depression in, 69; war brides' hostel, 215

CAMC. *See* Canadian Army Medical Corps (CAMC)

Cameron, Charles, 193

Campbell, Martha, 162

Camrose (AB): fundraising in, 177

Canadian Annual Review, 179-80, 183

Canadian Army Medical Corps (CAMC), 165-6, 213, 226; and MHC, 165-7

Canadian Army Pay Corps (CAPC), 28, 43, 46

Canadian Association of Returned Soldiers (CARS), 156

Canadian Association of Soldiers' and Sailors' Mothers and Wives League of the British Army and Navy, 193

Canadian Corps, 167, 171, 201; Hundred Days campaign, 198, 208-9; postwar mutinies, 212; at Vimy, 198

Canadian Defence League, 8

Canadian Expeditionary Force (CEF): administrative problems with new battalions, 45-6; Associated Kin of, 183; east-west distinction in allowances, 91-2; First Contingent, 21, 31, 39, 107, 198; formed at Valcartier, 26; Hughes' announcement of formation, 3; medical screening, 148; Militia pay arrangements adapted for, 27; numbers joining, 116, 133; numbers returning, 133; pay scales for, 23, 29; previous employment of volunteers, 91; proposed trust fund for demobilization, 35; retention of convalescents in, 137, 139; Second Contingent, 43; separation allowances for dependant, 64; Third Contingent, 43-4; voluntarism of, and of CPF, 120; wives and children of recruits, 24

Canadian Forestry Corps, 174

Canadian Legion, 235, 237

Canadian Mounted Rifles, 43

Canadian Northern railway, 23

Canadian Pacific Railway, 23-4, 119, 212

Canadian Patriotic Fund (CPF), 239-40; active service, definition of, 108; and aged parents of soldiers, 222; Alberta criticism of, 196-7; allowance stoppage for returned soldiers, 138; Ames' role in, 62; attacks on, 194-8; BC labour movement and, 191, 194; beneficiaries of, 61; beneficiaries to be resident in Canada, 205-6; *Bulletin,* 122, 125, 131, 180, 198; as bureaucracy, 47; as a charity, 103; as charity, 160; charity vs, 94, 95; class of visitor vs of beneficiary, 131; comparison with American benefits, 173; connection with Separation Allowance Board, 49; as controversial, 186; created by Ames, 54; creation of, 53, 55-7; in Crimean War, 53; day's wages scheme, 117; definitions of need and dependency, 62-4; delivery of Federal Emergency Relief Allocation, 223-4; and demobilization of married soldiers, 211; dependants as debtors, 101; and deserters, 104-5; deserving vs undeserving, 65; differences in cost of living between cities and small towns, 91-2, 173; differentiation among levels of need, 90; and disabled soldiers, 149-50; disbursements, 121; as disincentive to recruitment, 185; Eastern Conference, 128-9; and Emergency Appropriation, 223-4; enlistment and, 95; executive, 60-1; and families moving to Britain, 204; and families of disabled soldiers, 109-10; and families of soldiers, 37; and families returning from Britain, 198; family policy and, 24; *Federationist* campaign against, 191-2; final appeal, 203; finance committee, 56-7; financial targets and quotas, 117; financing of, 115-16; formation of, 19, 24; fraud and, 102-3, 112; funding through taxes, 115-16, 186, 205; fundraising, 116-21, 132, 174, 199-200, 202-3; fundraising campaigns, 116-21, 132 *(see also under names of provinces and cities);* as GONGO, 88; government funding for, 186-7, 205; guidelines for maximum allowances, 91; help to disabled, 139; and Home Service families, 111; home visits *(see* home visits); incorporation of, 60; Indian donations, 118; Inuit donations, 118; and Italians in Canada, 107; joint fundraising with Red Cross, 174, 177; legislation regarding, 60; local branches, 54, 128; maternalism of, 89, 102; maternity benefits, 111; on money management, 126-7; Morris's role in, 62; and mothers, 19-20, 24, 27, 37, 42, 44, 50, 59, 60; national coverage, 103; numbers of recipients, 95-6; officers as beneficiaries, 98; official launch, 59-60; Oliver's

criticism, 185; opposition criticism, 185; patriotism and, 78; postwar role, 222-3; proposed beneficiaries, 61; racism in decisions, 97; record-keeping, 104, 112; records, 46; regional variations in supplements, 90; repatriated dependants referred to, 215; repatriation of British wives and families, 107; and reservists' families, 42, 106; responsibilities for children, 100; and returning soldiers, 138-9; and separation allowances, 27; surplus funds, 95, 220-1; taxes to finance, 202; territorial limits, 106-7; "third responsibility," 121-2, 207; voluntarism of, and of CEF, 120; and voluntary enlistment, 116; volunteer visitors, 115; VTLC opposition, 192-3; and wartime marriages, 102; and wives in Britain, 108; for wives married after enlistment, 41. *See also subheading* CPF *under names of provinces and cities*

Canadian Patriotic Fund Act, 77
Canadian Patriotic Fund Association (CPFA), 53
Canadian Peace Centenary Commission (CPCC), 136
Canadian Pension Commission, 237, 241
Canadian Public Health Journal, 15
Canadian Railway Troops, 174, 202
Canadian Veteran, 237
Canadian Women's Army Corps, 241
CAPC. *See* Canadian Army Pay Corps (CAPC)
Capricieuse, 77
Carabiniers de Mont-Royal: 65th, 2, 78
Cardwell, Sir Edward, 7-8, 10
Carey, Edith Pearl, 47
Carman, Albert, 214, 215
Carolan, John, 154
Carson, John Wallace, 11, 41
Cartwright, Sir Richard, 13
Casgrain, Thomas Chase, 60, 176
Cassels, J. Hamilton, 183
casualties: in 1918, 201; preparation for, 133; rate of, and infant mortality, 16; in Somme offensive, 131, 171, 172; women and, 6
CEF. *See* Canadian Expeditionary Force (CEF)
Chamberlain, S.F., 73

Charity Organization Society, 19
Charlottetown: cost of living in, 27
Chartrand, Précille, 103
Chatham (ON): Relief Fund, 57
Chester (NS), 98
Chikchagalook, 118
children: BPC as guardian to, 231; as
    contributors to CPF fundraising, 118;
    foster care, 100; of immoral mothers,
    100; as military asset, 16; mortality, 124;
    in orphanages, 100; pensions for, 144;
    separation allowances for, 39; of soldiers,
    10; support of aging parents, 63; of
    widowers in CEF, 39; working, 91, 96
Childs, William, 153, 163
Christian, Curly, 148
Christie, Maj., 225
Christie, Nancy, 181
Church, Tommy, 156, 167, 168-9, 226, 227
civil servants: in CEF, 26; contributions to
    CPF, 67-8; day's pay schemes, 188-9; paid
    peacetime salary, 26, 38, 52; positions
    kept open for, 152; and separation
    allowances, 38, 98
Civil Service Commission, 164, 165
Clements, Mrs., 44
Clements, W.J., 148
Cleveland, Grover, 143
Clymer, Mr. and Mrs. A., 40
Coburg (ON): Soldiers' Wives Club, 181
Cole, F. Minden, 55, 181
Cole, Florence, 56, 65, 138, 181
Collingwood (ON): Fund contributions
    in, 185
Comacchio, Cynthia, 14-15, 16
common-law relationships: separation
    allowances and, 39. *See also* unmarried
    wives
compassionate discharges, during demobi-
    lization, 135
compassionate leave, 133-5, 208; conditions
    for, 134-5; for fatal illnesses, 133-4, 135; for
    officers vs soldiers, 134; sentimental
    grounds, 134-5
compulsory military service, 5
Connacher, W.M., 69
Connaught and Strathearn, Arthur, Duke
    of, 59, 62, 83, 84, 116, 117, 120
conscription, 165, 172, 209; age-based, 158,
    159; and Borden's visit to Britain, 174;

and CPF as disincentive to recruiting,
    185; and labour movement, 168; Militia
    Act and, 26; single men included, 112;
    and vandalism in Montreal, 178;
    voluntarism vs, 26, 116; and voluntary
    recruiting, 48, 174
conscripts, 5; pay of, 5; in Russia, 216-17
Consolidated Mining and Smelting, 194
convalescents, 109-10; camp at Valcartier,
    133, 135; discipline problems, 137; homes,
    136; hospitals, 76, 137; retention in CEF,
    137, 139; vocational training for, 140
convoy system, 205
Cooke, Mrs. S.M., 204
Cooksville (ON): Women's Patriotic
    League, 81
Copp, A.B., 185-6
Corps of Military Staff Clerks, 28
cost of living: appointment of cost of
    living commissioner, 183-4; in BC, 187,
    191; in cities vs small towns, 91-2; and
    family size, 27; and inflation, 95, 179-80;
    in Newfoundland, 76; in 1918, 201; and
    prewar depression, 178; regional
    variations in, 27, 63, 75, 90
Couche, J.A., 91
Courtney, J.M., 53, 98
cowardice, 151-2
CPF. *See* Canadian Patriotic Fund (CPF)
Craig, Richmond, 195
Creighton, Donald, 240
Crimean War, 7, 10, 53, 170
Cronyn, Hume, 230
Cummings, Mrs. Willoughby, 17
Curran, Margaret, 123
Currie, J.A., 227
Currie, Sir Arthur, 11, 151, 198, 212, 218,
    235, 237
Cushing & Hodgson, 113
Cushman, Blanche, 48

Dale, R.J., 55
Dandurand, Raoul, 20, 55, 59, 60, 85, 119,
    176, 230, 235
Dandurand, Ucal-H., 85, 119, 120, 175,
    176, 177
Darling, Frank, 145
Davidson, Lady, 76
Davis, Mortimer, 85, 175, 177
Dawley, H.B., 189

Day, Mrs. R.S., 72
day's pay collection scheme, 78-9, 82, 85, 117, 188-90
Dayton, Bert, 30
de Lesseps, Comte, 7
de Sola, Clarence, 2, 7, 20, 56
de Watteville, Herman Gaston, 9
death(s): confirmation of, 144; rates in Montreal, 51; from Spanish flu, 207. *See also* casualties; infants: mortality
Delage, Cyrille F., 79
demobilization: benefits after Second World War, 242; compassionate discharges during, 135; compulsory savings for, 35; demand for, 209, 210; department of, 166; of married men, 211; "pivotal men," 211; riots in Britain, 209. *See also* returned soldiers
Denison, Flora, 17
Denmark: Prussian defeat of, 5
Dennis, J.S., 69
Department of Demobilization, 157
Department of Immigration, 205
Department of Immigration and Colonization, 213
Department of Justice, on compulsory pay assignment, 93
Department of Labour, 191
Department of Soldiers' Civil Re-establishment (DSCR), 166, 233
dependants: of BC workers in Britain, 191; benefits for, 173; in Britain, 205, 212-13; as debtors, 101; double sets of, 101; pensions, 147, 149; repatriation, 212-16; separation allowances granted by CEF, 64; shipped back to Canada, 205; Vancouver meeting regarding, 206-7
Dependants' Allowance Board, 241
dependants' allowances, Second World War, 241
dependency, definitions of, 62-4
dependent mothers, 38, 63, 90; pensions for, 149; separation allowances for, 174
depression (1930s), 237
depression (prewar), 24, 178; in British Columbia, 70, 187; in Calgary, 69; cost of living and, 95; and enlistment, 29; in Montreal, 52; in Toronto, 58
DesBarres, F.W., 75
desertion (marital), 113

desertion (military), 4; and CPF, 104-5; and French-Canadian volunteers, 112; pay stoppage for, 47-8, 99
destitution: of disabled and families, 145; of families, 46-7; of parents of soldiers, 101; wives facing, 20. *See also* poverty
Devlin, Emmanuel Berchmans, 61, 64
Le Devoir, 2, 52, 53, 77, 119, 174, 175, 177
Devonshire, Duke of, 175, 176
Dexter, Robert, 87-8, 114
Dickinson, Katie, 109
Diefenbaker, John, 148
Diprose, Mrs., 49
disabilities: attributability of, 147-8, 241; defined, 141; functional, 154; levels of, 146; most returned soldiers with, 228; types of, 138
disability pensions, 144, 146-7; child allowance, 173; families depending on, 228, 229; importance of, 142; increases in, 147; and levels of disability, 146; for officers, 12; and poverty, 158; and private charity, 54; for privates, 12-13; rates, 147, 173, 229; and vocational training, 139
disabled soldiers: before BPC, 154; and CPFA, 53; developing new disabilities, 232-3; employment for, 139; employment income, 149; families of, 138; gratuities for, 149; GWVA concern for, 226, 228; marriage of, 231; pensions for (*see* disability pensions); political difficulties for help for, 54; rehabilitation of, 141; and separation allowances, 98-9, 109-10; vocational training, 139-40, 141
divorce, 23, 39, 162
Dobbin, F.H., 128
Doble, Arthur R., 55, 83, 155
Dominion Lands Act (1908), 38
Donaldson, Edith and Sam, 31
Dorchester (NB), 218-19
Dorval Jockey Club, 84
Doucet, Lude, 210
Douglas, Elizabeth, 220
Doullens, 208
Downing, James Joseph, 144
Drayton, Sir Henry, 222
Drummond, George, 51
Drummond, Julia, 51, 56
Drummond, Mrs. Huntly R., 175
Duguid, A. Fortescue, 33

Duke, W.R., 109
Dundas (ON), 82

Eaton, John C., 59
Eaton, Sir John, 60
Edmonton: Bijou Theatre, 196; cost of
 living in, 27; finance committee, 69;
 fundraising campaign in, 68; IODE in,
 21, 57; Next of Kin Association, 182, 197;
 Nutcracker, 196; relief committee, 69
Edmonton Bulletin, 68
Edwards, Mr. and Mrs. Frank, 192
Edwards, Mrs. (wife of Permanent Force
 soldier), 34
Edwards, Sidney, 40
Egan, Sir Henry, 223
Eggleton, H.T., 31
Elgin County (ON): CPF, 121
Elliott, G.W., 102, 113, 126
Ellis, Mayor (of Wetaskiwin), 70
emigration, and military service, 6
enlistment, 239; CPF and, 95; as escape
 from family responsibilities, 23;
 marriage and, 41; marriages after, 40,
 102, 107-8; separation allowances and,
 40-1; soldiers' wives' permission for, 23,
 30, 44, 133; targets, 44-5; of unionists,
 168; voluntary, and CPF, 116
Erindale (ON), 81
Evans, Mr. and Mrs. Austen, 98
Évard, Marie, 97
Everley, Emma, 44
Everywoman's World, 17
Ewart, T.S., 156
Ewing, A.F., 68
Excess Profits Tax, 199

Fahey, William, 12
Falk, T. Howard, 240
Falklands, battle of the, 37, 108
families: abandonment of, 162; in Belgium,
 106; depending on disability pensions,
 228, 229; destitute, 46-7; emergencies in,
 101-2; farm, 127, 135, 210; in France, 106;
 of Home Service soldiers, 37-8, 61-2, 111,
 116; husbands/fathers as breadwinner, 23,
 40; income, 34-5, 180; of internees, 87-8;
 of invalids, 137-8; in last year of war, 202;
 moving to Britain, 204-6; organizations

for, 181; psychological considerations,
 239-40; repatriation of, 212-16; of
 reservists, 20-1, 22-3, 106; of returned
 soldiers, 109-10; returning from Britain,
 198; returning to Canada, 204-5;
 reunions, 162, 218; size of, 96, 106, 184,
 221; societal responsibility toward, 24;
 of volunteers, 31-2
families of disabled, 109-10, 138; destitution
 of, 145; pensions for, 144
family wage vs military pay, 19, 54, 89
Farmer, Louisa, 97
farms: family, 127, 135, 210; labour on, 202;
 veterans' establishing, 227-8
Farthing, Bishop, 55, 56, 65, 85, 225
fathers: family responsibilities, 23, 63, 172;
 of soldiers, 39, 42-3. *See also* husbands;
 parents
Fawcett, Millicent, 17
Federal Emergency Appropriation, 223-5
Federal Emergency Relief Allocation
 (FERA), 223-4
feminists: solution to poverty, 18; women's
 equality and, 14
Fenian Raids, 12, 143
Fennix, Martha E., 123
Ferris, Dr., 69
Ferris, Mrs. W.D., 68, 69
Ferry, Mr. and Mrs. Howard, 36
File Hills Indian Reserve, 66
Finance Act, 60
Fink, Mrs. M., 193
First World War: cost of, 40; financing of,
 179; outbreak of, 1-3; regenerative nature,
 142
Fiset, Sir Eugène, 103-4, 156
Flavelle, Sir Joseph, 132, 179, 183-4, 199
Fleming, Sir Sanford, 53
Flemming, Horace A., 73
Flint, G.A. and Annie, 99
Flumerfelt, Alfred Cornelius, 72
Flynn, J. Harry, 226
Foch, Ferdinand, 199, 208, 209
Forestry Corps, 202
Forster, Mrs. W.D., 75
Fort Garry, 142
Fort MacLeod (AB): Next of Kin Associa-
 tion in, 182
Fort William (ON): CPF in, 82

France: army, 4; birth rate, 16; casualties, 142; defeat by Prussia, 5; families in, 106; French Revolution, 4; military service in, 5; pensions in, 141; privates' base pay in, 23; reserve in, 5; vocational training for disabled in, 141. *See also names of battlefields*
Francq, Gustave, 20, 55, 65
Franz Ferdinand, Archduke, 1
Fraser, Private, 151
fraud, 102-3, 112
Frederick the Great, 4
Fredericton: CPF, 75
Freed, Alma (later Sharpe), 102
French, John and Mary, 13
Frid, Roy, 210
Friedman, David, 55, 85, 175
Frink, J.H., 57, 75
Frontenac County (ON), 81
Fuisse, Pte., 48
Fyfe Smith, Mrs. J., 72

Gagnon, Amédée, 103-4
Gale, Charles, 206
Galt, John, 66
Galt (ON), 122
garrison towns, 5
Gaunt, Hamilton, 21
Gauvreau, A., 224
Geddes, Helen, 30
Genin, J.R., 55, 65, 175
George A. Touche & Co., 113
Georgeson, Agnes and Daniel, 105
Germans: deporting of, 87; as immigrants, 86-7; internment of, 87, 109
Germany: British ultimatum to, 2-3, 25; emigration from, 6; Far East squadron, 37, 70, 108; internment in, 87; outbreak of war, 1-3; submarine warfare, 107, 205, 211; universal military service in, 4-5
Gibbon, J. Murray, 83, 175
Gibbons, George, 119
Gildea, James, 8
Giolma, Frank, 206
Glover, Richard, 9
Gooderham, Mrs. A.E., 17
Goodwin, Albert, 168
Goodwin, Ginger, 194
Gordon, Nathan, 85

Gordon Highlanders, 50th, 11
Gouin, Sir Lomer, 78, 119, 177
Gouttes de lait, 15, 51
Graham, George, 185
Graham, Sir Hugh, 55, 178
Grand Army of Canada, 226
Grand Army of the Empire, 156
Grand Army of United Veterans, 227
Grand Trunk Railway, 23, 212
Grant, Mr. and Mrs. John, 43, 50
Gray, A.W., 72
Great Britain: Board of Trade, 191; Brigade of Guards, 10; British wives returning to, 107; conscription and, 7; demobilization riots, 209; dependants in, 14; disability pensions in, 229; employment in munitions factories, 191; food shortages in, 107, 205; free passage for returning soldiers' dependants, 213; labour shortage in, 191; military charities, 22; Ministry of Munitions, 191; Ministry of Pensions, 166; National Relief Fund, 108; National Service, 8; officers' wives in, 203-4; pensions for veterans, 142-3; pensions in, 141; poor laws, 9, 18; provision for soldiers' widows, 14; Royal Hospital, Chelsea, 142; Royal Navy, 7, 22; separation allowances in, 22-3, 106; Short Service Act, 8; soldiers' families moving to, 204-6; soldiers' pay assignments in, 106; soldiers' wives in, 14; ultimatum to Germany, 2-3, 25; War Charities Act, 178; War Office, 10; widow's pensions in, 145; workhouses, 18
Great War Veterans' Association (GWVA), 157, 158, 159, 168-9, 195, 206, 212, 226, 227, 228, 232, 235
Green, Charles, 41-2
Green, Doris (later Simpson), 41-2
Greenwood (BC): opposition to CPF, 194-5
Grenadier Guards, 11
Griesbach, W.A., 151, 235
Growell, Mrs., 9-10
Guelph (ON): fundraising in, 117; prison in, 136
Guerin, John James Edward, 176
Guilbault, J.A., 79
Guilfoyle, E.W., 159
Gunn, J.A., 219

Gutteridge, Helena, 190, 191
Gwatkin, Willoughby, 38

Hague Conventions, 16, 17
Haig, Douglas, Earl, 199, 208, 209, 235
Haileyburian, 36
Hains, Frances, 215
Haldane, Sir Richard, 22
Halifax: Belgian Relief, 74; Camp Hill
   veterans' hospital, 136, 165, 233; coastal
   fortifications in, 73, 74; cost of living in,
   27; CPF, 73-4; explosion, 130, 180, 211;
   fundraising in, 73; garrison in, 73; home
   visits, 130; Khaki League, 155; Knights of
   Columbus, 155; Reception Committee,
   155; reception of immigrants, 214; Red
   Cross, 155; relief committee, 74; veterans'
   agencies in, 155; working class, 130;
   YMCA, 155
Hall, Lt., 30
Hamilton: average CPF payments in, 92;
   Boer War Fund, 82; CPF, 131; fundraising
   in, 177; hospitals in, 125-6; services
   provided, 125-6; working wives, 113
Hamilton, Ernest, 95, 128, 161, 202, 218
Hamilton, L.A., 81
Hamilton, Sara, 128, 202, 218
Harding, Florence, 105
Harding, Pte., 154
Hart, Sydney, 31
Harvey, Mrs. Frank, 44
Haultain, Sir Frederick, 66, 140
Hay, A.C., 153
Hay, Angus, 156
Hay, E.W., 79
Hazen, J.D., 74, 145
Hedley (BC), 132; CPF in, 71; fundraising
   in, 86, 117-18
Henderson, George, 152
Henderson, Mrs. J.A., 56
Hendrie, Sir John, 82, 229
Herbert, G.H., 159
Hersey, Milton, 56, 57
Hespeler (ON), 127
high school cadet corps, 8, 25
Hill, Jane, 210
Hill, W.B., 97
Hobson, Robert, 82
Hocken, H.C., 58
Hodgetts, C.A., 15

Holder, Mrs. Gordon, 214
Holmes à Court, W.A.R., 133
Holt, Herbert, 83, 85
Home Service, 26, 108-9; and CPF, 37-8; CPF
   benefits and, 64, 109, 111; families of sol-
   diers, 37-8, 61-2, 111, 116; pay rates, 108; pay
   rates in, 37; and separation allowances,
   37-8, 108; subsistence allowances, 37
home visits, 65, 94, 103, 111, 115, 122, 125, 126,
   130-1, 163, 173, 223
homesickness, 202
homesteading, and military service, 38-9
Hood, John, 97
Horwood, Dora and Fred, 105-6, 219-20
House, Jane, 130
How, Douglas, 218-19
Howl, Nora, 44
Hudleston, F.H., 138
Hughes, John, 40
Hughes, Sam: announcement of CEF, 3;
   on base pay for privates, 23; career of,
   25; on disabled, 54; and hospital at
   Valcartier, 135; as minister of militia, 25;
   on not pampering returned soldiers,
   156; opening of Toronto fundraising
   campaign, 202-3; and pay assignment,
   35, 93; raising of battalions, 43-4, 45, 78,
   116; reaction to outbreak of war, 25; at
   Valcartier, 21; on volunteers vs con-
   scripts, 26
Hull (PQ): fundraising in, 117
Humley, Mrs. H.M., 109
Humphreys, Mrs. Tom, 30
Humphries, Charles, 173
Hundred Days campaign, 198
Hunter, A.T., 169
Hunter, Mr. and Mrs. Roy, 31
Hurdman, R.A., 126
Huron County (ON): compulsory savings
   accounts, 127
husbands: as family breadwinner, 23, 40;
   family responsibilities, 23. *See also*
   fathers
Hyatt, Fred, 152
Hyndman, J.D., 237

immigrants, 86-7, 215, 216; French, 2
Imperial Munitions Board (IMB), 132,
   183-4, 199
Imperial Munitions Board (IMB), 179, 180

Imperial Order Daughters of the Empire (IODE), 57, 178; Beaver House branch, 68, 69; Calgary, 57; Edmonton, 21, 57; Montreal branch, 124; Toronto, 17, 58; Vancouver, 193; Victoria, 21, 57, 72; Winnipeg, 136; Yukon, 73
Imperial Pension Office, 22
Imperial Tobacco (Montreal), 85
imposture, 112
industrial training, 140
infants: milk for, 15-16; mortality, 14-15, 51, 170
inflation, 50, 95, 109, 132, 147, 157, 159, 165, 167-8, 179
Ingall, Col., 106
Ingalls, C.M., 34, 45-6, 48-9
Ingersoll (ON), 81
insurance principle, 148, 232, 233, 234, 241
Intercolonial Railway, 212
International Court of Justice, 16
internment camps, 87, 108, 109, 190
Invalided Soldiers Commission (ISC), 166
invalids: families of, 137-8; relapses among, 137
Ionian, 7
Iron Cross, 175
Irwin, D.T., 53
Irwin, Robert, 97
Italians, 107
Ives, Jean, 204

Jackson, Walter, 104-5
James, Edward, 158
Jarvis, Aemilius, 183
Jarvis, F.S., 127
Jarvis, Herbert, 163
Jeckell, G.A., 73
Jennings, Harry, 133
Johnston, Ellen, 104
Joliette (PQ): CPF, 79
Jones, G.P., 71
Justice, Daisy, 126

Kapuskasing (ON): internment camp in, 87, 109
Kealey, Linda, 182
Kellogg, Paul, 89
Kemp, Albert Edward, 104
Kemp, Janet, 193
Kemp, Sir Edward, 151, 166, 216

Kennedy, J.A., 81
Kerr, Elizabeth, 110
Kerr, Mr. and Mrs. Walter, 42
Khaki Convalescent Home, 37-8
Khaki League, 155
Kidd, F.H., 94
King, Dorothy, 72
King, William Lyon Mackenzie, 59, 60, 226, 232, 236
Kingston (ON): fundraising in, 81; as military centre, 81; relief committee, 121
Kinmel mutiny, 212
Kitchener, Lord, 93
Knight, J.C., 196-7
Knight, Mary, 230
Knight, Norman, 154, 155, 158, 161, 163
Koch, Robert, 15
Komagata Maru, 70
Kyte, George, 104

Labatt, R.H., 146, 164-5
Labelle, A.E., 55, 56, 85, 175, 223
labour: and enlistment, 168; on farms, 202; opposition to CPF, 197; shortages, 87, 96, 141, 180, 191
Labour Gazette, 27, 63, 90, 95, 96, 179, 180
labour movement, 190-5; in BC, 190-5, 206; and conscription, 168; opposition to CPF, 197
Lachapelle, Emmanuel-Persillier, 20, 55, 65, 176
Lacoste, Sir Alexandre, 85
LaFlèche, Léo, 223-4, 235, 240
Lafontaine, Judge, 176
Laidlaw, William, 156
Lake, Sir Percy, 235
Lallicheur, Louis, 152
Lambert, A.O., 34
Lamer, Letitia and Joseph, 138
land grants, to veterans, 157, 166, 227-8
Langtry, Sgt.-Maj., 153
L'Annonciation (PQ): CPF, 79
Lansdowne, Lord, 171
LaPointe, Alderman, 120
Laporte, Hormisdas, 52, 176
Laurier, Sir Wilfrid, 1, 23, 26, 83, 143, 160, 170, 176
Laycock, Elizabeth and George, 102
Lazier, S.S., 57
Lemieux, Rodolphe, 61, 84

Lemieux, Sir Rodolphe, 200, 205-6, 230
Lessard, François, 177
Lesten, Mrs., 234
Lethbridge (AB): Next of Kin Association in, 182
Lévis, 21
Lewis, C.J., 189
Lighthall, W.D., 156
Livingstone, Judge, 128
Lloyd George, David, 172
Lodwick, Mr. and Mrs. Geoffrey, 189
Logie, Maj.-Gen., 109, 110
Longtin, J.-M., 79
Longwy, 2
Lorimer, Mrs. John, 206, 207
Lorne Park (ON), 81
Lougheed, Sir James, 38, 135, 158, 160, 165, 166, 230
Loughnan, David, 169
Love, Bertha, 97
Lovering, W.H., 82, 128
Loyal and Patriotic Society of Upper Canada, 53
Ludendorff, Erich von, 208
Lunenburg (NS): CPF in, 98
Lusitania, 87
Lynn, Bert and Mary, 162

MacDonald, E.M., 46-7, 61
Macdonald, Sir John A., 26
Macdonald, Wilson, 6
MacEachren, Caroline and Malcolm, 12
MacGregor, J.D., 73
Macgregor, Lyllian, 37-8
Machin, H.A.C., 41
Macken, Jean K., 193, 206
Mackenzie, Alexander, 143
Mackenzie, Sir William, 7
MacLean, H.H., 231
Maclennan, Mr. Justice, 102-3
Macmillan, Ernest, 87
MacMurchy, Helen, 15
MacNeil, C. Grant, 226, 231, 232, 233, 234, 235
Macphail, Sir Andrew, 151, 167
Macpherson, Kenneth, 159
Magrath, Charles, 57-8, 98
Maheux, Frank and Angeline, 216-18
Mahoney, Agnes, 49
Mail and Empire, 58

Maisonneuve, 119
Manitoba: Bill 7, 60; fundraising in, 67; Mothers Allowances Bill, 19; mothers' allowances in, 220; Norris government, 19; Patriotic Fund (MPF), 57, 66-7, 103, 106, 220; per capita quota, 117; unemployment in, 67; wood camp in, 67
Margeson, J.W., 36, 49
Marion, Napoléon, 137
Marler, Herbert, 232, 233
Marlow, Frederick, 166
Marois, Octavie, 13
Marois, Théo, 13
marriage(s): in Britain, 205; and enlistment, 40, 41, 102, 107-8; "on the strength," 9, 11; and pensions, 230; and remarriages, 230; separations of, 39; wartime, 102 (*see also* war brides). *See also* bigamy; divorce
Marsh Report, 241
Martin, John Clovis, 36
Martin, Médéric, 20-1, 52, 55, 65, 84, 176, 177
Martin, Mrs. John Clovis, 36
Massey-Harris, 58
maternalism, 14, 239. *See also* mothers
McAdams, Roberta, 182
McBride, Sir Richard, 70, 71
McClung, Nellie, 122-3
McConnell, John Wilson, 84-5, 85, 120, 175-6, 177
McCreath, Bert, 96-7, 118, 177, 203
McDougall, David, 140
McGill College of British Columbia, 72
McGill University, school of social work, 240
McInnes, Hector, 73-4
McKenzie, D.D., 61
McLean, H.H., 60-1
McLean, W.F., 227
McNab, Alex, 81
McNaught, W.K., 15
McQueen, John, and family, 101
McRae, James, 153
McVety, J.H., 190, 191
McWilliams, Jean, 182, 183
Medicine Hat (AB): Next of Kin Association in, 182
Megatama, 136, 164
Ménard, Alderman, 120
Mercier, Florida, 102-3, 123
Merrill, Helen, 17

Mewburn, Sidney, 134, 164, 210
middle classes, as home visitors, 19-20, 131
Midgley, Victor, 168
Military Family Resource Centres, 150
Military Hospitals Commission (MHC),
    160, 172-3; and ailing recruits, 136;
    allowances, 173; and CAMC, 165-7;
    convalescent homes, 110, 136; creation
    of, 135-6, 165-7; discipline problems, 137;
    liaison with Militia Department, 136-7;
    and *Megatama* invalids, 136; and Militia
    Department, 165; responsibilities of, 135-
    6; treatment of veterans as civilians, 137;
    and tuberculosis, 136
Military Police, 110
Military Service Act, 45, 48, 158, 168, 177,
    178, 181, 185, 194, 196, 198, 201, 202
military spending, 26; of First World War,
    35, 40, 179
Military Voters Act, 160, 196
Militia: British Army as model for, 10-11;
    departmentalization of stores and
    finances, 27-8; earnings, 27; married
    members, 11; pay rates, 90-1; paymasters,
    28; pensions, 12; size of, 11; summer
    camps, 27
Militia Act, 26
Militia Council, 11
Militia Department: and advent of war, 25;
    deserted wives and, 99; on home leave,
    134; and invalided soldiers, 135; marriage
    and, 11, 102; and MHC, 136-7, 165;
    notification of deaths, 144; organization
    of volunteers, 28; separation allowances,
    115, 123
milk, for children, 15-16, 51
Miller, John, 134
Mills, E.R.R., 154
Ministry of Overseas Military Forces, 213
Molson, Mrs. Denholm, 155
Molson, Percy, 85
Moltke, Helmut von, 5
Le Monde Ouvrier, 177
Mons, 209
Mont Blanc (steamer), 130
Montgomery, Lucy Maud, 17
Montpetit, Édouard, 85, 176
Montreal: Baron de Hirsch Institute, 51;
    beneficiaries' debts in, 127; Board of
    Trade, 55, 56; bonne ententism in, 171,

175, 176, 177, 178; bread tickets in, 112;
Canadian Club, 83; CARS in, 156; Charity
Organization Society, 51, 65, 87-8, 111, 114;
child mortality in, 124; city council, 120;
city deficit, 120; coal prices, 180; Comité
de Secours, 20; compared with Toronto,
50; corruption in, 52; cost of living in, 27,
52; CPF, 59, 64-5, 215; criteria for assistance, 111; day's pay collection scheme,
78-9, 85; death rates, 51; depression in,
52; disapproval of Emergency Appropriation, 223-4; education in, 50; end of
social work, 225; financial state at end of
war, 221; Franco-Belgian Committee,
55, 112; Franco-Belgian office, 111, 113;
French-Canadian participation in
fundraising, 175-6; French-Canadian
visitors, 119; French-English tensions,
118-20; fundraising in, 83-6, 118-21, 174-7,
203; *Gazette*, 176, 178; Germania Club, 2;
Grey Nuns Convalescent Hospital, 137;
Grey Nuns convent, 136; Home Service
families, 111; home visits, 111, 113-14, 125;
housing conditions, 51; immigrant
reception, 214-15; immigrants in, 50;
income disparities in, 51; infant mortality in, 51; inflation in, 50; IODE in, 124;
Khaki League, 155; Ladies' Auxiliary, 113,
124-5; Last Post Fund, 157; Lebanese
community, 121; loan from banks, 52-3;
Local Council of Women, 56; Loyola
College, 136; Manufacturers Association,
57; monthly relief payments, 111-12;
Mount Sinai Sanitorium, 101-2, 124;
office expenses, 112; paid staff, 113;
poverty in, 50-3; public works, 53; Relief
Committee, 103, 110-15, 126; reservist city
employees, 52; Royal Victoria Hospital,
111; Salvation Army, 84; sanitary problems, 124; "servant problem," 113; social
services in, 51; Société de Saint-Vincent-
de-Paul, 51; Soldiers' Wives League, 56,
57, 111, 138, 181; St. Andrew's Society, 51;
"trouble committee," 84; unemployment
in, 50; water rates, assistance with, 112;
Westmount Heating and Plumbing, 85;
Whirlwind Campaign, 83-6, 110;
Windsor Hotel, 2, 84-5, 119, 175; women
volunteers, 113-14; working-class
districts, 51; working-class life, 125

Montreal Daily Star, 56, 110, 177, 178
Montreal Garrison Artillery, 181
Moo-che-we-in-es, 118
Moor, Evelyn, 40
Morgan, Esther Ann Hill, 143
Morin, Mayor, 229
Morley, Alan, 191
Morphy, Hugh, 205, 206
Morris, May, 49
Morris, Mrs. E., 126
Morris, Philip: on Ames's visit to Edmonton, 68-9; commissioned to write report on CPF, 239; on CPF assistance to veterans, 222; on CPF's responsibilities, 64; on CPF's unemployment relief, 225; on debtors, 101; on deserted wives, 221-2; on erring wives and their children, 100; on exhaustion of CPF funds, 223; on families' moving to Britain, 205; on families travelling by rail, 215; on federal government support of dependants, 115; on independence of some places from CPF, 83; on labour hostility to CPF, 197; on marital desertion, 221-2; on officers and CPF, 98; on Prince Edward Island's contributions, 76; role in CPF, 62; on Saskatchewan River tragedy, 50; on Separation Allowance Board, 49; on separation allowances for unmarried mothers, 97; on Special Service companies, 110; on variations in cost of living, 92; on Windsor and Halton County, 80
Morris, W.S., 150
Morton, John, 13
mothers: allocation of support to, 97; allowances, 19, 240; dependent upon soldier sons (*see* dependent mothers); fatal illnesses of, 133-4; imperfections of, 24; poor, 19; Silver Cross of Sacrifice for, 228; of volunteers, 30-1; working, 15, 63, 124, 183, 231, 239. *See also* dependent mothers; maternalism; parents; widowed mothers
Mulloy, Lorne, 53, 54
Mulock, Mr. Justice, 203
Mulock, Sir William, 58
Murmansk, 216, 217
Murphy, Emily, 17
Murphy, Mrs. Arthur, 17
Murray, George H., 73

Murray, Mrs., 30
Murray, Mrs. Walter C., 182
Murray, W.C., 66
Murray Bay House, 124

Nanaimo (BC), 70, 187, 194
Nanton, Augustus M., 66
Nanton, Mrs., 67
Napoleonic wars, 4, 170
Nation, Fred, 117, 188
National Council of the Women of Canada (NCWC), 19, 65, 145, 181
National Registration cards, 174
nationalism, 4
Le Nationaliste, 120-1
Naylor, Joe, 194
need: definitions of, 62-4, 91; differentiation among levels of, 90; tailoring of allowances to, 115
Neely, George and Maria, 13
nervous exhaustion, 151
Nesbitt, E. Wallace, 107, 150
neurasthenia, 151
New Brunswick: average CPF payments in, 92; CPF, 74-5; economic conditions, 74; fundraising in, 121; government funding of CPF, 186; levy on counties and municipalities, 75; per capita quota, 117; volunteers from, 74, 75
New Glasgow (NS): CPF, 221
New Westminster: War Relief Fund, 72
New Zealand: free passage for returning soldiers' dependants, 213; universal military training, 8; volunteers from, 170; widow's pensions in, 145
Newfoundland: cost of living, 76; CPF territorial limits extended to, 106-7; fundraising, 77; Patriotic Association, 76-7; Patriotic Association of the Women of Newfoundland, 76; separation allowances, 77; volunteers from, 76
Next of Kin Associations (NOKAs), 48, 182
Nicholson, George, 230
Nickle, Hugh C., 121, 129
Nickle, William F., 162, 163, 184, 222, 224
Nightingale, Florence, 6, 10
Niobe, 61
North West Mounted Police, 26
Northern Enterprise (Bliss), 179

Northland (steamer), 212, 213
North-West campaign, 229; pensions in, 12-13
Norton, Bessie, 130
Norton, Mr. and Mrs. W.H., 130
Notman & Son, 84
Nova Scotia: beneficiaries' debts in, 127; and Federal Emergency Appropriation, 224-5; fundraising in, 121; Home Service in, 109; party patronage in, 104; per capita quota, 117; 2nd (Coloured) Construction Battalion, 97
nurses, 6-7, 10; soldiers' wives as, 9, 10; visiting, 16
Nutcracker, 196
NYD-N (not yet diagnosed – nervous), 151

O'Brien, Katherine, 129
O'Connor, W.F., 183, 184
officers: annual leave, 204; compassionate leave for, 134; disabled, 12; married, 30; needy, 98; pay rates, 29; pensions, 12, 163-4; purchase of commissions, 12, 98; rates of pay, 11; treatment pay, 163-4; widows of, 12; widows' pensions, 144, 145, 229 (*see also* widows' pensions); wives in Britain, 203-4
old-age pensions, 63
Oliver, Frank, 68, 185-6
Oliver, Mrs. W.E., 72
Olympic, 212
O'Meara, Mary, 31
One Big Union, 182
Ontario: average CPF payments in, 92; branches in, 80, 92; county governments, 80; CPF, 79-83; CPF donations, 203; CPF supplements, 90; Dairy Standards Act, 15; Home Service in, 109; Hydro Electric Power Commission, 114; lieutenant governor, 79-80; life insurance in, 173; Milk Commission, 15; per capita quota, 117; Regulation 17, 119; Soldiers' Aid Commission, 80, 81, 155; veterans' agencies in, 155; volunteers from, 79; Women's Christian Temperance Union, 178
orphans: GWVA and, 226; poverty of, 158; of Spanish flu, 207
Ostell, J.T., 2

Ottawa: anticonscription meetings in, 161; average CPF payments in, 92; CARS in, 156; Catholic clergy in, 120; fundraising in, 117, 177; IODE chapters, 155; veterans' agencies in, 155
Our National Benefaction, 94
outdoor relief, 18
Owen Sound: average CPF payments in, 92
Oxford County (ON): Patriotic Association, 81, 130; returned soldiers in, 160

Paradis, Philippe, 79
parents: children's support of, 63; siblings' support of, 63. *See also* fathers; mothers
parents of soldiers: CPF concern for, 222; destitution among, 101; support for, 229
Parker, Gordon, 210
Passchendaele, 208
Paterson, Thomas Wilson, 71, 72
Patriotic Fund: War of 1812, 12. *See also* Canadian Patriotic Fund (CPF)
Patriotic Fund Act (1901), 60
pauperism, 18
Pauzé, Alderman, 120
Pay and Record Office, 34
pay system: administrative problems, 32-4, 36; delays in, 154; in London, 37; pay offices, 46; performance of, 36-7, 44; regulations and, 46
paymasters: appointment of, 32; documentation, 33; in Militia, 28; rates of pay, 29; on Salisbury Plain, 34; training of, 32
paymasters general, 35, 46, 93; and assigned pay, 93
Pearson, Lester (Mike), 148
Peel County Council (ON): taxes used for fundraising, 80-1
Pension Act, 159, 235; Section II, 232, 234
Pension Appeal Court, 236, 237
Pension Board, 141, 152
Pension Commission. *See* Canadian Pension Commission
pensions: South African War, 53; for British veterans, 142-3; and deaths on active service, 98-9; for dependent mothers, 149; for disabled (*see* disability pensions); increases in, 48, 147, 159; insurance principle, 148, 232, 233, 234, 241; Militia, 12; North-West campaign, 12-13; as obligation vs charity, 145; for officers vs other

ranks, 12, 163-5; old-age, 63; political difficulties with, 54; as postwar liability, 228,
232; and rehabilitation of the disabled,
141; for reservists, 149; restructuring of,
228-9; scientific approach, 146; separation allowances and, 98-9; special committees on, 115, 144-5, 147, 163; trade
learning and, 145-6; for veterans, 140-1;
War of 1812, 12, 143; widows (*see* widows'
pensions)
Pensions and Claims Board, 142, 164
Pensions Appeal Board, 234, 235
Perley, Sir George, 41-2, 107-8, 213
Permanent Force: British reservists in, 8;
earnings, 27; as low-status occupation,
91; married members, 11; married
quarters, 11; pay for skilled tradesmen
in, 27; size of, 11
Perrault, O.S., 175
Perry, A.B., 66
Perry, Mr. and Mrs., 99
Petawawa (ON): CEF at, 28
Peterborough (ON): average CPF payments
in, 92
Peters, Wesley, 36
Pettipiece, R. Parm, 193
Pictou (NS), 97
Plume, Mr. and Mrs. H., 45
Plummer, Harry, 82
Plumptre, Mrs. H.P., 118, 203
pneumonia, 207
Poirier, Private, 159
Poles, as immigrants, 86
poor relief, 24
poorhouses, 18
Port Arthur (ON): average CPF payments
in, 92; CPF in, 82
Port Elgin (ON), 81
Portland (ME), 212
post-traumatic stress disorder (PTSD), 150,
240
Potts, Sybella, 202
poverty, 15, 168, 239; in British Columbia,
70-1; CPF role in ending, 126; disability
pensions and, 158; entitlement, and blame
for, 158; of parents of soldiers, 39-40;
relief of, 57-8; of returned soldiers, 157-8;
wages and, 18-19; widows' pensions and,
158; of working classes, 101. *See also*
destitution

Power, C.G., 230, 236
Préfontaine, Raymond, 52
Presnail, Marion, 30
La Presse, 2, 20, 53, 85, 121, 175, 177
Primrose, Alexander, 219
Prince Edward Island: average CPF
payments in, 92; CPF, 75-6; CPF
supplements in, 90; finance committee,
75; fundraising, 75-6; fundraising in, 121;
Ladies Auxiliary, 75; living costs, 75; per
capita quota, 117; relief committee, 75;
volunteers from, 75
Princess Patricia's Canadian Light Infantry
(PPCLI), 21, 133
privates: base pay for, 23; contribution to
separation allowances, 22-3; disabled,
12-13; pay rates, 29; pay rates for, 26-7;
pensions, 12; widows of, 12
Progressive movement, 114
Prussia, 4, 7, 8; defeat of Denmark, 5;
defeat of France, 5; defeat of Hapsburg
Empire, 5
public health and welfare, and health of
recruits, 5
Pugsley, William, 60
Purney, Willard, 157, 159, 160, 169, 226

Quebec: attitude toward France and
Belgium, 77; attitude toward South
African War, 77; average CPF payments
in, 92; CPF in, 103-4; fundraising target,
119; Khaki League, 155; per capita quota,
117; volunteers from, 77-8
Quebec City: CPF in, 57, 79, 214; fundraising in, 177; IODE, 214; reception of
repatriated families, 214-15; YWCA, 214
Queen Charlotte's Lying-In Hospital, 204
Quinney, Mrs. John, 30-1

railways, 23-4, 52, 82, 157, 211, 215
Rainbow, 61, 70
Ralston, J.L., 233-5, 236
Raun, Mrs. S.H., 109
Raynauld, Louis, 2, 7, 20
recruitment, 131-2; CPF as disincentive, 185;
employment and, 174; French-Canadian
resistance, 174; and separation allowances, 174; of unmarried men, 241;
voluntary, 48, 167, 171-2, 174, 201; widespread, 89

Red Cross, 175; American, 108, 173, 215; joint fundraising with CPF, 174, 177
Red Deer (AB): Soldiers' Wives Club, 181
Redmond, John, 83
Reford, R.W., 55
regiments: Carignan-Salières, 227; Prince of Wales, 11; Royal Canadian, 73, 74; Royal Montreal, 77-8; 85th, 2
Regina: CPF in, 66; war brides' hostel, 215
Reid, Helen: at American conferences, 173; background of, 65; on cooperation with Emergency Appropriation, 223; and CPF Health Clinic, 224; on CPF surplus funds, 221; defence of donors, 110-11; and health standards in Montreal, 124; on home visits, 113-14; and imposture and fraud, 112; later career of, 240; on Laycock case, 102; and Montreal's postwar relief, 225; on mothers in child's home, 183; at 1916 Eastern Conference, 128-9; role in CPF, 110-11; and school attendance, 124; on schooling in Quebec, 120; on soldiers' pay system, 46; "third responsibility" of, 181; on US funding of family support, 184-5; on volunteer workers, 203; and volunteers' visits, 111; on women's way of life, 99-100, 123; work with poor, 122, 123-5; on working mothers, 124; on working wives, 113
reservists: Belgian, 6, 7, 20, 21, 55-6, 106, 205; British, 7, 8, 21, 56, 70, 71, 106, 107, 142-3, 188; conflict between country and family, 23; families of, 20-1, 22-3, 106; French, 2, 6, 7, 20, 21, 55-6, 106, 205; pensions for, 149; Russian, 7
returned soldiers: changes in, 161, 218-19, 240; convalescent (*see* convalescents); CPF allowances, 138; disabilities of, 228 (*see also* disabilities); disabled, 109-10 (*see also* disabled soldiers); employment of, 141, 219; families of, 109-10, 162-3; impatience of, 218-19; as imperfect heroes, 162; organizations, 157; poverty of, 157-8; 168; restlessness of, 218-19; seasonal unemployment, 223; transfer to Special Service companies, 110. *See also* veterans
Returned Soldiers' Gratuity League, 226
Returned Soldiers' Insurance, 228, 232, 233, 236
Rhodes, Edgar N., 73

Richardson, Pte., 155
Riel, Louis, 12
Rioux, Émile, 103-4
Roberts, Lord, 8
Robidoux, Alfred, 79
Robinson, George, 42-3
Robinson, Jimmy, 195
Robson, H.A., 66
Robson, Mr. and Mrs., 97
Rogers, Bob, 60, 61
Rogers, Edith, 220
Roland, Charles, 66, 106
Ross, A.E., 223
Ross, John Kenneth Leveson, 60, 146
Ross, John W., 55, 56, 65, 83-4, 113, 165, 175, 177-8, 221, 223, 224, 225, 240
Rough, N., 65
Rowell, Newton W., 58, 163, 165, 228, 230
Royal Canadian Air Force: rates of pay, 241
Royal Canadian Rifles, 142
Royal Highlanders, 11
Royal Scots, 5th, 11
Russell, Colin, 151, 163
Russia, 1, 2; conscripts in, 216-17; privates' base pay in, 23; reservists in Canada, 7; revolution in, 168; Treaty of Brest-Litovsk, 198
Russo-Japanese war, 3
Rwanda, mass murder in, 150
Ryan, John F. and Mary, 13

sailors: marriage of, 8; separation allowances for wives, 22
Saint John: CPF, 214; CPF in, 57, 214; disabled soldiers in, 152-3; Khaki League, 155; reception of repatriated families, 214; Soldiers' and Families CPF, 75; women's auxiliary, 75
Salisbury Plain, 34
Sandon (BC): opposition to CPF, 194
Saskatchewan: average CPF payments in, 92; compulsory trust savings accounts, 127; and CPF allowances, 173; CPF in, 65-6, 66; CPF provincial convention, 129-30; Dependants' League, 66; fundraising in, 121; government funding of CPF, 186; Patriotic Purposes Tax, 130; per capita quota, 117; prices in, 200; Provincial Equal Franchise Board, 186; Returned Soldiers' Employment Commission, 155;

229th Battalion, 45; veterans' agencies in, 155; volunteers from, 66; Welcome and Aid League, 155

Saskatchewan River (AB): CPF in, 50

Saul, J.B., 134

Sault Ste-Marie: CPF, 50, 82; day's pay scheme, 82; relief committee, 82; steel industry, 82

Sayles, E. Roy, 81

Scammell, Ernest Henry, 136, 137, 139, 145-6, 149, 155, 167, 235

Scandinavian, 213, 214

Schreiber (ON): CPF in, 82

Scott, B.A., 79

Scott, Duncan Campbell, 118

Scott, Walter, 66

Second World War, 240-2

Segsworth, Walter E., 140, 149, 167

Separation Allowance and Assigned Pay Division, 48-9

Separation Allowance Board, 36, 49

separation allowances, 14, 19; British Army, 22; bureaucracy of, 48-9; civil servants and, 38, 98; cohabitation and, 39; and common-law relationships, 39; complexity of, 38; CPF vs, 54-5; and deaths on active service, 98-9; delays in cheques, 32, 34; and demobilization of married men, 211; for dependent mothers, 174; and disabled soldiers, 98-9, 109-10; double vs single sets of beneficiaries, 39, 101; employees, 48-9; and enlistment, 40-1; and family size, 106; granted by CEF, 64; in Great Britain, 22-3, 106; and Home Service, 37, 108; increases in, 48, 95, 173, 184; introduction of, 32; and marriages after enlistment, 40, 41; maternalism and, 183; Militia Department, 123; and need, 115; numbers of applications, 49; and overseas war brides, 42; paid by Militia Department, 115; payment after departure overseas, 105, 112; pensions and, 98-9; and pre-enlistment earnings, 27; rates of pay, 32; recruitment and, 174; for sailors' wives, 22; and soldiers' assigned pay, 93-4; and soldiers' dual families, 39; for unmarried wives, 22, 63, 64, 99-100; in US, 173; for widowed mothers, 38, 39-40; for widowers' children, 39; for wives, 22-3,

217; women's way of life and, 97, 100, 122-3

Serbia, 1

servants, domestic, 113, 129, 183

Shannon, L.W., 44

Sharpe, Colour-Sergeant, 102

Shaughnessy, Sir Thomas, 84, 85

Shelburne (NS), 97

Shell Committee, 179

Shell Scandal, 145

shell shock, 151, 154, 163-5

Sherbrooke (PQ): CPF, 57, 79

Shorncliffe, 148, 216

Shortt, Mrs. Adam, 145, 182

Sifton, Arthur L., 67-8, 69-70

Sifton, Clifford, 86

Silver Cross of Sacrifice, 228

Simpson, W.H., 41

Sims, Anna, 216

Slocan Star mine, 194

Smith, Clarence, 65, 110, 112, 113, 123, 128, 136, 223, 225

Smith, George P., 70

Smith, Mrs., 49

Smith, Obed, 212, 213, 214

Smith, Ralph, 188-9

Smith, Rufus, 52, 65, 111, 114

Sneesly, Mrs., 220

Snow, Mrs. Ezra, 208

social workers, 19-20; volunteers vs, 114

Société St-Jean-Baptiste, 2

Sola, Clarence de. *See* de Sola, Clarence

Soldier Settlement Act, 227-8

soldiers: absent without leave, 112; annual leave, 204; civilians and, 4; compassionate leave for, 134, 208; compulsory savings for demobilization, 35; confirmation of deaths, 144; convalescent (*see* convalescents); death on active service, 98-9; demobilization of married, 211 (*see also* demobilization); earnings compared to those of labouring men, 27; education and, 5; in 18th century, 4; employers covering peacetime wages, 56, 57; enfranchisement, 196; families in both Canada and England, 39; families of (*see* families); furloughs for, 198; health of, 5; income, cf. to British, 35; invalided from France to England, 46 (*see also* invalids); letters from, 161, 173;

letters to, 131; life insurance, 126, 173; life insurance policies, 126; marriage of, 8-9; medical screening, 148; missing, 210; mothers dependent upon (*see* dependent mothers); as overpaid, 35, 93; payment of (*see* soldiers' pay); prewar positions kept open for, 152; re-establishment of, 152, 158, 162; repatriation, 212, 213-16; reputation in Britain, 35; returned (*see* returned soldiers); veterans; shipping standards for returning, 212; trench, 157, 161, 170-1, 172, 219; widows of (*see* widows); wives of (*see* wives); wounded, and homesteading, 38-9
Soldiers' and Sailors' Families Association (SSFA), 22, 42, 204
Soldiers' and Sailors' Families Patriotic Fund, 57
Soldiers' Associated Kith and Kin, 181
soldiers' pay: assignment of, 92-4, 106, 217; base, 23; deferment of half, 35; and inflation, 109; in 1939, 241; scales, 90; stoppages, 47-8, 99; as unskilled labour, 27, 157; when disabled, 98-9
Soldiers' Wives and Mothers League, 182
Somme offensive, 131, 171, 172, 179
South Africa: free passage for returning soldiers' dependants, 213
South African War: and British Army model, 11; British Army's performance in, 22; CPF in, 53, 60; duration, 170; Hughes in, 25; Mulloy case, 54; Patriotic Fund Committee, 56; Quebec's attitude toward, 77; veterans, 138, 139, 143; veterans' land grants, 227; widows' pensions and, 14
Southampton (ON): White School CPF, 178
Spanish influenza, 125-6, 167, 207-8, 209, 221
Special Committee on Pensions, 90
Special Committee on Returned Men, 157
Special Committee on Returned Soldiers, 100, 148
Special Service companies, 110
Spee, Admiral von, 37
Speenhamland system, 18
St. Catharine's (ON): fundraising in, 177
St. John's: Naval and Military Convalescent Hospital, 76; Waterford Hall, 76

St. John's Ambulance Society, 133, 150
Stanstead County (PQ): CPF, 79
Starke, Col., 56
Stellarton (NS), 97
Stephens, George Washington, 52
Stevens, Harry H., 164
St-Pierre, Alderman, 120
strikes, 180; BC Electric, 191; BC Sugar Refineries, 191; against war, 168; Winnipeg general, 182
Strong-Boag, Veronica, 19
submarine blockade, 107, 205, 211
Sullivan, Sir William, 75
Swinerton, Robert H., 72
Swinford, Lt., 13
Sykes, Mr. and Mrs. Harry, 130

Taché, Étienne-Paschal, 53
Tarut, Alfred, 55
Taschereau, L.-A., 79
Taylor, Fawcett, 237
Taylor, Mrs. F.J., 37
Tessier, J.A., 79
Thacker, T.L., 189
Thibaudeau, Mme Rosaire, 175
Thirty Years War, 3
Thompson, Alfred E., 165
Thompson, John, 230, 232, 233
Thompson, W.J., 30-1
Thorne, W.H., 74
Thyn, Elizabeth, 102
Todd, John Launcelot, 140-1, 145, 146-8, 153, 155, 158, 163, 172, 229, 232, 234, 236
Todd, Marjory (Clouston), 140-1
Tooke, Arthur, 164
Toronto: anticonscription meetings in, 161; Bank of Commerce, 58-9; base hospital, 167; Citizens' Association, 58; city council, 58; cost of living in, 27; CPF subscriptions, 202-3; depression in, 58; disabled soldiers in, 153; economic conditions, 50; 50,000 Club, 86-7, 118, 177, 203; fundraising in, 58-9, 118, 177, 202-3; General Hospital, 136; Greek restaurant riots, 168-9; infant mortality rate, 15; IODE in, 17, 58; Knox College, 136; life insurance in, 173; Massey Hall, 58; Montreal compared with, 50; national meeting in, 128-9; population, 50; schoolchildren's contributions, 118;

unemployment in, 58; war brides' hostel, 215; White City Café, 168; women's committee, 118
Toronto and York County Patriotic Fund Association, 110
Toronto Daily Star, 58
Toronto Saturday Night, 162
Toronto Women's Patriotic League, 17
Touche, George A., & Co., 113
Treaty of Brest-Litovsk, 198
Trois-Rivières (PQ): CPF, 79
Trotsky, Leon, 87
tuberculosis, 136, 148
Tupper, Sir Charles, 156
Tupper, W.J., 160
Turley, W.E. (Bill), 153, 154, 226
Turner, Sir Richard, 204
Turriff, J.G., 200, 205, 206
Tweedie, T.M., 69

Ukrainians: as immigrants, 86; internment of, 87
unemployment, 23-4, 57, 67, 168, 191, 223, 235; relief, 223-5
United Empire Loyalists of Canada, 17
United States: Civil War, 5, 170; Civil War veterans, 143; disability pensions in, 229; entry into war, 172-3, 180, 201; Grand Army of the Republic, 143, 156; military pensions in, 143; pensions in, 164; professional social workers in, 114; Progressive movement, 114; Red Cross, 108, 173, 215; separation allowances in, 173; widows' pensions in, 143, 231; wives in, 173
universal military service, 4
University of Toronto: Hart House, 140; School of Mining Engineering, 140
unmarried wives: separation allowances for, 22, 63, 64, 99-100; widows' pensions for, 145, 230, 231

Valcartier (PQ): CAPC at, 32; CEF formed at, 21, 26; convalescents' camp at, 133, 135; militia volunteers to, 3; volunteers' camp, 28-9
Vancouver: anticonscription meetings in, 161; Canadian Club, 155; Citizens' War Fund, 71, 190; cost of living in, 27; CPF supplements in, 90; fundraising campaign, 71; IODE in, 193; Labour Temple, 168; Local Council of Women, 182, 190; meeting on dependants, 206-7; Returned Soldiers' Club, 155; Soldiers' and Sailors' Wives and Mothers' Association, 193; Soldiers' Wives and Dependants Protective League, 193; South Vancouver Soldiers' and Sailors' Wives and Mothers Association, 182-3; Trades and Labour Council (VTLC), 190, 192-3; veterans' agencies in, 155; veterans in, 206; war brides' hostel, 215; Win-the-War rally, 195; Wives, Mothers and Widows of Great Britain's Heroes, 193; Women's Employment League, 190; Women's Patriotic Guild, 72
Vancouver Daily World, 195
Vankoughnet, Gertrude, 166
venereal diseases, 47-8, 147, 162
Vernon (BC): internment camp in, 87
Versailles, 209
Versailles, Joseph, 175
Vert, A.E., 72
The Veteran, 169
veterans: advocacy for, 155; agencies for, 155-6; appearance before BPC, 159; benefits to, 223-5; bonuses for, 226-7; clubs for, 155; as farmers, 227-8; Federal Emergency Appropriation for, 223; interment for, 157; land grants for, 157, 166, 227-8; organizations, 206; restlessness of, 163; self-supporting, 141; training of, 141. *See also* returned soldiers
Veterans' Bureau, 237
Veterans' Charter, 228
Veterans' Guard of Canada, 217
Veterans' Land Act, 228
Victoria: Board of Trade, 202; Capital City Labour Council, 195; *Colonist*, 194; home visits in, 72; Hospital Ship Fund, 72; IODE in, 21, 57, 72; League of Frontiersmen, 155; Patriotic Aid Society, 72; Patriotic Service Committee, 72; veterans' agencies in, 155
Victoria, Queen, 10, 14, 171
Victoria Daily Times, 200, 206, 225
Victoria Rifles, 3rd, 181
Victorian, 7
Victorian Order of Nurses, 65
Victory Bonds, 127, 202

Vimy Ridge, 162, 198, 208
Vladivostok, 216
vocational training, 139-40, 165, 166
Voice (Winnipeg), 182
voluntarism: postwar, 225; and Somme
    offensive, 131-2
volunteers (domestic), 62, 113-14
volunteers (military), 62, 203; criteria for,
    26; families of, 31-2; French-Canadian,
    112; organization of, 28-9

wages: average, 63; civilian vs military, 110;
    day's pay scheme, 78-9, 82, 85, 117;
    employers covering, 56, 57; and poverty,
    18-19; rise in, 180
Waistell, George, 226
Walker, Sir Edmund, 59, 60
Walkerton (ON), 81
War Appropriation Act, 60
war brides, 9, 42, 107. *See also* wives
War Charities Branch, 178
War Income Tax, 195, 199
War Measures Act, 24, 60, 183, 202
War of 1812, 12, 143
War Savings Bonds, 199
War Savings Certificates, 127
War Service Gratuity, 217, 218, 226-7
War Veterans Allowance, 236-7
Ward, A.A., 189
Ward, W.R., 32, 33-4, 36, 93
Warmington, Mrs., 231
Warner, Mrs. Eden G., 150
wars: casualties, 3; deaths from infections,
    3; in 18th century, 3-4; wounded, 3
Wartime Elections Act, 48, 196
Watts, Alice, 45
Waugh, R.D., 67, 155
Welland Canal Protective Force, 109
Wentworth County (ON), 82
West, F.S., 214, 215
Wharton, Mrs. Gerald, 31
Whitby (ON): mental hospital in, 136
White, Sir Thomas, 62, 178, 222
Whitton, Sgt.-Maj., 153
widowed mothers: and demobilization,
    210; pensions for, 229-30; separation
    allowances for, 38, 39-40; of soldiers, 90
widowers, children of, 39
widows: British provision for, 14; GWVA
    concern for, 226; of officers, 12; of

privates, 12; remarriage of, 230; Silver
    Cross of Sacrifice for, 228; working, 231
widows' pensions, 144-5; bonuses added to,
    228-9; and death of disabled soldiers, 233;
    in 1885, 12, 13; entitlement, 149; financial
    need as base, 13; importance of, 142;
    increases in, 147; levels of, 145; lifestyle
    and, 13, 145, 230-1; means testing, 229, 230;
    for navy, 144; needs testing and, 145; and
    poverty, 158; rates, 94-5, 147, 173; remar-
    riage and, 230; as state charity, 13; for
    unmarried wives, 145, 230, 231; in US, 143
Wilhelm II, Kaiser, 7, 17
William Davies (packing firm), 184
Williams, A.T.H., 13
Williams, Dr. C.A., 85
Williams, Mrs. A.T.H., 229
Williams, Victor, 26
Wilson, E.W., 156
Winch, Ernest, 207
Windsor (ON): Fund contributions in, 185
Winnipeg: anticonscription meetings in,
    161; Army and Navy Veterans, 157, 159-60;
    Associated Charities, 19; creation of
    Canadian Legion, 235; Deer Lodge Hotel,
    136; disabled soldiers in, 153; general
    strikes, 182; Great War Veterans' Associ-
    ation, 157; Industrial Bureau, 21, 57, 66-7;
    IODE in, 136; Mothers' Association, 19;
    Next of Kin Association, 182; Returned
    Soldiers' Association, 155-6, 156; Social
    Workers' Club, 19; veterans' agencies in,
    155-6; veterans' meeting in, 156; *Voice*,
    182; war brides' hostel, 215
wives: in Britain, 203-4; childless, 41, 96,
    129, 183; definition of, 42; deserted, 221-2;
    discontent among, 206; economic status,
    20, 178; fatal illnesses of, 133-4, 135; fathers'
    duties assumed by, 172; infidelity, 162;
    and life insurance policies, 126; lifestyle,
    122-3; loneliness of, 173; meetings of, 124;
    militancy among, 206; ordering hus-
    bands' discharge, 44; permission for
    husbands to enlist, 23, 30, 44, 133; preg-
    nancies, 100, 102; return to Britain, 107;
    savings accounts, 126-8; separation allow-
    ances, 22-3, 217; unmarried (*see* unmar-
    ried wives); in US, 173; use of assigned
    pay, 94; working, 63, 96, 113, 129, 183
Wolfe, Herbert, 173

women: and battlefield casualties, 6;
immunity from conscription, 6; life
expectancy, 170; and peace, 16-17; poverty
of, 18-20; role in national defence, 6-7,
17; single, 63; as social workers, 19-20;
way of life, and separation allowances,
97, 99-100, 122-3. *See also* mothers; wives
Women's Century, 96
Wood, Bella, 105
Wood, E.R., 58
Wood, Josiah, 74
Woods, Walter, 236
Woodstock (ON), 81
workhouses, 18
working classes: in Halifax, 130; incomes
of, 101; in Montreal, 125; poverty and, 15

Workman, Mr. and Mrs. W.F., 204-5
Wray, Mary, 208, 209, 210
Wright, Mr. and Mrs. Gordon, 183

Yarmouth (NS), 225
Yealland, Lewis, 151
Young, Viola, 40
Young Men's Christian Association
(YMCA), 58, 214
Ypres, 144, 169
Yukon: CPF, 73; fundraising, 73; gold
mining, 72; IODE in, 73; population, 72;
Red Cross, 73

Zarsky, Mrs., 210
Zwingli, Mrs. Wineas, 123

Printed and bound in Canada by Friesens
Set in Minion and Helvetica Condensed by Artegraphica Design Co. Ltd.
Copy Editor: Sarah Wight
Proofreader: Gail Copeland
Indexer: Noeline Bridge